W9-DIW-406

Selected Essays of

MONTAIGNE

RIVERSIDE EDITIONS

RIVERSIDE EDITIONS

UNDER THE GENERAL EDITORSHIP OF

Gordon N. Ray

Selected Essays of
MONTAIGNE

IN THE TRANSLATION OF JOHN FLORIO

EDITED WITH AN INTRODUCTION BY

Walter Kaiser

HARVARD UNIVERSITY

HOUGHTON MIFFLIN COMPANY · BOSTON

The Riverside Press Cambridge

This new edition of an old book
is dedicated to

PETER BURTON DOW

*car, de même qu'il me surpasse
d'une distance infinie en toute
autre suffisance et vertu, aussi
fait-il au devoir de l'amitié.*

Preface

Like most name-droppers, she sometimes gets them slightly wrong. But when that loquacious prototype of the Book-of-the-Month-Club reader, Lady Politick Would-be, observes to Volpone that "all our English writers" steal from the Italian poet Guarini "almost as much as from Montaignié," she at least has her facts right; and those facts attest to the seminal influence of the present work on late-Renaissance England. For, as Lady Politick's mispronunciation may also suggest, the enormous popularity of Montaigne's essays among her compatriots was largely the result of their accessibility in John Florio's English translation. To compile even a partial list of those seventeenth-century writers who were directly influenced by Florio's Montaigne is to recite the names of some of the greatest authors of that age: this is the book used not only by Ben Jonson but also by his Scottish friend Drummond of Hawthornden, by Shakespeare and Webster, by Marston, Daniel, and Donne, by Bacon, Burton, and Taylor; this is the book Sir Walter Raleigh took with him to the Tower. Not only has it remained one of the enduring monuments of English prose, but it is as well one of the great translations of all time. After three and a half centuries, no other rendering has been achieved which is quite so congenial or which more faithfully preserves the idiosyncratic spirit and tone of Montaigne's French. It is true that Florio's language is somewhat more exuberant and artificially wrought than Montaigne's colloquial simplicity, and subsequent translations have, to be sure, generally been more accurate. Yet it is indicative of Florio's accomplishment that even the best of these later versions returns whenever possible to his original choice of words and ordering of phrases. At the same time, there is something paradoxical about Florio's success as a translator; for he regularly violates almost every principle of that difficult craft we take for granted. He does not always properly understand the original French; he occasionally omits or suppresses; he often expands and interpolates. When he could not find the word he wanted in English, he made one up; when he did not agree with Montaigne — as, for example, on such matters as religion — he simply changed the text. Most surprising, perhaps, neither the language from which nor that into which he translated was his own. Yet for all that, he has somehow managed to capture what has eluded his more scholarly and more conscientious rivals, and what George Saintsbury wrote over seventy years ago remains true today: "Those who can will of course always read him [Montaigne] in the original: for those who cannot there is certainly no English version, despite its occasional inaccuracies, which can be recommended with half the warmth and sincerity which can be lent to the claims of Florio."[1]

Though Florio's book was entered in the Stationer's Register in 1600, it was not published until 1603. It would appear, however, that the translation had circulated in manuscript prior to its publication, for Sir William Cornwallis' *Essayes*, published in 1600–1, indicate that he had some knowledge of Florio's work. The first modern recension, based upon a collation of the three earliest editions of Florio's book, was edited by J. I. M. Stewart in 1931 for The Nonesuch Press; I am indebted to Sir Francis Meynell for having graciously permitted me to base this modernized version on that text. In attempting to remove some of the patina of age for the benefit of the modern reader, I have been as gentle and cautious as possible. Spelling and punctuation have been modernized, paragraphs have been introduced, and difficult words and phrases (signalized with an asterisk) have been glossed at the back. Occasional minor corrections have been made and are normally indicated with brackets; when it has seemed unavoidable, I have supplied a footnote, but these have deliberately been kept to a minimum. To save space, the original Greek, Latin, Italian, and French of Montaigne's many quotations from earlier authors have reluctantly been suppressed and only the translations retained. In the rare cases where Florio neglected to supply such translations, I have made my own, and these have been placed within brackets. The citations for these quotations, usually erroneous in Florio's text, have been silently corrected to give precise, accurate references to the accepted modern texts. Florio acknowledges that he was helped with these quotations ("which as bugbears affrighted my unacquaintance with them") by his friend Matthew Gwinne, but it is unclear from what he says whether Gwinne merely traced or also translated these tags. In any case, I must confess that I am generally unable to share Saintsbury's pleasure in these verse renderings and have retained them, rather than replacing them with more modern if less poetic ones, only out of piety.

[1] George Saintsbury, introd., *The Essays of Montaigne Done Into English by John Florio*, The Tudor Translations, ed. W. E. Henley (3 vols.; London, 1892–3), I.xxix. In addition to Saintsbury's essay, the reader may wish to consult the standard study by Frances A. Yates, *John Florio: The Life of an Italian in Shakespeare's England* (Cambridge, 1934), and also the relevant sections in F. O. Matthiessen, *Translation: An Elizabethan Art* (Cambridge, Mass., 1931), and Douglas Bush, *English Literature in the Earlier Seventeenth Century, 1600–1660* (2nd ed.; Oxford, 1962).

To make a satisfactory selection from Montaigne is an almost impossible task, and one is inevitably bothered by what has had to be left out. Like all selections, this one naturally reflects the preferences and prejudices of the editor; but such exercises are bound to rely, in the end, upon the subjective principle of *suum cuique*. Nonetheless, I have made a conscious effort to represent the different stages of Montaigne's thought and to illustrate the diversity of his concerns. Because each of the essays is an organic whole and because it is important to see how Montaigne's thought exfoliates within a given essay, I have insisted, even in the case of the lengthy *Apology of Raymond Sebond,* upon printing each of these essays entire. By adopting the unorthodox method of arranging the essays in roughly the order of their composition (so far as that can be determined), I have hoped to enable the reader to perceive more clearly the general patterns of Montaigne's thought as it developed through his lifetime. For the same reason, I have also indicated the three main levels of text. Montaigne published the first two books of his essays in 1580. In 1588 he republished these two books in a considerably revised text and added a third book. For the rest of his life, he continued to make changes and additions in his own copy of the 1588 edition, and these were incorporated into the text published by Mlle. de Gournay after his death. With the publication in 1919 of the first great modern edition of the *Essais,* based on a careful examination of the so-called "exemplaire de Bordeaux," these three levels of text were sorted out, and subsequent editions have been careful to indicate them. The present selection follows the conventional practice of signalizing with a superscripted A the text published in 1580, with B the text published in 1588, and with C the additions and corrections made after 1588. To the best of my knowledge, this is the first time these three levels have been indicated in Florio's version.

It was my good fortune to have been introduced to the *Essais* by Professor Herbert Dieckmann of Harvard University, and I have never forgot the sympathy, perception, and humane learning with which he first elucidated these texts for me. How many of his ideas I have unwittingly appropriated without acknowledgment only he can tell, but I hope at least that I have not seriously betrayed any of them. Every student of Montaigne is under vast obligation to the great *Édition municipale de Bordeaux* of Fortunat Strowski and François Gebelin and to the pioneer studies of Pierre Villey; I must acknowledge as well my special indebtedness to the work of Albert Thibaudet, Hugo Friedrich, and Donald M. Frame. It is a particular pleasure to be able to thank once again the Henry P. Kendall Foundation, and also the Clark

Fund of the Harvard Foundation, for financial assistance. I am grateful to Miss Bette Anne Farmer, Mrs. William Kates, and Mrs. Patricia Cumming for many invaluable services. Many of the ideas in the Introduction were first explored in conversations with Stephen Graubard, who patiently listened to me talk them out and was kind enough to read and comment on an early draft. This book owes most, however, to Harry Levin, who has encouraged my study of Montaigne over a number of years; he first suggested this edition, and throughout its preparation he has made many significant contributions to it with unfailing generosity.

Finally, the dedication of this volume is made both in acknowledgment of my greatest personal obligation and in testimony of an abiding friendship, which it pleases me to think might have been admired by Montaigne himself.

W. K.

Eliot House
Cambridge, Massachusetts

Contents

Introduction

by Walter Kaiser

If, as the famous exhortation carved on the temple at Delphi suggested and as thoughtful men have reiterated in all ages, the greatest wisdom is to know oneself, few men have been wiser than Michel de Montaigne. It is for that wisdom, as it gradually emerges from a lifetime's painstaking effort to know himself, that we return again and again to his pages and listen with increasing fascination as he tries to tell us who he is and what it means to live as a man. These are questions that properly trouble all of us, but not many of us are able to face them with such an honest, persistent, unblinking gaze; and indeed, history offers only a handful of examples of men who have managed to pursue the quest of self-knowledge quite so far and, as a result, achieve so profound an understanding of "the human condition." Significantly enough, the very phrase we use is his.

From Montaigne's own century, one can think of only two others with equally serious claims to such a high order of wisdom, and they are the towering figures of Desiderius Erasmus and William Shakespeare. To bring these three names together, however, may even help us to define what we mean by wisdom, to perceive the ways in which it differs from rational intelligence or pure intuition or mere learning, to recognize that it invariably illumines the same few simple truths, and to admit that it always has its origins in an acceptance of what has been unforgettably called "the foul rag-and-bone shop of the heart." At the very least, the mention of these three names ought to remind us of a specific literary and ideological genealogy. For when Montaigne, at the end of his life, examined the lessons of his experience and concluded that "a man must learn that he is but a fool," we are aware that he was thinking back to and repeating the message of Erasmus' greatest book; and when, later, Shakespeare sat down to write the play that seems to express his final vision of mankind, the one book that we know for a certainty he had at his elbow was John Florio's translation of the *Essays* of Montaigne.

To be sure, in this particular instance Shakespeare read Montaigne only to disagree with him, just as, later in the seventeenth century, Blaise Pascal was to derive a great portion of his thought from a much more profound disagreement with the author of the *Essays*. Yet we cannot imagine that either argument, Shakespeare's temporal or Pascal's eternal one, would have seriously offended a man who all his life had so ruthlessly argued with himself. One imagines instead the wry amusement he would have taken in pointing out that both authors had stolen many of his remarks for their own writings; for as T. S. Eliot has observed, "by the time a man knew Montaigne well enough to attack him, he would already be thoroughly infected by him." Unquestionably Montaigne would have respected both arguments as honest attempts to arrive at truth, that truth which, as he says, "is of so great consequence that we ought not disdain any induction* that may bring us unto it." He never asks that we agree with him, for he is never sure that he agrees with himself, and whatever he tells us he tells us tentatively, as an observation not as a dogma: "I teach not," he insisted, "I report." Dogmatism and assertiveness, he maintained, are really signs of stupidity; for the ways of truth are both various and devious, and we must follow whatever path we can, but always prepared to retrace our steps, to take the other fork, to try again. That is why he called his own journeys essays. "Were my mind settled," he explains, "I would not essay, but resolve myself; it is still a prentice and a probationer." Yet as he himself tried now one road and now another, one fact became increasingly clear: experience gradually taught him that while there may indeed be many roads to truth, the traveler is always the same man. And so it is to that man that, more and more, he turned his attention.

No author, he claimed, ever knew more about his subject than he did; for that subject was nothing other than himself. One may add that no author has ever told us more about that subject. We shall always wish, as men have wished for centuries, that we had some better idea of who Erasmus and Shakespeare really were, and we pathetically grasp after the smallest facts about their personal lives, hoping always that we may achieve some clearer image of the man behind the book. But with Montaigne we know that the book *is* the man, and we feel that he has already told us everything there is to know. Perhaps there is no other author — not even Rousseau — with whom we feel quite so well acquainted, whom we should recognize quite so instantly were he to walk into the room, to whom we should better know what to say, with whom we should feel more at home. This sense of intimate familiarity with him is, however, not merely the result of his having told us so much and so candidly about himself; it is also the result of the curious fact that as we look at him we seem to recognize something of ourselves. For as he holds his self-portrait up for our scrutiny, that canvas miraculously becomes a mirror. "As the centuries go by," Virginia Woolf has said, "there is always a crowd before that picture, gazing into its depths, seeing their own faces reflected in it, seeing more the longer they look, never being able to say quite what it is that they see."

In the last analysis, Montaigne himself was never quite sure what he saw in his own portrait, because within his single subject there were "so bottomless a depth and infinite variety" — so many different men. I cannot keep my subject still, he complained; "it goeth so unquietly and staggering, with a natural drunkenness." He observed that everything in the world was in perpetual movement and that he was no less mutable. Now I am one man, he realized, now another, changing from minute to minute. How can I portray who I am if I am always different? How can I see who I really am when my peasants think I am one person and the king another? How can I tell others who I am if I am unsure myself? What, in fact, *do* I know? The simplest things are so uncertain, so infinitely complex; they too are constantly changing and present themselves in such different lights. If the objects of our perception are unsteady and our perception itself unreliable, what certainty can a man have? Perhaps one can only keep asking at every moment, with every new experience, "What do I know?" But that question in turn depends upon another: "Who am *I*?" For "he who hath no understanding of himself, what can he have understanding of?" One can only try. One can only experiment. One can only make essays.

And one must be honest. If few authors have ever seemed quite so honest as Montaigne, that is perhaps because few people have experienced quite such a visceral revulsion at the idea of falsehood. "My mind," he said, "of her own complexion detesteth falsehood and hateth to think on it. I feel an inward bashfulness and a stinging remorse if at any time it escape me, as sometimes it doth if unpremeditated occasions surprise me." Above all, he was intolerant of hypocrisy, lying about oneself: "It is a coward and servile humor for a man to disguise and hide himself under a mask and not dare to show himself as he is." The result of such sentiments is that extraordinary candor which so beguiles us in his essays and which makes no admission, however frank, offensive; for we honor the respect in which he held truth, and this in turn confers a kind of dignity on the grossest of his self-revelations. Rousseau, of course, was to claim the same thing for himself, yet we feel an essential difference: Rousseau is always self-consciously straining after honesty and congratulating himself when he attains it in his most daring confessions, whereas for Montaigne truthful candor was as natural as breath. No one has ever more successfully achieved Coleridge's ideal that the heart should have fed upon truth, as insects on a leaf, until it become tinged with the color and show its food in every minutest fiber. Truth, indeed, is the ultimate subject of these essays — or, more precisely, their ultimate object; but truth, as Montaigne reminds us again and again, is never simple, is always elusive. What is more, truth is organic and not abstract, and like the monsters of fable it attempts to escape us by changing its shape as we grapple with it. "Reason hath so many shapes that we know not which to take hold of. Experience hath as many." Since we can never be sure in which of its metamorphoses truth has revealed its real self, perhaps all we can do is depict successively each of these shapes as it appears, hoping that if we assemble enough we may be able to perceive by extrapolation the lineaments of its essence.

If men have found Montaigne so congenial and sympathetic a companion, if he has seemed to speak so directly to so many different men, that is because each of us is perpetually engaged in just such a struggle. We all share Montaigne's poignant longing for the permanence of truth; yet we all find ourselves caught in the impermanence of human existence. It is because he so frankly acknowledges his own humanity, with all its impermanence and uncertainty, frailty and vulnerability, and yet refuses to abandon that struggle, that we look to him for consolation and encouragement. Just as we participate in his hopes, so, if we are honest with ourselves, we must share his great doubts; but we find something salutary in the example of a man who, for all those doubts, continued to try, to "essay."

It is no accident that Western civilization has found one of its profoundest myths in the story of Jacob wrestling with the angel. For every man has his own angel, whether he calls him God or Truth or simply Life itself; each man knows that he can never hope to force the angel to any final submission; to each the angel makes his impatient demand, "Let me go, for the day breaketh." Montaigne's response to that demand is Jacob's: "I will not let thee go except thou bless me." It is the claim of human persistence for recognition. For Jacob, the achievement of that blessing takes the form of the bestowal of a name; similarly, for Montaigne it is a final sense of his own identity as a man. That, in the end, is what each of us shares with him, his deep sense of humanity. And it is for that, as it is gradually achieved in these essays, that we listen to him so attentively as he rambles on, from candid detail to witty speculation to painful doubt to tentative assertion, perfecting what has been called "the art of stating himself."

[2]

"I was born," Montaigne himself tells us, "between eleven of the clock and noon, the last of February, 1533." His birthplace was the family estate from which he takes his name, a small château on one of the vine-covered hills in the rich, undulating countryside of Périgord, not far from Bordeaux. The family had been prosperously engaged in the fish, wine, and woad trades for several generations, and it was his great-grandfather, Ramon Eyquem, who had purchased the estate in the preceding century, thereby giving his heirs the status of minor nobility. Like Marcel Proust, whose mind his resembles in so many subtle ways, Montaigne had a Jewish mother, descended from a distinguished family of Spanish or Portuguese merchants who had moved to Toulouse at the end of the fifteenth century; quite unlike Proust, however, and for reasons that we can only conjecture, he never once refers to his mother in his book, though we know that after her husband's death she continued to live with Montaigne and his wife in the family château and was, in fact, to outlive her son by nine years. Of his father, Pierre Eyquem, on the other hand, Montaigne speaks often and affectionately in the essays, calling him "the best and most indulgent father that ever was" and claiming that he continued to embrace his memory long after his death. From the description Montaigne gives us, we see his father as a small, wiry man, gentle and decorous in his conduct, precise in dress and code of honor alike. To judge from the amusing accounts of his athletic bravado given in the essay *Of Drunkenness* and elsewhere, it would appear that he had something of the Gascon spirit in him as well. He was the first of his family to abandon trade and live like a nobleman on his estate, where he began a program of building and improvement which his son attempted to continue, as he explains, "because I had rather a respect to his intention than a regard to my contentment."

Pierre Eyquem had served in the Italian wars in the campaign of 1515, and he brought back from that country some of the new ideas about education that had been formulated and put into practice by the *quattrocento* humanists; yet one feels that the humane intelligence and tender solicitude which characterize the education given Montaigne were as much as anything else simply the expression of his father's benign, enlightened nature. As a child, Montaigne was always awakened to the soft sounds of music so that he would not be startled; he was put out to nurse among the peasants so that he would always have sympathy for the lower classes; and he remembered having been beaten only twice. From an early age he was taught that honesty which, all his life, was to be one of his predominant characteristics; and though he was taught to practice it first in his childish games, he himself wisely reminds us that to children such games are not merely sports, but "their most serious actions." His father intended to have him taught Greek as though it were a game like chess, but he later confessed that he had never been able to learn it very well. Latin, on the other hand, was literally his first language; for his father, realizing how difficult it was to learn that language later in life, allowed him to hear no other until he was six years old. As a result, we have the entertaining picture of the entire household at Montaigne having to learn enough Latin to communicate with the young boy, and, as he says, "we were all so Latinized that the towns round about us had their share of it, insomuch as even at this day many Latin names both of workmen and of their tools are yet in use among them." He admits that as he grew older he began to lose some of his familiarity with Latin — an experience which most of us have shared; yet in fact he is here only referring to his ability to speak the language fluently, for he continued to read it with ease all his life. And though he did not speak it for forty years, he notes with interest in the essay *Of Repenting* that in the two or three great crises of his life, as when his father fainted in his arms, the first words to spring to his lips were in Latin.

Montaigne's subsequent schooling was at the Collège de Guyenne at Bordeaux, "then the most flourishing and reputed the best in France," where we are surprised to learn that this man, who we should think incapable of playing any part but himself, took delight in acting in Latin plays and was considered "if not a chief master, yet a principal actor in them." The main impression the Collège de Guyenne seems to have left with him, however, was one of regimentation and punishment. He insists that he was too idle to be a scholar, which may bear some relation to his remarks about beatings; and later in life, unconsciously echoing what Gargantua had written to Pantagruel, he claimed with excessive modesty that a mere schoolboy was more learned than he. Presumably he went on from the Collège de Guyenne to study law at one of the universities, but he does not speak of it, and we do not know where.

In 1554, the king, Henri II, established at Périgueux a sort of tax court called the Cour des Aides, and Pierre Eyquem bought himself a position as one of the general counselors. When, shortly afterwards, he was elected mayor of Bordeaux, he turned his position in the Cour des Aides over to his son, who was then twenty-one years of age. For various political reasons, the new court lasted only three years and was, in 1557, incorporated into the Parlement of Bordeaux. Montaigne was to serve there in the Chambre des Enquêtes for the next thirteen years, working on the legal cases pertaining to that court; but the uncongeniality of such occupation to a man who could readily perceive the law's inadequacies and inequalities can be seen from such later observations as the following, from the lengthy attack on the law at the beginning of his last essay:

> Authority of law is given to infinite doctors, to infinite arrests,* and to as many interpretations. Find we for all that any end of need of interpreters? Is there any advancement or progress towards tranquillity seen therein? Have we now less need of advocates and judges than when this huge mass of law was yet in her first infancy? Clean contrary! We obscure and bury understanding. We discover it no more but at the mercy of so many courts, bars, or plea-benches.

During this period, from 1558 to 1565, we find Montaigne journeying often to the royal court at Paris, and some have supposed that he did so in the hope of finding a career there which would enable him to escape from his legal duties at Bordeaux. In 1559 he accompanied the king to Bar-le-Duc, and a chance remark in one of his essays suggests the fortuitous importance of that visit:

> Being at Bar-le-Duc, I saw, for the commendation of René, King of Sicily's memory, a picture, which with his own hands he had made of himself, presented unto our King Francis II. Why is it not as lawful for every man to portray himself with his pen as it was for him to do it with a pencil?

In 1562 he went on another trip with the king which was to prove of considerable importance to him; for he met then at Rouen those natives from the New World who gave him some of the information on which he was to base his famous essay *Of the Cannibals.* Yet life at the court was scarcely more satisfactory to a man of Montaigne's temperament than his legal career, and he was subsequently to refer to its wearying servitude and pointless gregariousness. And when, several years after he had left the court, he was given its highest honor, the Order of St. Michael, he observed with some disillusionment in his *Apology of Raymond Sebond:*

> Being yet very young, I besought Fortune above all things that she would make me a knight of the Order of Saint Michael, which in those days was very rare and the highest type of honor the French nobility aimed at. She very kindly granted my request. I had it. In lieu of raising and advancing me from my place for the attaining of it, she hath much more graciously entreated me: she hath debased and depressed it, even unto my shoulders and under.

Montaigne's most important experience during these years — indeed, it was the greatest single experience of his entire life — was the friendship he shared with his fellow-counselor at Bordeaux, Étienne de la Boétie. La Boétie, who was a few years older than Montaigne, was already known as the author of a treatise against tyranny and was considered a magistrate of promise. The bonds of friendship that they forged, which are described by Montaigne in his great essay on the subject, were abruptly broken, however, by the sudden death of La Boétie on August 18, 1563. It was presumably after the death of his friend that he indulged in those youthful love-affairs to which he frankly refers in his essays, as he himself would seem to suggest when, writing on the subject of diversion, he says:

> I was once nearly* touched with a heavy displeasure, according to my complexion, and yet more just than heavy. I had peradventure lost myself in it had I only relied upon mine own strength. Needing a vehement diversion to withdraw me from it, I did by art and study make myself a lover, whereto my age assisted me. Love discharged and diverted me from the inconvenience which good-will and amity had caused in me.

In 1565, at the age of 33, Montaigne married Françoise de la Chassagne, the daughter of one of his fellow-counselors at Bordeaux, and though she was to give him six children, only one, a girl named Léonor, lived beyond infancy. Though he claims that he was a dutiful husband, it is obvious from the few remarks he makes about marriage that it did not provide him with a relationship anywhere near so meaningful as his friendship had been, and he frankly admits that he was drawn into marriage by custom rather than by his own will: "Of mine own disposition, would Wisdom itself have had me, I should have refused to wed her; but we may say our pleasure, the custom and use of life overbeareth us." Yet it would be rash to assume that his was an unhappy marriage, or even that it was less successful than most marriages in his day, when marriages tended to be arranged by parents rather than made in heaven. Marriage and love, he said, "have affinity but therewithal great difference: their names and titles should not thus be commixed; both are wronged so to be confounded." His tribute to his wife in an epistle dedicatory to one of the treatises of La Boétie that he had published suggests that, in any event, he felt it more decorous to be reticent about his marital relations; the same letter, however, betrays a considerable affection for her.

Three years after his marriage, in 1568, Montaigne's father died, leaving him as the head of the family. The following year, he published his first work, a translation which his father had requested him to make of Raymond Sebond's *Natural Theology*. In 1570 he resigned his post at Bordeaux and went to Paris, where he published most of the remaining works of La Boétie, whose literary executor he was. And then, in 1571, he retired to his tower.

[3]

In the year of Christ 1571, at the age of thirty-eight, on the eve of the calends of March, the anniversary of his birth, Michel de Montaigne, long weary of the servitude of the court and public duties, while he was still in good health, retired to the bosom of the learned muses where, in calm and freedom from all cares, he will live out however many days are left to him. In the hope that the Fates will permit him to perfect this ancestral home and this sweet retreat, he has dedicated it to his liberty, his tranquillity, and his leisure.

These words, inscribed in Latin on a wall of his study, solemnly announce Montaigne's decision to retire from public life to a life of study, contemplation, and ease. Above them, we are told, hung a painting of the amorous encounter of Mars and Venus, a story commonly interpreted in the Renaissance as a symbol for the abandonment of the active life. Yet paradoxically, it is here, in this tower and in this year 1571, that the significant part of Montaigne's life was actually to begin. That he decided to retire to his estate at what may seem an unduly early age was presumably in part the result of his sense of loss at the deaths of his father and La Boétie. Certainly it was in part also the result of his disillusionment with the life he had lived in the courts of law and those of kings — a life of which, as the inscription declares, he was long weary. But it is also true that, in returning to live in "this ancestral home" of which he was now lord, he was doing nothing more than what was common for the landed gentry of his time. Nor is it surprising to find a man of Montaigne's background and sensibility choosing to withdraw from the confused world of wars and politics and palace intrigue to order his thoughts and meditate upon the wisdom of the past. The outstanding example for such a retirement in Montaigne's own time had been the celebrated abdication of the Emperor Charles V, who, to the surprise of all Europe, had publicly divested himself of his insignia of office on October 22, 1555, and retired to a monastery at Yuste in Spain. Unexpected though the decision was on the part of a Holy Roman Emperor, men had come to look upon such a course of action as paradigmatic of the ideal life; for, as one of Castiglione's courtiers had prescribed, invoking a Renaissance commonplace, "the contemplative life should be the goal of the active life, as peace is of war and as repose is of toil."

Montaigne's retirement, if less dramatic, was equally purposeful, as he explains in his essay *Of Solitariness*. Before turning to that essay, however, we should listen to his description of the life he led in retirement; for it is a vivid picture of the man as he is remembered, not in the corridors of palaces, but in the solitude of his tower:

> [When I am] at home, I betake me somewhat the oftener to my library, whence all at once I command and survey all my household. It is seated in the chief entry of my house; thence I behold under me my garden, my base-court, my yard, and look even into most rooms of my house. There, without order, without method, and by piecemeal, I turn over and ransack now one book and now another. Sometimes I muse and rave, and walking up and down I indite and enregister these my humors, these my conceits. It is placed on the third storey of a tower. The lowermost is my chapel, the second a chamber with other lodgings where I often lie . . . [In my library, on the third floor,] I pass the greatest part of my life's days and wear out most hours of the day. I am never there a-nights. Next unto it is a handsome, neat cabinet, able and large enough to receive fire in winter, and very pleasantly windowe[d] . . . The form [of the library] is round and hath no flat side but what serveth for my table and chair, in which bending or circling manner at one look it offereth me the full sight of all my books, set round about upon shelves or desks, five ranks one upon another. It hath three bay windows of a far-extending, rich, and unresisted prospect, and is in diameter sixteen paces void.* In winter I am less continually there; for my house, as the name of it importeth, is perched upon an over-peering* hillock and hath no part more subject to all weathers than this; which pleaseth me the more, both because the access unto it is somewhat troublesome and remote, and for the benefit of the exercise, which is to be respected, and that I may the better seclude myself from company and keep encroachers from me. There is my seat; there is my throne.

The library, he tells us elsewhere, contained "a thousand books," which is, of course, only a round number. Yet it is a large number for a private library in Montaigne's day and confirms his claim that books were the best provision he had found for this human journey. Favorite phrases and sentences from those books he had painted on the beams of the library ceiling, and we fortunately possess a fairly complete record of which phrases (some of which can still be seen there today) were so especially meaningful to him as to deserve such a place of predominance. It is interesting to note from his description that he often composed his essays while pacing back and forth, perhaps dictating some of them to an amanuensis, and no doubt this method of composition had an influence on the dynamic, extended rhythms of his prose, as it did on the late prose of Henry James. Moreover, it may also help to explain his obsession in the essays with the idea of motion, which is one of his dominant images. What should be especially noted in this passage, however — and what has too often been tacitly overlooked or forgotten — is Montaigne's emphasis on the windows in the tower and the wide view they gave him of the surrounding countryside. The popular picture of Montaigne as a bookish recluse in a remote tower room is only partially accurate; for that room, as the essays amply demonstrate, was very much a room with a view.

Similarly, one must not overestimate Montaigne's bookishness. While it is true that he was widely read, it is also true that he was highly skeptical of books, not only of the value of what one could learn from them, but also of the dangers of an excessive preoccupation with them:

> This plodding occupation of books is as painful as any other, and as great an enemy unto health, which ought principally to be considered. And a man should not suffer himself to be inveigled by the pleasure he takes in them: it is the same pleasure that loseth the thriving husbandman, the greedy-covetous, the sinning-voluptuous, the puffed-up ambitious . . . Books are delightful, but if by continual frequenting them we in the end lose both health and cheerfulness, our best parts, let us leave them. I am one of those who think their fruit can no way countervail this loss.

These remarks are made, appropriately enough, in the essay on solitude, where Montaigne candidly examines the kind of life he has chosen for himself and frankly admits that it may not be quite such an easy or naturally congenial mode of existence as it might appear. Since what evidence there is points to its having been composed, at least in a first draft, very soon after Montaigne's retirement (probably as early as 1572), and since it specifically discusses such retirement, *Of Solitariness* is one of the best places to enter his *Essays*. Here we have what one admirer has called "the true pages of the tower," where Montaigne, sitting down with himself, examines whether that self can be a sufficient companion.

It is characteristic of his eagerness to sweep aside clichés and face matters directly that Montaigne should begin his discussion by dismissing the dialectical context in which it had traditionally been placed — the long argument over the merits of the active *versus* those of the contemplative life. And as for the equally traditional position, that those who avoid public service are truants to the responsibilities every man has *pro bono publico*, he boldly challenges us to look carefully at those who are "in the dance" and decide whether they are really there for the public good or rather for their personal gain. Nor, he goes on to point out, is solitude any simple escape; because even in solitude we must live with ourselves, and "though we have freed ourselves from the court and from the market, we are not free from the principal torments of our life." "A man may as well fail in solitariness as in company: there are ways for it." Some fifteen years later he was to repeat the same lesson:

> To gain a battle, perform an ambassage, and govern a people are noble and worthy actions; to chide, laugh, sell, pay, love, hate, and mildly and justly to converse both with his own and with himself, not to relent, and not gainsay himself, are things more rare, more difficult, and less remarkable. Retired lives sustain that way (whatever some say) offices as much more crabbed and extended than other lives do. And private men, saith Aristotle, serve virtue more hardly, and more highly attend her, than those which are magistrates or placed in authority.

The point is, of course, that the vices of the soul — ambition, avarice, irresolution, fear, lust — all follow us even into the strictest solitude; we drag our fetters along with us. How vivid this truth was to Montaigne is suggested by the minatory imagery in the classical quotations he assembles to support his remarks: images of ponderous chains and inextricable, fatal arrows and the Goyaesque figure of black care riding inescapably behind us on our fleeing horse. What is more, the attentive reader will recognize that just as Montaigne admits the difficulties of learning to live with himself, so he also hints that it was not quite as easy as appearances might suggest for him to abandon a more gregarious life in order to do so. If the verbs of the following passage indicate nothing else, they at least indicate how strongly attached he was to the world about him:

> *Shake we off* these violent hold-fasts* which elsewhere engage us and estrange us from ourselves. These so strong bonds *must be untied,* and a man may eftsoons love this or that, but *wed* nothing but himself; that is to say, let the rest be our own, yet not so *combined and glued together* that it may not be *sundered* without *flaying us* and therewithal *pull away* some piece of our own.

Later in his life, in the essay *Of Three Commerces or Societies* where he again considers the relation of the individual to society, he once more examines his retirement, and his analysis of it is even more subtle:

> My essential form is fit for communication and proper for production; I am all outward and in appearance, born for society and unto friendship. The solitude I love and commend is especially but to retire my affections and redeem my thoughts unto myself, to restrain and close up not my steps, but my desires and my cares, resigning all foreign

> solicitude and trouble and mortally shunning all manner of servitude and obligation, and not so much the throng of men as the importunity of affairs. Local solitariness, to say truth, doth rather extend and enlarge me outwardly; I give myself to state business and to the world more willingly when I am alone.

Nevertheless, Montaigne does acknowledge that a life of solitude is easier for a man of his temperament than for many others who, as he describes them, "embrace all, everywhere engage and in all things passionate themselves, that offer, that present, and yield themselves to all occasions." And one must admit, as he did, that he was by nature always somewhat standoffish, that his was a dispassionate temperament, that his cool, critical, rational gaze generally prevented him from committing himself wholeheartedly to any single issue or individual. The qualifying clause is his most distinctive stylistic feature; "*distinguo*," he said, "is the most universal member of my logic." It was this same quality that made him inevitably suspicious of what he was later to call "transcending humors," and accordingly he also realized that he was not made for the austerer retreats of the religious zealot or the self-mortifying philosopher. Intentionally to seek hardships and to furnish solitude with difficulties and painful discomforts are, he says, for "sterner and more vigorous complexions" than his: "there is work enough for me to do without going so far."

How to organize that solitude and what its goal should be are the central preoccupations of the essay *Of Solitariness*, and Montaigne insists again and again that we must not go into a life of solitude with any ulterior motives. The justification of the withdrawal must be found in the withdrawal itself, not in the outer world, and hence we must especially avoid any thoughts of deriving glory from solitude: the man who goes into retirement to write or merely even to read books is wrong, because he is probably really doing so to enhance his reputation in the world. Instead, we must turn to solitude simply for the sake of solitude, for the opportunity of learning how to live alone with ourselves and of coming to some understanding and acceptance of the self. "The greatest thing of the world is for a man to know how to be his own." Those external comforts upon which we rely — family, friends, goods, health — will one day all desert us, and against that time we must prepare ourselves to be self-sufficient. Montaigne's description of what a life of solitude should ideally be like provides the rationale for his own retreat, and it is one of the most celebrated and significant passages in the *Essays:*

> A man that is able may have wives, children, goods, and chiefly health, but not so tie himself unto them that his felicity depend on them. We should reserve a storehouse for ourselves, what need soever chance,

> altogether ours and wholly free, wherein we may hoard up and establish our true liberty and principal retreat and solitariness, wherein we must go alone to ourselves to take our ordinary entertainment, and so privately that no acquaintence or communication of any strange thing may therein find place; there to discourse, to meditate and laugh, as without wife, without children and goods, without train or servants, that if by any occasion they be lost it seem not strange to us to pass it over. We have a mind moving and turning in itself; it may keep itself company; it hath wherewith to offend and defend, wherewith to receive and wherewith to give. Let us not fear that we shall faint and droop through tedious and mind-trying idleness in this solitariness.

The image of what Florio translates as the "storehouse" is basic to any understanding of Montaigne's life after he retired to his tower, but often it has been incompletely or erroneously interpreted. Montaigne's phrase for it is "une arrière boutique," which has sometimes been rendered as "a back shop"; but in this case Florio's word, though not wholly satisfactory, is closer to what Montaigne means, for he is talking about *a room behind the shop*, a place to which we can retire from the business of the day. It is essential to perceive, however, that a room behind the shop assumes that there is also a shop: it is not a cave in the wilderness. We must never forget that Montaigne's tower was not an isolated structure, but an integral part of his estate, and though the room in which he sat was removed, it had an extensive view of his house, his lands, and the surrounding villages and countryside. The main part of life takes place not in the back room but out in the shop itself; the storehouse is, in the end, only meaningful if there is a store. Life for Montaigne did not merely consist of sitting in a tower writing essays; it was primarily made up of wife and children, goods and health, the people who daily came into the shop and the transactions that took place there. He studied men, as Carlyle pointed out, "not only in the closet but in the world." But he felt that one must not become overly involved in those transactions, that one should preserve the capacity of standing somewhat apart, or of stepping into the back room, in order better to contemplate, evaluate, and understand these transactions. Such solitary examination, which inevitably leads to self-examination, is possible precisely because, as he discovered, we have "une âme contournable en soi," a phrase misleadingly translated by Florio which literally means "a soul which is capable of being turned back upon itself." It is this realization, that the mind or soul can question itself and engage in a fruitful dialectic, that makes the retirement to the back room — or to the tower — possible. It is, moreover, the very source of all the essays.

[4]

The composition of those essays was certainly no part of Montaigne's original design when he retired to his estate in 1571. His purpose then was simply, as he says, "to live more at leisure and better at ease," and though aware that such a purpose would provide occasion for extensive meditation, he did not plan that it should also result in his writing down the thoughts that came to him in the tower. Yet the mind is naturally predatory, and, deprived of other food, it will, precisely because it is "contournable en soi," feed on itself. Once he had settled into his tower room, Montaigne experienced what each of us has at one time or another experienced in similar situations — the mind (in Yeats' beautiful simile) moving upon silence like a long-legged fly upon the stream: the vagaries of the restless spirit as it follows the anfractuous paths of memory and anticipation, learning and conjecture, the heart's proud assertions and base betrayals, the haunting phantoms of the psyche, the hunger, as Samuel Johnson called it, of the imagination. And it was, Montaigne tells us in the brief essay *Of Idleness,* merely to keep a register of "so many extravagant chimeras and fantastical monsters" that he first started to write down his thoughts, hoping, as he characteristically puts it, to make them ashamed of themselves one day.

Thus he commenced to put into writing whatever thoughts he had on whatever subject, whether that subject came to him from observation or from memory or from something he had read. "I take my first argument by fortune," he explains in the essay *Of Democritus and Heraclitus*, meaning that he turns to the first subject chance presents to him; "all are alike unto me, and I never purpose to handle them thoroughly." It is in this same essay that we have what is probably his first use of the word he was to adopt as a description of these exercises:

> Judgment is an instrument for all subjects, and meddleth everywhere. And therefore in the *essays* I make of it, there is no manner of occasion I seek not to employ therein.

Though one can be less certain of a date for this particular essay than for some of the others, it is not unlikely that it was begun soon after 1572. Yet to claim that his essays are exercises of his judgment is already a more sophisticated concept of what he is writing than Montaigne's first description of them simply as random jottings. Already he has begun to perceive the potentialities of his form for rationally examining the problems that concern him. He is to reiterate this new conception of his work once again in an essay probably written around 1579–80, just before their first publication, where he says "it is sufficient that my judgment is not dismayed or distracted, whereof these be the essays." Twice again in this early period before 1580 he uses the word *essay*, and both occasions clarify further what he means. He refers to them here as essays of his natural faculties, that is to say, trials or experiments of his reason: "concerning the natural faculties that are in me (whereof behold here an essay) . . ." and "here is simply an essay of my natural faculties, and no whit of those I have acquired."

This attempt to examine the mind's artifacts with only the mind's faculties, to "try out" his reason, to speak, as he says elsewhere, of everything that strikes his fancy without using anything but his own natural resources, is the basic principle that controls all of Montaigne's writing. He resolved to present us with exactly what he thought, honestly and directly, and with only what his reason could determine on any subject that happened to cross his mind. At the same time, few men have come to such a vivid recognition of the limits of that reason. He knew, for example, that his rational judgment would often lead him into absurdities, yet he deliberately chose not to conceal those absurdities:

> Whatsoever come of it, for so much as they are but follies, my intent is not to smother them, no more than a bald and hoary picture of mine where a painter hath drawn not a perfect visage but mine own. For howsoever, these are but my humors and opinions, and I deliver them but to show what my conceit is, and not what ought to be believed. Wherein I aim at nothing but to display myself, who peradventure, if a new prenticeship change me, shall be another tomorrow. I have no authority to purchase belief, neither do I desire it, knowing well that I am not sufficiently taught to instruct others.

He recounts, not teaches, what his mind's eye can see, aware of the possible distortions and partial vision of that eye; and since he himself introduces the subject of painting, we may find it suggestive to compare this deliberately human perspective with the development of visual perspective that was taking place in the fine arts at the same time. Both specifically attempt to look on and to present reality from a human "point of view" — with the eye of man, not of God. It was this attitude, of course, that Pascal condemned as "a carelessness about salvation."

To recognize the essential secularity of Montaigne's approach, however, is not to deny, as some have, that he believed in God. He himself insists on his own belief in many places, and he appears, indeed, to have been a traditionalist in religious matters, claiming as he does at the end of his essay *It Is Folly to Refer Truth or Falsehood to Our Sufficiency* that if a man professes Christian belief he must then "wholly submit himself to the authority of our ecclesiastical policy." We should never forget that the first floor of his tower was a chapel, that every morning and evening a bell on his estate rang out the *Ave Maria*, that he never failed to say his bedtime prayers, and that he rose up from his deathbed to kiss the cross in the moment before he expired. His reason told him, however, that such matters were, by their very nature, beyond the realm of human reason, and that "there is no greater folly in the world than to reduce them to the measure of our capacity and bounds of our sufficiency." In another essay, he ridicules with graphic impatience those who attempt to go so far with their reason: "Those which a-cock-horse will perch themselves upon the epicycle of Mercury and see so far into heaven, they even pull out my teeth!"

Accepting, then, the fact that there were certain things — God, life after death, the secrets of the universe, metaphysical truth — about which his reason could give him no understanding, he deliberately chose to restrict his inquiry to what his reason might examine with some profit. In the essay he wrote on prayer he is quite explicit about this:

> I have also in my time heard certain writings complained of forsomuch as they are merely human and philosophical without meddling with divinity. He that should say to the contrary (which a man might do with reason) that heavenly doctrine, as a queen and governess, doth better keep her rank apart, that she ought to be chief ruler and principal head everywhere and not suffragant* and subsidiary . . . that this fault is oftener seen, which is that divines write too humanly, than this other, that humanists write not theologically enough . . . I propose human fantasies and mine own, simply as human conceits and severally considered, not as settled, concluded, and directed by heavenly ordinance, incapable of any doubt or alteration: a matter of opinion and not of faith, what I discourse according to myself, not what I believe according unto God.

To the end of his life he continued to insist that what he had produced were essays not results, experiments not conclusions.

This probing, experimental, inconclusive character of Montaigne's thought is mirrored in the very style and structure of his essays, where both form and content reflect, in his words, "a continual agitation or incessant alteration of my thoughts." Just as he is prepared to take up any subject that comes along, so he is prepared to follow it wherever it may lead him, willing to risk difficult bypaths and obscure side-roads and even dead-ends in the hope of finding a passage through to the truth; for truth is always his goal. Like those explorers of his day who sought a northwest passage to the wealth of the orient, he knew where his destination lay but was uncertain which road would take him there; like them also, he realized that the essential thing was to try out — to essay — any path that presented itself and, above all, to keep moving on. Since the essays register a precise, accurate map of that journey, they trace no direct, broad highway, but labyrinthine paths through the wilderness. In his meditations one subject will suggest another, just as one path may lead into another; one observation may bring us to a further observation which, in its qualification of the first, will seem a turning back; certain landmarks are recognizable from the descriptions given of them by ancient writers of Greece and Rome who had traveled the same road, but other directions suggested by antiquity are found to be no longer viable, having been obliterated by time or proved false by experience.

Yet Montaigne tries them all, and he gives us a detailed account of each attempt. At times, he confesses, "I straggle out of the path; yet it is rather by license than by unadvisedness: my fantasies follow one another, but sometimes afar-off, and look one at another, but with an oblique look." Further complexity is provided by the fact that Montaigne made many later additions to his original words, additions that often indicate quite a different direction from that he initially appeared to be following. Another writer would have carefully erased his earlier footsteps, but not Montaigne; he lets the new ones stand beside the former ones, contradictory though they may be, because "my understanding doth not always go forward; it sometimes goes backward. I in a manner distrust mine own fantasies as much though second or third as I do when they are first, or present as past." As a result, we may find it difficult at times to follow his uncertain footsteps or to understand exactly where they are leading, and we may be confused to see that he is always prepared to disclaim what he has said, to qualify it, or even to contradict it. He was aware that we should experience such difficulties, but he emphatically insists that the journey, whichever direction it may *seem* to take, is always in quest of truth, and that while he may contradict himself, the truth he does not contradict. My book, he says,

> is a counter-roll* of divers and variable accidents and irresolute imaginations and sometimes contrary, whether it be that myself am other or that I apprehend subjects by other circumstances and considerations. Howsoever, I may perhaps gainsay myself, but truth, as Demades said, I never gainsay.

Even the titles of his essays are unreliable signposts if we seek from them an indication of what direction he intends to pursue at that particular moment. He confesses that they "embrace not always the matter" but often only glance at it. Yet at least they *do* glance at it, and one must not fail to recognize that behind the apparently haphazard, confused, irrelevant jumble of ideas in any given essay there is invariably a controlling thought. "It is the unheedy and negligent reader that loseth my subject and not myself; some word or other shall ever be found in a corner that hath relation to it, though closely* couched." The most indulgent and attentive reader in the world, however, may still be forgiven for wondering if such a claim can validly be made for an essay like *Of Coaches*, where an initial discussion of coaches and chariots leads to a description of the circuses provided for the people by Roman emperors and then, quite unexpectedly, to a bitter polemic against the brutalities of the Spaniards in the New World. Nevertheless, even here the disorder is only apparent; in fact it is carefully calculated to achieve certain ends and to shock the reader into certain truths. For there is a subject which tacitly unites all three, that of "proud pomp and glorious magnificence"; and all is so carefully, if unobtrusively, planned that at the very end of his essay Montaigne is able, by means of a grim anecdote, to reintroduce into his description of the sufferings of the King of Peru the subject of coaches with which he began.

The colloquial style in which the essays are written — a casual style which intensifies our experience of the meandering course of Montaigne's thought — is as deliberate as the lack of formal, logical order in the arrangement of ideas. He claimed that it was actually no style at all, but "a formless and abrupt speech, a popular gibberish, and proceeding without definition, without partition, and sans* conclusion." Earlier in the century, Erasmus' great fool had made the same claim for her speech; both she and Montaigne insist that an unadorned, spontaneous language is "the least mendacious mirror of the mind." Accordingly, the author of the essays composed them in the same language he spoke, without affectation, without polish, making no attempt to avoid slang or gross terms, in order to communicate with us as honestly and as directly as he could; for eloquence, he claimed, not only falsifies our thoughts but draws attention to itself rather than to the content of those thoughts. He chose therefore to write in the language of the Paris marketplace, and he observed that "most of those that converse with me speak like unto these essays" (though he could not refrain from adding that whether or not they thought like them was another question). "My language," he confessed, "is harsh and sharp, having free and unsinewy dispositions; and so it liketh me, if not by my judgment, yet by my inclination." It is precisely this that gives us the powerful impression as we read his words that we are listening to a man thinking aloud — and we may recall, in this connection, Alfred North Whitehead's observation that the highest form of teaching is simply an intelligent man thinking aloud. This is also why we come to feel we know the author of these essays so intimately; for we can perceptibly hear, even across Florio's translation, the tone of his voice, the cadences of his thought, and the very pauses in his breathing. "Cut these words," exclaimed his admirer Emerson, "and they would bleed; they are vascular and alive." Yet if the artlessness of his style is as deliberate an attempt to be honest as the disorganization of his ideas, it is also at times as calculated, and Montaigne disarmingly confesses that there may also be an affectation in avoiding affectation. "I perceive that sometimes I wade too far into it, and that, forcing myself to avoid art and affectation, I fall into it another way."

In the end, he himself was uncertain of what value to give to these trials or experiments of his reason: "As for me, I judge not the worth of another's work more obscurely than of mine own, and place my essays sometime low, sometimes high, very inconstantly and doubtfully." He even claimed, with typical frankness, that such writings as his were nothing more than an indication of the sickness of the age in which he lived and that they probably ought to be forbidden by law:

> But there should be some correction appointed by the laws against foolish and unprofitable writers, as there is against vagabonds and loiterers; so should both myself and a hundred others of our people be banished. It is no mockery. Scribbling seemeth to be a symptom or passion of an irregular and licentious age . . . The corruption of the times we live in is wrought by the particular contribution of every one of us: some confer treason unto it, some injustice, other some irreligion, tyranny, avarice, and cruelty, according as they are more or less powerful; the weaker sort, whereof I am one, impart foolishness, vanity, and idleness unto it.

[5]

In the inscription on his study wall, Montaigne described his retirement in 1571 as a retirement "to the bosom of the learned muses," and it is evident from his early essays that he read extensively during his first years in the tower. As we think of him seated there among the books of his library — a library constituted largely of the classics of Greek and Roman thought — we summon up an image that had characterized the humanist since Petrarch; and we may recall such diverse expressions of this Renaissance ideal as Dürer's etchings of St. Jerome in his study, or the intarsia-covered *studiolo* of Federico da Montefeltro at Urbino, or that well-known letter in which Machiavelli describes his refuge in "the ancient courts of ancient men." Indeed, Machiavelli's description of how he conversed with the authors of antiquity, he questioning and they answering him, how he there forgot his troubles and boredom, poverty and the fear of death, and how he "transferred" himself "wholly into them" is equally appropriate as a description of Montaigne in his library. Like all humanists, he turned to the literature of antiquity not simply for pleasure, but for instruction and wisdom — "to find out the knowledge that teacheth or handleth the knowledge of myself, and which may instruct me how to die well and how to live well."

In Plutarch's *Lives*, which had been translated into French by Jacques Amyot in 1559, Montaigne found numerous accounts of how the great men of the ancient world had lived and died, and if he continually turned to these accounts for guidance in his own life, it was because he considered Plutarch "so perfect and excellent a judge of human actions." Both the *Lives* and the *Moralia* remained two of his favorite books all his life; he claimed that he could hardly be without Plutarch, and the essays are filled with quotations from his works:

> He is so universal and so full that upon all occasions and whatsoever extravagant subject you have undertaken he intrudeth himself into your work and gently reacheth you a help-affording hand, fraught with rare embellishments and inexhaustible of precious riches . . . He can no sooner come in my sight, or if I cast but a glance upon him, but I pull some leg or wing from him.

In addition to Plutarch, however, Montaigne appears to have been particularly drawn to the writings of the Roman Stoics during his first years of retirement, especially to the works of the man Erasmus had bitterly called "that double-Stoic," Seneca, and, to a lesser extent, to the poetry of his nephew Lucan.

Reflecting as they do the ideals of life expounded by these Romans, Montaigne's early essays have commonly been classified as Stoical, and the adjective is appropriate so long as we recognize that in this case it refers to Seneca rather than to Zeno and that it is here not meant to imply a systematic adoption of the Stoic philosophy, but rather an eclectic endorsement of certain Stoic ideals. Most of the essays written during the years 1572–74 consist largely of quotations, anecdotes, and *sententiae* from such writers; they tend to be brief and impersonal, bookish and objective, and they quite obviously reflect the fact that Montaigne is still feeling his way into his form, as yet unaware of what was to become his true subject. Consequently, they have always been considered the least important part of his work and are largely neglected in the present selection; were we to possess nothing else from Montaigne's pen, it is unlikely that he would be much remembered. Nonetheless, it is essential to an appreciation of how his thought developed to realize that this is where he began — to understand, that is, that in his quest for self-knowledge he turned first to those authors who held an ideal vision of man and man's potentialities.

The Stoic ideals expounded in the early essays are ideals which, attempting to lift man above himself, prescribe such virtues as self-restraint, temperance, moderation, the tranquillity of the passions, the glory of reason, nobility of conduct, and courage in the face of death. To Montaigne, such ideals seemed actually to have found their embodiment in the historical figure of Cato the Younger, who is not only the subject of one of the early essays but stands throughout these essays as the hero of Montaigne's initial speculations on the nature of man. Generally, however, in exalting the proper use of right reason in the daily conduct of a man's life and in insisting that a man should preserve an impassive calm when confronted with the blows of Fortune, the Stoic philosophers may be said to have spoken of the ideal rather than the actual, of the artificial rather than the natural. Certainly their emphasis was, in Machiavelli's terminology, upon how men *ought* to live rather than upon how men *do* live. But any philosophy so deeply concerned with life, however hypothetically, must also come to terms with the negation of that life which is death, and the Stoics, in addition to prescribing how a man ought to live, prescribed how he ought to die. More precisely, the Stoics believed that the whole of life was essentially a *praeparatio ad mortem* and that philosophy itself was, as Cicero said, nothing more than the knowledge of how to die.

The longest of the essays composed during this early phase of Montaigne's thought takes this basic tenet of Stoicism for its subject and cites Cicero's aphorism in its opening sentence. In its original form (that written, as he specifically tells us, in March, 1572), the essay *That to Philosophy is to Learn How to Die* appears to have been little more than a *montage* of commonplace precepts on the subject of death — how it is inevitable, how it may take us by surprise at any moment, how it will only happen to us once, how we should learn to meet it courageously by "practicing" it and accustoming ourselves to the idea, how we must strip it of its mask of terror. The essay expounds its Stoic principle at the very outset, "that all the wisdom and discourse of the world doth in the end resolve upon this point, to teach us not to fear to die"; all the rest of the discussion is merely an amplification and explanation of this aphorism, to which Montaigne brings a host of examples and maxims culled from the traditional Stoic considerations of death.

What is interesting, however, is the way in which the author's own personality, which is to figure forth so predominantly in his later essays, already begins to be perceptible here behind his imitative, orthodox treatment of the subject. For while in one sense Montaigne's essay, starting out from Stoic sources, remains essentially Stoical in the calmness with which it contemplates death, in another sense the essay moves away from Stoicism by being deliberately unheroic and uncourageous about death, by admitting its author's personal fears. Death itself, as the essay progresses, becomes a very personal matter, a part of the author's own biography, not just a general phenomenon. What happens in this early essay is symptomatic of what is to happen to all of Montaigne's thought: his ideas, as they develop, invariably describe the same trajectory from the general, objective thought of classical antiquity to the personal, subjective thought of one man.

Though it is to anticipate somewhat, one must also point out at this juncture that, later, Montaigne's thoughts about death changed completely. For as he drew nearer to his own death, he came to realize more and more that it was life — the pleasures of living and not the pains of death — that really mattered. One may observe this tendency within this very essay, where almost without exception the additions made to the text after 1588 are about life, not death. As he goes on thinking about the problem and adding to his original discussion, thoughts of life and pleasure seep into Montaigne's somber meditation on death, visibly changing its color. The very first addition he makes announces that pleasure is our goal in life, and this is almost immediately followed by the long passage on the virtue of pleasure — a word, he *now* confesses, with which he takes malicious delight in boxing the ears of the Stoics. Originally, the purpose of his essay was to teach men to live so that they would know how to die; but now, in another late addition, he says he would like to compose a book "which, in teaching men to die, should after teach them to live." And it is a poignant warning from old age that cries out in an addition near the end:

> The profit of life consists not in the space but rather in the use. Some man hath lived long that hath had a short life. Follow it whilst you have time! It consists not in number of years, but in your will, that you have lived long enough.

Even the most celebrated Stoical remark in the essay undergoes a remarkable change from its initial version as a result of an addition made late in Montaigne's life:

> [A]I would have a man to be doing, [C]*and to prolong his life's offices as much as lieth in him,* [A]and let death seize upon me whilst I am setting my cabbages, careless of her dart but more of my unperfect garden.

In one of his last essays, *Of Physiognomy,* he returns to the subject of death once more and gives us what is perhaps his final opinion. But by now he is much more familiar with death, being closer to it himself and having witnessed the ravages of the plague and the horrors of the religious wars from the very windows of his tower. Whereas he had formerly said that we should constantly have death before our eyes and had ridiculed those who did not prepare for it in advance, here he recognizes that we may "trouble life with the care of death," and he deems a lack of concern about the approach of death to be the highest philosophy. He has come to look upon the meditation on death in quite a different light, and he is critical of the very sentence from Cicero upon which he had based his earlier discussion:

> They may brag as much as they please. "The whole life of a philosopher is the meditation of his death" (Cic. *Tusc.* I.30). But methinks it is indeed the end, yet not the scope of life. It is her last, it is her extremity, yet not her object. Herself must be unto herself, her aim, her drift, and her design. Her direct study is to order, to direct, and to suffer herself.

And in another of the late essays he sums up his feelings by saying: "The happy life, in my opinion, not (as said Antisthenes) the happy death, is it that makes man's happiness in this world."

[6]

If the idea of death seems to have had such a vivid personal importance for Montaigne, that is not simply because of his own personality or because he saw so much death about him, but above all because death had deprived him of his closest friend, Étienne de la Boétie. This was the greatest single blow of Montaigne's life, and compared to it every other adversity seemed to him slight and insignificant. Montaigne had actually been present at his deathbed and had heard La Boétie call to him with his last breath; in a moving letter to his father which we still possess he recounts in detail the Stoic fortitude with which his friend faced the approach of death. Montaigne's own interest in Stoicism in the years immediately following La Boétie's death seems, in fact, to have been in emulation of his friend, who had explicitly attempted to pattern his life after the precepts of that philosophy. Yet the effect of the acquaintance with La Boétie extended far beyond mere philosophical emulation: the memory of this profound friendship remained with Montaigne all his life, and the experience tinged the very fiber of his being. Indeed, we cannot begin to understand either the author or the content of the *Essays* until we have managed to achieve some understanding of the significance of this relationship.

Yet there is a serious question as to how much of it we actually can hope to understand. Montaigne himself, considering the relationship to be without parallel, was exceedingly dubious of the ability of anyone else to comprehend it: I should wish, he remarked, "to speak to such as had tried what I speak of; but knowing how far such an amity is from the common use and how seld* seen and rarely found, I look not to find a competent judge." Even the celebrated accounts of friendship left to us by classical antiquity seemed to him pale and weak in comparison with the feeling he had for La Boétie. He was also aware that one could not even approach an understanding of their relationship if one had not enjoyed the experience of some sort of close friendship, however inferior; for such relationships become comprehensible only insofar as we can interpret them out of our own personal experience, not through abstract explanations — "even as he that was found riding upon an hobby-horse, playing with his children, besought him who thus surprised him not to speak of it until he were a father himself."

Moreover, it seems probable that the modern reader will find the experience Montaigne describes even more remote and incomprehensible than his own contemporaries would have; for we live in an age which no longer confers the same value upon friendship between two men and in which such friendships as that described by Montaigne may in fact be hardly possible, as D. H. Lawrence suggests in one of the most penetrating works of modern fiction. To reread the last page of *Women in Love* is to be reminded of the effort of historical imagination required of us if we would comprehend the significance his friendship with La Boétie had for Montaigne. For what may seem to us something of an oddity — what seems to Ursula Brangwen "false, impossible" — was to the Renaissance the highest ideal of human relationship, and of the many things from the world of Greece and Rome that age tried to revive and emulate, not the least was the classical concept of perfect friendship — a fact attested to by a large portion of Renaissance literature, especially drama, and by such expressions as the proud boast of Fulke Greville's famous epitaph. That such friendships no longer represent the ideal they did either to Montaigne's or the ancient world is, of course, the result of the far greater value we place on perfect marriage; yet we must remember that the ideal concept of marriage invoked today is a modern phenomenon which was still only inchoate in the late Renaissance. To Thomas Aquinas, marriage was only one form, and a rather subordinate form at that, of *amicitia*. He derived this disposition, like so much else, from Aristotle; but acknowledging his source only emphasizes the fact that whenever the Middle Ages or the Renaissance looked to the classical world for emulative models of perfection in human relationships they found there almost no models for ideal marriage, but instead models for ideal friendship. Accordingly, Montaigne himself calls friendship the ultimate point in the perfection of society. The kind of communion we now hope for from marriage was almost inconceivable to earlier ages, which aspired instead to achieve an analogous relationship in friendship; and while we may not regret the change that has taken place, we must nevertheless recognize that it is a change if we are to see Montaigne's friendship with La Boétie in its proper perspective.

Like love, friendship of this order demands a basic surrender of the self to the other person. If we wish to appreciate the intensity of this experience for Montaigne, we must also try to imagine what such a surrender must have meant to a person of his particular temperament. The man who could so easily be alone in a crowd, who admitted to a certain "coolness" in his dealings with the world, who claimed that he "lent," not gave himself to others — when such a man finally did give himself to another, he must have given himself completely. Whether out of fear or pride, embarrassment or insecurity, each of us inevitably reserves a part of himself, however small, to himself alone; because we guard it so anxiously, we are only able to reveal or bestow it, if at all, in the ultimate generosity of love. And the heart, defensive in its vulnerability, does not often take the risk such commitments involve. Montaigne himself was presumably more wary than many of taking such risks. Yet once in his life he made such a commitment; to one person he opened the door of the room behind the shop and bade him come in, and there they shared that complete communication which is the profoundest relationship one man can have with another.

The experience of such a friendship was so overwhelming for Montaigne that he could never forget it; similarly, the termination of that experience with the death of his friend was so shattering a blow that he never really recovered from it. A quarter of a century later he wrote that "a wise man seeth little less his friend dying at the end of five and twenty years than at the beginning of the first year"; and he was to claim that what consolation he had found was simply that of knowing that he had not forgotten to tell his friend anything, that he had had "a perfect and free communication" with him. For, as he had said earlier, "friendship is nourished by communication." And in his old age he wrote into the margin of his book, in a passage that was later mysteriously crossed out by another hand and hence was unknown to Florio, this moving *cri du coeur:*

> Three and four times happy is the man who can entrust his pitiful old age to the hands of a friend . . . O my friend! Am I better off for having tasted it [friendship], or am I worse off? Surely I am better off. Missing him consoles and honors me. Is it not a pious and pleasant duty of my life to be forever performing his obsequies? Is there any enjoyment which is worth this deprivation?

It has been said, however, that we owe the existence of the essays to this very deprivation — that they are, in effect, the letters Montaigne would have written to his friend had Étienne de la Boétie lived. As if in confirmation, he himself explains in one of the essays that he would have cast his thoughts into the form of letters if he had had someone to whom he might have addressed them. It may indeed help us to understand the nature of these essays if we see them as letters that attempt to continue after death the perfect communication these two men had shared in life — letters, in the image of the modern Greek poet Seferis, "cast into the void of separation to fill it."

What is particularly important for an understanding of Montaigne's thought, however, is not simply the fact that this unforgettable experience stands behind everything he wrote, but that it was an experience he could not rationally understand. "If a man urge me to tell wherefore I loved him," he confessed, "I feel it cannot be expressed but by answering: because it was he, because it was myself." He cannot explain it; he can only acknowledge it. In this respect, his friendship with La Boétie takes on a special significance as perhaps the only experience of his life which he was unable to subject to the analytic powers of his reason. He was forced to recognize that this overwhelming experience was beyond the comprehension or analysis of reason, that, as Pascal was later aphoristically to put it, the heart has its reasons that reason does not know. It was, in the last analysis, the major and fundamental experience of his life which provided him with an awareness of metaphysical truth. Everything else he attempted to understand from his observation, but this he could not; he could only stand back and admit that it had happened. And his only explanation of why or how it had happened, ineffably moving though it is, is in effect no explanation at all: "because it was he, because it was myself."

Though he could give no explanation of this experience and was unable himself to understand it in any rational way, Montaigne does attempt to describe it in his great essay *Of Friendship*, which is in many respects the most beautiful of all the essays. There is no way of determining with any precision when this essay was composed, but one is tempted to conjecture that Montaigne wrote it sometime nearer 1580 than 1571. It would, in any case, seem to provide some sort of transition from the bookish, Stoic essays of the early period; for unlike them, it draws its force from lived experience and suggests the first outlines of that personal portrait which is to become the central subject of the later essays. Despite the title, this is not a discussion of friendship in general so much as a description of one particular friendship which was unique and intensely personal. It is one of the finest tributes to a human relationship in the world's literature.

At the outset, Montaigne attempts to distinguish carefully between friendship and other forms of love, and these distinctions are important insofar as they help to define, if negatively, this experience which he found ultimately undefinable. Although he himself had been exceptionally close to his father, he realized that familial relationships were not always dictated by love. The love of children for their fathers, he says, "may rather be termed respect"; that between brothers is largely created by custom. Kinship, in fact, does not necessarily cause love, and we may have to admit that "he is my son, he is my kinsman; but he may be a fool, a bad, or a peevish-minded fellow." The difference between erotic love and friendship is fundamental, and Montaigne's analysis of it is at once psychologically penetrating and revealing:

> the affection toward women . . . is a rash and wavering fire, waving and diverse: the fire of an ague subject to fits and stints and that hath but slender hold-fast* of us. In true friendship it is a general and universal heat and equally tempered, a constant and settled heat, all pleasure and smoothness, that hath no pricking or stinging in it.

And as for marriage, it cannot be compared with friendship because one cannot hope to achieve the same kind of communication with a woman that one can with a man. This passage, which, we are amused to discover, so troubled George Sand, not only makes explicit the different concept of women and marriage held in the sixteenth century, but also explains a great deal about Montaigne's own attitude toward his wife: "the ordinary sufficiency of women," he explains, "cannot answer this conference and communication, the nurse of this sacred bond; nor seem their minds strong enough to endure the pulling of a knot so hard, so fast and durable." Nor finally, he says, should friendship be confused with homosexuality, in favor of which the only thing that can be said is that sometimes "it was a love ending in friendship." Occasionally readers of Montaigne, confronted with the exceptional quality of his friendship, have attempted, whether out of predilection or lack of comprehension, to suggest that the relationship between him and La Boétie was essentially an erotic, homosexual one. But even to entertain this possibility is to miss the point entirely, for part of what Montaigne explicitly esteemed in their relationship was the absence of the storms of physical desire; and we should always recall the strictures he expresses about this "Greek license . . . justly abhorred by our customs."

When he turns to evoke the love he had actually experienced in friendship, he comes face to face with the realization that he can never articulate all he felt nor hope fully to be understood by his reader. Though one may indeed not wholly comprehend in the deepest sense, nevertheless one cannot fail to be impressed by the completeness of the rapport he claims to have enjoyed with La Boétie — not simply a total communication, but an actual sharing and intermingling of minds and wills:

> In the amity I speak of [our minds] intermix and confound themselves one in the other, with so universal a commixture that they wear out and can no more find the seam that hath conjoined them together . . . Our minds have jumped so unitedly together, they have with so fervent an affection considered each other, and with like affection so discovered and sounded, even to the very bottom of each other's entrails, that I did not only know his as well as mine own, but I would verily rather have trusted him concerning any matter of mine than myself.

In this respect, he finds even the exemplary story of Blossius and Gracchus recounted by Cicero in his discussion of friendship to be deficient as an analogue, and he concludes that the friendship he shared with La Boétie has no other model than itself and can be compared only with itself.

Equally impressive is his description of the generosity such love engendered between them, a generosity so complete that in any interchange it would be the recipient who conferred the favor upon the donor, "giving his friend that contentment to effect towards him what he desireth most." Yet in the end, since there was in fact no *meum* and *tuum*, there was actually no possibility of giving or lending; the essential gift, that of the self, had already been made by both. Accordingly, there is a profound selflessness experienced by Montaigne in this relationship, the surest measure of which is found not in this but in one of the last essays, where he returns once more to this subject:

> In truly perfect friendship, wherein I presume to have some skill and well-grounded experience, I give myself more unto my friend than I draw him unto me. I do not only rather love to do him good than he should do any to me, but also, that he should rather do good unto himself than unto me; for then doth he me most good when he doth it to himself. And if absence be either pleasing or beneficial unto him, it is to me much more pleasing than his presence.

All love essentially involves a kind of giving; but it is a rare form of love which is so selfless as to be willing to give the other person away if it will benefit him. However generous, love and friendship customarily ask at least the presence of the other person; but Montaigne's feeling was so deep that he was prepared to forego even that.

And death, of course, did finally deprive him of that presence, leaving him alone in "a dark and irksome night." In the concluding pages of his tribute he attempts to communicate his sense of loss, explaining that there is no thought or action in his life in which he does not miss his friend, and that "I was so accustomed ever to be two, and so inured to be never single, that methinks I am but half myself." In a world where he felt everything was uncertain and unstable, where life itself, he said, "is a motion unequal, irregular, multiform," his friendship with La Boétie had seemed to him the one fixed, immutable, transcendent point to which all else could be referred. To the end, he was unsure even of himself, but not of this friendship. That is why the memory of it remained with him always and informed everything he ever wrote.

One small, but poignant, indication of the powerful persistence of that memory is found, years later, in an entry of his travel journal. It is Thursday, the 11th of May, 1581, eighteen years after La Boétie's death, and Montaigne is in Tuscany, at the baths of La Villa near Lucca, attempting to find a cure for the agonizing kidney stones that so tormented his last years. In the midst of the most frank, dispassionate, clinical description of the progress of his cure — so characteristic of this honest man — nostalgia for his lost friend suddenly sweeps over him:

> Thursday morning I drank five more pounds of the water, in some fear that it might do me harm and that I might not be able to pass it. It caused me to have a bowel movement and to urinate a very little, and this same morning, while writing to M. Ossat, I fell to thinking of M. de la Boétie, and the thought was so bitter and held me so long without my being able to shake it off that it caused me great pain.

[7]

In late 1579 or early 1580, writing to Madame Diane de Foix on the subject of how children should be educated, Montaigne prescribed that "this great universe, which some multiply as species under one genus, is the true looking-glass wherein we must look if we will know whether we be of a good stamp or in the right bias; to conclude, I would have this world's frame be my scholar's choice book." It is a remark that reminds us of the windows in the tower, of the shop in front of the "storehouse." If the intense introspection of the meditations on solitude and death and friendship has a tendency to emphasize the seclusion of the room behind the shop, there are other essays which make us much more conscious of the shop itself. Whereas in the one kind of essay we seem to see Montaigne sitting in his tower conversing with himself and with the dead authors of classical antiquity, in the other we have an image of him going out into the world, conversing with the members of his household and the peasants on his estate, with the nobles who came to visit him, with the soldiers fighting nearby, with the king himself. For we should recall that during this period he held the title of Gentleman of the Chamber to Henri III and had a similar title bestowed upon him by Henri of Navarre; we also know that sometime after the dreadful Massacre of St. Bartholomew's Day in 1572 he had attempted to mediate between the Protestant and Catholic leaders. He was, in fact, extremely conscious of the world around him and endlessly fascinated by what he saw in the looking-glass of "this great universe." His allusion, in speaking of the universe, to the possible plurality of worlds may remind us as well that in his time a whole new world actually had been discovered, and it is in meditating upon this fact, in such essays as *Of the Cannibals* and *Of Coaches,* that his gaze looks farthest out from those windows in the tower.

"This discovery of so infinite and vast a country seemeth worthy of consideration," he announces as he turns his attention to the New World. Far more important than the geographical discovery, however, was the discovery that this new world was inhabited, that there had been a whole civilization existing of which men had known nothing. It is exactly as if we were to discover tomorrow that there was life on the moon, but a life quite different from ours. Now, such sudden confrontations of civilizations and cultures are always momentous events; for to find that there are other people living in quite a different way from ourselves, relying upon quite different assumptions and aspirations, can do enormous damage to one's beliefs about the very nature of man. Moreover, as cultural anthropologists know, nothing is more disturbing in such confrontations than the discovery of variations in eschatology: what we think about death and what we do with our dead form some of our profoundest beliefs and go to the depths of our cultural consciousness. This is, of course, less true of us today, precisely because those cultural anthropologists have given us a certain relativistic sophistication. We acknowledge that some people burn their dead and others bury theirs, and the disparity does not especially disturb us; to find that the natives of New Guinea use their fathers' skulls as pillows is to us more interesting than upsetting. But to less sophisticated peoples, the concept of right and wrong immediately enters in, and any variation in eschatology is horribly wrong.

A story recounted by Herodotus supplies an archetypal illustration of such cultural confrontations:

> When Darius had become king he summoned certain Greeks who happened to be present and asked them how much money they would take to eat the corpses of their fathers. They replied that no amount could make them do such a thing. Darius then summoned certain Indians named Callatians and asked them, in the presence of the Greeks, who understood by means of an interpreter, how much money they would take to burn the corpses of their fathers. But they cried aloud and bade him not speak of such a dreadful thing.

The impact of such an experience, beyond the immediate shock it occasioned, can easily be imagined. When they had returned to their homes, neither the Greeks nor the Callatians could have felt quite the same about how they disposed of their dead; having assumed that what they did was natural, they had come to discover that it actually had nothing to do with human nature, but merely with human customs. Each would no doubt have continued to call the other's custom barbarous, but the word could not have had the same force.

Originally, the Greek word *barbaros* had meant simply "non-Greek"; and though the word came to have more highly charged emotional connotations, it could still, upon examination, be demonstrated to have remained essentially chauvinistic: "men," observes Montaigne, "call that barbarism which is not common to them." That is why, in the famous essay *Of the Cannibals,* he questions whether or not we have a right to call the savages of the New World barbarians. "Lo," he counsels, "how a man ought to take heed lest he overweeningly follow vulgar opinions, which should be measured by the rule of reason and not by the common report." Applying that rule of reason — the natural faculties within him — he finds, of course, that the inhabitants of the New World are in many respects more noble and humane and virtuous than their French counterparts. Those forms of civilization of which the Frenchman boasts at the expense of the Indian have perhaps only corrupted and weakened him; and we can only call these savages "wild" in the same sense that we call wild those products of nature man has not artificially changed. As for their most barbarous quality, that they eat their dead enemies, well, says Montaigne in a bitter outcry,

> I am not sorry we note the barbarous horror of such an action, but grieved that, prying so narrowly into their faults we are so blinded in ours. I think there is more barbarism in eating men alive than to feed upon them being dead; to mangle by tortures and torments a body full of lively sense; to roast him in pieces; to make dogs and swine to gnaw and tear him in mammocks* (as we have not only read but seen very lately, yea and in our own memory, not amongst ancient enemies but our neighbors and fellow-citizens; and, which is worse, under pretense of piety and religion), than to roast and eat him after he is dead . . . We may then well call them barbarous in regard of reason's rules, but not in respect of us that exceed them in all kinds of barbarism.

He echoes a verse from Lucretius which was on the lips of many men during the time of these brutal wars of religion: *tantum religio potuit suadere malorum!*

As the essay progresses, Montaigne speaks more and more about the beauty of the lives of these people, their natural simplicity, their valor in warfare, their loves and friendships, the nobility of their characters. "Surely," he exclaims with acerb irony, "in respect of us these are very savages; for either they must be so in good sooth, or we must be so indeed: there is a wondrous difference between their form and ours!" Yet there is one basic difference between the Frenchman and the Indian which Montaigne very carefully does not mention, though it tacitly lurks behind everything he says. What are those "vulgar opinions" he asks us to question at the beginning of his essay? That the Indians are barbarians because they eat their dead, to be sure. But there is another "vulgar opinion" which is far more important, so important that he does not dare emphasize it; for it is nothing less than the Christian doctrine that these people are not only barbarians but eternally damned because they have not been baptized.

Less than three hundred years earlier, Dante had speculated about similar Indians. Let us imagine, he proposed to the eagle of God's justice in the heaven of Jupiter, that a man is born on the banks of the Indus River, where Christ is completely unknown and there is no possibility for him to be a Christian. Let us further suppose that this man is a good man, "as far as human reason can see," in all his wishes and acts, unsinning in his deeds or his words. But he dies unbaptized, without faith. "Where," demanded Dante, "is the justice that damns him? What fault is it of his if he does not believe?" The response given by the eagle is somewhat startling, for it does not attempt to answer the question but is instead an injunction that Dante should, so to speak, mind his own business:

> Who do you think you are, wishing to sit in the seat of judgment and judge over a distance of a thousand miles with the short sight of but a span? Truly, if the Scripture were not over you, to the man who would investigate subtleties with me the occasion for doubt would be marvelous to behold. O earthbound animals! O ignorant minds!

Such matters, the eagle explains, are not for the human mind to decide; what is more, one must not even ask if God's decrees are just, because God *is* Justice and justice is defined *by* whatever God decrees.

Though he is not arguing about the ultimate salvation of the inhabitants of the New World, in a sense Montaigne is trying to do exactly what Dante had been told he must not do: he is attempting to decide about the cannibals solely on the basis of his own reason, avoiding the salient fact that they are not Christians. Doubtless he is also suggesting, in the manner of Thomas More's *Utopia,* that if the inhabitants of a world where Christianity is unknown can be so good and virtuous, the Christians of Europe, with the advantage of divine grace, ought to be that much better. Yet Montaigne has put God aside for the moment, asking us to judge these people "as far as human reason can see"; he has taken the issue out from under the canopy of Scripture of which the eagle had spoken. And as the eagle had predicted, this creates a powerful occasion for doubt. When the cannibals are placed next to the Frenchmen without the third point of reference which is God's word, we experience the same relativistic phenomenon we all have known in railway stations when the train next to ours begins to move. For a moment, until we have consulted some third point of reference — the platform or the station — we do not know which train is moving; similarly, with the cannibal and the Frenchman it is hard to tell who is really the barbarian.

As it attempts to read in the book of "this world's frame" and decide "whether we be of a good stamp or in the right bias," reason, relying solely upon itself, unaided by belief or dogma or Scripture, finds that there are many variant readings in that text between which it is at a loss to decide. The lesson it derives is more often one of doubt than of certainty. Not only is the text itself complex, confused, contradictory, but our natural faculties for apprehending the truth of that book are often either insufficient or themselves confused, because, as Montaigne explains in another essay written at this time, "we taste nothing pure." There has rarely been a time when the world presented more basic questions to reason than Montaigne's own age, and the relativistic confrontation of the New World with the old is merely one example of the many dilemmas that reason was called upon to resolve. The very nature of belief had been brought into question by the Protestant Reformation. In the wars of religion two mutually exclusive truths confronted each other in bitter battle, and even that Scripture which might have decided the issue was found to be capable of two contrary interpretations. If earth presented the paradox of cannibal *versus* Frenchman, heaven presented the even greater paradox of Protestant *versus* Catholic. Even the physical order of that heaven and that earth was doubtful, and reason was asked to decide whether the book of this great universe in which it was reading was Ptolemaic or Copernican, whether man the reader stood at the center of that universe or whether he himself was caught up in its endless, unstable motion. It is not surprising to learn that Montaigne, who was so obsessed with the idea of motion, appears to have been one of the first thinkers to take Copernicus seriously. "The world," he was later to conclude in despair, "runs all on wheels. All things therein move without intermission, yea, the earth, the rocks of Caucasus, and the pyramids of Egypt, both with the public and their own motion. Constancy itself is nothing but a languishing and wavering dance."

Faced with such relativistic uncertainty, Montaigne became increasingly dubious of his reason's capacity to determine or resolve anything, and this dubiety is symbolized by the medallion he had struck for himself in January or February of 1576, on one side of which was shown a pair of scales in perfect balance and the word ἐπέχω (I suspend my judgment) and on the other side his best remembered motto, *Que Sçay je?* (What do I know?). How can one judge when one can be sure of almost nothing, when, as he was to admit several years later, "there is almost nothing that I wot I know"? How can one hope to arrive at truth with reason alone, which in itself is defective and uncertain, at best "a two-edged, dangerous sword"? The very complexity of human experience demonstrated that any dogmatic assertion was bound to be a gross oversimplification. As he tried, and failed, to sort out such complexities with his rational powers, the noble claims made for human reason by the Stoics began to seem more and more overly ambitious and unjustified to Montaigne. "Let him be as wise as he can," he says of the philosopher, "in the end he is but a man: what is more frail, more miserable, or more vain?" In the essay *Of Drunkenness*, where this remark appears, Montaigne has already begun to express considerable dissatisfaction and impatience with that Stoic concept of man to which he had originally been attracted. Less tempted now by theories of what man ought to be, he turns his attention instead to a consideration of what man actually is. To his despair, he is forced to conclude that man is nothing.

This conclusion appears to have been in large part the result of Montaigne's discovery at this time, around 1576, of the classical statement of skepticism, Sextus Empiricus' *Pyrrhonian Hypotyposes,* which had been translated into French by Henri Étienne in 1562. The intense skepticism of this book served to confirm Montaigne's growing doubts and lead him into that Pyrrhonism for which he was later to be best known, especially in the nineteenth century: it is with reference to this phase of Montaigne's philosophical development that Herman Melville coined the verb "to Montaignize" and the noun "Montaignism," and it is this Pyrrhonist who is host to the hero of Walter Pater's unfinished romance *Gaston de Latour*. If we are less disposed today to see this as the final phase of Montaigne's thought, we must nonetheless acknowledge its central, catalytic importance. Emphasizing the relativism of all things and the impotence of human reason, Pyrrhonism claims that there is no absolute truth attainable by man and that hence no moral judgments of right and wrong are possible. As a result, it is a skepticism so extreme that it will not even assert (since no assertions are possible) that man cannot know; it remains instead in an attitude of perpetual ephectic suspension by insisting that man cannot even know whether he knows or not. It is above all by restating for the modern world this classical skepticism that Montaigne has managed to have such a predominant influence on later thought — an influence so great that T. S. Eliot has claimed, "it is hardly too much to say that Montaigne is the most essential author to know if we would understand the course of French thought during the last three hundred years."

Montaigne gave his most extensive expression of this Pyrrhonism in the longest of his essays, *An Apology of Raymond Sebond,* which was presumably begun about 1576. It was probably at this time as well that he had the inscriptions placed on the beams of his library ceiling, a large proportion of which are skeptical in content and over a third of which found their way into the text of the *Apology.*

About a century and a half earlier, at the height of *quattrocento* optimism about the nature of man, the Spanish theologian Raymond Sebond had written the treatise *Natural Theology* which, earlier in his life, Montaigne had translated at his father's request. Sebond's book, which, according to Montaigne, "undertaketh by human and natural reasons to establish and verify all the articles of Christian religion against atheists," had exalted the powers of human reason, claiming that reason was capable of understanding everything, of comprehending even the Christian mysteries and, in effect, God Himself. By thus transferring to reason what had been traditionally ascribed to faith, Sebond left himself open to attack, and Montaigne begins his defense by answering what he considers the two major objections that had been made to Sebond. The first charge leveled against him by his detractors amounted to an accusation of heresy: matters of belief, they said, must be based upon faith and divine inspiration, not upon human reason. The second objection made to Sebond's argument was that he had failed to demonstrate what he had claimed, that his book had not, in the end, been able to prove the truths of faith simply by the light of reason. Montaigne's rejoinder to the first is brief but gives important indications about his own religious position: he admits that reason alone cannot prove the truths of religion, but he insists that the Christian ought nevertheless to employ his reason as far as he can — though just how far that is seems dubious in view of his subsequent observations. As for the second objection, it may be true, he says, that Sebond failed to prove his case by reason; but it is also true that reason cannot prove he did not. The fault lies not with Sebond but with reason itself; for, as he proceeds to demonstrate, reason can prove nothing.

Having reached this point in his defense, Montaigne turns aside from the subject of Sebond and takes up the true subject of this extended meditation, which is nothing less than the abject feebleness and insufficiency of human reason. "Let us now but consider man alone," he begins, "without other help, armed but with his own weapons, and unprovided of the grace and knowledge of God, which is all his honor, all his strength, and all the ground of his being." In the famous passage that follows — a passage which Hamlet would appear to have read — he boldly strips man of all his pretenses and presumption and reduces him to the level of other animals. Just as he had invidiously compared the French to the cannibals, so here he compares rational man to his irrational fellow-creatures, and man emerges no better than the Frenchmen had. Assembling an astonishing number of anecdotes about the behavior of beasts, he demonstrates that they are just as good and just as bad as man himself; if there is a demonstrable difference, it is generally in the animals' favor, and Montaigne cites numerous cases where they have demonstrated better faith, honor, kindness, and love than their human brothers. Even our concept of an anthropomorphic God is brilliantly ridiculed as an example of unwarranted human pride:

> Therefore Xenophanes said pleasantly that if beasts frame any gods unto themselves, as likely it is that they do, they surely frame them like unto themselves and glorify themselves as we do. For why may not a goose say thus: "All parts of the world behold me: the earth serveth me to tread upon, the sun to give me light, the stars to inspire me with influence; this commodity I have of the winds, and this benefit of the waters; there is nothing that this world's vault doth so favorably look upon as myself; I am the favorite of nature. Is it not man that careth for me, that keepeth me, lodgeth me, and serveth me? For me it is he soweth, reapeth, and grindeth. If he eats me, so doth man feed on his fellow, and so do I on the worms that consume and eat him."

Turning from the comparison between man and animals, he proceeds to consider knowledge itself, examining our claims for it. We pride ourselves on our knowledge and our understanding. But what, he asks, *do* we understand? We possess no certain truth, and even our science admits that it really does not understand. Knowledge also causes us more pain than happiness, annoys us more than it helps us; and in a passage added just after his return from Italy in 1581 he cites the terrible example of Torquato Tasso, whose madness he had witnessed with horror at Ferrara, claiming that it was the "killing vivacity" of his mind that had destroyed him — and, incidentally, thus drawing the first sketch of that Romantic portrait which was later to be executed in more lavish detail by Goethe and Baudelaire, Daumier and Cherbuliez. The weakness of the knowledge we boast of, he goes on, is that it is based on reason, and reason is nothing: it is contradictory and uncertain, changing from man to man, from minute to minute. As for that knowledge which is derived from the senses, it is evident that our senses often deceive us. We only have five, and that is probably not enough; the sensory capacities of animals are generally better than our own. Man can, in short, have no knowledge. How can he hope to comprehend the changing universe when he is caught up in that very mutability? Even more, how can he hope to comprehend the immutability of God?

All we can hope to know, Montaigne concludes, is the Socratic lesson that we know nothing. Caught as we are in the endlessly changing motion of all things, if we can achieve any transcendence it is not through our own powers but through the grace of God. At the end of several hundred pages of this deeply skeptical, pessimistic essay, we are left with a miserable picture of helpless man, which reminds us of nothing so much as Lear's painful cry of recognition when he confronts the naked figure of mad Tom o' Bedlam cowering on the stormy heath of the world:

> Is man no more than this? Consider him well. Thou ow'st the worm no silk, the beast no hide, the sheep no wool, the cat no perfume. Ha! here's three on 's are sophisticated; thou art the thing itself; unaccommodated man is no more but such a poor, bare, forked animal as thou art.

That we should be reminded of this poignant passage from *King Lear* is no accident; for Shakespeare found his source for these words in Florio's translation of *An Apology of Raymond Sebond.*

[8]

In 1580, nine years after he had retired to his tower, Montaigne published at Bordeaux the first two books of his essays, prefixing to them the charming preface to the reader in which he already admits that he himself is the real subject of his book and advises its would-be buyer that "it is then no reason thou shouldst employ thy time about so frivolous and vain a subject." Several months later, after having taken part in the seige of the Protestant-held town of La Fère, where he presented a copy of his book to the king, Henri III, he set out, accompanied by his brother, several friends, and servants, on a prolonged trip to Germany, Switzerland, and Italy, which was to occupy the next seventeen months. The purpose of the trip was twofold: he went for pleasure, because he was, as he tells us, exceedingly fond of travel, and he also hoped, by visiting the various spas of Europe, to find some relief from the terrible malady of kidney stones which had first struck him in 1578 and of which he gives a painful, detailed description in his essay *Of the Resemblance Between Children and Fathers.* The journal he kept of this voyage, part in French and part in Italian, some of it in his own hand and some of it dictated to a secretary, was never intended for publication and was actually not discovered until 1770.

The *Travel Journal* provides an intimate picture of Montaigne *en voyage,* though, interestingly enough, hardly more intimate than the portrait he prepared for publication. There are no surprises in these notes he kept only for himself, and he is franker here about only one thing, the intense suffering that his illness caused him. Though he alludes to this from time to time in the *Essays,* it is only from the journal that we realize just how constant and severe his pain was and how tormented it made his sleepless nights; at one moment he appears even to have contemplated suicide as a release. Throughout, these pages are informed with that acute observation and intense interest in the world about him that are so characteristic of this man and which, as a result, make him an exceptionally fine cicerone. Accordingly, they are of as much interest to the social historian as to the student of Montaigne, and we come away from them with a much more vivid picture of what daily life in the late sixteenth century was like. The descriptions of his sojourn in Rome are perhaps the most interesting, and in retrospect one remembers best his accounts of the Papal court and his encounters with the Vatican censors, his interest in the famous Roman prostitutes, his attendance at the execution of a thief and at the circumcision of a Jewish child, his description of the Russian ambassador, and, above all, his meditations upon the ruins of Rome, which, he said, were not its ruins but its sepulcher, for he maintained that there was nothing left of that great city but the plan of its site and the sky under which it had stood. Sainte-Beuve, in an essay on this journal, has summed up what every reader has felt when he wrote:

> What a charming, agreeable, pleasant traveler this man of the study was, who had in him the stuff of many men. How naturally happy and curious he was, open to everything, detached from himself and his household, astute, purged of all foolishness and every prejudice! And what serenity — indeed, what cheerfulness — even in suffering and difficulty, what courtesy to all comers, what good sense everywhere, what strength of intellect, what a feeling for grandeur when the occasion demanded, what boldness and also what shrewdness in him! I call Montaigne "the wisest Frenchman who ever lived."

During his second stay at the baths of Lucca in September, 1581, he received word that he had been elected Mayor of Bordeaux, an office he had not sought but which he accepted at the urging of the king himself. The term of office was for two years, but at the end of his first term he was re-elected for a second, and in the essay *How*

One Ought to Govern His Will he describes his attitude towards this office. As his re-election would seem to confirm, he appears to have been an excellent mayor, and the few letters we have from this period reveal him as a busy, conscientious public servant. Though it was a demanding position, especially because of problems arising from the wars of religion, he managed nevertheless to spend a great deal of time at his estate, where he was visited in 1584 by Henri of Navarre, the heir to the French throne; and when, near the end of his second term, the plague broke out in Bordeaux, he did not re-enter the city — an action for which he was severely criticized in the nineteenth century, but about which there is something to be said on both sides. A few months later he was forced to take his household away from Montaigne, where the plague had also struck, and he speaks in one of the essays of the wretchedness of these six months of fearful peregrination. Upon his return to his château, probably at the end of 1586, he discovered that the war was raging all around his estate, and because he held a moderate position in this conflict he found that he was considered suspect by the extremists in both camps. In a passage that may remind us of a modern poet who watched another civil war from another tower, Montaigne describes in the essay *Of Physiognomy* the despair with which he witnessed the soldiers and marauders on his lands. Nevertheless, his friendship with both the Catholic and Protestant leaders and his wise refusal to billet the troops of either side ensured him a certain safety, and he was later to speak of the miraculous way in which his estate and household had escaped the ravages of this devastating conflict.

By 1588 Montaigne had completed the essays of the third book and had made over six hundred additions to the earlier ones, largely quotations from other authors. "My book," he insisted, "is always one; except that" — he went on to explain — "according as the printer goes about to renew it, that the buyers depart not altogether empty-handed, I give myself law to add thereto, as it is but uncoherent, checky, or ill-joined inlaid work, some supernumeral emblem. They are but overweights, which disgrace not the first form but give some particular price unto every one of the succeeding, by an ambitious, petty subtlety." In another place he explains why the essays of the third book are so much longer than the earlier ones:

> Forsomuch as the often breaking of my chapters I so much used in the beginning of my book seemed to interrupt attention before it be conceived, disdaining for so little a while to collect and there seat itself, I have betaken myself to frame them longer, as requiring proposition and assigned leisure. In such an occupation, he to whom you will not grant one hour, you will allow him nothing.

He went to Paris in this year, presumably to supervise the publication of the first three-volume edition of the *Essays,* but perhaps also on some governmental mission of negotiation between the Protestants and Catholics about which we are ill-informed. We do know that he was briefly imprisoned in the Bastille by the League on July 10, 1588, but he was released almost immediately upon the orders of the Queen Mother, Catherine de' Medici. It was at this time also that he first met his devoted admirer, Marie de Gournay, whom he subsequently made his "daughter by alliance" and who became his literary executrix. Three years after his death, she was responsible for the first complete edition of the *Essays* in 1595, into which were incorporated Montaigne's late marginalia — and also a paragraph of doubtful authenticity in praise of Mlle. de Gournay herself which, one reluctantly suspects, may have been by her own hand.

[9]

When, at the top of the mountain of Purgatory, Beatrice appears to Dante in order to lead him through the rest of his journey, she addresses him by name. It is the first and the only time that name is mentioned in the *Divine Comedy,* and the author feels obliged to apologize, explaining that "my name . . . is recorded here out of necessity." Employing a strategy that was to be copied much later by Marcel Proust, Dante withholds the name of his first-person narrator until two-thirds of the way into his book, aware, as Proust was, that the device of anonymity contributes to the effect of universality. Yet unlike the modern writer, the medieval poet, when he does reveal his identity, feels constrained to justify himself; for he knows that the artist should ideally remain anonymous, since his art was created for the glory of God, not that of the individual author. Such an attitude reflects the basic difference between the medieval concept of the poet as scribe, copying down what God dictates, and the Renaissance concept of the poet as maker or creator, fashioning what Philip Sidney was to call a golden world out of the imagination. More generally, however, it also reflects the difference between the medieval and modern attitudes toward the importance of the individual. By 1580, when Sidney's treatise was probably composed, we are already well into the modern world, and when we read the preface to the reader that Montaigne, in the same year, prefixes to the first edition of his book, we are made conscious of nothing so much as the remoteness of Dante's medieval world. For here the author tells us from the very beginning who he is and that his purpose is wholly personal. Not only is there no longer any cause for embarrassment at the revelation of the author's identity, but he can even boldly assert that the very subject of his book is nothing more nor less than himself.

Montaigne's first realization that "myself am the groundwork of my book" appears to have come to him shortly before 1580. In an essay reluctantly omitted from the present selection, *Of Presumption,* which was apparently composed sometime between 1578 and 1580, Montaigne gives the earliest extended portrait of himself and is at considerable pains to justify the "presumption" of having chosen such a subject. Elsewhere he claims, with somewhat misleading modesty, that having originally taken up writing to ease the melancholy of his solitude, "and finding myself afterward wholly unprovided of subject and void of other matter, I have presented myself unto myself for a subject." Bookish learning, never very highly esteemed by Montaigne, becomes even more insignificant in comparison with what can be learned from the observation of the self: "I had rather," he was later to say, "understand myself well in myself than in Cicero." At the same time he was aware of the difficulty, as well as the importance, of the enterprise: "There is no description so hard nor so profitable as the description of a man's own life." Initially, his purpose seems simply to have been to provide a portrait of himself for his family and friends, so that, as he explains in his preface, "losing me (which they are likely to do ere long), they may therein find some lineaments of my conditions and humors, and by that means reserve more whole and more lively foster the knowledge and acquaintance they have had of me." He laments at one point that his ancestors have not left such portraits for him, because he would like to have known better who they were — their habits, their faces, their expressions, their characteristic phrases. Because of this, he insists that his own self-portrait should be an accurate, not a glorified one:

> I erect not here a statue to be set up in the marketplace of a town or in a church or in any other public place . . . it is for the corner of a library, or to amuse a neighbor, a kinsman, or a friend of mine withal, who by this image may haply take pleasure to renew acquaintance and to reconverse with me.

During the eight years between the two-volume and three-volume editions of his book, the idea of portraying himself became increasingly important to Montaigne, and he grew more and more fascinated with the potentialities latent in his subject. Of the more than six hundred additions, most of them inserted quotations from his reading, that Montaigne made to his original essays during the period from 1580 to 1588, one hundred and eighty are, according to the count of one authority, original; but of these one hundred and eighty, one hundred and ten are about himself. "I greedily long to make myself known," he confessed, "nor care I at what rate, so it be truly; or, to say better, I hunger for nothing, but I hate mortally to be mistaken by such as shall happen to know my name." The more he told about himself, the more impossible he found it to lie about anything or to leave anything out: "the worst of my actions or conditions seem not so ugly unto me as I find it both ugly and base not to dare to avouch them." As a result, he discovered, somewhat to his own amazement, that he could be more candid in his book than he would dare to be in conversation:

> Many things I would be loath to tell a particular man I utter to the whole world. And concerning my most secret thoughts and inward knowledge, I send my dearest friends to a stationer's shop.

In the preface he wrote in 1580, he had expressed the wish that he could have lived at a time when and in a place where it would have been possible for him to appear completely naked to the world. He subsequently discovered, however, that such nakedness was more of a possibility than he had imagined. "Each of my pieces are equally mine, one as another," he explained in justification of his frankness. And, he adds, having just described the behavior and size of his penis, "no other doth more properly make me a man than this. My whole portraiture I universally owe unto the world."

These last sentences were written sometime after 1588, however, and they suggest an important revision in Montaigne's original purpose of depicting himself. If nothing else, the popular success of his first two books, which went into four editions during the eight years in which he was composing the essays of the third book, demonstrated to him that the spectators who stood before his self-portrait comprised a larger audience than merely his family and friends. He realized that he was indeed writing "unto the world." As a result, the very composition and colors of his portrait begin to change. Before, when he had been describing himself simply to leave a memento for his friends, he had emphasized those qualities that were unique to him; but now he turns to examine and articulate those qualities in him that are not merely personal but universal. Yet it is far more than an awareness of his book's popularity and enlarged audience that causes this new interpretation of his purpose: this is the result of nothing less than the final and greatest vision of Montaigne's thought. For now, as John Middleton Murry has observed, "the Man is not exploring the Truth, but the Truth is exploring Man." In the end, his interest is not so much in what makes him Michel de Montaigne as in what "doth . . . make me a man." The distinction, however, is only apparent; for he came to realize that in a very profound sense the two were identical, that "every man," as he unforgettably put it, "beareth the whole stamp of the human condition." "A Man's life of any worth is a continual allegory," said Keats, "and very few eyes can see the Mystery of his life." Somehow Montaigne had managed to perceive this mystery and recognize the extent to which his was a life of allegory in which all men could read the story of their existence.

This great new theme, which is to be fugally developed and elaborated in the monumental last essays, is announced in the opening pages of the second essay of the third book, *Of Repenting*.

> I propose a mean* life, and without luster. 'Tis all one. They fasten all moral philosophy as well to a popular and private life, as to one of richer stuff. Every man beareth the whole stamp of the human condition. Authors communicate themselves unto the world by some special and strange mark; I the first, by my general disposition, as Michel de Montaigne; not as a grammarian, or a poet, or a lawyer. If the world complain that I speak too much of myself, I complain that it thinks no more of itself . . . I speak truth, not my belly-full, but as much as I dare; and I dare the more, the more I grow into years, for it seemeth custom alloweth old age more liberty to babble and indiscretion to talk of itself. It cannot herein be as in trades where the craftsman and his work do often differ . . . Here my book and myself march together and keep one pace. Elsewhere one may commend or condemn the work without the workman; here not. Who toucheth one toucheth the other.

As the essays follow their course from objective to subjective, from being a kind of commonplace book of the thought of antiquity to become an intimate journal of one man's existence, they trace the outlines of that allegorical life — allegorical, because every man experiences, in the course of his own life, the progression from an awareness of external reality to an increasing consciousness of the self. In adding year after year to this written record of his meditations, Montaigne gradually came to the discovery that what he had written down was simply himself, that he had formed "a book consubstantial to his author," and that if it could be said that he had made his book, it could also be said that his book had made him:

> And if it happen no man read me, have I lost my time to have entertained myself so many idle hours about so pleasing and profitable thought? In framing this portrait of myself, I have so often been fain to frizzle and trim me that so I might the better extract myself, that

> the pattern is thereby confirmed and in some sort formed. Drawing myself for others, I have drawn myself with purer and better colors than were my first. I have no more made my book than my book hath made me — a book consubstantial to his author, of a peculiar and fit occupation, a member of my life; not of an occupation and end strange and foreign, as all other books. Have I misspent my time to have taken an account of myself so continually and so curiously? For those who only run themselves over by fantasy and by speech for some hours examine not themselves so primely* and exactly, nor enter they into themselves, as he doth who makes his study his work and occupation of it, who with all his might and with all his credit engageth himself to a register of continuance.

It is in order to achieve this "register of continuance" that Montaigne's purpose becomes, in the end, simply that of telling us all that he can about himself.

"What an idiotic project Montaigne had in portraying himself!" exclaimed Pascal with annoyance. "What a charming project Montaigne had in portraying himself so naturally," answered Voltaire; "for he has portrayed human nature." The apparent egotism of Montaigne's undertaking, which was so to annoy Pascal, Scaliger, Coleridge, and others, is actually redeemed, as Voltaire suggests, by his perception that a book about one man, if it is scrupulously honest, is really a book about all men; because through the process of recording and examining as much as possible about one life, however humble and "without luster," a man may learn a great deal about life in general. One of the subtlest paradoxes in Montaigne is the fact that in turning to the self he attained a kind of selflessness. Precisely because he came to accept the self in a way that Pascal, who claimed that the self is always to be hated, never could, Montaigne is able to look upon the self with a dispassionate objectivity that Pascal never achieved. In prescribing that a man should know himself, the Delphic Oracle had not counseled egotism but had rather suggested that by knowing himself a man might thereby know humanity and understand what it means to live as a man.

To ask outright, "what does it mean to be a man?", is perhaps too ambitious an undertaking for the human mind, which is so caught up in the mutable process of becoming that it cannot make the leap directly to the abstraction of being. An understanding of being can perhaps only be derived from a careful observation of becoming. Therefore, Montaigne advises, let a man first look at what he can know, his own, changing, uncertain course through life, which is difficult enough; for "it is a thorny and crabbed enterprise, and more than it makes show of, to follow so strange and vagabond a path as that of our spirit, to penetrate the shady and enter the thick, covered depths of these internal winding cranks,* to choose so many and settle so several airs of his agitations." One cannot generalize about where the path will lead; one can only follow it step by step, asking at every moment, "what does it mean to me, at this particular moment, to be alive?"

> I describe not the essence, but the passage; not a passage from age to age, or as the people reckon, from seven years to seven years, but from day to day, from minute to minute. My history must be fitted to the present. I may soon change, not only fortune but intention. It is a counter-roll* of divers and variable accidents and irresolute imaginations, and sometimes contrary . . . Were my mind settled, I would not essay, but resolve myself.

The very meaning of the word *essay* changes for Montaigne as he revises his purpose in writing them. While he had originally meant it to indicate that he was trying out his rational powers, the years of Pyrrhonic doubt had shown him that reason was only a feeble, useless instrument. As a result, he now claims that "all this gallimaufry* which I huddle up here is but a register of my life's essays." Instead of being trials of his reason or judgment, the essays become simply records of his life's experiences. That they are such penetrating, universal records is because Montaigne possessed to a degree that has rarely been equaled what Walter Bagehot, speaking of Shakespeare, called "an experiencing nature."

Almost symbolically, it is this word that he chooses for the title of his last and greatest essay. In French, however, *expérience* has two meanings: it is the word for both "experience" and "experiment." In this latter sense it is exactly synonymous with the word *essay.* At the end of his life, Montaigne's purpose becomes one of experimenting with all that life offers him, trying out each of life's experiences, and registering the data he derives from his observation. He is, of course, supremely aware of the fallibility of the instruments at his disposal in conducting such experiments, and that is why he insists that they are only "attempts" — tentative and inconclusive.

> There is no desire more natural than that of knowledge. We attempt all means that may bring us unto it. When reason fails us, we employ experience, which is a mean by much more weak and vile. But truth is of so great consequence that we ought not disdain any induction* that may bring us unto it. Reason hath so many shapes that we know not which to take hold of. Experience hath as many. The consequences we seek to draw from the conference* of events is unsure, because they are ever dissemblable.*

When reason had failed him he had expressed that failure with the question *Que Sçay je?* Pyrrhonism's perpetual suspension in uncertainty is not, however, the final stage of Montaigne's thought. In these last essays he miraculously manages to go beyond that doubt and find an answer to his question. That answer is simply "myself." What do I know? Nothing, except that I know nothing: "it is by my experience I accuse* human ignorance, which (in mine opinion) is the surest part of the world's school." What can I know? Not very much. But I can perhaps know a little bit, tentative and ephemeral though it may be, about one man, Michel de Montaigne, and what experiences he has had of life.

The essays of the third book, longer, richer, infinitely more suggestive than most of the earlier essays, are largely concerned with the individual as he confronts his experience: *Of Repenting* examines the response of the individual conscience to experience; *Of Three Commerces or Societies* deals with the kinds of life the individual may lead in society; *How One Ought to Govern His Will* goes on to question what responsibilities the individual has to society and what responsibilities to the self; *Of Physiognomy* asks who the individual really is behind his outward appearance and ponders the role of philosophy in shaping that individual; *Of Experience* catalogues the details of one life and affirms the complexity and universality of each human experience. Other essays treat such subjects as love and diversion and vanity. Each of them displays not only a new emphasis upon the self but also a new and more profound acceptance of that self, neither overlooking nor pardoning its frailties, but acknowledging that they too are a part of man's very being. One of the inscriptions in Montaigne's library was Terence's famous statement: "I am a man, and I deem nothing human alien to me." He himself says the same thing in his last essay:

> There is nothing so goodly, so fair, and so lawful as to play the man well and duly, nor science so hard and difficult as to know how to live his life well and naturally; and of all the infirmities we have, the most savage is to despise our being.

Not to despise one's being, but to accept the whole self, means to accept the body as well as the soul, the senses as well as the mind, and Montaigne always rebelled against those who would separate the two and thus attempt to "escape from the man." It is false to disavow our bodily functions or passions in an attempt to seem better than we are: they are an ineradicable, inseparable part of us. We are neither all soul nor all body; we are neither, as he put it, angels nor horses, but men. There is no point in our trying to deny the body and "get upon stilts; for be we upon them yet must we go with our own legs. And sit we upon the highest throne in the world, yet sit we upon our own tail." Just as he was insistent in his desire to see life whole, without denying any of its contradictory or paradoxical experiences, so he determined to see man whole, his shame and his glory forming one seamless fabric. Once again we may think of the late Yeats, of whom he so often reminds us; for like Yeats he believed that the body should not be "bruised to pleasure soul," but that the soul should assist and favor the body, "and not refuse to be partaker of his natural pleasures." It is because of this that we find such a persistent emphasis upon pleasure — upon "the virtue of pleasure" — in these last essays and his late marginalia. The long addition about pleasure that he interpolates into the beginning of his early essay *That to Philosophy Is to Learn How to Die* is symptomatic of many others. "I hate," he says elsewhere, "a wayward and sad disposition that glideth over the pleasures of life." He knew that the pains of existence and cares of the soul cannot be avoided, but he believed that this was all the more reason not to deny life's joys and the pleasures of the body. Indeed, as he watched the advancing years snatch away one bodily pleasure after another, he came to feel that pleasure and life were almost synonymous; but joy, he felt, was philosophy's finest flower: "the most evident token and apparent sign of true wisdom is a constant and unconstrained rejoicing."

In this last phase of his thought, Montaigne, admitting that he can be "neither angel nor Cato," arrives at the opposite shore from that austere Stoicism whence he had set out and embraces a joyous, quasi-Epicurean philosophy which does not attempt to elevate man or correct his nature, but rather accepts man as he is and urges him to obey the dictates of his own nature. Nature generally and human nature specifically become the guiding criteria of Montaigne's last years. "I have, as elsewhere I noted," he says, "taken for my regard this ancient precept, very rawly and simply: that we cannot err in following nature, and that the sovereign document is for a man to conform himself to her." Through an excessive confidence in the powers of his reason, man has tried to channel or mold or "improve" nature with human laws and institutions. Such attempts to derive principles from nature as legal codes or the precepts of medicine, he argues in his last essay, are essentially a falsification of our nature; for our codifications are abstract and immutable, whereas nature is organic and constantly changing, a greater, more protean thing than any construct of the mind. Consequently, man in his natural state, like the savages of the New World, is both better and happier:

> There is but little relation between our actions, that are in perpetual motion, and the fixed and unmovable laws. The most to be desired are the rarest, the simplest, and the most general. And yet I believe it were better to have none at all than so infinite a number as we have. Nature gives them ever more happy than those we give ourselves. Witness the image of the Golden Age that poets feign, and the state wherein we see divers nations to live which have no other.

"We have forsaken nature," he complains in another place, "and yet we will teach her her lesson, she that led us so happily and directed us so safely."

This praise of what is natural does not, however, imply either moral or social anarchy. Nature, in Montaigne's conception, is not lawless, but has her own, better laws than our artificial, abstract ones. Similarly, she has her own wisdom, which is a greater wisdom than anything philosophers can achieve through the use of their reason; and although many philosophers have claimed they were urging us to follow nature, their concept of nature "present[s] her to us with a painted face, too high in color, and over-much sophisticated." She herself is a much simpler, more easy law-giver:

> As she hath given us feet to go withal, so hath she endowed us with wisdom to direct our life; a wisdom not so ingenious, sturdy, and pompous as that of their invention, but yet easy, quiet, and salutary, and that in him who hath the hap* to know how to employ it orderly and sincerely, effecteth very well what the other saith, that is to say, naturally. For a man to commit himself most simply unto nature is to do it most wisely.

This wisdom is the wisdom Montaigne found in Socrates, who replaces Cato as the hero of the essays in these final years. The Athenian's soul, says Montaigne, moved "with a natural and common motion," whereas with Cato it was "an outright proceeding, far above and beyond the common." The greatness of Socrates, as opposed to Cato, is that he "brought human wisdom from heaven again, where for a long time it had been lost, to restore it unto man, where her most just and laborious work is." In the essay *Of Physiognomy* Montaigne presents his most extended tribute to this "sacred image of human form," this "interpreter of natural simplicity," who had become for him, as he had been for Erasmus, the great saint of pagan antiquity. Montaigne's esteem of Socrates is not only based upon his natural wisdom and his recognition that the true wisdom is to know one's ignorance, but also upon the exemplary life he led and his equally exemplary death. It is on that death in particular that Montaigne, at the end of his own life, concentrates, because it exemplifies for him the fact that if we have known how to live we shall know how to die, that nature will teach us how to do both. In his last years, Montaigne faces the approach of death with an equanimity he had earlier feared he might lack; but now he finds himself ready for it when it will come, making no plans, he says, more than a year in advance, "ready booted to take his journey"; for now he accepts death as simply the final fact of nature: "I have seen the leaves, the blossoms, and the fruit, and now see the drooping and withering of it, happily, because naturally."

Yet it is life, not death, that comes flooding into these last essays — life in all its infinite complexity, in all its sunshine and shadow, happiness and pain, hope and fear, life in all its myriad details. And it is upon those little details of life that Montaigne turns his final gaze. Even "a piece of turf torn from a meadow," says a recent writer, John Updike, "becomes a *gloria* when drawn by a Dürer. Details. Details are the giant's fingers. He seizes the stick and strips the bark and shows, burning beneath, the moist white wood of joy." One senses just this joy in Montaigne as his fingers reveal the smallest details of his existence. And no detail is too trivial, because each is a part of life, each a part of what it means to be a man, each a part of the little a man can know. He can only know that, really, about one man, and when all the details are added up it may not seem like very much; but it *is* something, and to know one man is to know all. "A generous mind," Montaigne had written shortly before 1580, "ought not to belie his thoughts but make show of his inmost parts"; and, he added at the end of his life, "there all is good — or, at least, all is human." This impressive sense of humanity, after so many ranging pages, chooses to return at last to the man himself, and to tell us simply that he cannot stand to have his hair cut after dinner, that he hates smoky rooms, that he loves melons and radishes, oysters and salted meat (but not salted bread), that he has good teeth and small ears, that he wears silk stockings in both winter and summer, that he cannot make a child except before going to bed, that he cannot sleep by day and finds it difficult to get up before seven in the morning, that he does not need spectacles, that he eats so fast he sometimes bites his tongue and fingers, that he has a poor memory and itching eyes, that he needs curtains around his bed and goes to the bathroom upon arising, that he has a loud, strained voice, that originally he preferred white wine, later came to like claret, and now prefers white wine again. Simply this. This, and one more thing: that we are, as he says, great fools:

> "He hath passed his life in idleness," say we; "Alas, I have done nothing this day." What? Have you not lived? It is not only the fundamental but the noblest of your occupation[s]. "Had I been placed or thought fit for the managing of great affairs, I would have showed what I could have performed." Have you known how to meditate and manage your life? You have accomplished the greatest work of all. For a man to show and exploit himself, nature hath no need of fortune; she equally shows herself upon all grounds, in all suits, before and behind, as it were, without curtains, welt,* or guard. Have you known how to compose your manners? You have done more than he who hath composed books. Have you known how to take rest? You have done more than he who hath taken empires and cities. The glorious masterpiece of man is to live to the purpose.

Among the last words he wrote was the simple affirmation: "My art and profession is to live."

[10]

Montaigne's last years were spent quietly and uneventfully on his estate. He corresponded with his old friend Henri of Navarre, now King Henri IV, and had lengthy conversations with Pierre Charron who was later to write a treatise on wisdom which was much indebted to Montaigne's thought. He also came to know some of the most learned men of his day, Justus Lipsius, Jacques-Auguste de Thou, Pierre de Brach, Estienne Pasquier. On May 7, 1590, his one surviving child, Léonor, married at the age of nineteen, and a year later she presented him with a granddaughter, named after his wife. We think of him mostly, however, sitting in his tower, continuing to read and to meditate, making his final marginal additions to the essays in preparation for a new edition, which was not to appear until after his death. As always, we think of him also looking out of those windows at the world around him; and once again we may recall Yeats and those mandarins of his great poem "Lapis Lazuli" whom he delights to imagine seated looking out on all the tragic scene of life spread before them: as Montaigne's surely were, "their ancient, glittering eyes, are gay." Though he had hoped, when younger, that he might die away from home, or at least while planting his cabbages, so that he would be spared the mourners and ceremonies that accompany the dying, he actually died in his bed, at Saint-Michel de Montaigne, on September 13, 1592, in his sixtieth year.

Selected Essays of

MONTAIGNE

The Author to the Reader

[A]Reader, lo here a well-meaning book. It doth at the first entrance forewarn thee that in contriving the same, I have proposed unto myself no other than a familiar and private end. I have no respect or consideration at all, either to thy service or to my glory; my forces are not capable of any such design. I have vowed the same to the particular commodity of my kinsfolks and friends, to the end that, losing me (which they are likely to do ere long), they may therein find some lineaments of my conditions and humors, and by that means reserve more whole and more lively foster the knowledge and acquaintance they have had of me. Had my intention been to forestall and purchase the world's opinion and favor, I would surely have adorned myself more quaintly or kept a more grave and solemn march. I desire therein to be delineated in mine own genuine, simple, and ordinary fashion, without contention, art, or study; for it is myself I portray. My imperfections shall therein be read to the life, and my natural form discerned, so far-forth as public reverence hath permitted me. For if my fortune had been to have lived among those nations which yet are said to live under the sweet liberty of nature's first and uncorrupted laws, I assure thee I would most willingly have portrayed myself fully and naked.

Thus, gentle reader, myself am the groundwork of my book. It is then no reason thou shouldest employ thy time about so frivolous and vain a subject. Therefore farewell. From Montaigne, the first of March, 1580.

Of Solitariness

❧ I. 39 ✧ c. 1572 ☙

[A]Let us leave apart this outworn comparison between a solitary and an active life. And touching that goodly saying under which ambition and avarice shroud themselves — that we are not born for our particular, but for the public good — let us boldly refer ourselves to those that are engaged [in the dance]. And let them beat their conscience if, on the contrary, the states, the charges, and this trash of the world are not rather sought and sued for to draw a private commodity from the public. The bad and indirect means where-through in our age men canvass* and toil to attain the same do manifestly declare the end thereof to be of no great consequence. Let us answer ambition that herself gives us the taste of solitariness. For what doth she shun so much as company? What seeketh she more than elbow-room? There is no place but there are means and ways to do well or ill. Nevertheless, if the saying of Bias be true, that the worst part is the greatest, or that which Ecclesiastes saith, that of a thousand there is not one good —

> [B]Good men are rare, so many scarce, I fear,
> As gates of Thebes, mouths of rich Nilus were.
>
> Juv. XIII.26.

— [A]contagion is very dangerous in a throng. A man must imitate the vicious or hate them. Both are dangerous; for to resemble them is perilous, because they are many, and to hate many is hazardous, because they are disemblable.*

[C]And merchants that travel by sea have reason to take heed that those which go in the same ship be not dissolute, blasphemers, and wicked, judging such company unfortunate. Therefore Bias said pleasantly to those that together with him passed the danger of a great storm and called to the gods for help: "Peace, my masters, lest they should hear that you are here with me." And, of a more military example, Albuquerque, viceroy in India for Emanuel, King of Portugal, in an extreme danger of a sea-tempest took a young boy upon his shoulders for this only end, that in the common peril his innocency might be his warrant and recommending to God's favor to set him on shore.

AYet may a wise man live everywhere contented, yea, and alone in the throng of a palace; but if he may choose, he will (saith he) avoid the sight of it. If need require, he will endure the first; but if he may have his choice, he will choose the latter. He thinks he hath not sufficiently rid himself from vices if he must also contest with other men's faults. BCharondas punished those for wicked that were convicted to have frequented lewd companies.

CThere is nothing so dissociable* and sociable as man, the one for his vice, the other for his nature. And I think Antisthenes did not satisfy him that upbraided him with his conversation with the wicked, saying that physicians live amongst the sick; who, if they stead* sick men's healths, they impair their own by the infection, continual visiting, touching, and frequenting of diseases.

ANow, as I suppose, the end is both one, thereby to live more at leisure and better at ease. But man does not always seek the best way to come unto it, who often supposeth to have quit affairs when he hath but changed them. There is not much less vexation in the government of a private family than in the managing of an entire state: wheresoever the mind is busied, there it is all. And though domestical occupations be less important, they are as importunate. Moreover, though we have freed ourselves from the court and from the market, we are not free from the principal torments of our life:

> Reason and wisdom may set cares aside,
> Not place, the arbiter of seas so wide.
> Hor. *Epist.* I.ii.25.

Shift we, or change we places never so often, ambition, avarice, irresolution, fear, and concupiscences never leave us.

> Care, looking grim and black, doth sit
> Behind his back that rides from it.
> Hor. *Odes* III.i.40.

They often follow us, even into immured cloisters and into schools of philosophy; nor do hollow rocks nor wearing of hair-shirts nor continual fastings rid us from them.

> The shaft that death implied
> Sticks by the flying side.
> Virg. *Aen.* IV.73.

It was told Socrates that one was no whit amended by his travel. "I believe it well," saith he, "for he carried himself with him."

Why change we soils warm'd with another sun?
Who, from home banish'd, hath himself out-run?
Hor. *Odes* II.xvi.18.

If a man do not first discharge both himself and his mind from the burthen that presseth her, removing from place to place will stir and press her the more — as in a ship, wares well stowed and closely piled take up least room. You do a sick man more hurt than good to make him change place: you settle an evil in removing the same — as stakes of poles, the more they are stirred and shaken, the faster they stick and sink deeper into the ground. Therefore it is not enough for a man to have sequestered himself from the concourse of people: it is not sufficient to shift place; a man must also sever himself from the popular conditions that are in us. A man must sequester and recover himself from himself.

[B]You will say haply, "I my bonds have quit."
Why, so the striving dog the knot hath bit;
Yet when he flies, much chain doth follow it.
Pers. *Sat.* V.158.

We carry our fetters with us; it is not an absolute liberty; we still cast back our looks towards that we have left behind. Our mind doth still run on it; our fancy is full of it.

Unless our breast be purg'd, what wars must we,
What perils then, though much displeased, see?
How great fears, how great cares of sharp desire
Do careful man distract, torment, enfire?
Uncleanness, wantonness, sloth, riot, pride —
How great calamities have these implied?
Lucr. V.44.

[A]Our evil is rooted in our mind, and it cannot escape from itself.

The mind in greatest fault must lie,
Which from itself can never fly.
Hor. *Epist.* I.xiv.13.

Therefore must it be reduced and brought into itself: it is the true solitariness, and which may be enjoyed even in the frequency of peopled cities and kings' courts; but it is more commodiously enjoyed apart.

Now sithence* we undertake to live solitary and without company, let us cause our contentment to depend of ourselves. Let us shake off all bonds that tie us unto others. Gain we that victory over us, that in good earnest we may live solitary and therein live at our ease.

Stilpo, having escaped the combustion of his city wherein he had lost both wife and children and all his goods, Demetrius Poliorcetes, seeing him in so great a ruin of his country with an unaffrighted countenance, demanded of him whether he had received any loss. He answered, no; and that, thanks given to God, he had lost nothing of his own. [C]It is that which Antisthenes the philosopher said very pleasantly, that man ought to provide himself with munitions that might float upon the water, and by swimming escape the danger of shipwreck with him.

[A]Verily, a man of understanding hath lost nothing if he yet have himself. When the city of Nola was overrun by the barbarians, Paulinus, bishop thereof, having lost all he had there and being their prisoner, prayed thus to God: "Oh Lord, deliver me from feeling of this loss; for thou knowest as yet they have touched nothing that is mine." The riches that made him rich and the goods which made him good were yet absolutely whole. Behold what it is to choose treasures well that may be freed from injury, and to hide them in a place where no man may enter and which cannot be betrayed but by ourselves.

A man that is able may have wives, children, goods, and chiefly health, but not so tie himself unto them that his felicity depend on them. We should reserve a storehouse[1] for ourselves, what need soever chance, altogether ours, and wholly free, wherein we may hoard up and establish our true liberty and principal retreat and solitariness. Wherein we must go alone to ourselves to take our ordinary entertainment, and so privately that no acquaintance or communication of any strange thing may therein find place, there to discourse, to meditate and laugh, as without wife, without children and goods, without train or servants, that if by any occasion they be lost it seem not strange to us to pass it over. We have a mind moving and turning in itself: it may keep itself company; it hath wherewith to offend and defend, wherewith to receive, and wherewith to give. Let us not fear that we shall faint and droop through tedious and mind-trying idleness in this solitariness:

[B]Be thou, when with thee is not any,
As good unto thyself as many.
Tibul. IV.xiii.12.

[C]Virtue, [says Antisthenes,] is contented with itself, without discipline, without words, and without effects.

[A]In our accustomed actions, of a thousand there is not one found that regards us. He whom thou seest so furiously and, as it were, beside himself to clamber or crawl up the city walls or breach as a

1 *"Il se faut reserver une arrière-boutique . . ."* An *arrière-boutique* is, more precisely, a room in back of the shop. Cf. Introduction.

point-blank to a whole volley of shot, and another all wounded and scarred, crazed and faint and well-nigh hunger-starven, resolved rather to die than to open his enemy the gate and give him entrance — dost thou think he is there for himself? No, verily, it is peradventure for such a one whom neither he nor so many of his fellows ever saw and who haply takes no care at all for them, but is therewhilst wallowing up to the ears in sensuality, sloth, and all manner of carnal delights. This man whom, about midnight, when others take their rest, thou seest come out of his study meagre-looking, with eyes trilling,* phlegmatic, squalid, and spawling* — dost thou think that, plodding on his books, he doth seek how he shall become an honester man, or more wise, or more content? There is no such matter. He will either die in his pursuit or teach posterity the measure of Plautus' verses and the true orthography of a Latin word. Who doth not willingly chop and counter-change his health, his ease, yea, and his life for glory and for reputation, the most unprofitable, vain, and counterfeit coin that is in use with us? Our death is not sufficient to make us afraid, let us also charge ourselves with that of our wives, of our children, and of our friends and people. Our own affairs do not sufficiently trouble and vex us; let us also drudge, toil, vex, and torment ourselves with our neighbors' and friends' matters.

> Fie, that a man should cast that aught than he
> Himself of himself more belov'd should be.
>
> Ter. *Adel.* I.i.13.

C Solitariness meseemeth hath more apparance* and reason in those which have given their most active and flourishing age unto the world, in imitation of Thales.

AWe have lived long enough for others, live we the remainder of our life unto ourselves. Let us bring home our cogitations and inventions unto ourselves and unto our ease. It is no easy matter to make a safe retreat; it doth over-much trouble us with[out] joining other enterprises unto it. Since God gives us leisure to dispose of our dislodging, let us prepare ourselves unto it; pack we up our baggage; let us betimes bid our company farewell; shake we off these violent hold-fasts* which elsewhere engage us and estrange us from ourselves. These so strong bonds must be untied, and a man may eftsoons* love this or that but wed nothing but himself. That is to say, let the rest be our own, yet not so combined and glued together that it may not be sundered without flaying us and therewithal pull away some piece of our own. The greatest thing of the world is for a man to know how to be his own.

CIt is high time to shake off society, since we can bring nothing to it. And he that cannot lend, let him take heed of borrowing. Our forces fail us; retire we them and shut them up into ourselves. He that can suppress and confound in himself the offices of so many amities and of the company, let him do it. In this fall, which makes us inutile, irksome, and importunate to others, let him take heed he be not importunate, irksome and unprofitable to himself. Let him flatter, court, and cherish himself and above all let him govern himself, respecting his reason and fearing his conscience, so that he may not without shame stumble or trip in their presence. "For it is a rare matter that every man sufficiently should stand in awe and reverence of himself" [Quintilian X.7.].

Socrates saith that young men ought to be instructed, and men exercised in well-doing, and old men withdraw themselves from all civil and military negotiations, living at their own discretion, without obligation to any certain office.

ᴬThere are some complexions more proper for these precepts ᶜof retreat ᴬthan others. Those which have a tender and demiss* apprehension, a squeamish affection, a delicate will, and which cannot easily subject or employ itself (of which both by natural condition and propense* discourse I am one) will better apply themselves unto this counsel than active minds and busy spirits, which embrace all, everywhere engage, and in all things passionate themselves, that offer, that present, and yield themselves to all occasions. A man must make use of all these accidental commodities and which are without us so long as they be pleasing to us, but not make them our principal foundation. It is not so; nor reason nor nature permit it. Why should we against their laws subject our contentment to the power of others? Moreover, to anticipate the accidents of fortune; for a man to deprive himself of the commodities he hath in possession, as many have done for devotion and some philosophers by discourse; to serve themselves; to lie upon the hard ground; to pull out their own eyes; to cast their riches into the sea; to seek for pain and smart, some by tormenting this life for the happiness of another, othersome placing themselves on the lowest step, thereby to warrant themselves from a new fall — is the action of an excessive virtue. Let sterner and more vigorous complexions make their lurking* glorious and more exemplar.

> When riches fail, I praise the safe estate,
> Though small; base things do not high thoughts abate.
> But when 'tis better, finer with me, I,
> "They only live well and are wise," do cry,
> "Whose coin in fair farms doth well-grounded lie."
>
> Hor. *Epist.* I.xv.42.

There is work enough for me to do without going so far. It sufficeth me under fortune's favor to prepare myself for her disfavor and, being at ease, as far as imagination may attain unto to represent the evil to come unto myself — even as we enure ourselves to tilts and tourneys and counterfeit war in time of peace.

[C]I esteem not Arcesilaus the philosopher less reformed because I know him to have used household implements of gold and silver, according as the condition of his fortune gave him leave. I rather value him the more than if he had not done it, forsomuch as he both moderately and liberally made use of them. [A]I know unto what limits natural necessity goeth, and I consider the poor almsman begging at my door to be often more plump-cheeked, in better health and liking than I am. Then do I enter into his estate and assay to frame and suit my mind unto his bias. And so, over-running other examples, albeit I imagine death, poverty, contempt, and sickness to be at my heels, I easily resolve myself not to apprehend any fear of that which one of less worth than myself doth tolerate and undergo with such patience. And I cannot believe that the baseness or shallowness of understanding can do more than vigor and far-seeing, or that the effects and reason of discretion cannot reach to the effects of custom and use. And knowing what slender hold-fast* these accessory commodities have, I omit not in full jovissance* of them humbly to beseech God of his mercy (as a sovereign request) to make me contented with myself and with the goods proceeding from me. I see some gallantly disposed young men who, notwithstanding their fair-seeming show, have many boxes full of pills in their coffers at home, to take when the rheum shall assail them, which so much the less they fear when they think the remedy to be at hand. So must a man do; as also, if he feel himself subject to some greater infirmity, to store himself with medicaments that may assuage, supple, and stupefy the part grieved. The occupation a man should choose for such a life must neither be painful nor tedious. Otherwise, in vain should we account to have sought our abiding there, which depends from the particular taste of every man. Mine doth no way accommodate itself to husbandry. Those that love it must with moderation apply themselves unto it.

> Endeavor they things to them to submit,
> Not them to things (if they have Horace's wit).
>
> Hor. *Epist.* I.i.19.

Husbandry is otherwise a servile office, as Sallust termeth it. It hath more excusable parts, as the care of gardening, which Xenophon ascribeth to Cyrus. A mean or mediocrity may be found between this base and vile-carking* care, extended and full of toiling labor, which we see in men that wholly plunge themselves therein, and that profound and extreme rechlessness* to let all things go at six and seven, which is seen in others.

Cattle destroyed Democritus his sets,*
While his mind bodiless vagaries fets.*
Hor. *Epist.* I.xii.12.

But let us hear the counsel which Pliny the younger giveth to his friend Cornelius Rufus touching this point of solitariness: "I persuade thee, in this full-gorged and fat retreat wherein thou art, to remit this base and abject care of husbandry unto thy servants and give thyself to the study of letters, whence thou mayest gather something that may be altogether thine own." He meaneth reputation — like unto Cicero's humor, who saith that he will employ his solitariness and residence from public affairs to purchase unto himself by his writings an immortal life.

[B]Is it then nothing worth that thou dost know,
Unless what thou dost know, thou others show?
Pers. *Sat.* I.23.

[C]It seemeth to be reason, when a man speaketh to withdraw himself from the world, that one should look beyond him. These do it but by halves. Indeed, they set their match against the time they shall be no more, but pretend to reap the fruit of their designs when they shall be absent from the world, by a ridiculous contradiction. The imagination of those who through devotion seek solitariness, filling their minds with the certainty of heavenly promises in the other life, is much more soundly consorted. They propose God as an object infinite in goodnesses and incomprehensible in power unto themselves. The soul hath therein in all free liberty wherewith to glut herself. Afflictions and sorrows redound to their profit, being employed for the purchase and attaining of health and eternal gladness. Death, according to one's wish, is a passage to so perfect an estate. The sharpness of their rules is presently made smooth and easy by custom, and carnal concupiscences rejected, abated, and lulled asleep by refusing them; for nothing entertaineth them but use and exercise. This only end of another life blessedly immortal doth rightly merit we should abandon the pleasures and commodities of this our life. And he that can enlighten his soul with the flame of a lively faith and hope, really and constantly, in his solitariness doth build unto himself a voluptuous and delicious life, far surmounting all other lives.

[A]Therefore doth neither the end nor middle of this counsel please me. We are ever falling into a relapse, from an ague to a burning fever. This plodding occupation of books is as painful as any other, and as great an enemy unto health, which ought principally to be considered. And a man should not suffer himself to be inveigled by the pleasure he takes in them: it is the same pleasure that loseth the thriving husbandman, the greedy-covetous, the sinning-voluptuous, and the puffed-up-ambitious. The wisest men teach us sufficiently to beware and shield us from the treasons of our appetites and to discern true and perfect pleasures from delights blended and intermingled with more pain. For most pleasures, they say, tickle, fawn upon, and embrace us with purpose to strangle us, as did the thieves whom the Egyptians termed Philistas. And if the headache would seize upon us before drunkenness, we would then beware of too much drinking; but sensuality, the better to entrap us, marcheth before and hideth her track from us. Books are delightful; but if by continual frequenting them we in the end lose both health and cheerfulness (our best parts), let us leave them. I am one of those who think their fruit can no way countervail this loss. As men that have long time felt themselves enfeebled through some indisposition do in the end yield to the mercy of physic and by art have certain rules of life prescribed them which they will not transgress, so he that withdraws himself as distasted and over-tired with the common life ought likewise to frame and prescribe this unto the rules of reason, direct and range the same by premeditation and discourse. He must bid all manner of travel farewell, what show soever it bear, and in general shun all passions that any way impeach the tranquillity of mind and body, [B]and follow the course best agreeing with his humor.

> His own way every man
> Tread out directly can.
>
> Propert. *El.* II.xxv.38.

[A]A man must give to thriving husbandry, to laborious study, to toilsome hunting, and to every other exercise the utmost bounds of pleasure and beware he engage himself no further if once pain begin to intermeddle itself with her. We should reserve business and negotiations only for so much as is behooveful to keep us in breath and to warrant us from the inconveniences which the other extremity of a base, faint-hearted idleness draws after it. There are certain barren and thorny sciences which, for the most part, are forged for the multitude; they should be left for those who are for the service of the world. As for myself, I love no books but such as are pleasant and easy and which tickle me, or such as comfort and counsel me to direct my life and death.

> Silently creeping midst the wholesome wood
> With care what's for a wise man and a good.
>
> Hor. *Epist.* I.iv.4.

The wiser sort of men, having a strong and vigorous mind, may frame unto themselves an altogether spiritual life. But mine being common, I must help to uphold myself by corporal commodities. And age having eftsoons* despoiled me of those that were most suitable to my fantasy, I instruct and sharpen my appetite to those remaining most sortable* this other season. We must tooth and nail retain the use of this life's pleasures, which our years snatch from us, one after another:

> BPluck we sweet pleasures; we thy life give thee.
> Thou shalt a tale, a ghost, and ashes be.
> Pers. *Sat.* V.151.

ANow concerning the end of glory, which Pliny and Cicero propose unto us, it is far from my discourse. The most opposite humor to solitary retiring is ambition. Glory and rest are things that cannot squat in one same form. As far as I see, these have nought but their arms and legs out of the throng; their mind and intent is further and more engaged in them than it ever was.

> BGatherest thou, dotard, at these years,
> Fresh baits, fine food, for others' ears?
> Pers. *Sat.* I.19.

AThey have gone back that they might leap the better and with a stronger motion make a nimbler offer amidst the multitude. Will you see how they shoot short by a corn's breadth? Let us but counterpoise the advice of two philosophers,[2] and of two most different sects: the one writing to Idomeneus, the other to Lucilius, their friends, to divert them from the managing of affairs and greatness unto a solitary kind of life. "You have," say they, "lived hitherto swimming and floating adrift: come and die in the haven. You have given the past of your life unto light: give the remainder unto darkness. It is impossible to give over occupations if you do not also give over the fruits of them. Therefore, clear yourself from all care and glory. There is great danger lest the glittering of your fore-passed actions should over much dazzle you, yea, and follow you even to your den. Together with other concupiscences, shake off that which cometh from the approbation of others. And touching your knowledge and sufficiency, take you no care of them; they will lose no whit of their effect if yourself be anything the better for them. Remember but him who, being demanded to what purpose he toiled so much about an art which could by no means come to the knowledge of many, 'few are enough for me, one will suffice, yea, less than one will content me,' answered he.

"He said true. You and another are a sufficient theatre one for

2 Epicurus and Seneca.

another, or you to yourself alone. Let the people be one unto you, and one be all the people to you. It is a base ambition to go about to draw glory from one's idleness and from one's lurking* hole. A man must do as some wild beasts which at the entrance of their caves will have no manner of footing seen. You must no longer seek what the world saith of you, but how you must speak unto yourself. Withdraw yourself into yourself, but first prepare yourself to receive yourself; it were folly to trust to yourself if you cannot govern yourself. A man may as well fail in solitariness as in company; there are ways for it. Until such time as you have framed yourself such that you dare not halt before yourself and that you shall be ashamed of and bear a kind of respect unto yourself, [C]'let honest Ideas still represent themselves before your mind' (Cic. *Tusc. Qu.* II.22.). [A]Ever present Cato, Phocion, and Aristides unto your imagination, in whose presence even fools would hide their faults, and establish them as controllers of all your intentions. If they be disordered and untuned, their reverence will order and tune them again. They will contain you in a way to be contented with yourself, to borrow nothing but from yourself, to settle and stay your mind in assured and limited cogitations, wherein it may best please itself; and, having gotten knowledge of true felicities which, according to the measure a man understands them, he shall accordingly enjoy, and with them rest satisfied, without wishing a further continuance either of life or name."[3]

Lo, here the counsel of truly pure and purely true philosophy, not of a vainglorious, boasting, and prating philosophy, as is that of the two first.[4]

[3] This "letter" is largely made up of phrases taken from Seneca's epistles, especially epistles 7, 19, 21, 22, 25, and 68.

[4] Pliny and Cicero.

Of Idleness

☙§ I. 8 ◇ c. 1572 ❧

[A]As we see some idle, fallow grounds, if they be fat and fertile, to bring forth store* and sundry roots of wild and unprofitable weeds, and that to keep them in ure* we must subject and employ them with certain seeds for our use and service; and as we see some women, though single and alone, often to bring forth lumps of shapeless flesh, whereas to produce a perfect and natural generation they must be manured with another kind of seed; so is it with minds which, except they be busied about some subject that may bridle and keep them under, they will here and there wildly scatter themselves through the vast fields of imaginations.

[B]As trembling light reflected from the sun
Or radiant moon on water-filled brass lavers*
Flies over all, in air upraised soon
Strikes housetop beams, betwixt both strangely wavers.
Virg. *Aen.* VIII.22.

[A]And there is no folly or extravagant raving they produce not in that agitation:

Like sick men's dreams that feign
Imaginations vain.
Hor. *Ars poet.* 7.

The mind that hath no fixed bound will easily lose itself; for, as we say, to be everywhere is to be nowhere:

[B]Good sir, he that dwells everywhere
Nowhere can say that he dwells there.
Mart. VII.lxxiii.

[A]It is not long since I retired myself unto mine own house, with full purpose as much as lay in me not to trouble myself with any business, but solitarily and quietly to wear out the remainder of my well-nigh-spent life; where methought I could do my spirit no greater favor than to give him the full scope of idleness and entertain him as he best pleased, and, withal, to settle himself as he best liked, which

I hoped he might now, being by time become more settled and ripe, accomplish very easily. But I find —

> Evermore idleness
> Doth wavering minds address.
>
> Lucan IV.704.

— that contrariwise, playing the skittish and loose-broken jade, he takes a hundred times more cariere* and liberty unto himself than he did for others, and begets in me so many extravagant chimeras and fantastical monsters, so orderless and without any reason, one huddling upon another, that at leisure to view the foolishness and monstrous strangeness of them, I have begun to keep a register of them, hoping, if I live, one day to make him ashamed and blush at himself.

Of Democritus and Heraclitus

❧ I. 50 ◇ 1572–80 ❧

[A]Judgment is an instrument for all subjects, and meddleth everywhere. And therefore in the essays I make of it, there is no manner of occasion I seek not to employ therein. If it be a subject I understand not myself, therein I make trial of it, sounding afar off the depth of the ford; and finding the same over-deep for my reach, I keep myself on the shore. And to acknowledge not to be able to wade through is a part of its effect, yea, of such whereof he vaunteth most. If I light upon a vain and idle subject, I assay to try, and endeavor to see, whether I may find a good ground to work upon and matter to frame a body and wherewith to build and under-lay it. Sometimes I address my judgment and contrive it to a noble and outworn subject wherein is nothing found subsisting of itself, the highway to it being so bare-trodden that it cannot march but in other steps. There he pleaseth himself in choosing the course he thinks best, and [of] a thousand paths sometimes he saith this or that was best chosen.

I take my first argument of fortune. All are alike unto me. And I never purpose to handle them throughly. [C]For there is nothing wherein I can perceive the full perfection — which they do not that promise to show it us. Of a hundred parts and visages that everything hath, I take one, which sometimes I slightly run over and other times but cursorily glance at. And yet otherwhilst I pinch it to the quick and give it a stoccado,* not the widest, but the deepest I can. And for the most part I love to seize upon them by some unwonted luster. I would adventure to treat and discourse of some matter to the depth, knew I myself less or were I deceived in mine own impuissance. Scattering here one and there another word — scantlings* taken from their main groundwork, disorderly dispersed, without any well-grounded design and promise — I am not bound to make it good nor, without varying, to keep myself close-tied unto it whensoever it shall please me to yield myself to doubt, to uncertainty, and to my mistress-form, which is ignorance.

Each motion showeth and discovereth what we are. [A]The very same mind of Caesar we see in directing, marshalling, and setting the battle of Pharsalia is likewise seen to order, dispose, and contrive idle, trifling, and amorous devices. We judge of a horse not only by seeing him ridden and cunningly managed, but also by seeing him trot or pace, yea, if we but look upon him as he stands in the stable.

ᶜAmongst the functions of the soul, some are but mean and base. He that seeth her no further can never know her thoroughly. And he that seeth her march her natural and simple pace doth peradventure observe her best. The winds of passions take her most in her highest pitch, seeing she entirely coucheth herself upon very matter and wholly therein exerciseth herself, and handleth but one at once, not according to it, but according to herself. Things several in themselves have peradventure weight, measure, and condition; but inwardly, in us, she cuts it out for them as she understandeth the same herself. Death is fearful and ugly unto Cicero, wished for and desired of Cato, and indifferent unto Socrates. Health, welfare, conscience, authority, riches, glory, beauty, and their contraries are despoiled at the entrance and receive a new vesture at the soul's hand, yea, and what color she pleaseth, brown, bright, green, sad, or any hue else, sharp or sweet, deep or superficial, and what each of them pleaseth. For none of them did ever verify their styles, their rules, or forms in common: each one severally is a queen in her own estate. Therefore let us take no more excuses from external qualities of things. To us it belongeth to give ourselves account of it. Our good and our evil hath no dependency but from ourselves. Let us offer our vows and offerings unto it, and not to fortune. She hath no power over our manners.

Why shall I not judge of Alexander sitting and drinking at table, and talking in good company?[1] Or if he were playing at chess? What string of his wit doth not touch or harp on this fond, childish, and time-consuming play? I loathe and shun it, only because there is not sport enough in it and that in his recreation he is over-serious with us, being ashamed I must apply that attention thereunto as might be employed on some good subject. He was no more busied in levying his forces and preparing for his glorious passage into India, nor this other in disentangling and discovering of a passage whence dependeth the welfare and safety of mankind. See how much our mind troubleth this ridiculous amusing if all her sinews bandy* not. How amply she giveth everyone law in that to know and directly to judge of himself! I do not more universally view and feel myself in any other posture. What passion does not exercise us thereunto: choler, spite, hatred, impatience, and vehement ambition to overcome in a matter wherein it were haply more excusable to be ambitious for to be vanquished.

1 Florio slightly misunderstands this sentence, and I have silently corrected his mistranslation.

For a rare pre-excellency, and beyond the common reach, in so frivolous a thing is much misseeming a man of honor. What I say of this example may be spoken of all others. Every parcel, every occupation of a man, accuseth and showeth him equal unto another.

[A]Democritus and Heraclitus were two philosophers, the first of which, finding and deeming human condition to be vain and ridiculous, did never walk abroad but with a laughing, scornful, and mocking countenance. Whereas Heraclitus, taking pity and compassion of the very same condition of ours, was continually seen with a sad, mournful, and heavy cheer, and with tears trickling down his blubbered eyes.

> [B]One from his door, his foot no sooner passed
> But straight he laughed; the other wept as fast.
>
> Juven. *Sat.* X.28.

[A]I like the first humor best, not because it is more pleasing to laugh than to weep, but for it is more disdainful and doth more condemn us than the other. And methinks we can never be sufficiently despised according to our merit. Bewailing and commiseration are commixed with some estimation of the thing moaned and wailed. Things scorned and contemned are thought to be of no worth. I cannot be persuaded there can be so much ill luck in us as there is apparent vanity, nor so much malice as sottishness. We are not so full of evil as of voidness and inanity. We are not so miserable as base and abject.

Even so Diogenes, who did nothing but trifle, toy, and dally with himself in rumbling and rolling of his tub and flirting* at Alexander, accounting us but flies and bladders puffed with wind, was a more sharp, a more bitter, and a more stinging judge, and, by consequence, more just and fitting my humor than Timon, surnamed the hater of all mankind. For look what a man hateth, the same thing he takes to heart. Timon wished all evil might light on us; he was passionate in desiring our ruin; he shunned and loathed our conversation as dangerous and wicked and of a depraved nature. Whereas the other so little regarded us that we could neither trouble nor alter him by our contagion; forsook our company not for fear but for disdain of our commerce.

Of the same stamp was the answer of Statilius, to whom Brutus spake to win him to take part and adhere to the conspiracy against Caesar. He allowed the enterprise to be very just, but disallowed of the men that should perform the same as unworthy that any man should put himself in any adventure for them: [C]conformable to the discipline of Hegesias, who said that a wise man ought never to do anything but for himself, forasmuch as he alone is worthy to have any action performed for him; and to that of Theodorus, who thought it an injustice that a wise man should in any case hazard himself for the good and benefit of his country or to endanger his wisdom for fools.

Our own condition is as ridiculous, as risible, as much to be laughed at as able to laugh.

It Is Folly to Refer Truth or Falsehood to Our Sufficiency

☙ I. 27 ✧ 1572–80 ❧

[A]It is not peradventure without reason that we ascribe the facility of believing and easiness of persuasion unto simplicity and ignorance. For meseemeth to have learned heretofore that belief was, as it were, an impression conceived in our mind, and according as the same was found either more soft or of less resistance, it was easier to imprint anything therein. [C]"As it is necessary a scale must go down the balance when weights are put into it, so must a mind yield to things that are manifest" (Cic. *Acad. Qu.* II.12). Forasmuch, therefore, as the mind being most empty and without counterpoise, so much the more easily doth it yield under the burden of the first persuasion. [A]And that's the reason why children, those of the common sort, women, and sick folk are so subject to be misled, and so easy to swallow gudgeons.* Yet, on the other side, it is a sottish presumption to disdain and condemn that for false which unto us seemeth to bear no show of likelihood or truth, which is an ordinary fault in those who persuade themselves to be of more sufficiency than the vulgar sort. So was I sometimes wont to do, and if I heard anybody speak, either of ghosts walking, of foretelling future things, of enchantments, of witchcrafts, or any other thing reported which I could not well conceive or that was beyond my reach,

> Dreams, magic terrors, witches, uncouth wonders,
> Night-walking sprites, Thessalian conjured-thunders.
>
> Hor. *Epist.* II.208.

I could not but feel a kind of compassion to see the poor and silly* people abused with such follies. And now I perceive that I was as much to be moaned myself. Not that experience hath since made me to discern anything beyond my former opinions. Yet was not my curiosity the cause of it. But reason hath taught me that so resolutely to condemn a thing for false and impossible is to assume unto himself the advantage to have the bounds and limits of God's will, and of the power of our common mother, Nature, tied to his sleeve. And that there is no greater folly in the world than to reduce them to the measure of our capacity and bounds of our sufficiency. If we term those things monsters or miracles to which our reason cannot attain, how many such do daily present themselves unto our sight? Let us consider through what clouds and how blindfold we are led to the knowledge of most things that pass our hands. Verily we shall find it is rather custom, than science, that removeth the strangeness of them from us:

> [B]Now no man tired with glut of contemplation,
> Deigns to have heaven's bright church in admiration.
>
> Lucr. II.1037.

[A]And that those things, were they newly presented unto us, we should doubtless deem them as much, or more, unlikely and incredible than any other.

> If now first on a sudden they were here
> 'Mongst mortal men, object to eye or ear,
> Nothing, than these things, would more wondrous be,
> Or that, men durst less think, ever to see.
>
> Lucr. II.1032.

He who had never seen a river before, the first he saw he thought it to be the ocean; and things that are the greatest in our knowledge, we judge them to be the extremest that nature worketh in that kind.

> [B]A stream none of the greatest, may so seem
> To him that never saw a greater stream.
> Trees, men, seem huge, [A]and all things of all sorts,
> The greatest one hath seen, he huge reports.
>
> Lucr. VI.674.

[C]"Minds are acquainted by custom of their eyes, nor do they admire or inquire the reason of those things which they continually behold" (Cic. *Nat. De.* II.38). The novelty of things doth more incite us to search out the causes than their greatness. [A]We must judge of this infinite power of nature with more reverence and with more acknowledgment of our own ignorance and weakness. How many things of small likelihood are there, witnessed by men worthy of credit, whereof, if we cannot be persuaded, we should at least leave them in suspense? For to deem them impossible is by rash presumption to presume and know how far possibility reacheth. [C]If a man did well understand what difference there is between impossibility and that which is unwonted, and between that which is against the course of nature and the common opinion of men, in not believing rashly and in not disbelieving easily, the rule of *Nothing too much* commanded by Chilon should be observed.

[A]When we find in Froissart that the Earl of Foix (being in Béarn) had knowledge of the defeature at Inberoth of King John of Castile the morrow next it happened and the means he allegeth for it, a man may well laugh at it. And of that which our annals report, that Pope Honorius, the very same day that King Philip Augustus died [B]at Mantes, [A]caused his public funerals to be solemnized and commanded them to be celebrated throughout all Italy. For the authority of the witnesses hath peradventure no sufficient warrant to restrain us. But what if Plutarch, besides divers examples which he allegeth of antiquity, saith to have certainly known that in Domitian's time the news of the battle lost by Antonius in Germany, many days' journey thence, was published at Rome and divulged through the world the very same day it succeeded? And if Caesar holds that it hath many times happened that report hath foregone the accident? Shall we not say that those simple people have suffered themselves to be cozened and seduced by the vulgar sort because they were not as clear-sighted as we? Is there anything more dainty, more unspotted and more lively than Pliny's judgment, whensoever it pleaseth him to make show of it? Is there any farther from vanity? I omit the excellency of his learning and knowledge, whereof I make but small reckoning. In which of those two parts do we exceed him? Yet there is no scholar so meanly learned but will convince* him of lying, and read a lecture of contradiction against him upon the progress of nature's works.

When we read in Bouchet the miracles wrought by the relics of Saint Hilary, his credit is not sufficient to bar us the liberty of contradicting him. Yet at random to condemn all suchlike histories seemeth to me a notable impudency. That famous man Saint Augustine witnesseth to have seen a blind child to recover his sight over the relics of Saint Gervase and Protasius at Milan; and a woman at Carthage to have been cured of a canker by the sign of the holy cross, which a woman newly baptized made unto her; and Hesperius, a familiar friend of his, to have expelled certain spirits that molested his house with a little of the earth of our Saviour's sepulcher, which earth being afterwards transported into a church, a paralytic man was immediately therewith cured; and a woman going in procession, having, as she passed by, with a nosegay touched the case wherein Saint Stephen's bones were, and with the same afterward rubbed her eyes, she recovered her sight, which long before she had utterly lost; and divers other examples where he affirmeth to have been an assistant himself. What shall we accuse him of, and two other holy bishops, Aurelius and Maximinus, whom he calleth for his witnesses? Shall it be of ignorance, of simplicity, of malice, of facility, or of imposture? Is any man living so impudent that thinks he may be compared to them, whether it be in virtue or piety, in knowledge or judgment, in wisdom or sufficiency? [C]"Who, though they alleged no reason, yet might subdue me with their very authority" (Cic. *Tusc.* I.21.). [A]It is a dangerous fondhardiness* and of consequence, besides the absurd temerity it draws with it, to despise what we conceive not. For after that, according to your best understanding, you have established the limits of truth and bounds of falsehood, and that it is found you must necessarily believe things wherein is more strangeness than in those you deny, you have already bound yourself to abandon them.

Now, that which methinks brings as much disorder in our consciences, namely in these troubles of religion wherein we are, is the dispensation Catholics make of their belief. They suppose to show themselves very moderate and skillful when they yield their adversaries any of those articles now in question. But besides that they perceive not what an advantage it is for him that chargeth you, if you but once begin to yield and give them ground, and how much that encourageth him to pursue his point; those articles which they choose for the lightest are oftentimes most important. Either a man must wholly submit himself to the authority of our ecclesiastical policy or altogether dispense himself from it. It is not for us to determine what part of obedience we owe unto it. And moreover, I may say it, because I have made trial of it, having sometimes used this liberty of my choice and particular election, not regarding certain points of the observance of our Church, which seem to bear a face either more vain or more strange. Coming to communicate them with wise men, I have found that those things have a most solid and steady foundation, and that it is but foolishness and ignorance makes us receive them with less respect and reverence than the rest. Why remember we not what and how many contradictions we find and feel even in our own judgment? How many things served us but yesterday as articles of faith which today we deem but fables? Glory and curiosity are the scourges of our souls. The latter induceth us to have an oar in every ship, and the former forbids us to leave anything unresolved or [un]decided.

Of the Inconstancy of Our Actions

II. 1 ◇ c. 1572

[A]Those which exercise themselves in controlling human actions find no such let* in any one part as to piece them together and bring them to one same luster.[1] For they commonly contradict one another so strangely as it seemeth impossible they should be parcels of one warehouse. Young Marius is sometimes found to be the son of Mars, and other times the child of Venus. Pope Boniface the Eighth is reported to have entered into his charge as a fox, to have carried himself therein as a lion, and to have died like a dog. And who would think it was Nero, that lively* image of cruelty, who being required to sign (as the custom was) the sentence of a criminal offender that had been condemned to die, that ever he should answer, "Oh, would to God I could never have written!" So near was his heart grieved to doom a man to death.

The world is so full of such examples that every man may store himself; and I wonder to see men of understanding trouble themselves with sorting these parcels, sithence* (meseemeth) irresolution is the most apparent and common vice of our nature, as witnesseth that famous verse of Publius the comedian:

> The counsel is but bad,
> Whose change may not be had.
> Quoted in Aulus-Gellius XVII.14.

[B]There is some apparence* to judge a man by the most common conditions of his life, but seeing the natural instability of our customs and opinions, I have often thought that even good authors do ill and take a wrong course willfully to opinionate themselves about framing a constant and solid contexture of us. They choose an universal air and, following that image, range and interpret all a man's actions; which, if they cannot wrest sufficiently, they remit them into dissimulation. Augustus hath escaped their hands, for there is so apparent, so sudden

1 Florio's translation of this sentence is somewhat obscure. Montaigne is saying that "those who engage in comparing human actions never find anything so frustrating as when they try to fit them together and see them in the same light."

and continual a variety of actions found in him through the course of his life that even the boldest judges and strictest censurers have been fain to give him over and leave him undecided. There is nothing I so hardly believe to be in man as constancy, and nothing so easy to be found in him as inconstancy. He that should [C]distinctly and part by part [B]judge of him, should often jump* to speak truth. View all antiquity over, and you shall find it a hard matter to choose out a dozen of men that have directed their life unto one certain, settled, and assured course, which is the surest drift of wisdom. For to comprehend all in one word, saith an ancient writer, and to embrace all the rules of our life into one, it is at all times to will and not to will one same thing. I would not vouchsafe (saith he) to add anything, always provided the will be just; for if it be unjust, it is impossible it should ever continue one. Verily I have heretofore learned that vice is nothing but a disorder and want of measure, and by consequence it is impossible to fasten constancy unto it. It is a saying of Demosthenes (as some report) that consultation and deliberation is the beginning of all virtue, and constancy, the end and perfection. If by reason or discourse we should take a certain way, we should then take the fairest; but no man hath thought on it.

He scorns that which he sought, seeks that he scorned of late,
He flows, ebbs, disagrees in his life's whole estate.
Hor. *Epist.* I.i.98.

Our ordinary manner is to follow the inclination of our appetite this way and that way, on the left and on the right hand, upward and downward, according as the wind of occasions doth transport us. We never think on what we would have but at the instant we would have it, and change as that beast that takes the color of the place wherein it is laid. What we even now purposed, we alter by and by, and presently return to our former bias. All is but changing, motion, and inconstancy:

So are we drawn, as wood is shoved,
By others' sinews each way moved.
Hor. *Sat.* II.vii.82.

We go not but we are carried; as things that float, now gliding gently, now hulling* violently, according as the water is either stormy or calm.

[B]See we not, every man in his thoughts' height
Knows not what he would have, yet seeks he straight
To change place, as he could lay down his weight?
Lucr. III.1070.

[A]Every day new toys, each hour new fantasies, and our humors move and fleet with the fleetings and movings of time.

> Such are men's minds, as that great God of might
> Surveys the earth with increase-bearing light.
> *Odyssey* XVIII.135, trans. by Cicero.

[C]We float and waver between diverse opinions. We will nothing freely, nothing absolutely, nothing constantly. [A]Had any man prescribed certain laws or established assured policies in his own head, in his life should we daily see to shine an equality of customs, an assured order, and an infallible relation from one thing to another. [C]Empedocles noted this deformity to be amongst the Agrigentines, that they gave themselves so over unto delights as if they should die tomorrow next, and built as if they should never die. [A]The discourse thereof were easy to be made, as is seen in young Cato: he that touched but one step of it, hath touched all. It is a harmony of well-according tunes and which cannot contradict itself. With us it is clean contrary, so many actions, so many particular judgments are there required. The surest way (in mine opinion) were to refer them unto the next circumstances, without entering into further search and without concluding any other consequence of them.

During the late tumultuous broils of our mangled estate,[2] it was told me that a young woman, not far from me, had headlong cast herself out of a high window with intent to kill herself, only to avoid the ravishment of a rascally-base soldier that lay in her house, who offered to force her. And perceiving that with the fall she had not killed herself, to make an end of her enterprise, she would have cut her own throat with a knife, but that she was hindered by some that came in to her. Nevertheless having sore wounded herself, she voluntarily confessed that the soldier had yet but urged her with importunate requests, suing-solicitations, and golden bribes, but she feared he would in the end have obtained his purpose by compulsion. By whose earnest speeches, resolute countenance, and gored blood (a true testimony of her chaste virtue), she might appear to be the lively* pattern of another Lucretia. Yet know I certainly that both before that time and afterward, she had been enjoyed of others upon easier composition. And as the common saying is: "Fair and soft, as squeamish-honest as she seems, although you miss of your intent, conclude not rashly an inviolable chastity to be in your mistress; for a groom or a horsekeeper may find an hour to thrive in; and a dog hath a day."

Antigonus, having taken upon him to favor a soldier of his by reason

[2] The religious civil wars in France during the latter half of the sixteenth century.

of his virtue and valor, commanded his physicians to have great care of him and see whether they could recover him of a lingering and inward disease which had long tormented him. Who being perfectly cured, he afterward perceiving him to be nothing so earnest and diligent in his affairs, demanded of him how he was so changed from himself, and become so [cowardish]: "Yourself, good Sir (answered he), have made me so by ridding me of those infirmities which so did grieve me that I made no account of my life."

A soldier of Lucullus, having by his enemies been robbed of all he had, to revenge himself undertook a notable and desperate attempt upon them; and having recovered his losses, Lucullus conceived a very good opinion of him, and with the greatest shows of assured trust and loving kindness he could bethink himself, made especial account of him, and in any dangerous enterprise seemed to trust and employ him only:

> With words, which to a coward might
> Add courage, had he any spright.
> Hor. *Epist.* II.ii.36.

"Employ (said he unto him) some wretch-stripped and robbed soldier;"

> (None is, saith he, so clownish, but will on,
> Where you will have him, if his purse be gone.)
> Hor. *Epist.* II.ii.39.

and absolutely refused to obey him.

[C]When we read that Mohammed, having outrageously rated Hassan, chief leader of his Janissaries, because he saw his troop well-nigh defeated by the Hungarians, and he to behave himself but faintly in the fight, Hassan, without making other reply, alone as he was and without more ado, with his weapon in his hand rushed furiously in the thickest throng of his enemies that he first met withal, of whom he was instantly slain. This may haply be deemed rather a rash conceit than a justification, and a new spite than a natural prowess.

[A]He whom you saw yesterday so boldly venturous, wonder not if you see him a dastardly meacock* tomorrow next, for either anger or necessity, company or wine, a sudden fury or the clang of a trumpet, might rouse up his heart and stir up his courage. It is no heart nor courage so framed by discourse or deliberation. These circumstances have settled the same in him. Therefore it is no marvel if by other contrary circumstance he become a craven and change copy. [C]This supple variation and easy yielding contradiction, which is seen in us, hath made some to imagine that we had two souls, and others two faculties, whereof everyone as best she pleaseth accompanieth and doth agitate us; the one towards good, the other towards evil. Forsomuch as such a rough diversity cannot well sort and agree in one simple subject.

[B]The blast of accidents doth not only remove me according to his inclination; for besides, I remove and trouble myself by the instability of my posture, and whosoever looketh narrowly about himself, shall hardly see himself twice in one same state. Sometimes I give my soul one visage, and sometimes another, according unto the posture or side I lay her in. If I speak diversely of myself, it is because I look diversely upon myself. All contrarieties are found in her, according to some turn or removing, and in some fashion or other. Shamefaced, bashful, insolent, [C]chaste, luxurious,* peevish, [B]prattling, silent, fond, doting, laborious, nice, delicate, ingenious, slow, dull, froward, humorous, debonaire, [C]wise, ignorant, [B]false in words, true-speaking, [C]both liberal, covetous, and prodigal.[3] [B]All these I perceive in some measure or other to be in me, according as I stir or turn myself. And whosoever shall heedfully survey and consider himself, shall find this volubility and discordance to be in himself, yea and in his very judgment. I have nothing to say entirely, simply, and with solidity of myself, without confusion, disorder, blending, mingling; and in one word, *Distinguo* is the most universal part of my logic.

[A]Although I ever purpose to speak good of good, and rather to interpret those things that will bear it unto a good sense, yet is it that the strangeness of our condition admitteth that we are often urged to do well by vice itself, if well doing were not judged by the intention only. Therefore may not a courageous act conclude a man to be valiant. He that is so when just occasion serveth, shall ever be so and upon all occasions. If it were a habitude of virtue and not a sudden humor, it would make a man equally resolute at all assays, in all accidents. Such alone as in company, such in a single combat as in a set battle. For whatsoever some say, valor is all alike, and not one in the street or town, and another in the camp or field. As courageously should a man bear a sickness in his bed as a hurt in the field, and fear death no more at home in his house than abroad in an assault. We should not then see one same man enter the breach, or charge his enemy with an assured and undoubted fierceness, and afterward, having escaped that, to vex, to grieve and torment himself like unto a silly* woman, or faint-hearted milksop, for the loss of a suit or death of a child. [C]If one chance to be carelessly base-minded in his [infamy]

3 Florio has, characteristically, expanded Montaigne's list of adjectives. *Bashful, peevish, fond, doting, nice, slow,* and *froward* are not found in the French text.

and constantly resolute in poverty; if he be timorously fearful at sight of a barber's razor, and afterward stoutly undismayed against his enemies' swords, the action is commendable, but not the man. Divers Grecians (saith Cicero) cannot endure to look their enemy in the face, yet are they most constant in their sicknesses; whereas the Cimbrians and Celtiberians are mere contrary. "For nothing can bear itself even which proceedeth not from resolved reason" (Cic. *Tusc. Qu.* II.27.).

BThere is no valor more extreme in his kind than that of Alexander; yet it is but in species, nor everywhere sufficiently full and universal. CAs incomparable as it is, it hath his blemishes, Bwhich is the reason that, in the idlest suspicions he apprehendeth at the conspiracies of his followers against his life, we see him so earnestly to vex and so desperately to trouble himself. In search and pursuit whereof he demeaneth himself with so vehement and indiscreet an injustice and with such a demiss* fear that even his natural reason is thereby subverted. Also, the superstition wherewith he is so thoroughly tainted beareth some show of pusillanimity. CAnd the unlimited excess of the repentance he showed for the murder of Clitus is also a witness of the inequality of his courage.

AOur matters are but parcels huddled up and pieces patched together,[4] and we endeavor to acquire honor by false means and untrue tokens. Virtue will not be followed but by herself. And if at any time we borrow her mask, upon some other occasion she will as soon pull it from our face. It is a lively hue and strong dye, if the soul be once dyed with the same perfectly, and which will never fade or be gone except it carry the skin away with it. Therefore to judge a man we must a long time follow and very curiously mark his steps; whether constancy do wholly subsist and continue upon her own foundation in him, C"Who hath forecast and considered the way of life" (Cic. *Parad.* V.1.); Awhether the variety of occurrences make him change his pace (I mean his way, for his pace may either be hastened or slowed) let him run on; such a one (as sayeth the emprise* of our good Talbot) goeth before the wind.

It is no marvel (saith an old writer) that hazard hath such power over us, since we live by hazard. It is impossible for him to dispose of his particular actions that hath not in gross directed his life unto one certain end. It is impossible for him to range all pieces in order that hath not a plot or form of the total frame in his head. What availeth the provision of all sorts of colors unto one that knows not what he is to draw? No man makes any certain design of his life, and we

[4] Florio omits the following quotation added by Montaigne: C"They look down on pleasure, but they are cowardly in pain; they pay no attention to fame, but they are broken in spirit by infamy" [Cic. *De officiis,* I.21.]

deliberate of it but by parcels. A skillful archer ought first to know the mark he aimeth at, and then apply his hand, his bow, his string, his arrow, and his motion accordingly. Our counsels go astray because they are not rightly addressed and have no fixed end. No wind makes* for him that hath no intended port to sail unto.

As for me, I allow not greatly of that judgment which some made of Sophocles, and to have concluded him sufficient in the managing of domestical matters, against the accusation of his own son, only by the sight of one of his tragedies. [C]Nor do I commend the conjecture of the Parians, sent to reform the Milesians, as sufficient to the consequence they drew thence. In visiting and surveying the isle, they marked the lands that were best husbanded and observed the country houses that were best governed. And having registered the names of their owners, and afterward made an assembly of the townsmen of the city, they named and instituted those owners as new governors and magistrates, judging and concluding that being good husbands and careful of their houshold affairs, they must consequently be so of public matters.

[A]We are all framed of flaps and patches and of so shapeless and diverse a contexture that every piece and every moment playeth its part. And there is as much difference found between us and ourselves as there is between ourselves and other. [C]"Esteem it a great matter to play but one man" [Sen. *Epist.* CXX.].

[A]Since ambition may teach men both valor, temperance, liberality, yea, and justice; sith covetousness may settle in the mind of a shop-apprentice-boy, brought up in ease and idleness, a dreadless assurance to leave his homebred ease and forgo his place of education and in a small bark to yield himself unto the mercy of blustering waves, merciless winds, and wrathful Neptune; and that it also teacheth discretion and wisdom; and that Venus herself ministreth resolution and hardness unto tender youth as yet subject to the discipline of the rod, and teacheth the ruthless soldier the soft and tenderly effeminate heart of women in their mothers' laps—

> [B]The wench by stealth her lodged guards having stripped,
> By this guide, sole, in the dark, to the yonker* skipped.
>
> Tib. *El.* II.i.75.

—[A]it is no part of a well-grounded judgment simply to judge ourselves by our exterior actions. A man must thoroughly sound himself and dive into his heart and there see by what wards* or springs the motions stir. But forasmuch as it is a hazardous and high enterprise, I would not have so many to meddle with it as do.

That to Philosophy Is to Learn How to Die

❧ I. 20 ◇ 1572–80 ❧

[A]Cicero saith that to philosophy* is no other thing than for a man to prepare himself to death; which is the reason that study and contemplation doth in some sort withdraw our soul from us and severally employ it from the body, which is a kind of apprenticeage and resemblance of death; or else it is that all the wisdom and discourse of the world doth in the end resolve upon this point, to teach us not to fear to die. Truly either reason mocks us, or it only aimeth at our contentment, and, in fine, bends all her travail to make us live well and, as the holy Scripture saith, at our ease. All the opinions of the world conclude [C]that pleasure is our end, [A]howbeit they take divers means unto and for it, else would men reject them at their first coming. For who would give ear unto him that for its end would establish our pain and disturbance? [C]The dissensions of philosophical sects in this case are verbal: "Let us run over such overfine fooleries, and subtle trifles" [Sen. *Epist.* CXVII.]. There is more willfulness and wrangling among them than pertains to a sacred profession. But what person a man undertakes to act, he doth ever therewithal personate his own.

Although they say that in virtue itself the last scope of our aim is voluptuousness.[1] It pleaseth me to importune their ears still with this word, which so much offends their hearing. And if it imply any chief pleasure or exceeding contentments, it is rather due to the assistance of virtue than to any other supply; voluptuousness being more strong, sinewy, sturdy, and manly, is but more seriously voluptuous. And we should give it the name of pleasure, more favorable, sweeter, and more natural, and not term it vigor, from which it hath his denomination. Should this baser sensuality deserve this fair name, it should be by competency and not by privilege. I find it less void of incommodities and crosses than virtue. And besides that, her taste is more fleeting, momentary, and fading; she hath her fasts, her eves, and her

[1] This sentence should read: "Whatever they say, in virtue itself the last scope of our aim is voluptuousness."

travails, and both sweat and blood. Furthermore she hath particularly so many wounding passions, and of so several sorts, and so filthy and loathsome a s[a]ciety* waiting upon her, that she is equivalent to penitency. We are in the wrong to think her incommodities serve her as a provocation and seasoning to her sweetness, as in nature one contrary is vivified by another contrary, and to say, when we come to virtue, that like successes and difficulties overwhelm it and yield it austere and inaccessible. Whereas, much more properly than unto voluptuousness, they ennoble, sharpen, animate, and raise that divine and perfect pleasure which it [mediates] and procureth us. Truly he is very unworthy her acquaintance that counterbalanceth her cost to his fruit, and knows neither the graces nor use of it. Those who go about to instruct us how her pursuit is very hard and laborious, and her jovissance* well pleasing and delightful, what else tell they us but that she is ever unpleasant and irksome? For what human mean did ever attain unto an absolute enjoying of it? The perfectest have been content but to aspire and approach her, without ever possessing her. But they are deceived, seeing that of all the pleasures we know, the pursuit of them is pleasant. The enterprise is perceived by the quality of the thing which it hath regard unto; for it is a good portion of the effect, and consubstantial. That happiness and felicity which shineth in virtue replenisheth her approaches and appurtenances, even unto the first entrance and utmost bar.*

Now, of all the benefits of virtue, the contempt of death is the chiefest, a mean that furnisheth our life with an easeful tranquillity and gives us a pure and amiable taste of it, without which every other voluptuousness is extinguished. [A]Lo, here the reasons why all rules encounter and agree with this article. And albeit they all lead us with a common accord to despise grief, poverty, and other accidental crosses to which man's life is subject, it is not with an equal care, as well because accidents are not of such a necessity — for most men pass their whole life without feeling any want or poverty, and othersome without feeling any grief or sickness, as Xenophilus the musician, who lived a hundred and six years in perfect and continual health — as also if the worst happen, death may at all times and whensoever it shall please us cut off all other inconveniences and crosses. But as for death, it is inevitable.

> [B]All to one place are driven, of all
> Shaken is the lot-pot, where-hence shall
> Sooner or later drawn lots fall,
> And to death's boat for aye enthrall.
>
> Hor. *Odes* III.iii.25.

[A]And by consequence, if she make us afeard, it is a continual subject of torment and which can no way be eased. [C]There is no starting hole will hide us from her: she will find us wheresoever we are; we may, as in a suspected country, start and turn here and there: "Which evermore hangs like the stone over the head of Tantalus" (Cic. *De finib.* I.xviii.). [A]Our laws do often condemn and send malefactors to be executed in the same place where the crime was committed. To which, whilst they are going, lead them along the fairest houses, or entertain them with the best cheer you can,

> [B]Not all King Denys' dainty fare,
> Can pleasing taste for them prepare:
> No song of birds, no music's sound
> Can lullaby to sleep profound.
> Hor. *Odes* III.i.18.

[A]Do you think they can take any pleasure in it? Or be anything delighted? And that the final intent of their voyage, being still before their eyes, hath not altered and altogether distracted their taste from all these commodities and allurements?

> [B]He hears his journey, counts his days, so measures he
> His life by his way's length, vexed with the ill shall be.
> Claud. *In Ruff.* II.137.

[A]The end of our career is death; it is the necessary object of our aim. If it affright us, how is it possible we should step one foot further without an ague? The remedy of the vulgar sort is not to think on it. But from what brutal stupidity may so gross a blindness come upon him? He must be made to bridle his ass by the tail,

> Who doth a course contrary run
> With his head to his course begun.
> Lucr. IV.472.

It is no marvel if he be so often taken tripping. Some do no sooner hear the name of death spoken of but they are afraid; yea the most part will cross themselves as if they heard the Devil named. And because mention is made of it in men's wills and testaments, I warrant you there is none will set his hands to them till the physician have given his last doom and utterly forsaken him. And God knows, being then between such pain and fear, with what sound judgment they endure him. [B]For so much as this syllable sounded so unpleasantly in their ears, and this voice seemed so ill-boding and unlucky, the Romans had learned to allay and dilate the same by a periphrasis. In lieu of saying "He is dead" or "He hath ended his days," they would say "He hath lived." So it be life, be it past or no, they are comforted; from whom we have borrowed our phrases *quondam, alias,* or *late such a one.*[2]

[A]It may haply be, as the common saying is, "The time we live is worth the money we pay for it." I was born between eleven of the clock and noon, the last of February, 1533, according to our computation,[3] the year beginning the first of January. It is but a fortnight since I was thirty-nine years old. I want at least as much more. If in the meantime I should trouble my thoughts with a matter so far from me, it were but folly. But what? we see both young and old to leave their life after one selfsame condition. [C]No man departs otherwise from it than if he but now came to it, [A]seeing there is no man so crazed, bedrell,* or decrepit, so long as he remembers Methuselah but thinks he may yet live twenty years. Moreover, silly* creature as thou art, who hath limited the end of thy days? Happily thou presumest upon physicians' reports. Rather consider the effect and experience. By the common course of things, long since thou livest by extraordinary favor. Thou hast already over-passed the ordinary terms of common life. And to prove it, remember but thy acquaintances and tell me how many more of them have died before they came to thy age than have either attained or outgone the same. Yea, and of those that through renown have ennobled their life, if thou but register them, I will lay a wager I will find more that have died before they came to five and thirty years than after. It is consonant with reason and piety to take example by the humanity of Jesus Christ, who ended his human life at three and thirty years. The greatest man that ever was being no more than a man, I mean Alexander the Great, ended his days and died also of that age.

How many several means and ways hath death to surprise us!

> A man can never take good heed,
> Hourly what he may shun and speed.
>
> Hor. *Odes* II.xiii.13.

I omit to speak of agues and pleurisies. Who would ever have imagined that a duke of Brittany should have been stifled to death in a throng of people, as whilom was a neighbor of mine at Lyons when Pope Clement made his entrance there?[4] Hast thou not seen one of our late kings[5] slain in the midst of his sports? And one of his ancestors

[2] "*feu Maistre Jehan.*" Montaigne appears to believe that *feu* (late) comes from the Latin *fuit* (he was).

[3] In 1565 Charles IX decreed that the year should begin on January 1, rather than at Easter. It was not until two years later, however, that this decree took effect, and the year 1567 began on January 1.

[4] Florio mistranslates here. Montaigne says: "Who would even have imagined that a duke of Brittany should have been stifled to death in a throng of people,

die miserably by the chuck* of a hog? Æschylus, forethreatened by the fall of a house, when he stood most upon his guard, strucken dead by the fall of a tortoise shell, which fell out of the talons of an eagle flying in the air? And another choked with the kernel of a grape? And an emperor die by the scratch of a comb, whilst he was combing his head. And Æmilius Lepidus with hitting his foot against a doorsill? And Aufidius with stumbling against the council-chamber door as he was going in thereat? And Cornelius Gallus the prætor, Tigillinus, captain of the Roman watch, Ludovico, son of Guido Gonzaga, marquis of Mantua, end their days between women's thighs? And of a far worse example, Speusippus the Platonian philosopher and one of our Popes? Poor Bebius, a judge, whilst he demurreth the suit of a plaintiff but for eight days, behold his last expired. And Caius Julius, a physician, whilst he was anointing the eyes of one of his patients, to have his own sight closed forever by death. And if amongst these examples I may add one of a brother of mine called Captain Saint-Martin, a man of three and twenty years of age, who had already given good testimony of his worth and forward valor, playing at tennis, received a blow with a ball that hit him a little above the right ear, without appearance of any contusion, bruise, or hurt, and never sitting or resting upon it, died within six hours after of an apoplexy which the blow of the ball caused in him.

These so frequent and ordinary examples, happening and being still before our eyes, how is it possible for a man to forgo or forget the remembrance of death? And why should it not continually seem unto us that she is still ready at hand to take us by the throat?

What matter is it, will you say unto me, how and in what manner it is, so long as a man do not trouble and vex himself therewith? I am of this opinion, that howsoever a man may shroud or hide himself from her dart, yea were it under an ox-hide, I am not the man would shrink back. It sufficeth me to live at my ease; and the best recreation I can have, that do I ever take; in other matters, as little vainglorious and exemplary as you list.

> A dotard I had rather seem, and dull,
> So me my faults may please make me a gull,
> Than to be wise, and beat my vexed skull.
>
> Hor. *Epist.* II.ii.126.

But it is folly to think that way to come unto it. They come, they go, they trot, they dance; but no speech of death. All that is good

---

as whilom that one was when Pope Clement, my neighbor, made his entrance into Lyon." Clement V had formerly been Archbishop of Bordeaux, and thus Montaigne calls him "my neighbor."

[5] Henri II.

sport. But if she be once come, and on a sudden and openly surprise either them, their wives, their children, or their friends, what torments, what outcries, what rage, and what despair doth then overwhelm them? Saw you ever anything so drooping, so changed, and so distracted? A man must look to it, and in better times foresee it. And might that brutish carelessness lodge in the mind of a man of understanding (which I find altogether impossible), she sells us her ware at an over-dear rate: were she an enemy by man's wit to be avoided, I would advise men to borrow the weapons of cowardliness. But since it may not be, [B]and that be you either a coward or a runaway, an honest or valiant man, she overtakes you —

> [A]She persecutes the man that flies,
> She spares not weak youth to surprise,
> But on their hams and back turned plies.
>
> Hor. *Odes* III.ii.14.

— [B]and that no temper of cuirass may shield or defend you —

> Though he with iron and brass his head impale,
> Yet death his head enclosed thence will hale.
>
> Prop. *El.* IV.xviii.25.

— [A]let us learn to stand, and combat her with a resolute mind. And [to] begin to take the greatest advantage she hath upon us from her, let us take a clean contrary way from the common, let us remove her strangeness from her, let us converse, frequent, and acquaint ourselves with her, let us have nothing so much in mind as death, let us at all times and seasons and in the ugliest manner that may be, yea with all faces shape and represent the same unto our imagination. At the stumbling of a horse, at the fall of a stone, at the least prick with a pin, let us presently ruminate and say with ourselves, "What if it were death itself?" And thereupon let us take heart of grace and call our wits together to confront her. Amidst our banquets, feasts, and pleasures, let us ever have this restraint or object before us, that is, the remembrance of our condition; and let not pleasure so much mislead or transport us that we altogether neglect or forget how many ways our joys or our feastings be subject unto death, and by how many hold-fasts she threatens us and them. So did the Egyptians, who in the midst of their banquetings and in the full of their greatest cheer caused the anatomy* of a dead man to be brought before them as a memorandum and warning to their guests.

> Think every day shines on thee as thy last,
> Welcome it will come, whereof hope was past.
>
> Hor. *Epist.* I.iv.13.

It is uncertain where death looks for us; let us expect her everywhere. The premeditation of death is a forethinking of liberty. He who hath learned to die, hath unlearned to serve. [C]There is no evil in life for him that hath well conceived how the privation of life is no evil. To know how to die doth free us from all subjection and constraint. [A]Paulus Aemilius answered one whom that miserable king of Macedon, his prisoner, sent to entreat him he would not lead him in triumph, "Let him make that request unto himself." Verily, if Nature afford not some help, in all things it is very hard that art and industry should go far before. Of myself, I am not much given to melancholy, but rather to dreaming and sluggishness. There is nothing wherewith I have ever more entertained myself than with the imaginations of death, yea in the most licentious times of my age,

> [B]When my age flourishing
> Did spend its pleasant spring,
> Catul. LXVIII.16.

[A]being amongst fair ladies and in earnest play, some have thought me busied, or musing with myself how to digest some jealousy, or meditating on the uncertainty of some conceived hope, when God he knows I was entertaining myself with the remembrance of someone or other that but few days before was taken with a burning fever, and of his sudden end, coming from such a feast or meeting where I was myself, and with his head full of idle conceits, of love and merry glee; supposing the same, either sickness or end, to be as near me as him.

> [B]Now time would be, no more
> You can this time restore.
> Lucr. III.915.

[A]I did no more trouble myself or frown at such a conceit than at any other. It is impossible we should not apprehend or feel some motions or startings at such imaginations at the first, and coming suddenly upon us. But doubtless he that shall manage and meditate upon them with an impartial eye, they will assuredly, in tract of time, become familiar to him. Otherwise, for my part, I should be in continual fear and agony, for no man did ever more distrust his life nor make less account of his continuance. Neither can health, which hitherto I have so long enjoyed and which so seldom hath been crazed, lengthen my hopes nor any sickness shorten them of it. At every minute methinks I make an escape. [C]And I uncessantly record unto myself that whatsoever may be done another day, may be effected this day. [A]Truly, hazards and dangers do little or nothing approach us at our end. And if we consider how many more there remain besides this accident, which in number more than millions seem to threaten us and hang over us, we shall find that be we sound or sick, lusty or weak, at sea or at land, abroad or at home, fighting or at rest, in the midst of a battle or in our beds, she is ever alike near unto us. [C]"No man is weaker than other; none surer of himself (to live) till tomorrow [Sen. *Epist.* XCI.]. [A]Whatsoever I have to do before death, all leisure to end the same seemeth short unto me, yea were it but of one hour. Somebody, not long since turning over my writing tables, found by chance a memorial of something I would have done after my death. I told him (as indeed it was true) that being but a mile from my house and in perfect health and lusty, I had made haste to write it because I could not assure myself I should ever come home in safety. [C]As one that am ever hatching of mine own thoughts, and place them in myself, I am ever prepared about that which I may be. Nor can death (come when she please) put me in mind of any new thing. [A]A man should ever, as much as in him lieth, be ready booted to take his journey, and above all things, look he have then nothing to do but with himself.

> [B]To aim why are we ever bold,
> At many things in so short hold?
> Hor. *Odes.* II.xvi.17.

[A]For then we shall have work sufficient, without any more accrease.* Some man complaineth more that death doth hinder him from the assured course of an hoped-for victory than of death itself; another cries out he should give place to her before he have married his daughter or directed the course of his children's bringing up; another bewaileth he must forgo his wife's company; another moaneth the loss of his children, the chiefest commodities of his being. [C]I am now, by means of the mercy of God, in such a taking that without regret or grieving at any worldly matter, I am prepared to dislodge whensoever he shall please to call me. I am everywhere free. My farewell is soon taken of all my friends, except of myself. No man did ever prepare himself to quit the world more simply and fully, or more generally [shake] off all thoughts of it, than I am fully assured I shall do. The deadest deaths are the best.

> [B]O wretch, O wretch, (friends cry) one day,
> All joys of life hath ta'en away!
> Lucr. III.898.

[A]And the builder,

> The works unfinished lie,
> And walls that threatened high.
> Virg. *Aen.* IV.88.

A man should design nothing so long aforehand, or at least with such an intent, as to passionate himself to see the end of it. We are all born to be doing.

> When dying I myself shall spend,
> Ere half my business come to end.
> Ovid. *Am.* II.x.36.

I would have a man to be doing, [C]and to prolong his life's offices as much as lieth in him, [A]and let death seize upon me whilst I am setting my cabbages, careless of her dart, but more of my unperfect garden. I saw one die who, being at his last gasp, uncessantly complained against his destiny and that death should so unkindly cut him off in the midst of a history which he had in hand and was now come to the fifteenth or sixteenth of our kings.

> [B]Friends add not that in this case, now no more
> Shalt thou desire, or want things wished before.
> Lucr. III.900.

[A]A man should rid himself of these vulgar and hurtful humors. Even as churchyards were first placed adjoining unto churches and in the most frequented places of the city, to inure (as Lycurgus said) the common people, women and children, not to be scared at the sight of a dead man, and to the end that continual spectacle of bones, souls, tombs, graves, and burials, should forewarn us of our condition and fatal end.

> [B]Nay more, the manner was to welcome guests,
> And with dire shows of slaughter to mix feasts
> Of them that fought at sharp, and with boards tainted
> Of them with much blood, who o'er full cups fainted.
> Sil. Ital. XI.51.

[C]And even as the Egyptians, after their feastings and carousings, caused a great image of death to be brought in and showed to the guests and bystanders, by one that cried aloud, "Drink and be merry, for such shalt thou be when thou art dead," [A]so have I learned this custom or lesson, to have always death not only in my imagination but continually in my mouth. And there is nothing I desire more to be informed of than of the death of men: that is to say, what words, what countenance, and what face they show at their death; and in reading of histories, which I so attentively observe. [C]It appeareth by the shuffling and huddling up of my examples, I affect no subject so particularly as this. Were I a composer of books, I would keep a register commented of the diverse deaths, which in teaching men to die should after teach them to live. Dicaearchus made one of that title, but of another and less profitable end.

[A]Some man will say to me, the effect exceeds the thought so far that there is no fence so sure or cunning so certain but man shall either lose or forget if he come once to that point. Let them say what they list. To premeditate on it giveth no doubt a great advantage. And [is it] nothing, at the least to go so far without dismay or alteration, or without an ague? There belongs more to it: nature herself lends her hand and gives us courage. If it be a short and violent death, we have no leisure to fear it; if otherwise, I perceive that according as I engage myself in sickness, I do naturally fall into some disdain and contempt of life. I find that I have more ado to digest this resolution, that I shall die, when I am in health than I have when I am troubled with a fever; forsomuch as I have no more such fast hold on the commodities of life, whereof I begin to lose the use and pleasure, and view death in the face with a less daunted look, which makes me hope that the further I go from that and the nearer I approach to this, so much more easily do I enter in composition for their exchange. Even as I have tried in many other occurrences, which Caesar affirmed, that often some things seem greater, being far from us, than if they be near at hand, I have found that being in perfect health, I have much more been frightened with sickness than when I have felt it. The jollity wherein I live, the pleasure and the strength, make the other seem so disproportionable from that, that by imagination I amplify these commodities by one moiety,* and apprehended them much more heavy and burdensome than I feel them when I have them upon my shoulders. The same, I hope, will happen to me of death.

[B]Consider we by the ordinary mutations and daily declinations which we suffer, how nature deprives us of the [sight] of our loss and empairing.* What hath an aged man left him of his youth's vigor and of his forepast life?

> Alas to men in years how small
> A part of life is left in all?
>
> Maxim. I.16.

[C]Caesar, to a tired and crazed soldier of his guard who in the open street came to him to beg leave he might cause himself to be put to death, viewing his decrepit behavior, answered pleasantly, "Dost thou think to be alive then?" [B]Were man all at once to fall into it, I do not think we should be able to bear such a change, but being fair and gently led on by her hand in a slow and, as it were, unperceived descent, by little and little, and step by step, she rolls us into that miserable state, and day by day seeks to acquaint us with it. So that when youth fails in us, we feel, nay we perceive, no shaking or transchange* at all in ourselves; which in essence and verity is a harder death than that of a languishing and irksome life or that of age. Forsomuch as the leap from an ill being unto a not being is not so dangerous or steepy as it is from a delightful and flourishing being unto a painful and sorrowful condition. [A]A weak-bending, and faint-[stooping] body hath less strength to bear and undergo a heavy burden. So hath our soul. She must be roused and raised against the violence and force of this adversary. For as it is impossible she should take any rest whilst she feareth, whereof if she be assured (which is a thing exceeding human condition) she may boast that it is impossible unquietness, torment, and fear, much less the least displeasure, should lodge in her.

> [B]No urging tyrant's threatening face,
> Where mind is sound can it displace,
> No troublous wind the rough seas' master,
> Nor Jove's great hand, the thunder-caster.
>
> Hor. *Odes* III.iii.3.

[A]She is made mistress of her passions and concupiscence, lady of indulgence, of shame, of poverty, and of all fortune's injuries. Let him that can, attain to this advantage. Herein consists the true and sovereign liberty, that affords us means wherewith to jest and make a scorn of force and injustice, and to deride imprisonment, gyves, or fetters.

> In gyves and fetters I will hamper thee,
> Under a jailer that shall cruel be:
> Yet, when I will, God me deliver shall,
> He thinks, I shall die: death is end of all.
>
> Hor. *Epist.* I.xvi.76.

Our religion hath had no surer human foundation than the contempt of life. Discourse of reason doth not only call and summon us unto it. For why should we fear to lose a thing which, being lost, cannot be moaned? But also, since we are threatened by so many kinds of death, there is no more inconvenience to fear them all than to endure one. [C]What matter is it when it cometh, since it is unavoidable? Socrates answered one that told him, "The thirty tyrants have condemned thee to death." "And nature them," said he. What fondness is it to cark* and care so much at that instant and passage from all exemption of pain and care? As our birth brought us the birth of all things, so shall our death the end of all things. Therefore is it as great folly to weep we shall not live a hundred years hence, so to wail we lived not a hundred years ago. Death is the beginning of another life. So wept we, and so much did it cost us to enter into this life; and so did we spoil us of our ancient veil in entering into it. Nothing can be grievous that is but once. Is it reason so long to fear a thing of so short time? Long life or short life is made all one by death. For long or short is not in things that are no more. Aristotle saith there are certain little beasts alongst the river Hypanis that live but one day; she which dies at eight o'clock in the morning, dies in her youth, and she that dies at five in the afternoon, dies in her decrepitude. Who of us doth not laugh when we shall see this short moment of continuance to be had in consideration of good or ill fortune? The most and the least in ours, if we compare it with eternity, or equal it to the lasting of mountains, rivers, stars, and trees, or any other living creature, is no less ridiculous.

[A]But nature compels us to it. "Depart," saith she, "out of this world even as you came into it. The same way you came from death to life, return without passion or amazement from life to death. Your death is but a piece of the world's order, and but a parcel of the world's life.

> [B]Mortal men live by mutual intercourse:
> And yield their life-torch, as men in a course.
>
> Lucr. II.76, 79.

[A]"Shall I not change this goodly contexture of things for you? It is the condition of your creation: death is a part of yourselves: you fly from yourselves. The being you enjoy is equally shared between life and death. The first day of your birth doth as well address you to die as to live.

> The first hour that to men
> Gave life, strait cropped it then.
>
> Sen. *Her. Fur.* Chor. III.874.

> As we are born to die; the end
> Doth of the original depend.
>
> Manil. *Ast.* IV.16.

[C]"All the time you live, you steal it from death; it is at her charge. The continual work of your life is to contrive death; you are in death during the time you continue in life: for you are after death, when you are no longer living. Or if you had rather have it so, you are dead after life, but during life you are still dying; and death doth more rudely touch the dying than the dead, and more lively and essentially. [B]If you have profited by life, you have also been fed thereby; depart then satisfied.

Why like a full-fed guest
Depart you not to rest?
Lucr. III.938.

"If you have not known how to make use of it, if it were unprofitable to you, what need you care to have lost it? To what end would you enjoy it longer?

Why seek you more to gain, what must again
All perish ill, and pass with grief or pain?
Lucr. III.941.

[C]"Life in itself is neither good nor evil: it is the place of good or evil, according as you prepare it for them. [A]And if you have lived one day, you have seen all: one day is equal to all other days. There is no other light, there is no other night. This sun, this moon, these stars, and this disposition, is the very same which your forefathers enjoyed and which shall also entertain your posterity.

[C]No other saw our Sires of old,
No other shall their sons behold.
Manil. I.522.

[A]"And if the worst happen, the distribution and variety of all the acts of my comedy is performed in one year. If you have observed the course of my four seasons, they contain the infancy, the youth, the virility, and the old age of the world. He hath played his part: he knows no other wiliness belonging to it but to begin again. It will ever be the same, and no other.

[B]We still in one place turn about,
Still there we are, now in, now out.
Lucr. III.1080.

The year into itself is cast
By those same steps, that it hath passed.
Virg. *Georg.* II.402.

[A]"I am not purposed to devise you other new sports.

Else nothing, that I can devise or frame,
Can please thee, for all things are still the same.
Lucr. III.944.

"Make room for others, as others have done for you. [C]Equality is the chief groundwork of equity; who can complain to be comprehended where all are contained? [A]So may you live long enough, you shall never diminish anything from the time you have to die: it is bootless; so long shall you continue in that state, which you fear, as if you had died being in your swathing* clothes and when you were sucking.

Though years you live, as many as you will,
Death is eternal, death remaineth still.
Lucr. III.1090.

B"And I will so please you that you shall have no discontent.

Thou knowest not there shall be not other thou,
When thou art dead indeed, that can tell how
Alive to wail thee dying,
Standing to wail thee lying.
Lucr. III.885.

"Nor shall you wish for life, which you so much desire.

For then none for himself himself or life requires:
Nor are we of ourselves affected with desires.
Lucr. III.919, 922.

"Death is less to be feared than nothing, if there were anything less than nothing.

Death is much less to us, we ought esteem,
If less may be, than what doth nothing seem.
Lucr. III.926.

C"Nor alive, nor dead, it doth concern you nothing. Alive, because you are; dead, because you are no more. AMoreover, no man dies before his hour. The time you leave behind was no more yours than that which was before your birth, Band concerneth you no more.

For mark, how all antiquity foregone
Of all time e'er we were, to us was none.
Lucr. III.972.

A"Wheresoever your life endeth, there is it all. CThe profit of life consists not in the space but rather in the use. Some man hath lived long that hath had a short life. Follow it whilst you have time. It consists not in number of years, but in your will, that you have lived long enough. ADid you think you should never come to the place where you were still going? CThere is no way but hath an end. AAnd if company may solace you, doth not the whole world walk the same path?

BLife past, all things at last
Shall follow thee as thou hast passed.
Lucr. III.968.

[A]"Do not all things move as you do, or keep your course? Is there anything grows not old together with yourself? A thousand men, a thousand beasts, and a thousand other creatures die in the very instant that you die.

> [B]No night ensued daylight, no morning followed night,
> Which heard not moaning mixed with sick men's groaning,
> With deaths and funerals joined was that moaning.
>
> Lucr. II.578.

[C]"To what end recoil you from it, if you cannot go back? You have seen many who have found good in death, ending thereby many, many miseries. But have you seen any that hath received hurt thereby? Therefore is it mere simplicity to condemn a thing you never proved, neither by yourself nor any other. Why dost thou complain of me and of destiny? Do we offer thee any wrong? Is it for thee to direct us, or for us to govern thee? Although thy age be not come to her period, thy life is. A little man is a whole man as well as a great man. Neither men nor their lives are measured by the ell. Chiron refused immortality, being informed of the conditions thereof, even by the god of time and of continuance, Saturn, his father. Imagine truly how much an everduring life would be less tolerable and more painful to a man than is the life which I have given him. Had you not death, you would then uncessantly curse and cry out against me that I had deprived you of it. I have of purpose and wittingly blended some bitterness amongst it, that so seeing the commodity of its use, I might hinder you from over-greedily embracing or indiscreetly calling for it. To continue in this moderation, that is, neither to fly from life nor to run to death (which I require of you), I have tempered both the one and other between sweetness and sourness. I first taught Thales, the chiefest of your sages and wise men, that to live and die were indifferent, which made him answer one very wisely, who asked him wherefore he died not. "Because," said he, "it is indifferent." The water, the earth, the air, the fire, and other members of this my universe, are no more the instruments of thy life than of thy death. Why fearest thou thy last day? He is no more guilty and conferreth no more to thy death than any of the others. It is not the last step that causeth weariness; it only declares it. All days march towards death; only the last comes to it."

[A]Behold here the good precepts of our universal mother, Nature.

I have oftentimes bethought myself whence it proceedeth that in times of war, the visage of death (whether we see it in us or in others) seemeth without all comparison much less dreadful and terrible unto us than in our houses or in our beds — otherwise it should be an army of physicians and whiners — and she ever being one, there must needs be much more assurance amongst country people and of base condition, than in others. I verily believe these fearful looks and astonishing countenances wherewith we encompass it are those that more amaze and terrify us than death: a new form of life; the outcries of mothers; the wailing of women and children; the visitation of dismayed and swooning friends; the assistance of a number of pale-looking, distracted, and whining servants; a dark chamber, tapers burning round about; our couch beset round with physicians and preachers; and, to conclude, nothing but horror and astonishment on every side of us: are we not already dead and buried? The very children are afraid of their friends when they see them masked, and so are we. The mask must as well be taken from things as from men, which being removed, we shall find nothing hid under it but the very same death that a silly* varlet or a simple maidservant did lately suffer without amazement or fear. Happy is that death which takes all leisure from the preparations of such an equipage.

Of Drunkenness

☙ II. 2 ⟡ 1572–80 ❧

[A]The world is nothing but variety and dissemblance. Vices are all alike, inasmuch as they are all vices — and so do haply the Stoics mean it. But though they are equally vices, they are not equal vices. And that he who hath started a hundred steps beyond the limits,

> On this side, or beyond the which
> No man can hold a right true pitch,
> Hort. *Sat.* I.i.107.

is not of worse condition than he that is ten steps short of it, is no whit credible; and that sacrilege is not worse than the stealing of a colewort* out of a garden.

> No reason can evict, as great or same sin taints,
> Him that breaks in another's garden tender plants,
> And him that steals by night things consecrate to saints.
> Hor. *Sat.* I.iii.115.

There is as much diversity in that as in any other thing. [B]The confusion of order and measure of crimes is dangerous. Murderers, traitors, and tyrants have too much gain by it. It is no reason their conscience should be eased, in that some is either idle or lascivious or less assiduous unto devotion. Every man poiseth* upon his fellow's sin and elevates his own. Even teachers do often range it ill, in my conceit. [C]As Socrates said that the chiefest office of wisdom was to distinguish goods and evils, we others, to whom the best is ever in vice, should say the like of [the] knowledge to distinguish vices. Without which, and that very exact, both virtuous and wicked men remain confounded and unknown.

[A]Now drunkenness, amongst others, appeareth to me a gross and brutish vice. The mind hath more part elsewhere. And some vices there are which (if it may lawfully be spoken) have a kind of I wot not what generosity in them. Some there are that have learning, diligence, valor, prudence, wit, cunning, dexterity, and subtlety joined with them; whereas this is merely corporal and terrestrial. And the grossest and rudest nation that liveth amongst us at this day is only that which keepeth it in credit. Other vices but alter and distract the understanding, whereas this utterly subverteth the same, [B]and astonieth* the body.

> When once the force of wine hath inly pierced,
> Limbs' heaviness is next: legs fain would go,
> But reeling cannot; tongue drawls; mind's dispersed;
> Eyes swim; cries, hiccoughs, brables* grow.
>
> Lucr. III.475.

[C]The worst estate of man is where he loseth the knowledge and government of himself. [A]And amongst other things, it is said that as must-wine boiling and working in a vessel works and sends upward whatever it containeth in the bottom, so doth wine cause those that drink excessively of it [to] work up and break out their most concealed secrets.

> [B]Thou, wine-cup, dost by wine reveal
> The cares which wise men would conceal
> And close drifts at a merry meal.
>
> Hor. *Odes* III.xxi.14.

[A]Josephus reporteth that by making an ambassador to tipple-square,* whom his enemies had sent unto him, he wrested all his secrets out of him. Nevertheless, Augustus having trusted Lucius Piso, that conquered Thrace, with the secretest affairs he had in hand, had never cause to be discontented with him; nor Tiberius with Cossus, to whom he imparted all his seriousest counsels, although we know them both to have so given themselves to drinking of wine that they were often fain to be carried from the Senate, and both were reputed notable drunkards.

> Veins puffed up, as is used alway,
> By wine which was drunk yesterday.
>
> Virg. *Buc.* VI.15.

[C]And as faithfully [w]as the complot* and purpose to kill Caesar committed unto Cimber, who would daily be drunk with quaffing of wine, as unto Cassius, that drunk nothing but water; whereupon he answered very pleasantly, "What? Shall I bear a tyrant, that am not able to bear wine?" [A]We see our carousing toss-pot German soldiers, when they are most plunged in their cups and as drunk as rats, to have perfect remembrance of their quarter, of the watchword, and of their files.

> [B]Nor is the conquest easy of men soused,
> Lisping, and reeling with wine they caroused.
>
> Juven. *Sat.*XV.47.

[C]I would never have believed so sound, so deep, and so excessive drunkenness had I not read in histories that Attalus, having invited to sup with him (with intent to do him some notable indignity) the same Pausanias who for the same cause killed afterward Philip, King of Macedon, (a king who by the eminent fair qualities that were in him bore a testimony of the education he had learned in the house and company of Epaminondas) made him so dead drunk that, insensibly and without feeling, he might prostitute his beauty as the body of a common hedge-harlot to muleteers, grooms, and many of the abject servants of his house.

And what a lady whom I much honor and highly esteem told me, protesting that, near Bordeaux, towards Castres, where her house is, a widow countrywoman, reputed very chaste and honest, suspecting herself to be with child, told her neighbors that, had she a husband, she should verily think she were with child. But the occasion of this suspicion increasing more and more, and perceiving herself so big-bellied that she could not longer conceal it, she resolved to make the parish priest acquainted with it, whom she entreated to publish in the church that, whosoever he were that was guilty of the fact and would avow it, she would freely forgive him and, if he were so pleased, take him to her husband. A certain swain or hine-boy* of hers, emboldened by this proclamation, declared how that, having one holiday found her well tippled with wine and so sound asleep by the chimney-side, lying so fit and ready for him, that without awaking her he had the full use of her body. Whom she accepted for her husband, and both live together at this day.

[A]It is assured that antiquity hath not greatly described this vice. The compositions of divers philosophers speak but sparingly of it. Yea, and some of the Stoics deem it not amiss for man sometimes to take his liquor roundly and drink drunk, thereby to recreate his spirits.

> [B]They say, in this too, Socrates the wise,
> And great in virtue's combats, bare the prize.
> Pseudo-Gallus I.47.

[A]Cato, [C]that strict censurer and severe corrector of others, [A]hath been reproved for much drinking,

> [B]'Tis said, by use of wine repeated
> Old Cato's virtue oft was heated.
> Hor. *Odes* III.xxi.11.

[A]Cyrus, that so far-renowned king, amongst his other commendations, meaning to prefer himself before his brother Artaxerxes and get the start of him, allegeth that he could drink better and tipple more than he. And amongst the best policed and formalest nations, the custom of drinking and pledging of healths was much in use. I have heard Silvius, that excellent physician of Paris, affirm that, to preserve the vigor of our stomach from empairing,* it is not amiss once a month to rouse up the same by this excess of drinking; and lest it should grow dull and stupid, thereby to stir it up. [B]And it is written that the Persians, after they had well tippled, were wont to consult of their chiefest affairs.

[A]My taste, my relish, and my complexion are sharper enemies unto this vice than my discourse. For, besides that I captivate more easily my conceits under the authority of ancient opinions, indeed I find it to be a fond, a stupid, and a base kind of vice, but less malicious and hurtful than others, all which shock and, with a sharper edge, wound public society. And if we cannot give ourselves any pleasure except (as they say) it cost us something, I find this vice to be less chargeable unto our conscience than others. Besides, it is not hard to be prepared, difficult to be found — a consideration not to be despised.

[C]A man well advanced in years and dignity, amongst three principal commodities he told me to have remaining in life, counted this. And where shall a man more rightly find it than amongst the natural? But he took it ill. Delicateness and the choice of wines is therein to be avoided. If you prepare your voluptuousness to drink it with pleasure and daintily neat, you tie yourself unto an inconvenience to drink it other than is always to be had. A man must have a milder, a loose, and freer taste. To be a true drinker, a man should not have so tender and squeamish a palate. The Germans do in a manner drink equally of all sorts of wine with like pleasure. Their end is rather to gulp it down freely than to taste it kindly. And to say truth, they have it better cheap. Their voluptuousness is more plenteous and fuller. Secondarily, to drink after the French manner, as two draughts and moderately, is over-much to restrain the favors of that god. There is more time and constancy required thereunto. Our forefathers were wont to spend whole nights in that exercise; yea, oftentimes they joined whole long days unto them. And a man must proportion his ordinary more large and firm. I have in my days seen a principal lord and man of great employment and enterprises and famous for good success who, without straining himself and eating but an ordinary meal's meat, was wont to drink little less than five bottles of wine; yet at his rising seemed to be nothing distempered, but rather, as we have found to our no small cost in managing of our affairs, over-wise and considerate. The pleasure of that whereof we would make account in the course of our life ought to be employed longer space. It were necessary, as shop-boys or laboring people, that we should refuse no occasion to drink, and continually to have this desire in our mind. It seemeth that we daily shorten the use of this, and that in our houses (as I have seen in mine infancy) breakfasts, nunchions,* and beavers* should be more frequent and often used than nowadays they are. And should we thereby in any sort proceed towards amendment? No, verily. But it may be that we have much more given ourselves over unto paillardise* and all manner of luxury than our fathers were. They are two occupations that inter-hinder one another in their vigor. On the one side, it hath empaired* and weakened our stomach, and on the other sobriety serveth to make us more jolly-quaint, lusty, and wanton for the exercise of love matters.

It is a wonder to think on the strange tales I have heard my father report of the chastity of his times. He might well speak of it, as that he was both by art and nature proper for the use and solace of ladies. He spake little and well, few words but to the purpose, and was ever wont to intermix some ornament taken from vulgar* books and, above all, Spanish amongst his common speeches. And of all Spanish authors, none was more familiar unto him than Marcus Aurelius.[1] His demeanor and carriage was ever mild, meek, gentle, and very modest, and above all grave and stately. There is nothing he seemed to be more careful of than of his honesty, and [to] observe a kind of decency of his person and orderly decorum in his habits, were it on foot or on horseback. He was exceeding nice in performing his word or promise, and so strictly conscientious and obsequious in religion that generally he seemed rather to incline toward superstition than the contrary. Though he were but a little man, his courage and vigor was great. He was of an upright and well-proportioned stature, of a pleasing, cheerful-looking countenance, of a swarthy hue, nimbly addicted, and exquisitely nimble unto all noble and gentleman-like exercises. I have seen some hollow staves of his filled with lead which he wont to use and exercise his arms withal, the better to enable himself to pitch the bar, to throw the sledge, to cast the pole, and to play at fence, and shoes with leaden soles, which he wore to inure himself to leap, to vault, and to run. I may without blushing say that in memory of himself he hath left certain petty* miracles amongst us. I have seen him when he was past three-score years of age mock at all our sports and out-countenance our youthful pastimes, with a heavy, furred gown about him to leap into his saddle, to make the pommada* round about a table upon his thumb, and seldom to ascend any stairs without skipping three or four steps at once. And concerning my discourse, he was wont to say that in a whole province

1 This was an historical romance by Antonio de Guevara (1480?–1545) entitled *Reloj de príncipes o Libro áureo del emperador Marco Aurelio.* First published in 1529, it was translated into French as early as 1531.

there was scarce any woman of quality that had an ill name. He would often report strange familiarities, namely of his own, with very honest women without any suspicion at all. And protested very religiously that when he was married he was yet a pure virgin. Yet had he long time followed wars beyond the mountains and therein served long, whereof he hath left a journal-book of his own collecting, wherein he hath particularly noted whatsoever happened day by day worthy the observation so long as he served, both for the public and his particular use. And he was well strucken in years when he took a wife. For, returning out of Italy in the year of our Lord one-thousand-five-hundred-eight-and-twenty, and being full three and thirty years old, by the way he chose himself a wife. But come we to our drinking again.

[A]The incommodities of age, which need some help and refreshing, might with some reason beget in me a desire or longing of this faculty; for it is in a man the last pleasure which the course of our years stealeth upon us. Good fellows say that natural heat is first taken in our feet. That properly belongeth to infancy. From thence it ascendeth unto the middle region, where it is settled and continueth a long time; and, in mine opinion, there produceth the only true and moving pleasures of this corporal life. [C]Other delight and sensualities, in respect of that, do but sleep. [A]In the end, like unto a vapor which by little and little exhaleth and mounteth aloft, it comes unto the throat and there makes her last [a]bode.

[B]Yet could I never conceive how any man may either increase or prolong the pleasure of drinking beyond thirst and in his imagination frame an artificial appetite and against nature. My stomach could not well reach so far: it is very much troubled to come to an end of that which it takes for his need. [C]My constitution is, to make an account of drinking but to succeed meat; and therefore do I ever make my last draught the greatest. And, forasmuch as in age we have the roof of our mouths commonly furred with rheum or distempered, distasted, and altered through some other evil constitution, wine seemeth better unto us and of a quicker relish, according as our pores be either more or less open and washed; at least I seldom relish the same very well, except it be the first draught I take.[2] Anacharsis wondered to see the Grecians drink in greater glasses at the end of their meals than in the beginning. It was (as I imagine) for the very same reason that the Germans do it, who never begin to carouse but when they have well fed. Plato forbiddeth children to drink any wine before they be eighteen years of age and to be drunk before they

[2] This sentence, printed in the edition of 1595, is omitted in the Bordeaux *exemplaire* and is generally not to be found in modern translations.

come to forty. But to such as have once attained the age of forty, he is content to pardon them if they chance to delight themselves with it, and alloweth them somewhat largely to blend the influence of Dionysus in their banquets, that good god, who bestoweth cheerfulness upon men and youth unto aged men, who layeth and assuageth the passions of the mind, even as iron is made flexible by the fire. And in his profitable *Laws* [he finds] drinking-meetings or quaffing-companies as necessary and commendable (always provided there be a chief leader amongst them to contain and order them) — drunkenness being a good and certain trial of every man's nature and therewithal proper to give aged men the courage to make merry in dancing and in music, things allowable and profitable and such as they dare not undertake being sober and settled; that wine is capable to supply the mind with temperance and the body with health. Notwithstanding, these restrictions, partly borrowed of the Carthaginians, please him well. Let those forbear it that are going about any expedition of war. Let every magistrate and all judges abstain from it at what time they are to execute their charge and to consult of public affairs. Let none bestow the day in drinking, as the time that is due unto more serious negotiations, nor the nights wherein a man intendeth to get children. It is reported that Stilpo the philosopher, finding himself surcharged with age, did purposely hasten his end by drinking of pure wine. The like cause (though not wittingly) did also suffocate the vital forces, crazed through old age, of the philosopher Arcesilaus. [A]But it is an old and pleasant question whether a wise man's mind were like to yield unto the force of wine.

> If unresisted force it bends,
> 'Gainst wisdom which itself defends.
> Hor. *Odes* III.xxviii.4.

Unto what vanity doth the good opinion we have of ourselves provoke us! The most temperate and perfectest mind of the world finds it too great a task to keep herself upright, lest she fall by her own weakness. Of a thousand there is not one perfectly righteous and settled but one instant of her life; and question might be made whether, according to her natural condition, she might at any time be so. But to join constancy unto it [is] her last perfection — I mean, if nothing should shock her, which a thousand accidents may do. Lucretius, that famous poet, may philosophy* and bandy at his pleasure: lo, where he lieth senseless of an amorous potion. Thinks any man that an apoplexy cannot as soon astonish* Socrates as a poor laboring man? Some of them have by the force of a sickness forgot their own names, and a slight hurt have overthrown the judgment of others. Let him be as wise as he can, in the end he is but a man. What is more frail, more miserable, or more vain? Wisdom forceth not our natural conditions.

> [B]We see, therefore, paleness and sweats o'er-grow
> Our bodies; tongues do falter; voice doth break;
> Eyes dazzle; ears buzz; joints do shrink below.
> Lastly we swoon by heart-fright, terrors weak.
> Lucr. III. 155.

[A]He must [s]eel his eyes against the blow that threateneth him; being near the brim of a precipice, he must cry out [C]like a child. Nature having purposed to reserve these light marks of her authority unto herself, inexpugnable unto our reason and to the Stoic virtue, to teach him his mortality and our insipidity. [A]He waxeth pale for fear; he blusheth for shame; he groaneth feeling the colic, if not with a desperate and loud-roaring voice, yet with a low, smothered, and hoarse-sounding noise.

> He thinks that nothing strange be can
> To him, that longs to any man.
> Ter. *Heaut.* I.i.25.

Giddy-headed poets, [C]that fain what they list, [A]dare not so much as discharge their heroes from tears.

> So said he weeping, and so said,
> Himself hand to the steerage laid.
> Virg. *Aen.* VI.1.

Let it suffice him to bridle his affections and moderate his inclinations; for it is not in him to bear them away. Plutarch himself, who is so perfect and excellent a judge of human actions, seeing Brutus and Torquatus to kill their own children, remaineth doubtful whether virtue could reach so far and whether such men were not rather moved by some other passion. All actions beyond the ordinary limits are subject to some sinister interpretation — forasmuch as our taste doth no more come unto that which is above it than to that which is under it.

[C]Let us omit that other sect,[3] which maketh open profession of fierceness. But when, in the very same sect[4] which is esteemed the most demiss,* we hear the brags of Metrodorus: "Fortune, I have prevented, caught, and overtaken thee: I have mured and rammed up all thy passages whereby thou mightest attain unto me" (Cic. *Tusc.* V.9.). When Anaxarchus by the appointment of Nicocreon the tyrant of Cyprus, being laid along in a trough of stone and smoten

3 The Stoics. 4 The Epicureans.

with iron sledges, ceaseth not to cry out: "Strike, smite, and break; it is not Anaxarchus, it is but his veil* you martyr so. [A]When we hear our martyrs in the midst of a flame cry aloud unto the tyrant, "This side is roasted enough; chop it, eat it; it is full roasted; now begin on the other." When in Josephus we hear a child all to-rent* with biting snippers and pierced with the breath[5] of Antiochus, to defy him to death, cry with a loud-assured, and undismayed voice, "Tyrant, thou losest time: lo, I am still at mine ease. Where is that smarting pain, where are those torments wherewith whilom thou didst so threaten me? My constancy doth more trouble thee than I have feeling of thy cruelty. O faint-hearted varlet! Dost thou yield when I gather strength? Make me to faint or shrink; cause me to moan or lament; force me to yield and sue for grace if thou canst; encourage thy satellites; hearten thy executioners. Lo, how they droop and have no more power! Arm them; strengthen them; flesh them!" Verily we must needs confess there is some alteration and some fury (how holy soever) in those minds. When we come unto these Stoic evasions: "I had rather be furious than voluptuous" [C](the saying of Antisthenes) — [A]*Μανείην μᾶλλον ἢ ἡσθείην* (Diogenes Laertius VI.iii.) — "Rather would I be mad than merry"; when Sextius telleth us he had rather be surprised with pain than sensuality; when Epicurus undertakes to have the gout, to wantonize and fawn upon him and, refusing ease and health, with a hearty cheerfulness defy all evils, and, scornfully despising less sharp griefs, disdaining to grapple with them, he blithely desireth and calleth for sharper, more forcible, and worthy of him —

He wished, 'mongst heartless beasts, some foaming boar
Or mountain lion would come down and roar.
Virg. *Aen.* IV.158.

— who would not judge them to be pranks of a courage removed from his wonted seat? Our mind cannot out of her place attain so high. She must quit it and raise herself aloft and, taking the bridle in her teeth, carry and transport her man so far that afterward he wonder at himself and rest amazed at his actions. As, in exploits of war, the heat and earnestness of the fight doth often provoke the noble-minded soldiers to adventure on so dangerous passages that afterward, being better advised, they are the first to wonder at it. As also poets are often surprised and rapt with admiration at their own labors and forget the trace by which they passed so happy a career. It is that which some term a fury or madness in them. And as Plato saith, that a settled and reposed man doth in vain knock at

[5] Florio here misreads as *haleine* (breath) Montaigne's word *aleines* (awls).

poesy's gate. Aristotle likewise saith that no excellent mind is freely exempted from some or other intermixture of folly. And he hath reason to call any starting or extraordinary conceit (how commendable soever) and which exceedeth our judgment and discourse, folly — forsomuch as wisdom is an orderly and regular managing of the mind and which she addresseth with measure and conducteth with proportion and take her own word for it.[6] CPlato disputeth thus: that the faculty of prophesying and divination is far above us, and that when we treat it we must be beside ourselves: our wisdom must be darkened and overshadowed by sleep, by sickness, or by drowsiness, or by some celestial fury ravished from her own seat.

6 *"et s'en respond:"* that is, "and is responsible for it."

Of Friendship

⁂ I. 28 ◇ 1572–76, 1578–80 ⁂

[A]Considering the proceeding of a painter's work I have, a desire hath possessed me to imitate him. He maketh choice of the most convenient place and middle of every wall, there to place a picture labored with all his skill and sufficiency; and all void places about it he filleth up with antic* boscage* or crotesko* works, which are fantastical pictures having no grace but in the variety and strangeness of them. And what are these my compositions, in truth, other than antic* works and monstrous bodies, patched and huddled up together of divers members, without any certain or well-ordered figure, having neither order, dependency, or proportion, but casual and framed by chance?

A woman fair for parts superior,
Ends in a fish for parts inferior.
Hor. *Ars Poet.* 4.

Touching this second point, I go as far as my painter; but for the other and better part I am far behind. For my sufficiency reacheth not so far as that I dare undertake a rich, a polished, and according to true skill and artlike table.* I have advised myself to borrow one of Stephen de la Boétie, who with this kind of work shall honor all the world.[1] It is a discourse he entitled *Voluntary Servitude,* but those who have not known him have since very properly rebaptized the same, *The Against One.* In his first youth he writ, by way of essay, in honor of liberty against tyrants. It hath long since been dispersed amongst men of understanding, not without great and well-deserved commendations; for it is full of wit and containeth as much learning as may be; yet doth it differ much from the best he can do. And if in the age I knew him in he would have undergone my design to set his fantasies down in writing, we should doubtless see many rare things, and which would very nearly approach the honor of antiquity. For, especially touching that part of nature's gifts, I know none may

1 "*qui honorera tout le reste de cette besongne*": more accurately, "which will confer honor on all the rest of this work."

be compared to him. But it was not long* of him that ever this treatise came to man's view, and I believe he never saw it since it first escaped his hands, with certain other notes concerning the Edict of January, famous by reason of our intestine* war, which haply may in other places find their deserved praise.

It is all I could recover of his reliques [C](whom, when death seized, he, by his last will and testament, left with so kind remembrance heir and executor of his library and writings) [A]besides the little book I since caused to be published. To which his pamphlet I am particularly most bounden, forsomuch as it was the instrumental mean of our first acquaintance. For it was showed me long time before I saw him, and gave me the first knowledge of his name, addressing, and thus nourishing that unspotted friendship which we (so long as it pleased God) have so sincerely, so entire and inviolably maintained between us, that truly a man shall not commonly hear of the like; and amongst our modern men no sign of any such is seen. So many parts are required to the erecting of such a one that it may be counted a wonder if fortune once in three ages contract the like.

There is nothing to which nature hath more addressed us than to society. [C]And Aristotle saith that perfect law-givers have had more regardful care of friendship than of justice. [A]And the utmost drift of its perfection is this. For [C]generally, all those amities which are forged and nourished by voluptuousness or profit, public or private need, are thereby so much the less fair and generous, and so much the less true amities in that they intermeddle other causes, scope, and fruit with friendship than itself alone. Not do those four ancient kinds of friendships, natural, social, hospitable, and venerean, either particularly or conjointly beseem the same.

[A]That from children to parents may rather be termed respect. Friendship is nourished by communication which, by reason of the over-great disparity cannot be found in them and would haply offend the duties of nature; for neither all the secret thoughts of parents can be communicated unto children, lest it might engender an unbeseeming familiarity between them, nor the admonitions and corrections (which are the chiefest offices of friendship) could be exercised from children to parents. There have nations been found where, by custom, children killed their parents, and others where parents slew their children, thereby to avoid the hindrance of inter-bearing* one another in aftertimes; for naturally one dependeth from the ruin of another. There have philosophers been found disdaining this natural conjunction: witness [C]Aristippus, [A]who, being urged with the affection he ought* his children, as proceeding from his loins, began to spit, saying that also that excrement proceeded from him and that also we engendered worms and lice. And that other man, whom Plutarch would have persuaded to agree with his brother, answered, "I care not a straw the more for him, though he came out of the same womb I did."

Verily, the name of brother is a glorious name, and full of loving kindness; and therefore did he and I term one another sworn brother. But this commixture, dividence, and sharing of goods, this joining wealth to wealth, and that the riches of one shall be the poverty of another, doth exceedingly distemper and distract all brotherly alliance and lovely conjunction. If brothers should conduct the progress of their advancement and thrift in one same path and course, they must necessarily oftentimes hinder and cross one another. Moreover, the correspondency and relation that begetteth these true and mutually perfect amities, why shall it be found in these? The father and the son may very well be of a far differing complexion, and so may brothers. He is my son, he is my kinsman; but he may be a fool, a bad, or a peevish-minded man. And then, according as they are friendships which the law and duty of nature doth command us, so much the less of our own voluntary choice and liberty is there required unto it. And our genuine liberty hath no production more properly her own than that of affection and amity. Sure I am that, concerning the same, I have assayed all that might be, having had the best and most indulgent father that ever was, even to his extremest age, and who from father to son was descended of a famous house and, touching this rare-seen virtue of brotherly concord, very exemplary:

[B]To his brothers known so kind,
As to bear a father's mind.
Hor. *Odes* II.ii.6.

[A]To compare the affection toward women unto it, although it proceed from our own free choice, a man cannot; nor may it be placed in this rank. Her fire, I confess it

(Nor is that goddess ignorant of me,
Whose bitter-sweets with my cares mixed be)
Catul. *Epigr.* LXVIII.17.

to be more active, more fervent, and more sharp. But it is a rash and wavering fire, waving and divers, the fire of an ague subject to fits and stints, and that hath but slender hold-fast* of us. In true friendship it is a general and universal heat and equally tempered, a constant and settled heat, all pleasure and smoothness, that hath no pricking or stinging in it, which, the more it is in lustful love, the more is it but a ranging and mad desire in following that which flies us:

> Ev'n as the huntsman doth the hare pursue,
> In cold, in heat, on mountains, on the shore,
> But cares no more, when he her ta'en espies,
> Speeding his pace, only at that which flies.
>
> Ariosto X.7.

As soon as it creepeth into the terms of friendship, that is to say in the agreement of wills, it languisheth and vanisheth away; enjoying doth lose it, as having a corporal end and subject to saciety.* On the other side, friendship is enjoyed according as it is desired: it is neither bred nor nourished nor increaseth but in jovissance,* as being spiritual and the mind being refined by use and custom. Under this chief amity these fading affections have sometimes found place in me, lest I should speak of him who in his verses speaks but too much of it. So are these two passions entered into me in knowledge one of another, but in comparison never: the first, flying a high and keeping a proud pitch, disdainfully beholding the other to pass her points far under it.

Concerning marriage — besides that it is a covenant which hath nothing free but the entrance, the continuance being forced and constrained, depending elsewhere than from our will, and a match ordinarily concluded to other ends — a thousand strange knots are therein commonly to be unknit, able to break the web and trouble the whole course of a lively affection; whereas in friendship there is no commerce or business depending on the same but itself. Seeing (to speak truly) that the ordinary sufficiency of women cannot answer this conference and communication, the nurse of this sacred bond; nor seem their minds strong enough to endure the pulling of a knot so hard, so fast, and durable. And truly, if without that, such a genuine and voluntary acquaintance might be contracted where not only minds had this entire jovissance,* but also bodies a share of the alliance, [C]and where a man might wholly be engaged, [A]it is certain that friendship would thereby be more complete and full; but this sex could never yet by any example attain unto it, [C]and is by ancient schools rejected thence.

[A]And this other Greek license is justly abhorred by our customs. [C]Which notwithstanding, because according to use it had so necessary a disparity of ages and difference of offices between lovers, did no more sufficiently answer the perfect union and agreement which here we require. "For, what love is this of friendship? Why doth no man love either a deformed young man or a beautiful old man?"

(Cic. *Tusc.* IV.33.). For even the picture the Academy makes of it will not (as I suppose) disavow me to say thus in her behalf: that the first fury inspired by the son of Venus in the lover's heart upon the object of tender youth's flower (to which they allow all insolent and passionate violences an immoderate heat may produce) was simply grounded upon an external beauty, a false image of corporal generation; for in the spirit it had no power, the sight whereof was yet concealed, which was but in his infancy and before the age of budding. For if this fury did seize upon a base-minded courage, the means of its pursuit were riches, gifts, favor to the advancement of dignities, and such-like vile merchandise, which they reprove. If it fell into a most generous mind, the interpositions were likewise generous: philosophical instructions, documents to reverence religion, to obey the laws, to die for the good of his country; examples of valor, wisdom, and justice; the lover endeavoring and studying to make himself acceptable by the good grace and beauty of his mind (that of his body being long since decayed), hoping by this mental society to establish a more firm and permanent bargain.

When this pursuit attained the effect in due season, (for by not requiring in a lover he should bring leisure and discretion in his enterprise, they require it exactly in the beloved; forasmuch as he was to judge of an internal beauty, of a difficile* knowledge and abstruse discovery) then by the interposition of a spiritual beauty was the desire of a spiritual conception engendered in the beloved. The latter was here chiefest; the corporal, accidental and second, altogether contrary to the lover. And therefore do they prefer the beloved and verify that the gods likewise prefer the same; and greatly blame the poet Aeschylus who, in the love between Achilles and Patroclus, ascribeth the lover's part unto Achilles, who was in the first and beardless youth of his adolescency and the fairest of the Grecians.

After this general community, the mistress and worthiest part of it predominant and exercising her offices, they say the most availful commodity did thereby redound both to the private and public; that it was the force of countries received the use of it, and the principal defense of equity and liberty: witness the comfortable loves of Hermodius and Aristogeiton. Therefore name they it sacred and divine, and it concerns not them whether the violence of tyrants or the demisness* of the people be against them. To conclude, all that can be alleged in favor of the Academy is to say that it was a love ending in friendship, a thing which hath no bad reference unto the Stoical definition of love, that "love is an endeavor of making friendship by the show of beauty" (Cic. *Tusc.* IV.34.).

I return to my description in a more equitable and equal manner. "Clearly friendships are to be judged by wits and ages already strengthened and confirmed" (Cic. *Amic.* XX.).

[A]As for the rest, those we ordinarily call friends and amities are but acquaintances and familiarities, tied together by some occasion or commodities, by means whereof our minds are entertained. In the amity I speak of, they intermix and confound themselves one in the other, with so universal a commixture that they wear out and can no more find the seam that hath conjoined them together. If a man urge me to tell wherefore I loved him, I feel it cannot be expressed [C]but by answering, "Because it was he, because it was myself."

[A]There is, beyond all my discourse and besides what I can particularly report of it, I know not what inexplicable and fatal power, a mean and mediatrix of this indissoluble union. [C]We sought one another before we had seen one another, and by the reports we heard one of another, which wrought a greater violence in us than the reason of reports may well bear. I think by some secret ordinance of the heavens we embraced one another by our names. And at our first meeting, which was by chance at a great feast and solemn meeting of a whole township, we found ourselves so surprised, so known, so acquainted, and so combinedly bound together, that from thence forward nothing was so near unto us as one unto another. He writ an excellent Latin satire, since published, by which he excuseth and expoundeth the precipitation of our acquaintance, so suddenly come to her perfection. Sithence* it must continue so short a time, and begun so late (for we were both grown men, and he some years older than myself), there was no time to be lost. And it was not to be modelled or directed by the pattern of regular and remiss friendship, wherein so many precautions of a long and preallable* conversation are required. This hath no other Idea than of itself, and can have no reference but to itself. [A]It is not one especial consideration, nor two, nor three, nor four, nor a thousand: it is I wot not what kind of quintessence of all this commixture which, having seized all my will, induced the same to plunge and lose itself in his; [C]which likewise having seized all his will, brought it to lose and plunge itself in mine with a mutual greediness and with a semblable concurrence. [A]I may truly say "lose," reserving nothing unto us that might properly be called our own, nor that was either his or mine.

When Laelius, in the presence of the Roman consuls — who, after the condemnation of Tiberius Gracchus, pursued all those that had been of his acquaintance — came to inquire of Caius Blosius, who was one of his chiefest friends, what he would have done for him, and that he answered, "all things"; "What? All things?" replied he, "And what if he had willed thee to burn our temples?"; Blosius answered, "He would never have commanded such a thing." "But what if he had done it?" replied Laelius. The other answered, "I would have obeyed him." If he were so perfect a friend to Gracchus as histories report, he needed not offend the consuls with this last and bold confession and should not have departed from the assurance he had of Gracchus his mind. But yet those who accuse this answer as seditious understand not well this mystery, and do not presuppose in what terms he stood and that he held Gracchus his will in his sleeve, both by power and knowledge. [C]They were rather friends than citizens, rather friends than [friends and] enemies of their country or friends of ambition and trouble. Having absolutely committed themselves one to another, they perfectly held the reins of one another's inclination; and let this yoke be guided by virtue and conduct of reason, because without them it is altogether impossible to combine and proportion the same, the answer of Blosius was such as it should be. If their affections miscarried, according to my meaning, they were neither friends one to other nor friends to themselves.

As for the rest, [A]this answer sounds no more than mine would do to him that would in such sort inquire of me, "if your will should command you to kill your daughter, would you do it?", and that I should consent unto it. For that beareth no witness of consent to do it, because I am not in doubt of my will, and as little of such a friend's will. It is not in the power of the world's discourse to remove me from the certainty I have of his intentions and judgments of mine. No one of its actions might be presented unto me, under what shape soever, but I would presently find the spring and motion of it. Our minds have jumped so unitedly together, they have with so fervent an affection considered of each other, and with like affection so discovered and sounded even to the very bottom of each other's heart and entrails, that I did not only know his as well as mine own, but I would verily rather have trusted him concerning any matter of mine than myself.

Let no man compare any of the other common friendships to this. I have as much knowledge of them as another, yea of the perfectest of their kind; [B]yet will I not persuade any man to confound their rules, for so a man might be deceived. In these other strict friendships a man must march with the bridle of wisdom and precaution in his hand; the bond is not so strictly tied but a man may in some sort distrust the same. "Love him," said Chilo, "as if you should one day hate him again. Hate him as if you should love him again." This precept, so abominable in this sovereign and mistress amity, is necessary and wholesome in the use of vulgar* [C]and customary [B]friendships,

[C]toward which a man must employ the saying Aristotle was wont so often to repeat: "O you my friends, there is no perfect friend."

[A]In this noble commerce, offices and benefits (nurses of other amities) deserve not so much as to be accounted of; this confusion so full of our wills is cause of it. For even as the friendship I bear unto myself admits no accrease* by any succor I give myself in any time of need, whatsoever the Stoics allege, and as I acknowledge no thanks unto myself for any service I do unto myself, so the union of such friends, being truly perfect, makes them lose the feeling of such duties and hate and expel from one another these words of division and difference: benefit, good deed, duty, obligation, acknowledgment, prayer, thanks, and such their like. All things being by effect common between them — wills, thoughts, judgments, goods, wives, children, honor, and life — [C]and their mutual agreement being no other than one soul in two bodies, according to the fit definition of Aristotle, [A]they can neither lend or give aught to each other. See here the reason why lawmakers, to honor marriage with some imaginary resemblance of this divine bond, inhibit donations between husband and wife, meaning thereby to infer that all things should peculiarly be proper to each of them and that they have nothing to divide and share together.

If in the friendship whereof I speak one might give unto another, the receiver of the benefit should bind his fellow. For, each seeking more than any other thing to do each other good, he who yields both matter and occasion is the man showeth himself liberal, giving his friend that contentment to effect towards him what he desireth most. [C]When the philosopher Diogenes wanted money, he was wont to say that he redemanded the same of his friends, and not that he demanded it. [A]And to show how that is practiced by effect, I will relate an ancient singular example.

Eudamidas the Corinthian had two friends, Charixenus, a Sicyonian, and Aretheus, a Corinthian. Being upon his deathbed, and very poor, and his two friends very rich, thus made his last will and testament. "To Aretheus, I bequeath the keeping of my mother, and to maintain her when she shall be old. To Charixenus the marrying of my daughter, and to give her as great a dowry as he may. And in case one of them shall chance to die before, I appoint the survivor to substitute his charge and supply his place." Those that first saw this testament laughed and mocked at the same; but his heirs, being advertised* thereof, were very well pleased and received it with singular contentment. And Charixenus, one of them, dying five days after Eudamidas, the substitution being declared in favor of Aretheus, he carefully and very kindly kept and maintained his mother; and of five talents that he was worth, he gave two and a half in marriage to one only daughter he had, and the other two and a half to the daughter of Eudamidas, whom he married both in one day.

This example is very ample, if one thing were not, which is the multitude of friends. For this perfect amity I speak of is indivisible: each man doth so wholly give himself unto his friend that he hath nothing left him to divide elsewhere. Moreover, he is grieved that he is [not] double, triple, or quadruple, and hath not many souls or sundry wills, that he might confer them all upon this subject. Common friendship may be divided. A man may love beauty in one, facility of behavior in another, liberality in one, and wisdom in another, paternity in this, fraternity in that man, and so forth. But this amity which possesseth the soul and sways it in all sovereignty, it is impossible it should be double. [C]If two at one instant should require help, to which would you run? Should they crave contrary offices of you, what order would you follow? Should one commit a matter to your silence, which if the other knew would greatly profit him, what course would you take? Or how would you discharge yourself? A singular and principal friendship dissolveth all other duties and freeth all other obligations. The secret I have sworn not to reveal to another, I may without perjury impart it unto him, who is no other but myself. It is a great and strange wonder for a man to double himself; and those that talk of tripling know not nor cannot reach unto the height of it. Nothing is extreme that hath his like. And he who shall presuppose that of two I love the one as well as the other, and that they inter-love one another, and love me as much as I love them, he multiplieth in brotherhood a thing most singular and a lonely one, and than which one alone is also the rarest to be found in the world.

[A]The remainder of this history agreeth very well with what I said; for Eudamidas giveth as a grace and favor to his friends to employ them in his need. He leaveth them as his heirs of his liberality, which consisteth in putting the means into their hands to do him good. And doubtless the force of friendship is much more richly shown in his deed than in Aretheus'.

To conclude, they are unimaginable effects, to him that hath not tasted them, [C]and which makes me wonderfully to honor the answer of that young soldier to Cyrus, who, inquiring of him what he would take for a horse with which he had lately gained the prize of a race, and whether he would change him for a kingdom, "No, surely, my liege," said he; "yet would I willingly forgo him to gain a true friend, could I but find a man worthy of so precious an alliance." He said not ill in saying "could I but find." For a man shall easily find men fit for a superficial acquaintance; but in this, wherein men negotiate from the very center of their hearts and make no spare of anything, it is most requisite all the wards* and springs be sincerely wrought and perfectly true.

In confederacies which hold but by one end, men have nothing to provide for but for the imperfections which particularly do interest and concern that end and respect. It is no great matter what religion my physician and lawyer is of: this consideration hath nothing common with the offices of that friendship they owe me. So do I in the familiar acquaintances that those who serve me contract with me. I am nothing inquisitive whether a lackey be chaste or no, but whether he be diligent; I fear not a gaming muleteer so much as if he be weak; nor a hot-swearing cook, as one that is ignorant and unskillful. I never meddle with saying what a man should do in the world — there are over many others that do it — but what myself do in the world.

> So is it requisite for me;
> Do thou as needful is for thee.
> Ter. *Heaut.* I.i.28.

Concerning familiar table-talk, I rather acquaint myself with and follow a merry-conceited humor than a wise man. And in bed I rather prefer beauty than goodness. And in society or conversation of familiar discourse, I respect rather sufficiency, though without *prud'homie**; and so of all things else. ᴬEven as he that was found riding upon a hobby-horse, playing with his children, besought him who thus surprised him not to speak of it until he were a father himself, supposing the tender fondness and fatherly passion which then would possess his mind should make him an impartial judge of such an action, so would I wish to speak to such as had tried what I speak of. But knowing how far such an amity is from the common use, and how seld* seen and rarely found, I look not to find a competent judge. For even the discourses which stern antiquity hath left us concerning this subject seem to me but faint and forceless in respect of the feeling I have of it. And in that point the effects exceed the very precepts of philosophy:

> For me, be I well in my wit,
> Nought as a merry friend so fit.
> Hor. *Sat.* I.v.44.

Ancient Menander accounted him happy that had but met the shadow of a true friend: verily he had reason to say so, especially if he had tasted of any. For truly, if I compare all the rest of my forepassed life, which although I have, by the mere* mercy of God, passed at rest and ease and, except the loss of so dear a friend, free from all grievous affliction, with an ever-quietness of mind, as one that have taken my natural and original commodities in good payment without searching any others — if, as I say, I compare it all unto the four years I so happily enjoyed the sweet company and dear, dear society of that worthy man, it is nought but a vapor, nought but a dark and irksome [night]. Since the time I lost him,

> Which I shall ever hold a bitter day,
> Yet ever honor'd (so my God t'obey),
> Virg. *Aen.* V.49.

I do but languish, I do but sorrow. And even those pleasures all things present me with, instead of yielding me comfort, do but redouble the grief of his loss. We were co-partners in all things. All things were with us at half; methinks I have stolen his part from him.

> I have set down no joy enjoy I may,
> As long as he my partner is away.
> Ter. *Heaut.* I.i.97.

I was so accustomed to be ever two, and so inured to be never single, that methinks I am but half myself.

> [B]Since that part of my soul riper fate reft me,
> Why stay I here the other part he left me?
> Nor so dear, nor entire, while here I rest.
> That day hath in one ruin both oppressed.
> Hor. *Odes* II.xvii.5.

[A]There is no action can betide me, or imagination possess me, but I hear him saying, as indeed he would have done to me:[2] for even as he did excel me by an infinite distance in all other sufficiencies and virtues, so did he in all offices and duties of friendship.

> What modesty or measure may I bear
> In want and wish of him that was so dear?
> Hor. *Odes* I.xxiv.1.

> A brother reft from miserable me,
> All our delights are perished with thee
> Which thy sweet love did nourish in my breath.
> Thou all my good hast spoiled in thy death;

2 Montaigne's sentence read: *"Il n'est action ou imagination où je ne le trouve à dire, comme si eut-il bien faict à moy."* A more accurate translation than Florio's would be: "There is no deed or thought where I do not miss him, as he would indeed have missed me."

With thee my soul is all and whole enshrin'd,
At whose death I have cast out of mind
All my mind's sweetmeats, studies of this kind.
Never shall I hear thee speak, speak with thee?
Thee brother, than life dearer, never see?
Yet shalt thou ever be belov'd of me.
Catul. LXVIII. 20; LXV.9.

But let us a little hear this young man speak, being but sixteen years of age.

Because I have found this work to have since been published (and to an ill end) by such as seek to trouble and subvert the state of our commonwealth, nor caring whether they shall reform it or no, which they have fondly inserted among other writings of their invention, I have revoked my intent, which was to place it here.[3] And lest the author's memory should any way be interessed* with those that could not thoroughly know his opinions and actions, they shall understand that this subject was by him treated of in his infancy only by way of exercise, as a subject common, bare-worn, and wire-drawn* in a thousand books. I will never doubt but he believed what he writ, and writ as he thought: for he was so conscientious that no lie did ever pass his lips, yea, were it but in matters of sport or play. And I know that, had it been in his choice, he would rather have been born at Venice than at Sarlat, and good reason why.[4] But he had another maxim deeply imprinted in his mind, which was carefully to obey and religiously to submit himself to the laws under which he was born. There was never a better citizen, nor more affected* to the welfare and quietness of his country, nor a sharper enemy of the changes, innovations, new-fangles, and hurly-burlies of his time. He would more willingly have employed the utmost of his endeavors to extinguish and suppress than to favor or furthen them. His mind was modelled to the pattern of other best ages. But yet, in exchange of his serious treatise, I will here set you down another, more pithy, material, and of more consequence, by him likewise produced in that tender age.[5]

[3] La Boétie's *Servitude volontaire,* for which this essay was to serve as a preface, was partially published by the Protestants in a seditious context in 1574, after Montaigne had written the greater part of his essay. In 1576, La Boétie's entire treatise was again published by the Protestants in another seditious book, and it was presumably after this that Montaigne decided to "revoke his intent."

[4] In the *Servitude volontaire* there is a long comparison made by La Boétie between the government of Venice and that of the Turks.

[5] In the following essay, Montaigne originally published 29 sonnets by La Boétie and dedicated them to Madame de Gramont, the Countess of Guissen.

Of the Cannibals

☙ I. 31 ✧ 1579–80 ❧

[A]At what time King Pyrrhus came into Italy, after he had surveyed the marshalling of the army which the Romans sent against him: "I wot not," said he, "what barbarous men these are (for so were the Grecians wont to call all strange nations), but the disposition of this army which I see is nothing barbarous." So said the Grecians of that which Flaminius sent into their country, [C]and Philip, viewing from a tower the order and distribution of the Roman camp in his kingdom under Publius Sulpitius Galba. [A]Lo how a man ought to take heed lest he overweeningly follow vulgar opinions, which should be measured by the rule of reason and not by the common report.

I have had long time dwelling with me a man who for the space of ten or twelve years had dwelled in that other world which in our age was lately discovered, in those parts where Villegaignon first landed and surnamed Antarctic France. This discovery of so infinite and vast a country seemeth worthy great consideration. I wot not whether I can warrant myself that some other be not discovered hereafter, sithence* so many worthy men, and better learned than we are, have so many ages been deceived in this. I fear me our eyes be greater than our bellies, and that we have more curiosity than capacity. We embrace all, but we fasten nothing but wind. Plato maketh Solon to report that he had learned of the priests of the city of Saïs in Egypt that, whilom and before the general deluge, there was a great island called Atlantis situated at the mouth of the strait of Gibraltar, which contained more firm land than Africa and Asia together. And that the kings of that country, who did not only possess that island but had so far entered the mainland that of the breadth of Africa they held as far as Egypt, and of Europe's length, as far as Tuscany. And that they undertook to invade Asia and to subdue all the nations that compass the Mediterranean Sea, to the gulf of Mare Maggiore; and to that end they traversed all Spain, France, and Italy, so far as Greece, where the Athenians made head against them. But that a while after, both the Athenians themselves and that great island were swallowed up by the deulge. It is very likely this extreme ruin of waters wrought strange alterations in the habitations of the earth, as some hold that the sea hath divided Sicily from Italy,

> [B]Men say sometimes this land by that forsaken,
> And that by this, were split and ruin-shaken,
> Whereas till then both lands as one were taken.
> Virg. *Aen.* III.414–416.

[A]Cyprus from Syria, the island of Negroponte from the mainland of Bœotia, and in other places joined lands that were sundered by the sea, filling with mud and sand the channels between them.

> The fen long barren, to be rowed in, now
> Both feeds the neighbor towns and feels the plow.
> Hor. *Ars Poet.* 65.

But there is no great apparence* the said island should be the new world we have lately discovered; for it well-nigh touched Spain, and it were an incredible effect of inundation to have removed the same more than twelve hundred leagues, as we see it is. Besides, our modern navigations have now almost discovered that it is not an island but rather firm land and a continent, with the East Indies on one side and the countries lying under the two poles on the other; from which if it be divided, it is with so narrow a strait and interval that it no way deserveth to be named an island. [B]For it seemeth there are certain motions in these vast bodies, [C]some natural and othersome [B]febricitant,* as well as in ours. When I consider the impression my river of Dordogne worketh in my time toward the right shore of her descent, and how much it hath gained in twenty years, and how many foundations of divers houses it hath overwhelmed and violently carried away, I confess it to be an extraordinary agitation. For should it always keep one course or had it ever kept the same, the figure of the world had ere this been overthrown. But they are subject to changes and alterations. Sometimes they overflow and spread themselves on one side, sometimes on another; and other times they contain themselves in their natural beds or channels. I speak not of sudden inundations, whereof we now treat the causes. In Médoc, alongst the seacoast, my brother the Lord of Arsac may see a town of his buried under the sands which the sea casteth up before it; the tops of some buildings are yet to be discerned. His rents and domains have been changed into barren pastures. The inhabitants thereabouts affirm that, some years since, the sea encroacheth so much upon them that they have lost four leagues of firm land. These sands are her forerunners. [C]And we see great hillocks of gravel moving, which march half a league before it and usurp on the firm land.

[A]The other testimony of antiquity, to which some will refer this discovery, is in Aristotle (if at least that little book, *Of Unheard-of Wonders,* be his), where he reporteth that certain Carthaginians having sailed athwart the Atlantic Sea without the strait of Gibraltar, after long time they at last discovered a great fertile island, all replenished with goodly woods and watered with great and deep rivers, far distant from all land; and that both they and others, allured by the goodness and fertility of the soil, went thither with their wives, children, and household, and there began to inhabit and settle themselves. The lords of Carthage, seeing their country by little and little to be dispeopled, made a law and express inhibition that upon pains of death no more men should go thither, and banished all that were gone thither to dwell, fearing (as they said) that in success* of time they would so multiply as they might one day supplant them and overthrow their own estate. This narration of Aristotle hath no reference unto our new-found countries.

This servant I had was a simple and rough-hewn fellow, a condition fit to yield a true testimony. For subtle people may indeed mark more curiously and observe things more exactly, but they amplify and gloss them; and, the better to persuade and make their interpretations of more validity, they cannot choose but somewhat alter the story. They never represent things truly, but fashion and mask them according to the visage they saw them in; and to purchase credit to their judgment and draw you on to believe them, they commonly adorn, enlarge, yea, and hyperbolize the matter. Wherein is required either a most sincere reporter or a man so simple that he may have no invention to build upon and to give a true likelihood unto false devices, and be not wedded to his own will. Such a one was my man, who, besides his own report, hath many times showed me divers mariners and merchants whom he had known in that voyage. So am I pleased with his information that I never inquire what cosmographers say of it. We had need of topographers to make us particular narrations of the places they have been in. For some of them, if they have the advantage of us that they have seen Palestine, will challenge a privilege to tell us news of all the world besides. I would have every man write what he knows and no more, not only in that but in all other subjects. For one may have particular knowledge of the nature of one river and experience of the quality of one fountain, that in other things knows no more than another man, who nevertheless, to publish this little scantling,* will undertake to write of all the physics. From which vice proceed divers great inconveniences.

Now (to return to my purpose), I find (as far as I have been informed) there is nothing in that nation that is either barbarous or savage, unless men call that barbarism which is not common to them. As indeed we have no other aim of truth and reason than the example and Idea of the opinions and customs of the country we live in. There is ever perfect religion, perfect policy, perfect and complete use of all things. They are even savage, as we call those fruits wild which nature of herself and of her ordinary progress hath produced; whereas indeed they are those which ourselves have altered by our artificial devices and diverted from their common order, we should rather term savage. In those are the true and most profitable virtues and natural properties most lively and vigorous, which in these we have bastardized, applying them to the pleasure of our corrupted taste. [C]And if, notwithstanding, in divers fruits of those countries that were never tilled we shall find that in respect of ours they are most excellent and as delicate unto our taste, [A]there is no reason art should gain the point of honor of our great and puissant mother nature. We have so much by our inventions surcharged the beauties and riches of her works that we have altogether overchoked her. Yet, wherever her purity shineth she makes our vain and frivolous enterprises wonderfully ashamed.

> [B]Ivies spring better of their own accord,
> Unhaunted plots much fairer trees afford.
> Birds by no art much sweeter notes record.
> Prop. *El.* I.ii.10.

[A]All our endeavor or wit cannot so much as reach to represent the nest of the least birdlet, its contexture, beauty, profit, and use, no nor the web of a silly* spider. [C]"All things," saith Plato, "are produced either by nature, by fortune, or by art: the greatest and fairest by one or other of the two first, the least and imperfect by the last" (*Laws* X.). [A]Those nations seem, therefore, so barbarous unto me, because they have received very little fashion from human wit and are yet near their original naturality. The laws of nature do yet command them, which are but little bastardized by ours; and that with such purity as I am sometimes grieved the knowledge of it came no sooner to light, at what time there were men that better than we could have judged of it. I am sorry Lycurgus and Plato had it not, for meseemeth that what in those nations we see by experience doth not only exceed all the pictures wherewith licentious poesy hath proudly embellished the golden age and all her quaint inventions to feign a happy condition of man, but also the conception and desire of philosophy. They could not imagine a genuity* so pure and simple as we see it by experience, nor ever believe our society might be maintained with so little art and human combination. It is a nation, would I answer Plato, that hath no kind of traffic, no knowledge of letters, no intelligence of numbers, no name of magistrate nor of politic superiority, no use of service, of riches or of poverty, no contracts, no successions, no partitions, no occupation but idle, no respect of kindred but common, no apparel but natural, no manuring of lands, no use of wine, corn, or metal. The very words that import lying, falsehood, treason, dissimulations, covetousness, envy, detraction, and pardon, were never heard of amongst them. How dissonant would he find his imaginary commonwealth from this perfection![1]

> [B]Nature at first uprise,
> These manners did devise.
> Virg. *Georg.* II.20.

[A]Furthermore, they live in a country of so exceeding pleasant and temperate situation that, as my testimonies have told me, it is very rare to see a sick body amongst them; and they have further assured me they never saw any man there either shaking with the palsy, toothless, with eyes dropping, or crooked and stooping through age. They are seated alongst the sea-coast, encompassed toward the land with huge and steepy mountains, having between both a hundred leagues or thereabout of open and champain* ground. They have great abundance of fish and flesh that have no resemblance at all with ours, and eat them without any sauces or skill of cookery, but plain boiled or broiled. The first man that brought a horse thither, although he had in many other voyages conversed with them, bred so great a horror in the land that before they could take notice of him they slew him with arrows.

Their buildings are very long, and able to contain two or three hundred souls, covered with barks of great trees, fastened in the ground at one end, interlaced and joined close together by the tops, after the manner of some of our granges; the covering whereof hangs down to the ground and steadeth* them as a flank. They have a kind of wood so hard that, riving and cleaving the same, they make blades, swords, and gridirons to broil their meat with. Their beds are of a kind of cotton cloth, fastened to the house roof, as our ship cabins. Everyone hath his several couch, for the women lie from their husbands.

They rise with the sun, and feed for all day as soon as they are up, and make no more meals after that. They drink not at meal, as Suidas reporteth of some other people of the East which drank after meals, but drink many times a day and are much given to pledge carouses. Their drink is made of a certain root, and of the color of our claret

1 Florio omits the following quotation added by Montaigne: [C]"Men fresh sprung from gods" (Sen. *Epist.* XC.)

wines, which lasteth but two or three days. They drink it warm. It hath somewhat a sharp taste, wholesome for the stomach, nothing heady, but laxative for such as are not used unto it, yet very pleasing to such as are accustomed unto it. Instead of bread, they use a certain white composition, like unto corianders confected. I have eaten some, the taste whereof is somewhat sweet and wallowish.*

They spend the whole day in dancing. Their young men go ahunting after wild beasts with bows and arrows. Their women busy themselves therewhilst with warming of their drink, which is their chiefest office. Some of their old men, in the morning before they go to eating, preach in common to all the household, walking from one end of the house to the other, repeating one selfsame sentence many times till he have ended his turn (for their buildings are a hundred paces in length). He commends but two things unto his auditory: first, valor against their enemies; then lovingness unto their wives. They never miss (for their restraint) to put men in mind of this duty, that it is their wives which keep their drink lukewarm and well-seasoned. The form of their beds, cords, swords, blades, and wooden bracelets (wherewith they cover their hand wrists when they fight) and great canes, open at one end (by the sound of which they keep time and cadence in their dancing) are in many places to be seen, and namely in mine own house. They are shaven all over, much more close and cleaner than we are, with no other razors than of wood or stone. They believe their souls to be eternal, and those that have deserved well of their gods to be placed in that part of heaven where the sun riseth, and the cursed toward the west, in opposition. They have certain prophets and priests, which commonly abide in the mountains and very seldom show themselves unto the people. But when they come down, there is a great feast prepared and a solemn assembly of many townships together (each grange as I have described maketh a village, and they are about a French league one from another). The prophet speaks to the people in public, exhorting them to embrace virtue and follow their duty. All their moral discipline containeth but these two articles: first, an undismayed resolution to war; then an inviolable affection to their wives. He doth also prognosticate of things to come and what success they shall hope for in their enterprises. He either persuadeth or dissuadeth them from war; but if he chance to miss of his divination, and that it succeed otherwise than he foretold them, if he be taken, he is hewn in a thousand pieces and condemned for a false prophet. And therefore he that hath once misreckoned himself is never seen again.

[C]Divination is the gift of God, the abusing whereof should be a punishable imposture. When the divines amongst the Scythians had foretold an untruth, they were couched along upon hurdles full of heath or brushwood, drawn by oxen, and so, manacled hand and foot, burned to death. Those which manage matters subject to the conduct of man's sufficiency are excusable, although they show the utmost of their skill. But those that gull and cony-catch us with the assurance of an extraordinary faculty and which is beyond our knowledge, ought to be double punished: first, because they perform not the effect of their promise; then for the rashness of their imposture and unadvisedness of their fraud.

[A]They war against the nations that lie beyond their mountains, to which they go naked, having no other weapons than bows or wooden swords, sharp at one end as our broaches* are. It is an admirable thing to see the constant resolution of their combats, which never end but by effusion of blood and murder; for they know not what fear or routs are. Every victor brings home the head of the enemy he hath slain as a trophy of his victory and fasteneth the same at the entrance of his dwelling place. After they have long time used and treated their prisoners well and with all commodities they can devise, he that is the master of them, summoning a great assembly of his acquaintance, tieth a cord to one of the prisoner's arms, [C]by the end whereof he holds him fast, with some distance from him for fear he might offend him, [A]and giveth the other arm, bound in like manner, to the dearest friend he hath, and both in the presence of all the assembly kill him with swords. Which done, they roast and then eat him in common and send some slices of him to such of their friends as are absent. It is not, as some imagine, to nourish themselves with it (as anciently the Scythians wont to do), but to represent an extreme and inexpiable revenge. Which we prove thus: Some of them perceiving the Portugals, who had confederated themselves with their adversaries, to use another kind of death when they took them prisoners — which was to bury them up to the middle, and against the upper part of the body to shoot arrows, and then being almost dead, to hang them up — they supposed that these people of the other world (as they who had sowed the knowledge of many vices amongst their neighbors and were much more cunning in all kinds of evils and mischief than they) undertook not this manner of revenge without cause, and that consequently it was more smartful and cruel than theirs, and thereupon began to leave their old fashion to follow this.

I am not sorry we note the barbarous horror of such an action, but grieved that, prying so narrowly into their faults, we are so blinded in ours. I think there is more barbarism in eating men alive than to feed upon them being dead; to mangle by tortures and torments a body full of lively sense, to roast him in pieces, to make dogs and swine to gnaw and tear him in mammocks* (as we have not only read but seen very lately, yea and [in] our own memory, not amongst ancient enemies but our neighbors and fellow-citizens; and, which is worse, under pretense of piety and religion), than to roast and eat him after he is dead.

Chrysippus and Zeno, archpillars of the Stoic sect, have supposed that it was no hurt at all, in time of need and to what end soever, to make use of our carrion bodies and to feed upon them, as did our forefathers who, being besieged by Caesar in the city of Alexia, resolved to sustain the famine of the siege with the bodies of old men, women, and other persons unserviceable and unfit to fight.

[B]Gascons (as fame reports)
Lived with meats of such sorts.
Juven. *Sat.* XV.93.

[A]And physicians fear not, in all kinds of compositions availful to our health, to make use of it, be it for outward or inward applications. But there was never any opinion found so unnatural and immodest that would excuse treason, treachery, disloyalty, tyranny, cruelty, and suchlike, which are our ordinary faults.

We may then well call them barbarous in regard of reason's rules, but not in respect of us that exceed them in all kind of barbarism. Their wars are noble and generous and have as much excuse and beauty as this human infirmity may admit; they aim at nought so much, and have no other foundation amongst them, but the mere jealousy of virtue. They contend not for the gaining of new lands; for to this day they yet enjoy that natural uberty* and fruitfulness which without laboring toil doth in such plenteous abundance furnish them with all necessary things that they need not enlarge their limits. They are yet in that happy estate as they desire no more than what their natural necessities direct them. Whatsoever is beyond it is to them superfluous. Those that are much about one age do generally intercall one another brethren, and such as are younger they call children, and the aged are esteemed as fathers to all the rest. These leave this full possession of goods in common and without division to their heirs, without other claim or title but that which nature doth plainly impart unto all creatures, even as she brings them into the world. If their neighbors chance to come over the mountains to assail or invade them, and that they get the victory over them, the victors' conquest is glory and the advantage to be and remain superior in valor and virtue; else have they nothing to do with the goods and spoils of the vanquished, and so return into their country, where they neither want any necessary thing nor lack this great portion, to know how to enjoy their condition happily, and are contented with what nature affordeth them. So do these when their turn cometh. They require no other ransom of their prisoners but an acknowledgment and confession that they are vanquished. And in a whole age a man shall not find one that doth not rather embrace death than either by word or countenance remissly to yield one jot of an invincible courage. There is none seen that would not rather be slain and devoured than sue for life or show any fear. They use their prisoners with all liberty, that they may so much the more hold their lives dear and precious, and commonly entertain them with threats of future death, with the torments they shall endure, with the preparations intended for that purpose, with mangling and slicing of their members, and with the feast that shall be kept at their charge. All which is done to wrest some remiss and exact some faint-yielding speech of submission from them, or to possess them with a desire to escape or run away; that so they may have the advantage to have daunted and made them afraid and to have forced their constancy. For certainly true victory consisteth in that only point.

> CNo conquest such, as to suppress
> Foes' hearts, the conquest to confess.
> Claud. *Cons. Hon. Pan.* 248.

The Hungarians, a most warlike nation, were whilom wont to pursue their prey no longer than they had forced their enemy to yield unto their mercy. For having wrested this confession from him, they set him at liberty without offense or ransom, except it were to make him swear never after to bear arms against them.

AWe get many advantages of our enemies that are but borrowed and not ours. It is the quality of porterly* rascal and not of virtue, to have stronger arms and sturdier legs. Disposition is a dead and corporal quality. It is a trick of fortune to make our enemy stoop and to blear his eyes with the sun's light. It is a prank of skill and knowledge to be cunning in the art of fencing, and which may happen unto a base and worthless man. The reputation and worth of a man consisteth in his heart and will; therein consists true honor. Constancy is valor, not of arms and legs, but of mind and courage; it consisteth not in the spirit and courage of our horse nor of our arms, but in ours. He that obstinately faileth in his courage, C"if he slip or fall, he fights upon his knee" (Sen. *De provid.* II.). AHe that in danger of imminent death is no whit daunted in his assuredness, he that in yielding up his ghost beholding his enemy with a scornful and fierce look, he is vanquished, not by us, but by fortune; he is slain but not conquered. BThe most valiant are often the most unfortunate. CSo are there triumphant losses in envy of victories. Not those four sister victories — the fairest that ever the sun beheld with his all-seeing eye — of Salamis, of Platæa, of Mycale, and of Sicily, durst ever dare to oppose all their glory together to the glory of the King Leonidas his discomfiture and of his men at the passage of Thermopylæ. What man did ever run with so glorious an envy or more ambitious desire to the goal of a combat than Captain Ischolas to an evident loss and overthrow? Who so ingeniously or more politicly did ever assure himself of his welfare than he of his ruin? He was appointed to defend a certain passage of Peloponnesus against the Arcadians, which finding himself altogether unable to perform, seeing the nature of the place and inequality of the forces, and resolving that whatsoever should present itself unto his enemy must necessarily be utterly defeated. On the other side, deeming it unworthy both his virtue and magnanimity and the Lacedemonian name to fail or faint in his charge, between these two extremities he resolved upon a mean and indifferent course, which was this. The youngest and best-disposed of his troop he reserved for the service and defense of their country, to which he sent them back; and with those whose loss was least and who might best be spared, he determined to maintain that passage, and by their death to force the enemy to purchase the entrance of it as dear as possibly he could; as indeed it followed. For being suddenly environed round by the Arcadians, after a great slaughter made of them, both himself and all his were put to the sword. Is any trophy assigned for conquerors that is not more duly due unto these conquered? A true conquest respecteth rather an undaunted resolution and honorable end than a fair escape, and the honor of virtue doth more consist in combating than in beating.

[A]But, to return to our history, these prisoners, howsoever they are dealt withal, are so far from yielding that, contrariwise, during two or three months that they are kept, they ever carry a cheerful countenance and urge their keepers to hasten their trial; they outrageously defy and injure them. They upbraid them with their cowardliness and with the number of battles they have lost against theirs. I have a song made by a prisoner wherein is this clause, "Let them boldly come all together and flock in multitudes to feed on him, for with him they shall feed upon their fathers and grandfathers, that heretofore have served his body for food and nourishment. These muscles (saith he), this flesh, and these veins, are your own; fond men as you are, know you not that the substance of your forefathers' limbs is yet tied unto ours? Taste them well, for in them shall you find the relish of your own flesh." An invention that hath no show of barbarism. Those that paint them dying and that represent this action when they are put to execution, delineate the prisoners spitting in their executioners' faces and making mows* at them. Verily, so long as breath is in their body, they never cease to brave and defy them, both in speech and countenance. Surely, in respect of us these are very savage men; for either they must be so in good sooth, or we must be so indeed. There is a wondrous distance between their form and ours.

Their men have many wives, and by how much more they are reputed valiant, so much the greater is their number. The manner and beauty in their marriages is wondrous strange and remarkable. For the same jealousy our wives have to keep us from the love and affection of other women, the same have theirs to procure it. Being more careful for their husbands' honor and content than of anything else, they endeavor and apply all their industry to have as many rivals as possibly they can, forasmuch as it is a testimony of their husbands' virtue. [C]Our women would count it a wonder, but it is not so. It is virtue properly matrimonial, but of the highest kind. And in the Bible, Leah, Rachel, Sarah, and Jacob's wives brought their fairest maiden-servants unto their husbands' bed. And Livia seconded the lustful appetites of Augustus, to her great prejudice. And Stratonice, the wife of King Deiotarus, did not only bring a most beauteous chamber-maid that served her to her husband's bed, but very carefully brought up the children he begot on her, and by all possible means aided and furthered them to succeed in their father's royalty. [A]And lest a man should think that all this is done by a simple and servile or awful duty unto their custom, and by the impression of their ancient custom's authority, without discourse or judgment and because they are so blockish and dull-spirited that they can take no other resolution, it is not amiss we allege* some evidence of their sufficiency. Besides what I have said of one of their warlike songs, I have another amorous canzonet, which beginneth in this sense: "Adder, stay; stay, good adder, that my sister may by the pattern of thy parti-colored coat draw the fashion and work of a rich lace for me to give unto my love; so may thy beauty, thy nimbleness or disposition be ever preferred before all other serpents." The first couplet is the burden of the song. I am so conversant with poesy that I may judge this invention hath no barbarism at all in it, but is altogether Anacreontic. Their language is a kind of pleasant speech, and hath a pleasing sound and some affinity with the Greek terminations.

Three of that nation, ignorant how dear the knowledge of our corruptions will one day cost their repose, security, and happiness, and how their ruin shall proceed from this commerce, which I imagine is already well advanced (miserable as they are to have suffered themselves to be so cozened by a desire of new-fangled novelties, and to have quit the calmness of their climate to come and see ours), were at Rouen in the time of our late King Charles the Ninth, who talked with them a great while. They were shown our fashions, our pomp, and the form of a fair city. Afterward some demanded their advice and would needs know of them what things of note and admirable they had observed amongst us. They answered three things, the last of which I have forgotten and am very sorry for it; the other two I yet remember. They said, first, they found it very strange that so many tall men with long beards, strong and well-armed, as it were, about the king's person (it is very likely they meant the Switzers of his guard) would submit themselves to obey a beardless child, and that we did not rather choose one amongst them to command the rest. Secondly (they have a manner of phrase whereby they call men but a moiety* one of another), they had perceived there were men amongst us full-gorged with all sorts of commodities, and others which, hunger-starved and bare with need and poverty, begged at their gates; and found it strange these moieties* so needy could endure such an injustice, and that they took not the others by the throat or set fire on their houses. I talked a good while with one of them, but I had so bad an interpreter, and who did so ill apprehend my meaning, and who through his foolishness was so troubled to conceive my imaginations, that I could draw no great matter from him. Touching that point wherein I demanded of him what good he received by the superiority he had amongst his countrymen (for he was a captain and our mariners called him King), he told me it was to march foremost in any charge of war. Further, I asked him, how many men did follow him. He showed me a distance of place, to signify they were as many as might be contained in so much ground, which I guessed to be about four or five thousand men. Moreover I demanded if, when wars were ended, all his authority expired; he answered that he had only this left him, which was that when he went on progress and visited the villages depending of him, the inhabitants prepared paths and highways athwart* the hedges of their woods, for him to pass through at ease.

All that is not very ill; but what of that? They wear no kind of breeches nor hosen.

We Taste Nothing Purely

❧ II. 20 ◇ 1578–80 ☙

[A]The weakness of our condition causeth that things in their natural simplicity and purity cannot fall into our use. The elements we enjoy are altered; metals likewise. Yea, gold must be impaired with some other stuff to make it fit for our service. [C]Nor virtue so simple, which Aristo, Pyrrho, and the Stoics made the end of their life, hath been able to do no good without composition. Nor the Cyrenaic sensuality or Aristippian voluptuousness. [A]Of the pleasures and goods we have, there is none exempted from some mixture of evil and incommodity.

> [B]From middle spring of sweets, some bitter springs,
> Which in the very flower smartly stings.
>
> Lucr. IV.1133.

Our exceeding voluptuousness hath some air of groaning and wailing. Would you not say it dieth with anguish? Yea when we forge its image in her excellency, we deck it with epithets of sickish and dolorous qualities: languor, effeminacy, weakness, fainting, and *morbidezza,** a great testimony of their consanguinity and consubstantiality. [C]Excessive joy hath more severity than jollity; extreme and full content, more settledness than cheerfulness. "Felicity itself, unless it temper itself, distempers us" (Sen. *Epist.* LXXIV.). Ease consumeth us. [A]It is that which an old Greek verse saith of such a sense: "The Gods sell us all the goods they give us"; that is to say, they give us not one pure and perfect, and which we buy not with the price of some evil. [C]Travail and pleasure, most unlike in nature, are notwithstanding followed together by a kind of I wot not what natural conjunction. Socrates saith that some god attempted to huddle up together and confound sorrow and voluptuousness, but being unable to effect it, he bethought himself to couple them together at least by the tail. [B]Metrodorus said that in sadness there is some alloy of pleasure. I know not whether he meant anything else, but I imagine that for one to inure himself to melancholy there is some kind of purpose, of consent and mutual delight; I mean besides ambition, which may also be joined unto it. There is some shadow of delicacy and quaintness which smileth and fawneth upon us even in the lap of melancholy. Are there not some complexions that of it make their nourishment?

> It is some pleasure, yet,
> With tears our cheeks to wet.
> Ovid. *Trist.* IV.iii.27.

[C]And one Attalus, in Seneca, saith the remembrance of our l[o]st friends is as pleasing to us as bitterness in wine that is over old;

> Sir boy, my servitor of good old wine,
> Bring me my cup thereof bitter, but fine,
> Catul. XXV.1.

and as of sweetly sour apples. [B]Nature discovereth* this confusion unto us. Painters are of opinion that the motions and wrinkles in the face which serve to weep, serve also to laugh. Verily, before one or other be determined to express which, behold the picture's success; you are in doubt toward which one inclineth. And the extremity of laughing intermingles itself with tears. [C]"There is no evil without some obligation" (Sen. *Epist.* LXIX.).

When I imagine man fraught with all the commodities may be wished — let us suppose all his several members were forever possessed with a pleasure like unto that of generation, even in the highest point that may be — I find him to sink under the burthen of his ease, and perceive him altogether unable to bear so pure, so constant, and so universal a sensuality. Truly he flies when he is even upon the nick and naturally hasteneth to escape it, as from a step whereon he cannot stay or contain himself and feareth to sink into it.

[B]When I religiously confess myself unto myself, I find the best good I have, hath some vicious taint. And I fear that Plato in his purest virtue (I that am as sincere and loyal an esteemer thereof, and of the virtues of such a stamp, as any other can possibly be) if he had merely* listened unto it (and sure he listened very near) he would therein have heard some harsh tune of human mixture, but an obscure tune and only sensible unto himself. Man all in all is but a botching and parti-colored work. [A]The very laws of justice cannot subsist without some commixture of injustice. And Plato saith, they undertake to cut off Hydra's heads, that pretend to remove all incommodities and inconveniences from the laws. "Every great example hath some touch of injustice which is requited by the common good against particulars," saith Tacitus (Tac. *Ann.* XIV.xliv.).

[B]It is likewise true that for the use of life and service of public society there may be excess in the purity and perspicuity of our spirits. This piercing brightness hath over-much subtlety and curiosity. They should be made heavy and dull, to make them the more obedient to example and practice; and they must be thickened and obscured, to proportion them to this shady and terrestrial life. Therefore are vulgar and less-wiredrawn* wits found to be more fit and happy in the conduct of affairs, and the exquisite and high-raised opinions of philosophy, unapt and unfit to exercise. This sharp vivacity of the spirit, and this supple and restless volubility, troubleth our negotiations. Human enterprises should be managed more grossly and superficially, and have a good and great part of them left for the rights of fortune. Affairs need not be sifted so nicely and so profoundly. A man loseth himself about the considerations of so many contrary lusters and diverse forms. [C]"Their minds were astonished* while they revolved things so different" (Livy XXXII. 20.). It is that which our elders report of Simonides. Because his imagination concerning the question Hiero the King had made unto him (which the better to answer he had divers days allowed him to think of it) presented sundry subtle and sharp considerations unto him; doubting which might be the likeliest, he altogether despaireth of the truth. [B]Whosoever searcheth all the circumstances and embraceth all the consequences thereof, hindereth his election. A mean engine doth equally conduct and sufficeth for the executions of great and little weights.

It is commonly seen that the best husbands* and the thriftiest are those who cannot tell how they are so, and that these cunning arithmeticians do seldom thrive by it. I know a notable prattler and an excellent blazoner of all sorts of husbandry and thrift, who hath most piteously let ten thousand pounds sterling a year pass from him. I know another who saith he consulteth better than any man of his counsel, and there cannot be a properer man to see unto or of more sufficiency; notwithstanding when he cometh to any execution, his own servants find he is far otherwise. This I say without mentioning or accounting his ill luck.

An Apology of Raymond Sebond

☙ II. 12 ✧ 1575–76, 1578–80 ❧

[A]Knowledge is, without all contradiction, a most profitable and chief ornament. Those who despise it declare evidently their sottishness. Yet do not I value it at so excessive a rate as some have done; namely Herillus the philosopher, who grounded his chief felicity upon it, and held that it lay in her power to make us content and wise, which I cannot believe, nor that which others have said, that knowledge is the mother of all virtue and that all vice proceedeth of ignorance — which, if it be, it is subject to a large interpretation. My house hath long since ever stood open to men of understanding and is very well known to many of them; for my father, who commanded the same fifty years and upward, set on fire by that new kind of earnestness wherewith King Francis the First embraced letters and raised them unto credit, did with great diligence and much cost endeavor to purchase the acquaintance of learned men, receiving and entertaining them as holy persons and who had some particular inspiration of divine wisdom, collecting their sentences and discourses as if they had been oracles; and with so much more reverence and religious regard by how much less authority he had to judge of them, for he had no knowledge of letters, no more than his predecessors before him. As for me, I love them indeed, but yet I worship them not.

Amongst others, Peter Bunel[1] (a man in his time, by reason of his learning, of high esteem) having sojourned a few days at Montaigne with my father and others of his coat, being ready to depart thence, presented him with a book entitled *Theologia naturalis, sive liber creaturarum magistri Raimondi de Sabonde.*[2] And for so much as the Italian and Spanish tongues were very familiar unto him and that the book was written in a kind of latinized Spanish whereof divers words had Latin terminations, he hoped that with little aid he might reap no small profit by it, and commended the same very much unto

[1] A humanist scholar of Toulouse, famous for his elegant Latin (1499–1546).

[2] First published in 1487, Sebond's book was reprinted many times during the sixteenth century.

him as a book most profitable and fitting the days in which he gave it him. It was even at what time the new fangles of Luther began to creep in favor and in many places to shake the foundation of our ancient belief. Wherein he seemed to be well advised, as he who by discourse of reason foresaw that this budding disease would easily turn to an execrable atheism. For the vulgar,* wanting the faculty to judge of things by themselves, suffering itself to be carried away by fortune and led on by outward appearances, if it once be possessed with the boldness to despise and malapertness* to impugn the opinions which to-fore it held in awful reverence (as are those wherein consisteth their salvation) and that some articles of their religion be made doubtful and questionable, they will soon and easily admit an equal uncertainty in all other parts of their belief, as they that had no other grounded authority or foundation but such as are now shaken and weakened, and immediately reject (as a tyrannical yoke) all impressions they had in former times received by the authority of laws or reverence of ancient custom —

[B]That which we fear'd before too much,
We gladly scorn when 'tis not such.
Lucr. V.1139.

—[A]undertaking thence forward to allow of nothing, except they have first given their voice and particular consent to the same.

My father, a few days before his death, lighting by chance upon this book, which before he had neglected, amongst other writings commanded me to translate the same into French. It is easy to translate such authors where nothing but the matter is to be represented, but hard and dangerous to undertake such as to have added much to the grace and elegancy of the language —[C]namely, to reduce them into a weaker and poorer tongue. [A]It was a strange task and new occupation for me; but by fortune being then at leisure and unable to gainsay the commandment of the best father that ever was, I came ere long (as well as I could) to the end of it; wherein he took singular delight and commanded the same to be printed, which accordingly was after his decease performed.

I found the conceits of the author to be excellent, the contexture of his work well followed, and his project full of piety. Now forasmuch as divers amuse themselves to read it, and especially ladies, to whom we owe most service, it hath often been my hap* to help them, when they were reading it, to discharge the book of two principal objections which are brought against the same. His drift is bold, and his scope adventurous; for he undertaketh by human and natural reasons to establish and verify all the articles of Christian religion against atheists.

Wherein, to say truth, I find him so resolute and so happy, as I deem it a thing impossible to do better in that argument and think that none equalleth him. Which book seeming to me both over-rich and exquisite, being written by an author whose name is so little known and of whom all we know is that he was a Spaniard who about two hundred years since professed physic in Toulouse, I demanded once of Adrianus Turnebus, a man who knew all things, what such a book might be; who answered that he deemed the same to be some quintessence extracted from out Saint Thomas Aquinas. For, in good truth, only such a spirit fraught with so infinite erudition and so full of admirable subtlety was capable of such and so rare imaginations. So it is that, whosoever be the author or deviser of it (the title whereof ought not without further reason to be taken from Sebond), he was a very sufficient, worthy man and endowed with sundry other excellent qualities.

The first thing he is reproved for in his book is that Christians wrong themselves much in that they ground their belief upon human reasons, which is conceived but by faith and by a particular inspiration of God. Which objection seemeth to contain some zeal of piety by reason whereof we ought with so much more mildness and regard endeavor to satisfy them that propose it. It were a charge more befitting a man conversant, and suitable to one acquainted, with the Holy Scriptures than me, who am altogether ignorant in them. Nevertheless, I think that, even as to a matter so divine and high and so much exceeding all human understanding as is this verity wherewith it hath pleased the goodness of God to enlighten us, it is most requisite that he afford and lend us his help, and that, with an extraordinary and privileged favor, that so we may the better conceive and entertain the same. For I suppose that means merely human can no way be capable of it, which, if they were, so many rare and excellent minds and so plenteously stored with natural faculties as have been in times past would never by their discourse have missed the attaining of this knowledge. It is faith only which lively and assuredly embraceth the high mysteries of our religion.

And no man can doubt but that it is a most excellent and commendable enterprise properly to accommodate and fit to the service of our faith the natural helps and human implements which God hath bestowed upon us. And no question is to be made but that it is the most honorable employment we can put them unto, and that there is no occupation or intent more worthy a good Christian than by all means, studies, and imaginations carefully to endeavor how to embellish, amplify, and extend the truth of his belief and religion. It is not enough for us to serve God in spirit and soul; we owe Him besides, and we yield unto Him a corporal worshipping: we apply our limbs, our motions, and all external things to honor Him. The like ought to be done, and we should accompany our faith with all the reason we possess. Yet always with this proviso: that we think it doth not depend of us and that all our strength and arguments can never attain to so supernatural and divine a knowledge, except it seize upon us and, as it were, enter into us by an extraordinary infusion; and unless it also enter into us not only by discourse, but also by human means, she is not in her dignity nor in her glory. And verily I fear therefore that except in this way we should not enjoy it. Had we fast-hold on God by the interposition of a lively faith, had we hold-fast* on God by Himself and not by us, had we a divine foundation, then should not human and worldly occasions have the power so to shake and totter us as they have. Our hold would not then yield to so weak a battery; the love of novelty, the constraint of princes, the good success of one party, the rash and casual changing of our opinions, should not then have the power to shake and alter our belief. We should not suffer the same to be troubled at the will and pleasure of a new argument and at the persuasion, no, not of all the rhetoric that ever was. We should withstand these boisterous billows with an inflexible and unmovable constancy:

> As huge rocks do regorge th'invective waves,
> And dissipate the billows' brawling braves,
> Which these 'gainst those still bellow out,
> Those being big and standing stout.
>
> Anon.

If this ray of divinity did in any sort touch us, it would everywhere appear; not only our words, but our actions would bear some show and luster of it. Whatsoever should proceed from us might be seen enlightened with this noble and matchless brightness. We should blush for shame that in human sects there was never any so factious, what difficulty or strangeness soever his doctrine maintained, but would in some sort conform his behaviors and square his life unto it; whereas so divine and heavenly an institution never marks Christians but by the tongue.

BAnd will you see whether it be so? Compare but our manners unto a Turk or a pagan, and we must needs yield unto them; whereas in respect of our religious superiority we ought by much, yea, by an incomparable distance, out-shine them in excellency. And well might a man say, "Are they so just, so charitable, and so good? Then must they be Christians."

CAll other outward show and exterior appearances are common to all religions, as hope, affiance,* events, ceremonies, penitence, and martyrdom. The peculiar badge of our truth should be virtue, as it is the heavenliest and most difficult mark and worthiest production of verity itself.

BAnd therefore was our good Saint Louis in the right, when that Tartarian King who was become a Christian intended to come to Lyons to kiss the Pope's feet and there to view the sanctity he hoped to find in our lives and manners, instantly to divert him from it, fearing lest our dissolute manners and licentious kind of life might scandalize him and so alter his opinion fore-conceived of so sacred a religion. Howbeit the contrary happened to another, who for the same effect being come to Rome and there viewing the dissoluteness of the prelates and people of those days was so much the more confirmed in our religion, considering with himself what force and divinity it must of consequence have, since it was able, amidst so many corruptions and so viciously polluted hands, to maintain her dignity and splendor.

AHad we but one only grain of faith, we should then be able to remove mountains from out their place, saith the Holy Writ. Our actions, being guided and accompanied with divinity, should not then be merely human but, even as our belief, contain some wonder-causing thing. C"The institution of an honest and blessed life is but short if a man believe" (Quint. XII.xi.). Some make the world believe that they believe things they never do. Others (and they are the greater number) persuade themselves they do so, as unable to conceive what it is to believe. AWe think it strange if in wars, which at this time do so oppress our state, we see the events to float so strangely and with so common and ordinary a manner to change and alter. The reason is, we add nothing unto it but our own. Justice, which is on the one side, is used but for a cloak and ornament; she is indeed alleged,* but nor received, nor harbored, nor wedded. She is as in the mouth of a lawyer and not, as she ought, in the heart and affection of the party. God oweth His extraordinary assistance unto faith and religion, and not to our passions. Men are but directors unto it, and use religion for a show; it ought to be clean contrary.

CDo but mark it: we [do] handle it as it were a piece of wax, from out so right and so firm a rule to draw so many contrary shapes. When was this better seen than nowadays in France? Those which have taken it on the left and those who have taken it on the right hand, such as speak the false and such who speak the truth of it, do so alike employ and fit the same to their violent and ambitious enterprises, proceed unto it with so conformable a proceeding in riotousness and injustice, they make the diversity they pretend in their opinions doubtful and hard to be believed in a thing from which depends the conduct and law of our life. Can a man see one same school and discipline more united and like customs and fashions to proceed? View but the horrible impudency wherewith we toss divine reasons to and fro, and how irreligiously we have both rejected and taken them again, according as fortune hath in these public storms transported us from place to place. This solemn proposition, whether it be lawful for a subject, for the defense of religion, to rebel and take arms against his prince — call but to mind in what mouths but a twelve-month ago the affirmative of the same was the chief pillar of the one part, the negative was the main underprop of the other; and listen now from whence cometh the voice and instruction of one and other, and whether arms clatter and clang less for this than for that cause.[3] And we burn those men which say that truth must be made to abide the yoke of our need. And how much worse doth France than speak it?

[A]Let us confess the truth: he that from out this lawful army should cull out first those who follow it for mere zeal of a religious affection than such as only regard the defense and protection of their country's laws or service of their prince, whether he could ever erect a complete company of armed men? How comes it to pass that so few are found who have still held one same will and progress in our public revolutions, and that we see them now and then but faintly, and sometimes as fast as they can headlong to run into the action? And the same men, now by their violence and rashness, and now through their slowness, demissness,* and heaviness to spoil and as it were overthrow our affairs, but that they are thrust into them by casual motives and particular consideration, according to the diversities wherewith they are moved?

[C]I plainly perceive, we lend nothing unto devotion but the offices that flatter our passions. There is no hostility so excellent as that which is absolutely Christian. Our zeal worketh wonders whenever it secondeth our inclination toward hatred, cruelty, ambition, avarice, detraction, or rebellion. Towards goodness, benignity, or temperance it goeth but slowly and against the hair; except miraculously some rare complexion lead him unto it, it neither runs nor flieth to it. Our religion was ordained to root out vices, but it shroudeth, fostereth, and provoketh them.

[A]As commonly we say, we must not make a fool of God. Did we believe in Him — I say not through faith, but with a simple belief — yea, I speak it to our confusion, did we but believe and know Him as we do another story or as one of our companions, we should then love

[3] Written after the assassination of Henri III in 1589. The right to revolt was claimed by the Protestants under the Catholic King, but then denied by them under his Protestant successor.

Him above all other things by reason of the infinite goodness and unspeakable beauty that is and shines in Him. Had He but the same place in our affections that riches, pleasures, glory, and our friends have!

[C]The best of us doth not so much fear to wrong Him as he doth to injury his neighbor, his kinsman, or his master. Is there so simple a mind, who on the one side having before him the object of one of our vicious pleasures and on the other to his full view, perfect knowledge, and assured persuasion the state of an immortal glory, that would enter into contention of one for the other? And [yet] we often refuse it through mere contempt; for what draws us to blaspheming unless it be at all adventures the desire itself of the offense? The philosopher Antisthenes, when he was initiated in the mysteries of Orpheus, the priest saying unto him that such as vowed themselves to that religion should after death receive eternal and perfect felicities, replied, "if thou believe it why dost thou not die thyself?" Diogenes more roughly, as his manner was, and further from our purpose, answered the priest who persuaded him to be one of his order that so he might come unto and attain the happiness of the other world: "Wilt thou have me believe that those famous men Agesilaus and Epaminondas shall be miserable and that thou, who art but an ass and dost nothing of any worth, shalt be happy because thou art a priest?"

[A]Did we but receive these large promises of everlasting blessedness with like authority as we do a philosophical discourse, we should not then have death in that horror as we have:

> [B]He would not now complain to be dissolved dying,
> But rather more rejoice that now he is forth-flying,
> Or as a snake his coat out-worn,
> Or as old harts, doth cast his horn.
>
> Lucr. III.612.

[A]I will be dissolved, should we say, and be with Jesus Christ. The forcible power of Plato's discourse of the immortality of the soul provoked divers of his scholars unto death that so they might more speedily enjoy the hopes he told them of.

All which is a most evident token that we receive our religion but according to our fashion and by our own hands and no otherwise than other religions are received. We are placed in the country where it was in use, where we regard her antiquity or the authority of those who have maintained her, where we fear the menaces wherewith she threateneth all misbelievers or follow her promises. The considerations ought to be applied and employed to our belief, but as subsidiaries; they are human bonds. Another country, other testimonies, equal promises, alike menaces, might semblably imprint a clean contrary religion in us. [B]We are Christians by the same title as we are either Perigordians or Germans. [A]And as Plato saith: there are few so confirmed in atheism but some great danger will bring unto the knowledge of God's divine power. The part doth not touch or concern a good Christian; it is for mortal and worldly religions to be received by a human convoy. What faith is that like to be which cowardice of heart doth plant and weakness establish in us? [C]A goodly faith, that believes that which it believeth only because it wanteth the courage not to believe the same! [A]A vicious passion, as that of inconstancy and astonishment is, can it possibly ground any regular production in our minds or souls?

[C]They establish, saith he, by the reason of their judgment, that whatsoever is reported of hell or of after-coming pains is but a fiction. But the occasions to make trial of it, offering itself at what time age or sickness doth summon them to death, the [terror] of the same, through the horror of their future condition, doth then replenish them with another kind of belief. And because such impressions make men's hearts fearful, he by his *Laws* inhibiteth all instruction of such threats and the persuasion that any evil may come unto man from the gods except for his greater good and for a medicinable effect whensoever he falleth into it. [They] report of Bion that, being infected with the atheisms of Theodorus, he had for a long time made but a mockery of religious men; but when death did once seize upon him, he yielded unto the extremest superstitions; as if the gods would either be removed or come again according to Bion's business.

Plato and these examples conclude that we are brought to believe in God either by reason or by compulsion. Atheism being a proposition as unnatural and monstrous as it is hard and uneasy to be established in any man's mind, how insolent and unruly soever he may be. Many have been seen to have conceived either through vanity or fierceness strange and seld*-known opinions, as if they would become reformers of the world by affecting a profession only in countenance; who, though they be sufficiently foolish, yet are they not powerful enough to ground or settle it in their consciences. Yet will not such leave to lift up their joined hands to heaven, give them but a stoccado* on their breast; and when fear shall have suppressed or sickness vanquished this licentious fervor of a wavering mind, then will they suffer themselves gently to be reclaimed and discreetly to be persuaded to give credit unto true belief and public examples. A decree seriously digested is one thing, and these shallow and superficial impressions another, which, bred by the dissoluteness of a loose spirit, do rashly and uncertainly float up and down the fantasy of a man. Oh men most brain-sick and miserable, that endeavor to be worse than they can!

[B]The error of paganism and the ignorance of our sacred truth was the cause of this great soul's fall (but only great in worldly greatness) also in this next abuse, which is, that children and old men are found to be more susceptible or capable of religion, as if it were bred and had her credit from our imbecility.

[A]The bond which should bind our judgment, tie our will, enforce and join our souls to our creator, should be a bond taking his doubling and forces not from our considerations, reasons, and passions, but from a divine and supernatural compulsion, having but one form, one countenance, and one grace, which is the authority and grace of God. Now our heart being ruled and our soul commanded by faith, reason willeth that she draws all our other parts to the service of her intent, according to their power and faculty. Nor is it likely but that this vast world's frame must bear the impression of some marks therein imprinted by the hand of this great, wondrous architect, and that even in all things therein created there must be some image somewhat resembling and having coherency with the workman that wrought and framed them. He hath left imprinted in these high and mysterious works the characters of His divinity, and only our imbecility is the cause we can nor discover nor read them. It is that which Himself telleth us, that by His visible operations He doth manifest those that are invisible to us.

Sebond hath much travailed about this worthy study, and showeth us that there is no parcel of this world that either belieth or shameth his maker. It were a manifest wronging of God's goodness if all this universe did not consent and sympathize with our belief. Heaven, earth, the elements, our bodies, our soul, yea, all things else conspire and agree unto it; only the means how to make use of them must be found out. They will instruct us sufficiently, be we but capable to learn and apt to understand. [B]For this world is a most holy temple into which man is brought, there to behold statues and images not wrought by mortal hand, but such as the secret thought of God hath made sensible, as the sun, the stars, the waters, and the earth, thereby to represent the intelligible unto us. [A]The invisible things of God, saith Saint Paul, do evidently appear by the creation of the world, judging of His eternal wisdom and divinity by His works.

> God to the world doth not heav'n's face envy,
> But by still moving it doth notify
> His face and essence, doth Himself apply,
> That He may well be known, and teach by seeing,
> How He goes, how we should mark His decreeing.
>
> Manil. IV.907.

Now our reason and human discourse is as the lumpish and barren matter, and the grace of God is the form thereof. 'Tis that which giveth both fashion and worth unto it. Even as the virtuous actions of Socrates and Cato are but frivolous and [un]profitable, because they had not their end and regarded not the love and obedience of the true creator of all things, and namely because they were ignorant of the true knowledge of God, so is it of our imagination and discourse. They have a kind of body, but a shapeless mass without light or fashion unless faith and the grace of God be joined thereunto.

Faith, giving as it were a tincture and luster unto Sebond's arguments, make[s] them the more firm and solid; they may well serve for a direction and guide to a young learner, to lead and set him in the right way of this knowledge. They in some sort fashion and make him capable of the grace of God, by means whereof our belief is afterward achieved and made perfect. I know a man of authority, brought up in letters, who confessed unto me that he was reclaimed from the errors of misbelieving by the arguments of Sebond. And if it happen they be despoiled of this ornament and of the help and approbation of faith, and taken but for mere human fantasies, yet to combat those that headlong are fallen into the dreadful error and horrible darkness of irreligion, even then shall they be found as firm and forcible as any other of that condition that may be opposed against them; so that we shall stand upon terms to say unto our parties,

> If you have any better, send for me,
> Or else that I bid you contented be.
> Hor. *Epist.* I.v.6.

Let them either abide the force of our proofs or show us some others upon some other subject, better compact and more full.

I have in a manner unawares half engaged myself in the second objection to which I had purposed to frame an answer for Sebond.

Some say his arguments are weak, and simple to verify what he would (the second objection), and undertake to front him easily. Such fellows must somewhat more roughly be handled; for they are more dangerous and more malicious than the first. [C]Man doth willingly apply other men's sayings to the advantage of the opinions he hath fore-judged in himself: to an atheist all writings make for atheism; he with his own venom infecteth the innocent matter. [A]These have some preoccupation of judgment that makes their taste wallowish* and tasteless to conceive the reasons of Sebond. As for the rest, they think to have fair play offered them if they have free liberty to combat our religion with mere worldly weapons, which they durst not charge did they behold her in her majesty, full of authority and commandment.

The means I use to suppress this frenzy, and which seemeth the fittest for my purpose, is to crush and trample this human pride and fierceness under foot, to make them feel the emptiness, vacuity, and no worth of man, and violently to pull out of their hands the silly weapons of their reason, to make them stoop and bite and snarl at the ground under the authority and reverence of God's majesty. Only to her belongeth science and wisdom; it is she alone can judge of herself, and from her we steal whatsoever we repute, value, and count ourselves to be.

> Of greater, better, wiser mind than He,
> God can abide no mortal man should be.
> Herodot. VII.10.

CLet us suppress this over-weening, the first foundation of the tyranny of the wicked spirit. "God resisteth the proud, but giveth grace to the humble" (I *Peter*, V.5.). Plato saith that intelligence is in all the gods, but little or nothing at all in men.

A Meanwhile it is a great comfort unto a Christian man to see our mortal implements and fading tools so fitly sorted to our holy and divine faith that when they are employed to the mortal and fading subjects of their Nature, they are never more forcibly nor more jointly appropriated unto them. Let us then see whether man hath any other stronger reasons in his power than Sebond's, and whether it lie in him by argument or discourse to come to any certainty.

CFor Saint Augustine, pleading against these kind of men, [has cause to] upbraid them with their injustice, in that they hold the parts of our belief to be false and that our reason faileth in establishing them. And to show that many things may be and have been whereof our discourse can never ground the nature and the causes, he proposeth and setteth down before them certain known and undoubted experiments wherein man confesseth to see nothing; which he doth as all things else, with a curious and ingenious search. More must be done, and they must be taught that to convince the weakness of their reason we need not go far to cull out rare examples, and that it is so defective and blind as there is no facility so clear that is clear enough unto her; that easy and uneasy is all one to her; that all subjects equally and nature in general disavoweth her jurisdiction and interposition.

A What preacheth truth unto us, when it biddeth us fly and shun worldly philosophy, when it so often telleth us that all our wisdom is but folly before God; that of all vanities man is the greatest; that man, who presumeth of his knowledge, doth not yet know what knowledge is; and that man, who is nothing, if he but think to be something seduceth and deceiveth himself? These sentences of the Holy Ghost do so lively and manifestly express what I would maintain, as I should need no other proof against such as with all submission and obeisance would yield to his authority. But these will needs be whipped to their own cost, and cannot abide their reason to be combatted but by itself.

Let us now but consider man alone without other help, armed but with his own weapons, and unprovided of the grace and knowledge of God which is all his honor, all his strength, and all the ground of his being. Let us see what hold-fast* or free-hold he hath in this gorgeous and goodly equipage. Let him with the utmost power of his discourse make me understand upon what foundation he hath built those great advantages and odds he supposeth to have over other creatures. Who hath persuaded him that this admirable moving of heaven's vaults, that the eternal light of these lamps so fiercely rolling over his head, that the horror-moving and continual motion of this infinite, vast ocean, were established and continue so many ages for his commodity and service? Is it possible to imagine anything so ridiculous as this miserable and wretched creature, which is not so much as master of himself, exposed and subject to offenses of all things, and yet dareth call himself master and emperor of this universe, in whose power it is not to know the least part of it, much less to command the same? And the privilege, which he so fondly challengeth, to be the only absolute creature in this huge world's frame, perfectly able to know the absolute beauty and several parts thereof, and that he is only of power to yield the great architect thereof due thanks for it, and to keep account both of the receipts and layings-out of the world. Who hath sealed him this patent? Let him show us his letters of privilege for so noble and so great a charge.

[C]Have they been granted only in favor of the wise? Then concern they but a few. Are the foolish and wicked worthy of so extraordinary a favor? Who, being the worst part of the world, should they be preferred before the rest? Shall we believe him? "For whose cause then shall a man say that the world was made? In sooth, for those creatures' sake which have the use of reason: those are gods and men, than whom assuredly nothing is better" (Cic. *De nat. deor.* II.liv.). We shall never sufficiently baffle the impudency of this conjoining.

[A]But, silly wretch, what hath he in him worthy such an advantage? To consider the incorruptible life of the celestial bodies, their beauty, greatness, and agitation, continued with so just and regular a course:

> When we of this great world the heavenly temples see
> Above us, and the skies with shine-stars fixed to be,

And mark in our discourse
Of sun and moon the course;
Lucr. V.1203.

to consider the power and domination these bodies have, not only upon our lives and condition of our fortune,

For on the stars he doth suspend
Of men the deeds, the lives, and end,
Manil. III.58.

but also over our disposition and inclinations, our discourses and wills, which they rule, provoke, and move at the pleasure of their influences, as our reason finds and teacheth us,

By speculation it from far discerns,
How stars by secret laws do guide our sterns,
And this whole world is mov'd by intercourse
And by sure signs of fates to know the course,
Manil. I.60.

seeing that not a man alone, nor a king only, but monarchies and empires, yea, and all this world below is moved at the shaking of one of the least heavenly motions;

How little motions makes, how different affection,
So great this kingdom is, that hath kings in subjection,
Manil. IV.93.

if our virtue, vices, sufficiency and knowledge, and the same discourse we make of the power of the stars and the comparison between them and us, cometh, as our reason judgeth, by their mean and through their favor;

One with love madded, his love to enjoy,
Can cross the seas and overturn all Troy;
Another's lot is to set laws severe.
Lo, sons kill fathers, fathers sons destroy,
Brothers for mutual wounds their arms do bear.
Such war is not our own, forc'd are we to it,
Drawn to our own pains, our own limbs to tear.
Fates so t' observe, 'tis fatal we must do it.
Manil. IV.78, 118.

if we hold that portion of reason which we have from the distribution of heaven, how can she make us equal unto it? How can she submit his essence and conditions unto our knowledge? Whatsoever we behold in those huge bodies doth affright us. C"What workmanship, what iron braces, what main beams, what engines, what masons and carpenters, were to so great a work?" (Cic. *De nat. deor.* I.viii.).

[A]Why do we then deprive them of soul, of life, and of discourse? Have we discovered or known any unmovable or insensible stupidity in them — we, who have no commerce but of obedience with them? [C]Shall we say we have seen the use of a reasonable soul in no other creature but in man? What? Have we seen anything comparable to the sun? Leaveth he to be because we have seen nothing semblance unto it? And doth he leave his moving because his equal is no where to be found? If that which we have not seen is not, our knowledge is wonderfully abridged. "What narrowness of my heart is such?" (Cic. *De nat. deor.* I.xxxi.). [A]Be they not dreams of human vanity, to make a celestial earth or world of the moon, as Anaxagoras did, and therein to plant worldly habitations and, as Plato and Plutarch do, erect their colonies for our use? And to make of our known earth a bright shining planet? [C]"Among other discommodities of our mortality this is one: there is darkness in our minds and in us not only necessity of erring, but a love of errors" (Sen. *De ira* II.9.). "Our corruptible body doth overload our soul, and our dwelling on earth weighs down our sense that is set to think of many matters" (Wisdom of Solomon IX.15, quoted in Augustine, *Civ. Dei* XII.xv.).

[A]Presumption is our natural and original infirmity. Of all creatures man is the most miserable and frail, and therewithal the proudest and disdainfullest, who perceiveth and seeth himself placed here, amidst their filth and mire of the world, fast tied and nailed to the worst, most senseless, and drooping part of the world, in the vilest corner of the house and farthest from heaven's cope,* with those creatures that are the worst of the three conditions; and yet dareth imaginarily place himself above the circle of the moon and reduce heaven under his feet. It is through the vanity of the same imagination that he dare equal himself to God, that he ascribeth divine conditions unto himself, that he selecteth and separateth himself from out the rank of other creatures, to which his fellow-brethren and compeers he cuts out and shareth their parts and allotteth them what portions of means or forces he thinks good. How knoweth he by the virtue of his understanding the inward and secret motions of beasts? By what comparison from them to us doth he conclude the brutishness he ascribeth unto them?

[C]When I am playing with my cat, who knows whether she have more sport in dallying with me than I have in gaming with her? We entertain one another with mutual apish tricks; if I have my hour to begin or to refuse, so hath she hers. Plato, in setting forth the golden age under Saturn, amongst the chief advantages that man had then reporteth the communication he had with beasts, of whom inquiring and taking instruction he knew the true qualities and differences of every one of them; by and from whom he got an absolute understanding and perfect wisdom, whereby he led a happier life than we can do. Can we have a better proof to judge of man's impudency touching beasts? This notable author was of opinion that in the greatest part of the corporal form which nature hath bestowed on them she hath only respected the use of the prognostications which in his days were thereby gathered.

[A]That defect which hindreth the communication between them and us, why may it not as well be in us as in them? It is a matter of divination to guess in whom the fault is that we understand not one another; for we understand them no more than they us. By the same reason may they as well esteem us beasts as we them. It is no great marvel if we understand them not: no more do we the Cornish, the Welsh, or Irish. Yet have some boasted that they understood them, as Apollonius Tyaneus, [B]Melampus, Tiresias, Thales, [A]and others. [B]And if it be, as cosmographers report, that there are nations who receive and admit a dog to be their king, it must necessarily follow that they give a certain interpretation to his voice and moving. [A]We must note the parity that is between us. We have some mean understanding of their senses; so have beasts of ours — about the same measure. They flatter and fawn upon us; they threat and entreat us; so do we them. Touching other matters, we manifestly perceive that there is a full and perfect communication amongst them, and that not only those of one same kind understand one another, but even such as are of different kinds.

> [B]Whole herds (though dumb) of beasts, both wild and tame,
> Use diverse voices different sounds to frame,
> As joy, or grief, or fear,
> Upspringing passions bear.
>
> Lucr. V.1058.

[A]By one kind of barking of a dog the horse knoweth he is angry; by another voice of his he is nothing dismayed. Even in beasts that have no voice at all, by the reciprocal kindness which we see in them we easily infer there is some other mean of intercommunication: [C]their gestures treat, and their motions discourse.

> [B]No otherwise than for they cannot speak,
> Children are drawn by signs their minds to break.
>
> Lucr. V.1029.

[A]And why not, as well as our dumb men dispute, argue, and tell histories by signs? I have seen some so ready and excellent in it that, in good sooth, they wanted nothing to have their meaning perfectly understood. Do we not daily see lovers with the looks and rolling of their eyes plainly show when they are angry or pleased, and how they entreat and thank one another, assign meetings, and express any passion?

> Silence also hath a way
> Words and prayers to convey.
> Tasso *Aminta* II. chor. 34.

[C]What do we with our hands? Do we not sue and entreat, promise and perform, call men unto us and discharge them, bid them farewell and be gone, threaten, pray, beseech, deny, refuse, demand, admire, number, confess, repent, fear, be ashamed, doubt, instruct, command, incite, encourage, swear, witness, accuse, condemn, absolve, injury, despise, defy, despite, flatter, applaud, bless, humble, mock, reconcile, recommend, exalt, show gladness, rejoice, complain, wail, sorrow, discomfort, despair, cry out, forbid, declare silence and astonishment, and what not, with so great variation and amplifying as if they would contend with the tongue? And with our head, do we not invite and call to us, discharge and send away, avow, disavow, belie, welcome, honor, worship, disdain, demand, direct, rejoice, affirm, deny, complain, cherish, blandish, chide, yield, submit, brag, boast, threaten, exhort, warrant, assure, and inquire? What do we with our eyelids? And with our shoulders? To conclude, there is no motion nor gesture that doth not speak, and speaks in a language very easy, and without any teaching to be understood. Nay, which is more, it is a language common and public to all; whereby it followeth, seeing the variety and several use it hath from others, that this must rather be deemed the proper and peculiar speech of human nature. I omit that which necessity in time of need doth particularly instruct and suddenly teach such as need it, and the alphabets upon fingers, and grammars by gestures, and the sciences which are only exercised and expressed by them, and the nations Pliny reporteth to have no other speech.

[B]An ambassador of the city of Abdera, after he had talked a long time unto Agis, King of Sparta, said thus unto him: "O King, what answer wilt thou that I bear back unto our citizens?" Thus answered he: "That I have suffered thee to speak all thou wouldst and as long as thou pleasedst without ever speaking one word." Is not this a kind of speaking silence, and easy to be understood? [A]And as for other matters, what sufficiency is there in us that we must not acknowledge from the industry and labors of beasts? Can there be a more formal and better ordered policy, divided into so several charges and offices, more constantly entertained, and better maintained, than that of bees? Shall we imagine their so orderly disposing of their actions and managing of their vacations* have so proportioned and formal a conduct without discourse, reason, and forecast?

Some by these signs, by these examples moved,
Said that in bees there is and may be proved
Some taste of heavenly kind,
Part of celestial mind.
Virg. *Georg.* IV.219.

The swallows which at the approach of spring time we see to pry, to search and ferret all the corners of our houses, is it without judgment they seek or without discretion they choose from out a thousand places that which is fittest for them to build their nests and lodging? And in that pretty, cunning contexture and admirable framing of their houses, would birds rather fit themselves with a round than a square figure, with an obtuse than a right angle, except they knew both the commodities and effects of them? Would they, suppose you, first take water and then clay, unless they guessed that the hardness of the one is softened by the moistness of the other? Would they floor their palace with moss or down, except they foresaw that the tender parts of their young ones shall thereby lie more soft and easy? Would they shroud and shelter themselves from stormy weather, and build their cabins toward the east, unless they knew the different conditions of winds and considered that some are more healthful and safe for them than some others? Why doth the spider spin her artificial web thick in one place and thin in another? And now useth one and then another knot, except she had an imaginary kind of deliberation, forethought, and conclusion? We perceive by the greater part of their works what excellency beasts have over us, and how weak our art and short our cunninng is, if we go about to imitate them. We see notwithstanding, even in our grossest works, what faculties we employ in them and how our mind employeth the uttermost of her skill and forces in them. Why should we not think as much of them? Wherefore do we attribute the works which excel whatever we can perform either by nature or art unto a kind of unknown, natural, and servile inclination? Wherein, unawares, we give them a great advantage over us to infer that nature, led by a certain loving-kindness, leadeth and accompanieth them as it were by the hand unto all the actions and commodities of their life; and that she forsaketh and leaveth us to the hazard of fortune, and by art to quest and find out those things that are behooveful and necessary for our preservation, and therewithal denieth us the means to attain by any institution and contention of spirit to the natural sufficiency of brute beasts. So that their brutish stupidity doth in all commodities exceed whatsoever our divine intelligence can effect.

Verily, by this account we might have just cause and great reason to term her a most injust and partial stepdame. But there is no such thing; our policy is not so deformed and disordered. Nature hath generally embraced all her creatures. And there is not any but she hath amply stored with all necessary means for the preservation of their being. For the daily plaints which I often hear men make (when the license of their conceits doth sometimes raise them above the clouds, and then headlong tumbling them down even to the antipodes) exclaiming that man is the only forsaken and outcast creature, naked on the bare earth, fast bound and swathed, having nothing to cover and arm himself withal but the spoil of others; whereas nature hath clad and mantled all other creatures, some with shells, some with husks, with rinds, with hair, with wool, with stings, with bristles, with hides, with moss, with feathers, with scales, with fleeces, and with silk, according as their quality might need or their condition require; and hath fenced and armed them with claws, with nails, with talons, with hooves, with teeth, with stings, and with horns, both to assail others and to defend themselves; and hath moreover instructed them in everything fit and requisite for them, as to swim, to run, to creep, to fly, to roar, to bellow, and to sing. Whereas man only (Oh silly,* wretched man!) can neither go, nor speak, nor shift, nor feed himself, unless it be to whine and weep only, except he be taught.

> [B]An infant, like a shipwreck ship-boy cast from seas,
> Lies naked on the ground and speechless, wanting all
> The helps of vital spirit, when nature with small ease
> Of throes, to see first light, from her womb lets him fall;
> Then, as is meet, with mournful cries he fills the place,
> For whom so many ills remain in his life's race.
> But divers herds of tame and wild beasts forward spring,
> Nor need they rattles, nor of nurses cock'ring-kind*
> The flattering broken speech their lullaby need sing.
> Nor seek they divers coats, as divers seasons bind.
> Lastly, no armor need they, nor high-reared wall
> Whereby to guard their own, since all things unto all
> Work-masters nature doth produce,
> And the earth largely to their use.
>
> Lucr. V.222.

[A]Such complaints are false: there is a greater equality and more uniform relation in the policy of the world. Our skin is as sufficiently provided with hardness against the injuries of the weather as theirs — witness divers nations which yet never knew the use of clothes. [B]Our ancient Gauls were but slightly appareled; no more are the Irishmen, our neighbors, in so cold a climate. [A]Which we may better judge by ourselves; for all those parts of our body we are pleased to leave bare to wind and weather are by experience found able to endure it. If there be any weak part in us which in likelihood should seem to fear cold, it ought to be the stomach, where digestion is made; our forefathers used to have it bare, and our ladies, as dainty-nice as they be, are many times seen to go open-breasted as low as their navel. The bundles and swathes about our children are no more necessary; and the mothers of Lacedemonia brought up theirs in all liberty and looseness of moving their limbs without swathing or binding. Our whining, our puling, and our weeping is common to most creatures, and divers of them are often seen to wail and groan a long time after their birth, forsomuch as it is a countenance fitting the weakness wherein they feel themselves. As for the use of eating and feeding, it is in us, as in them, natural and without teaching:

> [B]For everyone soon understanding is
> Of his own strength, which he may use amiss.
> Lucr. V.1032.

[A]Who will make question that a child, having attained the strength to feed himself, could not quest for his meat and shift for his drink? The earth without labor or tilling doth sufficiently produce and offer him as much as he shall need. And if not at all times, no more doth she unto beasts — witness the provision we see the ants and other silly* creatures to make against the cold and barren seasons of the year. The nations that have lately been discovered, so plenteously stored with all manner of natural meat and drink, without care or labor, teach us that bread is not our only food, and that without toiling, our common mother Nature hath with great plenty stored us with whatsoever should be needful for us; yea, as it is most likely, more richly and amply than nowadays she doth that we have added so much art unto it:

> The earth itself at first of th' own accord
> Did men rich vineyards and clean fruit afford.
> It gave sweet off-springs food from sweeter soil
> Which yet scarce greater grow for all our toil.
> Yet tire therein we do,
> Both ploughmen's strength and oxen too;
> Lucr. II.1157.

the gluttonous excess and intemperate lavishness of our appetite exceeding all the inventions we endeavor to find out wherewith to glut and cloy the same.

As for arms and weapons, we have more that be natural unto us than the greatest part of other beasts. We have more several motions of limbs, and naturally, without teaching; we reap more serviceable use of them than they do. Those which are trained up to fight naked are seen headlong to cast themselves into the same hazards and dangers as we do. If some beasts excel us in this advantage, we exceed many others. And the industry to enable, the skill to fortify, and the wit to shelter and cover our body by artificial means, we have it by a kind of natural instinct and teaching. Which to prove: the elephant doth whet and sharpen his teeth he useth in war (for he hath some he only useth for that purpose), which he heedfully spareth and never puts them to other service; when bulls prepare themselves to fight, they raise, scatter, and with their feet cast the dust about them; the wild boar whets his tusks; when the ichneumon is to grapple with the crocodile, he walloweth his body in the mire, then lets the same dry and harden upon him, which he doth so often that at last the same becomes as hard and tough as any well-compact crust, which serveth him instead of a cuirass. Why shall we not say that it is as natural for us to arm ourselves with wood and iron?

As for speech, sure it is that if it be not natural it is not necessary. I believe nevertheless that if a child bred in some uncouth solitariness, far from haunt of people, (though it were a hard matter to make trial of it) would no doubt have some kind of words to express and speech to utter his conceits; and it is not to be imagined that nature hath refused [u]s that mean and barred us that help which she hath bestowed upon many and divers other creatures. For what is that faculty we see in them when they seem to complain, to rejoice, to call one unto another for help, and bid one another to loving copulation (as commonly they do) by the use of their voice, but a kind of speech? [B]And shall not they speak among themselves that speak and utter their mind unto us and we to them? How many ways speak we unto our dogs, and they seem to understand and answer us? With another language and with other names speak we unto and call them than we do our birds, our hogs, our oxen, our horses, and such like; and according to their different kinds we change our idiom:

> [A]So ants amidst their sable-colored band
> One with another mouth to mouth confer,
> Haply their way or state to understand.
> Dante, *Purg.* XXVI.34–6.

Me seemeth that Lactantius doth not only attribute speech unto beasts, but also laughing. And the same difference of tongues which, according to the diversity of countries, is found amongst us is also found amongst beasts of one same kind. Aristotle to that purpose allegeth the divers calls or purrs of partridges according to the situation of their place of breeding:

> [B]And divers birds send forth much divers sounds
> At divers times, and partly change the grounds
> Of their hoarse-sounding song
> As seasons change along.
>
> Lucr. V.1077, 1080, 1082, 1083.

[A]But it would be known what language such a child should speak; and what some report by divination hath no great likelihood. And if, against this opinion, a man would allege unto me that such as are naturally deaf speak not at all, I answer that it is not only because they could not receive the instruction of the world by their ears, but rather inasmuch as the sense of hearing, whereof they are deprived, hath some affinity with that of speaking, both which with a natural kind of ligament or seam hold and are fastened together: in such sort as what we speak, we must first speak it unto ourselves, and before we utter and send the same forth to strangers we make it inwardly to sound unto our ears.

I have said all this to maintain the coherency and resemblance that is in all human things, and to bring us unto the general throng. We are neither above nor under the rest. Whatever is under the cope* of heaven, saith the wise man, runneth one law and followeth one fortune.

> [B]All things infolded are
> In fatal bonds as fits their share.
>
> Lucr. V.874.

[A]Some difference there is; there are orders and degrees; but all is under the visage of one same nature:

> [B]All things proceed in their course, natures all
> Keep difference, as in their league doth fall.
>
> Lucr. V.921.

[A]Man must be forced and marshalled within the lists of this policy. Miserable man with all his wit cannot in effect go beyond it; he is embraced and engaged, and, as other creatures of his rank are, he is subjected in like bonds and without any prerogative or essential pre-excellence: whatever privilege he assume unto himself, he is of very mean condition. That which is given by opinion or fantasy hath neither body nor taste. And if it be so that he alone above all other creatures hath this liberty of imagination and this license of thoughts which represent unto him both what is and what is not and what him pleaseth, falsehood and truth, it is an advantage bought at a very high rate and whereof he hath little reason to glory; for thence springs the chiefest source of all the mischiefs that oppress him, as sin, sickness, irresolution, trouble, and despair.

But to come to my purpose, I say therefore, there is no likelihood we should imagine the beasts do the very same things by a natural inclination and forced genuity* which we do of our own free will and industry. Of the very same effects we must conclude alike faculties; and by the richest effects infer the noblest faculties; and consequently acknowledge that the same discourse and way we hold in working, the very same, or perhaps some other better, do beasts hold. Wherefore shall we imagine that natural compulsion in them that prove no such effect ourselves? Since it is more honorable to be addressed to act and tied to work orderly by and through a natural and unavoidable condition, and most approaching to divinity, than regularly to work and act by and through a casual and rash liberty. And it is safer to leave the reigns of our conduct unto nature than unto ourselves. The vanity of our presumption maketh us rather to be beholding and, as it were, indebted unto our own strength for our sufficiency than unto her liberality; and enrich other creatures with natural gifts and yield those unto them, that so we may ennoble and honor ourselves with gifts purchased, as methinketh, by a very simple humor; for I would prize graces and value gifts that were altogether mine own and natural unto me, as much as I would those I had begged and with a long prenticeship shifted for. It lieth not in our power to obtain a greater commendation than to be favored both of God and Nature.

By that reason, the fox which the inhabitants of Thrace use when they will attempt to march upon the ice of some frozen river, and to that end let her go loose afore the[m], should we see her running alongst the river-side, approach her ear close to the ice to listen whether by any far or near distance she may hear the noise of roaring of the water running under the same, and according as she perceiveth the ice thereby to be thick or thin to go either forward or backward — might we not lawfully judge that the same discourse possesseth her head as in like case it would ours? And that it is a kind of debating reason and consequence, drawn from natural sense: "whatsoever maketh a noise moveth, whatsoever moveth is not frozen, whatsover is not frozen is liquid, whatsoever is liquid yields under any weight"? For the impute that only to a quickness of the sense of hearing, without discourse or consequence, is but a fond conceit and cannot enter into my imagination. The like must be judged of so many wiles and inventions wherewith beasts save themselves from the snares and scape the baits we lay to entrap them.

And if we will take hold of any advantage tending to that purpose, that it is in our power to seize upon them, to employ them to our service, and to use them at our pleasure, it is but the same odds we have one upon another. To which purpose we have our slaves or bondmen. [B]And were not the Climacides certain women in Syria which, creeping on all four, upon the ground, served the ladies instead of footstools or ladders to get up into their coaches? [A]Where the greater part of free men for very slight causes abandon both their life and being to the power of others. [C]The wives and concubines of the Thracians strive and contend which of them shall be chosen to be slain over her husband's or lover's tomb. [A]Have tyrants ever failed to find many men vowed to their devotion, where some for an over-plus or supererogation have added this necessity, that they must necessarily accompany them as well in death as in life? [B]Whole hosts of men have thus tied themselves unto their captains. The tenor of the oath ministered unto the scholars that entered and were admitted the rude school of Roman gladiators implied these promises, which was this: "We vow and swear to suffer ourselves to be enchained, beaten, burned, and killed with the sword, and endure whatsoever any lawful fencer ought to endure for his master, most religiously engaging both our body and soul to the use of his service:"

> Burn, tyrant, if thou wilt, my head with fire, with sword
> My body strike, my back cut with hard-twisted cord.
>
> Tibul. I.ix.21.

Was not this a very strict convenant? Yet were there some years ten thousand found that entered and lost themselves in those schools.

[C]When the Scythians buried their king, they strangled over his dead body first the chiefest and best beloved of his concubines, then his cupbearer, the master of his horse, his chamberlain, the usher of his chamber, and his master cook. And in his anniversary killed fifty horse mounted with fifty pages, whom before they had slain with thrusting sharp stakes into their fundament, which going up along their chine-bone came out at their throat; whom, thus mounted, they set in orderly ranks about the tomb.

[A]The men that serve us do it better-cheap and for a less curious and favorable entreating than we use unto birds, unto horses, and unto dogs. [C]What cark* and toil apply we not ourselves unto for their sakes? Methinks the vilest and basest servants will never do that so willingly for their masters which princes are glad to do for their beasts. Diogenes, seeing his kinsfolks to take care how they might redeem him out of thraldom, "they are fools," said he, "for it is my master that governeth, keepeth, feedeth, and serveth me;" and such as keep or entertain beasts may rather say they serve them than that they are served of them.

And if they have that natural greater magnanimity, that never lion was seen to subject himself unto another lion, nor one horse unto another horse, for want of heart. As we hunt after beasts, so tigers and lions hunt after men, and have a like exercise one upon another, hounds over the hare, the pike or luce over the tench, the swallows over the grasshoppers, and the sparrow-hawks over blackbirds and larks.

> [B]The stork her young ones feeds with serpents prey
> And lizards found somewhere out of the way.
> Jove's servants, eagles, hawks of nobler kind,
> In forests hunt, a hare or kid to find.
>
> Juven. XIV.74, 81.

We share the fruits of our prey with our dogs and hawks as a meed of their pain and reward of their industry; as about Amphipolis in Thrace falconers and wild hawks divide their game equally; and as about the Maeotid fens if fishers do not very honestly leave behind them an even share of their fishings for the wolves that range about those coasts they presently run and tear their nets.

[A]And as we have a kind of fishing rather managed by sleight than strength, as that of hook and line about our angling rods, so have beasts amongst themselves. Aristotle reporteth that the cuttle-fish casteth a long gut out of her throat which, like a line, she sendeth forth and at her pleasure pulleth it in again, according as she perceiveth some little fish come near her who, being close-hidden in the gravel or strand, letteth him nibble or bite the end of it and then by little and little draws it in unto her, until the fish be so near that with a sudden leap she may catch it. Touching strength, there is no creature in the world open to so many wrongs and injuries as a man. He need not a whale, an elephant, nor a crocodile, nor any such other wild beast, of which one alone is of power to defeat a great number of men. Silly* lice are able to make Sulla give over his dictatorship. The heart and life of a mighty and triumphant emperor is but the breakfast of a silly* little worm.

Why say we that skill to discern and knowledge to make choice (gotten by art and acquired by discourse) of things good for this life and availful against sickness, and so distinguish of those which are hurtful, and to know the virtue of rhubarb, quality of oak fern, and operation of polypodium, is only peculiar unto man? When we see the goats of Candia, being shot with an arrow, to choose from out a million of simples the herb dittany, or garden-ginger, and therewith cure themselves; and the tortoise, having eaten of a viper, immediately to seek for origanum, or wild marjoram, to purge herself; the dragon to run and clear his eyes with fennel; the cranes with their bills to minister glisters of sea-water unto themselves; the elephants to pull out, not only from themselves and their fellows but also from their masters (witness that of King Porus whom Alexander defeated), such javelins or darts as in fight have been thirled* or shot at them, so nimbly and so cunningly as ourselves could never do it so easily and with so little pain — why say we not likewise that that is science and prudence in them? For, if to depress them some allege it is by the only instruction and instinct of nature they know it, that will not take the name of science and title of prudence from them: it is rather to ascribe it unto them than to us, for the honor of so assured a schoolmistress.

Chrysippus, albeit in other things as disdainful a judge of the condition of beasts as any other philosopher, considering the earnest movings of the dog who, coming into a path that led three several ways, in search or quest of his master whom he had lost, or in pursuit of some prey that hath escaped him, goeth scenting first one way and then another and, having assured himself of two because he findeth not the track of what he hunteth for, without more ado furiously betakes himself to the third, he is enforced to confess that such a dog must necessarily discourse thus with himself: "I have followed my master's footing hitherto; he must of necessity pass by one of these three ways; it is neither this nor that; then consequently he is gone this other." And, by this conclusion or discourse assuring himself, coming to the third path, he useth his sense no more nor sounds it any longer, but by the power of reason suffers himself violently to be carried through it. This mere logical trick and this use of divided and conjoined propositions and of the sufficient numbering of parts, is it not as good that the dog know it by himself as by Trapezuntius[4] his logic?

Yet are not beasts altogether unapt to be instructed after our manner. We teach blackbirds, starlings, ravens, piots,* and parrots to chat; and that facility we perceive in them, to lend us their voice so supple and their wind so tractable that so we may frame and bring it to a certain number of letters and syllables, witnesseth they have a kind of inward reason which makes them so docile and willing to learn. I think every man is cloyed and wearied with seeing so many apish and mimic tricks that jugglers teach their dogs, as the dances where they miss not one cadence of the sounds or notes they hear: mark but the divers turnings and several kinds of motions which by the commandment of their bare words they make them perform. But I wonder not a little at the effect, which is ordinary amongst us, and

[4] George of Trebizond (1396–1486), a logician who wrote a commentary on Aristotle.

that is the dogs which blind men use both in city and country. I have observed how suddenly they will stop when they come before some doors where they are wont to receive alms, how carefully they will avoid the shock of carts and coaches, even when they have room enough to pass by themselves. I have seen some, going along a town ditch, leave a plain and even path and take a worse, that so they might draw their master from the ditch. How could a man make the dog conceive his charge was only to look to his master's safety, and for his service to despise his own commodity and good? And how should he have the knowledge that such a path would be broad enough for him but not for a blind man? Can all this be conceived without reason? We must not forget what Plutarch affirmeth to have seen a dog in Rome do before the Emperor Vespasian the father, in the theatre of Marcellus. This dog served a juggler, who was to play a fiction of many faces and sundry countenances, where he also was to act a part. Amongst other things, he was for a long while to counterfeit and feign himself dead, because he had eaten of a certain drug. Having swallowed a piece of bread which was supposed to be the drug, he began suddenly to stagger and shake as if he had been giddy; then, stretching and laying himself along as stiff as if he were stark dead, suffered himself to be dragged and haled from one place to another, according to the subject and plot of the play; and when he knew his time, first he began fair and softly to stir, as if he were roused out of a dead slumber; then, lifting up his head, he looked and stared so ghastly that all the bystanders were amazed.

The oxen which in the king's garden of Susa were taught to water them and to draw water out of deep wells turned certain great wheels, to which were fastened great buckets (as in many places of Languedoc is commonly seen); and being every one appointed to draw just a hundred turns a day, they were so accustomed to that number as it was impossible by any compulsion to make them draw one more, which task ended, they would suddenly stop. We are grown striplings before we can tell a hundred, and many nations have lately been discovered that never knew what numbers meant.

More discourse is required to teach others than to be taught. And, omitting what Democritus judged and proved — which is, that beasts have instructed us in most of our arts, as the spider to weave and sew, the swallow to build, the swan and the nightingale music, and divers beasts, by imitating them, the art of physic — Aristotle is of opinion that nightingales teach their young ones to sing, wherein they employ both long time and much care, when it followeth that those which we keep tame in cages and have not had leisure to go to their parents' school lose much grace in their singing. [B]Whereby we may conclude they are much amended by discipline and study. And amongst those that run wild, their song is not all one, nor alike. Each one hath learned either better or worse, according to his capacity. And so jealous are they in their prenticeship that to excel one another they will so stoutly contend for the mastery that many times such as are vanquished die, their wind and strength sooner failing than their voice. They young ones will very sadly sit recording their lesson, and are often seen laboring how to imitate certain song-notes. The scholar listeneth attentively to his master's lesson and carefully yieldeth account of it; now one and then another shall hold his peace; mark but how they endeavor to amend their faults, and see how the elder striveth to reprove the youngest.

Arrius protesteth to have seen an elephant who, on every thigh having a cymbal hanging and one fastened to his trunk, at the sound of which all other elephants danced in a round, now rising aloft, then louting* full low at certain cadences, even as the instrument directed them; and was much delighted with the harmony. [A]In the great shows of Rome, elephants were ordinarily seen taught to move and dance at the sound of a voice certain dances, wherein were many strange shifts, interchanges, caperings, and cadences, very hard to be learned. Some have been noted to con and practice their lessons using much study and care, as being loath to be chidden and beaten of their masters.

But the tale of the piot* is very strange which Plutarch confidently witnesseth to have seen. This jay was in a barber's shop of Rome, and was admirable in counterfeiting with her voice whatsoever she heard. It fortuned one day that certain trumpeters stayed before this shop, and there sounded a good while; and being gone, all that day and the next after the piot began to be very sad, silent, and melancholy; whereat all men marvelled and surmised that the noise or clang of the trumpets had thus affrighted and dizzied her and that with her hearing she had also lost her voice. But at last they found she was but in a deep study and dumpish,* retracting into herself, exercising her mind, and preparing her voice to represent the sound and express the noise of the trumpets she had heard. And the first voice she uttered was that, wherein she perfectly expressed their strains, their closes, and their changes, having by her new prenticeship altogether quit and, as it were, scorned whatever she could prattle before.

I will not omit to allege another example of a dog, which Plutarch also saith to have seen (as for any order or method, I know very well I do but confound it, which I observe no more in ranging these examples than I do in all the rest of my business), who, being in a ship, noted that this dog was in great perplexity how to get some oil out of a deep pitcher which, by reason of its narrow mouth, he could not reach with his tongue, got him presently some pebble stones and put so many into the jar that he made the oil come up so near the brim as he could easily reach and lick some. And what is that but the effect of a very subtle spirit? It is reported that the ravens of Barbary will do the like when the water they would drink is too low.

This action doth somewhat resemble that which Juba, a king of that nation, relateth of their elephants, that when, through the wiles of those who chase them, anyone chanceth to fall into certain deep pits which they prepare for them and to deceive them they cover over with reeds, shrubs, and boughs, his fellows will speedily with all diligence bring great store of stones and pieces of timber that so they may help to recover him out again. But this beast hath in many other effects such affinity with man's sufficiency that, would I particularly trace out what experience hath taught, I should easily get an affirmation of what I so ordinarily maintain, which is that there is more difference found between such and such a man than between such a beast and such a man. An elephant's keeper in a private house of Syria was wont every meal to steal away half of the allowance which was allotted him. It fortuned on a day his master would needs feed him himself and, having poured that just measure of barley which for his allowance he had prescribed into his manger, the elephant, sternly eyeing his master, with his trunk divided the provender in two equal parts and laid the one aside, by which he declared the wrong his keeper did him. Another, having a keeper who, to increase the measure of his provender, was wont to mingle stones with it, came one day to the pot which, with meat in it for his keeper's dinner, was seething over the fire, and filled it up with ashes.

These are but particular effects; but that which all the world hath seen and all men know, which is that in all the armies that came out of the East their chiefest strength consisted in their elephants, by whom they reaped without comparison far greater effects than nowadays we do by our great ordnance, which in a manner holds their place in a ranged battle (such as have any knowledge in ancient histories may easily guess it to be true):

> [B]Their elders used great Hannibal to steed,
> Our leaders, and Molossian kings at need,
> And on their back to bear strong guarding knights,
> Part of the war, and troops addressed to fights.
>
> Juven. XII.107.

[A]A man must needs rest assured of the confidence they had in these beasts and of their discourse, yielding the front of a battle unto them, where the least stay they could have made, by reason of the hugeness and weight of their bodies, and the least amazement that might have made them turn head upon their own men, had been sufficient to lose all. And few examples have been noted that ever it fortuned they turned upon their own troops, whereas we headlong throng one upon another and so are put to rout. They had charge given them not only of one simple moving, but of many and several parts in combat; [B]as the Spaniards did to their dogs in their new conquest of the Indies, to whom they gave wages and imparted their booties; which beasts showed as much dexterity in pursuing and judgment in staying their victory, in charging or retreating, and, as occasion served, in distinguishing their friends from their enemies, as they did earnestness and eagerness.

[A]We rather admire and consider strange than common things; without which I should never so long have amused myself about this tedious catalogue. For in my judgment, he that shall nearly check what we ordinarily see in those beasts that live amongst us shall in them find as wonderful effects as those which with so much toil are collected in far countries and past ages. [C]It is one same nature, which still doth keep her course. He that throughly should judge her present estate might safely conclude both what shall happen and what is past.

[A]I have seen amongst us men brought by sea from distant countries, whose language, because we could in no wise understand, and that their fashions, their countenance, and their clothes did altogether differ from ours, who of us did not deem them brutish and savage? Who did not impute their muteness unto stupidity or beastliness, and to see them ignorant of the French tongue, of our kissing the hands, of our low-louting* courtesies, of our behavior and carriage, by which, without contradiction, human nature ought to take her pattern? Whatsoever seemeth strange unto us and we understand not, we blame and condemn. The like befalleth us in our judging of beasts. They have diverse qualities which somewhat symbolize* with ours; from which we may comparatively draw some conjecture. But of such as are peculiar unto them, what know we what they are? Horses, dogs, oxen, sheep, birds, and the greater number of sensitive creatures that live amongst us know our voice, and by it suffer themselves to be directed. So did the lamprey which Crassus had, and came to him when he called it; so did the eels that breed in Arethusa's fountain. [B]And myself have seen some fish-ponds where, at a certain cry of those that kept them, the fish would presently come to shore, where they were wont to be fed.

> [A]They have their proper names, and every one
> Comes at his master's voice, as call'd upon.
>
> Mart. IV.xxix.6.

By which we may judge, and conclude that elephants have some apprehension of religion, forsomuch as after divers washings and purifications they are seen to lift up their trunk as we do our arms, and at certain hours of the day, without any instruction, of their own accord, holding their eyes fixed towards the sun-rising, fall into a long meditating contemplation. Yet because we see no such appearance in other beasts, may we rightly conclude that they are altogether void of religion, and may not take that in payment which is hidden from us. As we perceive something in that action which the philosopher Cleanthes well observed, because it somewhat draws near unto ours. He saw, as himself reporteth, a company of emmets* go from their nest, bearing amongst them the body of a dead ant, toward another emmets' nest, from which many other ants came as it were to meet them by the way to parley with them; who, after they had continued together awhile, they which came last returned back to consult, as you may imagine, with their fellow-citizens; and because they could hardly come to any capitulation, they made two or three voyages to and fro. In the end, the last come brought unto the other a worm from their habitation as for a ransom of the dead; which worm the first company took upon their backs and carried it home, leaving the dead body unto the other. Lo, here the interpretation that Cleanthes gave it, witnessing thereby that those creatures which have no voice at all have nevertheless mutual commerce and interchangeable communication, whereof if we be not partakers it is only our fault; and therefore do we fondly* to censure it.

And they yet produce divers other effects, far surpassing our capacity and so far out of the reach of our imitation that even our thoughts are unable to conceive them. Many hold opinion that in the last and famous sea-fight which Antony lost against Augustus his admiral-galley was in her course stayed by that little fish the Latins call *remora* and the English a suck-stone, whose property is to stay any ship he can fasten himself unto. And the emperor Caligula, sailing with a great fleet along the coast of Romania, his own galley was suddenly stayed by such a fish, which he caused to be taken sticking fast to the keel; moodily raging that so little a creature had the power to force both sea and wind and the violence of all his oars only with her bill sticking to his galley (for it is a kind of shell-fish); and was much more amazed when he perceived the fish, being brought aboard his ship, to have no longer that powerful virtue which it had being in the sea.

A certain citizen of Cyzicus whilom purchased unto himself the reputation to be an excellent mathematician because he had learned the quality of the hedgehog, whose property is to build his hole or den open divers ways and toward several winds, and, foreseeing rising storms, he presently stopped the holes that way. Which thing the foresaid citizen heedfully observing, would in the city foretell any future storm and what wind should blow.

The chameleon taketh the color of the place wherein he is. The fish called a pourcontrel* or many-feet changeth himself into what color he lists, as occasion offereth itself, that so he may hide himself from what he feareth and catch what he seeketh for. In the chameleon it is a change proceeding of passion, but in the pourcontrel a change in action. We ourselves do often change our color and alter our countenance through sudden fear, choler, shame, and suchlike violent passions which are wont to alter the hue of our faces, but it is by the effect of sufferance, as in the chameleon. The jaundice hath power to make us yellow, but it is not in the disposition of our wills. The effects we perceive in other creatures, greater than ours, witness some more excellent faculty in them which is concealed from us, as it is to be supposed divers others of their conditions and forces are, [C]whereof no appearance or knowledge cometh to us.

[A]Of all former predictions, the ancientest and most certain were such as were drawn from the flight of birds. We have nothing equal unto it nor so admirable. The rule of fluttering and order of shaking their wings by which they conjecture the consequences of things to ensue must necessarily be directed to so noble an operation by some excellent and supernatural mean; for it is a wresting of the letter to attribute so wondrous effects to any natural decree, without the knowledge, consent, or discourse of him that causeth and produceth them, and is a most false opinion. Which to prove, the torpedo or cramp-fish hath the property to benumb and astonish* not only the limbs of those that touch it, but also theirs that with any long pole or fishing line touch any part thereof. She doth transmit and convey a kind of heavy numbing into the hands of those that stir or handle the same. Moreover, it is averred that if any matter be cast upon them the astonishment* is sensibly felt to gain upward until it come to the hands, and even through the water it astonisheth* the feeling sense. Is not this a wonderful power? Yet is it not altogether unprofitable for the cramp-fish; she both knows and makes use of it; for to catch prey she pursueth she is seen to hide herself under the mud that, other fishes swimming over her, strucken and benumbed with her exceeding coldness, may fall into her claws.

The cranes, swallows, and other wandering birds, changing their abode according to the seasons of the year, show evidently the knowledge they have of their fore-divining faculty, and often put the same in use. Hunters assure us that to choose the best dog and which they purpose to keep from out a litter of other young whelps, there is no better mean than the dam herself; for if they be removed from out their kennel, him that she first brings thither again shall always prove the best. Or if one but encompass her kennel with fire, look which of her whelps she first seeketh to save is undoubtedly the best. Whereby it appeareth they have a certain use of prognosticating that we have not, or else some hidden virtue to judge of their young ones, different and more lively than ours.

The manner of all beasts' breeding, engendering, nourishing, working, moving, living, and dying being so near to ours, whatever we abridge from their moving causes and add to our condition above theirs can no way depart from our reason's discourse. For a regiment of our health physicians propose the example of beasts' manner of life, and proceeding unto us; for this common saying is always in the people's mouth:

> Keep warm ('tis meet) thy head and feet;
> In all the rest, live like a beast.

Generation is the chiefest natural action. We have a certain disposition of some members fittest for that purpose; nevertheless, they bid us range ourselves unto a brutish situation and disposition as most effectual:

> [It seems that women conceive best in the manner of beasts, like quadrupeds, because thus the seed can easily reach its goal when the breasts are low and the loins high;][5]
>
> Lucr. IV.1261.

and reject those indiscreet and insolent motions which women have so luxuriously found out, as hurtful, conforming them to the example and use of beasts of their sex, as more modest and considerate:

> [For a woman may forbid and oppose conception if she assists the man's action with the writhing of her hips and the motion of her breast; for she turns the plough away from the furrow and causes the seed to miss its mark.][6]
>
> Lucr. IV.1266.

If it be justice to give every one his due, beasts which serve, love, and defend their benefactors, pursue and outrage strangers and such as offend them, by so doing they represent some show of our justice, as also in reserving a high kind of equality in dispensing of what they have to their young ones. Touching friendship, without all comparison they profess it more lively and show it more constantly than men.

[5] Not translated by Florio.

[6] Not translated by Florio.

Hircanus, a dog of Lysimachus the king, his master being dead, without eating or drinking would never come from off his bed, and when the dead corpse was removed thence, he followed it, and lastly flung himself into the fire where his master was burned. As did also the dog of one called Pyrrhus, who, after he was dead, would never budge from his master's couch, and when he was removed suffered himself to be carried away with him, and at last flung himself into the fire wherein his master was consumed. There are certain inclinations of affection which without counsel of reason arise sometimes in us, proceeding of a casual temerity, which some call sympathy: beasts as well as men are capable of it. We see horses take a kind of acquaintance one of another so that often, travelling by the highway or feeding together, we have much ado to keep them asunder; we see them bend and apply their affections to some of their fellows' colors as if it were upon a certain visage; and when they meet with any such, with signs of joy and demonstration of good will to join and accost them, and to hate and shun other forms and colors. Beasts, as well as we, have choice in their loves and are very nice in choosing of their mates. They are not altogether void of our extreme and unappeasable jealousies. Lustful desires are either natural and necessary, as eating and drinking, or else natural and not necessary, as the acquaintance of males and females, or else neither necessary nor natural. Of this last kind are almost all men's; for they are all superfluous and artificial. It is wonderful to see with how little nature will be satisfied, and how little she hath left for us to be desired. The preparations in our kitchens do nothing at all concern her laws. The Stoics say that a man might very well sustain himself with one olive a day. The delicacy of our wines is no part of her lesson; no more is the surcharge and relishing which we add unto our lecherous appetites:

> [Nor does she require a wench born of some great consul.][7]
>
> Hor. *Sat.* I.ii.69.

These strange, lustful longings, which the ignorance of good and a false opinion have possessed us with, are in number so infinite that in a manner they expel all those which are natural; even as if there were so many strangers in a city that should either banish and expel all the natural inhabitants thereof or utterly suppress their ancient power and authority and, absolutely usurping the same, take possession of it. Brute beasts are much more regular than we, and with more moderation contain themselves within the compass which nature hath prescribed them; yet not so exactly but that they have some coherency without riotous licentiousness. And even as there have been found

[7] Not translated by Florio.

certain furious longings and unnatural desires which have provoked men unto the love of beasts, so have divers times some of them have been drawn to love us and are possessed with monstrous affections from one kind to another. Witness the elephant that in the love of an herb-wife* in the city of Alexandria was co-rival with Aristophanes the grammarian, who in all offices pertaining to an earnest wooer and passionate suitor yielded nothing unto him; for, walking through the fruit market, he would here and there snatch up some with his trunk and carry them unto her; as near as might be he would never lose the sight of her; and now and then over her band put his trunk into her bosom and feel her breasts. They also report of a dragon that was exceedingly in love with a young maiden; and of a goose in the city of Aesop which dearly loved a young child; also of a ram that belonged to the musician Glaucia. Do we not daily see monkeys ragingly in love with women, and furiously to pursue them? And certain other beasts given to love the males of their own sex? Oppianus and others report some examples to show the reverence and manifest the awe some beasts in their marriages bear unto their kindred, but experience makes us often see the contrary:

> To bear her sire the heifer shameth not;
> The horse takes his own filly's maidenhead;
> The goat gets them with young whom he begot;
> Birds breed by them, by whom themselves were bred.
>
> Ovid, *Metam.* X.325.

Touching a subtle prank and witty trick, is there any so famous as that of Thales the philosopher's mule which, laden with salt, passing through a river chanced to stumble, so that the sacks she carried were all wet and, perceiving the salt (because the water had melted it) to grow lighter, ceased not, as soon as she came near any water, together with her load to plunge herself therein; until her master, being aware of her craft, commanded her to be laden with wool, which, being wet, became heavier. The mule, finding herself deceived, used her former policy no more.

There are many of them that lively represent the visage of our avarice, who with a greedy kind of desire endeavor to surprise whatsoever comes within their reach and, though they reap no commodity nor have any use of it, to hide the same very curiously.

As for husbandry, they exceed us not only in foresight to spare and gather together for times to come, but have also many parts of the skill belonging thereunto. As the ants, when they perceive their corn to grow musty and grain to be sour, for fear it should rot and putrefy spread the same abroad before their nests that so it may air and dry.

But the caution they use in gnawing and prevention they employ in paring their grains of wheat is beyond all imagination of man's wit. Because wheat doth not always keep dry nor wholesome, but moisten, melt, and dissolve into a kind of whey, namely, when it beginneth to bud, fearing it should turn to seed and lose the nature of a storehouse for their sustenance, they part and gnaw off the end whereat it wonts to bud.

As for war, which is the greatest and most glorious of all human actions, I would fain know if we will use it for an argument of some prerogative or otherwise for a testimony of our imbecility and imperfection; as in truth the science we use to defeat and kill one another, to spoil and utterly to overthrow our own kind, it seemeth it hath not much to make itself to be wished for in beasts that have it not:

> [B]When hath a greater lion damnified
> A lion's life? In what wood ever died
> A boar by tusks and gore
> Of any greater boar?
>
> Juven. XV.160.

[A]Yet are not they altogether exempted from it. Witness the furious encounters of bees and the hostile enterprises of the princes and leaders of the two contrary armies:

> Ofttimes 'twixt two no great kings, great dissension
> With much ado doth set them at contention;
> The vulgar minds straight may you see from far,
> And hearts that tremble at the thought of war.
>
> Virg. *Georg.* IV.67.

I never mark this divine description but methinks I read human foolishness and worldly vanity painted in it. For, these motions of war which out of their horror and astonishment* breed this tempest of cries and clang of sounds in us:

> [B]Where lightning raiseth itself to the skies,
> The earth shines round with armor, sounds do rise
> By men's force under feet, wounded with noise
> The hills to heav'n reverberate their voice,
>
> Lucr. II.325.

[A]this horror-causing array of so many thousands of armed men, so great fury, earnest fervor, and undaunted courage, it would make one laugh to see by how many vain occasions it is raised and set on fire, and by what light means it is again suppressed and extinct:

> For Paris' lustful love, as stories tell,
> All Greece to direful war with Asia fell.
>
> Hor. *Epist.* I.ii.645.

The hatred of one man, a spite, a pleasure, a familiar suspect, or a jealousy—causes which ought not to move two scolding fishwives to scratch one another—is the soul and motive of all this hurly-burly. Shall we believe them that are the principal authors and causes thereof? Let us but hearken unto the greatest and most victorious emperor and the mightiest that ever was, how pleasantly he laughs and wittingly he plays at so many battles and bloody fights, hazarded both by sea and land, at the blood and lives of five hundred thousand souls which followed his fortune, and the strength and riches of two parts of the world consumed and drawn dry for the service of his enterprise:

> [Because Antony made love to Glaphyra, Fulvia has appointed me this penalty, that I should make love to her as well. Sleep with Fulvia? What if Manius begged me to bugger him? Should I do it? I should hardly think so if I'm wise. Either sleep with me or let's fight, she says. And what if my member is dearer to me than my life? Let the trumpets sound!][8]
>
> Mart. XI.xxi.3.

(I use my Latin somewhat boldly, but it is with that leave which you[9] have given me.)

This vast, huge body hath so many faces and several motion, which seem to threat both heaven and earth:

> BAs many waves as roll in Afric marble-sounds*
> When fier[c]e Orion hides in winter waves his head,
> Or when thick ears of corn are parch'd by sun new-spread,
> In Hermus' fruitful fields or Lycia's yellow grounds,
> With noise of shields and feet the trembling earth so sounds.
>
> Virg. *Aen.* VII.718.

AThis manyheaded, divers-armed, and furiously-raging monster is man, wretched, weak, and miserable man; whom if you consider well, what is he but a crawling and ever-moving ants' nest?

> The sable-colored band
> Marches along the land.
>
> Virg. *Aen.* IV.404.

A gust of contrary winds, the croaking of a flight of ravens, the false pace of a horse, the casual flight of an eagle, a dream, a sudden voice, a false sign, a morning's mist, an evening fog, are enough to overthrow, sufficient to overwhelm, and able to pull him to the ground. Let the sun but shine hot upon his face, he faints and swelters with

8 Not translated by Florio.

9 The essay is dedicated to a princess, perhaps Marguerite de Valois. See note 26.

heat. Cast but a little dust in his eyes, as to the bees mentioned by our poet, all our ensigns, all our legions, yea, great Pompey himself in the forefront of them is overthrown and put to rout. For as I remember it was he whom Sertorius vanquished in Spain with all those goodly arms. [B]This also served Eumenes against Antigonus, and Surena against Crassus:

> [A]These stomach-motions, these contentions great,
> [Calm'd] with a little dust, straight lose their heat.
>
> Virg. *Georg.* IV.86.

[C]Let us but uncouple some of our ordinary flies and let loose a few gnats amongst them: they shall have both the force to scatter and courage to consume him. The Portugals not long since beleaguering the city of Tamly in the territory of Xiatine, the inhabitants thereof brought great store of hives (whereof they have plenty upon their walls) and with fire drove them so forcible upon their enemies, who, as unable to abide their assaults and endure their stingings, left their enterprise. Thus by this new kind of help was the liberty of the town gained and victory purchased, with so happy success that in their retreating there was not one townsman found wanting.

[A]The souls of emperors and cobblers are all cast in one same mold. Considering the importance of princes' actions and their weight, we persuade ourselves they are brought forth by some as weighty and important causes. We are deceived. They are moved, stirred, and removed in their motions by the same springs and wards that we are in ours. The same reason that makes us chide and brawl and fall out with any of our neighbors causeth a war to follow between princes. The same reason that makes us whip or beat a lackey maketh a prince (if thee apprehend it) to spoil and waste a whole province. [B]They have as easy a will as we, but they can do much more. [A]Alike desires perturb both a skin-worm and an elephant.

Touching trust and faithfulness, there is no creature in the world so treacherous as man. Our histories report the earnest pursuit and sharp chase that some dogs have made for the death of their masters. King Pyrrhus, finding a dog that watched a dead man, and understanding he had done so three days and nights together, commanded the corpse to be interred and took the dog along with him. It fortuned one day as Pyrrhus was surveying the general musters of his army, the dog perceiving in that multitude the man who had murdered his master, loud barking and with great rage ran furiously upon him; by which signs he furthered and procured his master's revenge, which by way of justice was shortly executed. Even so did the dog belonging to Hesiod, surnamed the wise, having convicted the children of Ganistor of Naupactus of the murder committed on his master's person. Another dog, being appointed to watch a temple in Athens, having perceived a sacrilegious thief to carry away the fairest jewels therein, barked at him so long as he was able; and seeing he could not awaken the sextons or temple-keepers, followed the thief whithersoever he went. Daylight being come, he kept himself aloof-off, but never lost the sight of him; if he offered him meat, he utterly refused it; but if any passenger chanced to come by, on them he fawned with wagging his tail, and took whatever they offered him; if the thief stayed to rest himself, he also stayed in the same place. The news of this dog being come to the temple-keepers, they, as they went along inquiring of the dog's hair and color, pursued his track so long that at last they found both the dog and the thief in the city of Cromyon, whom they brought back to Athens, where for his offense he was severely punished. And the judges, in acknowledgment of the dog's good office, at the city's charge appointed him for his sustenance a certain daily measure of corn and enjoined the priests of the temple carefully to look unto him. Plutarch affirmeth this story to be most true, and to have happened in his time.

Touching gratitude and thankfulness (for methinks we have need to further this word greatly), this only example shall suffice, of which Apion reporteth to have been a spectator himself. One day, saith he, that the senate of Rome to please and recreate the common people caused a great number of wild beasts to be baited, namely huge, great lions, it so fortuned that there was one amongst the rest who, by reason of his furious and stately carriage, of his unmatched strength, of his great limbs, and of his loud and terror-causing roaring, drew all bystanders' eyes to gaze upon him. Amongst other slaves that in sight of all the people were presented to encounter with these beasts, there chanced to be one Androdus[10] of Dacia, who belonged unto a Roman lord who had been consul. This huge lion, having eyed him afar off, first made a sudden stop, as strucken into a kind of admiration; then with a mild and gentle countenance, as if he would willingly have taken acquaintance of him, fair and softly approached unto him. Which done, and resting assured he was the man he took him for, begun fawningly to wag his tail, as dogs do that fawn upon their new-found masters, and lick the poor and miserable slave's hands and thighs, who through fear was almost out of his wits and half dead. Androdus at last taking heart of grace and by reason of the lion's mildness, having roused up his spirits, and wishly* fixing his eyes upon him to see whether he could call him to remembrance, it was to all beholders a singular pleasure to observe the love, the joy, and blandishments each endeavored to inter-show one another. Whereat the people

10 Generally called Androcles.

raising a loud cry and by their shouting and clapping of hands seeming to be much pleased, the emperor willed the slave to be brought before him, as desirous to understand of him the cause of so strange and seld*-seen an accident; who related this new and wonderful story unto him:

"My master," said he, "being proconsul in Africa, forsomuch as he caused me every day to be most cruelly beaten and held me in so rigorous bondage, I was constrained, as being weary of my life, to run away. And, safely to scape from so eminent a person and who had so great authority in the country, I thought it best to get me into the desert and most unfrequented wildernesses of that region, with a full resolution if I could not compass the means to sustain myself to find one way or other with violence to make myself away. One day, the sun about noon-tide being extremely hot and the scorching heat thereof intolerable, I fortuned to come unto a wild, unhaunted* cave hidden amongst crags and almost inaccessible and where I imagined no footing had ever been; therein I hid myself. I had not long been there but in comes this lion with one of his paws sore hurt and bloody-gored, wailing for the smart and groaning for the pain he felt; at whose arrival I was much dismayed; but he, seeing me lie close-cowering in a corner of his den, gently made his approaches unto me, holding forth his gored paw toward me, and seemed with showing the same humbly to sue and suppliantly to beg for help at my hands. I, moved with ruth, taking it into my hand, pulled out a great splint which was gotten into it and, shaking off all fear, first I wrung and crushed his sore and caused the filth and matter which therein was gathered to come forth; then, as gently as for my heart I could, I cleansed, wiped, and dried the same. He, feeling some ease in his grief and his pain to cease, still holding his foot between my hands, began to sleep and take some rest. Thenceforward he and I lived together the full space of three years in his den with such meat as he shifted for; for, what beasts he killed or what prey soever he took, he ever brought home the better part and shared it with me, which for want of fire I roasted in the sun, and therewith nourished myself all that while. But at last wearied with this kind of brutish life, the lion being one day gone to purchase his wonted prey, I left the place, hoping to mend my fortunes; and having wandered up and down three days, I was at last taken by certain soldiers which from Africa brought me into this city to my master again, who immediately condemned me to death and to be devoured by wild beasts. And as I now perceive, the same lion was also shortly after taken, who, as you see, hath now requited me of the good turn I did him, and the health which by my means he recovered."

Behold here the history Androdus reported unto the emperor, which after he caused to be declared unto all the people, at whose general request he was forthwith set at liberty and quit of his punishment, and by the common consent of all had the lion bestowed upon him. Apion saith further that Androdus was daily seen to lead the lion up and down the streets of Rome, tied only with a little twine and, walking from tavern to tavern, received such money as was given him, who would gently suffer himself to be handled, touched, decked, and strewed with flowers all over and over; many saying when they met him, "Yonder is the lion that is the man's host, and yonder is the man that is the lion's physician."

[B]We often mourn and weep for the loss of those beasts we love; so do they many times for the loss of us:

> Next Aethon, horse of war, all ornaments laid down,
> Goes weeping, with great drops bedews his cheeks adown.
>
> Virg. *Aen.* XI.89.

As some of our nations have wives in common, and some in several, each man keeping himself to his own, so have some beasts; [yea,] some there are that observe their marriages with as great respect as we do ours. [A]Touching the mutual society and reciprocal confederation which they devise amongst themselves that so they may be fast combined together and in times of need help one another, it is apparent that if oxen, hogs, and other beasts, being hurt by us, chance to cry, all the herd runs to aid him and in his defense will join all together. The fish called of the Latins *scarus* having swallowed the fisher's hook, his fellows will presently flock about him and nibble the line in sunder; and if any of them happen to be taken in a bow-net, some of his fellows, turning his head away, will put his tail in at the neck of the net, who with his teeth fast holding the same, never leave him until they have pulled him out. The barble fishes, if one of them chance to be engaged, will set the line against their backs and, with a fin they have toothed like a sharp saw, presently saw and fret the same asunder.

Concerning particular offices which we for the benefit of our life draw one from another, many like examples are found amongst them. It is assuredly believed that the whale never swimmeth unless she have a little fish going before her as her vanguard; it is in shape like a gudgeon, and both the Latins and we call it the whale's-guide. For she doth ever follow him, suffering herself as easily to be led and turned by him as a ship is directed and turned by a stern;* for requital of which good turn, whereas all things else, be it beast, fish, or vessel, that comes within the horrible chaos of this monstrous mouth is presently lost and devoured, this little fish doth safely retire himself therein and there sleeps very quietly; and as long as he sleeps the whale never stirs, but as soon as he awaketh and goeth his way, wherever he takes his course she always followeth him; and if she fortune to lose him, she wanders here and there and often striketh upon the rocks, as a ship that hath nor mast nor rudder. This Plutarch witnesseth to have seen in the island of Anticyra.

There is such a like society between the little bird called a wren and the crocodile; for the wren serveth as a sentinel to so great a monster. And if the ichneumon, which is his mortal enemy, approach to fight with him, the little birdlet, lest he might surprise him whilst he sleepeth, with his singing and pecking him with his bill awakens him and gives him warning of the danger he is in. The bird liveth by the scraps and feedeth upon the leavings of that monster, who gently receiveth him into his mouth and suffers him to peck his jaws and teeth for such mammocks* of flesh as stick between them. And if he purpose to close his mouth, he doth first warn him to be gone, fair and easy closing it by little and little, without any whit crushing or hurting him.

The shellfish called a nacre liveth even so with the pinnothere, which is a little creature like unto a crabfish and as his porter or usher waits upon him, attending the opening of the nacre which he continually keeps gaping until he sees some little fish enter in fit for their turn; then he creeps into the nacre and leaves not pinching his quick flesh until he makes him close his shell; and so they both together, fast in their hold, devour their prey.

In the manner of the tunny's life may be discovered a singular knowledge of the three parts of the mathematics. First for astrology, it may well be said that man doth learn it of them; for wheresoever the winter solstitium doth take them, there do they stay themselves and never stir till the next equinoctium, and that is the reason why Aristotle doth so willingly ascribe that art unto them. Then for geometry and arithmetic, they always frame their shoal of a cubic figure, every way square, and so form a solid, close, and well-ranged battalion encompassed round about of six equal sides. Thus orderly marshalled, they take their course and swim whither their journey tends, as broad and wide behind as before; so that he that seeth and telleth but one rank may easily number all the troop, forsomuch as the number of the depth is equal unto the breadth, and the breadth unto the length.

Touching magnanimity and haughty courage, it is hard to set it forth more lively and to produce a rarer pattern than that of the dog which from India was sent unto Alexander; to whom was first presented a stag, then a wild boar, and then a bear, with each of which he should have foughten, but he seemed to make no account of them and would not so much as remove out of his place for them; but when he saw a lion, he presently roused himself, showing evidently he meant only so noble a beast worthy to enter combat with him.

[B]Concerning repentance and acknowledging of faults committed, it is reported that an elephant, having through rage of choler slain his governor, conceived such an extreme inward grief that he would never afterward touch any food and suffered himself to pine to death.

[A]Touching clemency, it is reported of a tiger, the fiercest and most inhuman beast of all, who having a kid given her to feed upon endured the force of gnawing hunger two days together rather than she would hurt him; the third day with main strength she broke the cage wherein she was kept pent and went elsewhere to shift for feeding, as one unwilling to seize upon the silly* kid, her familiar and guest.

And concerning privileges of familiarity and sympathy caused by conversation, is it not oft seen how some make cats, dogs, and hares so tame, so gentle, and so mild that, without harming one another, they shall live and continue together?

But that which experience teacheth seafaring men, especially those that come into the seas of Sicily, of the quality and condition of the halcyon bird or, as some call it, alcedo or king's-fisher, exceeds all men's conceit. In what kind of creature did ever nature so much prefer both their hatching, sitting, brooding, and birth? Poets feign that the island of Delos, being before wandering and floating up and down, was for the delivery of Latona made firm and settled. But God's decree hath been that all the watery wilderness should be quiet and made calm, without rain, wind, or tempest, during the time the halcyon sitteth and bringeth forth her young ones, which is much about the winter solstitium and shortest day in the year. By whose privilege, even in the heart and deadest time of winter we have seven calm days and as many nights to sail without any danger. Their hens know no other cock but their own; they never forsake him all the days of their life; and if the cock chance to be weak and crazed, the hen will take him upon her neck and carry him with her wheresoever she goeth, and serve him even until death. Man's wit could never yet attain to the full knowledge of that admirable kind of building or structure which the halycon useth in contriving of her nest, no, nor devise what it is of. Plutarch, who hath seen and handled many of them, thinks it to be made of certain fish-bones, which she so compacts and conjoineth together, interlacing some long and some crosswise, adding some foldings and roundings to it, that in the end she frameth a round kind of vessel, ready to float and swim upon the water; which done, she carrieth the same where the sea-waves beat most. There the sea, gently beating upon it, shows her how to daub and patch up the parts not well closed, and how to strengthen those places and fashion those ribs that are not fast but stir with the sea-waves; and on the other side, that which is closely wrought, the sea beating on it doth so fasten and conjoin together that nothing, no, not stone nor iron, can any way loosen, divide, or break the same except with great violence. And what is most to be wondered at is the proportion and figure of the concavity within; for it is so composed and proportioned that it can receive or admit no manner of thing but the bird that built it; for to all things else it is so impenetrable, close, and hard that nothing can possibly enter in, no, not so much as the sea-water. Lo, here a most plain description of this building or construction taken from a very good author; yet methinks it doth not fully and sufficiently resolve us of the difficulty in this kind of architecture. Now, from what vanity can it proceed we should so willfully contemn and disdainfully interpret those effects which we can neither imitate nor conceive?

But to follow this equality or correspondency between us and beasts somewhat further: the privilege whereof our soul vaunts to bring to her condition whatsoever it conceiveth and to despoil what of mortal and corporal qualities belongs unto it, to marshal those things which she deemed worthy her acquaintance, to disrobe and deprive their corruptible conditions and to make them leave as superfluous and base garments thickness, length, depth, weight, color, smell, roughness, smoothness, hardness, softness, and all sensible accidents else, to fit and appropriate them to her immortal and spiritual condition; so that Rome and Paris which I have in my soul, Paris which I imagine, yes, I imagine and conceive the same without greatness and place, without stone and mortar and without wood — then say I unto myself, the same privilege seemeth likewise to be in beasts. For a horse accustomed to hear the sound of trumpets, the noise of shot, and the clattering of arms, whom we see to snort, to startle, and to neigh in his sleep as he lies along upon his litter, even as he were in the hurly-burly: it is most certain that in his mind he apprehends the sound of a drum without any noise and an army without arms or body:

> You shall see warlike horses, when in sleep
> Their limbs lie, yet sweat, and a snorting keep,
> And stretch their utmost strength
> As for a goal at length.
>
> Lucr. IV.988.

That hare which a greyhound imagineth in his dream, after whom as he sleepeth we see him bay, quest, yelp, and snort, stretch out his tail, shake his legs, and perfectly represent the motions of his course, the same is a hare without bones, without hair:

> Ofttimes the hunters' dogs in easy rest
> Stir their legs suddenly open, and quest,
> And send from nostrils thick, thick snuffing scent,
> As if on trail they were of game full bent;
> And wakened so, they follow shadows vain
> Of deer in chase, as if they fled amain,
> Till, their fault left, they turn to sense again.
> Lucr. IV.992.

Those watching dogs which in their sleep we sometimes see to grumble and then, barking, to startle suddenly out of their slumber as if they perceived some stranger to arrive — that stranger which their mind seemeth to see is but an imaginary man, and not perceived, without any dimension, color, or being:

> The fawning kind of whelps at home that lives,
> From eyes to shake light, swift sleep often strives,
> And from the ground their starting bodies hie,
> As if some unknown stranger they did spy.
> Lucr. IV.999.

Touching corporal beauty, before I go any further, it were necessary I knew whether we are yet agreed about her description. It is very likely that we know not well what beauty either in nature or in general is, since we give so many and attribute so divers forms to human beauty, yea, and to our beauty; [C]of which, if there were any natural or lively description, we should generally know it as we do the heat of fire. We imagine and feign her forms as our fantasies lead us:

> [B]A Dutch frau's color hath no grace
> Seen in a Roman lady's face.
> Proper. II.xviii.26.

[A]The Indians describe it black and swarthy, with blabbered, thick lips, with a broad and flat nose, [B]the inward gristle whereof they load with great gold rings, hanging down to their mouth, and their nether lips with great circlets beset with precious stones which cover all their chins, deeming it an especial grace to show their teeth to the roots. In Peru, the greatest ears are ever esteemed the fairest, which, with all art and industry, they are continually stretching out; [C]and a man who yet liveth sweareth to have seen in a province of the East Indies the people so careful to make them great and so to load them with heavy jewels that at ease he could have thrust his arm through one of their ear-holes. [B]There are other nations who endeavor to make their teeth as black as jet, and scorn to have them white; and in other places they dye them red.

[C]Not only in the province of Basque, but in other places, women are accounted fairest when their heads are shaven; and, which is strange, in some of the northerly, frozen countries, as Pliny affirmeth. [B]Those of Mexico esteem the littleness of their foreheads as one of the chiefest beauties and, whereas they shave their hair over all their body besides, by artificial means they labor to nourish and make it grow only in their foreheads; and so love to have great dugs that they strive to have their children suck over their shoulders. [A]So would we set forth ill-favoredness.

The Italians proportion it big and plump; the Spaniard spiny* and lank; and amongst us, one would have her white, another brown, one soft and delicate, another strong and lusty; some desire wantonness and blitheness and others some sturdiness and majesty to be joined with it. [C]Even as the pre-eminence in beauty which Plato ascribeth unto the spherical figure, the Epicureans refer the same unto the pyramidal or square, and say they cannot swallow a god made round like a bowl. [A]But howsoever it is, nature hath no more privileged us in that than in other things concerning her common laws. And if we impartially enter into judgment with ourselves, we shall find that if there be any creature or beast less favored in that than we, there are others, and that in great numbers, to whom nature hath been more favorable than to us. [C]"We are excelled in comeliness by many living creatures" (Seneca, *Epist.* CXXIV.). Yea, of terrestrial creatures that live with us. For concerning those of the sea, omitting their figure, which no proportion can contain, so much doth it differ both in color, in neatness, in smoothness, and in disposition, we must give place unto them; which in all qualities we must likewise do to the airy ones. [A]And that prerogative which poets yield unto our upright stature, looking toward heaven whence her beginning is —

> Where other creatures on earth look and lie,
> A lofty look God gave man, bad him pry
> On heav'n, rais'd his high count'nance to the sky
>
> Ovid. *Metam.* I.84.

— is merely poetical; for there are many little beasts that have their sight directly fixed toward heaven: I find the camel's and the ostrich's neck much more raised and upright than ours.

[C]What beasts have not their face aloft and before, and look not directly opposite, as we, and in their natural posture descry not as much of heaven and earth as man doth? And what qualities of our corporal constitution, both in Plato and Cicero, cannot fit and serve a thousand beasts? [A]Such as most resemble man are the vilest and filthiest of all the rout: as for outward appearance and true shape of the visage, it is the monkey or the ape—

> [C]An ape, a most ill-favored beast,
> How like to us in all the rest?
> Ennius, in Cic. *De nat. deor.* I.xxxv.

—[A]as for inward and vital parts, it is the hog.

Truly, when I consider man all naked, yea, be it in that sex which seemeth to have and challenge the greatest share of eye-pleasing beauty, and view his defects, his natural subjection, and manifold imperfections, I find we have had much more reason to hide and cover our nakedness than any creature else. We may be excused for borrowing those which nature had therein favored more than us, with their beauties to adorn us and under their spoils of wool, of hair, of feathers, and of silk to shroud us.

Let us moreover observe that man is the only creature whose wants offends his own fellows, and he alone that in natural actions must withdraw and sequester himself from those of his own kind. Verily, it is an effect worthy consideration that the skilfullest masters of amorous dalliances appoint for a remedy of venerean passions a free and full survey of the body which one longeth and seeks after; and that to cool the longing and assuage the heat of friendship, one need but perfectly view and thoroughly consider what he loveth:

> The love stood still that ran in full cariere,*
> When bare it saw parts that should not appear.
> Ovid. *De rem. amor.* 429.

And although this remedy may haply proceed from a squeamish and cold humor, yet is it a wonderful sign of our imbecility that the use and knowledge should so make us to be cloyed one of another. [B]It is not bashfulness so much as art and foresight makes our ladies so circumspect and unwilling to let us come into their closets before they are fully ready and throughly painted to come abroad and show themselves:

> [A]Our mistresses know this, which makes them not disclose
> Parts to be played within, especially from those
> Whom they would servants hold and in their love-bands close;
> Lucr. IV.1182.

whereas in other creatures there is nothing but we love and pleaseth our senses, so that even from their excrements and ordure we draw not only dainties to eat, but our richest ornaments and perfumes.

This discourse of beauty touches only our common order and is not so sacrilegious as it intendeth or dareth to comprehend those divine, supernatural, and extraordinary beauties which sometimes are seen to shine amongst us even as stars under a corporal and terrestrial veil.

Moreover, that part of nature's favors which we impart unto beasts is, by our own confession, much more advantageous unto them. We assume unto ourselves imaginary and fantastical goods, future and absent goods, which human capacity can no way warrant unto herself; or some other which, by the overweening of our own opinion, we falsely ascribe unto ourselves, as reason, honor, and knowledge. And to them as their proper share we leave the essential, the manageable, and palpable goods, as peace, rest, security, innocency, and health — health, I say, which is the goodliest and richest present nature can impart unto us. So that even Stoic philosophy dareth to affirm that if Heraclitus and Pherecydes could have changed their wisdom with health, and by that means the one to have rid himself of the dropsy and the other of the lousy evil, which so tormented them, they would surely have done it. Whereby they also yield so much more honor unto wisdom, by comparing and counterpeising* the same unto health than they do in this other proposition of theirs where they say that if Circe had presented Ulysses with two kinds of drink, the one to turn a wise man into a fool, the other to change a fool into a wise man, he would rather have accepted that of folly than have been pleased that Circe should transform his human shape into a beast's. And they say that wisdom herself would thus have spoken unto him: "Meddle not with me, but leave me rather than thou shouldst place me under the shape and body of an ass." What? This great and heavenly wisdom? Are philosophers contented then to quit it for a corporal and earthly veil? Why, then it is not for reason's sake, nor by discourse, and for the soul we so much excel beasts; it is for the love we bear unto our beauty, unto our fair hue and goodly disposition of limbs that we reject and set our understanding at nought, our wisdom, and what else we have.

Well, I allow of this ingenious and voluntary confession. Surely they knew those parts we so much labor to pamper to be mere fantasies. Suppose beasts had all the virtue, the knowledge, the wisdom and sufficiency of the Stoics, they should still be beasts; nor might they ever be compared unto a miserable, wretched, and senseless man.

[C]For, when all is done, whatsoever is not as we are is not of any worth. And God, to be esteemed of us, must, as we will show anon, draw somewhat near it. Whereby it appeareth that [A]it is not long of a true discourse, but of a foolish hardiness and self-presuming obstinacy we prefer ourselves before other creatures and sequester ourselves from their condition and society.

But to return to our purpose, we have for our part inconstancy, irresolution, uncertainty, sorrow, superstition, carefulness for future things, yea, after our life, ambition, covetousness, jealousy, envy, inordinate, mad and untamed appetites, war, falsehood, disloyalty, detraction, and curiosity. Surely we have strangely overpaid this worthy discourse whereof we so much glory and this readiness to judge or capacity to know, if we have purchased the same with the price of so infinite passions to which we are incessantly enthralled. [B]If we be not pleased, as Socrates is, to make this noble prerogative over beasts to be of force, that whereas nature hath prescribed them certain seasons and bounds for their natural lust and voluptuousness, she hath given us at all hours and occasions the full reins of them. [C]"As it is better not to use wine at all in sick persons, because it seldom doth them good, but many times much hurt, than in hope of doubtful health to run into undoubted danger; so do I not know whether it were better that this swift motion of the thought, this sharpness, this conceitedness, which we call reason, should not at all be given to mankind, because it is pernicious unto many and healthful to very few, than that it should be given so plentifully and so largely" (Cic. *De nat. deor.* III.xxvii.).

[A]What good or commodity may we imagine this far-understanding of so many things brought ever unto Varro, and to Aristotle? Did it ever exempt, or could it at any time free them from human inconveniences? Were they ever discharged of those accidents that incidentally follow a silly* laboring man? Could they ever draw any ease for the gout from logic? And howbeit they knew the humor engendering the same to lodge in the joints, have they felt it the less? Did they at any time make a covenant with death, although they knew full well that some nations rejoice at her coming? As also of cuckoldship, because they knew women to be common in some countries? But contrariwise, having both held the first rank in knowledge, the one amongst the Romans, the other among the Grecians, yea, and at such times wherein sciences flourished most, we could never learn they had any special excellency in their life. We see the Grecian hath been put to his plunges* in seeking to discharge himself from some notable imputations in his life.

BWas it ever found that sensuality and health are more pleasing unto him that understands astrology and grammar?

> As stiff unlearned sinews stand,
> As theirs that much more understand.
> Hor. *Epod.* VIII.17

Or shame and poverty less importunate and vexing?

> Thou shalt be from disease and weakness free,
> From moan, from care, long time of life to thee
> Shall by more friendly fate afforded be.
> Juven. XIV.156.

I have in my days seen a hundred artificers and as many laborers more wise and more happy than some rectors in the university, and whom I would rather resemble. Methinks learning hath a place amongst things necessary for man's life, as glory, nobleness, dignity, Cor at most as riches, Aand such other qualities which indeed stead* the same, but afar-off and more in conceit than by nature.

CWe have not much more need of offices, of rules, and laws how to live in our commonwealth than the cranes and ants have in theirs. Which notwithstanding, we see how orderly and without instruction they maintain themselves. If man were wise he would value everything according to its worth, and as it is either more profitable or more necessary for life.

AHe that shall number us by our actions and proceedings shall doubtless find many more excellent ones amongst the ignorant than among the wiser sort: I mean in all kind of virtues. My opinion is that ancient Rome brought forth many men of much more valor and sufficiency, both for peace and war, than this late-learned Rome which, with all her wisdom, hath overthrown her erst-flourishing estate. If all the rest were alike, then should honesty and innocency at least belong to the ancient; for she was exceedingly well placed with simplicity.

But I will shorten this discourse, which haply would draw me further than I would willingly follow; yet thus much I will say more, that only humility and submission is able to make a perfect honest man. Everyone must not have the knowledge of his duty referred to his own judgment, but ought rather to have it prescribed unto him and not be allowed to choose it at his pleasure and free-will; otherwise, according to the imbecility of our reasons and infinite variety of our opinions, we might peradventure forge and devise such duties unto ourselves as would induce us, as Epicurus saith, to endeavor to destroy and devour one another.

The first law that ever God gave unto man was a law of pure obedience. It was a bare and simple commandment whereof man should inquire and know no further; [C]forasmuch as to obey is the proper duty of a reasonable soul, acknowledging a heavenly and superior benefactor. From obeying and yielding unto him proceed all other virtues, even as all sins derive from self-overweening. [B]Contrariwise, the first temptation that ever seized on human nature was disobedience, by the devil's instigation, whose first poison so far insinuated itself into us, by reason of the promises he made us of wisdom and knowledge: "You shall be like gods, knowing both good and evil" [Genesis III.5.]. [C]And the Sirens, to deceive Ulysses, and alluring him to fall into their dangerous and counfounding snares, offer to give him the full fruition of knowledge. [A]The opinion of wisdom is the plague of man. That is the occasion why ignorance is by our religion recommended unto us, as an instrument fitting belief and obedience. [C]"Take heed lest any man deceive you by philosophy and vain seducements according to the rudiments of the world" (Colossians II.8.).

[A]All the philosophers of all the sects that ever were do generally agree in this point, that the chiefest felicity, or *summum bonum*, consisteth in the peace and tranquillity of the soul and body. [B]But where shall we find it?

> [A]In sum, who wise is known
> Is less than Jove alone,
> Rich, honorable, free, fair, king of kings,
> Chiefly in health, but when phlegm trouble brings.
>
> Hor. *Epist.* I.i.106.

It seemeth, verily, that nature, for the comfort of our miserable and wretched condition hath allotted us no other portion but presumption. It is therefore, as Epictetus saith, that man hath nothing that is properly his own but the use of his opinions. Our hereditary portion is nothing but smoke and wind. [B]The gods, as saith philosophy, have health in true essence and sickness in conceit; man, clean contrary, possesseth goods in imagination and evils essentially. [A]We have had reason to make the powers of our imagination to be of force; for all our felicities are but in conceit and, as it were, in a dream.

Hear but this poor and miserable creature vaunt himself: "there is nothing," saith Cicero, "so delightful and pleasant as the knowledge of letters, of letters I say, by whose means the infinity of things, the incomprehensible greatness of nature, the heavens, the earth, and all the seas of this vast universe are made known unto us. They have taught us religion, moderation, stoutness of courage, and redeemed our soul out of darkness to make her see and distinguish of all things, the high as well as the low, the first as the last, and those between both. It is they that store and supply us with all such things as may make us live happily and well, and instruct us how to pass our time without sorrow or offense." Seemeth not this goodly orator to speak of the Almighty's and everliving God's condition? And touching effects, a thousand poor silly* women in a country town have lived and live a life much more reposed, more peaceable, and more constant than ever he did.

> Good sir, it was God, God it was first found
> That course of man's life which is now renown'd
> By name of wisdom, who by art repos'd
> Our life in so clear light, calm so compos'd,
> From so great darkness, so great waves oppos'd.
>
> Lucr. V.8.

Observe what glorious and noble words these be; yet but a slight accident brought this wise man's understanding to a far worse condition than that of a simple shepherd, notwithstanding this divine teacher,[11] and this heavenly wisdom.

Of like impudence is [C]the promise of Democritus his book, "I will now speak of all things"; and that fond title which Aristotle gives us of "mortal gods"; and [A]that rash judgment of Chrysippus, that Dion was as virtuous as God. And my Seneca saith he acknowledgeth that God hath given him life, but how to live well, that he hath of himself; [C]like unto this other: "We rightly vaunt us of virtue, which we should not do if we had it of God, not of ourselves" (Cic. *De nat. deor.* III.36.). This also is Seneca's, that the wise man hath a fortitude like unto God's, but [in human] weakness, wherein he excelleth him.

[A]There is nothing more common than to meet with such passages of temerity. There is not any of us that will be so much offended to see himself compared to God, as he will deem himself wronged to be depressed in the rank of other creatures. So much are we more jealous of our own interest than of our creator's. But we must tread this foolish vanity under foot and bodly shake off and lively reject those fond,* ridiculous foundations whereon these false opinions are built. So long as man shall be persuaded to have means or power of himself, so long will he deny and never acknowledge what he oweth unto his master; he shall always (as the common saying is) make shift with his own. He must be stripped [u]nto his shirt.

11 Epicurus.

Let us consider some notable example of the effect of philosophy. Posidonius, having long time been grieved with a painful, lingering disease which with the smarting pain made him to wring his hands and gnash his teeth, thought to scorn grief with exclaiming and crying out against it: "Do what thou list, yet will I never say that thou are evil or pain." He feeleth the same passions that my lackey doth, but he boasteth himself that at least he containeth his tongue under the laws of his sect. [C]"It was not for him to yield in deeds, who had so braved it in words" (Cic. *Tusc.* II.xiii.).

Arcesilaus lying sick of the gout, Carneades coming to visit him and seeing him frown, supposing he had been angry, was going away again, but he called him back and, showing him his feet and breast, said unto him, "There is nothing come from thence hither." This hath somewhat a better garb; for he feeleth himself grieved with sickness and would fain be rid of it; yet is not his heart vanquished or weakened thereby, the other stands upon his stiffness, as I fear, more verbal than essential. And Dionysius Heracleotes, being tormented with a violent smarting in his eyes, was at last persuaded to quit these Stoic resolutions.

[A]Be it supposed that learning and knowledge should work those effects they speak of — that is, to blunt and abate the sharpness of those accidents or mischances that follow and attend us — doth she any more than what ignorance effecteth much more evidently and simply? The philosopher Pyrrho, being at sea and by reason of a violent storm in great danger to be cast away, presented nothing unto those that were with him in the ship to imitate but the security of a hog which was aboard, who, nothing at all dismayed, seemed to behold and outstare the tempest. Philosophy, after all her precepts, gives us over to the examples of a wrestler, or of a muleteer, in whom we ordinarily perceive much less feeling of death, of pain, of grief, and other inconveniences, and more undaunted constancy, than ever learning or knowledge could store a man withal, unless he were born and of himself through some natural habitude prepared unto it. What is the cause the tender members of a child [C]or limbs of a horse [A]are much more easy and with less pain cut and incised than ours if it be not ignorance? How many only through the power of imagination have fallen into dangerous diseases? We ordinarily see divers that will cause themselves to be let blood, purged, and dieted, because they would be cured of diseases they never felt but in conceit. When essential and true maladies fail us, then science and knowledge lends us hers. This color or complexion, saith she, presageth some rheumatic defluxion will ensue you; this sultry, hot season menaceth you with some febricant* commotion; this cutting of the vital line of your left hand warneth you of some notable and approaching indisposition. And at last she will roundly address herself unto perfect health, saying, this youthly vigor and sudden joy cannot possibly stay in one place; her blood and strength must be abated, for fear it turn you to some mischief. Compare but the life of a man subject to these like imaginations unto that of a day-laboring swain, who follows his natural appetites, who measureth all things only by the present sense, and hath neither learning nor prognostications, who feeleth no disease but when he hath it; whereas the other hath often the stone imaginarily, before he have it in his reins.* As if it were not time enough to endure the sickness when it shall come, he doth in his fancy prevent the same and headlong runneth to meet with it.

What I speak of physic, the same may generally be applied and drawn to all manner of learning. Thence came this ancient opinion of those philosophers who placed chief felicity in the acknowledging of our judgment's weakness. My ignorance affords me as much cause of hope as of fear, and having no other regimen for my health than that of other men's examples and of the events, I see elsewhere in like occasions whereof I find some of all sorts, and rely upon the comparisons that are most favorable unto me. I embrace health with open arms, free, plain, and full, and prepare my appetite to enjoy it, by how much more it is now less ordinary and more rare unto me; so far is it from me that I with the bitterness of some new and forced kind of life trouble her rest and molest her ease. Beasts do manifestly declare unto us how many infirmities our mind's agitation bring us.

[C]That which is told us of those that inhabit Brazil, who die only through age, which some impute to the clearness and calmness of their air, I rather ascribe to the calmness and clearness of their minds, void and free from all passions, cares, toiling, and unpleasant labors, as a people that pass their life in a wonderful kind of simplicity and ignorance without letters, or laws, and without kings or any religion.

[A]Whence comes it, as we daily see by experience, that the rudest and grossest clowns are more tough, strong, and more desired in amorous executions, and that the love of a muleteer is often more accepted than that of a perfumed, quaint courtier? Because in the latter the agitation of his mind doth so distract, trouble, and weary the force of his body; as it also troubleth and wearieth itself. Who doth belie, or more commonly cast the same down even into madness, but her own promptitude, her point, her agility, and, to conclude, her proper force? [B]When proceeds the subtlest folly, but from the subtlest wisdom? As from the extremest friendships proceed the extremest enmities, and from the soundest healths, the mortallest diseases, so from the rarest and quickest agitations of our minds ensue the most distempered and outrageous frenzies. There wants but half a peg's turn to pass from the one to the other. [A]In mad men's actions, we see how fitly folly suiteth and meets with the strongest operations of our mind. Who knows not how unperceivable the neighborhood between folly with the liveliest elevations of a free mind is, and the effects of a supreme and extraordinary virtue? Plato affirmeth that melancholy minds are more excellent and disciplinable; so are there none more inclinable unto folly.

Divers spirits are seen to be overthrown by their own force and proper nimbleness. What a start hath one of the most judicious, ingenious, and most fitted unto the air of true ancient poesy (Torquato Tasso) lately gotten by his own agitation and self-gladness above all other Italian poets that have been of a long time? Hath not he wherewith to be beholding unto this his killing vivacity? unto this clearness that hath so blinded him? unto his exact and far-reaching apprehension of reasons which hath made him void of reason? unto the curious and laborious pursuit of sciences that have brought him unto sottishness? unto this rare aptitude to the exercises of the mind which hath made him without mind or exercise? I rather spited than pitied him when I saw him at Ferrara in so piteous a plight, that he survived himself, misacknowledging both himself and his labors which, unwitting to him and even to his face, have been published both uncorrected and maimed. Will you have a man healthy, will you have him regular and in constant and safe conditions? Overwhelm him in the dark pit of idleness and dullness. [C]We must be besotted ere we can become wise, and dazzled before we can be led.

[A]And if a man shall tell me that the commodity to have the appetite cold to griefs and wallowish* to evils draws this incommodity after it, it is also consequently the same that makes us less sharp and greedy to the enjoying of good and of pleasures, it is true; but the misery of our condition beareth that we have not so much to enjoy as to shun, and that extreme voluptuousness doth not so much pinch us as a light smart. [C]"Men have a duller feeling of a good turn than of an ill" (Livy XXX.xxi.). [A]We have not so sensible a feeling of perfect health as we have of the least sickness:

> A light stroke that doth scarce the top-skin wound,
> Grieves the gall'd body, when in health to be
> Doth scarce move any. Only ease is found
> That neither side not foot tormenteth me;
> Scarce any in the rest can feel he's sound.
>
> La Boétie.

Our being in health is but the privation of being ill. See wherefore the sect of philosophy that hath most preferred sensuality hath also placed the same but to indolency or unfeeling of pain. To have no infirmity at all is the chiefest possession of health that man can hope for; [C]as Ennius said:

> He hath but too much good,
> Whom no ill hath withstood.
>
> Ennius, in Cic. *De fin.* II.xiiii.

[A]For the same tickling and pricking which a man doth feel in some pleasures and seems beyond simple health and indolency, this active and moving sensuality, or, as I may term it, itching and tickling pleasure, aims but to be free from pain as her chiefest scope. The lustful longing which allures us to the acquaintance of women seeks but to expel that pain which an earnest and burning desire doth possess us with, and desireth but to allay it thereby to come to rest and be exempted from this fever; and so of others.

I say therefore that if simplicity directeth us to have no evil, it also addresseth us according to our condition to a most happy estate. [C]Yet ought it not to be imagined so dull and heavy that it be altogether senseless. And Crantor had great reason to withstand the unsensibleness of Epicurus, if it were so deeply rooted that the approaching and birth of evils might gainsay it. I commend not that unsensibleness which is neither possible nor to be desired. I am well pleased not to be sick, but if I be I will know that I am so; and if I be cauterized or cut, I will feel it. Verily, he that should root out the knowledge of evil should therewithal extirp the knowledge of voloptuousness and at last bring man to nothing. "This very point, not to be offended or grieved with anything, befalls not freely to a man without either inhumanity in his mind or senselessness in his body" (Cic. *Tusc.* III.vi.).

Sickness is not amiss unto man, coming in her turn; nor is he always to shun pain nor ever to follow sensuality.

[A]It is a great advantage for the honor of ignorance that science itself throws us into her arms when she finds herself busy to make us strong against the assaults of evils; she is forced to come to this composition, to yield us the bridle and give us leave to shroud ourselves in her lap and submit ourselves unto her favor, to shelter us against the assaults and injuries of fortune. For what meaneth she else when she persuades us to [C]withdraw our thoughts from the evils that possess us and entertain them with foregone pleasures, and [A]stead us as a comfort of present evils with the remembrance of forepast felicities, and call a vanished content to our help for to oppose it against that which vexeth us? C"Eases of griefs he reposeth either in calling from the thought of offense or calling to the contemplations of some pleasures" (Cic. *Tusc.* III.xv.). AUnless it be that where force fails her she will use policy and show a trick of nimbleness and turn away where the vigor both of her body and arms shall fail her. For not only to a strict philosopher, but simply to any settled man, when he by experience feeleth the burning alteration of a hot fever, what current payment is it to pay him with the remembrance of the sweetness of Greek wine? BIt would rather impair his bargain,

For to think of our joy
Redoubles our annoy.
(Italian saying)

AOf that condition is this other counsel which philosophy giveth, only to keep forepast felicities in memory and thence blot out such griefs as we have felt; as if the skill to forget were in our power, Cand counsel, of which we have much less.

Of labors overpast
Remembrance hath sweet taste.
Eurip., in Cic. *De fin.* II.xxxii.

AWhat? shall philosophy, which ought to put the weapons into my hands to fight against fortune, which should harden my courage to suppress and lay at my feet all human adversities, will she so faint as to make me like a fearful cunny* creep into some lurking*-hole, and like a craven to tremble and yield?

For memory representeth unto us not what we choose, but what pleaseth her. Nay, there is nothing so deeply imprinteth anything in our remembrance as the desire to forget the same. It is a good way to commend to the keeping and imprint anything in our mind, to solicit her to lose the same. CAnd that is false: "This is engrafted in us, or at least in our power, that we both bury in perpetual oblivion things past against us, and record with pleasure and delight whatsoever was for us" (Cic. *De fin.* I.xvii.). And this is true: "I remember even those things I would not, and cannot forget what I would" (Cic. *De fin.* II.xxxii.). AAnd whose counsel is this? CHis "who only durst profess himself a wise man" (Cic. *De fin.* II.iii.).

AWho from all mankind bare for wit the prize,
And dimm'd the stars, as when sky's sun doth rise.[12]
Lucr. III.1056.

12 He is speaking of Epicurus.

To empty and diminish the memory, is it not the ready and only way to ignorance?

> [C]Of ills a remedy by chance,
> And very dull is ignorance.
> Seneca *Oedip.* III.vii.

[A]We see divers like precepts by which we are permitted to borrow frivolous appearances from the vulgar sort, where lively and strong reason is not of force sufficient, always provided they bring us content and comfort. Where they cannot cure a sore, they are pleased to stupefy and hide the same. I am persuaded they will not deny me this, that if they could possibly add any order or constancy to a man's life, that it might thereby be still maintained in pleasure and tranquillity, by or through any weakness or infirmity of judgment, but they would accept it:

> I will begin to strew flowers, and drink free,
> And suffer witless, thriftless, held to be.
> Hor. *Epist.* I.v.14.

There should many philosophers be found of Lycas his opinion. This man in all other things being very temperate and orderly in his demeanors, living quietly and contentedly with his family, wanting of no duty or office both toward his own household and strangers', very carefully preserving himself from all hurtful things, notwithstanding, through some alteration of his senses or spirits, he was so possessed with this fantastical conceit or obstinate humor that he ever and continually thought to be amongst the theatres, where he still saw all manner of spectacles, pastimes, sports, and the best comedies of the world. But being at last by the skill of physicians cured of this malady, and his offending humor purged, he could hardly be held from putting them in suit, to the end they might restore him to the former pleasures and contents of his imagination.

> You have not saved me, friends, but slain me quite,
> (Quoth he) from whom so rest is my delight
> And error purg'd, which best did please my sprite.
> Hor. *Epist.* II.ii.138.

Of a raving like unto that of Thrasilaus, son unto Pythodorus, who verily believed that all the ships that went out from the haven of Piraeus, yea and all such as came into it, did only travel about his business, rejoicing when any of them had made a fortunate voyage and welcomed them with great gladness. His brother Crito, having caused him to be cured and restored to his better senses, he much bewailed and grieved the condition wherein he had formerly lived in such joy and so void of all care and grief. It is that which that ancient Greek verse saith, that not to be so advised brings many commodities with it:

> The sweetest life I wis,
> In knowing nothing is.
> Soph. *Ajax,* 552.

And as Ecclesiates witnesseth, "In much wisdom, much sorrow; and who getteth knowledge purchaseth sorrow and grief."

Even that to which philosophy doth in general terms allow this last remedy which she ordaineth for all manner of necessities, that is, to make an end of that life which we cannot endure: [C]"Doth it like you? Obey. Doth it not like you? Get out as you will (adapted from Sen. *Epist.* LXX). Doth grief prick you? And let it pierce you too. If you be naked, yield your throat, but if you be covered with the armor of Vulcan — that is, with fortitude — resist" (Cic. *Tusc.* II.xiv.). And that saying used of the Grecians in their banquets which they apply unto it, "Either let him carouse, or carry him out of the house" (Cic. *Tusc.* V.xli.), which rather fitteth the mouth of a Gascon than that of Cicero, who very easily doth change the letter B into V:[13]

> [A]Live well you cannot; them that can give place.
> Well have you sported, eaten well, drunk well;
> 'Tis time you part, lest wanton youth with grace
> Laugh at and knock you with that swilling swell.
> Hor. *Epist.* II.ii.213.

What is it but a confession of his insufficiency and a sending one back not only to ignorance, there to be shrouded, but unto stupidity itself, unto unsensibleness and not-being?

> When ripe age put Democritus in mind
> That his mind's motions fainted, he to find
> His death went willing, and his life resigned.
> Lucr. III.1052.

It is that which Antisthenes said that a man must provide himself either of wit to understand or of a halter to hang himself; and that which Chrysippus alleged* upon the speech of the poet Tyrtaeus:

> Or virtue to approach,
> Or else let death encroach.
> (Quoted by Plutarch)

[C]And Crates said, that love was cured with hunger; if not, by time; and in him that liked not these two means, by the halter.

[13] By means of which the Latin *bibat* ("let him carouse") would become *vivat* (let him live).

[B]That Sextius to whom Seneca and Plutarch give so much commendation, having given over all things else and betaken himself to the study of philosophy, seeing the progress of his studies so tedious and slow, purposed to cast himself into the sea; ran unto death for want of knowledge. Read here what the law saith upon this subject: If peradventure any great inconvenience happen which cannot be remedied, the haven is not far off, and by swimming may a man save himself out of his body, as out of a leaking boat; for it is fear to die, and not desire to live, which keeps a fool joined to his body.

[A]As life through simplicity becometh more pleasant, so (as I erewhile began to say) becometh it more innocent and better. The simple and the ignorant, saith St. Paul, raise themselves up to heaven and take possession of it, whereas we, with all the knowledge we have, plunge ourselves down to the pit of hell. I rely neither upon Valentinianus, a professed enemy to knowledge and learning, nor upon Licinius, both Roman emperors, who named them the venom and plague of all politic estates; nor on Mohammet, who, [C]as I have heard, [A]doth utterly interdict all manner of learning to his subjects. But the example of that great Lycurgus and his authority ought to bear chief sway, and the reverence of that divine Lacedaemonian policy, so great, so admirable, and so long time flourishing in all virtue and felicity without any institution or exercise at all of letters. Those who return from that new world which of late hath been discovered by the Spaniards, can witness unto us how those nations, being without magistrates or law, live much more regularly and formally than we, who have amongst us more officers and laws than men of other professions or actions:

> Their hands and bosoms with writs and citations,
> With papers, libels, proxies, full they bear,
> And bundles great of strict examinations,
> Of glosses, counsels, readings here and there.
> Whereby in towns poor men of occupations
> Possess not their small goods secure from fear;
> Before, behind, on each sides, advocates,
> Proctors, and notaries hold up debates.
>
> Ariosto XIV.84.

It was that which a Roman senator said, that their predecessors had their breath stinking of garlic and their stomach perfumed with a good conscience; and contrary, the men of his times outwardly smelt of nothing but sweet odors, but inwardly they stunk of all vices.

Which, in mine opinion, is as much to say they had much knowledge and sufficiency, but great want of honesty. Incivility, ignorance, simplicity, and rudeness are commonly joined with innocency; curiosity, subtlety, and knowledge are ever followed with malice; humility, fear, obedience, and honesty, which are the principal instruments for the preservation of human society, require a single docile soul and which presumeth little of herself.

Christians have a peculiar knowledge how curiosity is in a man a natural and original infirmity. The care to increase in wisdom and knowledge was the first overthrow of minkind; it is the way whereby man hath head-long cast himself down into eternal damnation. Pride is his loss and corruption: it is pride that misleadeth him from common ways, that makes him to embrace all newfangles and rather choose to be chief of a straggling troop and in the path of perdition, and be regent of some erroneous sect and a teacher of falsehood, than a disciple in the school of truth and suffer himself to be led and directed by the hand of others in the ready beaten high way. It is haply that which the ancient Greek proverb implieth: "Superstition obeyeth pride as a father" (attributed by Stobaeus to Socrates).[14]

[C]O overweening, how much doest thou hinder us? Socrates, being advertised that the god of wisdom had attributed the name of wise unto him, was thereat much astonished, and diligently searching and rousing up himself and ransacking the very secrets of his heart, found no foundation or ground for this divine sentence. He knew some that were as just, as temperate, as valiant, and as wise as he, and more eloquent, more fair, and more profitable to their country. In fine, he resolved that he was distinguished from others and reputed wise only because he did not so esteem himself, and that his god deemed the opinion of science and wisdom a singular sottishness in man, and that his best doctrine was the doctrine of ignorance, and simplicity his greatest wisdom.

[A]The Sacred Writ pronounceth them to be miserable in this world that esteem themselves. "Dust and ashes," saith he, "what is there in thee thou shouldst so much glory of?" (Eccles. X.9.). And in another place, "God had made man like unto a shadow, of which who shall judge when, the light being gone, it shall vanish away?"[15] Man is a thing of nothing.

So far are our faculties from conceiving that high deity that of our Creator's works those bear his mark best and are most his own which we understand least. It is an occasion to induce Christians to believe when they chance to meet with any incredible thing; that it is so

[14] This quotation was inscribed on the ceiling of Montaigne's library.
[15] These two inscriptions were also on the library ceiling.

much the more according unto reason, by how much more it is against human reason. [B]If it were according unto reason, it were no more a wonder; and were it to be matched, it were no more singular. [C]"God is better known by our not knowing him," saith St. Augustine (*De ordin.* II.16.); and Tacitus, "It is a course of more holiness and reverence to hold belief than to have knowledge of God's actions" (*De mor. German.* XXXIV.). And Plato deems it to be a vice of impiety over-curiously to inquire after God, after the world, and after the first causes of things. "Both it is difficult to find out the father of this universe, and, when you have found him, it is unlawful to reveal him to the vulgar," saith Cicero (after Plato, *Tim.* II.).

[A]We easily pronounce puissance, truth, and justice; they be words importing some great matter; but that thing we neither see nor conceive. [B]We say that God feareth, that God will be angry, and that God loveth,

> Who, with terms of mortality,
> Note things of immortality.
>
> Lucr. V.122.

They be all agitations and [emotions] which, according to our form, can have no place in God, nor we imagine them according to his. [A]It only belongs to God to know himself and interpret his own works.

[C]And in our tongues he doth it improperly, to descend and come down to us that are and lie groveling on the ground. How can wisdom, which is the choice between good and evil, beseem him, seeing no evil doth touch him? How reason and intelligence, which we use to come from obscure to apparent things, seeing there is no obscure thing in God? Justice, which distributeth unto every man what belongs unto him, created for the society and conversation of man, how is she in God? How temperance, which is the moderation of corporal sensualities, which have no place at all in his God-head? Fortitude patiently to endure sorrows and labors and dangers appertaineth as little unto him, these three things no way approaching him, having no access unto him. And therefore Aristotle holds him to be equally exempted from virtue and from vice. "Nor can he be possessed with favor and anger; for all that is so is but weak" (Cic. *De nat. deor.* I. 17.).

[A]The participation which we have of the knowledge of truth, whatsoever she is, it is not by our own strength we have gotten it. God hath sufficiently taught it us in that he hath made choice of the simple, common, and ignorant to teach us his wonderful secrets. Our faith hath not been purchased by us; it is a gift proceeding from the liberality of others. It is not by our discourse or understanding that we have received our religion; it is by a foreign authority and commandment. The weakness of our judgment helps us more than our strength to compass the same, and our blindness more than our clear-sighted eyes. It is more by the means of our ignorance than of our skill that we are wise in heavenly knowledge. It is no marvel if our natural and terrestrial means cannot conceive the supernatural or apprehend the celestial knowledge. Let us add nothing of our own unto it but obedience and subjection. For, as it is written, "I will confound the wisdom of the wise and destroy the understanding of the prudent. Where is the wise? Where is the scribe? Where is the disputer of this world? Hath not God made the wisdom of this world foolishness? For, seeing the world by wisdom knew not God in the wisdom of God, it hath pleased him by the vanity of preaching to save them that believe" (I *Cor.* 1.19.).

Yet must I see at last whether it be in man's power to find what he seeks for, and if this long search wherein he hath continued so many ages hath enriched him with any new strength or solid truth. I am persuaded, if he speak in conscience, he will confess that all the benefit he hath gotten by so tedious a pursuit hath been that he hath learned to know his own weakness. That ignorance which in us was natural we have with long study confirmed and averred. It hath happened unto those that are truly learned, as happeneth unto ears of corn which, as long as they are empty, grow and raise their head aloft, upright, and stout; but if they once become full and big with ripe corn, they begin to humble and droop downward. So, men having tried and sounded all, and in all this chaos and huge heap of learning and provision of so infinite different things, and found nothing that is substantial, firm, and steady, but all vanity, having renounced their presumption and too late known their natural condition.

[C]It is that which Velleius upbraids Cotta and Cicero withal, that they have learned of Philo to have learned nothing. Pherecydes, one of the seven wise, writing to Thales even as he was yielding up the ghost, "I have," saith he, "appointed my friends, as soon as I shall be laid in my grave, to bring thee all my writings. If they please thee and the other sages, publish them; if not, conceal them. They contain no certainty, nor do they any whit satisfy me. My profession is not to know the truth nor to attain it. I rather open than discover things."

[A]The wisest that ever was, being demanded what he knew, answered: he knew that he knew nothing. He verified what some say, that the greatest part of what we know is the least part of what we know not; that is, that that which we think to know is but a parcel, yea, and a small particle of our ignorance.

[C]We know things in a dream, saith Plato, and we are ignorant of them in truth. "Almost all the ancients affirmed nothing may be known, nothing perceived, nothing understood; that our senses are narrow, our minds are weak, and the race of our life is short" (Cic. *Academ.* I.xii.).

[A]Cicero himself, who ought* all he had unto learning, Valerius saith that in his age he began to disesteem letters. [C]And whilst he practiced them, it was without bond to any special body, following what seemed probable unto him, now in the one and now in the other sect, ever holding himself under the Academy's doubtfulness. "Speak I must, but so as I avouch nothing, question all things, for the most part in doubt and distrust of myself" (Cic. *De divin.* II.iii.).

[A]I should have too much ado if I would consider man after his own fashion and in gross; which I might do by his own rule, who is wont to judge of truth not by the weight or value of voices, but by the number. But leave we the common people,

> Who snore while they are awake . . .
> Whose life is dead while yet they see,
> And in a manner living be.
>
> Lucr. III.1061, 1059.

who feeleth not himself, who judgeth not himself, who leaves the greatest part of his natural parts idle.

I will take man even in his highest estate. Let us consider him in this small number of excellent and choice men who, having naturally been endowed with a peculiar and exquisite wit, have also fostered and sharpened the same with care, with study and with art, and have brought and strained unto the highest pitch [C]of wisdom [A]it may possible reach unto. They have fitted their soul unto all senses and squared the same to all biases; they have strengthened and under-propped it with all foreign helps that might any way fit or stead* her, and have enriched and adorned her with whatsoever they have been able to borrow, either within or without the world for her avail. It is in them that the extreme height of human nature doth lodge. They have reformed the world with policies and laws. They have instructed the same with arts and sciences, as also by example of their wonderful manners and life. I will but make account of such people, of their witness and of their experience. Let us see how far they have gone and what holdfast they have held by. The maladies and defects which we shall find in that college, the world may boldly allow them to be his.

Whosoever seeks for anything cometh at last to this conclusion and sayeth that either he hath found it, or that it cannot be found, or that he is still in pursuit after it. All philosophy is divided into these three kinds. Her purpose is to seek out the truth, the knowledge, and the certainty. The Peripatetic, the Epicureans, the Stoics, and others have thought they had found it. These have established the sciences that we have, and as of certain knowledges have treated of them. Clitomachus, Carneades, and the Academics have despaired the finding of it and judged that truth could not be conceived by our means. The end of these is weakness and ignorance. The former had more followers and the worthiest sectaries. Pyrrho and the other Sceptics, or Epechists, [C]whose doctrine or manner of teaching many ancient learned men have thought to have been drawn from Homer, from the seven wise men, from Archilochus, and Euripides, to whom they join Zeno, Democritus, and Xenophanes, [A]say that they are still seeking after truth. These judge that those are infinitely deceived who imagine they have found it, and that the second degree is over boldly vain in affirming that man's power is altogether unable to attain unto it. For to establish the measure of our strength, to know and distinguish of the difficulty of things, is a great, a notable and extreme science, which they doubt whether man be capable thereof or no:

> Who thinks nothing is known, knows not that whereby he
> Grants he knows nothing if it known may be.
>
> Lucr. IV.470.

That ignorance which knoweth, judgeth, and condemneth itself is not an absolute ignorance. For, to be so, she must altogether be ignorant of herself. So that the profession of the Pyrrhonians is ever to waver, to doubt, and to inquire, never to be assured of anything, nor to take any warrant of himself. Of the three actions or faculties of the soul, that is to say the imaginative, the concupiscible, and the consenting, they allow and conceive the two former; the last they hold and defend to be ambiguous, without inclination or approbation either of one or other side, be it never so light.

[C]Zeno in gesture painted forth his imagination upon this division of the soul's faculties: the open and outstretched hand was appearance; the hand half shut and fingers somewhat bending, consent; the fist close[d], comprehension; if the fist of the left hand were closely clinched together, it signified science.

[A]Now this situation of their judgment,[16] straight and inflexible, receiving all objects with application or consent, leads them unto their ataraxy, which is the condition of a quiet and settled life, exempted from the agitations which we receive by the impression of the opinion and knowledge we imagine to have of things. Whence proceed fear, avarice, envy, immoderate desires, ambition, pride, superstition, love

16 The Pyrrhonians.

of novelties, rebellion, disobedience, obstinacy, and the greatest number of corporal evils. Yea, by that mean they are exempted from the jealousy of their own discipline, for they contend but faintly. They fear nor revenge nor contradiction in the disputations. When they say that heavy things descend downward, they would be loath to be believed, but desire to be contradicted thereby to engender doubt and suspense of judgment, which is their end and drift. They put forth their propositions but to contend with those they imagine we hold in our conceit.

If you take theirs, then will they undertake to maintain the contrary; all is one to them; nor will they give a penny to choose. If you propose that snow is black, they will argue on the other side, that it is white. If you say it is neither one not other, they will maintain it to be both. If by a certain judgment you say that you cannot tell, they will maintain that you can tell. Nay, if by an affirmative axiom you swear that you stand in some doubt, they will dispute that you doubt not of it, or that you cannot judge or maintain that you are in doubt. And by this extremity of doubt, which staggereth itself, they separate and divide themselves from many opinions, yea, from those which divers ways have maintained both the doubt and the ignorance.

[B]Why shall it not be granted then, say they, as to dogmatists or doctrine-teachers for one to say green and another yellow, so for them [also] to doubt? Is there anything can be proposed unto you either to allow or refuse which may not lawfully be considered as ambiguous and doubtful? And whereas others be carried — either by the custom of their country, or by the institution of their parents, or by chance — as by a tempest, without choice or judgment, yea, sometimes before the age of discretion, to such or such another opinion, to the Stoic or Epicurean sect, to which they find themselves more engaged, subjected, or fast-tied as to a prize they cannot let go —[C]"being carried, as it were, by a tempest to any kind of doctrine, they stick close to it as it were to a rock" (Cic. *Academ.* II.iii.) — [B]why shall not these likewise be permitted to maintain their liberty and consider things without duty or compulsion? [C]"They are so much the freer and at liberty for that their power of judgment is kept entire" (Cic. *Academ.* II.iii.).

Is it not some advantage for one to find himself disengaged from necessity which bridleth others? [B]Is it not better to remain in suspense than to entangle himself in so many errors that human fantasy hath brought forth? Is it not better for a man to suspend his own persuasion than to meddle with these seditious and quarrelous divisions? [C]What shall I choose? Marry, what you list, so you choose! A very foolish answer, to which it seemeth nevertheless that all dogmatism arriveth, by which it is not lawful for you to be ignorant of that we know not.

[B]Take the best and strongest side, it shall never be so sure but you shall have occasion to defend the same, to close and combat a hundred and a hundred sides? Is it not better to keep out of this confusion? You are suffered to embrace as your honor and life Aristotle's opinion upon the eternity of the soul, and to belie and contradict whatsoever Plato saith concerning that; and shall they be interdicted to doubt of it?

[C]If it be lawful for Panaetius to maintain his judgment about haruspices, dreams, oracles, and prophecies, whereof the Stoics make no doubt at all, wherefore shall not a wise man dare that in all things which this man dareth in such as he hath learned of his masters, confirmed and established by the general consent of the school whereof he is a sectary and a professor? [B]If it be a child that judgeth, he wots not what it is; if a learned man, he is forestalled. They have reserved a great advantage for themselves in the combat, having discharged themselves of the care how to shroud themselves. They care not to be beaten, so they may strike again; and all is fish that comes to net with them. If they overcome, your proposition halteth; if you, theirs is lame; if they fail they verify ignorance; if you, she is verified by you; if they prove that nothing is known, it is very well; if they cannot prove it, it is good alike. [C]"So as when the same matter, the like weight and moment is found on divers parts, we may the more easily withhold avouching on both parts" (Cic. *Academ.* I.xii.).

And they suppose to find out more easily why a thing is false than true, and that which is not than that which is, and what they believe not than what they believe. [A]Their manner of speech is: "I confirm nothing; it is no more so than thus, or neither; I conceive it not; appearances are everywhere alike; the law of speaking *pro* or *contra* is all one. [C]Nothing seemeth true that may not seem false." [A]Their sacramental word is ἐπέχω, which is as much to say as, "I hold and stir not." Behold the burdens of their songs and other such like. Their effects are a pure, entire, and absolute surceasing and suspense of judgment. They use their reason to inquire and to debate, and not to stay and choose. Whosoever shall imagine a perpetual confession of ignorance and a judgment upright and without staggering to what occasion soever may chance, that man conceives the true Pyrrhonism.

I expound this fantasy as plain as I can, because many deem it hard to be conceived; and the authors themselves represent it somewhat obscurely and diversely.

Touching the actions of life, in that they are after the common sort, they are lent and applied to natural inclinations, to the impulsion and constraint of passions, to the constitutions of laws and customs, and to the tradition of arts. [C]"For God would not have us know these things, but only use them" (Cic. *De divin.* I.xviii.). [A]By such means they suffer their common actions to be directed without any conceit or judgment, which is the reason that I cannot well sort unto this discourse what is said of Pyrrho. They feign him to be stupid and unmovable, leading a kind of wild and unsociable life, not shunning to be hit with carts, presenting himself unto downfalls, refusing to conform himself to the laws. It is an endearing* of his discipline. He would not make himself a stone or a block, but a living, discoursing, and reasoning man, enjoying all pleasures and natural commodities, busying himself with, and using, all his corporal and spiritual parts [C]in rule and right. [A]The fantastical and imaginary and false privileges which man hath usurped unto himself to sway, to appoint, and to establish, he hath absolutely renounced and quit them.

[C]Yet is there no sect but is enforced to allow her wise sectary in chief to follow divers things nor comprised, nor perceived, nor allowed, if he will live. And if he take shipping, he follows his purpose, not knowing whether it shall be profitable or no, and yields to this, that the ship is good, that the pilot is skillful, and that the season is fit — circumstances only probable. After which he is bound to go and suffer himself to be removed by apparances,* always provided they have no express contrariety in them. He hath a body; he hath a soul; his senses urge him forward; his mind moveth him. Although he find not this proper and singular mark of judging in himself, and that he perceive he should not engage his consent, seeing some falsehood may be like unto this truth, he ceaseth not to direct the offices of his life fully and commodiously.

How many arts are there which profess to consist more in conjecture than in the science, that distinguish not between truth and falsehood, but only follow seeming? There is both true and false, say they, and there are means in us to seek it out, but not to stay it when we touch it. It is better for us to suffer the order of the world to manage us without further inquisition. A mind warranted from prejudice hath a marvelous preferment to tranquillity. Men that censure and control their judges do never duly submit themselves unto them. How much more docile and tractable are simple and uncurious minds found both towards the laws of religion and politic decrees than these over-vigilant and nice wits, teachers of divine and human causes!

[A]There is nothing in man's invention wherein is so much likelihood, possibility, and profit. This representeth man bare and naked, acknowledging his natural weakness, apt to receive from above some strange power, disfurnished of all human knowledge, and so much the more fit to harbor divine understanding, [B]disannulling his judgment, that so he may give more place unto faith; [C]neither misbelieving [A]nor establishing any doctrine or opinion [B]repugnant unto common laws and observances; humble, obedient, disciplinable, and studious; a sworn enemy to heresy, [A]and by consequence exempting himself from all vain and irreligious opinions invented and brought up by false sects. [B]It is a white sheet prepared to take from the finger of God what form soever it shall please him to imprint therein. The more we address and commit ourselves to God and reject ourselves, the better it is for us. [A]"Accept," said Ecclesiastes, "in good part things both in show and taste, as from day to day they are presented unto thee; the rest is beyond thy knowledge." [C]"The Lord knows the thoughts of men, that they are vain" (Psal. XCIII.ii).

[A]See how of three general sects of philosophy two make express profession of doubt and ignorance; and in the third, which is the dogmatists, it is easy to be discerned that the greatest number have taken the face of assurance only because they could set a better countenance on the matter. They have not so much gone about to establish any certainty in us as to show how far they had waded in seeking out the truth: [C]"which the learned do rather conceit than know."

Timaeus, being to instruct Socrates of what he knows of the gods, of the world, and of men, purposeth to speak of it as one man to another, and that it sufficeth if his reasons be as probable as another man's; for exact reasons are neither in his hands not in any mortal man. Which one of his sectaries hath thus imitated: "As I can, I will explain them; yet not as Apollo giving oracles, that all should be certain and set down, that I say, but as a mean man, who follows likelihood by his conjecture" (Cic. *Tusc.* I.ix.). And that upon the discourse of the contempt of death, a natural and popular discourse. Elsewhere he hath translated it upon Plato's very words: "It will be no marvel if, arguing of the nature of gods and original of the world, we scarcely reach to that which in our mind we comprehend; for it is meet we remember that both I am a man who am to argue and you who are to judge; so as you seek no further if I speak but things likely" (Cic. trans. of Plato's *Timaeus* III.).

[A]Aristotle ordinarily hoardeth us up a number of other opinions and other beliefs, that so he may compare his unto it and make us see how far he hath gone further and how near he comes unto true likelihood. For truth is not judged by authority nor by others' testimony. [C](And therefore did Epicurus religiously avoid to allege* any in his compositions.) [A]He is the prince of dogmatists, and yet we learn of him that to know much breeds an occasion to doubt more. He is often seen seriously to shelter himself under so inextricable obscurity that his meaning cannot be perceived. In effect, it is a Pyrrhonism under a resolving form.

[C]Listen to Cicero's protestation, who doth declare us others' fantasies by his own: "They that would know what we conceit of everything use more curiosity than needs. This course in philosophy to dispute against all things, to judge expressly of nothing, derived from Socrates, renewed by Arcesilaus, confirmed by Carneades, is in force till our time. We are those that aver some falsehood intermixed with every truth, and that with such likeness as there is no set note in those things for any assuredly to give judgment or assent" (Cic. *De nat. deor.* I.v.).

[B]Why hath not Aristotle alone, but the greatest number of philosophers affected difficulty unless it be to make the vanity of the subject to prevail and to amuse the curiosity of our mind, seeking to feed it by gnawing so raw and bare a bone? [C]Clitomachus affirmed that he could never understand by the writings of Carneades what opinion he was of. [B]Why hath Epicurus interdicted facility unto his sectaries? And wherefore hath Heraclitus been surnamed σκοτεινός, a dark, misty, clouded fellow? Difficulty is a coin [C]that wise men make use of as jugglers do with pass and repass, because they will not display the vanity of their art, and [B]wherewith human foolishness is easily appaid:*

> For his dark speech much prais'd, but of th' unwise;
> For fools do all still more admire and prize
> That under words turn'd topsy-turvy lies.
>
> Lucr. I.640.

[C]Cicero reproveth some of his friends because they were wont to bestow more time about astrology, law, logic, and geometry than such arts could deserve, and diverted them from the devoirs* of their life more profitable and more honest. The Cyrenaic philosophers equally contemned natural philosophy and logic. Zeno, in the beginning of his books of the *Commonwealth,* declared all the liberal sciences to be unprofitable. [A]Chrysippus said that which Plato and Aristotle had written of logic they had written the same in jest and for exercise's sake, and could not believe that ever they spoke in good earnest of so vain and idle a subject. [C]Plutarch saith the same of the metaphysics. [A]Epicurus would have said it of rhetoric, of grammar, [C]of poesy, of the mathematics, and, except natural philosophy, of all other sciences. [A]And Socrates of all but of the art of civil manners and life. [C]Whatsoever he was demanded of any man he would ever first inquire of him to give an account of his life, both present and past, which he would seriously examine and judge of, deeming all other apprenticeships as subsequents and of supererogation in regard of that.

"That learning pleaseth me but a little which nothing profiteth the teachers of it unto virtue" (Sallust. *Bell. Jug.* LXXXV.). [A]Most of the arts have thus been contemned by knowledge itself; for they thought it not amiss to exercise their minds in matters wherein was no profitable solidity. As for the rest, some have judged Plato a dogmatist, others a doubter, some a dogmatist in one thing and some a doubter in another. [C]Socrates, the foreman of his dialogues, doth ever ask and propose his disputation, yet never concluding, nor ever satisfying; and saith he hath no other science but that of opposing. Their author Homer hath equally grounded the foundations of all sects of philosophy, thereby to show how indifferent he was which way we went. Some say that of Plato arose ten diverse sects. And, as I think, never was instruction wavering and nothing avouching if his be not.

Socrates was wont to say that when midwives begin once to put in practice the trade to make other women bring forth children, themselves become barren; that he, by the title of wise which the gods had conferred upon him, had also in his man-like and mental love shaken off the faculty of begetting, being well pleased to afford all help and favor to such as were engenderers, to open their nature, to supple their passages, to ease the issue of their child-bearing, to judge thereof, to baptize the same, to foster it, to strengthen it, to swathe it, and to circumcise it, exercising and handling his instrument at the peril and fortune of others.

[A]So it is with most authors of this third kind, [B]as the ancients have well noted by the writings of Anaxagoras, Democritus, Parmenides, Xenophanes, and others. [A]They have a manner of writing doubtful both in substance and intent, rather inquiring than instructing, albeit here and there they interlace their style with dogmatical cadences. And is not that as well seen [C]in Seneca and [A]in Plutarch? [C]How much do they speak sometimes of one face and sometimes of another, for such as look near unto it? Those who reconcile lawyers ought first to have reconciled them every one unto himself. Plato hath, in my seeming, loved this manner of philosophying* dialogue-wise in good earnest, that thereby he might more decently place in sundry mouths the diversity and variation of his own conceits.

Diversely to treat of matters is as good and better as to treat them conformably; that is to say, more copiously and more profitably. Let us take example by ourselves. Definite sentences make the last period of dogmatical and resolving speech; yet see we that those which our parliaments present unto our people as the most exemplary and fittest to nourish in them the reverence they owe unto this dignity, especially by reason of the sufficiency of those persons which exercise the same, taking their glory not by the conclusion, which to them is daily and is common to all judges, as much as the debating of divers and agitations of contrary reasonings of law causes will admit.

And the largest scope for reprehensions of some philosophers against others draweth contradictions and diversities with it, wherein every one of them findeth himself so entangled, either by intent to show the wavering of man's mind above all matters, or ignorantly forced by the volubility and incomprehensibleness of all matters.

[A]What meaneth this burden: "In a slippery and gliding place let us suspend our belief"? For, as Euripides saith,

> God's works do traverse our imaginations
> And cross our works in divers different fashions.
> [quoted from Amyot's Plutarch]

[B]Like unto that which Empedocles was wont often to scatter amongst his books, as moved by divine fury and forced by truth: "No, no, we feel nothing, we see nothing; all things are hid from us; there is not one that we may establish how and what it is;" [C]but returning to this holy word: "The thoughts of mortal men are fearful; our devices and foresights are uncertain" (*Book of Wisdom* IX.xiv.).

[A]It must not be thought strange if men, despairing of the goal, have yet taken pleasure in the chase of it; study being in itself a pleasing occupation — yea, so pleasing that amid sensualities the Stoics forbid also that which comes from the exercise of the mind and require a bridle to it [C]and find intemperance in over-much knowledge.

[A]Democritus, having at his table eaten some figs that tasted of honey, began presently in his mind to seek out whence this unusual sweetness in them might proceed; and to be resolved, rose from the board to view the place where those figs had been gathered. His maidservant, noting this alteration in her master, smilingly said unto him that he should no more busy himself about it: the reason was, she had laid them in a vessel where honey had been. Whereat, he seemed to be wroth in that she had deprived him of the occasion of his intended search and robbed his curiosity of matter to work upon. "Away!" quoth he unto her, "Thou hast much offended me; yet will I not omit to find out the cause as if it were naturally so." [C]Who perhaps would not have missed to find some likely or true reason for a false and supposed effect.

[A]This story of a famous and great philosopher doth evidently represent unto us this studious passion which so doth amuse us in pursuit of things, of whose obtaining we despair. Plutarch reporteth a like example of one who would not be resolved of what he doubted, because he would not lose the pleasure he had in seeking it; as another that would not have his physician remove the thirst he felt in his ague because he would not lose the pleasure he took in quenching the same with drinking. [C]"It is better to learn more than we need than nothing at all" (Sen. *Epist.* 88.). Even as in all feeding, pleasure is always alone and single, and all we take that is pleasant is not ever nourishing and wholesome; so likewise what our mind draws from learning leaveth not to be voluptuous, although it neither nourish nor be wholesome.

[B]Note what their saying is: "The consideration of nature is a food proper for our minds; it raiseth and puffeth us up; it makes us by the comparison of heavenly and high things to disdain base and low matters; the search of hidden and great causes is very pleasant, yea, unto him that attains naught but the reverence and fear to judge of them." These are the very words of their profession.

The vain image of this crazed curiosity is more manifestly seen in this other example, which they for honor's sake have so often in their mouths. Eudoxus wished and prayed to the gods that he might once view the sun near at hand, to comprehend his form, his greatness, and his beauty, on condition he might immediately be burnt and consumed by it. Thus with the price of his own life would [h]e attain a science whereof both use and possession shall therewith be taken from him; and for so sudden and fleeting knowledge lose and forgo all the knowledges he either now hath or ever hereafter may have.

[A]I cannot easily be persuaded that Epicurus, Plato, or Pythagoras have sold us their Atoms, their Ideas, and their Numbers for ready payment. They were over-wise to establish their articles of faith upon things so uncertain and disputable. But in this obscurity and ignorance of the world, each of these notable men hath endeavored to bring some kind of show or image of light, and have busied their minds about inventions that might at least have a pleasing and wily appearance, [C]provided (notwithstanding it were false) it might be maintained against contrary oppositions. "These things are conceited by every man as his wit serves, not as his knowledge stretches and reaches" (Sen. *Suasor.* IV.).

[A]An ancient philosopher, being blamed for professing that philosophy, whereof in his judgment he made no esteem, answered that that was true philosophizing. They have gone about to consider all, to balance all, and have found that it was an occupation fitting the natural curiosity which is in us. Some things they have written for the behoof of common society, as their religions; and for this consideration was it reasonable that they would not throughly unfold common opinions, that so they might not breed trouble in the obedience of laws and customs of their countries.

[C]Plato treateth this mystery in a very manifest kind of sport. For where he writeth according to himself, he prescribeth nothing for certainty. When he institutes a lawgiver, he borroweth a very swaying and avouching kind of style, wherein he boldly intermingleth his most fantastical opinions, as profitable to persuade the common sort, as ridiculous to persuade himself; knowing how apt we are to receive all impressions, and chiefly the most wicked and enormous. And therefore is he very careful in his *Laws* that nothing be sung in public but poesies the fabulous fictions of which tend to some profitable end, being so apt to imprint all manner of illusion in man's mind that it is injustice not to feed them rather with commodious lies than with lies either unprofitable or damageable. He flatly saith in his *Commonwealth*[17] that for the benefit of men it is often necessary to deceive them.

It is easy to distinguish how some sects have rather followed truth and some profit, by which the latter have gained credit. It is the misery of our condition that often what offers itself unto our imagination for the likeliest presents not itself unto it for the most beneficial unto our life. The boldest sects, both Epicurean, Pyrrhonian, and New Academic, when they have cast their account, are compelled to stoop to the civil law.

[A]There are other subjects which they have tossed, some on the left and some on the right hand, each one laboring and striving to give it some semblance were it right or wrong; for having found nothing so secret whereof they have not attempted to speak, they are many times forced to forge divers feeble and fond* conjectures; not that themselves took them for a groundwork, nor to establish a truth, but for an exercise of their study. [C]"They seem not so much to have thought as they said, as rather willing to exercise their wits in the difficulty of the matter."

[A]And if it were not so taken, how should we cloak so great an inconstancy, variety, and vanity of opinions which we see to have been produced by these excellent and admirable spirits? As, for example, what greater vanity can there be than to go about by our proportions and conjectures to guess at God, and to govern both him and the world according to our capacity and laws, and to use this small scantling* of sufficiency which he hath pleased to impart unto our natural condition at the cost and charges of divinity? And, because we cannot extend our sight so far as his glorious throne, to have removed him down to our corruption and miseries? Of all human and ancient opinions concerning religion, I think that to have had more likelihood and excuse which [ac]knowledged and confessed God to be an incomprehensible power, chief beginning, and preserver of all

17 I.e., *The Republic*.

things, all goodness, all perfection, accepting in good part the honor and reverence which mortal men did yield him, under what usage, name, and manner soever it was:

> [C]Almighty Jove is parent said to be
> Of things, of kings, of gods, both he and she.
> Valer. Soranus, in Aug. *De civ. Dei* VII.xi.

This zeal hath universally been regarded of heaven with a gentle and gracious eye. All policies have reaped some fruit by their devotion: men and impious actions have everywhere had correspondent events. Heathen histories acknowledge dignity, order, justice, prodigies, and oracles, employed for their benefit and instruction, in their fabulous religion; God, of his mercy, deigning peradventure to foster by his temporal blessings the budding and tender beginnings of such a brute knowledge as natural reason gave them of him athwart the false images of their deluding dreams. Not only false but impious and injurious are those which man hath forged and devised by his own invention.

[A]And of all religions Saint Paul found in credit at Athens, that which they had consecrated unto a certain hidden and unknown divinity seemed to be most excusable.

[C]Pythagoras shadowed the truth somewhat nearer, judging that the knowledge of this first cause and *ens entium** must be undefined, without any prescription or declaration; that it was nothing else but the extreme endeavor of our imagination towards perfection, every-one amplifying the idea thereof according to his capacity. But if Numa undertook to conform the devotion of his people to this project, to join the same to a religion merely mental, without any prefixed object or material mixture, he undertook a matter to no use. Man's mind could never be maintained if it were still floating up and down in this infinite deep of shapeless conceits. They must be framed unto her to some image, according to her model.

The majesty of God hath in some sort suffered itself to be circum-scribed to corporal limits; his supernatural and celestial sacraments bear signs of our terrestrial condition; his adoration is expressed by offices and sensible words; for it is man that believeth and prayeth.

I omit other arguments that are employed about this subject. But I could hardly be made believe that the sight of our crucifixes and pictures of that pitiful torment, that the ornaments and ceremonious motions in our churches, that the voices accommodated and suited to our thoughts' devotions, and this stirring of our senses, doth not greatly inflame the people's souls with a religious passion of wondrous beneficial good.

[A]Of those to which they have given bodies, as necessity required, amid this general blindness — as for me, I should rather have taken part with those who worshipped the sun:

the common light,
The world's eye; and if god bear eyes in his chief head,
His most resplendent eyes the sun-beams may be said,
Which unto all give life, which us maintain and guard,
And in this world of men the works of men regard;
This great, this beauteous sun, which us our seasons makes,
As in twelve houses he ingress or egress takes;
Who with his virtues known doth fill this universe;
With one cast of his eyes doth us all clouds disperse;
The spirit and the soul of this world, flaming, burning,
Round about heav'n in course of one day's journey turning;
Of endless greatness full, round, moveable, and fast;
Who all the world for bounds beneath himself hath plac'd;
In rest, without rest, and still more staid without stay,
Of Nature th' eldest child, and father of the day.
Ronsard, *Remonstrances au peuple de France,* 64–78.

Forasmuch as besides this greatness and matchless beauty of his, it is the only glorious piece of this vast world's frame which we perceive to be furthest from us, and by that mean so little known as they are pardonable that entered into admiration and reverence of it.

[C]Thales, who was the first to inquire and find out this matter, esteemed God to be a spirit who made all things of water. Anaximander thought the gods did die and were new-born at divers seasons, and that the worlds were infinite in number. Anaximenes deemed the air to be a god, which was created immense and always moving. Anaxagoras was the first that held the description and manner of all things to be directed by the power and reason of a spirit infinite. Alcmaeon hath ascribed divinity unto the sun, unto the moon, unto the stars, and unto the soul. Pythagoras hath made God a spirit dispersed through the nature of all things, whence our souls are derived. Parmenides, a circle circumpassing the heavens, and by the heat of light maintaining the world. Empedocles said the four natures, whereof all things are made to be gods. Protagoras that he had nothing to say, whether they were or were not, or what they were. Democritus would sometimes say that the images and their circuitions were gods, and other times this nature, which disperseth these images, and then our knowledge and intelligence. Plato scattereth his belief after divers semblances: in his *Timaeus* he saith that the world's father could not be named; in his *Laws,* that his being must not be inquired after; and elsewhere in the said books he maketh the world, the heaven, the stars, the earth, and our souls to be gods; and besides, admitteth those that by ancient institutions have been received in every commonwealth. Xenophon reporteth a like difference of Socrates his discipline: sometimes that God's form ought not to be inquired after; then he makes him infer that the sun is a god and the soul a god; other times that there is but one, and then more. Speusippus, nephew unto Plato, makes God to be a certain power, governing all things and having a soul. Aristotle saith sometimes that it is the spirit, and sometimes the world; other times he appointeth another ruler over this world, and sometimes he makes God to be the heat of heaven. Xenocrates makes eight: five named amongst the planets, the sixth composed of all the fixed stars, as of his own members, the seventh and eighth the sun and moon. Heraclides Ponticus doth but roam among his opinions, and in fine depriveth God of sense and makes him remove and transchange himself from one form to another, and then saith that is both heaven and earth. Theophrastus in all his fantasies wandereth still in like irresolutions, attributing the world's superintendency now to the intelligence, now to the heaven, and now to the stars. Strato, that it is nature having power to engender, to augment, and to diminish, without form or sense. Zeno, the natural law, commanding the good and prohibiting the evil, which law is a breathing creature; and removeth the accustomed gods, Jupiter, Juno, and Vesta. Diogenes Apolloniates, that it is age. Xenophanes makes God round, seeing, hearing, not breathing, and having nothing common with human nature. Aristo deemeth the form of God to be incomprehensible and depriveth him of senses, and wotteth not certainly whether he be a breathing soul or something else. Cleanthes, sometimes reason, other times the world, now the soul of nature, and other while the supreme heat, enfolding and containing all. Perseus, Zeno's disciple, hath been of opinion that they were surnamed gods who had brought some notable good or benefit unto human life, or had invented profitable things. Chrysippus made a confused huddle of all the foresaid sentences, and amongst a thousand forms of the gods which he feigneth, he also accounteth those men that are immortalized. Diagoras and Theodorus flatly denied that there were any gods. Epicurus makes the gods bright-shining, transparent, and perflable,* placed as it were between two forts, between two worlds, safely sheltered from all blows, invested with a human shape, and with our members, which unto them are of no use.[18]

> I still thought and will say, of gods there is a kind;
> But what our mankind doth, I think they nothing mind.
> Ennius, in Cic. *De divin.* II.50

18 This paragraph is adapted from a passage in Cicero's *De natura deorum.*

Trust to your philosophy; boast to have hit the nail on the head or to have found out the bean of this cake,[19] to see this coil and hurly-burly of so many philosophical wits!

The trouble or confusion of worldly shapes and forms hath gotten this of me, that customs and conceits differing from mine do not so much dislike me as instruct me; and at what time I confer or compare them together, they do not so much puff me up with pride as humble me with lowliness. And each other choice, except that which cometh from the express hand of God, seemeth to me a choice of small prerogative or consequence. The world's policies are no less contrary one to another in this subject than the schools; whereby we may learn that fortune herself is no more divers, changing, and variable than our reason, nor more blind and inconsiderate.

[A]Things most unknown are fittest to be deified. [C]Wherefore, to make gods of ourselves, [A]as antiquity hath done, it exceeds the extreme weakness of discourse. I would rather have followed those that worshipped the serpent, the dog, and the ox, forsomuch as their nature and being is least known to us, and we may more lawfully imagine what we list of those beasts and ascribe extraordinary faculties unto them. But to have made gods of our condition, whose i[m]perfections we should know, and to have attributed desire, choler, revenge, marriages, generation, alliances, love, and jealousy, our limbs and our bones, our infirmities, our pleasures, [C]our deaths, and our sepulchres [A]unto them hath of necessity proceeded from a mere and egregious sottishness or drunkenness of man's wit:

> [B]Which from divinity so distant are,
> To stand in rank of gods unworthy far.
> Lucr. V.123.

[C]"Their shapes, their ages, their apparel, their furnitures are known; their kinds, their marriages, their kindred, and all translated to the likeness of man's weakness; for they are also brought in with minds much troubled; for we read of the lustfulness, the grievings, the angriness of the gods" (Cic. *De nat. deor.* II.xxviii.).

[A]As to have ascribed divinity [C]not only unto faith, virtue, honor, concord, liberty, victory, and piety, but also unto voluptuousness, fraud, death, envy, age, and misery, [A]yea, unto fear, unto ague, and unto evil fortune, and such other injuries and wrongs to our frail and transitory life:

> [B]What boots it into temples to bring manners of our kinds?
> O crooked souls on earth, and void of heavenly minds!
> Pers. *Sat.* II.62, 61

19 On Twelfth Night, the person who finds a bean in his cake becomes King of the Bean.

[C]The Egyptians, with an impudent wisdom, forbade upon pain of hanging that no man should dare to say that Serapis and Isis, their gods, had whilom been but men, when all knew they had been so. And their images or pictures drawn with a finger across their mouths imported, as Varro saith, this mysterious rule unto their priests, to conceal their mortal offspring, which by a necessary reason disannulled all their veneration.

[A]Since man desired so much to equal himself to God, it had been better for him, saith Cicero, to draw those divine conditions unto himself and bring them down to earth, than to send his corruption and place his misery above in heaven; but to take him aright, he hath divers ways and with like vanity of opinion doth both the one and other.

When philosophers blazon and display the hierarchy of their gods and to the utmost of their skill endeavor to distinguish their alliances, their charges, and their powers, I cannot believe they speak in good earnest. When Plato deciphereth unto us the orchard of Pluto and the commodities or corporal pains which even after the ruin and consumption of our body wait for us, and applieth them to the apprehension or feeling we have in this life —

> Them paths aside conceal, a myrtle grove
> Shades them round; cares in death do not remove
>
> Virg. *Aen.* VI.443.

— when Mohamet promiseth unto his followers a paradise all tapestried, adorned with gold and precious stones, peopled with exceeding beauteous damsels, stored with wines and singular cates,* I will perceive they are but scoffers which suit and apply themselves unto our foolishness, thereby to enhoney* and allure us to these opinions and hopes fitting our mortal appetite.

[C]Even so are some of our men fallen into like errors by promising unto themselves after their resurrection a terrestrial and temporal life, accompanied with all sorts of pleasure and worldly commodities.

[A]Shall we think that Plato, who had so heavenly conceptions and was so well aquainted with divinity, as of most he purchased the surname of divine, was ever of opinion that man, this silly* and wretched creature man, had any one thing in him which might in any sort be applied and suited to this incomprehensible and unspeakable power? Or ever imagined that our languishing hold-fasts* were capable, or the virtue of our understanding of force, to participate or be partakers, either of the blessedness or eternal punishment? He ought, in the behalf of human reason, be answered:

"If the pleasures thou promisest us in the other life are such as I have felt here below, they have nothing in them common with infinity. If all my five natural senses were even surcharged with joy and gladness and my soul possessed with all the contents and delights it could possibly desire or hope for, and we know what it either can wish or hope for, yet were it nothing. If there be anything that is mine, then there is nothing that is divine. If it be nothing else but what may appertain unto this our present condition, it may not be accounted of. [C]All mortal men's contentment is mortal. [A]The acknowledging of our parents, of our children, and of our friends, if it cannot touch, move, or tickle us in the other world, if we still take hold of such a pleasure, we continue in terrestrial and transitory commodities. We cannot worthily conceive of these high, mysterious, and divine promises; if we can but in any sort conceive them and so imagine them aright, they must be thought to be unimaginable, unspeakable, and incomprehensible, [C]and absolutely and perfectly other than those of our miserable experience. [A]'No eye can behold,' saith Saint Paul, 'the hap that God prepareth for his elect, nor can it possibly enter into the heart of man' (I Cor. ii.9).

"And if, to make us capable of it (as thou saith, Plato, by thy purifications), our being is reformed and essence changed, it must be by so extreme and universal a change that, according to philosophical doctrine, we shall be no more ourselves:

> [B]Hector he was, when he in fight us'd force;
> Hector he was not, drawn by th' enemy's horse.
>
> Ovid. *Trist.* III.ii.27.

[A]It shall be some other thing that shall receive these recompenses:

> [B]What is chang'd, is dissolved, therefore dies,
> Translated parts in order fall and rise.
>
> Lucr. III.756.

[A]For in the metempsychosis, or transmigration of the souls, of Pythagoras, and the change of habitation which he imagined the souls to make, shall we think that the lion in whom abideth the soul of Caesar doth wed the passions which concerned Caesar, [C]or that it is he? And if it were he, those had some reason who, debating this opinion against Plato, object that the son might one day be found committing with his mother under the shape of a mule's body, and such-like absurdities.

"And shall we imagine [A]that in the transmigrations which are made from the bodies of some creatures into others of the same kind, the new, succeeding ones are not other than their predecessors were? Of a phoenix's cinders, first (as they say) is engendered a worm and then another phoenix. Who can imagine that this second phoenix be no other and different from the first? Our silk-worms are seen to die and then to wither dry, and of that body breedeth a butterfly, and of that a worm: were it not ridiculous to think the same to be the first silk-worm? What hath once lost his being, is no more:

> If time should recollect, when life is past,
> Our stuff, and it replace as now 'tis plac'd,
> And light of life were granted us again,
> Yet nothing would that deed to us pertain,
> When interrupted were our turn again.
>
> Lucr. III.847.

And, Plato, when in another place thou sayest that it shall be the spiritual part of man that shall enjoy the recompenses of the other life, thou tellest of things of as small likelihood:

> [B]Ev'n as no eye by th' roots pull'd out can see
> Ought in whole body several to be.
>
> Lucr. III.562.

[A]For by this reckoning, it shall no longer be man, nor consequently us, to whom this enjoying shall appertain; for we are built of two principal essential parts, the separation of which is the death and consummation of our being:

> [B]A pause of life is interpos'd; from sense
> All motions strayed are, far-wand'ring thence.
>
> Lucr. III.872.

[A]We do not say that man suffereth when the worms gnaw his body and limbs whereby he lived, and that the earth consumeth them:

> This nought concerns us, who consist of union
> Of mind and body join'd in meet communion.
>
> Lucr. III.857.

"Moreover, upon what ground of their justice can the gods reward man and be thankful unto him after his death, for his good and virtuous actions, since themselves addressed and bred them in him? And wherefore are they offended, and revenge his vicious deeds, when themselves have created him with so defective a condition, and that but with one twinkling of their will they may hinder him from sinning?"

Might not Epicurus with some show of human reason object that unto Plato, [C]if he did not often shroud himself under this sentence: "that it is impossible by mortal nature to establish any certainty of the immortal"?

[A]She[20] is ever straying, but especially when she meddleth with

[20] Reason.

divine matters. Who feels it more evidently than we? For, although we have ascribed unto her assured and infallible principles, albeit we enlighten her steps with the holy lamp of that truth which God hath been pleased to impart unto us, we notwithstanding see daily — how little soever she stray from the ordinary path and that she start or straggle out of the way traced and measured out by the Church — how soon she loseth, entangleth, and confoundeth herself, turning, tossing, and floating up and down in this vast, troublesome, and tempestuous sea of man's opinions, without restraint or scope. So soon as she loseth this high and common way, she divideth and scattereth herself a thousand diverse ways.

Man can be no other than he is, nor imagine but according to his capacity. [B]It is greater presumption, saith Plutarch, in them that are but men to attempt to reason and discourse of gods and demi-gods, than in a man merely ignorant of music to judge of those that sing, or for a man that was never in wars to dispute of arms and war, presuming by some light conjecture to comprehend the effects of an art altogether beyond his skill.

[A]As I think, antiquity imagined it did something for divine majesty when she compared the same unto man, attiring her with his faculties and enriching her with his strange humors [C]and most shameful necessities; [A]offering her some of our cates* to feed upon and [C]some of our dances, mummeries, and interludes to make her merry, [A]with our clothes to apparel her, and our houses to lodge her; cherishing her with the sweet odors of incense and sounds of music, adorning her with garlands and flowers; [C]and, to draw to our vicious passion, to flatter her justice with an inhuman revenge, gladding her with the ruin and dissipation of things created and preserved by her — as Tiberius Sempronius, who, for a sacrifice to Vulcan, caused the rich spoils and arms which he had gotten of his enemies in Sardinia to be burned; and Paulus Aemilius, those he had obtained in Macedonia, to Mars and Minerva; and Alexander, coming to the Ocean of India, cast in favor of Thetis many great rich vessels of gold into the sea, replenishing, moreover, her altars with a butcherly slaughter, not only of innocent beasts, but of men, [A]as divers nations, and among the rest ours, were wont to do. And I think none hath been exempted from showing the like essays*:

> [B]Four young men born of Sulmo, and four more
> Whom Ufens bred, he living over-bore,
> Whom he to his dead friend
> A sacrifice might send.
>
> Virg. *Aen.* X.517.

[C]The Getae deem themselves immortal and their death but the beginning of a journey to their god Zamolxis. From five to five years, they dispatch some one among themselves toward him to require* him of necessary things. This deputy of theirs is chosen by lots. And the manner to dispatch him, after they have by word of mouth instructed him of his charge, is that amongst those which assist his election, three hold so many javelins upright upon which the others by mere strength of arms throw him. If he chance to stick upon them in any mortal place, and that he die suddenly, it is to them an assured argument of divine favor; but if he escape, they deem him a wicked and execrable man, and then choose another.

Amestris, mother unto Xerxes, being become aged, caused at one time fourteen young striplings of the noblest houses in Persia, following the religion of her country, to be buried all alive, thereby to gratify some god of under earth.

Even at this day, the idols of Themistitan are cemented with the blood of young children, and love no sacrifice but of such infant and pure souls. O justice greedy of the blood of innocency!

> Religion so much mischief could
> Persuade, where it much better should.
>
> Lucr. I.102.

The Carthaginians were wont to sacrifice their own children unto Saturn, [B]and who had none was fain to buy some; and their fathers and mothers were enforced in their proper persons, with cheerful and pleasant countenance, to assist that office.

[A]It was a strange conceit with our own affliction to go about to please and appay* divine goodness, as the Lacedaemonians, who flattered and wantonized their Diana by torturing of young boys, whom often in favor of her they caused to be whipped to death. It was a savage kind of humor to think to gratify the architect with the subversion of his architecture, and to cancel the punishment due unto the guilty by punishing the guiltless; and to imagine that poor Iphigenia, in the port of Aulis, should by her death and sacrifice discharge and expiate towards God the Grecians' army of the offenses which they had committed:

> [B]She, a chaste offering, griev'd incestuously
> By father's stroke, when she should wed, to die;
>
> Lucr. I.99.

[C]and those two noble and generous souls of the Decii, father and son, to reconcile and appease the favor of the gods towards the Romans' affairs, should headlong cast their bodies athwart the thickest throng of their enemies. "What injustice of the gods was so great as they could not be appeased unless such men perished?" (Cic. *De nat. deor.* III.vi.).

[A]Considering that it lies not in the offender to cause himself to be whipped how and when he list, but in the judge, [B]who accounteth nothing a right punishment except the torture he appointeth, [C]and cannot impute that unto punishment which is in the free choice of him that suffereth. The divine vengeance presupposeth our full dissent, for his justice and our pain.

[B]And ridiculous was that humor of Polycrates, the tyrant of Samos, who, to interrupt the course of his continual happiness and to recompense it, cast the richest and most precious jewel he had into the sea, deeming that by this purposed mishap he should satisfy the revolution and vicissitude of fortune; [C]which, to deride his folly, caused the very same jewel, being found in a fish's belly, to return to his hands again.

[A]And [C]to what purpose are the manglings and dismemberings of the Corybantes, of the Maenads, and nowadays of the Mohammedans, who scar and gash their faces, their stomach, and their limbs, to gratify their prophet, seeing [A]the offense consisteth in the will, not [C]in the breast, nor eyes, nor in the genitories, health, [A]shoulders, or throat? [C]"So great is the fury of a troubled mind put from the state it should be in, as the gods must be so pacified as even men would not be so outrageous" (Aug. *Civ. Dei.* VI.x.).

This natural contexture[21] doth by her use not only respect us, but also the service of God and other men's. It is injustice to make it miscarry at our pleasure, as under what pretense soever it be to kill ourselves. It seemeth to be a great cowardice and manifest treason to abuse the stupid and corrupt the servile functions of the body, to spare the diligence unto the soul how to direct them according unto reason. "Where are they afeared of God's anger, who in such sort deserve to have his favor? Some have been gelded for princes' lustful pleasure; but no man at the Lord's command hath laid hands on himself to be less than a man" (Aug. *Civ. Dei.* VI.x.).

[A]Thus did they replenish their religion and stuff it with divers bad effects:

> Religion hath ofttimes in former times
> Bred execrable facts, ungodly crimes.
>
> Lucr. I.82.

Now can nothing of ours, in what manner soever, be either compared or referred unto divine nature that doth not blemish or defile

21 The body.

the same with as much imperfection. How can this infinite beauty, power, and goodness admit any correspondency or similitude with a thing so base and abject as we are, without extreme interest and manifest derogation from his divine greatness? [C]"The weakness of God is stronger than men, and the foolishness of God is wiser than men" (I Cor. i.25.).

Stilpo, the philosopher, being demanded whether the gods rejoice at our honors and sacrifices, "you are indiscreet," said he; "let us withdraw ourselves apart if you speak of such matters."

[A]Notwithstanding, we prescribe him limits; we lay continual siege unto his power by our reasons. (I call our dreams and our vanities reason, with the dispensation of philosophy, which saith that both the fool and the wicked do rave and dote by reason; but that it is a reason of several and particular form.) We will subject him to the vain and weak appearances of our understanding, him who hath made both us and our knowledge.

"Because nothing is made of nothing, God was not able to frame the world without matter." What? Hath God delivered unto our hands the keys and the strongest wards* of his infinite puissance? Hath he obliged himself not to exceed the bounds of our knowledge? Suppose, O man, that therein thou hast been able to mark some signs of his effects; thinkest thou he hath therein employed all he was able to do and that he hath placed all his forms and ideas in this piece of work? Thou seest but the order and policy of this little, little cell wherein thou art placed — the question is whether thou seest it. His divinity hath an infinite jurisdiction far beyond that; this piece is nothing in respect of the whole:

> All things that are, with heav'n, with sea, and land,
> To th' whole sum of th' whole sum as nothing stand.
>
> Lucr. VI.679.

This law thou allegest is but a municipal law, and thou knowest not what the universal is. Tie thyself unto that whereto thou art subject, but tie not him; he is neither thy companion, nor thy brother, nor thy fellow-citizen, nor thy copesmate*; if he in any sort have communicated himself unto thee, it is not to debase himself or stoop to thy smallness, or to give thee the controlment of his power.

Man's body cannot soar up unto the clouds; this is for thee. The sun uncessantly goeth his ordinary course; the bounds of the seas and of the earth cannot be confounded; the water is ever fleeting, wavering, and without firmness; a wall without breach or flaw, impenetrable unto a solid body; man cannot preserve his life amidst the flames; he cannot corporally be both in heaven and on earth, and in a thousand places together and at once.

It is for thee that he hath made these rules; it is thou they take hold of. He hath testified unto Christians that whenever it pleased him he hath outgone them all. And in truth, omnipotent as he is, wherefore should he have restrained his forces unto a limited measure? In favor of whom should he have renounced his privilege?

Thy reason hath in no one other thing more likelihood and foundation than in that which persuadeth thee a plurality of worlds:

> [B]The earth, the sun, the moon, the sea and all,
> In number numberless, not one they call.
> Lucr. II.1085.

[A]The famousest wits of former ages have believed it, yea, and some of our modern, as forced thereunto by the apparance* of human reason; forasmuch as whatsoever we see in this vast world's frame, there is no one thing alone, single and one:

> [B]Whereas in general sum, nothing is one,
> To be bred only one, grow only one,
> Lucr. II.1077.

[A]and that all several kinds are multiplied in some number. Whereby it seemeth unlikely that God hath framed this piece of work alone without a fellow, and that the matter of this form hath wholly been spent in this only *individuum:*

> [B]Wherefore you must confess, again, again,
> Of matter such-like meetings elsewhere reign
> As this, these skies in greedy grip contain;
> Lucr. II.1064.

[A]namely, if it be a breathing creature, as its motions make so likely [C]that Plato assureth it, and divers of ours either affirm it or dare not impugn it; no more than this old opinion that the heaven, the stars, and other members of the world are creatures composed both of body and soul, mortal in respect of their composition, but immortal by the creator's decree.

[A]Now if there be divers worlds, as [C]Democritus, [A]Epicurus, and well near all philosophy hath thought, what know we whether the principles and the rules of this one concern or touch likewise the others? Haply they have another semblance and another policy. [C]Epicurus imagineth them either like or unlike. [A]We see an infinite difference and variety in this world only by the distance of places. There is neither corn, nor wine, no, nor any of our beasts seen in that new corner of the world which our fathers have lately discovered: all things differ from ours. CAnd in the old time, mark but in how many parts of the world they had never knowledge nor of Bacchus nor of Ceres.

AIf any credit may be given unto Pliny Cor to Herodotus, Athere is in some places a kind of men that have very little or no resemblance at all with ours. BAnd there be mongrel and ambiguous shapes between a human and brutish nature. Some countries there are where men are born headless, with eyes and mouths in their breasts; where all are hermaphrodites; where they creep on all four; where they have but one eye in their forehead and heads more like unto a dog than ours; where from the navel downwards they are half fish and live in the water; where women are brought abed at five years of age and live but eight; where their heads and the skin of their brows are so hard that no iron can pierce them, but will rather turn edge; where men never have beards. COther nations there are that never have use of fire; others whose sperm is of a black color.

BWhat shall we speak of them who naturally change themselves into wolves, Cinto colts, Band then into men again? And if it be, Aas Plutarch saith, that in some part of the Indies there are men without mouths, and who live only by the smell of certain sweet odors, how many of our descriptions be then false? He is no more risible, nor perhaps capable of reason and society. The direction and cause of our inward frame should for the most part be to no purpose.

Moreover, how many things are there in our knowledge that oppugn* these goodly rules which we have allotted and prescribed unto nature! And we undertake to join God himself unto her. How many things do we name miraculous and against nature! CEach man and every nation doth it according to the measure of his ignorance. AHow many hidden properties and quintessences do we daily discover! For us to go according to nature is but to follow according to our understanding, as far as it can follow, and as much as we can perceive in it; whatsoever is beyond it is monstrous and disordered.

By this account all shall then be monstrous to the wisest and most sufficient; for even to such human reason hath persuaded that she had neither ground nor footing, Cno, not so much as to warrant snow to be white (and Anaxagoras said it was black); whether there be anything or nothing; whether there be knowledge or ignorance (which Metrodorus Chius denied that any man might say); or Awhether we live, as Euripides seemeth to doubt and call in question whether the life we live be a life or no, or whether that which we call death be a life:

> Who knows if thus to live be called death,
> And if it be to die thus to draw breath?
>
> **Eurip., in Stobaeus, 119.**

[B]And not without apparance.* For wherefore do we from that instant take a title of being which is but a twinkling in the infinite course of an eternal night and so short an interruption of our perpetual and natural condition; [C]death possessing whatever is before and behind this moment, and also a good part of this moment?

[B]Some others affirm there is no motion and that nothing stirreth, [C]namely, those which follow Melissus (for it there be but one, neither can this spherical motion serve him, nor the moving from one place to another, as Plato proveth); [B]that there is neither generation nor corruption in nature. [C]Protagoras saith there is nothing in nature but doubt; that a man may equally dispute of all things; and of that also, whether all things may equally be disputed of. Mansiphanes said that of things which seem to be, no one thing is no more than it is not; that nothing is certain but uncertainty. Parmenides, that of that which seemeth there is no one thing in general; that there is but one. Zeno, that oneself same is not, and that there is nothing. If one were he should either be in another or in himself: if he be in another, then are they two; if he be in himself, they are also two, the comprising and the comprised.

According to these rules or doctrines, the nature of things is but a false or vain shadow.

[A]I have ever thought this manner of speech in a Christian is full of indiscretion and irreverence: "God cannot die, God cannot gainsay himself, God cannot do this or that." I cannot allow a man should so bound God's heavenly power under the laws of our word. And that apparance* which in these propositions offers itself unto us ought to be represented more reverently and more religiously.

Our speech hath his infirmities and defects, as all things else have. Most of the occasions of this world's troubles are grammatical. Our suits and processes proceed but from the canvassing and debating the interpretation of the laws, and most of our wars from the want of knowledge in state counsellors that could not clearly distinguish and fully express the covenants and conditions of accords between prince and prince. How many weighty strifes and important quarrels hath the doubt of this one syllable *hoc* brought forth in the world?[22]

[B]Examine the plainest sentence that logic itself can present unto us. If you say, "it is fair weather," and in so saying say true, it is fair weather then. Is not this a certain form of speech? Yet will it deceive us. That it is so, let us follow the example. If you say, "I lie," and that you should say true, you lie then. The art, the reason, the force of the conclusion of this last are like unto the other; notwithstanding, we are entangled.

22 The debate between the Catholics, Lutherans, and Calvinists over the dogma of transubstantiation centered around the phrase, "Hoc est corpus meum."

[A]I see the Pyrrhonian philosophers, who can by no manner of speech express their general conceit; for they had need of a new language. Ours is altogether composed of affirmative propositions, which are directly against them. So that when they say, "I doubt," you have them fast by the throat to make them avow that at least you are assured and know that they doubt. So have they been compelled to save themselves by this comparison of physic, without which their conceit would be inexplicable and intricate: when they pronounce "I know not" or "I doubt," they say this proposition transports itself together with the rest, even as the rhubarb doth which scoured ill humors away and therewith is carried away himself.

[B]This conceit is more certainly conceived by an interrogation: "What can I tell?" [*Que Sçay je?*], as I bear it in an impresa* of a pair of balances.

[A]Note how some prevail with this kind of unreverent and unhallowed speech. In the disputations that are nowadays in our religion, if you overmuch urge the adversaries, they will roundly tell you that it lieth not in the power of God to make his body at once to be in paradise and on earth and in many other places together. And how that ancient scoffer[23] made profitable use of it! At least, saith he, it is no small comfort unto man to see that God cannot do all things: for he cannot kill himself if he would, which is the greatest benefit we have in our condition; he cannot make mortal men immortal, nor raise the dead to life again, nor make him that hath lived never to have lived and him who hath had honors not to have had them, having no other right over what is past but of forgetfulness. And that this society between God and man may also be combined with some pleasant examples, he cannot make twice ten not to be twenty. See what he saith, and which a Christian ought to abhor, that ever such and so profane words should pass his mouth. Whereas, on the contrary part, it seemeth that fond men endeavor to find out this foolish boldness of speech, that so they may turn and wind God Almighty according to their measure:

> Tomorrow let our father fill the sky
> With dark cloud, or with clear sun; he thereby
> Shall not make void what once is overpast,
> Nor shall he undo, or in new mold cast
> What time hath once caught, that flies hence so fast.
>
> Hor., *Odes*, III.xxix.43.

When we say that the infinity of ages as well past as to come is but an instant with God, that his wisdom, goodness, and power are one self-same thing with his essence, our tongue speaks it, but our under-

23 Pliny the Elder.

standing can no whit apprehend it. Yet will our self-overweening sift his divinity through our searce.* Whence are engendered all the vanities and errors wherewith the world is so full-fraught, reducing and weighing with his uncertain balance a thing so far from his reach and so distant from his weight. [C]"It is a wonder whither the perverse wickedness of man's heart will proceed if it be but called on with any little success" (Pliny *Hist. nat.* II.xxiii.).

How insolently do the Stoics charge Epicurus because he holds that to be perfectly good and absolutely happy belongs but only unto God, and that the wise man hath but a shadow and similitude thereof? [A]How rashly have they joined God unto destiny (which, at my request, let none that beareth the surname of a Christian do at this day!) and Thales, Plato, and Pythagoras have subjected him unto necessity! This over-boldness, or rather bold fierceness, to seek to discover God by and with our eyes hath been the cause that a notable man of our times[24] hath attributed a corporal form unto divinity, [B]and is the cause of that which daily happeneth unto us, which is, by a particular assignation to impute all important events to God; which, because they touch us, it seemeth they also touch him, and that he regardeth them with more care and attention than those that are but slight and ordinary unto us. [C]"The gods take some care for great things, but none for little" (Cic. *De nat. deor.* II.lxvi.). Note his example; he will enlighten you with his reason: "Nor do kings in their kingdoms much care for the least matters" (Cic. *De nat. deor.* III.xxxv.). As if it were all one to that King either to remove an empire or a leaf of a tree, and if his providence were otherwise exercised, inclining or regarding no more the success of a battle than the skip of a flea. The hand of his government affords itself to all things after a like tenure, fashion, and order; our interest addeth nothing unto it; our motions and our measures concern him nothing and move him no whit. "God is so great a workman in great things, as he is no less in small things" (Aug. *Civ. Dei* XI.xxii.).

Our arrogancy setteth ever before us this blasphemous equality. Because our occupations charge us, [Strato] hath presented the gods with all immunity of offices, as are their priests. He maketh nature to produce and preserve all things, and by her weights and motions to compact all parts of the world, discharging human nature from the fear of divine judgments. "That which is blessed and eternal, nor is troubled itself, nor troubleth others" (Cic. *De nat. deor.* I.xvii.). Nature willeth that in all things alike there be also like relation. Then the infinite number of mortal men concludeth a like number of im-

[24] The person Montaigne refers to is Tertullian, and Florio mistranslates *des nostres* as "of our times," whereas Montaigne means "of our religion."

mortal. The infinite things that kill and destroy presuppose as many that preserve and profit. As the souls of the gods, sans* tongues, sans* eyes, and sans* ears, have each one in themselves a feeling of that which the other feel[s], and judge of our thoughts; so men's souls, when they are free and severed from the body, either by sleep or any distraction, divine, prognosticate, and see things which, being conjoined to their bodies, they could not see. ^A^Men (saith St. Paul) when they professed themselves to be wise, they became fools; for they turned the glory of the incorruptible God to the similitude of the image of a corruptible man (Rom. I.22–3.).

^B^Mark, I pray you, a little the juggling of ancient deifications. After the great, solemn, and proud pomp of funerals, when the fire began to burn the top of the pyramid and to take hold of the bed or hearse wherein the dead corpse lay, even at that instant they let fly an eagle, which, taking her flight aloft upward, signified that the soul went directly to paradise. We have yet a thousand medals and monuments, namely of that honest woman Faustina, wherein that eagle is represented carrying a cockhorse up towards heaven those deified souls. It is pity we should so deceive ourselves with our own foolish devices and apish inventions —

> Of that they stand in fear
> Which they in fancy bear
> Lucan I.486.

— as children will be afeared of their fellow's visage which themselves have besmeared and blacked. ^C^"As though anything were more wretched than man over whom his own imaginations bear sway and domineer (Unknown).

To honor him whom we have made is far from honoring him that hath made us. ^B^Augustus had as many temples as Jupiter and served with as much religion and opinion of miracles. The Thracians, in requital of the benefits they had received of Agesilaus, came to tell him how they had canonized him. "Hath your nation," said he, "the power to make those whom it pleaseth gods? Then first, for example's sake, make one of yourselves; and ^C^when I shall have seen what good he shall have thereby, ^B^I will then thank you for your offer." ^C^O senseless man, who cannot possibly make a worm, and yet will make gods by dozens!

Listen to Trismegistus when he praiseth our sufficiency: "For man to find out divine nature, and to make it, hath surmounted the admiration of all admirable things." ^B^Lo, here arguments out of philosophy's schools itself,

Only to whom heav'ns deities to know,
Only to whom is giv'n, them not to know.
Lucan I.452.

"If God be, he is a living creature; if he be a living creature, he hath sense; and if he have sense he is subject to corruption. If he be without a body, he is without a soul, and consequently without action; and if he have a body he is corruptible." Is not this brave?

C"We are incapable to have made the world; then is there some more excellent nature that hath set her helping hand unto it. Were it not a sottish arrogancy that we should think ourselves to be the perfectest thing of this universe? Then surely there is some better thing, and that is God. When you see a rich and stately mansion house, although you know not who is owner of it, yet will you not say that it was built for rats. And this more than human frame and divine composition which we see of heaven's palace, must we not deem it to be the mansion of some lord greater than ourselves? Is not the highest ever the most worthy? And we are seated in the lowest place.

"Nothing that is without a soul and void of reason is able to bring forth a living soul capable of reason. The world doth bring us forth; then the world hath both soul and reason.

"Each part of us is less than ourselves; we are part of the world. Then the world is stored with wisdom and with reason, and that more plenteously than we are.

"It is a goodly thing to have a great government. Then the world's government belongeth to some blessed and happy nature.

"The stars annoy us not; then the stars are full of goodness.

B"We have need of nourishment. Then so have the gods, and feed themselves with the vapors arising here below.

C"Worldly goods are not goods unto God. Then are not they goods unto us.

"To offend and to be offended are equal witnesses of imbecility. Then it is folly to fear God.

"God is good by his own nature; man by his industry, which is more.

"Divine wisdom and man's wisdom have no other distinction but that the first is eternal. Now lastingness is not an accession unto wisdom; therefore are we fellows.

B"We have life, reason, and liberty; we esteem goodness, charity, and justice; these qualities are then in him."

In conclusion, the building and destroying the conditions of divinity are forged by man according to the relation to himself. Oh what a pattern and what a model! Let us raise and let us amplify human qualities as much as we please; puff up thyself, poor man, yea, swell and swell again —

> Swell till you break, you shall not be
> Equal to that great one, quoth he.
> Hor. *Sat.* II.iii.318.

[C]"Of a truth, they conceiting not God, whom they cannot conceive, but themselves instead of God, do not compare him but themselves, not to him but themselves" (Aug. *Civ. Dei* XII.xvii.).

[B]In natural things the effects do but half refer their causes. What this? It is above nature's order; its condition is too high, too far out of reach and overswaying to endure that our conclusions should seize upon or fetter the same. It is not by our means we reach unto it; this train is too low. We are no nearer heaven on the top of [Senis] mount than in the bottom of the deepest sea: consider of it that you may see with your astrolabe.

They bring God even to the carnal acquaintance of women, to a prefixed number of times, and to how many generations. Paulina, wife unto Saturnius, a matron of great reputation in Rome, supposing to lie with the god Serapis, by the maquerelage* of the priests of that temple found herself in the arms of a wanton lover of hers.

[C]Varro, the most subtle and wisest Latin author, in his books of divinity writeth that Hercules his sexton, with one hand casting lots for himself and with the other for Hercules, gaged a supper and a wench against him — if he won, at the charge of his offerings; but if he lost, as his own cost. He lost and paid for a supper and a wench. Her name was Laurentina, who by night saw that god in her arms, saying moreover unto her that the next day the first man she met withal should heavenly pay her her wages. It fortuned to be one Taruntius, a very rich young man, who took her home with him and in time left her absolute heir of all he had. And she, when it came to her turn, hoping to do that god some acceptable service, left the Roman heir-general of all her wealth. And therefore she had divine honors attributed unto her.

As if it were not sufficient for Plato to descend originally from the gods by a two-fold line and to have Neptune for the common author of his race, it was certainly believed at Athens that Ariston, desiring to enjoy fair Perictione, he could not, and that in his dream he was warned by god Apollo to leave her untouched and unpolluted until such time as she were brought a-bed; and these were the father and mother of Plato.

How many such-like cuckoldries are there in histories, procured by the gods against silly* mortal men! And husbands most injuriously blazoned* in favor of their children! In Mohammed's religion by the easy belief of that people are many Merlins found: that is to say, fatherless children, spiritual children conceived and borne divinely in the wombs of virgins; and that in their language bear names importing as much.

[B]We must note that nothing is more dear and precious to any thing than its own being [C](the lion, the eagle, and the dolphin esteem nothing above their kind); [B]each thing referreth the qualities of all other things unto her own conditions, which we may either amplify or shorten, but that is all; for besides this principle and out of this reference our imagination cannot go and guess further; and it is impossible it should exceed that or go beyond it. [C]Whence arise these ancient conclusions: of all forms that of man is the fairest; then God is of this form. No man can be happy without virtue, nor can virtue be without reason; and no reason can lodge but in a human shape. God is then invested with a human figure. "The prejudice forestalled in our minds is so framed as the form of a man comes to man's mind when he is thinking of God" (Cic. *De nat. deor.* I.xxvii.).

[B]Therefore Xenophanes said pleasantly that if beasts frame any gods unto themselves, as likely it is they do, they surely frame them like unto themselves and glorify themselves as we do. For why may not a goose say thus: "All parts of the world behold me; the earth serveth me to tread upon, the sun to give me light, the stars to inspire me with influence; this commodity I have of the winds, and this benefit of the waters; there is nothing that this world's vault doth so favorably look upon as myself; I am the favorite of nature. Is it not man that careth for me, that keepeth me, lodgeth me, and serveth me? For me it is he soweth, reapeth, and grindeth. If he eat me, so doth man feed on his fellow, and so do I on the worms that consume and eat him." As much might a crane say, yea, and more boldly, by reason of her flight's liberty and the possession of this goodly and high-bounding region. [C]"So flattering a broker and bawd, as it were, is nature to itself" (Cic. *De nat. deor.* I.xxvii.).

[B]Now by the same consequence, the destinies are for us, the world is for us; it shineth and thundereth for us; both the creator and the creatures are for us. It is the mark and point whereat the university of things aimeth. Survey but the register which philosophy hath kept, these two thousand years and more, of heavenly affairs. The gods never acted, and never spake, but for man; she ascribeth no other consultation nor imputeth other vacation* unto them. Lo, how they are up in arms against us:

And young earth-gallants tamed by the hand
Of Hercules, whereby the habitation
Of old Saturnus did in peril stand
And, shin'd it ne'er so bright, yet fear'd invasion.
Hor. *Odes.* II.xii.6.

See how they are partakers of our troubles, [C]that so they may be even with us, forsomuch as so many times we are partakers of theirs:

[B]Neptunus with his great three-forkèd mace
Shakes the weak wall and tottering foundation,
And from the site the city doth displace.
Fierce Juno first holds ope the gates t' invasion.
Virg. *Aen.* II.610.

[C]The Caunians, for the jealousy of their own gods' domination, upon their devotion day arm themselves and, running up and down, brandishing and striking their air with their glaives, and in this earnest manner they expel all foreign and banish all strange gods from out their territory.

[B]Their powers are limited according to our necessity. Some heal horses, some cure men, [C]some the plague, [B]some the scald,* some the cough, [C]some one kind of scab and some another: "this corrupt religion engageth and inserteth god even in the least matters" (Livy. XXVII. xxiii.); [B]some make grapes to grow, and some garlic, some have the charge of bawdry and uncleanness, and some of merchandise: [C]to every kind of tradesman a god. [B]Some one hath his province and credit in the east, and some in the west:

His armor here,
His chariots there appear.
Virg. *Aen.* I.16.

[C]Sacred Apollo, who enfoldest
The earth's set navel and it holdest.
Cic. *De div.* II.lvi.

Besmeared with blood and gore,
Th' Athenians Pallas, Minos' Candy coast
Diana, Lemnos Vulcan honors most;
Mycene and Sparta Juno think divine;
The coast of Maenalus Faun crowned with pine;
Latium doth Mars adore.
Ovid. *Fast.* III.81.

[B]Some hath but one borough or family in his possession; [C]some lodgeth alone, and some in company, either voluntarily or necessarily.

To the great grandsire's shrine
The nephews temples do combine.
Ovid. *Fast.* I.294.

BSome there are so silly* and popular (for their number amounteth to six and thirty thousand) that five or six of them must be shuffled up together to produce an ear of corn, and thereof they take their several names. CThree to a door, one to be the boards, one to be the hinges, and the third to the threshold; four to a child, as protectors of his bandels,* of his drink, of his meat, and of his sucking; some are certain, others uncertain, some doubtful; and some that come not yet into paradise:

Whom for as yet with heav'n we have not graced,
Let them on earth by our good grant be placed.
Ovid. *Metam.* I.194.

There are some philosophical, some poetical, and some civil; some of a mean condition between divine and human nature, mediators and spokesmen between us and God, worshipped in a kind of second or diminutive order of adoration; infinite in titles and offices; some good, some bad; Bsome old and crazed; and some mortal. For Chrysippus thought that in the last conflagration or burning of the world all the gods should have an end except Jupiter.

CMan feigneth a thousand pleasant societies between God and him. Nay, is he not his countryman?

The isle of famous Crete,
For Jove a cradle meet.
Ovid. *Metam.* VIII.99.

Behold the excuse that Scaevola, chief bishop, and Varro, a great divine, in their days, give us upon the consideration of this subject: "It is necessary (say they) that man be altogether ignorant of true things and believe many false." "Since they seek the truth whereby they may be free, let us believe it is expedient for them to be deceived" (Aug. *Civ. Dei* IV.xxxi.).

BMan's eye cannot perceive things but by the forms of his knowledge. CAnd we remember not the downfall of miserable Phaeton, forsomuch as he undertook to guide the reins of his father's steeds with a mortal hand. Our mind doth still relapse into the same depth, and by her own temerity doth dissipate and bruise itself.

BIf you inquire of philosophy what matter the sun is composed of, what will it answer but of iron and stone or other stuff for his use? CDemand of Zeno what nature is. "A fire," saith he, "an artist fit to engender, and proceeding orderly." BArchimedes, master of this science, and who in truth and certainty assumeth unto himself a precedency above all others, saith the sun is a god of inflamed iron. Is not this a quaint imagination, produced by the inevitable necessity of geometrical demonstrations? Yet not so unavoidable [C]and beneficial but Socrates hath been of opinion that it sufficed to know so much of it as that a man might measure out the land he either demised* or took to rent; and [B]that Polyaenus, who therein had been a famous and principal doctor, after he had tasted the sweet fruits of the lazy, idle, and delicious gardens of Epicurus, did not contemn them as full or falsehood and apparent vanity.

[C]Socrates in Xenophon, upon this point of Anaxagoras, allowed and esteemed of antiquity, well seen and expert above all others in heavenly and divine matters, saith that he weakened his brains much, as all men do who over nicely and greedily will search out those knowledges which hang not for their mowing nor pertain unto them. When he would needs have the sun to be a burning stone, he remembered not that a stone doth not shine in the fire and, which is more, that it consumes therein. And when he made the sun and fire to be all one, he forgot that fire doth not tan and black those he looketh upon; that we fixly* look upon the fire; and that fire consumeth and killeth all plants and herbs. According to the advice of Socrates and mine, the wisest judging of heaven is not to judge of it at all.

Plato, in his *Timaeus*, being to speak of demons and spirits, saith, "It is an enterprise far exceeding my skill and ability. We must believe what those ancient forefathers have said of them who have said to have been engendered by them. It is against reason not to give credit unto the children of the gods, although their sayings be neither grounded upon necessary nor likely reasons, since they tell us that they speak of familiar and household matters."

[A]Let us see whether we have a little more insight in the knowledge of human and natural things.

Is it not a fond* enterprise to those unto which, by our own confession, our learning cannot possibl[y] attain, to devise and forge them another body, and of our own invention to give them a false form? As is seen in the planetary motions unto which, because our mind cannot reach nor imagine their natural conduct, we lend them something of ours, that is to say, material, gross, and corporal springs and wards:*

> The axe-tree gold, the wheels' whole circle gold,
> The rank of rays did all of silver hold.
>
> Ovid. *Metam.* II.107.

You would say we have had coachmakers, carpenters, and painters who have gone up thither and there have placed engines with divers motions [C]and ranged the wheelings, the windings, and interlacements of the celestial bodies diapred* in colors, according to Plato, about the spindle of necessity.

> [B]The world, of things the greatest habitation,
> Which five high-thundering zones by separation
> Engird, through which a scarf depainted fair
> With twice six signs star-shining in the air,
> Obliquely rais'd the wain
> O' th' moon doth entertain.
>
> Varro, in the commentary of Valerius Probus on Virg. *Ecl.* VI.

They are all dreams and mad follies. Why will not nature one day be pleased to open her bosom to us and make us perfectly see the means and conduct of her motions, and enable our eyes to judge of them? O good God, what abuses and what distractions should we find in our poor understanding and weak knowledge! [C]I am deceived if she hold one thing directly in its point; and I shall part hence more ignorant of all other things than mine own ignorance. Have I not seen this divine saying in Plato, that nature is nothing but an enigmatical poesy? As a man might say an overshadowed and dark picture, intershining with an infinite variety of false lights, to exercise our conjectures. "All these things lie hid so veiled and environed with misty darkness as no edge of man is so piercent* as it can pass into heaven or dive into the earth" (Cic. *Acad.* II.xxxix.). And truly, philosophy is nothing else but a sophisticated poesy. Whence have these ancient authors all their authorities but from poets? And the first were poets themselves, and in their art treated the same. Plato is but a loose poet. All high and more than human sciences are decked and enrobed with a poetical style.

[A]Even as women, when their natural teeth fail them, use some of ivory, and instead of a true beauty or lively color lay on some artificial hue; and as they make trunk-sleeves* of wire and whale-bone bodies, backs of lathes, and stiff, bombasted* verdugales,* and to the open view of all men paint and embellish themselves with counterfeit and borrowed beauties; so doth learning [B](and our law hath, as some say, certain lawful fictions, on which it groundeth the truth of justice). [A]Which, in lieu of current payment and presupposition, delivereth us those things which she herself teacheth us to be mere inventions; for these epicycles, eccentrics, and concentrics which astrology useth to direct the state and motions of her stars, she giveth them unto us as the best she could ever invent to fit and suit unto this subject. As in all things else, philosophy presenteth unto us not that which is, or she believeth, but what she inventeth, as having most appearance, likelihood, or comeliness.

[C]Plato, upon the discourse of our body's estate and of that of beasts: "That what we have said is true, we would be assured of it had we but the confirmation of some oracle to confirm it; this only we warrant, that it is the likeliest we could say."

[A]It is not to heaven alone that she sendeth her cordages, her engines, and her wheels. Let us but somewhat consider what she saith of ourselves and of our contexture. There is no more retrogradation, trepidation, augmentation, recoiling, and violence in the stars and celestial bodies than they have feigned and devised in this poor silly* little body of man. Verily they have thence had reason to name it *microcosmos,* or little world, so many several parts and visages have they employed to fashion and frame the same. To accommodate the motions which they see in man, the divers functions and faculties that we feel in ourselves, into how many several parts have they divided our soul? Into how many seats have they placed her? Into how many orders, stages, and stations have they divided this wretched man beside the natural and perceptible? And to how many distinct offices and vacation*? They make a public imaginary thing of it.

It is a subject which they hold and handle. They have all power granted them to rip him, to sever him, to range him, to join and reunite him together again, and to stuff him every one according to his fantasy; and yet they neither have nor possess him. They cannot so order or rule him, not in truth only, but in imagination, but still some cadence or sound is discovered which escapeth their architecture, bad as it is, and botched together with a thousand false patches and fantastical pieces.

[C]And they have no reason to be excused. For to painters, when they portray the heaven, the earth, the seas, the hills, the scattered islands, we pardon them if they but represent us with some slight appearance of them; and, as of things unknown, we are contented with such feigned shadows. But when they draw us, or any subject that is familiarly known unto us, to the life, then seek we to draw from them a perfect and exact representation of theirs or our true lineaments or colors, and scorn if they miss never so little.

[A]I commend the Milesian wench who, seeing Thales the philosopher continually amusing himself in the contemplation of heaven's wide-bounding vault and ever holding his eyes aloft, laid something in his way to make him stumble, thereby to warn and put him in mind that he should not amuse his thoughts about matters above the clouds before he had provided for and well considered those at his feet. Verily she advised him well, and it better became him rather to look to himself than to gaze on heaven; [C]for as Democritus by the mouth of Cicero saith,

> No man looks what before his feet doth lie;
> They seek and search the climates of the sky.
>
> Cic. *De div.* II.xiii.

[A]But our condition beareth that the knowledge of what we touch with our hands, and have amongst us, is as far from us and above the clouds as that of the stars. [C]As saith Socrates in Plato, that one may justly say to him who meddleth with philosophy as the woman said to Thales, which is, he seeth nothing of that which is before him. For every philosopher is ignorant of what his neighbor doth, yea, he knows not what himself doth, and wots not what both are, whether beasts or men.

[A]These people who think Sebond's reasons to be weak and lame, who know nothing themselves, and yet will take upon them to govern the world and know all —

> What cause doth calm the sea, what clears the year;
> Whether stars forc'd or of self-will appear;
> What makes the moon's dark orb to wax or wane;
> What friendly feud of things both will and can.
>
> Hor. *Epist.* I.xii.16.

— did they never sound amid their books the difficulties that present themselves to them to know their own being? We see very well that our finger stirreth and our foot moveth, that some parts of our body move of themselves without our leave and other some that stir but at our pleasure; and we see that certain apprehensions engender a blushing red color, others a paleness; that some imagination doth only work in the milt,* another in the brain; some one induceth us to laugh, another causeth us to weep; some astonisheth* and stupefieth all our senses and stayeth the motion of all our limbs; [C]at some object the stomach riseth, and at some other the lower parts.

[A]But how a spiritual impression causeth or worketh such a dent or flaw in a massy and solid body or subject, and the nature of the conjoining and compacting of these admirable springs and wards,* man yet never knew. [C]"All uncertain in reason and hid in the majesty of nature," saith Pliny; and Saint Augustine, "The mean is clearly wonderful whereby spirits cleave to our bodies, nor can it be comprehended by man, and that is very man" (Pliny *Hist. nat.* II.xxxvii.; Aug. *Civ. Dei* XXI.x.). [A]Yet is there no doubt made of him; for men's opinions are received after ancient beliefs, by authority and upon credit, as if it were a religion and a law. What is commonly held of it is received as a gibberish or fustian* tongue. Thus truth with all her framing of arguments and proportioning of proofs is received as a firm and solid body, which is no more shaken, which is no more judged. On the other side, everyone, the best he can, patcheth up and comforteth this received belief with all the means his reason can afford him, which is an instrument very supple, pliable, and yielding to all shapes. Thus is the world filled with toys and overwhelmed in lies and leasings.*

The reason that men doubt not much of things is that common impressions are never thoroughly tried and sifted; their ground is not sounded, nor where the fault and weakness lieth. Men only debate and question of the branch, not of the tree. They ask not whether a thing be true, but whether it was understood or meant thus and thus. They inquire not whether Galen hath spoken anything of worth, but whether thus, or so, or otherwise. Truly there was some reason this bridle or restraint of our judgment's liberty and this tyranny over our beliefs should extend itself even to schools and arts.

The god of scholastical learning is Aristotle. It is religion to debate of his ordinances, as of those of Lycurgus in Sparta. His doctrine is to us as a canon law, which peradventure is as false as another. I know not why I should or might not as soon and as easy accept either Plato's Idea or Epicurus his atoms and indivisible things, or the fulness and emptiness of Leucippus and Democritus, or the water of Thales, or of Anaximander's infinite of nature, or the air of Diogenes, or the numbers of proportion of Pythagoras, or the infinite of Parmenides, or the single One of Musaeus, or the water and fire of Apollodorus, or the similary and resembling parts of Anaxagoras, or the discord and concord of Empedocles, or the fire of Heraclitus, or any other opinion of this infinite confusion of opinions and sentences which this goodly human reason, by her certainty and clear-sighted vigilancy brings forth in whatsoever it meddleth withal — as I should of Aristotle's conceit, touching this subject of the principles of natural things, which he frameth of three parts, that is to say, matter, form, and privation. And what greater vanity can there be than to make inanity itself the cause of the production of things? Privation is a negative. With what humor could he make it the cause and beginning of things that are? Yet durst no man move that but for an exercise of logic. Wherein nothing is disputed to put it in doubt, but to defend the author of the school from strange objections. His authority is the mark beyond which it is not lawful to inquire.

It is easy to frame what one list* upon allowed foundations; for according to the law and ordinance of this positive beginning the other parts of the frame are easily directed without crack or danger. By which way we find our reason well grounded, and we discourse without rub or let* in the way. For our masters preoccupate and gain aforehand as much place in our belief as they need to conclude afterward what they please, as geometricians do by their granted questions; the consent and approbation which we lend them giving them wherewith to draw us either on the right or left hand, and at their pleasure to wind and turn us. Whatsoever is believed in his presuppositions, he is our master and our god; he will lay the plot of his foundations so ample and easy that, if he list,* he will carry us up even unto the clouds.

In this practice or negotiation of learning, we have taken the saying of Pythagoras for current payment, which is that every expert man ought to be believed in his own trade. The logician referreth himself to the grammarian for the signification of words; the rhetorician borroweth the places of arguments from the logician; the poet his measures from the musician; the geometrician his proportions from the arithmetician; the metaphysics take the conjectures of the physics for a ground. For every art hath her presupposed principles by which man's judgment is bridled on all parts. If you come to the shock or front of this bar in which consists the principal error, they immediately pronounce this sentence: that there is no disputing against such as deny principles.

There can be no principles in men except divinity hath revealed unto them. All the rest, both beginning, middle, and end, is but a dream and a vapor. Those that argue by presupposition, we must presuppose against them the very same axiom which is disputed of. For each human presupposition and every invention, unless reason make a difference of it, hath as much authority as another. So must they all be equally balanced, and first the general and those that tyrannize us. [C]A persuasion of certainty is a manifest testimony of foolishness and of extreme uncertainty; and no people are less philosophers and more foolish than Plato's "philodoxes," or lovers of their own opinions.

[A]We must know whether fire be hot, whether snow be white, whether in our knowledge there be anything hard or soft. And touching the answers, whereof they tell old tales — as to him who made a doubt of heat, to whom one replied that to try he should cast himself into the fire; to him that denied the ice to be cold, that he should put some in his bosom — they are most unworthy the profession of a philosopher. If they had left us in our own natural estate, admitting of strange apparences* as they present themselves unto us by our senses, and had suffered us to follow our natural appetites, directed by the condition of our birth, they should then have reason to speak so. But from them it is that we have learned to become judges of the world. It is from them we hold this conceit, that man's reason is the general controller of all that is, both without and within heaven's vault, which embraceth all and can do all, by means whereof all things are known and discerned.

This answer were good among the cannibals, who without any of Aristotle's precepts or so much as knowing the name of natural philosophy, enjoy most happily a long, quiet, and a peaceable life. This answer might haply avail more, and be of more force, than all those they can borrow from their reason and invention. All living creatures, yea, beasts and all, where the commandment of the natural law is yet pure and simple, might with us be capable of this answer; but they have renounced it.

They shall not need to tell me, "It is true, for you both hear and see that it is so." They must tell me if what I think I feel, I feel the same in effect; and if I feel it, then let them tell me wherefore I feel it, and how, and what. Let them tell me the name, the beginning, the tennons* and the abuttings* of heat and of cold, with the qualities of him that is agent or of the patient; or let them quit me their profession, which is neither to admit nor approve anything but by the way of reason. It is their touchstone to try all kinds of essays;* but surely it is a touchstone full of falsehood, errors, imperfection, and weakness.

Which way can we better make trial of it than by itself? If she may not be credited speaking of herself, hardly can she fit to judge of strange matters. If she know anything it can be but her being and domicile. She is in the soul, and either a part or effect of the same. For the true and essential reason, whose name we steal by false signs, lodgeth in God's bosom. There is her home, and there is her retreat; thence she takes her flight, when God's pleasure is that we shall see some some glimpse of it, even as Pallas issued out of her father's head to communicate and impart herself unto the world.

Now let us see what man's reason hath taught us of herself and of the soul. [C]Not of the soul in general, whereof well nigh all philosophy maketh both the celestial and first bodies partakers; nor of that which Thales attributed even unto things that are reputed without soul or life, drawn thereunto by the consideration of the adamant stone; but of that which appertaineth to us and which we should know best:

> [B]What the soul's nature is we do not know—
> If it be bred, or put in those are bred,
> Whether by death divorced with us it go,
> Or see the dark vast lakes of hell below,
> Or into other creatures turn the head.
>
> Lucr. I.113.

[A]To Crates and Dicaearchus it seemed that there was none at all, but that the body stirred thus with and by a natural motion; to Plato, that it was a substance moving of itself; to Thales, a nature without rest; to Asclepiades, an exercitation of the senses; to Hesiodus and Anaximander, a thing composed of earth and water; to Parmenides, of earth and fire; to Empedocles, of blood:

> His soul of purple blood he vomits out.
> Virg. *Aen.* IX.349.

To Posidonius, Cleanthes, and Galen, a heat or hot complexion:

> A fiery vigor and celestial spring
> In their original they strangely bring.
> Virg. *Aen.* VI.730.

To Hippocrates, a spirit dispersed through the body; to Varro, an air received in at the mouth, heated in the lungs, tempered in the heart, and dispersed through all parts of the body; to Zeno, the quintessence of the four elements; to Heraclides Ponticus, the light; to Xenocrates and to the Egyptians, a moving number; to the Chaldaeans, a virtue without any determinate form.

> [B]There of the body is a vital frame,
> The which the Greeks a harmony do name.
> Lucr. III.100.

[A]And not forgetting Aristotle: that which naturally causeth the body to move, who calleth it entelechy, or perfection moving of itself — as cold an invention as any other, for he neither speaketh of the essence, nor of the beginning, nor of the soul's nature, but only noteth the effects of it. Lactantius, Seneca, and the better part amongst the dogmatists have confessed they never understood what it was.

[C]And after all this rabble of opinions — "Which of these opinions is true, let some god look unto it," saith Cicero (Cic. *Tusc.* I.xi.) — [A]"I know by myself," quoth Saint Bernard, "how God is incomprehensible, since I am not able to comprehend the parts of mine own being" (*De anima* I.). [C]Heraclitus, who held that every place was full of souls and demons, maintained nevertheless that a man could never go so far towards the knowledge of the soul as that he could come unto it, so deep and mysterious was her essence.

[A]There is no less dissension nor disputing about the place where she should be seated. Hippocrates and Hierophilus place it in the ventricle of the brain; Democritus and Aristotle, through all the body:

> [B]As health is of the body said to be,
> Yet is no part of him, in health we see;
> Lucr. III.103.

[A]Epicurus in the stomach:

> [B]For in these places fear doth domineer,
> And near these places joy keeps merry cheer.
> Lucr. III.142.

[A]The Stoics, within and about the heart; Erasistratus, joining the membrane of the epicranium; Empedocles, in the blood; as also Moses, which was the cause he forbad the eating of beasts' blood, unto which their soul is commixed. Galen thought that every part of the body had his soul; Strato hath placed it between the two upper eyelids.

[C]"We must not so much as inquire what face the mind bears or where it dwells," saith Cicero (Cic. *Tusc.* I.xxviii.). I am well pleased to let this man use his own words; for why should I alter the speech of eloquence itself, since there is small gain in stealing matter from his inventions: they are both little used, not forcible, and little unknown.

[A]But the reason why Chrysippus and those of his sect will prove the soul to be about the heart is not to be forgotten. "It is," saith he, "because when we will affirm or swear anything we lay our hand upon the stomach; and when we will pronounce ἐγώ, which signifieth *myself,* we put down our chin toward the stomach." This passage ought not to be passed over without noting the vanity of so great a personage; for besides that his considerations are of themselves very slight, the latter proveth but to the Grecians that they have their soul in that place. No human judgment is so vigilant or Argus-eyed but sometimes shall fall asleep or slumber.

[C]What shall we fear to say? Behold the Stoics, fathers of human wisdom, who devise that the soul of man overwhelmed with any ruin laboreth and panteth a long time to get out, unable to free herself from that charge, even as a mouse taken in a trap.

Some are of opinion that the world was made to give a body, in lieu of punishment, unto the spirits, which through their fault were fallen from the purity wherein they were created, the first creation having been incorporeal; and that according as they have more or less removed themselves from their spirituality, so are they more or less merrily and jovially, or rudely and saturnally, incorporated. Whence proceedeth the infinite variety of so much matter created. But the spirit who, for his chastisement, was invested with the body of the sun must of necessity have a very rare and particular measure of alteration.

The extremities of our curious search turn to a glimmering and all to a dazzling; as Plutarch saith of the offspring of histories, that after the manner of cards or maps the utmost limits of known countries are set down to be full of thick marrish* grounds, shady forests, desert and uncouth places. See here wherefore the grossest and most childish dotings are more commonly found in these which treat of highest and furthest matters, even confounding and overwhelming themselves in their own curiosity and presumption. The end and beginning of learning are equally accounted foolish.

Mark but how Plato taketh and raiseth his flight aloft in his poetical clouds, or cloudy poesies. Behold and read in him the gibberish of the gods. But what dreamed or doted he on when[A] he defined man to be a creature with two feet and without feathers, giving them that were disposed to mock at him a pleasant and scopeful occasion to do it? For, having plucked off the feathers of a live capon, they named him "the man of Plato."

And by what simplicity did the Epicureans first imagine that the atoms or motes which they termed to be bodies, having some weight and a natural moving downward, had framed the world; until such time as they were advised by their adversaries that by this description it was not possible they should join and take hold one of another, their fall being so downright and perpendicular, and every way engendering parallel lines? And therefore was it necessary they should afterward add a casual moving sidling unto them, and moreover to give their atoms crooked and forked tails, that so they might take hold of anything and clasp themselves.

[C]And even then, those that pursue them with this other consideration, do they not much trouble them? If atoms have by chance formed so many sorts of figures, why did they never meet together to frame a house, or make a shoe. Why should we not likewise believe that an infinite number of Greek letters confusedly scattered in some open place might one day meet and join together to the contexture of the *Iliads*?

That which is capable of reason, saith Zeno, is better than that which is not. There is nothing better than the world; then the world is capable of reason. By the same arguing Cotta maketh the world a mathematician, and by this other arguing of Zeno, he makes him a musician and an organist. The whole is more than the part; we are capable of wisdom, and we are part of the world: then the world is wise.

[A]There are infinite like examples seen not only of false but foolish arguments, which cannot hold and which accuse their authors not so much of ignorance as of folly, in the reproaches that philosophers charge one another with about the disagreeings in their opinions and sects. [C]He that should fardle* up a bundle or huddle of the fooleries of man's wisdom might recount wonders.

I willingly assemble some as a show or pattern by some means or bias no less profitable than the most moderate instructions. [A]Let us by that judge what we are to esteem of man, of his sense, and of his reason; since in these great men, and who have raised man's sufficiency so high, there are found so gross errors and so apparent defects. As for me, I would rather believe that they have thus casually treated learning even as a sporting child's baby and have sported themselves with reason as of a vain and frivolous instrument, setting forth all sorts of inventions, devices, and fantasies, sometimes more outstretched, and sometimes more loose. The same Plato who defineth man like unto a capon saith elsewhere, after Socrates, that in good sooth he knoweth not what man is, and that of all parts of the world there is none so hard to be known.

By this variety of conceits and instability of opinions they, as it were, lead us closely by the hand to this resolution of their irresolution. They make a profession not always to present their advice manifest and unmasked; they have oft concealed the same under the fabulous shadows of poesy, and sometimes under other vizards.* For our imperfection admitteth this also, that raw meats are not always good for our stomachs, but they must be dried, altered, and corrupted, and so do they who sometimes shadow their simple opinions and judgments; and that they may the better suit themselves unto common use, they many times falsify them. They will not make open profession of ignorance and of the imbecility of man's reason, [C]because they will not make children afraid; [A]but they manifestly declare the same unto us under the show of a troubled science and unconstant learning.

[B]I persuade[d] somebody in Italy, who labored very much to speak Italian, that always provided he desired but to be understood and not to seek to excel others therein, he should only employ and use such words as came first to his mouth, whether they were Latin, French, Spanish, or Gascon, and that adding the Italian terminations unto them, he should never miss to fall upon some idiom of the country, either Tuscan, Roman, Venetian, Piedmontese, or Neapolitan, and amongst so many several forms of speech to take hold of one. The very same I say of philosophy. She hath so many faces, and so much variety, and hath said so much, that all our dreams and devices are found in her. The fantasy of man can conceive or imagine nothing, be it good or evil, that is not to be found in her. [C]"Nothing may be spoken so absurdly but that it is spoken by some of the philosophers" (Cic. *De div.* II.lviii.). [B]And therefore do I suffer my humors or caprices more freely to pass in public; forasmuch as, though they are borne with and of me and without any pattern, well I wot they will be found to have relation to some ancient humor, and some shall be found that will both know and tell whence and of whom I have borrowed them.

[C]My customs are natural. When I contrived them, I called not for the help of any discipline. And weak and faint as they were, when I have had a desire to express them and to make them appear to the world a little more comely and decent, I have somewhat endeavored to aid them with discourse and assist them with examples. I have wondered at myself, that by mere chance I have met with them agreeing and suitable to so many ancient examples and philosophical discourses. What regimen my life was of I never knew nor learned but after it was much worn and spent. A new figure: an unpremeditated philosopher and a casual!

[A]But to return unto our soul. Where Plato hath seated reason in the brain, anger in the heart, lust in the liver, it is very likely that it was rather an interpretation of the soul's motions than any division or separation he meant to make of it, as of a body into many members. And the likeliest of their opinion is that it is always a soul, which by her rational faculty remembereth herself, comprehendeth, judgeth, desireth, and exerciseth all her other functions by divers instruments of the body, as the pilot ruleth and directeth his ship according to the experience he hath of it, now stretching, haling, or loosing a cable, sometimes hoisting the mainyard, removing an oar, or stirring the rudder, causing several effects with one only power. And that she abideth in the brain appeareth by this, that the hurts and accidents which touch that part do presently offend the faculties of the soul, whence she may without inconvenience descend and glide through other parts of the body —

> [C]Never the sun forsakes heav'n's middle ways,
> Yet with his rays he lights all, all surveys.
> Claudian *De sexto Cons. Hon.* V.411.

—[A]as the sun spreadeth his light and infuseth his power from heaven and therewith filleth the whole world.

> [B]Th'other part of the soul through all the body sent
> Obeys and moved is, by the mind's government.
> Lucr. III.144.

[A]Some have said that there was a general soul, like unto a great body, from which all particular souls were extracted and returned thither, always reconjoining and intermingling themselves unto that universal matter:

> For God through all the earth to pass is found,
> Through all sea-currents, through the heav'n profound;

Here hence men, herds, and all wild beasts that are
Short life in birth each to themselves do share.
All things resolved to this point restor'd
Return, nor any place to death afford.
Virg. *Georg.* IV.221.

Others, that they did but reconjoin and fasten themselves to it again; others, that they were produced by the divine substance; others, by the angels, of fire and air. Some, from the beginning of the world, and some, even at the time of need. Others make them to descend from the round of the moon and that they return to it again. The common sort of antiquity, that they are begotten from father to son, after the same manner and production that all other natural things are, arguing so by the resemblances which are between fathers and children:

Thy father's virtues be
Instilled into thee;
(Unknown)

Of valiant sires and good
There comes a valiant brood;
Hor. *Odes.* IV.iv.29.

and that from fathers we see descend unto children not only the marks of their bodies, but also a resemblance of humors, of complexions, and inclinations of the soul:

Why follows violence the savage lion's race?
Why craft the fox's? Why to deer to fly apace?
By parents it is given, when parents fear incites,
Unless because a certain force of inward spirits
With all the body grows,
As seed and seed-spring goes;
Lucr. III.741.

that divine justice is grounded thereupon, punishing the fathers' offenses upon the children; forsomuch as the contagion of the fathers' vices is in some sort printed in childrens' souls, and that the misgovernment of their will toucheth them.

Moreover, that if the souls came from any other place than by a natural consequence, and that out of the body they should have been some other thing, they should have some remembrance of their first being, considering the natural faculties which are proper unto him, to discourse, to reason, and to remember:

[B]If our soul at our birth be in our body cast,
Why can we not remember ages over-past,
Nor any marks retain of things done first or last?
Lucr. III.671.

[A]For to make our soul's condition to be of that worth we would, they must all be presupposed wise, even when they are in their natural simplicity and genuine purity. So should they have been such, being freed from the corporal prison as well before they entered the same as we hope they shall be when they shall be out of it. And it were necessary they should, being yet in the body, remember the said knowledge, as Plato said, that what we learned was but a new remembering of that which we had known before — a thing that any man may by experience maintain to be false and erroneous. First, because we do not precisely remember what we are taught, and that if memory did merely execute her function she would at least suggest us with something besides our learning. Secondly, what she knew being in her purity was a true understanding, knowing things as they are by her divine intelligence; whereas here, if she be instructed, she is made to receive lies and apprehend vice; wherein she cannot employ her memory, this image and conception having never had place in her.

To say that the corporal prison doth so suppress her natural faculties that they are altogether extinct in her, first, is clean contrary to this other belief, to acknowledge her forces so great and the operations which men in this transitory life feel of it so wonderful as to have thereby concluded this divinity, and forepast eternity, and the immortality to come:

> [B]If of our mind the power be so much altered,
> As of things done all hold, all memory is fled,
> Then, as I guess, it is not far from being dead.
>
> Lucr. III.674.

[A]Moreover, it is here with us and nowhere else that the soul's powers and effects are to be considered. All the rest of her perfections are vain and unprofitable unto her; it is by her present condition that all her immortality must be rewarded and paid, and she is only accountable for the life of man. It were injustice to have abridged her of her means and faculties and to have disarmed her against the time of her captivity and prison, of her weakness and sickness, of the time and season where she had been forced and compelled to draw the judgment and condemnation of infinite and endless continuance and to rely upon the consideration of so short a time, which is peradventure of one or two hours or, if the worst happen, of an age, which have no more proportion with [infinity] than a moment, definitively to appoint and establish of all her being by that instant of space. It were an impious disproportion to wrest an eternal reward in consequence of so short a life.

[C]Plato, to save himself from this inconvenience, would have future payments limited to a hundred years' continuance, relatively unto a human continuance; and many of ours have given them temporal limits.

[A]By this they judged that her generation followed the common condition of human things, as also her life, by the opinion of Epicurus and Democritus, which hath most been received, following these goodly apparances*: that her birth was seen when the body was capable of her; her virtue and strength was perceived as the corporal increased; in her infancy might her weakness be discerned, and in time her vigor and ripeness, then her decay and age, and in the end her decrepitude:

> The mind is with the body bred, we do behold;
> It jointly grows with it; with it it waxeth old.
>
> Lucr. III.445.

They perceived her to be capable of diverse passions and agitated by many languishing and painful motions, wherethrough she fell into weariness and grief, capable of alteration and change, of joy, stupefaction, and languishment; subject to her infirmities, diseases, and offenses, even as the stomach or the foot:

> [B]We see, as bodies sick are cur'd, so is the mind;
> We see how physic can it each way turn and wind;
>
> Lucr. III.510.

[A]dazzled and troubled by the force of wine; removed from her seat by the vapors of a burning fever; drowsy and sleepy by the application of some medicaments, and roused up again by the virtue of some others:

> [B]The nature of the mind must needs corporeal be;
> For with corporeal darts and strokes it's griev'd, we see.
>
> Lucr. III.176.

[A]She was seen to dismay and confound all her faculties by the only biting of a sick dog, and to contain no great constancy of discourse, no sufficiency, no virtue, no philosophical resolution, no contention of her forces, that might exempt her from the subjection of these accidents. The spittle or slavering of a mastiff dog shed upon Socrates his hands, to trouble all his wisdom, to distemper his great and regular imaginations, and so to vanquish and annul them, that no sign or show of his former knowledge was left in him:

> [B]The soul's force is disturbed, separated,
> Distraught by that same poison, alienated.
>
> Lucr. III.498.

[A]And the said venom to find no more resistance in his soul than in that of a child of four years old, a venom able to make all philosophy (were she incarnate) become furious and mad. So that Cato, who scorned both death and fortune, could not abide the sight of a looking-glass, or of water; overcome with horror and quelled with amazement, as if by the contagion of a mad dog, he had fallen into that sickness which physicians call hydrophobia, or fear of waters:

> [B]The force of the disease dispers'd through joints offends,
> Driving the soul, as in salt seas the wave ascends,
> Foaming by furious force which the wind raging lends.
>
> Lucr. III.491.

[A]Now concerning this point, philosophy hath indeed armed man for the enduring of all other accidents, whether of patience or, if it be over-costly to be found, of an infallible defeat, in conveying herself altogether from the sense. But they are means which serve a soul that is her own and in her proper force, capable of discourse and deliberation; not to this inconvenience where, with a philosopher, a soul becometh the soul of a fool troubled, vanquished, and lost; which divers occasions may produce, as in an over-violent agitation, which by some vehement passion the soul may beget in herself, or a hurt in some part of the body, or an exhalation from the stomach, casting us into some astonishment,* dazzling, or giddiness of the head:

> [B]The mind in body's sickness often wandering strays;
> For it enraged raves, and idle talk outbrays;
> Brought by sharp lethargy sometime to more than deep,
> While eyes and eyelids fall into eternal sleep.
>
> Lucr. III.464.

[A]Philosophers have in mine opinion but slightly harped upon this string.

[C]No more than another of like consequence. They have ever this dilemma in their mouth, to comfort our mortal condition: "The soul is either mortal or immortal; if mortal, she shall be without pain; if immortal, she shall mend." They never touch the other branch: "What if she impair and be worse?" And leave the menaces of future pains to poets. But thereby they deal themselves a good game. They are two omissions which, in their discourses, do often offer themselves unto me. I come to the first again.[25]

[A]The soul loseth the use of that Stoical chief felicity, so constant and so firm. Our goodly wisdom must necessarily in this place yield herself and quit her weapons. As for other matters, they also considered by the vanity of man's reason that the mixture and society of

[25] I.e., to the weakness of even the strongest soul.

two so different parts as is the mortal and the immortal is imaginable:

> For what immortal is, mortal to join unto
> And think they can agree and mutual duties do,
> Is to be foolish. For what think we stranger is,
> More disagreeable, or more disjoin'd than this,
> That mortal with immortal endless join'd in union
> Can most outrageous storms endure in their communion?
>
> Lucr. III.801.

Moreover, they felt their soul to be engaged in death, as well as the body:

> BIt jointly faints in one,
> Wearied as age is gone.
>
> Lucr. III.459.

CWhich thing, according to Zeno, the image of sleep doth manifestly show unto us. For he esteemeth that it is a fainting and declination of the soul, as well as of the body: "He thinks the mind is contracted and doth, as it were, slide and fall down" (Cic. *De div.* II.lviii.). AAnd that (which is perceived in some) its force and vigor maintaineth itself even in the end of life, they referred and imputed the same to the diversity of diseases, as men are seen in that extremity to maintain, some one sense, and some another, some their hearing, and some their smelling, without any alteration. And there is no weakness or decay seen so universal but some entire and vigorous parts will remain:

> BNo otherwise than if, when sick man's foot doth ache,
> Meantime, perhaps, his head no fellow-feeling take.
>
> Lucr. III.111.

Our judgment's sight referreth itself unto truth, as doth the owl's eyes unto the shining of the sun, as saith Aristotle. How should we better convince him than by so gross blindness in so apparent a light?

AFor the contrary opinion of the soul's immortality, Cwhich Cicero saith to have first been brought in, at least by the testimony of books, by Pherecydes Syrius, in the time of King Tullus (others ascribe the invention thereof to Thales, and other to others), Ait is the part of human knowledge treated most sparingly and with more doubt. The most constant dogmatists (namely in this point) are enforced to cast themselves under the shelter of the academic's wings. No man knows what Aristotle hath established upon this subject; Cno more than all the ancients in general, who handle the same with a very wavering belief: "who rather promise than approve a thing most acceptable" (Sen. *Epist.* CII.). AHe hath hidden himself under the clouds of intricate and ambiguous words and unintelligible senses, and hath left his sectaries as much cause to dispute upon his judgment as upon the matter.

Two things made this his opinion plausible to them: the one, that without the immortality of souls there should no means be left to ground or settle the vain hopes of glory, a consideration of wonderful credit in the world; the other, [C]as Plato saith, [A]that it is a most profitable impression that vices, when they steal away from out the sight and knowledge of human justice, remain ever as a blank before divine justice, which even after the death of the guilty will severely pursue them.

[C]Man is ever possessed with an extreme desire to prolong his being, and hath to the uttermost of his skill provided for it. Tombs and monuments are for the preservation of his body, and glory for the continuance of his name. He hath employed all his wit to frame himself anew, as impatient of his fortune, and to underprop or uphold himself by his inventions. The soul, by reason of her trouble and imbecility, as unable to subsist of herself, is ever and in all places questing and searching comforts, hopes, foundations, and foreign circumstances on which she may take hold and settle herself. And how light and fantastical soever his invention doth frame them unto him, he notwithstanding relieth more surely upon them and more willingly than upon himself.

[A]But it is a wonder to see how the most obstinate in this so just and manifest persuasion of our spirit's immortality have found themselves short and unable to establish the same by their human forces. [C]"These are dreams not of one that teacheth, but wisheth that he would have," said an ancient writer (Cic. *Acad.* II.xxxviii.). [A]Man may by his own testimony know that the truth he alone discovereth, the same he oweth unto fortune and chance; since even when she is fallen into his hands, he wanteth wherewith to lay hold on her and keep her; and that this reason hath not the power to prevail with it. All things produced by our own discourse and sufficiency, as well true as false, are subject to uncertainty and disputation. It is for the punishment of our temerity and instruction of our misery and incapacity that God caused the trouble, downfall, and confusion of Babel's tower.

Whatsoever we attempt without his assistance, whatever we see without the lamp of his grace, is but vanity and folly. With our weakness we corrupt and adulterate the very essence of truth (which is uniform and constant) when fortune giveth us the possession of it. What course soever man taketh of himself, it is God's permission that he ever cometh to that confusion, whose image he so lively representeth unto us, by the just punishment wherewith he framed the presumptuous over-weening of Nimrod and brought to nothing the frivolous enterprises of the building of his high-towering pyramids or heaven-menacing tower. C"I will destroy the wisdom of the wise, and reprove the providence of them that are most prudent" (I Cor. i.19.). AThe diversity of tongues and languages, wherewith he disturbed that work and overthrew that proudly raised pile — what else is it but this infinite altercation and perpetual discordance of opinions and reasons which accompanieth and entangleth the frivolous frame of man's learning or vain building of human science? CWhich he doth most profitably. Who might contain us had we but one grain of knowledge? This saint hath done me much pleasure: "The very concealing of the profit is either an exercise of humility or a beating down of arrogancy" (Aug. *Civ. Dei.* XI.xxiii.). Unto what point of presumption and insolency do we not carry our blindness and foolishness?

ABut to return to my purpose. Verily there was great reason that we should be beholding to God alone, and to the benefit of his grace, for the truth of so noble a belief, since from his liberality alone we receive the fruit of immortality, which consisteth in enjoying of eternal blessedness. CLet us ingenuously confess that only God and faith hath told it us; for it is no lesson of nature, nor coming from our reason. And he that shall both within and without narrowly sift and curiously sound his being and his forces without this divine privilege; he that shall view and consider man, without flattering him, shall not find nor see either efficacy or faculty in him that tasteth of any other thing but death and earth. The more we give, the more we owe; and the more we yield unto God, the more Christianlike do we.

That which the Stoic philosopher said, he held by the casual consent of the people's voice. Had it not been better he held it of God? "When we discourse of the immortality of souls, in my conceit the consent of those men is of no small authority who either fear or adore the infernal powers. This public persuasion I make use of" (Sen. *Epist.* CXVII.).

ANow the weakness of human arguments upon this subject is very manifestly known by the fabulous circumstances they have added unto the train of this opinion to find out what condition this our immortality was of. CLet us omit the Stoics — "they grant us use of life, as is unto ravens; they say our souls shall long continue, but they deny they shall last ever" (Cic. *Tusc.* I.xxxi.) — who give unto souls a life beyond this but finite. AThe most universal and received fantasy, and which endureth to this day, hath been that whereof Pythagoras is made author; not that he was the first inventor of it, but because it received much force and credit by the authority of his approbation. Which is, that souls at their departure from us did but pass and roll from one to another body, from a lion to a horse, from a horse to a king, incessantly wandering up and down, from house to mansion. CAnd himself said that he remembered to have been Aethalides, then Euphorbus, afterward Hermotimus, at last from Pyrrhus to have passed into Pythagoras; having memory of himself the space of two hundred and six years.

Some added, more, that the same souls do sometimes ascend up to heaven and come down again:

> Must we think, father, some souls hence do go,
> Raised to heav'n, thence turn to bodies slow?
> Whence doth so dire desire of light on wretches grow?
>
> Virg. *Aen.* VI.719.

Origen makes them eternally to go and come from a good to a bad estate. The opinion that Varro reporteth is that in the revolution of four hundred and forty years they reconjoin themselves unto their first bodies; Chrysippus, that that must come to pass after a certain space of time unknown and not limited; Plato, who saith that he holds this opinion from Pindarus and from ancient poesy, of infinite vicissitudes of alteration, to which the soul is prepared, having no pains nor rewards in the other world but temporal, as her life in this is but temporal, concludeth in her a singular knowledge of the affairs of heaven, of hell, and here below, where she hath passed, repassed, and sojourned in many voyages: a matter in his remembrance.

Behold her progress elsewhere: "He that hath lived well, reconjoineth himself unto that star or planet to which he is assigned; who evil, passeth into a woman, and if then he amend not himself he transchangeth himself into a beast of condition agreeing to his vicious customs, and shall never see an end of his punishments until he return to his natural condition and by virtue of reason he have deprived himself of those gross, stupid, and elementary qualities that were in him" (adapted from Plato's *Timaeus*).

ABut I will not forget the objection which the Epicureans make unto this transmigration from one body to another, which is very pleasant. They demand what order there should be if the throng of the dying should be greater than that of such as be born. For, the souls removed from their abode would throng and strive together who should get the best seat in this new case; and demand besides, what they would pass their time about whilst they should stay until any other mansion were made ready for them. Or contrariwise, if more creatures were born than should die, they say bodies should be in an ill taking, expecting the infusion of their soul, and it would come to pass that some of them should die before they had ever been living:

Lastly, ridiculous it is souls should be pressed
To Venus' meetings, and begetting of a beast;
That they to mortal limbs immortal be addressed
In number numberless, and over-hasty strive
Which of them first and chief should get in there to live.
Lucr. III.777.

Others have stayed the soul in the deceased bodies, therewith to animate serpents, worms, and other beasts, which are said to engender from the corruption of our members, yea, and from our ashes. Others divide it in two parts, one mortal, another immortal. Others make it corporeal and yet, notwithstanding, immortal. Others make it immortal without any science or knowledge. Nay, there are some of ours who have deemed that of condemned men's souls devils were made, as Plutarch thinks that gods are made of those souls which are saved; for there be few things that this author doth more resolutely aver than this, holding everywhere else an ambiguous and doubtful kind of speech. "It is to be imagined and firmly believed," saith he, "that the souls of men virtuous both according unto nature and divine justice become of men saints, and of saints demigods, and after they are once perfectly (as in sacrifices of purgation) cleansed and purified, being delivered from all passibility and mortality, they become of demigods — not by any civil ordinance, but in good truth and according to manifest reason — perfect and very, very gods, receiving a most blessed and thrice glorious end."

But whosoever shall see him, who is notwithstanding one of the most sparing and moderate of that faction, so undauntedly to skirmish and will hear him relate his wonders upon this subject, him I refer to his discourse of the moon and of Socrates his demon, where as evidently as in any other place may be averred that the mysteries of philosophy have many strange conceits common with those of poesy; man's understanding losing itself if it once go about to sound and control all things to the utmost end; as, tired and troubled by a long and wearisome course of our life, we return to a kind of doting childhood.

Note here the goodly and certain instructions which, concerning our soul's subject, we draw from human knowledge.

There is no less rashness in that which she teacheth us touching our corporal parts. Let us make choice but of one or two examples, else should we lose ourselves in this troublesome and vast ocean of physical errors.

Let us know whether they agree but in this one, that is to say, of what matter men are derived and produced one from another. [C]For, touching their first production, it is no marvel if in a thing so high and so ancient, man's wit is troubled and confounded. Archelaus, the physician, to whom, as Aristoxenus affirmeth, Socrates was disciple and minion, assevered that both men and beasts had been made of milky slime or mud, expressed by the heat of the earth.

^A^Pythagoras saith that our seed is the scum or froth of our best blood; Plato, the distilling of the marrow in the backbone, which he argueth thus: because that place feeleth first the weariness which followeth the generative business. Alcmaeon, a part of the brain's substance; which to prove, he saith, their eyes are ever most troubled that over-intemperately addict themselves to that exercise. Democritus, a substance extracted from all parts of the corporal mass. Epicurus, extracted from the soul and the body. Aristotle, an excrement drawn from the nourishment of the blood, the last [that] scattereth itself in our several members. Others, blood, concocted and digested by the heat of the genitories, which they judge because in the extreme, earnest, and forced labors, many shed drops of pure blood; wherein some apparance* seemeth to be, if from so infinite a confusion any likelihood may be drawn. But to bring this seed to effect, how many contrary opinions make they of it? Aristotle and Democritus hold that women have no sperm, that it is but a sweat, which by reason of the pleasure and frication* they cast forth, and availeth nothing in generation. Galen and his adherents contrariwise affirm that there can be no generation except two seeds meet together.

Behold the physicians, the philosophers, the lawyers, and the divines pell-mell together by the ears with our women about the question and disputation how long women bear their fruit in their womb. And as for me, by mine own example, I take their part that maintain a woman may go eleven months with child. The world is framed of this experience; there is no mean* woman so simple that cannot give her censure upon all these contestations, although we could not agree.

This is sufficient to verify that in the corporal part man is no more instructed of himself than in the spiritual. We have proposed himself to himself, and his reason to his reason, to see what she can tell us of it. Methinks I have sufficiently declared how little understanding she hath of herself. ^C^And he who hath no understanding of himself, what can he have understanding of? "As though he could take measure of anything, that knows not his own measure" (Pliny *Hist. nat.* II.i.).

Truly, Protagoras told us pretty tales when he makes man the measure of all things, who never knew so much as his own. If it be not he, his dignity will never suffer any other creature to have this advantage over him. Now he being so contrary in himself, and one judgment so incessantly subverting another, this favorable proposition was but a jest which induced us necessarily to conclude the nullity of the compass and the compasser.

When Thales judgeth the knowledge of man very hard unto man, he teacheth him the knowledge of all other things to be impossible unto him.

[A]You,[26] for whom I have taken the pains to enlarge so long a work (against my custom) will not shun to maintain your Sebond with the ordinary form of arguing whereof you are daily instructed, and will therein exercise both your mind and study. For this last trick of fence must not be employed but as an extreme remedy. It is a desperate thrust, 'gainst which you must forsake your weapons to force your adversary to renounce his, and a secret slight which must seldom and very sparingly be put in practice. It is a great fondhardness* to lose ourself for the loss of another. [B]A man must not be willing to die to revenge himself as Gobrias was, who being close by the ears with a lord of Persia, Darius chanced to come in with his sword in his hand and, fearing to strike for fear he should hurt Gobrias, he called unto him and bade him smite boldly although he should smite through both.

[C]I have heard arms and conditions of single combats being desperate, and in which he that offered them put both himself and his enemy in danger of an end inevitable to both, reproved as unjust and condemned as unlawful. The Portugals took once certain Turks prisoners in the Indian Seas, who, impatient of their captivity, resolved with themselves (and their resolution succeeded) by rubbing of shipnails one against another and causing sparkles of fire to fall amongst the barrels of powder which lay not far from them, with intent to consume both themselves, their masters, and the ship.

[A]Here we but touch the skirts and glance at the last closings of sciences, wherein extremity as well as in virtue is vicious. Keep yourselves in the common path; it is not good to be so subtle and so curious. Remember what the Italian proverb saith:

> Who makes himself too fine
> Doth break himself in fine.
> Petrarch *Canzon.* XXII.48.

I persuade you in your opinions and discourses as much as in your customs and in every other thing to use moderation and temperance

26 Though various possibilities have been suggested, most modern commentators feel that this essay was probably addressed to Marguerite de Valois, who was the daughter of Henri II and Catherine de' Medici and became the wife of Henri of Navarre, later King Henri IV.

and avoid all newfangled inventions and strangeness. All extravagant ways displease me. You, who by the authority and pre-eminence which your greatness hath laid upon you, and more by the advantages which the qualities that are most your own bestow on you, may with a nod command whom you please, should have laid this charge upon someone that had made profession of learning, who might otherwise have disposed and enriched this fantasy. Notwithstanding, here have you enough to supply your wants of it.

Epicurus said of the laws that the worst were so necessary unto us that without them men would inter-devour one another. [C]And Plato verifieth that without laws we should live like beasts.

[A]Our spirit is a vagabond, a dangerous and fondhardy* implement: it is very hard to join order and measure to it. In my time such as have any rare excellency above others or extraordinary vivacity, we see them almost all so lavish and unbridled in license of opinions and manners, as it may be counted a wonder to find anyone settled and sociable. There is great reason why the spirit of man should be so strictly embarred. In his study, as in all things else, he must have his steps numbered and ordered. The limits of his pursuit must be cut out by art. He is bridled and fettered with and by religions, laws, customs, knowledge, precepts, pains, and recompenses, both mortal and immortal; we see him by means of his volubility and dissolution escape all these bonds. It is a vain body that hath no way about him to be seized on or cut off; a diverse and deformed body on which neither knot nor hold may be fastened.

[B]Verily there are few souls so orderly, so constant, and so well born as may be trusted with their own conduct and may with moderation and without rashness sail in the liberty of their judgments beyond common opinions. It is more expedient to give somebody the charge and tuition of them.

The spirit is an outrageous glaive,* [C]yea, even to his own possessor, [A]except he have the grace very orderly and discreetly to arm himself therewith. [C]And there is no beast to whom one may more justly apply a blinding-board* to keep her sight in and force her look to her footing and keep from straying here and there without the track which use and laws trace her out.

[A]Therefore shall it be better for you to close and bound yourselves in the accustomed path, howsoever it be, than to take your flight to this unbridled licence. But if any one of these new doctors shall undertake to play the wise or ingenious before you at the charge of his and your health; to rid you out of this dangerous plague which daily more and more spreads itself in your courts, this preservative will in any extreme necessity be a let,* that the contagion of this venom shall neither offend you nor your assistance.*

The liberty, then, and the jollity of their ancient spirits brought forth many different sects of opinions in philosophy and human sciences, everyone undertaking to judge and choose so that he might raise a faction. But now [C]that men walk all one way — "who are addicted and consecrated to certain set and fore-decreed opinions, so as they are enforced to maintain those things which they prove or approve not" (Cic. *Tusc.* II.ii.) — and [A]that we receive arts by civil authority and appointment, [C]so that schools have but one pattern, alike circumscribed discipline and institution, [A]no man regardeth more what coins weigh and are worth, but every man in his turn receiveth them according to the value that common approbation and succession allotteth them. Men dispute no longer of the alloy, but of the use: so are all things spent and vented* alike. Physic is received as geometry; and juggling tricks, enchantments, bonds, the commerce of deceased spirits, prognostications, domifications,* yea, even this ridiculous wit- and wealth-consuming pursuit of the philosopher's stone — all is employed and uttered without contradiction.

It sufficeth to know that Mars his place lodgeth in the middle of the hand's triangle, that of Venus in the thumb, and Mercury's in the little finger; and when the table-line cutteth the teacher's rising it is a sign of cruelty, when it faileth under the middle finger and that the natural median-line makes an angle with the vital under the same side it is a sign of a miserable death; and when a woman's natural line is open and closes not at angle with the vital, it evidently denotes that she will not be very chaste. I call yourself to witness it, with this science only a man may not pass with reputation and favor among all companies.

Theophrastus was wont to say that man's knowledge, directed by the sense, might judge of the causes of things unto a certain measure; but being come to the extreme and first causes, it must necessarily stay and be blunted or abated, either by reason of its weakness or of the things' difficulty. It is an indifferent and pleasing kind of opinion to think that our sufficiency may bring us to the knowledge of some things and hath certain measures of power beyond which it's temerity to employ it. This opinion is plausible and brought in by way of composition; but it is hard to give our spirit any limits, being very curious and greedy and not tied to stay rather at a thousand than at fifty [paces.]

Having found by experience that if one had missed to attain unto some one thing another hath come unto it, and that which one age never knew the age succeeeding hath found out, and that sciences and arts are not cast in a mold, but rather by little and little formed and shaped by often handling and polishing them over, even as bears fashion their young whelps by often licking them, what my strength cannot discover I cease not to sound and try; and in handling and kneading this new matter and with removing and chafing it, I open some facility for him that shall follow me, that with more ease he may enjoy the same and make it more facile, more supple, and more pliable:

> As the best beeswax melteth by the sun,
> And handling into many forms doth run,
> And is made aptly fit
> For use by using it.
>
> Ovid. *Metam.* X.284.

As much will the second do for a third, which is a cause that difficulty doth not make me despair, much less my inability; for it is but mine own.

Man is as well capable of all things as of some. And if, as Theophrastus saith, he avow the ignorance of the first causes and beginnings, let him hardly quit all the rest of his knowledge. If his foundation fail him, his discourse is overthrown. The dispute hath no other scope and to inquire no other end but the principles. If this end stay not his course, he casteth himself into an infinite irresolution. [C]"One thing can neither more nor less be comprehended than another, since of all things there is one definition of comprehending" (Cic. *Acad.* II.xli.).

[A]Now it is likely that if the soul knew anything, she first knew herself; and if she knew any without and besides herself, it must be her veil and body before anything else. If even at this day the gods of physic are seen to wrangle about our anatomy—

> Apollo stood for Troy,
> Vulcan Troy to destroy,
>
> Ovid. *Trist.* I.ii.5.

—when shall we expect that they will be agreed? We are nearer unto ourselves than is whiteness unto snow, or weight unto a stone. If man know not himself, how can he know his functions and forces? It is not by fortune that some true notice doth not lodge with us, but by hazard. And forasmuch as by the same way, fashion, and conduct errors are received into our soul, she hath not wherewithal to distinguish them nor whereby to choose the truth from falsehood.

The Academics received some inclination of judgment and found it over-raw to say it was no more likely snow should be white than black, and that we should be no more assured of the moving of a stone, which goeth from our hand, than of that of the eighth sphere. And to avoid this difficulty and strangeness, which in truth cannot but hardly lodge in our imagination, howbeit they establish that we were in no way capable of knowledge and that truth is engulfed in the deepest abysses, where man's sight can no way enter, yet avowed they some things to be more likely and possible than others, and received this faculty in their judgment, that they might rather incline to one apparance* than to another. They allowed her this propension, interdicting her all resolution.

The Pyrrhonians' advice is more hardy, and therewithal more likely. For this Academical inclination and this pro[p]ension rather to one than another proposition, what else is it than a re-acknowledging of some apparent truth in this than in that? If our understanding be capable of the form, of the lineaments, of the behavior and face of truth, it might as well see it all complete as but half, growing and imperfect. For this appearance of versimilitude, which makes them rather take the left than the right hand, do you augment it; this one ounce of likelihood which turns the balance, do you multiply it by a hundred, nay, by a thousand ounces: it will in the end come to pass that the balance will absolutely resolve and conclude one choice and perfect truth.

But how do they suffer themselves to be made tractable by likelihood if they know not truth? How know they the semblance of that whereof they understand not the essence? Either we are able to judge absolutely, or absolutely we cannot. If our intellectual and sensible faculties are without ground or footing, if they but hull* up and down and drive with the wind, for nothing suffer we our judgment to be carried away to any part of their operation, what apparance* soever it seemeth to present us with. And the surest and most happy situation of our understanding should be that where without any tottering or agitation it might maintain itself settled, upright, and inflexible. [C]"There is no difference betwixt true and false visions concerning the mind's assent" (Cic. *Acad.* II.xxviii.).

[A]That things lodge not in us in their proper form and essence, and make not their entrance into us of their own power and authority, we see it most evidently. For if it were so, we would receive them all alike. Wine should be such in a sick man's mouth as in a healthy man's. He whose fingers are chapped through cold or stiff or benumbed with frost should find the same hardness in the wood or iron he might handle which another doth. Then strange subjects yield unto our mercy and lodge with us according to our pleasure.

Now if on our part we receive anything without alteration, if man's holdfasts were capable and sufficiently powerful by our proper means to seize on truth, those means being common to all, this truth would successively remove itself from one to another. And of so many things as are in the world, at least one should be found that by an universal consent should be believed of all. But that no proposition is seen which is not controversied and debated amongst us, or that may not be, declareth plainly that our judgment doth not absolutely and clearly seize on that which it seizeth; for my judgment cannot make my fellow's judgment to receive the same, which is a sign that I have seized upon it by some other mean than by a natural power in me or other men.

Leave we apart this infinite confusion of opinions which is seen amongst philosophers themselves, and this universal and perpetual disputation in and concerning the knowledge of things. For it is most truly presupposed that men (I mean the wisest, the best born, yea, and the most sufficient) do never agree, no, not so much that heaven is over our heads. For they who doubt of all do also doubt of this; and such as affirm that we cannot conceive anything say we have not conceived whether heaven be over our heads: which two opinions are in number, without any comparison, the most forcible.

Besides this diversity and infinite division, by reason of the trouble which our own judgment layeth upon ourselves and the uncertainty which every man finds in himself, it may manifestly be perceived that this situation is very uncertain and unstaid. How diversely judge we of things! How often change we our fantasies! What I hold and believe this day, I believe and hold with all my belief: all my implements, springs, and motions embrace and clasp this opinion, and to the utmost of their power warrant the same; I could not possibly embrace any verity, nor with more assurance keep it, than I do this. I am wholly and absolutely given to it. But hath it not been my fortune not once but a hundred, nay, a thousand times, my daily, to have embraced some other thing with the very same instruments and condition which upon better advice I have afterwards judged false?

A man should at the least become wise at his own cost, and learn by others' harms. If under this color I have often found myself deceived, if my touchstone be commonly found false and my balance uneven and unjust, what assurance may I more take of it at this time than at others? Is it not folly in me to suffer myself so often to be beguiled and cozened by one guide? Nevertheless, let fortune remove us five hundred times from our place, let her do nothing but incessantly empty and fill, as in a vessel, other and other opinions in our mind, the present and last is always supposed certain and infallible. For this must a man leave goods, honor, life, state, health, and all:

The latter thing destroys all found before
And alters sense at all things liked of yore.
Lucr. V.1413.

[B]Whatsoever is told us, and whatever we learn, we should ever remember it is man who delivereth and man that receiveth. It is a mortal hand that presents it and a mortal hand that receives it. Only things which come to us from heaven have right and authority of persuasion and marks of truth; which we neither see with our eyes nor receive by our means. This sacred and great image would be of no force in so wretched a mansion except God prepare it to that use and purpose, unless God by his particular grace and supernatural favor reform and strengthen the same.

[A]Our frail and defective condition ought at least make us demean ourselves more moderately and more circumspectly in our changes. We should remember that whatsover we receive in our understanding we often receive false things, and that it is by the same instruments which many times contradict and deceive themselves. And no marvel if they contradict themselves, being so easy to incline and upon very slight occasions subject to waver and turn. Certain it is that our apprehension, our judgment, and our soul's faculties in general do suffer according to the body's motions and alterations, which are continual. Have we not our spirits more vigilant, our memory more ready, and our discourses more lively in time of health than in sickness? Doth not joy and blitheness make us receive the subjects that present themselves unto our soul with another kind of countenance than lowering vexation and drooping melancholy doth? Do you imagine that Catullus' or Sappho's verses delight and please an old covetous chuffpenny* wretch as they do a lusty and vigorous young man?

[B]Cleomenes, the son of Anaxandridas, being sick, his friends reproved him saying he had new strange humors and unusual fantasies. "It is not unlikely," answered he, "for I am not the man I was wont to be in the time of health; but being other, so are my fantasies and my humors."

[A]In the rabble* case-canvassing of our plea-courts this byword, *Gaudeat de bona fortuna,* let him joy in his good fortune, is much in use, and is spoken of criminal offenders who happen to meet with judges in some mild temper or well-pleased mood. For it is most certain that in times of condemnation the judge's doom or sentence is sometimes perceived to be more sharp, merciless, and forward, and at other times more tractable, facile, and inclined to shadow or excuse an offense, according as he is well or ill pleased in mind. A man that cometh out of his house troubled with the pain of the gout, vexed with jealousy, or angry that his servant hath robbed him, and whose mind is overcome with grief and plunged with vexation and distracted with anger, there is not question to be made but his judgment is at that instant much distempered and much transported that way.

[B]That venerable senate of the Areopagites was wont to judge and sentence by night, for fear the sight of the suitors might corrupt justice. [A]The air itself and the clearness of the firmament doth forebode us some change and alteration of weather, as saith that Greek verse in Cicero:

> Such are men's minds as with increaseful light
> Our father Jove surveys the world in sight.
> Cic., after Homer, in Aug., *Civ. Dei* V.xxviii.

It is not only fevers, drinks, and great accidents that overwhelm our judgment: the least things in the world will turn it topsy-turvy. And although we feel it not, it is not to be doubted if a continual ague may in the end suppress our mind a tertian will also (according to her measure and proportion) breed some alteration in it. If an apoplexy doth altogether stupefy and extinguish the sight of our understanding, it is not to be doubted but a cold and rheum will likewise dazzle the same. And by consequence, hardly shall a man in all his life find one hour wherein our judgment may always be found in his right bias, our body being subject to so many continual alterations and stuffed with so divers sorts of gins and motions that, giving credit to physicians, it is very hard to find one in perfect plight and that doth not always mistake his mark and shoot wide.

As for the rest, this disease is not so easily discovered except it be altogether extreme and remediless; forasmuch as reason marcheth ever crooked, halting, and broken-hipped, and with falsehood as with truth; and therefore it is very hard to discover her mistaking and disorder. I always call reason that appearance or show of discourses which every man deviseth or forgeth in himself. That reason, of whose condition there may be a hundred, one contrary to another, about one selfsame subject, it is an instrument of lead and wax, stretching, pliable, and that may be fitted to all biases and squared to all measures. There remains nothing but the skill and sufficiency to know how to turn and wind the same.

How well soever a judge meaneth and what good mind soever he beareth, if diligent ear be not given unto him (to which few amuse themselves) his inclination unto friendship, unto kindred, unto beauty, and unto revenge, and not only matters of so weighty consequence, but this innated and casual instinct which makes us to favor one thing more than another and incline to one man more than to another, and which without any leave of reason giveth us the choice in two like subjects or some shadow of like vanity, may insensibly insinuate in his judgment the commendation and applause, or disfavor and disallowance, of a cause and give the balance a twitch.

I that nearest pry into myself and who have mine eyes incessantly fixed upon me, as one that hath not much else to do elsewhere —

Only secure who in cold coast
Under the North Pole rules the roost
And there is fear'd; or what would fright
And Tyridates put to flight,
Hor. *Odes* I.xxvi.3.

— dare very hardly report the vanity and weakness I feel in myself. My foot is so staggering and unstable, and I find it so ready to trip and so easy to stumble, and my sight is so dim and uncertain, that fasting I find myself other than full fed. If my health applaud me, or but the calmness of one fair day smile upon me, then am I a lusty gallant; but if a corn wring my toe, then am I pouting, unpleasant, and hard to be pleased. [B]One same pace of a horse is sometimes hard and sometimes easy unto me, and one same way, one time short, another time long and wearisome; and one same form now more, now less agreeable and pleasing to me. [A]Sometimes I am apt to do anything, and other times fit to do nothing. What now is pleasing to me, within a while after will be painful. There are a thousand indiscreet and casual agitations in me. Either a melancholy humor possesseth me, or a choleric passion swayeth me; which having shaken off, sometimes frowardness and peevishness hath predominancy, and other times gladness and blitheness overrule me.

If I chance to take a book in hand, I shall in some passages perceive some excellent graces, and which ever wound me to the soul with delight; but let me lay it by and read him another time, let me turn and toss him as I list, let me apply and manage him as I will, I shall find it an unknown and shapeless mass.

[B]Even in my own writings, I shall not at all times find the track or air of my first imaginations. I wot not myself what I would have said, and shall vex and fret myself in correcting and giving a new sense to them, because I have peradventure forgotten or lost the former, which happily was better.

I do but come and go; my judgment doth not always go forward, but is ever floating and wandering:

Much like a petty skiff that's taken short
In a grand sea, when winds do make mad sport.
Catul. XXV.12.

Many times (as commonly it is my hap to do) having for exercise and sport's sake undertaken to maintain an opinion contrary to mine, my mind applying and turning itself that way doth so tie me unto it as I find no more the reason of my former conceit, and so I leave it. Where I incline, there I entertain myself, howsover it be, and am carried away by mine own weight.

Every man could near-hand say as much of himself would he but look into himself as I do. Preachers know that the emotion which surpriseth them whilst they are in their earnest speech doth animate them towards belief and that, being angry, we more violently give ourselves to defend our proposition, imprint it in ourselves, and embrace the same with more vehemency and approbation than we did being in our temperate and reposed sense.

You relate simply your case unto a lawyer. He answers faltering and doubtfully unto it. Whereby you perceive it is indifferent unto him to defend either this or that side: all is one to him. Have you paid him well? Have you given him a good bait or fee to make him earnestly apprehend it? Begins he to be interested in the matter? Is his will moved or his mind inflamed? Then will his reason be moved and his knowledge inflamed with all. See then, an apparent and undoubted truth presents itself to his understanding, wherein he discovers a new light and believes it in good sooth, and so persuades himself.

Shall I tell you? I wot not whether the heat proceeding of spite and obstinacy, against the impression and violence of a magistrate and of danger, [C]or the interest of reputation, [B]have induced some man to maintain even in the fiery flames the opinion for which amongst his friends and at liberty he would never have been moved nor have ventured his finger's end.

[A]The motions and fits which our soul receiveth by corporal passions do greatly prevail in her; but more her own, with which it is so fully possessed as happily it may be maintained she hath no other way or motion than by the blast of her winds, and that without their agitation she should remain without action, as a ship at sea which the winds have utterly forsaken. And he who should maintain that, [C]following the Peripatetic faction, [A]should offer us no great wrong, since it is known that the greatest number of the soul's actions proceed and have need of this impulsion of passion. Valor, say they, cannot be perfected without the assistance of choler:

> [C]Ajax every valor had
> Most, then when he was most mad.
>
> Cic. *Tusc.* IV.xxiii.

Nor doth any man run violently enough upon the wicked or his enemies except he be throughly angry; and they are of opinion that an advocate or counsellor at the bar, to have the cause go on his side and to have justice at the judge's hands, doth first endeavor to provoke him to anger.

Longing desires moved Themistocles and urged Demosthenes and have provoked philosophers to long travels, to tedious watchings, and to lingering peregrinations, and lead us to honors, to doctrine, and to health — all profitable respects. And this demiseness* of the soul in suffering molestation and tediousness serveth to no other purpose but to breed repentance and cause penitence in our consciences, and for our punishment to feel the scourge of God and the rod of politic correction. ᴬCompassion serveth as a sting unto ᴮclemency, and wisdom to preserve and govern ourselves is by our own fear roused up; and how many noble actions by ambition, how many by presumption? ᴬTo conclude, no eminent or glorious virtue can be without some immoderate and irregular agitation.

May not this be one of the reasons which moved the Epicureans to discharge God of all care and thought of our affairs, forsomuch as the very effects of his goodness cannot exercise themselves towards us without disturbing his rest by means of the passions, which are as motives and solicitations, directing the soul to virtuous actions? ᶜOr have they thought otherwise and taken them as tempests which shamefully lead astray the soul from her rest and tranquillity? "As we conceive the sea's calmness when not so much as the least pirling* wind doth stir the waves, so is a peaceable, reposed state of the mind then seen, when there is no perturbation whereby it may be moved" (Cic. *Tusc.* V.vi.).

ᴬWhat differences of sense and reason, what contrariety of the imaginations doth the diversity of our passions present unto us! What assurance may we then take of so unconstant and wavering a thing, subject by its own condition to the power of trouble, ᶜnever marching but a forced and borrowed pace? ᴬIf our judgment be in the hands of sickness itself and of perturbation, if by rashness and folly it be retained to receive the impression of things, what assurance may we expect at his hands?

ᶜDares not philosophy think that men produce their greatest effects and nearest approaching to divinity when they are beside themselves, furious, and mad? We amend ourselves by the privation of reason, and by her drooping. The two natural ways to enter the cabinet of the gods and there to foresee the course of the destinies are fury and sleep. This is very pleasing to be considered. By the dislocation that passions bring unto our reason we become virtuous; by the extirpation which either fury or the image of death bringeth us, we become prophets and divines. I never believed it more willingly. It is a mere divine inspiration that sacred truth hath inspired in a philosophical spirit, which against his proposition exacteth from him that the quiet state of our soul, the best settled estate, yea, the healthfullest that philosophy can acquire unto is not the best estate. Our vigilancy is more drowsy than sleep itself; our wisdom less wise than folly; our dreams of more worth than our discourses. The worst place we can take is in ourselves.

But thinks it not that we have the foresight to mark that the voice which the spirit uttereth when he is gone from man, so clear-sighted, so great, and so perfect, and whilst he is in man, so earthly, so ignorant, and so overclouded, is a voice proceeding from the spirit, which is in earthly, ignorant, and overclouded man — and therefore a trustless and not-to-be-believed voice?

[A]I have no great experience in these violent agitations, being of a soft and dull complexion, the greatest part of which, without giving it leisure to acknowledge herself, do suddenly surprise our soul. But that passion which in young men's hearts is said to be produced by idleness, although it march but leisurely and with a measured progress, doth evidently present to those that have assayed to oppose themselves against her endeavor the power of the conversation and alteration which our judgment suffereth. I have sometimes enterprised to arm myself with a resolution to abide, resist, and suppress the same. For I am so far from being in their rank that call and allure vices that unless they entertain me I scarcely follow them. I felt it, mauger* my resistance, to breed, to grow, and to augment, and in the end, being in perfect health and clear-sighted, to seize upon and possess me in such sort that, as in drunkenness, the image of things began to appear unto me otherwise than it was wont. I saw the advantages of the subject I sought after evidently to swell and grow greater, and much to increase by the wind of my imagination; and the difficulties of my enterprise to become more easy and plain; and my discourse and conscience to shrink and draw back; but, that fire being evaporated all on a sudden as by the flashing of a lightning, my soul to reassume another sight, another state, and other judgment. The difficulty in my retreat seemed great and invincible, and the very same things of another taste and show, than the fervency of desire had presented them unto me.

And which more truly, Pyrrho cannot tell. We are never without some infirmity. Fevers have their heat and their cold; from the effects of a burning passion we fall into the effects of a chilling passion.

[B]So much as I had cast myself forward, so much do I draw myself back:

> As th' ocean, flowing, ebbing in due course,
> To land now rushes, foaming throws his source
> On rocks, therewith bedews the utmost sand,
> Now swift returns, the stones roll'd back from strand
> By tide resucks, foord* failing, leaves the land.
> Virg.*Aen.* XI.624.

[A]Now by the knowledge of my volubility I have by accidence engendered some constancy of opinions in myself; yea, have not so much altered my first and natural ones. For, what apparance* soever there be in novelty, I do not easily change, for fear I should lose by the bargain. And since I am not capable to choose, I take the choice from others and keep myself in the seat that God hath placed me in. Else could I hardly keep myself from continual rolling. Thus have I by the grace of God preserved myself whole, without agitation or trouble of conscience, in the ancient belief of our religion, in the midst of so many sects and divisions which our age hath brought forth.

The writings of the ancient fathers — I mean the good, the solid, and the serious — do tempt and in a manner remove me which way they list. Him that I hear seemeth ever the most forcible; I find them every one in his turn to have reason, although they contrary one another. That facility which good wits have to prove anything they please likely, and that there is nothing so strange but they will undertake to set so good a gloss on it as it shall easily deceive a simplicity like unto mine, doth manifestly show the weakness of their proof.

The heavens and the planets have moved these three thousand years, and all the world believed as much, until [C]Cleanthes the Samian, or else, according to Theophrastus, Nicetas the Syracusan, [A]took it upon him to maintain it was the earth that moved, [C]by the oblique circle of the zodiac, turning about her axle-tree. [A]And in our days Copernicus hath so well grounded this doctrine that he doth very orderly fit it to all astrological consequences. What shall we reap by it, but only that we need not care which of the two it be? And who knoweth whether a thousand years hence a third opinion will rise which happily shall overthrow these two precedent?

> So age to be pass'd over alters times of things:
> What erst was most esteem'd
> At last nought worth is deem'd;
> Another then succeeds, and from contempt upsprings,
> Is daily more desir'd, flow'reth as found but then
> With praise and wondrous honor amongst mortal men.
> Lucr. V.1275.

So when any new doctrine is represented unto us, we have great cause to suspect it and to consider how, before it was invented, the contrary unto it was in credit; and as that hath been reversed by this latter, a third invention may peradventure succeed in after-ages which in like sort shall front the second. Before the principles which Aristotle found out were in credit, other principles contented man's reason, as his do now content us. What learning have these men, what particular privilege, that the course of our invention should only rely upon them and that the possession of our belief shall forever hereafter belong to them? They are no more exempted from being rejected than were their forefathers.

If any man urge me with a new argument, it is in me to imagine that if I cannot answer it another can. For, to believe all apparances* which we cannot resolve is mere simplicity. It would then follow that all the common sort [C](whereof we are all part) [A]should have his belief turning and winding like a weathercock. For his soul, being soft and without resistance, should incessantly be enforced to receive new and admit other impressions, the latter ever defacing the precedent's trace. He that perceiveth himself weak ought to answer, according to law terms, that he will confer with his learned counsel or else refer himself to the wisest from whom he hath had his prenticeship.

How long is it since physic came first into the world? It is reported that a new start-up fellow, whom they call Paracelsus, changeth and subverteth all the order of ancient and so-long-time-received rules, and maintaineth that until this day it hath only served to kill people. I think he will easily verify it. But I suppose it were no great wisdom to hazard my life upon the trial of his newfangled experience.

We must not believe all men, saith the precept, since every man may say all things.

It is not long since that one of these professors of novelties and physical reformations told me that all our forefathers had notoriously abused themselves in the nature and motions of the winds, which, if I should listen unto him, he would manifestly make me perceive. After I had with some patience given attendance to his arguments, which were indeed full of likelihood, I demanded of him whether they that sailed according to Theophrastus his laws went westward when they bent their course eastward? Or whether they sailed sideling or backward? "It is fortune," answered he; "but so it is, they took their mark amiss." To whom I then replied that I had rather follow the effects than his reason.

They are things that often shock* together. And it hath been told me that in geometry, which supposeth to have gained the high point of certainty amongst all sciences, there are found unavoidable demonstrations, and which subvert the truth of all experience. As James Peletier told me in mine own house that he had found out two lines bending their course one towards another as if they would meet and join together; nevertheless he affirmed that even unto infinity they could never come to touch one another. And the Pyrrhonians use their arguments and reason but to destroy the apparance* of experience. And it is a wonder to see how far the suppleness of our reason hath in this design followed them to resist the evidence of effects. For, they affirm that we move not, that we speak not, that there is no weight, nor heat, with the same force of arguing that we aver the most likeliest things. Ptolemy, who was an excellent man, had established the bounds of the world. All ancient philosophers have thought they had a perfect measure thereof, except it were certain scattered islands which might escape their knowledge. It had been to Pyrrhonize a thousand years ago had any man gone about to make a question of the art of cosmography and the opinions that have been received thereof of all men in general. [B]It had been flat heresy to avouch that there were antipodes. [A]See how in our age an infinite greatness of firm land hath been discovered, not an island only nor one particular country, but a part in greatness very near equal unto that which we knew. Our modern geographers cease not to affirm that now all is found and all is discovered;

> For what is present here
> Seems strong, is held most dear.
> Lucr. V.1411.

The question is now, if Ptolemy was heretofore deceived in the grounds of his reason, whether it were not folly in me to trust what these late fellows say of it, [C]and whether it be not more likely that this huge body which we term the world is another manner of thing than we judge it.

Plato saith that it often changeth his countenance that the heaven, the stars, and the sun do sometimes re-inverse the motion we perceive in them, changing the east into the west. The Egyptian priests told Herodotus that since their first king, which was eleven thousand and odd years (when they made him to see the pictures of all their former kings, drawn to the life in statues), the sun had changed his course four times, that the sea and the earth do interchangeably change one into another, that the world's birth is undetermined. The like said Aristotle and Cicero. And some one amongst us[27] averreth that it is altogether eternal, mortal, and new-reviving again by many vicissi-

[27] Origen.

tudes, calling Solomon and Isaiah to witness to avoid these oppositions: that God hath sometimes been a creator without a creature, that he hath been idle, that he hath unsaid his idleness by setting his hand to this work, and that by consequence he is subject unto change.

In the most famous schools of Greece, the world is reputed a god, framed by another greater and mightier god, and is composed of a body and a soul which abideth in his center, spreading itself by musical numbers unto his circumference, divine, thrice-happy, very great, most wise, and eternal. In it are other gods, as the sea, the earth, and planets, which mutually entertain one another with an harmonious and perpetual agitation and celestial dance, sometime meeting, other times far-sundering themselves, now hiding, then showing themselves, and changing place, now forward, now backward.

Heraclitus firmly maintained that the world was composed of fire, and by the destinies' order it should one day burst forth into flames and so be consumed into cinders, and another day it should be new-born again. And Apuleius of men saith: "Severally mortal; altogether everlasting" (Apul. *De deo Socrat.*, in Aug. *Civ. Dei* XII.x.), Alexander writ unto his mother the narration of an Egyptian Priest drawn from out their monuments, witnessing the antiquity of that nation infinite and comprehending the birth and progress of [other] countries to the life. Cicero and Diodorus said in their days that the Chaldeans kept a register of four hundred thousand and odd years. Aristotle, Pliny, and others, that Zoroaster lived six thousand years before Plato. And Plato saith, that those of the city of Saïs have memories in writing of eight thousand years, and that the town of Athens was built a thousand years before the city of Saïs; [B]Epicurus, that at one same time all things that are look how we see them; they are all alike and in the same fashion in divers other worlds. Which he would have spoken more confidently had he seen the similitudes and correspondencies of this new-found world of the West Indies with ours, both present and past, by so many strange examples.

[C]Truly, when I consider what hath followed our learning by the course of this terrestrial policy, I have divers times wondered at myself to see in so great a distance of times and places the sympathy or jumping of so great a number of popular and wild opinions, and of extravagant customs and beliefs, and which by no means seem to hold with our natural discourse. Man's spirit is a wonderful worker of miracles. But this relation hath yet a kind of I wot not what more heteroclite,* which is found both in names and in a thousand other things.

[B]For there were found nations which, as far as we know, had never heard of us, where circumcision was held in request, where great states and commonwealths were maintained only by women and no men; where our fasts and lent was represented, adding thereunto the abstinence from women; where our crosses were several ways in great esteem. In some places they adorned and honored their sepulchres with them, and elsewhere, especially that of Saint Andrew, they employed to shield themselves from nightly visions and to lay them upon children's couches as good against enchantments and witchcrafts. In another place they found one made of wood of an exceeding height, worshipped for the god of rain, which was thrust very deep into the ground. There was found a very express and lively image of our penitentiaries*; the use of miters, the priests' single life, the art of divination by the entrails of sacrificed beasts, [C]the abstinence from all sorts of flesh and fish for their food, [B]the order amongst priests in saying of their divine service to use not a vulgar but a particular tongue. And this erroneous and fond* conceit that the first god was expelled his throne by a younger brother of his; that they were at first created with all commodities, which afterward, by reason of their sins, were abridged them; that their territory hath been changed; that their natural condition hath been much impaired; that they have heretofore been drowned by the inundation of waters come from heaven; that none were saved but a few families which cast themselves into the cracks or hollow of high mountains, which cracks they stopped very close so that the waters could not enter in, having before shut therein many kinds of beasts; that when they perceived the rain to cease and waters to fall they first sent out certain dogs, which returned clean-washed and wet, they judged that the waters were not yet much fallen; and that afterward sending out some other, which seeing to return all muddy and foul, they issued forth of the mountains to re-people the world again, which they found replenished only with serpents.

There were places found where they used the persuasions of the day of judgment, so that they grew wondrous wroth and offended with the Spaniards who, in digging and searching of riches in their graves, scattered here and there the bones of their deceased friends, saying that those dispersed bones could very hardly be reconjoined together again. They also found where they used traffic by exchange and no otherwise, and had fairs and markets for that purpose. They found dwarfs and such other deformed creatures used for the ornament of princes' tables. They found the use of hawking and fowling according to the nature of their birds; tyrannical subsidies and grievances upon subjects; delicate and pleasant gardens; dancing, tumbling, leaping, and juggling; music of instruments, armories, dicing-houses, tennis courts, and casting lots* or mum-chance,* wherein they are often so earnest and moody that they will play themselves and their liberty; using no other physic but by charms; the manner of writing by figures; believing in one first man, universal father of all people; the adoration of one god who heretofore lived man in perfect virginity, fasting, and penance, preaching the law of nature and the ceremonies of religion, and who vanished out of the world without any natural death; the opinion of giants; the use of drunkenness, with their manner of drinks and drinking and pledging of healths; religious ornaments painted over with bones and dead men's skulls; surplices, holy water, and holy-water sprinkles; women and servants which strivingly present themselves to be burned or interred with their deceased husbands or masters; a law that the eldest or first-born child shall succeed and inherit all; where nothing is reserved for punies* but obedience; a custom to the promotion of certain officers of great authority, and where he that is promoted takes upon him a new name and quitteth his own; where they used to cast lime upon the knees of new-born children, saying unto him: "From dust thou camest and to dust thou shall return again;" the arts of augurs or prediction.

These vain shadows of our religion, which are seen in some of these examples witness the dignity and divinity thereof. It hath not only in some sort insinuated itself among all the infidel nations on this side by some imitations, but amongst those barbarous nations beyond, as it were by a common and supernatural inspiration. For amongst them was also found the belief of purgatory, but after a new form: for what we ascribe unto fire they impute unto cold, and imagine that souls are both purged and punished by the vigor of an extreme coldness.

This example putteth me in mind of another pleasant diversity: for as there were some people found who took pleasure to unhood the end of their yard* and to cut off the foreskin, after the manner of the Mohammedans and Jews, some there were found that made so great a conscience to unhood it that with little strings they carried their foreskin very carefully outstretched and fastened above for fear that end should see the air. And of this other diversity also, that as we honor our kings and celebrate our holidays with decking and trimming ourselves with the best habiliments we have, in some regions there, to show all disparity and submission to their king, their subjects present themselves unto him in their basest and meanest apparel, and entering into his palace, they take some old torn garment and put it over their other attire, to the end all glory and ornament may shine in their sovereign and master. But let us go on.

[A]If nature enclose within the limits of her ordinary progress, as all other things, so the beliefs, the judgments, and the opinions of men; if they have their revolutions, their seasons, their birth, and their death, even as cabbages; if heaven doth move, agitate, and roll them at his pleasure, what powerful and permanent authority do we ascribe unto them? [B]If by uncontrolled experience we palpably touch that the form of our being depends of the air, of the climate, and of the soil wherein we are born — and not only the hue, the stature, the complexion, and the countenance, but also the soul's faculties: [C]"The climate helpeth not only for strength of body, but of mind's," saith Vegetius (I.ii.) — and that the goddess, foundress of the city of Athens, chose a temperature of a country to situate it in that might make the men wise, as the Egyptian priests taught Solon: "about Athens is a thin air, whereby those countrymen are esteemed the sharper witted; about Thebes the air is gross and therefore the Thebans were gross and strong of constitution" (Cic. *De fato* IV.); [B]in such manner that as fruits and beasts do spring up divers and different, so men are born either more or less warlike, martial, just, temperate, and docile — here subject to wine, there to theft and whoredom, here inclined to superstition, addicted to misbelieving, [C]here given to liberty, there to servitude, [B]capable of some one art or science, gross-witted or ingenious, either obedient or rebellious, good or bad, according as the inclination of the place beareth where they are seated — and being removed from one soil to another as plants are, they take a new complexion; which was the cause that Cyrus would never permit the Persians to leave their barren, rough, and craggy country for to transport themselves into another, more gentle, more fertile, and more plain, [C]saying that fat and delicious countries make men wanton and effeminate and fertile soils yield infertile spirits; [B]if sometime we see one art to flourish, or a belief, and sometimes another, by some heavenly influence; some ages to produce this or that nature and so to incline mankind to this or that bias; men's spirits one while flourishing, another while barren, even as fields are seen to be — what become of all those goodly prerogatives wherewith we still flatter ourselves? Since a wise man may mistake himself, yea, many men and whole nations, and as we say, man's nature either in one thing or other hath for many ages together mistaken herself, what assurance have we that at any time she leaveth her mistaking, [C]and that she continueth not even at this day in her error?

[A]Methinks amongst other testimonies of our imbecility this one ought not to be forgotten, that by wishing itself man cannot yet find out what he wanteth, that not by enjoying or possession but by imagination and full wishing we cannot all agree in one that we most stand in need of and would best content us. Let our imagination have free liberty to cut out and sew at her pleasure, she cannot so much as desire what is fittest to please Cand content her:

> BBy reason what do we fear or desire?
> With such dexterity what dost aspire
> But thou eftsoons repentest it,
> Though thy attempt and vow do hit?
>
> Juven. *Sat.* X.4.

AThat is the reason why CSocrates never requested the gods to give him anything but what they knew to be good for him. And the public and private prayer of the Lacedaemonians did merely imply that good and fair things might be granted them, remitting the election and choice of them to the discretions of the highest power:

> BWe wish a wife, wife's breeding; we would know
> What children. Shall our wife be sheep or shrow*?
>
> Juv. *Sat.* X.352.

AAnd the Christian beseecheth God that his will may be done, lest he should fall into that inconvenience which poets feign of King Midas, who requested of the gods that whatsoever he touched might be converted into gold; his prayers were heard, his wine was gold, his bread gold, the feathers of his bed, his shirt, and his garments were turned into gold, so that he found himself overwhelmed in the enjoying of his desire; and being enriched with an intolerable commodity, he must now unpray his prayers:

> Wretched and rich, amaz'd at so strange ill,
> His riches he would fly, hates his own will.
>
> Ovid, *Metam.* XI.128.

BLet me speak of myself. Being yet very young, I besought Fortune above all things that she would make me a knight of the Order of Saint Michael, which in those days was very rare, and the highest type of honor the French nobility aimed at. She very kindly granted my request; I had it. In lieu of raising and advancing me from my place for the attaining of it, she hath much more graciously entreated me; she hath debased and depressed it even unto my shoulders and under.

CCleobis and Biton, Trophonius and Agamedes, the first two having besought the goddess, the two latter their god, of some recompense worthy their piety, received death for a reward: so much are heavenly opinions different from ours concerning what we have need of.

AGod might grant us riches, honors, long life, and health; but many times to our own hurt. For whatsoever is pleasing to us is not always healthful for us. If in lieu of our former health he send us death or some worse sickness — "thy rod and thy staff hath comforted me" (Ps. xxiii) — he doth it by the reasons of his providence, which more certainly considereth and regardeth what is meet for us than we ourselves can do, and we ought to take it in good part, as from a most wise and thrice-friendly hand:

> [B]If you will counsel have, give the gods leave
> To weigh what is most meet we should receive
> And what for our estate most profit were:
> To them than to himself man is more dear.
> Juven. *Sat.* X.346.

For to crave honors and charges of them is to request them to cast you in some battle or play at hazard, or some such thing whereof the event is unknown to you and the fruit uncertain.

[A]There is no combat amongst philosophers so violent and sharp as that which ariseth upon the question of man's chief felicity, [C]from which, according to Varro's calculation, arose two hundred and four score sects. "But he that disagrees about the chiefest felicity calls in question the whole course of philosophy" (Cic. *De fin.* V.v.).

> [A]Three guests of mine do seem almost at odds to fall,
> Whilst they with divers taste for divers things do call.
> What should I give? What not? You will not what he will;
> What you would, to them twain is hateful, sour, and ill.
> Hor. *Epist.* II.ii.61.

Nature should thus answer their contestations and debates.

Some say that our felicity consisteth and is in virtue, others in voluptuousness, others in yielding unto nature; some others in learning, [C]others in feeling no manner of pain or sorrow, [A]others for a man never to suffer himself to be carried away by apparances.* And to this opinion seemeth this other [B]of ancient Pythagoras [A]to incline:

> Sir, nothing to admire is th' only thing
> That may keep happy and to happy bring;
> Hor. *Epist.* I.vi.1.

which is the end and scope of the Pyrrhonian sect.

[C]Aristotle ascribeth unto magnanimity to admire and wonder at nothing. [A]And Arcesilaus said that sufferance and an upright and inflexible state of judgment were true felicities, whereas consents and applications were vices and evils. True it is that where he establisheth it for a certain axiom he started from Pyrrhonism. When the Pyrrhonians say that ataraxy is the chief felicity, which is the immobility of judgment, their meaning is not to speak it affirmatively;

but the very wavering of their mind, which makes them to shun downfalls and to shroud themselves under the shelter of calmness, presents this fantasy unto them and makes them refuse another.

[B]Oh how much do I desire that whilst I live, either some learned men or Justus Lipsius, the most sufficient and learned man now living, of a most polished and judicious wit, true cousin-german* to my Turnebus, had both will, health, and leisure enough sincerely and exactly, according to their divisions and forms, to collect into one volume or register, as much as by us might be seen, the opinions of ancient philosophy concerning the subject of our being and customs, their controversies, the credit and partaking of factions and sides, the application of the authors' and sectators' lives to their precepts in memorable and exemplary accidents. Oh what a worthy and profitable labor would it be!

[A]Besides, if it be from ourselves that we draw the regimen of our customs, into what a bottomless confusion do we cast ourselves! For what our reason persuades us to be most likely for it, is generally for every man to obey the laws of his country, [B]as is the advice of Socrates, inspired, saith he, by a divine persuasion. [A]And what else meaneth she thereby but only that our devoir* or duty hath no other rule but casual?

Truth ought to have a like and universal visage throughout the world. Law and justice, if man knew any that had a body and true essence, he would not fasten it to the condition of this or that country's customs. It is not according to the Persians' or Indians' fantasy that virtue should take her form.

Nothing is more subject unto a continual agitation than the laws. I have since I was born seen those of our neighbors the Englishmen changed and rechanged three or four times, not only in politic subjects, which is that some will dispense of constancy, but in the most important subject that possibly can be, that is to say in religion. Whereof I am so much the more both grieved and ashamed because it is a nation with which my countrymen have heretofore had so inward and familiar acquaintance that even to this day there remain in my house some ancient monuments of our former alliance.

[C]Nay, I have seen amongst ourselves some things become lawful which erst were deemed capital; and we that hold some others are likewise in possibility, according to the uncertainty of warring fortune, one day or other to be offenders against the majesty both of God and man, if our justice chance to fall under the mercy of injustice; and, in the space of few years' possession, taking a contrary essence.

How could that ancient god[28] more evidently accuse in human knowledge the ignorance of divine essence and teach men that their

[28] Apollo.

religion was but a piece of their own invention, fit to combine their society, than in declaring, as he did, to those which sought the instruction of it by his sacred tripod, that the true worshipping of god was that which he found to be observed by the custom of the place where he lived?

O God, what bond or duty is it that we own not to our sovereign creator's benignity, in that he hath been pleased to clear and enfranchise our belief from those vagabonding and arbitrary devolutions and fixed it upon the eternal base of his holy word?

[A]What will philosophy then say to us in this necessity? That we follow the laws of our country; that is to say, this waving sea of a people's or of a prince's opinions, which shall paint me forth justice with as many colors, and reform the same into as many visages, as there are changes and alterations of passions in them. I cannot have my judgment so flexible. What goodness is that which but yesterday I saw in credit and esteem, and tomorrow to have lost all reputation, [C]and that [at] the crossing of a river is made a crime? What truth is that which these mountains bound and is a lie in the world beyond them?

[A]But they are pleasant when, to allow the laws some certainty, they say that there be some firm, perpetual, and immovable which they call natural, and by the condition of their proper essence are imprinted in mankind. Of which some make three in number, some four, some more, some less — an evident token that it is a mark as doubtful as the rest. Now are they so unfortunate (for how can I term that but misfortune that of so infinite a number of laws there is not so much as one to be found which the fortune [C]or temerity of chance [A]hath granted to be universally received and by the consent of unanimity of all nations to be admitted?), they are, I say, so miserable that of these three or four choice-selected laws there is not one alone that is not impugned or disallowed, not by one nation but by many. Now is the generality of approbation the only likely ensign by which they may argue some laws to natural. For what nature had indeed ordained us, that should we doubtless follow with one common consent; and not one only nation, but every man in particular, should have a feeling of the force and violence which he should urge him with that would incite him to contrary and resist that law. Let them all, for example's sake, show me but one of this condition.

Protagoras and Ariston gave the justice of the laws no other essence but the authority and opinion of the lawgiver, and, that excepted, both good and honest lost their qualities and remained but vain and idle names of indifferent things. Thrasymachus in Plato thinks there is no other right but the commodity of the superior.

There is nothing wherein the world differeth so much as in customs and laws. Some things are here accounted abominable which in another place are esteemed commendable, as in Lacedaemonia the sleight and subtlety in stealing. Marriages in proximity of blood are amongst us forbidden as capital; elsewhere they are allowed and esteemed:

> There are some people where the mother wedde[th]
> Her son, the daughter her own father beddeth,
> And so by doubling love their kindness spreadeth.
>
> Ovid. *Metam.* X.331.

The murdering of children and of parents, the communication with women, traffic of robbing and stealing, free license to all manner of sensuality — to conclude, there is nothing so extreme and horrible but is found to be received and allowed by the custom of some nation.

[B] It is credible that there be natural laws, as may be seen in other creatures; but in us they are lost; this goodly human reason engrafting itself among all men to sway and command, confounding and topsy-turving the visage of all things, according to her inconstant vanity and vain inconstancy. [C]"Therefore nothing more is ours: all that I call ours belongs to art" (Cf. Cic. *De fin.* V.xxi.).

[A]Subjects have divers lusters and several considerations, whence the diversity of opinions is chiefly engendered. One nation vieweth a subject with one visage, and thereon it stays; another with another.

Nothing can be imagined so horrible as for one to eat and devour his own father. Those which anciently kept this custom hold it nevertheless for a testimony of piety and good affection, seeking by that mean to give their fathers the worthiest and most honorable sepulchre, harboring their fathers' bodies and relics in themselves and their marrow, in some sort reviving and regenerating them by the transmutation made in their quick* flesh by digestion and nourishment. It is easy to be considered what abomination and cruelty it had been in men accustomed and trained in this inhuman superstition to cast the carcasses of their parents into the corruption of the earth as food for beasts and worms.

Lycurgus wisely considereth in theft the vivacity, diligence, courage, and nimbleness that is required in surprising or taking anything from one's neighbor, and the commodity which thereby redoundeth to the commonwealth that every man heedeth more curiously the keeping of that which is his own; and judged that by this twofold institution to assail and to defend much good was drawn for military dicipline (which was the principal science and chief virtue wherein he would enable that nation) of greater respect and more consideration than was the disorder and injustice of prevailing and taking other men's goods.

Dionysius the tyrant offered Plato a robe made after the Persian fashion, long, damasked, and perfumed; but he refused the same saying that being born a man he would not willingly put on a woman's garment. But Aristippus took it, with this answer, that no garment could corrupt a chaste mind. [C]His friends reproved his demiseness* in being so little offended that Dionysius had spitten in his face. "Tut," said he, "fishers suffer themselves to be washed over head and ears to get a gudgeon.*" Diogenes, washing of coleworts* for his dinner, seeing him pass by, said unto him, "If thou couldst live with coleworts,* thou wouldst not court and fawn upon a tyrant;" to whom Aristippus replied, "If thou couldst live among men, thou wouldst not wash coleworts."* [A]See here how reason yieldeth apparance* to divers effects. [B]It is a pitcher with two ears, which a man may take hold on either by the right or left hand:

> O stranger-harb'ring land, thou bringst us war:
> Steeds serve for war;
> These herds do threaten jar.
> Yet horses erst were wont to draw our wains,
> And harnessed matches bear agreeing reins,
> Hope is thereby that we
> In peace shall well agree.
>
> Virg. *Aen.* III.539.

[C]Solon being importuned not to shed vain and bootless tears for the death of his son, "That's the reason," answered he, "I may more justly shed them, because they are bootless and vain." Socrates his wife exasperated her grief by this circumstance: "Good Lord," said she, "how unjustly do these bad judges put him to death!" "What! Wouldst thou rather they should execute me justly?" replied he to her.

[A]It is a fashion amongst us to have holes bored in our ears; the Greek held it for a badge of bondage. We hide ourselves when we will enjoy our wives; the Indians do it in open view of all men. The Scythians were wont to sacrifice strangers in their temples, whereas in other places churches are sanctuaries for them.

> [B]The vulgar hereupon doth rage, because
> Each place doth hate their neighbors' sovereign laws,
> And only gods doth deem
> Those gods themselves esteem.
>
> Juv. *Sat.* XV.37.

[A]I have heard it reported of a judge who, when he met with any sharp conflict between Bartolus and Baldus,[29] or with any case admit-

29 Fourteenth-century Italian legal theorists.

ting contrariety, was wont to write in the margin of his book, "A question for a friend"; which is to say that the truth was so entangled and disputable that in such a case he might favor which party he should think good. There was no want but of spirit and sufficiency if he set not everywhere through his books, "A question for a friend."

The advocates and judges of our time find in all cases biases too, too many to fit them where they think good. To so infinite a science, depending on the authority of so many opinions and of so arbitrary a subject, it cannot be but that an exceeding confusion of judgments must arise. There are very few processes so clear but the lawyers' advices upon them will be found to differ. What one company had judged, another will adjudge the contrary, and the very same will another time change opinion. Whereof we see ordinary examples by this license, which wonderfully blemisheth the authority and luster of our law, never to stay upon one sentence, but to run from one to another judge to decide one same case.

Touching the liberty of philosophical opinions concerning vice and virtue, it is a thing needing no great extension and wherein are found many advices which were better unspoken than published [C]to weak capacities.

[B]Arcesilaus was wont to say that in paillardise* it was not worthy consideration [C]where, [B]on what side, and how it was done. [C]"Obscene pleasures, if nature require them, the Epicure esteemeth not to be measured by kind, place, or order, but by form, age and fashion" (Cic. *Tusc.* V.xxxiii.). "Nor doth he think that holy loves should be strange from a wise man" (Cic. *De fin.* III.xx.). "Let us then question to what years young folk may be beloved" (Sen. *Epist.* CXXIII.). These two last Stoic places, and upon this purpose the reproach of Diogarchus to Plato himself, show how many excessive licenses and out of common use soundest philosophy doth tolerate.

[A]Laws take their authority from possession and custom; it is dangerous to reduce them to their beginning. In rolling on, they swell and grow greater and greater, as do our rivers. Follow them upward unto their source, and you shall find them but a bubble of water, scarce to be discerned, which in gliding on swelleth so proud and gathers so much strength. Behold the ancient considerations which have given the first motion to this famous torrent, so full of dignity, of honor and reverence: you shall find them so light and weak that these men which will weigh all and complain of reason and who receive nothing upon trust and authority, it is no wonder if their judgments are often far distant from common judgment. Men that take nature's first image for a pattern, it is no marvel if in most of their opinions, they miss the common beaten path.

As, for example, few amongst them would have approved the forced conditions of our marriages, [C]and most of them would have had women in community and without any private respect.

[A]They refused our ceremonies. Chrysippus said that some philosophers would in open view of all men show a dozen of tumbling tricks, yea, without any slops* or breeches, for a dozen of olives. [C]He would hardly have persuaded Cleisthenes to refuse his fair daughter Agarista to Hippocleides because he had seen him graft the forked tree in her upon a table.[30] Metrocles somewhat indiscreetly, as he was disputing in his school in presence of his auditory, let a fart, for shame whereof he afterwards kept his house and could not be drawn abroad until such time as Crates went to visit him, who, to his persuasions and reasons adding the example of his liberty, began to fart avie* with him and to remove this scruple from off his conscience, and moreover, won him to his Stoical (the more free) sect from the Peripatetical (and more civil) one, which [unto that time] he had followed.

That which we call civility — not to dare to do that openly which amongst us is both lawful and honest being done in secret — they termed folly; and to play the wily fox in concealing and disclaiming what nature, custom, and our desire publish and proclaim of our actions, they deemed to be a vice. And thought it a suppressing of Venus her mysteries to remove them from out the private vestry of her temple and expose them to the open view of the people, and that to draw her sports from out the curtains was to lose them (shame is matter of some consequence; concealing, reservation, and circumspection are parts of estimation); that sensuality under the mask of virtue did very ingeniously procure not to be prostituted in the midst of highways, not trodden upon, and seen by the common sort, alleging the dignity and commodity of her wonted cabinets. Whereupon [A]some say that to forbid and remove the common brothel houses is not only to spread whoredom everywhere, which only was allotted to those places, but also to incite idle and vagabond men to that vice by reason of the difficulty:

> [Corvinus, you are now the lover of Aufidia who were formerly her husband; now she is the wife of the man who was your rival. Why does she please you, belonging to another, who did not please you when she was your wife? Are you impotent unless insecure?]
>
> Mart. III.lxx.

This experience is diversified by a thousand examples:

> [There wasn't one person in the whole town who wanted to touch your wife, Cecilianus, when they freely could; but now that you've

30 I.e., stand upon his hands on a table.

surrounded her with guards, there is a vast throng of lovers. You're a clever fellow.]

Mart. I.lxxiv.

A philosopher being taken with the deed was demanded what he did; answered very mildly, "I plant man," blushing no more being found so napping than if he had been taken setting of garlic.

CIt is, as I suppose, of a tender and respective opinion that a notable and religious author holds this action so necessarily bound to secrecy and shame that in Cynic embracements and dalliances he could not be persuaded that the work should come to her end, but rather that it lingered and stayed, only to represent wanton gestures and lascivious motions to maintain the impudency of their school's profession; and that to pour forth what shame had forced and bashfulness restrained they had also afterward need to seek some secret place. He had not seen far enough into their licentiousness. For Diogenes, in sight of all exercising his masturbation, bred a longing desire in the bystanders that in such sort they might fill their bellies by rubbing or clawing the same.[31] To those that asked him why he sought no fitter place to feed in than in the open, frequented highway, he made answer, "It is because I am hungry in the open, frequented highway."

The [women philosophers] which meddled with their sects did likewise in all places and without any discretion meddle with their bodies; and Crates had never received Hipparchia into his fellowship but upon condition to follow all the customs and fashions of his order.

These philosophers set an extreme rate on virtue and rejected all other disciplines except the moral; hence it is that in all actions they ascribed the sovereign authority to the election of their wise, yea, and above all laws, and appointed no other restraint unto voluptuousness Abut the moderation and preservation of others' liberty.

Heraclitus and Protagoras, forsomuch as wine seemeth bitter unto the sick and pleasing to the healthy, and an oar crooked in the water and straight to them that see it above the water, and suchlike contrary appearances which are found in some subjects, argued that all subjects had the causes of these appearances in them and that there was some kind of bitterness in the wine which had a reference unto the sick man's taste, in the oar a certain crooked quality having relation to him that seeth it in the water, and so of all things else. Which implieth that all is in all things and by consequence nothing in any; for either nothing is or all is. This opinion put me in mind of the experience we

31 Florio mistranslates. Montaigne says: "For Diogenes, practicing his masturbation in public, expressed the wish, in the presence of those who were standing nearby, that he might similarly satisfy his stomach by rubbing it."

have that there is not any one sense or visage either straight or crooked, bitter or sweet, but man's wit shall find in the writings which he undertaketh to run over. In the purest, most unspotted, and most absolutely perfect word that can possibly be, how many errors, falsehoods, and lies have been made to proceed from it? What heresy hath not found testimonies and ground sufficient both to undertake and to maintain itself? It is therefore that the authors of such errors will never go from this proof of the testimony of words' interpretation.

A man of worth, going about by authority to approve the search of the philosopher's stone (wherein he was overwhelmed) alleged* at least five or six several passages out of the Holy Bible unto me, upon which he said he had at first grounded himself for the discharge of his conscience (for he is a man of the ecclesiastical profession); and truly the invention of them was not only pleasant but also very fitly applied to the defence of this goodly and mind-enchanting science.

This way is the credit of divining fables attained to. There is no prognosticator, if he have but this authority, that anyone will but vouchsafe to read him over and curiously to search all the infoldings and lusters of his words; but a man shall make him say what he pleaseth, as the Sibyls. There are so many means of interpretation that it is hard, be it flat-long, side-long, or edge-long, but an ingenious and pregnant wit shall in all subjects meet with some air that will fit his turn.

[C]Therefore is a cloudy, dark, and ambiguous style found in so frequent and ancient custom. That the author may gain to draw, allure, and busy posterity to himself, which not only the sufficiency but the casual favor of the matter may gain as much or more; as for other matters, let him, be it either through foolishness or subtlety, show himself somewhat obscure and divers is no matter: care not he for that. A number of spirits sifting and tossing him over will find and express sundry forms, either according, or collaterally, or contrary to his own, all which shall do him credit. He shall see himself enriched by the means of his disciples, as the grammar school masters.

[A]It is that what hath made many things of nothing to pass very current, that hath brought divers books in credit, and charged with all sorts of matter that any hath but desired: one selfsame thing admitting a thousand and a thousand, and as many several images and divers considerations as it best pleaseth us.

[C]Is it possible that ever Homer meant all that which some make him to have meant, and that he prostrated himself to so many and so several shapes as divines, lawyers, captains, philosophers, and all sort of people else, which, how diversely and contrary soever it be they treat of sciences, do notwithstanding wholly rely upon him and refer themselves unto him as a general master for all offices, works, sciences, and tradesmen, and an universal counsellor in all enterprises? [A]Whosoever hath had need of oracles or predictions and would apply them to himself hath found them in him for his purpose. A notable man, and a good friend of mine, would make one marvel to hear what strange, far-fetched conceits and admirable affinities in favor of our religion he maketh to derive from him; and can hardly be drawn from this opinion but that such was Homer's intent and meaning (yet is Homer so familiar unto him as I think no man of our age is better acquainted with him). [C]And what he finds in favor of our religion many ancient learned men have found in favor of theirs.

See how Plato is tossed and turned over; every man endeavoring to apply [him] to his purpose giveth him what construction he list. He is wrested and inserted to all newfangled opinions that the world receiveth or alloweth of, and according to the different course of subjects is made to be repugnant unto himself. Everyone according to his sense makes him to disavow the customs that were lawful in his days inasmuch as they are unlawful in these times. All which is very lively and strongly maintained, according as the wit and learning of the interpreter is strong and quick.

[A]Upon the ground which Heraclitus had, and that sentence of his that all things had those shapes in them which men found in them, Democritus out of the very same drew a clean contrary conclusion, *id est,* that subjects had nothing at all in them of that which we found in them; and forasmuch as honey was sweet to one man and bitter to another, he argued that honey was neither sweet not bitter. The Pyrrhonians would say they know not whether it be sweet or bitter, or both, or neither; for they ever gain the highest point of doubting. [C]The Cyrenaics held that nothing was perceptible outwardly, and only that was perceivable which by the inward touch or feeling touched or concerned us, as grief and sensuality, distinguishing neither tune, nor colors, but only certain affections that came to us of them, and that man had no other seat of his judgment. Protagoras deemed that to be true to all men which to all men seemeth so. The Epicureans place all judgment in the senses and in the notice of things and in voluptuousness. Plato's mind was that the judgment of truth and truth itself drawn from opinions and senses belonged to the spirit and to cogitation.

[A]This discourse hath drawn me to the consideration of the senses, wherein consisteth the greatest foundation and trial of our ignorance. Whatsoever is known is without peradventure known by the faculty of the knower; for since the judgment cometh from the operation of him that judgeth, reason requireth that he perform and act this operation by his means and will and not by others' compulsion, as it would follow if we knew things by the force and according to the law of their essence.

Now all knowledge is addressed unto us by the senses; they are our masters:

> [B]Whereby a way for credit leads well-lined
> Into man's breast and temple of his mind.
>
> Lucr. V.103.

[A]Science begins by them and in them is resolved.

After all, we should know no more than a stone unless we know that here is sound, smell, light, savor, measure, weight, softness, hardness, sharpness, color, smoothness, breadth, and depth. Behold here the platform of all the frame and principles of the building of all our knowledge. [C]And according to some, science is nothing else but what is known by the senses. [A]Whosoever can force me to contradict my senses hath me fast by the throat and cannot make me recoil one foot backward. The senses are the beginning and end of human knowledge:

> You shall find knowledge of the truth at first was bred
> From our first senses, nor can senses be misled. . . .
> What than our senses should
> With us more credit hold?
>
> Lucr. IV.479, 483.

Attribute as little as may be unto them, yet must this ever be granted them, that all our instruction is addressed by their means and intermission. Cicero saith that Chrysippus, having assayed to abate the power of his senses and of their virtue, presented contrary arguments unto himself and so vehement oppositions that he could not satisfy himself. Whereupon Carneades, who defended the contrary part, boasted that he used the very same weapons and words of Chrysippus to combat against him, and therefore cried out upon him, "O miserable man! thine own strength hath foiled thee!"

There is no greater absurdity in our judgment than to maintain that fire heateth not, that light shineth not, that in iron there is neither weight nor firmness, which are notices our senses bring unto us, nor belief or science in man that may be compared unto that in certain.

The first consideration I have upon the senses' subject is that I make a question whether man be provided of all natural senses or no. I see divers creatures that live an entire and perfect life, some without sight, and some without hearing. Who knoweth whether we also want either one, two, three, or many senses more? For, if we want any one, our discourse cannot discover the want or defect thereof. It is the senses' privilege to be the extreme bounds of our perceiving. There is nothing beyond them that may stead* us to discover them; no one sense can discover another:

> [B]Can ears the eyes, or can touch reprehend
> The ears, or shall mouth's taste that touch amend?
> Shall our nose it confute,
> Or eyes 'gainst it dispute?
>
> Lucr. IV.487.

[A]They all make the extremest line of our faculty:

> To teach distinctly might
> Is shar'd; each hath its right.
>
> Lucr. IV.490.

It is impossible to make a man naturally blind, to conceive that he seeth not; impossible to make him desire to see and sorrow his defect. Therefore ought we not to take assurance that our mind is contented and satisfied with those we have, seeing it hath not wherewith to feel her own malady and perceive her imperfection, if it be in any. It is impossible to tell that blind man anything, either by discourse, argument, or similitude, that lodgeth any apprehension of light, color, or sight in his imagination. There is nothing more backward that may push the senses to any evidence. The blind-born, which we perceive desire to see, it is not to understand what they require; they have learned of us that something they want and something they desire, that is in us, [C]with the effects and consequences thereof, which they call good; [A]yet wot not they what it is, nor apprehend they it near or far.

I have seen a gentleman of a good house, born blind — at least blind in such an age that he knows not what sight is. He understandeth so little what he wanteth that, as we do, he useth words fitting sight and applieth them after a manner only proper and peculiar to himself. A child being brought before him to whom he was godfather, taking him in his arms, he said, "Good Lord, what a fine child this is! It is a goodly thing to see him: what a cheerful countenance he hath! How prettily he looketh!" He will say as one of us: "This hall hath a fair prospect; it is very fair weather; the sun shines clear." Nay, which is more, because hunting, hawking, tennis-play, and shooting at butts are our common sports and exercises (for so he hath heard) his mind will be so affected unto them, and he will so busy himself about them, that he will think to have as great an interest in them as any of us and show himself as earnestly passionate both in liking and disliking them as any else; yet doth he conceive and receive them but by hearing. If he be in a fair, champain* ground where he may ride, they will tell him, "yonder is a hare started," or, "the hare is killed"; he is as busily earnest of his game as he heareth others to be that have perfect sight. Give him a ball, he takes it in the left hand and with the right strikes it away with his racket. In a piece* he shoots at random and is well pleased with what his men tell him, be it high or wide.

Who knows whether mankind commit as great a folly for want of some sense and that by this default the greater part of the visage of things be concealed from us? Who knows whether the difficulties we find in sundry of nature's works proceed thence? And whether divers effects of beasts which exceed our capacity are produced by the faculty of some sense that we want? And whether some of them have by that mean a fuller and more perfect life than ours? We seize on an apple well nigh with all our senses: we find redness, smoothness, odor, and sweetness in it; besides which it may have other virtues, either drying or binding, to which we have no sense to be referred. The proprieties* which in many things we call secret, as in the adamant to draw iron — is it not likely there should be sensitive faculties in nature able to judge and perceive them, the want whereof breedeth in us the ignorance of the true essence of such things? It is happily some particular sense that unto cocks or chanticleers discovereth the morning and midnight hour and moveth them to crow; [C]that teacheth a hen before any use or experience to fear a hawk and not a goose or a peacock, far greater birds; that warneth young chickens of this hostile quality which the cat hath against them, and not to distrust a dog: to strut and arm themselves against the mewing of the one (in some sort a flattering and mild voice) and not against the barking of the other (a snarling and quarrelous voice); that instructeth rats, wasps, and emmets ever to choose the best cheese and fruit, having never tasted them before; [A]and that addresseth the stag, [C]the elephant, and the serpent [A]to the knowledge of certain herbs and simples which, being either wounded or sick, have the virtue to cure them.

There is no sense but hath some great domination and which by his mean affordeth not an infinite number of knowledges. If we were to report the intelligence of sounds, of harmony, and of the voice, it would bring an unimaginable confusion to all the rest of our learning and science. For, besides what is tied to the proper effect of every sense, how many arguments, consequences, and conclusions draw we unto other things by comparing one sense to another? Let a skillful wise man but imagine human nature to be originally produced without sight and discourse; how much ignorance and trouble such a defect would bring unto him, and what obscurity and blindness in our mind: by that shall we perceive how much the privation of one or two or three such senses, if there be any in us, doth import us about the knowledge of truth. We have by the consultation and concurrence of our five senses formed one verity, whereas peradventure there was required the accord and consent of eight or ten senses and their contribution to attain a perspicuous insight of her and see her in her true essence.

Those sects which combat man's science do principally combat the same by the uncertainty and feebleness of our senses; for since by their mean and intermission all knowledge comes unto us, if they chance to miss in the report they make unto us, if either they corrupt or alter that which from abroad they bring unto us, if the light which by them is transported into our soul be obscured in the passage, we have nothing else to hold by. From this extreme difficulty are sprung all these fantasies which every subject containeth, whatsoever we find in it: that it hath not what we suppose to find in it; and that of the Epicureans, which is that the sun is no greater than our sight doth judge it:

> BWhate'er it be, it in no greater form doth pass
> Than to our eyes, which it behold, it seeming was;
> Lucr. V.577.

Athat the appearances, which represent a great body, to him that is near unto it and a much lesser to him that is further from it, are both true:

> BYet grant we not in this our eyes deceiv'd or blind;
> Impute not then to eyes this error of the mind;
> Lucr. IV.380, 387.

Aand, resolutely, that there is no deceit in the senses; that a man must stand to their mercy, and elsewhere seek reasons to excuse the difference and contradiction we find in them, yea, invent all other untruths and raving conceits (so far come they) rather than excuse the causes.

CTimagoras swore that howsoever he winked or turned his eyes he could never perceive the light of the candle to double, and that this seeming proceeded from the vice of opinion and not from the instrument.

AOf all absurdities, the most absurd Camongst the Epicureans Ais to disavow the force and effect of the senses.

> What by the eyes is seen at any time is true.
> Though the cause reason could not render of the view,

Why what was square at hand afar off seemed round,
Yet it much better were that, wanting reason's ground,
The causes of both forms we harp on but not hit
Than let slip from our hands things clear and them omit,
And violate our first belief and rashly rend
All those groundworks whereon both life and health depend.
For not alone all reason falls; life likewise must
Fail out of hand, unless your senses you dare trust,
And breakneck places, and all other errors shun,
From which we in this kind most carefully should run.

Lucr. IV.500.

[C]This desperate and so little philosophical counsel represents no other thing but that human science cannot be maintained but by unreasonable, fond,* and mad reason; yet is it better that man use it to prevail, yea, and of all other remedies else how fantastical soever they be, rather than avow his necessary foolishness. So prejudicial and disadvantageous a verity he cannot avoid, but senses must necessarily be the sovereign masters of his knowledge; but they are uncertain and falsifiable to all circumstances. There must a man strike to the utmost of his power, and if his just forces fail him, as they are wont, to use and employ obstinacy, temerity, and impudency.

[B]If that which the Epicureans affirm be true, that is to say, we have no science if the appearances of the senses be false; and that which the Stoics say, if it is also true, that the senses' appearances are so false as they can produce us no science; we will conclude at the charges of these two great dogmatist sects that there is no science. [A]Touching the error and uncertainty of the senses' operation, a man may store himself with as many examples as he pleaseth, so ordinary are the faults and deceits they use towards us. And the echoing or reporting of a valley, the sound of a trumpet seemeth to sound before us which cometh a mile behind us:

[B]And hills, which from the main far off to kenning* stand,
Appear all one, though they far-distant be, at hand.
And hills and fields do seem unto our boat to fly,
Which we drive by our boat as we do pass thereby.
When in midst of a stream a stately horse doth stay,
The stream's o'erthwarting seems his body 'cross to sway
And swiftly 'gainst the stream to thrust him th' other way.

Lucr. IV.398, 390, 421

[A]To roll a bullet under the forefinger, the middlemost being put over it, a man must very much enforce himself to affirm there is but one, so assuredly doth our sense present us two. That the senses do often master our discourse, and force it to receive impressions which he knoweth and judgeth to be false, it is daily seen. I leave the sense of feeling, which hath his functions nearer, more quick and substantial, and which by the effect of the grief or pain it brings to the body doth so often confound and re-inverse all these goodly Stoical resolutions and enforceth to cry out of the bellyache him who hath with all resolution established in his mind this doctrine, that the colic, as every other sickness or pain, is a thing indifferent, wanting power to abate anything of sovereign good or chief felicity, wherein the wise man is placed by his own virtue.

There is no heart so demiss* but the rattling sound of a drum or the clang of a trumpet will rouse and inflame, nor mind so harsh and stern but the sweetness and harmony of music will move and tickle; nor any soul so skittish and stubborn that hath not a feeling of some reverence in considering the cloudy vastity and gloomy canopies of our churches, the eye-pleasing diversity of ornaments, and orderly order of our ceremonies, and hearing the devout and religious sound of our organs, the moderate, symphonical, and heavenly harmony of our voice. Even those that enter into them with an obstinate will and contemning mind have in their heart a feeling of remorse, of chillness and horror, that puts them into a certain diffidence of their former opinions.

[B]As for me, I distrust mine own strength to hear with a settled mind some of Horace's or Catullus' verses sung with a sufficiently well-tuned voice, uttered by and proceeding from a fair, young, and heart-alluring mouth. [C]And Zeno had reason to say that the voice was the flower of beauty.

Some have gone about to make me believe that a man who most of us Frenchmen know, in repeating certain verses he had made, had imposed upon me that they were not such in writing as in the air and that mine eyes would judge of them otherwise than mine ears, so much credit hath pronunciation to give price and fashion to those works that pass her mercy. Whereupon Philoxenus was not to be blamed when, hearing one to give an ill accent to some composition of his, he took in a rage some of his pots or bricks and, breaking them, trod and trampled them under his feet, saying unto him, "I break and trample what is thine, even as thou manglest and marrest what is mine."

[A]Wherefore did they who with an undaunted resolve have procured their own death, because they would not see the blow or stroke coming, turn their face away? And those who for their health's sake cause themselves to be cut and cauterized cannot endure the sight of the preparations, tools, instruments, and works of the chirugeon,* but because the sight should have no part of the pain or smart? Are not these fit examples to verify the authority which senses have over discourse?

We may long enough know that such a one's locks or flaring tresses are borrowed of a page or taken from some lackey, that this fair ruby-red came from Spain and this whiteness or smoothness from the ocean sea; yet must sight force us to find and deem the subject more lovely and more pleasing against all reason. For in that there is nothing of its own:

> We are misled by ornaments. What is amiss
> Gold and gems cover; least part of herself the maiden is.
> 'Mongst things so many you may ask where your love lies:
> Rich love by this Gorgonian shield deceives thine eyes.
> Ovid. *Remed. amor.* I.343.

How much do poets ascribe unto the virtue of the senses, which makes Narcissus to have even fondly* lost himself for the love of his shadow?

> He all admires, whereby himself is admirable;
> Fond* he, fond of himself, to himself amiable;
> He that doth like is lik'd; and while he doth desire
> He is desired; at once he burns and sets on fire.
> Ovid. *Metam.* III.424.

And Pygmalion's wits so troubled by the impression of the sights of his ivory statue, that he loveth and serves it, as if it had life:

> He kisses and thinks kisses come again;
> He sues, pursues, and holds, believes in vain
> His fingers sink where he doth touch the place,
> And fears lest black and blue touch'd limbs deface.
> Ovid. *Metam.* X.256.

Let a philosopher be put in a cage made of small and thin-set iron wire and hanged on the top of Our Lady's churchsteeple in Paris; he shall, by evident reason, perceive that it is impossible he shall fall down out of it, yet can he not choose, except he have been brought up in the trade of tilers or thatchers, but the sight of that exceeding height must needs dazzle his sight and amaze or turn his senses. For we have much ado to warrant ourselves in the walks or battlements of a high tower or steeple if they be battlemented and wrought with pillars and somewhat wide one from another, although of stone and never so strong. Nay, some there are that can scarcely think or hear of such heights. Let a beam or plank be laid across from one of those two steeples to the other, as big, as thick, as strong, and as broad as would suffice any man to walk safely upon it; there is no philosophical wisdom of so great resolution and constancy that is able to encourage and persuade us to march upon it as we would were it below on the ground.

I have sometimes made trial of it upon our mountains on this side of Italy, yet am I one of those that will not easily be affrighted with such things; and I could not without horror to my mind and trembling of legs and thighs endure to look on those infinite precipices and steepy downfalls, though I were not near the brim nor any danger within my length and more, and unless I had willingly gone to the peril I could not possibly have fallen. Where I also noted that how deep soever the bottom were, if but a tree, a shrub, or any out-butting crag of a rock presented itself unto our eyes upon those steepy and high alps, somewhat to uphold the sight and divide the same, it doth somewhat ease and assure us from fear, as if it were a thing which in our fall might either help or uphold us; and that we cannot without some dread and giddiness in the head so much as abide to look upon one of those even and downright precipices: [C]"So as they cannot look down without giddiness of both eyes and minds" (Livy XLIV.vi.); [A]which is an evident deception of the sight.

Therefore was it that a worthy philosopher pulled out his eyes that so he might discharge his soul of the seducing and diverting he received by them, and the better and more freely apply himself unto philosophy.[32] But by this account he should also have stopped his ears, [B]which, as Theophrastus said, are the most dangerous instruments we have to receive violent and sudden impressions to trouble and alter us, [A]and should, in the end, have deprived himself of all his other senses, that is to say, both of his being and life. For they have the power to command our discourses and sway our mind. [C]"It comes to pass that many times our minds are much moved with some shadows, many times with deep sounding or singing of voices, many times with care and fear" (Cic. *De div.* I.xxxvii.).

[A]Physicians hold that there are certain complexions which by some sounds and instruments are agitated even unto fury. I have seen some who, without infringing their patience, could not well hear a bone gnawn under their table; and we see few men but are much troubled at that sharp, harsh, and teeth-edging noise that smiths make in filing of brass or scraping of iron and steel together. Others will be offended if they but hear one chew his meat somewhat aloud; nay, some will be angry with or hate a man that either speaks in the nose or rattles in the throat. That piping prompter of Gracchus who mollified, raised, and wound his master's voice whilst he was making orations at Rome, what good did he if the motion and quality of the sound had not the force to move and efficacy to alter the auditory's judgment? Verily,

32 Democritus.

there is great cause to make so much ado and keep such a coil* about the constancy and firmness of this goodly piece,[33] which suffers itself to be handled, changed, and turned by the motion and accident of so light a wind.

The very same cheating and cozening that senses bring to our understanding, themselves receive it in their turns. Our mind doth likewise take revenge of it; ᶜthey lie, they cog,* and deceive one another avie.* ᴬWhat we see and hear, being passionately transported by anger, we neither see nor hear it as it is:

> That two suns do appear
> And double Thebes are there.
> Virg. *Aen.* IV.470.

The object which we love seemeth much more fair unto us than it is —

> ᴮWe therefore see that those who many ways are bad
> And foul are yet belov'd and in chief honor had
> Lucr. IV.1152

— ᴬand that much fouler which we loathe. To a pensive and heart-grieved man, a clear day seems gloomy and dusky. Our senses are not only altered but many times dulled by the passions of the mind. How many things see we which we perceive not if our mind be busied or distracted elsewhere!

> Ev'n in things manifest it may be seen,
> If you mark not, they are as they had been
> At all times sever'd far, removed clean.
> Lucr. IV.809.

The soul seemeth to retire herself into the inmost parts and amuseth the senses' faculties, so that both the inward and outward parts of man are full of weakness and falsehood.

ᴮThose which have compared our life unto a dream have happily had more reason so to do than they were aware. When we dream, our soul liveth, worketh, and exerciseth all her faculties, even and as much as when it waketh; and if more softly and obscurely, yet verily not so as that it may admit so great a difference as there is between a dark night and a clear day: yea, as between a night and a shadow. There it sleepeth; here it slumbereth, more or less. They are ever darknesses, yes, Cimmerian darknesses.

ᶜWe wake sleeping and sleep waking. In my sleep I see not so clear, yet can I never find my waking clear enough or without dimness. Sleep also in his deepest rest doth sometimes bring dreams

[33] The judgment.

asleep; but our waking is never so vigilant as it may clearly purge and dissipate the ravings or idle fantasies which are the dreams of the waking, and worse than dreams.

Our reason and soul receiving the fantasies and opinions which sleeping seize on them, and authorizing our dreams' actions with like approbation as it doth the day's, why make we not a doubt whether our thinking and our working be another dreaming, and our waking some kind of sleeping?

[A]If the senses be our first judges, it is not ours that must only be called to counsel; for in this faculty beasts have as much or more right as we. It is most certain that some have their hearing more sharp than man, others their sight, others their smelling, others their feeling or taste. Democritus said that gods and beasts had the sensitive faculties much more perfect than man. Now between the effects of their senses and ours the difference is extreme. Our spittle cleanseth and drieth our sores and killeth serpents:

> There is such distance and such difference in these things
> As what to one is meat t' another poison brings;
> For oft a serpent touched with spittle of a man
> Doth die and gnaw itself with fretting all he can.
>
> Lucr. IV.636.

What qualities shall we give unto spittle, either according to us or according to the serpent? By which two senses shall we verify its true essence which we seek for? Pliny saith that there are certain sea-hares in India that to us are poison and we bane to them, so that we die if we but touch them. Now whether is man or the sea-hare poison? Whom shall we believe, either the fish of man or the man of fish?

[B]Some quality of the air infecteth man which nothing at all hurteth the ox; some other the ox and not the man. Which of the two is either in truth or nature the pestilent quality?

[A]Such as are troubled with the yellow jaundice deem all things they look upon to be yellowish, which seem more pale and wan to them than to us:

> [B]And all that jaundic'd men behold
> They yellow straight or palish hold.
>
> Lucr. IV.330.

[A]Those which are sick of the disease which physicians call hyposphagma, which is a suffusion of blood under the skin, imagine that all things they see are bloody and red. Those humors that so change the sight's operation, what know we whether they are predominant and ordinary in beasts? For, we see some whose eyes are as yellow as theirs that have the jaundice, others that have them all blood-shotten with redness. It is likely that the object's color they look upon seemeth otherwise to them than to us. Which of the two judgments shall be true? For it is not said that the essence of things hath reference to man alone. Hardness, whiteness, depth, and sharpness touch the service and concern the knowledge of beasts as well as ours; nature hath given the use of them to them as well as to us.

When we wink a little with our eye, we perceive the bodies we look upon to seem longer and outstretched. Many beasts have their eye as winking as we. This length is then haply the true form of that body and not that which our eyes give it being in their ordinary seat. [B]If we close our eye above, things seem double unto us:

> The lights of candles double-flaming then,
> And faces twain, and bodies twain of men.
>
> Lucr. IV.451.

[A]If our ears chance to be hindered by anything, or that the passage of our hearing be stopped, we receive the sound otherwise than we were ordinarily wont. Such beasts as have hairy ears, or that in lieu of an ear have but a little hole, do not by consequence hear that we hear and receive the sound other than it is. We see at solemn shows or in theatres that, opposing any colored glass between our eyes and the torches' light, whatsoever is in the room seems or green or yellow or red unto us, according to the color of the glass:

> [B]And yellow, russet, rusty curtains work this feat
> In common sights abroad where over scaffolds great,
> Stretched on masts, spread over beams, they hang still waving.
> All the seats' circuit there, and all the stage's braving
> Of fathers, mother, gods, and all the circled show,
> They double-dye and in their colors make to flow.
>
> Lucr. IV.73.

[A]It is likely that those beasts' eyes which we see to be of divers colors produce the appearances of those bodies they look upon to be like their eyes.

To judge the senses' operation it were then necessary we were first agreed with beasts, and then between ourselves; which we are not; but ever and anon disputing about that one seeth, heareth, or tasteth something to be other than indeed it is, and contend as much as about anything else of the diversity of those images our senses report unto us. A young child heareth, seeth, tasteth otherwise, by nature's ordinary rule, than a man of thirty years; and he otherwise than another of threescore.

The senses are to some more obscure and dim and to some more open and quick. We receive things differently, according as they are and seem unto us. Things being then so uncertain and full of controversy, it is no longer a wonder if it be told us that we may avouch snow to be white unto us, but to affirm that it's such in essence and in truth we cannot warrant ourselves; which foundation being so shaken, all the science in the world must necessarily go to wrack.

What? Do our senses themselves hinder one another? To the sight a picture seemeth to be raised aloft, and in the handling flat. Shall we say that musk is pleasing or no, which comforteth our smelling and offendeth our taste? There are herbs and ointments which to some parts of the body are good and to othersome hurtful. Honey is pleasing to the taste but unpleasing to the sight. Those jewels wrought and fashioned like feathers or sprigs which in impresas* are called feathers without ends, no eye can discern the breadth of them, and no man warrant himself from this deception that on the one end or side it groweth not broader and broader, sharper and sharper, and on the other more and more narrow, especially being rolled about one's finger; when notwithstanding, in handling it seemeth equal in breadth and everywhere alike.

[B]Those who to increase and aid their luxury were anciently wont to use perspective or looking glasses fit to make the object they represented appear very big and great, so that the members they were to use might by that ocular increase please them the more, to whether of the two senses yielded they, either to the sight presenting those members as big and great as they wished them, or to the feeling that presented them little and to be disdained?

[A]Is it our senses that lend these diverse conditions unto subjects when, for all that, the subjects have but one? As we see in the bread we eat: it is but bread; but one using it, it maketh bones, blood, flesh, hair, and nails thereof:

> [B]As meat distributed into the members dies,
> Another nature yet it, perishing, supplies.
>
> Lucr. III.703.

[A]The moistness which the root of a tree sucks becomes a trunk, a leaf, and fruit; and the air, being but one, applied unto a trumpet becometh diverse in a thousand sorts of sounds. Is it our senses, say I, who likewise fashion of diverse qualities those subjects, or whether have they them so and such? And upon this doubt, what may we conclude of their true essence?

Moreover, since the accidents of sickness, of madness, or of sleep make things appear other unto us than they seem unto the healthy, unto the wise, and to the waking, is it not likely that our right seat and natural humors have also wherewith to give a being unto things, having reference unto their condition, and to appropriate them to itself, as do inordinate humors, and our health as capable to give them his visage as sickness? [C]Why hath not the temperate man some form of the objects relative unto himself as the intemperate? And shall not he likewise imprint his character in them? The distasted impute wallowishness* unto wine, the healthy good taste, and the thirsty briskness, relish, and delicacy.

[A]Now our condition appropriating things unto itself and transforming them to its own humor, we know no more how things are in sooth and truth; for nothing comes unto us but falsified and altered by our senses. Where the compass, the quadrant, or the ruler are crooked, all proportions drawn by them and all the buildings erected by their measure are also necessarily defective and imperfect. The uncertainty of our senses yields whatever they produce also uncertain.

> As in building, if the first rule be to blame
> And the deceitful square err from right form and frame,
> If any instrument want any jot of weight,
> All must needs faulty be and stooping in their height,
> The building naught, absurd, upward and downward bended,
> As if they meant to fall, and fall as they intended;
> And all this as betrayed
> By judgments foremost laid.
> Of things the reason therefore needs must faulty be
> And false, which from false senses draws its pedigree.
>
> Lucr. IV.514.

As for the rest, who shall be a competent judge in these differences? As we said in controversies of religion that we must have a judge inclined to neither party and free from partiality or affection, which is hardly to be had among Christians, so happeneth it in this; for if he be old, he cannot judge of age's sense, himself being a party in this controversy, and so if he be young, healthy, sick, sleeping, or waking — it is all one. We had need of somebody void and exempted from all these qualities that without any preoccupation of judgment might judge of these propositions as indifferent unto him, by which account we should have a judge that were no man.

To judge of the appearances that we receive of subjects, we had need have a judicatory instrument; to verify this instrument we should have demonstration; and to approve demonstration an instrument: thus are we ever turning round. Since the senses cannot determine our disputation, themselves being so full of uncertainty, it must then be reason; and no reason can be established without another reason: then are we ever going back unto infinity.

Our fantasy doth not apply itself to strange things but is rather conceived by the interposition of senses, and senses cannot comprehend a strange subject, nay, not so much as their own passions. And so, nor the fantasy nor the appearance is the subject's, but rather the passions only and sufferance of the sense; which passion and subject are divers things. Therefore, who judgeth by appearances judgeth by a thing different from the subject.

And to say that the senses' passions refer the quality of strange subjects by resemblance unto the soul, how can the soul and the understanding rest assured of that resemblance, having of itself no commerce with foreign subjects? Even as he that knows not Socrates, seeing his picture, cannot say that it resembleth him. And would a man judge by appearances, be it by all, it is impossible; for by their [contrarieties] and differences they hinder one another, as we see by experience. May it be that some choice appearances rule and direct the others? This choice must be verified by another choice, the second by a third, and so shall we never make an end.

In few, there is no constant existence, neither of our being nor of the objects. And we, and our judgment, and all mortal things else do incessantly roll, turn, and pass away. Thus can nothing be certainly established, nor of the one, nor of the other, both the judging and the judged being in continual alteration and motion.

We have no communication with being, for every human nature is ever in the middle between being born and dying, giving nothing of itself but an obscure appearance and shadow and an uncertain and weak opinion. And if perhaps you fix your thought to take its being it would be even as one should go about to grasp the water; for how much the more he shall close and press that which, by its own nature, is ever gliding, so much the more he shall lose what he would hold and fasten. Thus, seeing all things are subject to pass from one change to another, reason, which therein seeketh a real subsistence, finds herself deceived, as unable to apprehend anything subsistent and permanent; forsomuch as each thing either cometh to a being and is not yet altogether, or beginneth to die before it be born.

Plato said that bodies had never an existence, but indeed a birth; [c]supposing that Homer made the Ocean father and Thetis mother of the gods thereby to show us that all things are in continual motion, change, and variation — as he saith, a common opinion amongst all the philosophers before his time, only Parmenides excepted, who denied any motion to be in things, of whose power he maketh no small account. [A]Pythagoras, that each thing or matter was ever gliding and labile. The Stoics affirm there is no present time, and that which we call present is but conjoining and assembling of future time and past. Heraclitus averreth that no man ever entered twice one same river. [B]Epicharmus avoucheth that who erewhile borrowed any money doth not now owe it, and that he who yesternight was bidden to dinner this day cameth today unbidden, since they are no more themselves but are become others, [A]and that one mortal substance could not twice be found in one self estate; for by the suddenness and lightness of change sometimes it wasteth and other times it assembleth; now it comes and now it goes; in such sort that he who beginneth to be born never comes to the perfection of being. For this being born cometh never to an end, nor ever stayeth as being at an end; but after the seed proceedeth continually in change and alteration from one to another. As of man's seed there is first made a shapeless fruit in the mother's womb, then a shapen child, then, being out of the womb, a sucking babe; afterward he becometh a lad, than consequently a stripling, then a full-grown man, then an old man, and in the end an aged decrepit man. So that age and subsequent generation goeth ever undoing and wasting the precedent:

> [B]Of th' universal world age doth the nature change,
> And all things from one state must to another range;
> No one thing like itself remains; all things do pass;
> Nature doth change and drive to change each thing that was.
>
> Lucr. V.826.

[A]And when we do foolishly fear a kind of death, whenas we have already passed and daily pass so many others. For not only, as Heraclitus said, the death of fire is a generation of air, and the death of air a generation of water, but also we may most evidently see it in ourselves. The flower of age dieth, fadeth, and fleeteth when age comes upon us, youth endeth in the flower of a full-grown man's age, childhood in youth, and the first age dieth in infancy. And yesterday endeth in this day, and today shall die in tomorrow. And nothing remaineth or ever continueth in one state.

For to prove it, if we should ever continue one and the same, how is it then that now we rejoice at one thing and now at another? How comes it to pass we love things contrary, or we hate them, or we love them, or we blame them? How is it that we have different affections, holding no more the same sense in the same thought? For it is not likely that without alteration we should take other passions; and what admitteth alterations continueth not the same; and if it be not one self same, then *is* it not, but rather, with *being all one* the simple *being* doth also change, ever becoming other from other. And by consequence nature's senses are deceived and lie falsely, taking what appeareth for what is, for want of knowing what it is that is.

But then what is it that is indeed? That which is eternal: that is to say, that which never had birth nor ever shall have end and to which no time can bring change or cause alteration. For time is a fleeting thing, and which appeareth as in a shadow, with the matter ever gliding, always fluent, without ever being stable or permanent. To whom rightly belong these terms *before* and *after,* and it *hath been* or *shall be,* which at first sight doth manifestly show that it is not a thing which *is;* for it were great sottishness and apparent falsehood to say that that is which is not yet in being, or that already hath ceased from being. And concerning these words, *present, instant, even now,* by which it seems that especially we uphold and principally ground the intelligence of time, reason discovering the same doth forthwith destroy it; for presently it severeth it asunder and divideth it into future and past time, as willing to see it necessarily parted in two.

As much happeneth unto nature, which is measured according unto time which measureth her; for no more is there anything in her that remaineth or is subsistent; rather all things in her are either born or ready to be born, or dying. By means whereof it were a sin to say of God, who is the only that is, that he was or shall be; for these words are declinations, passages, or vicissitudes of that which cannot last nor continue in being. Wherefore we must conclude that only God *is,* not according to any measure of time, but according to an immovable and immutable eternity, not measured by time, nor subject to any declination, before whom nothing is nor nothing shall be after, nor more new or more recent, but one really being, which by one only *now* or *present* filleth the *ever;* and there is nothing that truly is but he alone — without saying "He hath been" or "He shall be — without beginning and sans* ending.

To this so religious conclusion of a heathen man I will only add this word taken from the testimony of the same condition,[34] for an end of this long and tedious discourse which might well furnish me with endless matter: "Oh what a vile and abject thing is man," saith he, "unless he raise himself above humanity!"

^C^Observe here a notable speech and a profitable desire, but likewise absurd. For ^A^ to make the handful greater than the hand, and the embraced greater than the arm, and to hope to straddle more than our leg's length, is impossible and monstrous. Nor that man should

34 From Seneca.

mount over and above himself or humanity; for he cannot see but with his own eyes nor take hold but with his own arms.

He shall raise himself up if it please God extraordinarily to lend him his helping hand. He may elevate himself by forsaking and renouncing his own means and suffering himself to be elevated and raised by mere heavenly means.

[C]It is for our Christian faith, not for his Stoic virtue, to pretend or aspire to this divine metamorphosis or miraculous transmutation.

Of Repenting

§ III. 2 ✧ 1585–88

[B]Others fashion man, I repeat him;[1] and represent a particular one, but ill-made, and whom were I to form anew, he should be far other than he is; but he is now made. And though the lines of my picture change and vary, yet lose they not themselves.

The world runs all on wheels. All things therein move without intermission; yea the earth, the rocks of Caucasus, and the pyramids of Egypt, both with the public and their own motion. Constancy itself is nothing but a languishing and wavering dance. I cannot settle my object; it goeth so unquietly and staggering, with a natural drunkenness. I take it in this plight, as it is at the instant I amuse myself about it. I describe not the essence, but the passage; not a passage from age to age, or as the people reckon, from seven years to seven, but from day to day, from minute to minute. My history must be fitted to the present. I may soon change, not only fortune but intention. It is a counter-roll* of divers and variable accidents and irresolute imaginations, and sometimes contrary; whether it be that myself am other, or that I apprehend subjects by other circumstances and considerations. Howsoever, I may perhaps gainsay myself, but truth (as Demades said) I never gainsay: Were my mind settled, I would not essay,* but resolve myself. It is still a prentice and a probationer.

I propose a mean* life, and without luster. 'Tis all one. They fasten all moral philosophy as well to a popular and private life, as to one of richer stuff. Every man beareth the whole stamp of human condition. [C]Authors communicate themselves unto the world by some special and strange mark; I the first, by my general disposition, as Michel de Montaigne; not as a grammarian, or a poet, or a lawyer. If the world complain I speak too much of myself, I complain it thinks no more of itself.

[B]But is it reason that, being so private in use, I should pretend to make myself public in knowledge? Or is it reason I should produce into the world, where fashion and art have such sway and command,

1 A more precise translation of this famous opening phrase would be: "Others form man; I tell of him."

the raw and simple effects of nature, and of a nature as yet exceeding weak? To write books without learning, is it not to make a wall without stone or suchlike thing? Conceits of music are directed by art; mine by hap. Yet have I this according to learning, that never man handled subject he understood or knew better than I do this I have undertaken, being therein the cunningest man alive. Secondly, that never man [C]waded further into his matter, nor more distinctly sifted the parts and dependences of it, nor [B]arrived more exactly and fully to the end he proposed unto himself. To finish the same, I have need of naught but faithfulness, which is therein as sincere and pure as may be found. I speak truth, not my belly-full, but as much as I dare; and I dare the more, the more I grow into years, for it seemeth custom alloweth old age more liberty to babble and indiscretion to talk of itself. It cannot herein be as in trades where the craftsman and his work do often differ: Being a man of so sound and honest conversation, writ he so foolishly? Are such learned writings come from a man of so weak a conversation? [C]Who hath but an ordinary conceit and writeth excellently, one may say his capacity is borrowed, not of himself. A skillful man is not skillful in all things. But a sufficient man is sufficient everywhere, even unto ignorance.

[B]Here my book and myself march together and keep one pace. Elsewhere one may commend or condemn the work without the workman; here not. Who toucheth one toucheth the other. He who shall judge of it without knowing him, shall wrong himself more than me; he that knows it, hath wholly satisfied me — happy beyond my merit if I get this only portion of public approbation, as I may cause men of understanding to think I had been able to make use and benefit of learning, had I been endowed with any; and deserved better help of memory.

Excuse we here what I often say, that I seldom repent myself, [C]and that my conscience is contented with itself; not of an angel's or a horse's conscience, but as of a man's conscience. [B]Adding ever this clause, not of ceremony but of true and essential submission; that I speak, inquiring and doubting, merely and simply referring myself, from resolution, unto common and lawful opinions. I teach not; I report.

No vice is absolutely vice which offendeth not and a sound judgment accuseth not. For the deformity and incommodity thereof is so palpable as peradventure they have reason who say it is chiefly produced by sottishness and brought forth by ignorance; so hard is it to imagine one should know it without hating it. [C]Malice sucks up the greatest part of her own venom, and therewith empoisoneth herself. [B]Vice leaveth, as an ulcer in the flesh, a repentance in the soul which still scratcheth and bloodieth itself. For reason effaceth other griefs and sorrows, but engendereth those of repentance, the more irksome because inward, as the cold and heat of agues is more offensive than that which comes outward. I account vice (but each according to their measure) not only those which reason disallows, and nature condemns, but such as man's opinion hath forged as false and erroneous, if laws and custom authorize the same.

In like manner there is no goodness but gladdeth an honest disposition. There is truly I wot not what kind of congratulation, of well doing, which rejoiceth in ourselves, and a generous jollity, that accompanieth a good conscience. A mind courageously vicious may happily furnish itself with security, but she cannot be fraught with this self-[joying] delight and satisfaction.

It is no small pleasure for one to feel himself preserved from the contagion of an age so infected as ours, and to say to himself, "Could a man enter and see even into my soul, yet should he not find me guilty either of the affliction or ruin of anybody, nor culpable of envy or revenge, nor of public offense against the laws, nor tainted with innovation, trouble, or sedition, nor spotted with falsifying of my word." And although the liberty of times allowed and taught it every man, yet could I never be induced to touch the goods or dive into the purse of any Frenchman, and have always lived upon mine own, as well in time of war, as peace. Nor did I ever make use of any poor man's labor without reward. These testimonies of an unspotted conscience are very pleasing, which natural joy is a great benefit unto us, and the only payment never faileth us.

To ground the recompense of virtuous actions upon the approbation of others, is to undertake a most uncertain or troubled foundation, [C]namely in an age so corrupt and times so ignorant as this is. The vulgar people's good opinion is injurious. Whom trust you in seeing what is commendable? God keep me from being an honest man, according to the description I daily see made of honor, each one by himself! "What erst were vices are now grown fashions" (Sen. *Epist.* XXXIX.). Some of my friends have sometimes attempted to school me roundly and sift me plainly, either of their own motion or invited by me, as to an office which to a well-composed mind, both in profit and lovingness, exceedeth all the duties of sincere amity. Such have I ever entertained with open arms of courtesy and kind acknowledgment. But now, to speak from my conscience, I often found so much false measure in their reproaches and praises, that I had not greatly erred if I had rather erred than done well after their fashion.

[B]Such as we especially, who live a private life not exposed to any gaze but our own, ought in our hearts establish a touchstone and thereto touch our deeds and try our actions, and accordingly now cherish and now chastise ourselves. I have my own laws and tribunal to judge of me, whither I address myself more than anywhere else. I restrain my actions according to other but extend them according to myself. None but yourself knows rightly whether you be demiss* and cruel, or loyal and devout. Others see you not, but guess you by uncertain conjectures. They see not so much your nature as your art. Adhere not, then, to their opinion, [C]but hold unto your own. "You must use your own judgment" (Cic. *Tusc.* I.xxiii.). "The weight of the very conscience of vice and virtues is heavy; take that away, and all is down" (Cic. *De nat. deor.* III.xxxv.).

[B]But whereas [what] is said, that repentance nearly followeth sin, seemeth not to imply sin placed in his rich array, which lodgeth in us as in his proper mansion. One may disavow and disclaim vices that surprise us and whereto our passions transport us. But those, which by long habit are rooted in a strong, and anchored in a powerful will, are not subject to contradiction. Repentance is but a denying of our will and an opposition of our fantasies, which diverts us here and there. It makes some disavow his former virtue and continency.

> Why was not in a youth same mind as now?
> Or why bears not this mind a youthful brow?
>
> Hor. *Odes* IV.x.7.

That is an exquisite life which even in his own private keepeth itself in awe and order. Everyone may play the juggler and represent an honest man upon the stage; but within, and in bosom, where all things are lawful, where all is concealed, to keep a due rule or formal decorum, that's the point. The next degree is to be so in one's own home and in his ordinary actions, whereof we are to give account to nobody, wherein is no study, nor art. And therefore Bias describing the perfect state of a family, "whereof (saith he) the master be such inwardly by himself as he is outwardly, for fear of the laws and respect of men's speeches." And it was a worthy saying of Julius Drusus, to those workmen which for three thousand crowns offered so to reform his house that his neighbors should no more overlook into it. "I will give you six thousand (said he) and contrive it so that on all sides every man may look into it." The custom of Agesilaus is remembered with honor, who in his travel was wont to take up his lodging in churches, that the people and gods themselves might pry into his private actions. Some have been admirable to the world, in whom nor his wife, nor his servants ever noted anything remarkable. Few men have been admired of their familiars. CNo man hath been a Prophet, not only in his house, but in his own country, saith the experience of histories.[2] Even so in things of nought. And in this base example is the image of greatness discerned. In my climate* of Gascony they deem it a jest to see me in print. The further the knowledge which is taken of me is from home, of so much more worth am I. In Guienne I pay printers; in other places they pay me. Upon this accident they ground, who living and present keep close-lurking,* to purchase credit when they shall be dead and absent. I had rather have less. And I cast not myself into the world but for the portion I draw from it. That done, I quit it. BThe people attend on such a man with wonderment, from a public act unto his own doors; together with his robes he leaves off his part, falling so much the lower by how much higher he was mounted. View him within; there all is turbulent, disordered, and vile. And were order and formality found in him, a lively, impartial, and well-sorted judgment is required to perceive and fully to discern him in these base and private actions; considering that order is but a dumpish and drowsy virtue. To gain a battle, perform an ambassage, and govern a people are noble and worthy actions. To chide, laugh, sell, pay, love, hate, and mildly and justly to converse both with his own and with himself, not to relent, and not gainsay himself, are things more rare, more difficult, and less remarkable.

Retired lives sustain that way, whatever some say, offices as much more crabbed and extended than other lives do. CAnd private men (saith Aristotle) serve virtue more hardly, and more highly attend her, than those which are magistrates or placed in authority. BWe prepare ourselves unto eminent occasions more for glory than for conscience. CThe nearest way to come unto glory were to do that for conscience which we do for glory. BAnd meseemeth the virtue of Alexander representeth much less vigor in her large theater, than that of Socrates in his base and obscure exercitation. I easily conceive Socrates in the room of Alexander; Alexander in that of Socrates, I cannot. If any ask the one what he can do, he will answer, *Conquer the world;* let the same question be demanded of the other, he will say, *Lead my life conformably to its natural condition.* A science much more generous, more important, and more lawful.

The worth of the mind consisteth not in going high, but in marching orderly. CHer greatness is not exercised in greatness; in mediocrity it is. As those which judge and touch us inwardly make no great account of the brightness of our public actions, and see they are but streaks and points of clear-water surging from a bottom

[2] Cf. Luke IV. 24.

otherwise slimy and full of mud; so those who judge us by this gay outward appearance conclude the same of our inward constitution, and cannot couple popular faculties as theirs are, unto these other faculties, which amaze them so far from their level. So do we attribute savage shapes and ugly forms unto devils. As who doth not ascribe high-raised eyebrows, open nostrils, a stern, frightful visage, and a huge body unto Tamburlaine, as is the form or shape of the imagination we have foreconceived by the bruit of his name? Had any heretofore shown me Erasmus, I could hardly have been induced to think, but whatsoever he had said to his boy or hostess, had been adages and apothegms. We imagine much more fitly an artificer upon his close-stool* or on his wife, than a great judge, reverend for his carriage and regardful for his sufficiency. We think that from those high thrones they should not abase themselves so low as to live.

[B]As vicious minds are often incited to do well by some strange impulsion, so are virtuous spirits moved to do ill. They must then be judged by their settled estate, when they are near themselves, and as we say, at home, if at any time they be so; or when they are nearest unto rest and in their natural seat. Natural inclinations are by institution helped and strengthened, but they neither change nor exceed. A thousand natures in my time have, athwart a contrary disipline, escaped toward virtue or toward vice.

So when wild beasts, disused from the wood,
Fierce looks laid down, grow tame, clos'd in a cage
Taught to bear man, if then a little blood
Touch their hot lips, fury returns and rage;
Their jaws by taste admonish'd swell with veins,
Rage boils, and from faint keeper scarce abstains.
Lucan IV.237.

These original qualities are not grubbed out; they are but covered and hidden. The Latin tongue is to me in a manner natural; I understand it better than French. But it is now forty years I have not made use of it to speak, nor much to write. Yet in some extreme emotions and sudden passions, wherein I have twice or thrice fallen since my years of discretion — and namely once, when my father, being in perfect health, fell all along upon me in a swoon — I have ever, even from my very heart, uttered my first words in Latin, [C]nature rushing and by force expressing itself against so long a custom. [B]The like example is alleged to divers others.

Those which in my time have attempted to correct the fashions of the world by new opinions, reform the vices of appearance; those of essence they leave untouched if they increase them not. And their increase is much to be feared. We willingly protract all other well-doing upon these external reformations, of less cost and of greater merit; whereby we satisfy good cheap, other natural consubstantial and intestine vices. Look a little into the course of our experience. There is no man (if he listen to himself) that doth not discover in himself a peculiar form of his, a swaying form, which wrestleth against the institution and against the tempests of passions, which are contrary unto him. As for me, I feel not myself much agitated by a shock; I commonly find myself in mine own place, as are sluggish and lumpish bodies. If I am not close and near unto myself, I am never far off. My debauches or excesses transport me not much. There is nothing extreme and strange. Yet have I sound fits and vigorous lusts. The true condemnation, and which toucheth the common fashion of our men, is, that their very retreat is full of corruption and filth, the Idea of their amendment blurred and deformed, their repentance crazed and faulty very near as much as their sin. Some, either because they are so fast and naturally joined unto vice, or through long custom, have lost all sense of its ugliness. To others (of whose rank I am) vice is burdenous, but they counterbalance it with pleasure, or other occasions; and suffer it and at a certain rate lend themselves unto it, though basely and viciously. Yet might haply so remote a disproportion of measure be imagined where with justice the pleasure might excuse the offense, as we say of profit; not only being accidental and out of sin, as in thefts, but even in the very exercise of it, as in the acquaintance or copulation with women, where the provocation is so violent, and as they say, sometime unresistible.

In a town of a kinsman of mine the other day, being in Armagnac, I saw a countryman commonly surnamed The Thief, who himself reported his life to have been thus: Being born a beggar, and perceiving that to get his bread by the sweat of his brow and labor of his hands would never sufficiently arm him against penury, he resolved to become a thief; and that trade had employed all his youth safely, by means of his bodily strength. For he ever made up harvest and vintage in other men's grounds, but so far off and in so great heaps that it was beyond imagination one man should in one night carry away so much upon his shoulders. And was so careful to equal the prey and disperse the mischief he did, that the spoil was of less import to every particular man.

He is now, in old years, indifferently rich for a man of his condition (Godamercy* his trade), which he is not ashamed to confess openly. And to reconcile himself with God, he affirmeth to be daily ready, with his gettings and other good turns, to satisfy the posterity of those he hath heretofore wronged or robbed; which if himself be not of ability to perform (for he cannot do all at once), he will charge his heirs withal, according to the knowledge he hath of the wrongs by him done to every man. By this description, be it true or false, he respecteth theft as a dishonest and unlawful action, and hateth the same; yet less than pinching want. He repents but simply; for in regard it was so counterbalanced and recompensed, he repenteth not. That is not that habit which incorporates us unto vice and confirmeth our understanding in it, nor is it that boisterous wind which by violent blasts dazzleth and troubleth our minds, and at that time confounds, and overwhelms both us, our judgment, and all, into the power of vice.

What I do is ordinarily full and complete, and I march (as we say) all in one pace. I have not many motions that hide themselves and slink away from my reason, or which very near are not guided by the consent of all my parts, without division or intestine sedition. My judgment hath the whole blame or commendation. And the blame it hath once, it hath ever; for almost from its birth it hath been one, of the same inclination, course, and force. And in matters of general opinions, even from my infancy, I ranged myself to the point I was to hold.

Some sins there are outrageous, violent, and sudden; leave we them. But those other sins, so often reassumed, determined, and advised upon, whether they be of complexion [C]or of profession and calling, [B]I cannot conceive how they should so long be settled in one same courage unless the reason and conscience of the sinner were thereunto inwardly privy and constantly willing. And how to imagine or fashion the repentence thereof, which he vaunteth doth sometimes visit him, seemeth somewhat hard unto me.

[C]I am not of Pythagoras' sect, that men take a new soul when, to receive oracles, they approach the images of gods, unless he would say withal that it must be a strange one, new, and lent him for the time, our own giving so little sign of purification and cleanness worthy of that office. [B]They do altogether against the Stoical precepts which appoint us to correct the imperfections and vices we find in ourselves but withal forbid us to disturb the quiet of our mind. They make us believe they feel great remorse and are inwardly much displeased with sin, but of amendment, correction, [C]or intermission, [B]they show us none. Surely there can be no perfect health where the disease is not perfectly removed. Were repentence put in the scale of the balance, it would weigh down sin. I find no humor so easy to be counterfeited as devotion, if one conform not his life and conditions to it. Her essence is abstruse and concealed, her appearance gentle and stately.

For my part, I may in general wish to be other than I am; I may condemn and mislike my universal form; I may beseech God to grant me an undefiled reformation and excuse my natural weakness. But meseemeth I ought not to term this repentence no more than the displeasure of being neither angel nor Cato. My actions are squared to what I am and conformed to my condition. I cannot do better. And repentance doth not properly concern what is not in our power; sorrow doth. I may imagine infinite dispositions of a higher pitch and better governed than mine, yet do I nothing better my faculties; no more than mine arm becometh stronger or my wit more excellent by conceiving some other's to be so. If to suppose and wish a more nobler working than ours might produce the repentance of our own, we should then repent us of our most innocent actions, forsomuch as we judge that in a more excellent nature they had been directed with greater perfection and dignity and ourselves would do the like.

When I consult with my age of my youth's proceedings, I find that commonly (according to my opinion) I managed them in order. This is all my resistance is able to perform. I flatter not myself; in like circumstances I should ever be the same. It is not a spot but a whole dye that stains me. I acknowledge no repentance [that] is superficial, mean, and ceremonious. It must touch me on all sides before I can term it repentance. It must pinch my entrails and afflict them as deeply and throughly as God himself beholds me.

When in negotiating, many good fortunes have slipped me for want of good discretion; yet did my projects make good choice, according to the occurrences presented unto them. Their manner is ever to take the easier and surer side. I find that in my former deliberations I proceeded, after my rules, discreetly, for the subject's state propounded to me; and in like occasions would proceed alike a hundred years hence. I respect not what now it is, but what it was when I consulted of it.

[C]The consequence of all designs consists in the seasons; occasions pass and matters change incessantly. I have in my time run into some gross, absurd, and important errors, not for want of good advice, but of good hap.* There are secret and indivinable parts in the objects men do handle, especially in the nature of men, and mute conditions, without show and sometimes unknown of the very possessors, produced and stirred up by sudden occasions. If my wit could neither find nor presage them, I am not offended with it; the function thereof is contained within its own limits. If the success [beat] me and [B]favor the side I refused, there is no remedy. I fall not out with myself. I accuse my fortune, not my endeavor. That's not called repentance. Phocion had given the Athenians some counsel, which was not followed; the matter, against his opinion, succeeding happily. "How now, Phocion (quoth one), art thou pleased the matter hath thrived so well?" "Yea (said he), and I am glad of it, yet repent not the advice I gave."

When any of my friends come to me for counsel, I bestow it frankly and clearly, not (as well-nigh all the world doth) wavering at the hazard of the matter whereby the contrary of my meaning may happen. That so, they may justly find fault with my advice, for which I care not greatly. For they shall do me wrong, and it became not me to refuse them that duty.

CI have nobody to blame for my faults or misfortunes but myself. For in effect I seldom use the advice of other unless it be for compliment's sake and where I have need of instruction or knowledge of the fact. Marry, in things wherein nought but judgment is to be employed, strange reasons may serve to sustain but not to divert me. I lend a favorable and courteous ear unto them all. But (to my remembrance) I never believed any but mine own. With me they are but flies and moths which distract my will. I little regard mine own opinions; other men's I esteem as little. Fortune pays me accordingly. If I take no counsel, I give as little. I am not much sought after for it, and less credited when I give it. Neither know I any enterprise, either private or public, that my advice hath directed and brought to conclusion. Even those whom fortune had someway tied thereunto, have more willingly admitted the direction of others' conceits than mine. As one that am as jealous of the rights of my quiet as of those of my authority, I would rather have it thus. Where leaving me, they jump with my profession, which is wholly to settle and contain me in myself. It is a pleasure unto me to be disinterested of other men's affairs and disengaged from their contentions. BWhen suits or businesses be over-past, howsoever it be, I grieve little at them. For the imagination that they must necessarily happen so, puts me out of pain. Behold them in the course of the universe, and enchained in Stoical causes. Your fantasy cannot by wish or imagination remove one point of them, but the whole order of things must reverse both what is past and what is to come.

Moreover, I hate that accidental repentance which old age brings with it. He[3] that in ancient times said he was beholden to years because they had rid him of voluptuousness, was not of mine opinion. I shall never give impuissance thanks for any good it can do me. C"Nor shall foresight ever be seen so averse from her own work that weakness be found to be one of the best things" (Quint. *Instit.* V.12.). BOur appetites are rare in old age. The blow over-past, a deep satiety

3 Socrates.

seizeth upon us. Therein I see no conscience. Fretting care and weakness imprint in us an effeminate and drowsy virtue.

We must not suffer ourselves so fully to be carried into natural alterations as to corrupt or adulterate our judgment by them. Youth and pleasure have not heretofore prevailed so much over me but I could ever (even in the midst of sensualities) discern the ugly face of sin. Nor can the distaste which years bring on me, at this instant, keep me from discerning that of voluptuousness in vice. Now I am no longer in it, I judge of it as if I were still there.

[C]I who lively and attentively examine my reason, find it [B]to be the same that possessed me in my most dissolute and licentious age — unless, perhaps, they being enfeebled and impaired by years, do make some difference —[C]and find that what delight it refuseth to afford me in regard of my bodily health, it would no more deny me, than in times past, for the health of my soul. [B]To see it out of combat, I hold it not the more courageous. My temptations are so mortified and crazed as they are not worthy of its oppositions; holding but my hand before me, I becalm them. Should one present that former concupiscence unto it, I fear it would be of less power to sustain it than heretofore it hath been. I see in it, by itself, no increase of judgment nor access of brightness; what it now judgeth, it did then. Wherefore if there be any amendment, 'tis but diseased.

[C]O miserable kind of remedy, to be beholden unto sickness for our health. It is not for our mishap, but for the good success of our judgment to perform this office. Crosses and afflictions make me do nothing but curse them; they are for people that cannot be awaked but by the whip. The course of my reason is the nimbler in prosperity; it is much more distracted and busied in the digesting of mischiefs than of delights. I see much clearer in fair weather. Health forewarneth me, as with more pleasure, so to better purpose than sickness. I approached the nearest I could unto amendment and regularity when I should have enjoyed the same. I should be ashamed and vexed that the misery and mishap of my old age could exceed the health, attention, and vigor of my youth; and that I should be esteemed, not for what I have been, but for what I am left to be.

The happy life (in my opinion), not (as said Antisthenes) the happy death, is it that makes man's happiness in this world. I have not preposterously busied myself to tie the tail of a philosopher unto the head and body of a varlet; nor that this paltry end should disavow and belie the fairest, soundest, and longest part of my life. I will present myself and make a general muster of my whole, everywhere uniformly. Were I to live again, it should be as I have already lived. I neither deplore what is past nor dread what is to come. And if I be not deceived, the inward parts have nearly resembled the outward. It is one of the chiefest points wherein I am beholden to fortune, that in the course of my body's estate, each thing hath been carried in season. I have seen the leaves, the blossoms, and the fruit; and now see the drooping and withering of it. Happily, because naturally, I bear my present miseries the more gently because they are in season and with greater favor make me remember the long happiness of my former life.

In like manner, my discretion may well be of like proportion in the one and the other time; but sure it was of much more performance and had a better grace, being fresh, jolly, and full of spirit, than now that it is worn, decrepit, and toilsome.

I therefore renounce these casual and dolorous reformations. [B]God must touch our hearts; our conscience must amend of itself, and not by reinforcement of our reason nor by the enfeebling of our appetites. Voluptuousness in itself is neither pale nor discolored, to be discerned by blear and troubled eyes. We should affect temperance and chastity for itself and for God's cause, who hath ordained them unto us. That which catarrhs bestow upon us, and which I am beholden to my colic [for, is] neither temperance nor chastity. A man cannot boast of contemning or combating sensuality if he see her not or know not her grace, her force, and most attractive beauties. I know them both, and therefore may speak it.

But methinks our souls in age are subject unto more importunate diseases and imperfections than they are in youth. I said so being young, when my beardless chin was upbraided me; and I say it again, now that my [C]gray [C]beard gives me authority. We entitle wisdom the frowardness of our humors and the distaste of present things. But in truth we abandon not vices so much as we change them, and in mine opinion for the worse. Besides a silly and ruinous pride, cumbersome tattle, wayward and unsociable humors, superstition, and a ridiculous carking* for wealth when the use of it is well-nigh lost, I find the more envy, injustice, and lewdness in it. It sets more wrinkles in our minds than on our foreheads. Nor are there any spirits, or very rare ones, which in growing old taste not sourly and mustily. Man marcheth entirely towards his increase and decrease. [C]View but the wisdom of Socrates and divers circumstances of his condemnation. I dare say he something lent himself unto it by prevarication of purpose, being so near, and at the age of seventy, to endure the benumbing of his spirit's richest pace and the dimming of his accustomed brightness. [B]What metamorphoses have I seen it daily make in divers of mine acquaintances! It is a powerful malady which naturally and imperceptibly glideth unto us. There is required great provision of study, heed, and precaution to avoid the imperfections wherewith it chargeth us, or at least to weaken their further progress.

I find that notwithstanding all my entrenchings, by little and little it getteth ground upon me. I hold out as long as I can, but know not whither at length it will bring me. Hap* what hap* will, I am pleased the world know from what height I tumbled.

Of Three Commerces or Societies

❧ III. 3 ✧ c. 1586 ☙

[B]We must not cleave so fast unto our humors and dispositions. Our chiefest sufficiency is to apply ourselves to divers fashions. It is a being, but not a life, to be tied and bound by necessity to one only course. The goodliest minds are those that have most variety and pliableness in them. [C]Behold an honorable testimony of old Cato: "He had a wit so turnable for all things alike, as one would say he had been only born for that he went about to do" (Liv. XXXIX.40.)

[B]Were I to dress myself after mine own manner, there is no fashion so good whereto I would be so affected or tied as not to know how to leave and loose it. Life is a motion unequal, irregular, and multiform. It is not to be the friend, less the master, but the slave of oneself to follow uncessantly and be so addicted to his inclinations as he cannot stray from them nor wrest them. This I say now, as being extremely pestered with the importunity of my mind, forsomuch as she cannot amuse herself but whereon it is busied, nor employ itself but bent and whole. How light soever the subject is one gives it, it willingly amplifieth, and wire-draws* the same, even unto the highest pitch of toil. Its idleness is therefore a painful trade unto me, and offensive to my health. Most wits have need of extravagant stuff to unbenumb and exercise themselves; mine hath need of it rather to settle and continue itself. "The vices of idleness should be shaken off with business" (Sen. *Epist*. LVI.). For the most laborious care and principal study of it is to study itself. [C]Books are one of those businesses that seduce it from study. [B]At the first thoughts that present themselves, it rouseth up and makes proof of all the vigor it hath. It exerciseth its function sometimes toward force, sometimes toward order and comeliness, [C]it rangeth, moderates and fortifieth. [B]It hath of itself to awaken the faculties of it — nature having given it, as unto all other, matter of its own for advantage, subjects fit enough whereon to devise and determine. [C]Meditation is a large and powerful study to such as vigorously can taste and employ themselves therein. I had rather forge than furnish my mind.

There is no office or occupation either weaker or stronger than that of entertaining of one's thoughts according to the mind, whatsoever it be. The greatest make it their vacation,* "to whom it is all one to live and to meditate" (Cic. *Tusc.* V.38.). Nature hath also favored it with this privilege, that there is nothing we can do so long, nor action, whereto we give ourselves more ordinarily and easily. It is the work of gods, said Aristotle, whence both their happiness and ours proceedeth. Reading serves me especially to awake my conceit by divers objects, to busy my judgment, not my memory.

[B]Few entertainments, then, stay me without vigor and force. 'Tis true that courtesy and beauty possess me as much or more than weight and depth. And because I slumber in all other communications and lend but the superficial parts of my attention unto them, it often befalleth me, in such kind of weak and absurd discourses (discourses of countenance), to blurt out and answer ridiculous toys and fond absurdities unworthy a child, or wilfully to hold my peace, therewithal more foolishly and uncivilly. I have a kind of raving fanciful behavior that retireth me into myself, and on the other side, a gross and childish ignorance of many ordinary things; by means of which two qualities I have in my days committed five or six as sottish tricks as anyone whosover, which to my derogation may be reported. But to follow my purpose, this harsh complexion of mine makes me nice in conversing with men (whom I must pick and cull out for the nonce) and unfit for common actions. We live and negotiate with the people. If their behavior importune us, if we disdain to lend ourselves to base and vulgar spirits, which often are as regular as those of a finer mold —[C]and all wisdom is unsavory that is not conformed to common insipience —[B]we are no longer to intermeddle either with our or other men's affairs; and both public and private forsake such kind of people.

The least wrested and most natural proceedings of our mind are the fairest; the best occupations, those which are least forced. Good God, how good an office doth wisdom unto those whose desires she squareth according to their power! There is no science more profitable. "As one may,"[1] was the burden and favored saying of Socrates: a sentence of great substance. We must address and stay our desires to things most easy and nearest. [Is it] not a fond*-peevish humor in me to disagree from a thousand to whom my fortune joineth me, without whom I cannot live, [and] to adhere unto one or two that are out of my commerce and conversation, or rather to a fantastical conceit or fanciful desire

[1] Cf. Xenophon, *Memorabilia,* I.iii.3. Montaigne used this phrase (*selon qu'on peut*) as one of his mottoes, and in the front of many of the books in his library he wrote it in Italian: *mentre si può.*

for a thing I cannot obtain? My soft behaviors and mild manners, enemies to all sharpness and foes to all bitterness, may easily have discharged me from envy and contention. To be beloved, I say not; but not to be hated never did man give more occasion. But the coldness of my conversation hath with reason robbed me of the good will of many; which may be excused, if they interpret the same to other or worse sense. I am most capable of getting rare amities and continuing exquisite acquaintances. For so much as with so greedy hunger I snatch at such acquaintances as answer my taste and square with my humor; I so greedily produce and headlong cast myself upon them, that I do not easily miss to cleave unto them and, where I light on, to make a steady impression. I have often made happy and successful trial of it.

In vulgar worldly friendships, I am somewhat cold and barren for my proceeding is not natural if not unresisted and with hoised-full* sails. Moreover, my fortune having inured and allured me even from my infancy to one sole singular and perfect amity, hath verily in some sort distasted me from others and over-deeply imprinted in my fantasy that it is a beast sociable and for company and not of troop, as said an ancient writer. So that it is naturally a pain unto me to communicate myself by halves and with modification and that servile or suspicious wisdom which in the conversation of these numerous and imperfect amities is ordained and proposed unto us — prescribed in these days especially, wherein one cannot speak of the world but dangerously or falsely. Yet I see that who (as I do) makes for his end the commodities of his life (I mean essential commodities) must avoid as a plague these difficulties and quaintness of humor.

I should commend a high-raised mind that could both bend and discharge itself that wherever her fortune might transport her she might continue constant, that could discourse with her neighbors of all matters, as of her building, of her hunting and of any quarrel, and entertain with delight a carpenter or a gardener. I envy those which can be familiar with the meanest of their followers, and vouchsafe to contract friendship, and frame discourse with their own servants.

[C]Nor do I like the advice of Plato, ever to speak imperiously unto our attendants, without blitheness and sans* any familiarity, be it to men or women servants. For, besides my reason, it is inhumanity and injustice to attribute so much unto that prerogative of fortune; and the government where less inequality is permitted between the servant and master is, in my conceit, the more indifferent. Some other[s] study to rouse and raise their mind; but I to abase and prostrate mine: it is not faulty but in extension.

You tell of Aeacus the pedigree;
The wars at sacred Troy you do display;
You tell not at what price a hogshead we
May buy of the best wine, who shall allay
Wine-fire with water, at whose house to hold,
At what a-clock I may be kept from cold.
Hor. *Odes.* III.xix.3.

Even as the Lacedaemonian valor had need of moderation and of sweet and pleasing sounds of flutes to flatter and allay it in time of war lest it should run headlong into rashness and fury, whereas all other nations use commonly piercing sounds and strong shouts which violently excite and inflame their soldiers' courage, so think I (against ordinary custom) that in the employment of our spirit we have for the most part more need of lead than wings, of coldness and quiet than of heat and agitation. Above all, in my mind, the only way to play the fool well is to seem wise among fools, to speak as though one's tongue were ever bent to "Favelar' in punta di forchetta" (Ital. Prov.), "To syllabize or speak mincingly." One must lend himself unto those he is with and sometimes affect ignorance. Set force and subtlety aside; in common employments 'tis enough to reserve order; drag yourself even close to the ground [if] they will have it so. The learned stumble willingly on this block, making continual muster and open show of their skill and dispersing their books abroad, and have in these days so filled the closets and possessed the ears of ladies that if they retain not their substance, at least they have their countenance, using in all sorts of discourse and subject how base or popular soever, a new, an affected and learned fashion of speaking and writing.

They in this language fear, in this they fashion
Their joys, their cares, their rage, their inward passion;
What more? they learned are in copulation.
Juven. *Sat.* VI.189.

And allege* Plato and Saint Thomas for things which the first man they meet would decide as well and stand for as good a witness. Such learning as could not enter into their mind hath stayed on their tongues. If the well-born will give any credit unto me, they shall be pleased to make their own and natural riches to prevail and be of worth. They hide and shroud their forms under foreign and borrowed beauties. It is great simplicity for any body to smother and conceal his own brightness, to shine with a borrowed light. They are buried and entombed under the art of C"[*de*] *capsula totae.*"[2] BIt is because they do not sufficiently know themselves. The wor[l]d con-

2 "Everything out of a box" (Sen. *Epist.* CXV.).

tains nothing of more beauty. It is for them to honor arts, and to beautify embellishment. What need they more than to live beloved and honored? They have and know but too much in that matter. There needs but a little rousing and inflaming of the faculties that are in them.

When I see them meddling with rhetoric, with law, and with logic, and suchlike trash, so vain and unprofitable for their use, I enter into fear that those who advise them to such things, do it that they may have more law to govern them under that pretense. For what other excuse can I devise for them? It is sufficient that without us they may frame or roll the grace of their eyes unto cheerfulness, unto severity, and unto mildness, and season a *No* with frowardness, with doubt, and with favor; and require not an interpreter in discourses made for their service. With this learning they command without control and overrule both regents and schools. Yet if it offend them to yield us any pre-eminence and would for curiosity['s] sake have part in books also, poesy is a study fit for their purpose, being a wanton, amusing, subtle, disguised, and prattling art, all in delight, all in show, like to themselves. They may also select divers commodities out of history. In moral philosophy they may take the discourses which enable them to judge of our humors, to censure our conditions, and to avoid our guiles and treacheries, to temper the rashness of their own desires, to husband their liberty, lengthen the delights of life, gently to bear the inconstancy of a servant, the peevishness or rudeness of a husband, the importunity of years, the unwelcomeness of wrinkles, and suchlike mind-troubling accidents. Lo, here the most and greatest share of learning I would assign them.

There are some particular, retired, and close dispositions. My essential form is fit for communication and proper for production: I am all outward and in appearance, born for society and unto friendship. The solitude I love and commend is especially but to retire my affections and redeem my thoughts unto myself, to restrain and close up not my steps, but my desires and my cares, resigning all foreign solicitude and trouble, and mortally shunning all manner of servitude and obligation, and not so much the throng of men as the importunity of affairs. Local solitariness (to say truth) doth rather extend and enlarge me outwardly; I give myself to state business and to the world more willingly when I am all alone. At the court and in press of people, I close and slink into mine own skin. Assemblies thrust me again into myself. And I never entertain myself so fondly, so licentiously, and so particularly as in places of respect and ceremonious discretion. Our follies make me not laugh, but our wisdoms do. Of mine own complexion, I am no enemy to the agitations and stirrings of our courts: I have there passed great part of my life and am inured to be merry in great assemblies, so it be by intermission and suitable to my humor.

But this tenderness and coyness of judgment whereof I speak doth perforce tie me unto solitariness. Yea, even in mine own house, in the midst of a numerous family and most frequented houses, I see people more than a good many, but seldom such as I love to converse or communicate withal. And there I reserve, both for myself and others, an unaccustomed liberty; making truce with ceremonies, assistance, and invitings, and such other troublesome ordinances of our courtesies (O servile custom and importunate manner!); there every man demeaneth himself as he pleaseth and entertaineth what his thoughts affect, whereas I keep myself silent, meditating, and close, without offense to my guests or friends.

The men whose familiarity and society I hunt after are those which are called honest, virtuous, and sufficient, the image of whom doth distaste and divert me from others. It is (being rightly taken) the rarest of our forms; and a form or fashion chiefly due unto nature.

The end or scope of this commerce is principally and simply familiarity, conference, and frequentation: the exercise of minds, without other fruit. In our discourses, all subjects are alike to me: I care not though they want either weight or depth; grace and pertinency are never wanting; all therein is tainted with a ripe and constant judgment and commixed with goodness, liberty, cheerfulness, and kindness. It is not only in the subject of laws and affairs of princes that our spirit showeth its beauty, grace, and vigor: it showeth them as much in private conferences. I know my people by their very silence and smiling, and peradventure discover them better at a table than sitting in serious council.

Hippomachus said he discerned good wrestlers but by seeing them march through a street. If learning vouchsafe to step into our talk, she shall not be refused; yet must not she be stern, mastering, imperious, and importunate, as commonly she is, but assistant and docile of herself. Therein we seek for nothing but recreation and pastime; when we shall look to be instructed, taught and resolved, we will go seek and sue to her in her throne. Let her if she please keep from us at that time; for, as commodious and pleasing as she is, I presume that for a need we could spare her presence and do our business well enough without her. Wits well-born, soundly bred and exercised in the practice and commerce of men, become gracious and plausible of themselves. Art is but the check-roll and register of the productions uttered, and conceits produced by them.

The company of [C]fair, and [B]society of honest women is likewise a sweet commerce for me, [C]"for we also have learned eyes" (Cic. *Parad.* V.2.). [B]If the mind have not so much to solace herself as in the former, the corporal senses, whose part is more in the second, bring it to a proportion near unto the other; although in mine opinion not equal. But it is a society wherein it behooveth a man somewhat to stand upon his guard, and especially those that are of a strong constitution and whose body can do much, as in me. In my youth I heated myself therein and was very violent and endured all the rages and furious assaults which poets say happen to those who without order or discretion abandon themselves over-loosely and riotously unto it. True it is indeed that the same lash hath since stood me instead of an instruction.

> Greek sailors that Capharean rocks did fly,
> From the Euboean seas their sails still ply.
> Ovid. *Trist.* I.i.83.

It is folly to fasten all one's thoughts upon it and with a furious and indiscreet affection to engage himself unto it. But on the otherside, to meddle with it without love or bond of affection, as comedians do, to play a common part of age and manners, without ought of their own but bare-conned* words, is verily a provision for one's safety; and yet but a cowardly one, as is that of him who would forgo his honor, his profit, or his pleasure for fear of danger. For it is certain that the practicers of such courses cannot hope for any fruit able to move or satisfy a worthy mind.

One must very earnestly have desired that whereof he would enjoy an absolute delight: I mean though fortune should unjustly favor their intention — which often happeneth, because there is no woman, how deformed and unhandsome soever, but thinks herself lovely, amiable, [C]and praiseworthy, either for her age, her hair or gait (for there are generally no more fair than foul ones). And the Brachmanian maids wanting other commendations, by proclamation for that purpose, made show of their matrimonal parts unto the people assembled, to see if thereby at least they might get them husbands.

[B]By consequence there is not one of them but upon the first oath one maketh to serve her will very easily be persuaded to think well of herself. Now this common treason and ordinary protestations of men in these days must needs produce the effects experience already discovereth, which is that either they join together and cast away themselves on themselves to avoid us, or on their side follow also the example we give them, acting their part of the play without passion, without care, and without love lending themselves to this intercourse: [C]"Neither liable to their own nor other folks' affection" (Tacit. *Ann.*

XIII.45.). Thinking, according to Lysias' persuasions in Plato, they may so much the more profitably and commodiously yield unto us by how much less we love them. [B]Wherein it will happen as in comedies, the spectators shall have as much or more pleasure as the comedians.

For my part, I no more acknowledge Venus without Cupid, than a motherhood without an offspring. They are things which inter-lend and inter-owe one another their essence. Thus doth this cozening rebound on him that useth it; and as it cost him little, so gets he not much by it. Those which made Venus a goddess have respected that her principal beauty was incorporeal and spiritual. But she whom these kind of people hunt after is not so much as human, nor also brutal, but such as wild beasts would not have her so filthy and terrestrial. We see that imagination inflames them, and desire or lust urgeth them before the body. We see in one and other sex, even in whole herds, choice and distinctions in their affections, and amongst themselves acquaintances of long-continued good-will and liking. And even those to whom age denieth bodily strength do yet bray, neigh, roar, skip, and wince* for love. Before the deed we see them full of hope and heat; and, when the body hath played his part, even tickle and tingle themselves with the sweetness of that remembrance. Some of them swell with pride at parting from it; others, all weary and glutted, ring out songs of glee and triumph. Who makes no more of it but to discharge his body of some natural necessity hath no cause to trouble others with so curious preparation. It is no food for a greedy and clownish hunger.

As one that would not be accounted better than I am, thus much I will display of my youth's wanton errors. Not only for the danger of [C]one's health that follows that game (yet could I not avoid two, though light and cursory assaults) [B]but also for contempt, I have not much been given to mercenary and common acquaintances. I have coveted to set an edge on that sensual pleasure by difficulty, by desire, and for some glory; and liked Tiberius his fashions, who in his amours was swayed as much by modesty and nobleness as by any other quality. And Flora's humor, who would prostitute herself to none worse than dictators, consuls, or censors and took delight in the dignity and greatness of her lovers, doth somewhat suit with mine. Surely glittering pearls and silken clothes add something unto it, and so do titles, nobility, and a worthy train. Besides which, I made high esteem of the mind, yet so as the body might not justly be found fault withal. For, to speak my conscience, if either of the two beauties were necessarily to be wanting, I would rather have chosen to want the mental, whose use is to be employed in better things. But in the subject of love — a subject that chiefly hath reference unto the two senses of seeing and touching — something may be done without the graces of the mind, but little or nothing without the corporal. Beauty is the true availful advantage of women. [C]It is so peculiarly theirs, that ours, though it require some features and different allurements, is not in her right cue* or true bias unless confused with theirs, childish and beardless. It is reported that such as serve the great Turk under the title of beauty (whereof the number is infinite) are di[s]missed at furthest when they once come to the age of two and twenty years. [B]Discourse, discretion, together with the offices of true amity, are better found amongst men; and therefore govern they the world's affairs.

These two commerces or societies are accidental and depending of others; the one is troublesome and tedious for its rarity; the other withers with old age: nor could they have sufficiently provided for my life's necessities. That of books, which is the third, is much more solid-sure and much more ours; some other advantages it yieldeth to the two former, but hath for her share constancy and the facility of her service. This accosteth and secondeth all my course, and everywhere assisteth me. It comforts me in age, and solaceth me in solitariness. It easeth me of the burthen of a wearisome sloth, and at all times rids me of tedious companies; it abateth the edge of fretting sorrow, on condition it be not extreme and over-insolent. To divert me from any importunate imagination or insinuating conceit, there is no better way than to have recourse unto books; with ease they allure me to them and with facility they remove them all. And though they perceive I neither frequent nor seek them, but wanting other more essential, lively, and more natural commodities, they never mutiny or murmur at me; but still entertain me with one and selfsame visage.

He may well walk a-foot that leads his horse by the bridle, saith the proverb. And our James, king of Naples and Sicily who, being fair, young, healthy and in good plight, caused himself to be carried abroad in a plain wagon or screen* lying upon an homely pillow of coarse feathers, clothed in a suit of homespun gray and a bonnet of the same, yet royally attended on by a gallant troop of nobles, of litters, coaches, and of all sorts of choice lead-horses, a number of gentlemen, and officers, represented a tender and wavering austerity. The sick man is not to be moaned that hath his health in his sleeve. In the experience and use of this sentence, which is most true, consisteth all the commodity I reap of books. In effect, I make no other use of them than those who know them not. I enjoy them, as a miser doth his gold, to know that I may enjoy them when I list; my mind is settled and satisfied with the right of possession. I never travel without books, nor in peace nor in war; yet do I pass many days and months without using them. It shall be anon, say I, or tomorrow, or when I please; in the meanwhile the time runs away and passeth without hurting me. For it is wonderful what repose I take and how I continue in this consideration, that they are at my elbow to delight me when time shall serve, and in acknowledging what assistance they give unto my life. This is the best munition I have found in this human peregrination, and I extremely bewail those men of understanding that want the same. I accept with better will all other kinds of amusements, how slight soever, forsomuch as this cannot fail me.

At home I betake me somewhat the oftener to my library, whence all at once I command and survey all my household. It is seated in the chief entry of my house; thence I behold under me my garden, my base court, my yard, and look even into most rooms of my house. There, without order, without method, and by piecemeals I turn over and ransack now one book and now another. Sometimes I muse and rave; and walking up and down I indite and enregister these my humors, these my conceits. [C]It is placed on the third story of a tower. The lowermost is my chapel, the second a chamber with other lodgings, where I often lie, because I would be alone. Above it is a great wardrobe. It was in times past the most unprofitable place of all my house. There I [pass] the greatest part of my life's days, and wear out most hours of the day. I am never there a-nights. Next unto it is a handsome neat cabinet, able and large enough to receive fire in winter and very pleasantly windowe[d]. And if I feared not care more than cost — care which drives and diverts me from all business — I might easily join a convenient gallery of a hundred paces long and twelve broad on each side of it and upon one floor, having already, for some other purpose, found all the walls raised unto a convenient height. Each retired place requireth a walk. My thoughts are prone to sleep if I sit long. My mind goes not alone as if legs did move it. Those that study without books are all in the same case. The form of it is round and hath no flat side, but what serveth for my table and chair; in which bending or circling manner, at one look it offereth me the full sight of all my books set round about upon shelves or desks, five ranks one upon another. It hath three bay-windows of a far-extending, rich, and unresisted prospect and is in diameter sixteen paces void.* In winter I am less continually there; for my house (as the name of it importeth) is perched upon an overpeering* hillock; and hath no part more subject to all weathers than this, which pleaseth me the more, both because the access unto it is somewhat troublesome and remote, and for the benefit of the exercise, which is to be respected, and that I may the better seclude myself from company and keep encroachers from me. There is my seat, there is my throne. I endeavor to make my rule therein absolute, and to sequester that only corner from the community of wife, of children, and of acquaintance. Elsewhere I have but a verbal authority of confused essence. Miserable in my mind is he who in his own home hath nowhere to be to himself, where he may particularly court and at his pleasure hide or withdraw himself. Ambition payeth her followers well to keep them still in open view, as a statue in some conspicuous place. "A great fortune is a great bondage" (Sen. *Cons. ad Pol.* XXVI.). They cannot be private so much as at their privy. I have deemed nothing so rude in the austerity of the life which our churchmen affect as that in some of their companies they institute a perpetual society of place and a numerous assistance amongst them in anything they do. And deem it somewhat more tolerable to be ever alone, than never able to be so.

[B]If any say to me, it is a kind of vilifying the Muses to use them only for sport and recreation, he wots not as I do what worth, pleasure, sport and pastime is of. I had well-nigh termed all other ends ridiculous. I live from hand to mouth and, with reverence be it spoken, I live but to myself: there end all my designs. Being young, I studied for ostentation; then a little to enable* myself and become wiser; now for delight and recreation, never for gain. A vain conceit and lavish humor I had after this kind of stuff, [C]not only to provide for my need, but somewhat further [B]to adorn and embellish myself withal. I have since partly left it.

Books have and contain divers pleasing qualities to those that can duly choose them. But no good without pains; no roses without prickles. It is a pleasure not absolutely pure and neat, no more than all others; it hath his inconveniences attending on it and sometimes weighty ones. The mind is therein exercised, but the body (the care whereof I have not yet forgotten) remaineth there-whilst without action, and is wasted, and ensorrowed. I know no excess more hurtful for me, nor more to be avoided by me, in this declining age.

Lo, here my three most favored and particular employments. I speak not of those I owe of duty to the world.

Of Coaches

III. 6 ✧ 1585–88

[B]It is easy to verify that excellent authors writing of causes do not only make use of those which they imagine true but eftsoons* of such as themselves believe not, always provided they have some invention and beauty. They speak sufficiently, truly, and profitably if they speak ingeniously. We cannot assure ourselves of the chief cause; we huddle up a many together to see whether by chance it shall be found in that number:

> Enough it is not one cause to devise,
> But more, whereof that one may yet arise.
> Lucr. VI.704.

Will you demand of me whence this custom ariseth to bless and say "God help!" to those that sneeze? We produce three sorts of wind. That issuing from below is too indecent; that from the mouth implieth some reproach of gourmandise; the third is sneezing. And because it cometh from the head and is without imputation we thus kindly entertain it. Smile not at this subtlety. It is, as some say, Aristotle's.

Meseemeth to have read in Plutach, who of all the authors I know hath best commixed art with nature and coupled judgment with learning, where he yieldeth a reason why those which travel by sea do sometimes feel such qualms and risings of the stomach, saying that it proceedeth of a kind of fear, having found out some reason by which he proveth that fear may cause such an effect. Myself, who am much subject unto it, know well that this cause doth nothing concern me. And I know it not by argument but by necessary experience, without alleging* what some have told me, that the like doth often happen unto beasts, namely unto swine, when they are farthest from apprehending any danger; and what an acquaintance of mine hath assured me of himself, and who is greatly subject unto it, that twice or thrice in a tempestuous storm, being surprised with exceeding fear, all manner of desire or inclination to vomit had left him. [C]As to that ancient good fellow: "I was worse vexed than that danger could help me"

[Sen. *Epist.* LIII.]. [B]I never apprehended fear upon the water nor anywhere else (yet have I often had just cause offered me, if death itself may give it) which either might trouble or astonish* me.

It proceedeth sometimes as well from want of judgment as from lack of courage. All the dangers I have had have been when mine eyes were wide open and my sight clear, sound, and perfect; for even to fear, courage is required. It hath sometimes steadied me in respect of others to direct and keep my flight in order that so it might be, [C]if not without fear, at least [B]without dismay and astonishment. Indeed, it was moved, but not amazed nor distracted.

Undaunted minds march further and represent flight not only temperate, settled, and sound, but also fierce and bold. Report we that which Alcibiades relateth of Socrates, his companion in arms. "I found," saith he, "after the rout and discomfiture of our army, both him and Laches in the last rank of those that ran away, and with all safety and leisure considered him; for I was mounted upon an excellent horse and he on foot, and so had we combatted all day. I noted first how in respect of Laches he showed both discreet judgment and undaunted resolution; then I observed the undismayed bravery of his march, nothing different from his ordinary pace, his look orderly and constant, duly observing and heedily judging whatever passed round about him, sometimes viewing the one and sometimes looking on the other, both friends and enemies, with so composed a manner that he seemed to encourage the one and menace the other, signifying that whosoever should attempt his life must purchase the same or his blood at a high-valued rate. And thus they both saved themselves; for men do not willingly grapple with these, but follow such as show fear or dismay." Lo, here the testimony of that renowned captain, who teacheth us what we daily find by experience, that there is nothing doth sooner cast us into dangers than an inconsiderate greediness to avoid them. [C]"The less fear there is, most commonly the less danger there is" (Livy, XXII.v.).

[B]Our people is to blame to say such a one feareth death when it would signify that he thinks on it and doth foresee the same. Foresight doth equally belong as well to that which concerneth us in good as touch us in evil. To consider and judge danger is in some sort not to be daunted at it.

I do not find myself sufficiently strong to withstand the blow and violence of this passion of fear or of any other impetuosity; were I once therewith vanquished and deterred I could never safely recover myself. He that should make my mind forego her footing could never bring her unto her place again. She doth over-lively sound and over-deeply search into herself, and therefore never suffers the wound which pierced the same to be throughly cured and consolidated. It hath been happy for me that no infirmity could ever yet displace her. I oppose and present myself in the best ward* I have against all charges and assaults that beset me. Thus the first that should bear me away would make me unrecoverable. I encounter not two: which way soever spoil should enter my hold, there am I open and remedilessly drowned.

[C]Epicurus saith that a wise man can never pass from one state to its contrary. I have some opinion answering his sentence: that he who hath once been a very fool shall at no time prove very wise.

[B]God sends my cold answerable to my clothes, and passions answering the means I have to endure them. Nature having discovered me on one side that covered me on the other. Having disarmed me of strength, she hath armed me with insensibility and a regular or soft apprehension.

I cannot long endure, and less could in my youth, to ride either in coach or litter or to go in a boat, and both in the city and country I hate all manner of riding but ahorseback. And can less endure a litter than a coach, and by the same reason more easily a rough agitation upon the water, whence commonly proceedeth fear, than the soft stirring a man shall feel in calm weather. By the same easy, gentle motion which the oars give conveying the boat under us, I wot not how I feel both my head intoxicated and my stomach distempered; as I cannot likewise abide a shaking stool under me. When as either the sail or the gliding course of the water doth equally carry us away, or that we are but towed, that gently gliding and even agitation doth no whit distemper or hurt me. It is an interrupted and broken motion that offends me, and more when it is languishing. I am not able to display its form. Physicians have taught me to bind and gird myself with a napkin or swathe round about the lower part of my belly as a remedy for this accident, which as yet I have not tried, being accustomed to wrestle and withstand such defects as are in me and tame them by myself.

[C]Were my memory sufficiently informed of them, I would not think my time lost here to set down the infinite variety which histories present unto us of the use of coaches in the service of war, divers according to the nations and different according to the ages, to my seeming of great effect and necessity. So that it is wondrously strange how we have lost all true knowledge of them. I will only allege this, that even lately in our fathers' time the Hungarians did very availfully bring them into fashion and profitably set them awork against the Turks, every one of them containing a targeteer and a musketeer, with a certain number of harquebuses or calivers* ready charged and so ranged that they might make good use of them, and all over-covered with a pavesado* after the manner of a galiot.* They made the front of their battle with three thousand such coaches, and after the cannon had played, caused them to discharge and shoot off a volley of small shot upon their enemies before they should know or feel what the rest of the forces could do, which was no small advancement. Or, if not this, they mainly drove those coaches amid the thickest of their enemy's squadrons, with purpose to break, disrout, and make way through them; besides the benefit and help they might make of them in any suspicious or dangerous place, to flank their troops marching from place to place, or in haste to encompass, to embarricado, to cover or fortify any lodgement or quarter. In my time a gentleman of quality in one of our frontiers, unwieldy and so burly of body that he could find no horse able to bear his weight, and having a quarrel or deadly feud in hand, was wont to travel up and down in a coach made after this fashion, and found much ease and good in it. But leave we these warlike coaches, as if their nullity were not sufficiently known by better tokens. The last kings of our first race were wont to travel in chariots drawn by four oxen.

[B]Mark Antony was the first that caused himself, accompanied with a minstrel harlot, to be drawn by lions fitted to a coach. So did Heliogabalus after him, naming himself Cybele, the mother of the gods, and also by tigers, counterfeiting god Bacchus; who sometimes would also be drawn in a coach by two stags and another time by four mastiff dogs; and by four naked wenches, causing himself to be drawn by them in pomp and state, he being all naked. The emperor Firmus made his coach to be drawn by estridges* of exceeding greatness, so that he rather seemed to fly than to roll on wheels. The strangeness of these inventions doth bring this other thing unto my fantasy, that it is a kind of pusillanimity in monarchs, and a testimony that they do not sufficiently know what they are, when they labor to show their worth and endeavor to appear unto the world by excessive and intolerable expenses — a thing which in a strange country might somewhat be excused; but amongst his native subjects, where he swayeth all in all, he draweth from his dignity the extremest degree of honor that he may possibly attain unto. As for a gentleman in his own private house to apparel himself richly and curiously, I deem it a matter vain and superfluous: his house, his household, his train, and his kitchen do sufficiently answer for him.

[C]The counsel which Isocrates giveth to his king in my conceit seemeth to carry some reason: when he willeth him to be richly stored and stately adorned with movables and household stuff, forsomuch as it is an expense of continuance and which descendeth even to his posterity or heirs; and to avoid all magnificences which presently vanish both from custom and memory.

BI loved, when I was a younger brother, to set myself forth and be gay in clothes, though I wanted other necessaries; and it became me well. There are some on whose backs their rich robes weep, or as we say, their rich clothes are lined with heavy debts. We have divers strange tales of our ancient kings' frugality about their own persons and in their gifts, great and far-renowned kings both in credit, in valor, and in fortune. Demosthenes mainly combats the law of his city, who assigned their public money to be employed about the stately setting forth of their plays and feasts. He willeth that their magnificence should be seen in the quantity of tall ships well manned and appointed, and armies well furnished.

CAnd they have reason to accuse Theophrastus, who in his book of riches established a contrary opinion and upholdeth such a quality of expenses to be the true fruit of wealth and plenty. They are pleasures, saith Aristotle, that only touch the vulgar and basest communality, which as soon as a man is satisfied with them vanish out of mind and whereof no man of sound judgment or gravity can make any esteem. The employment of it as more profitable, just, and durable would seem more royal, worthy, and commendable about ports, havens, fortifications, and walls, in sumptuous buildings, in churches, hospitals, colleges, mending of highways and streets, and such-like monuments, in which things Pope Gregory the Thirteenth shall leave aye-lasting and commendable memory unto his name, and wherein our Queen Catherine should witness unto succeeding ages her natural liberality and exceeding bounty if her means were answerable to her affection. Fortune hath much spited me to hinder the structure and break off the finishing of our New Bridge in our great city and before my death to deprive me of all hope to see the great necessity of it set forward again.[1]

BMoreover, it appeareth unto subjects, spectators of these triumphs, that they have a show made them of their own riches and that they are feasted at their proper charges; for the people do easily presume of their kings, as we do of our servants, that they should take care plenteously to provide us of whatsoever we stand in need of, but that on their behalf they should no way lay hands on it. And therefore the emperor Galba, sitting at supper, having taken pleasure to hear a musician play and sing before him, sent for his casket, out of which he took a handful of crowns and put them into his hand with these words: "Take this not as a gift of the public money, but of mine own

1 Montaigne is speaking of the Pont Neuf, which was not completed until 1604.

private store." So is it that it often cometh to pass that the common people have reason to grudge and that their eyes are fed with that which should feed their belly.

Liberality itself in a sovereign hand is not in her own luster; private men have more right, and may challenge more interest in her. For, taking the matter exactly as it is, a king hath nothing that is properly his own; he oweth even himself to others. [C]Authority is not given in favor of the authorizing, but rather in favor of the authorized. A superior is never created for his own profit, but rather for the benefit of the inferior, and a physician is instituted for the sick, not for himself. All magistracy, even as each art, rejecteth her end out of herself. "No art is all in itself" (Cic. *De finib.* V.vi.). [B]Wherefore the governors and overseers of princes' childhood or minority, who so earnestly endeavor to imprint this virtue of bounty and liberality in them and teach them not to refuse anything and esteem nothing so well employed as what they shall give (an instruction which in my days I have seen in great credit), either they prefer and respect more their own profit than their masters' or else they understand not aright to whom they speak. It is too easy a matter to imprint liberality in him that hath wherewith plenteously to satisfy what he desireth at other men's charges. [C]And his estimation being directed not according to the measure of the present, but according to the quality of his means that exerciseth the same, it cometh to prove vain in so puissant hands. They are found to be prodigal before they be liberal. [B]Therefore it is but of small commendation in respect of other royal virtues — and the only, as said the tyrant Dionysius, that agreed and squared well with tyranny itself. I would rather teach him the verse of the ancient laborer —

> Not whole sacks, but by the hand
> A man should sow his seed i' the land —
> Corinna.

that whosoever will reap any commodity by it must sow with his hand and not pour out of the sack, [C]that corn must be discreetly scattered and not lavishly dispersed, [B]and that being to give or, to say better, to pay and restore to such a multitude of people according as they have deserved, he ought to be a loyal, faithful, and advised distributor thereof. If the liberality of a prince be without heedy discretion and measure, I would rather have him covetous and sparing.

Princely virtue seemeth to consist most in justice; and of all parts of justice that doth best and most belong to kings which accompanieth liberality. For they have it particularly reserved to their charge, whereas all other justice they happily exercise the same by the intermission of others. Immoderate bounty is a weak mean to acquire them good will, for it rejecteth more people than it obtaineth. C"The more you have used it to many, the less may you use it to many more; and what is more fond than what you willingly would do to provide you can no longer do it?" (Cic. *De off*. II.xv.). BAnd if it be employed without respect of merit, it shameth him that receiveth the same and is received without grace. Some tyrants have been sacrificed to the people's hatred by the very hands of those whom they had rashly preferred and wrongfully advanced; such kind of men, meaning to assure the possession of goods unlawfully and indirectly gotten, if they show to hold in contempt and hatred him from whom they held them, and in that combine themselves unto the vulgar judgment and common opinion.

The subjects of a prince rashly excessive in his gifts become impudently excessive in begging; they adhere not unto reason but unto example. Verily we have often just cause to blush for our impudency. We are over-paid according to justice when the recompense equaleth our service. For do we not owe a kind of natural duty to our princes? If he bear our charge, he doth overmuch; it sufficeth if he assist it. The over-plus is called a benefit, which cannot be exacted; for the very name of liberality implieth liberty. After our fashion we have never done; what is received is no more reckoned of; only future liberality is loved. Wherefore the more a prince doth exhaust himself in giving, the more friends he impoverisheth. CHow should he satisfy intemperate desires, which increase according as they are replenished? Who so hath his mind on taking hath it no more on what he hath taken. Covetousness hath nothing so proper as to be ungrateful.

The example of Cyrus shall not ill fit this place for the behoof of our kings of these days as a touchstone to know whether their gifts be well or ill employed, and make them perceive how much more happily that emperor did wound and impress them than they do. Whereby they are afterward forced to exact and borrow of their unknown subjects, and rather of such as they have wronged and aggrieved than of those they have enriched and done good unto; and receive no aids where anything is gratitude except the name.

Croesus upbraided him with his lavish bounty and calculated what his treasure would amount unto if he were more sparing and close-handed. A desire surprised him to justify his liberality, and, dispatching letters over all parts of his dominions to such great men of his estate whom he had particularly advanced, entreated everyone to assist him with as much money as they could for an urgent necessity of his, and presently to send it him by declaration. When all these count-books or notes were brought him, each of his friends supposing that it sufficed not to offer him no more than they had received of his bounteous liberality but adding much of their own unto it, it was found that the said sum amounted unto much more than the niggardly sparing of Croesus. Whereupon Cyrus said, "I am no less greedy of riches than other princes, but I am rather a better husband of them. You see with what small adventure I have purchased the invaluable treasure of so many friends, and how much more faithful treasurers they are to me than mercenary men would be, without obligation and without affection; and my exchequer or treasury better placed than in paltry coffers, by which I draw upon me the hate, the envy, and the contempt of other princes."

[B]The ancient emperors were wont to draw some excuse for the superfluity of their sports and public shows, for so much as their authority did in some sort depend, at least in appearance, from the will of the Roman people, which from all ages are accustomed to be flattered by such kind of spectacles and excess. But they were particular ones who had bred this custom to gratify their concitizens and fellows, especially by their purse, by such profusion and magnificence. It was clean altered when the masters and chief rulers came once to imitate the same. [C]"The passing of money from right owners to strangers should not seem liberality" (Cic. *De off*. I.xiv.). Philip, because his son endeavored by gifts to purchase the good will of the Macedonians, by a letter seemed to be displeased, and chid him in this manner: "What? Wouldst thou have thy subjects to account thee for their purse-bearer and not repute thee for their king? Wilt thou frequent and practice them? Then do it with the benefits of thy virtue, not with those of thy coffers."

[B]Yet was it a goodly thing to cause a great quantity of great trees, all branchy and green, to be far brought and planted in plots yielding nothing but dry gravel, representing a wild, shady forest divided in due, seemly proportion, and the first day to put into the same a thousand estridges,* a thousand stags, a thousand wild boars, and a thousand bucks, yielding them over to be hunted and killed by the common people; the next morrow in the presence of all the assembly to cause a hundred great lions, a hundred leopards, and three hundred huge bears to be baited and tugged in pieces; and for the third day, in bloody manner and good earnest to make three hundred couple of gladiators or fencers to combat and murder one another, as did the emperor Probus.

It was also a goodly show to see those huge amphitheatres all enchased with rich marble, on the outside curiously wrought with carved statues and all the inner side glittering with precious and rare embellishments —

> A belt beset with gems behold,
> Behold a walk bedaub'd with gold
> Calipurnius, *Ecl.* VII.47.

— all the sides round about that great void replenished and environed from the ground unto the very top with three or four score ranks of steps and seats, likewise all of marble, covered with fair cushions —

> "If shame there be, let him be gone," he cries,
> "And from his knightly cushion let him rise
> Whose substance to the law doth not suffice"
> Juven. III.153.

— where might conveniently be placed an hundred thousand men and all sit at ease. And the plain groundwork of it, where sports were to be acted, first by art to cause the same to open and chap* in sunder with gaps and cranishes* representing hollow caverns which vomited out the beasts appointed for the spectacle; that ended, immediately to overflow it all with a main, deep sea, fraught with store of sea monsters and other strange fishes, all overlaid with goodly tall ships ready rigged and appointed to represent a sea fight; and thirdly, suddenly to make it smooth and dry again for the combat of gladiators; and fourthly, being forthwith cleansed, to strew it over with vermilion and storax instead of gravel for the erecting of a solemn banquet for all that infinite number of people — the last act of one only day.

> How oft have we beheld wild beasts appear
> From broken gulfs of earth upon some part
> Of sand that did not sink? How often there
> And thence did golden boughs o'er-saffon'd start?
> Nor only saw we monsters of the wood,
> But I have seen sea-calves whom bears withstood
> And such a kind of beast as might be named
> A horse, but in most foul proportion framed.
> Calp. *Ecl.* VII.64.

They have sometimes caused an high, steepy mountain to arise in the midst of the said amphitheatres, all overspread with fruitful and flourishing trees of all sorts, on the top whereof gushed out streams of water, as from out the source of a purling spring. Other times they have produced a great, tall ship floating up and down, which of itself opened and split asunder, and after it had disgorged from out its bulk four or five hundred wild beasts to be baited, it closed and vanished away of itself, without any visible help. Sometimes from out the bottom of it they caused streaks and purlings of sweet water to spout up, bubbling to the highest top of the frame and gently watering, sprinkling, and refreshing that infinite multitude. To keep and cover themselves from the violence of the weather, they caused that huge compass to be all over-spread, sometimes with purple sails all curiously wrought with the needle, sometimes of silk and of some other color; in the twinkling of an eye, as they pleased, they displayed and spread or drew and pulled them in again.

Though fervent sun make't hot to see a play,
When linen thieves come sails are kept away.
Mart. XII.xxix.15.

The nets likewise, which they used to put before the people to save them from harm and violence of the baited beasts, were woven with gold:

Nets with gold interlaced
Their shows with glittering graced.
Calp. *Ecl.* VII.53.

If anything be excusable in such lavish excess, it is where the invention and strangeness breedeth admiration, and not the costly charge.

Even in those vanities we may plainly perceive how fertile and happy those former ages were of other manner of wits than ours are. It happeneth of this kind of fertility as of all other productions of nature. We may not say [t]hat nature employed then the utmost of her power. We go not, but rather creep and stagger here and there: we go our pace. I imagine our knowledge to be weak in all senses; we neither discern far forward nor see much backward. It embraceth little and liveth not long. It is short both in extension of time and in ampleness of matter or invention.

Before great Agamemnon and the rest
Many liv'd valiant, yet are all suppressed,
Unmoan'd, unknown, in dark oblivion's nest.
Hor. *Odes* IV.ix.25.

Beside the Trojan war, Troy's funeral night,
Of other things did other poets write.
Lucr. V.327.

[C]And Solon's narration concerning what he had learned of the Egyptian priests of their state's long life, and manner how to learn and preserve strange or foreign histories, in mine opinion is not a testimony to be refused in this consideration. "If we behold an unlimited greatness on all sides both of regions and times, whereupon the mind casting itself and intentive doth travel far and near so as it sees no bounds of what is last, whereon it may insist, in this infinite immensity there would appear a multitude of innumerable other forms" (Cic. *De nat. deor.* I.xx.).

[B]If whatsoever hath come unto us by report of what is past were true and known of anybody, it would be less than nothing in respect of that which is unknown. And even of this image of the world which, whilst we live therein, glideth and passeth away, how wretched, weak, and how short is the knowledge of the most curious? Not only of the particular events which fortune often maketh exemplar and of consequence, but of the state of mighty commonwealths, large monarchies, and renowned nations there escapeth our knowledge a hundred times more than cometh unto our notice. We keep a coil* and wonder at the miraculous invention of our artillery and [are] amazed at the rare device of printing; when, as unknown to us, other men and another end of the world named China knew and had perfect use of both a thousand years before. If we saw as much of this vast world as we see but a least part of it, it is very likely we should perceive a perpetual multiplicity and ever-rolling vicissitude of forms.

Therein is nothing singular and nothing rare if regard be had unto nature, or, to say better, if relation be had unto our knowledge, which is a weak foundation of our rules and which doth commonly present us a right false image of things. How vainly do we nowadays conclude the declination and decrepitude of the world by the fond arguments we draw from our own weakness, drooping, and declination —

> And now both age and land
> So sick affected stand.
>
> Lucr. II.1136.

— and as vainly did conclude its birth and youth by the vigor he perceiveth in the wits of his time, abounding in novelties and invention of divers arts:

> But all this world is new, as I suppose,
> World's nature fresh, nor lately it arose;
> Whereby some arts refined are in fashion,
> And many things now to our navigation
> Are added, daily grown to augmentation.
>
> Lucr. V.331.

Our world hath of late discovered another (and who can warrant us whether it be the last of his brethren, since both the daemons, the sibyls, and all we have hitherto been ignorant of this?) no less large, fully peopled, all-things-yielding, and mighty in strength than ours, nevertheless so new and infantine that he is yet to learn his A B C. It is not yet full fifty years that he knew neither letters, nor weight, nor measures, nor apparel, nor corn, nor vines. But was all naked, simply pure in nature's lap, and lived but with such means and food as his mother nurse afforded him. If we conclude aright of our end, and the foresaid poet of the infancy of this age, this late world shall but come to light when ours shall fall into darkness. The whole universe shall fall into a palsy or convulsion of sinews; one member shall be maimed or shrunken, another nimble and in good plight. I fear that by our contagion we shall directly have furthered his declination and hastened his ruin, and that we shall too dearly have sold him our opinions, our new-fangles, and our arts. It was an unpolluted, harmless, infant world; yet have we not whipped and submitted the same unto our discipline, or schooled him by the advantage of our valour or natural forces, nor have we instructed him by our justice and integrity, nor subdued by our magnanimity. Most of their answers, and a number of the negotiations we have had with them, witness that they were nothing short of us nor beholding to us for any excellency of natural wit or perspicuity concerning pertinency.

The wonderful, or as I may call it, amazement-breeding magnificence of the never-like-seen cities of Cuzco and Mexico (and, amongst infinite such-like things, the admirable garden of that king, where all the trees, the fruits, the herbs and plants, according to the order and greatness they have in a garden, were most artificially framed in gold; as also, in his cabinet, all living creatures that his country or his seas produced were cast in gold) and the exquisite beauty of their works in precious stones, in feathers, in cotton, and in painting show that they yielded little unto us in cunning and industry. But concerning unfeigned devotion, awful observance of laws, unspotted integrity, bounteous liberality, due loyalty, and free liberty, it hath greatly availed us that we had not so much as they; by which advantage they have lost, cast away, sold, undone, and betrayed themselves.

Touching hardiness and undaunted courage, and as for matchless constancy, unmoved assuredness, undismayed resolution against pain, smarting, famine, and death itself, I will not fear to oppose the examples which I may easily find amongst them to the most famous ancient examples we may with all our industry discover in all the annals and memories of our known old world. For, as for those which have subdued them, let them lay aside the wiles, the policies and stratagems, which they have employed to cozen, to coney-catch, and to circumvent them, and the just astonishment which those nations might justly conceive by seeing so unexpected an arrival of bearded men, divers in language, in habit, in religion, in behavior, in form, in countenance, and from a part of the world so distant and where they never heard any habitation was, mounted upon great and unknown monsters against those who had never so much as seen any horse and less any beast whatsoever apt to bear or taught to carry either man or burden, covered with a shining and hard skin and armed with slicing, keen weapons and glittering armor against them who for the wonder of the glistering of a looking-glass or of a plain knife would have changed or given inestimable riches in gold, precious stones, and pearls, and who had neither the skill not the matter wherewith at any leisure they could have pierced our steel; to which you may add the flashing fire and thundering roar of shot and harquebuses — able to quell and daunt even Caesar himself had he been so suddenly surprised and as little experienced as they were — and thus to come unto and assault silly,* naked people, saving where the invention of weaving of cotton cloth was known and used, for the most altogether unarmed, except some bows, stones, staves, ᶜand wooden bucklers, ᴮunsuspecting poor people, surprised under color of amity and well-meaning faith, overtaken by the curiosity to see strange and unknown things — I say, take this disparity from the conquerors, and you deprive them of all the occasions and cause of so many unexpected victories.

When I consider that stern, untamed obstinacy and undaunted vehemence wherewith so many thousands of men, of women, and children, do so infinite times present themselves unto inevitable dangers for the defense of their gods and liberty, this generous obstinacy to endure all extremities, all difficulties, and death more easily and willingly than basely to yield unto their domination of whom they have so abominably been abused (some of them choosing rather to starve with hunger and fasting, being taken, than to accept food at their enemy's hands, so basely victorious), I perceive that whosoever had undertaken them man to man, without odds of arms, of experience, or of number, should have had as dangerous a war, or perhaps more, as any we see amongst us.

Why did not so glorious a conquest happen under Alexander, or during the time of the ancient Greeks and Romans? Or why befell not so great a change and alteration of empires and people under such hands as would gently have polished, reformed, and encivilized what in them they deemed to be barbarous and rude, or would have nourished and fostered those good seeds which nature had there brought forth, adding not only to the manuring of their grounds and ornaments of their cities such arts as we had, and that no further than had been necessary for them, but therewithal joining unto the original virtues of the country those of the ancient Grecians and Romans? What reparation and what reformation would all that far-spreading world have found if the examples, demeanors, and policies wherewith we first presented them had called and allured those uncorrupted nations to the admiration and imitation of virtue and had established between them and us a brotherly society and mutual correspondency! How easy a matter had it been profitably to reform and Christianly to instruct minds yet so pure and new, so willing to be taught, being for the most part endowed with so docile, so apt, and so yielding natural beginnings! Whereas, contrariwise, we have made use of their ignorance and inexperience [to] draw them more easily unto treason, fraud, luxury, avarice, and all manner of inhumanity and cruelty, by the example of our life and pattern of our customs. Who ever raised the service of merchandise and benefit of traffic to so high a rate? So many goodly cities ransacked and razed, so many nations destroyed and made desolate, so infinite millions of harmless people of all sexes, states, and ages massacred, ravaged, and put to the sword, and the richest, the fairest, and the best part of the world topsy-turvied, ruined and defaced for the traffic of pearls and pepper! Oh mechanical victories! Oh base conquest! Never did greedy revenge, public wrong, or general enmities so moodily enrage and so passionately incense men against men unto so horrible hostilities, bloody dissipations, and miserable calamities.

Certain Spaniards coasting alongst the sea in search of mines fortuned to land in a very fertile, pleasant, and well-peopled country, unto the inhabitants whereof they declared their intent and showed their accustomed persuasions, saying that they were quiet and well-meaning men, coming from far countries, being sent from the King of Castile, the greatest king of the habitable earth, unto whom the Pope, representing God on earth, had given the principality of all the Indies; that if they would become tributaries to him they should be most kindly used and courteously entreated. They required of them victuals for their nourishment and some gold for the behoof of certain physical experiments. Moreover, they declared unto them the believing in one only God and the truth of our religion, which they persuaded them to embrace, adding thereto some minatory threats.

Whose answer was this: That haply they might be quiet and well-meaning, but their countenance showed them to be otherwise. As concerning their king, since he seemed to beg he showed to be poor and needy. And for the Pope who had made that distribution, he expressed himself a man loving dissension in going about to give unto a third man a thing which was not his own, so to make it questionable and litigious amongst the ancient possessors of it. As for victuals, they should have part of their store. And for gold, they had but little and that it was a thing they made very small account of as merely unprofitable for the service of their life, whereas all their care was but how to pass it happily and pleasantly, and therefore what quantity soever they should find, that only excepted which was employed about the service of their gods, they might boldly take it. As touching one only God, the discourse of him had very well pleased them, but they would by no means change their religion under which they had for so long time lived so happily, and that they were not accustomed to take any counsel but of their friends and acquaintance. As concerning their menaces, it was a sign of want of judgment to threaten those whose nature, condition, power, and means was to them unknown. And therefore they should with all speed hasten to avoid their dominions, forsomuch as they were not wont to admit or take in good part the kindnesses and remonstrances of armed people, namely of strangers; otherwise they would deal with them as they had done with such others, showing them the heads of certain men sticking upon stakes about their city which had lately been executed.

Lo, here an example of the stammering of this infancy! But so it is, neither in this nor in infinite other places where the Spaniards found not the merchandise they sought for, neither made stay or attempted any violence, whatsoever other commodity the place yielded; witness my Cannibals.

Of two the most mighty and glorious monarchs of that world, and peradventure of all our western parts, kings over so many kings, the last they deposed and overcame, he of Peru, having by them been taken in battle and set at so excessive a ransom that it exceedeth all belief, and that truly paid, and by his conversation having given them apparent signs of a free, liberal, undaunted, and constant courage, and declared to be of a pure, noble, and well-composed understanding, a humor possessed the conquerors, after they had most insolently exacted from him a million, three hundred five and twenty thousand and five hundred weights of gold, besides the silver and other precious things which amounted to no less a sum (so that their horses were all shod of massive gold), to discover (what disloyalty or treachery soever it might cost them) what the remainder of this king's treasure might be [C]and without controlment enjoy whatever he might have hidden or concealed from them. [B]Which to compass, they forged a false accusation and proof against him, that he practiced to raise his provinces and intended to induce his subjects to some insurrection, so to procure his liberty. Whereupon, by the very judgment of those who had complotted this forgery and treason against him he was condemned to be publicly hanged and strangled, having first made him to redeem the torment of being burned alive by the baptism which, at the instant of his execution, in charity they bestowed upon him. A horrible and the like never-heard-of accident, which nevertheless he undismayedly endured with an unmoved manner and truly royal gravity, without ever contradicting himself either in countenance or speech. And then, somewhat to mitigate and circumvent those silly,* unsuspecting people, amazed and astonished at so strange a spectacle, they counterfeited a great mourning and lamentation for his death and appointed his funerals to be solemnly and sumptuously celebrated.

The other, King of Mexico, having a long time manfully defended his beseiged city and in the tedious siege showed whatever pinching sufferance and resolute perseverance can effect, if ever any courageous prince or warlike people showed the same, and his disastrous success having delivered him alive into his enemies' hands upon conditions to be used as beseemed a king; who during the time of his imprisonment did never make the least show of anything unworthy that glorious title. After which victory the Spaniards, not finding that quantity of gold they had promised themselves when they had ransacked and ranged all corners, they, by means of the cruellest tortures and horriblest torments they could possibly devise, began to wrest and draw some more from such prisoners as they had in keeping. But unable to profit anything that way, finding stronger hearts than their torments, they in the end fell to such moody outrages that, contrary to all law of nations and against their solemn vows and promises, they condemned the king himself and one of the chiefest princes of his court to the rank, one in presence of another. The prince, environed round with hot burning coals, being overcome with the exceeding torment, at last in most piteous sort turning his dreary eyes toward his master as if he asked mercy of him for that he could endure no longer, the king, fixing rigorously and fiercely his looks upon him, seeming to upbraid him with his remissness and pusillanimity, with a stern and settled voice uttered these few words unto him: "What? supposeth thou I am in a cold bath? Am I at more ease than thou art?" Whereat the silly* wretch immediately fainted under the torture and yielded up the ghost. The king, half-roasted, was carried away, not so much for pity (for what ruth could ever enter so barbarous minds, who upon the surmised information of some odd piece or vessel of gold they intended to get would broil a man before their eyes, and not a man only, but a king, so great in fortune and so renowned in desert?) but forasmuch as his unmatched constancy did more and more make their inhuman cruelty ashamed. They afterward hanged him, because he had courageously attempted by arms to deliver himself out of so long captivity and miserable subjection; where he ended his wretched life, worthy an high-minded and never-daunted prince.

At another time, in one same fire they caused to be burned all alive four hundred common men and three-score principal lords of a province, whom by the fortune of war they had taken prisoners.

These narratives we have out of their own books; for they do not only avouch but vauntingly publish them. May it be they do it for a testimony of their justice or zeal toward their religion? Verily, they are ways over-different and enemies to so sacred an end. Had they proposed unto themselves to enlarge and propagate our relgion, they would have considered that it is not amplified by possession of lands, but of men; and would have been satisfied with such slaughters as the necessity of war bringeth, without indifferently adding thereunto so bloody a butchery, as upon savage beasts, and so universal as fire or sword could ever attain unto, having purposely preserved no more than so many miserable bond-slaves as they deemed might suffice for the digging, working, and service of their mines: so that divers of their chieftains have been executed to death, even in the places they had conquered by the appointment of the kings of Castile, justly offended at the seld*-seen horror of their barbarous demeanors, and well-nigh all disesteemed, contemned, and hated. God hath meritoriously permitted that many of their great pillages and ill-gotten goods have either been swallowed up by the revenging seas in transporting them, or consumed by the intestine wars and civil broils wherewith themselves have devoured one another; and the greatest part of them have been overwhelmed and buried in the bowels of the earth, in the very places they found them, without any fruit of their victory.

Touching the objection which some make, that the receipt, namely in the hands of so thrifty, wary, and wise a prince,[2] doth so little answer the foreconceived hope which was given unto his predecessors and the said former abundance of riches they met withal at the first discovery of this new-found world (for although they bring home great quantity of gold and silver, we perceive the same to be nothing in respect of what might be expected thence), it may be answered that the use of money was there altogether unknown, and consequently that all their gold was gathered together, serving to no other purpose than for show, state, and ornament, as a movable reserved from father to son by many puissant kings, who exhausted all their mines to collect so huge a heap of vessels or statues for the ornament of their

2 Philip II of Spain.

temples and embellishing of their palaces; whereas all our gold is employed in commerce and traffic between man and man. We mince and alter it into a thousand forms; we spend, we scatter and disperse the same to several uses. Suppose our kings should thus gather and heap up all the gold they might for many ages hoard up together and keep it close and untouched.

Those of the kingdom of Mexico were somewhat more encivilized and better artists than other nations of that world. And as we do, so judged they, that this universe was near his end, and took the desolation we brought amongst them as an infallible sign of it. They believed the state of the world to be divided into five ages, as in the life of five succeeding suns, whereof four had already ended their course or time, and the same which now shined upon them was the fifth and last. The first perished together with all other creatures by an universal inundation of waters. The second by the fall of the heavens upon us, which stifled and overwhelmed every living thing; in which age they affirm the giants to have been, and showed the Spaniards certain bones of them, according to whose proportion the stature of men came to be of the height of twenty handfuls. The third was consumed by a violent fire, which burned and destroyed all. The fourth by a whirling emotion of the air and winds, which with the violent fury of itself removed and overthrew divers high mountains; saying that men died not of it, but were transformed into monkeys. (Oh what impressions doth not the weakness of man's belief admit!) After the consummation of this fourth sun the world continued five and twenty years in perpetual darkness; in the fifteenth of which one man and one woman were created who renewed the race of mankind. Ten years after, upon a certain day, the sun appeared as newly created, from which day beginneth ever since the calculation of their years. On the third day of whose creation died their ancient gods; their new ones have day by day been born since. In what manner this last sun shall perish my author could not learn of them. But their number of this fourth doth change, doth jump and meet with that great conjunction of the stars which, eight hundred and odd years since, according to the astrologians' supposition, produced divers great alterations and strange novelties in the world.

Concerning the proud pomp and glorious magnificence by occasion of which I am fallen into this discourse, nor Greece nor Rome nor Egypt can, be it in profit or difficulty or nobility, equal or compare sundry and divers of their works: the cawcy* or highway which is yet to be seen in Peru, erected by the kings of that country, stretching from the city of Quito unto that of Cuzco (containing three hundred leagues in length), straight, even, and fine, and twenty paces in breadth curiously paved, raised on both sides with goodly high masonry walls, all along which on the inner side there are two continual running streams, pleasantly beset with beauteous trees which they call *molly.* In framing of which, where they met any mountains or rocks, they have cut, razed, and leveled them and filled all hollow places with lime and stone. At the end of each day's journey, as stations, there are built stately great palaces, plenteously stored with all manner of good victuals, apparel, and arms, as well for daily wayfaring men as for such armies that might happen to pass that way.

In the estimation of which work I have especially considered the difficulty which in that place is particularly to be remembered. For they built with no stones that were less than ten foot square; they had no other means to carry or transport them than by mere strength of arms to draw and drag the carriage they needed; they had not so much as the art to make scaffolds, nor knew they other device than to raise so much earth or rubbish against their building according as the work riseth and afterward to take it away again.

But return we to our coaches. Instead of them and of all other carrying beasts, they caused themselves to be carried by men, and upon their shoulders. This last king of Peru, the same day he was taken, was thus carried upon rafters or beams of massive gold, sitting in a fair chair of state likewise all of gold, in the middle of his battle.* Look how many of his porters as were slain to make him fall (for all their endeavor was to take him alive), so many others, and as it were avie,* took and underwent presently the place of the dead, so that they could never be brought down or made to fall, what slaughter soever was made of those kind of people, until such time as a horseman furiously ran to take him by some part of his body and so pulled him to the ground.

How One Ought to Govern His Will

❧ III. 10 ✧ 1586–87 ☙

[B]In regard of the common sort of men, few things touch me, or (to speak properly), sway me. For it is reason they touch, so they possess us not. I have great need, both by study and discourse, to increase this privilege of insensibility, which is naturally crept far into me. I am not wedded unto many things, and, by consequence, not passionate of them. I have my sight clear, but tied to few objects; my senses delicate and gentle, but my apprehension and application hard and dull. I engage myself with difficulty. As much as I can, I employ myself wholly to myself. And in this very subject, I would willingly bridle and uphold my affection, lest it be too far plunged therein, seeing it is a subject I possess at the mercy of others, and over which fortune hath more interest than myself. So as even in my health, which I so much esteem, it were requisite not to desire, nor so carefully to seek it, as thereby I might light upon intolerable diseases. [C]We must moderate ourselves betwixt the hate of pain and the love of pleasure. Plato sets down a mean course of life between both.

[B]But to affections that distract me from myself and divert me elsewhere, surely to such I oppose myself with all my force. Mine opinion is that one should lend himself to others, and not give himself but to himself. Were my will easy to engage or apply itself, I could not continue. I am over-tender, both by nature and custom,

> Avoiding active business,
> And born to secure idleness.
> Ovid. *Trist.* III.ii.9.

Contested and obstinate debates, which in the end would give mine adversary advantage, the issue which would make my earnest pursuit ashamed, would perchance torment me cruelly. If I vexed as other men, my soul should never have strength to bear the alarms and emotions that follow such as embrace much. She would presently be displaced by this intestine agitation.

If at any time I have been urged to the managing of strange affairs, I have promised to undertake them with my hand, but not with my lungs and liver; to charge, and not to incorporate them into me; to have a care, but nothing at all to be over-passionate of them. I look to them, but I hatch them not. I work enough to dispose and direct the domestical troubles within mine own entrails and veins, without harboring, or importune myself with any foreign employments; and am sufficiently interested with my proper, natural, and essential affairs, without seeking others' businesses.

Such as know how much they owe to themselves, and how many offices of their own they are bound to perform, shall find that nature hath given them this commission fully ample and nothing idle. Thou hast business enough within thyself, therefore stray not abroad.

Men give themselves to hire. Their faculties are not their own, but theirs to whom they subject themselves: their inmates, and not themselves, are within them. This common humor doth not please me. We should thriftily husband our mind's liberty, and never engage it but upon just occasions, which, if we judge impartially, are very few in number. Look on such as suffer themselves to be transported and swayed: they do it everywhere, in little as well as in great matters; to that which concerneth, as easily as to that which toucheth them not. They thrust themselves indifferently into all actions, and are without life if without tumultuary agitation. [C]"They are busy that they may not be idle, or else in action for action's sake" (Sen. *Ep.* XXII). They seek work, but to be working.

It is not so much because they will go, as for that they cannot stand still. Much like to a rolling stone, which never stays until it come to a lying place. To some men, employment is a mark of sufficiency and a badge of dignity. [B]Their spirits seek rest in action, as infants repose in the cradle. They may be said to be as serviceable to their friends as importunate to themselves. No man distributes his money to others, but everyone his life and time. We are not so prodigal of anything, as of those whereof to be covetous would be both commendable and profitable for us.

I follow a clean contrary course. I am of another complexion. I stay at home and look to myself. What I wish for, I commonly desire the same but mildly, and desire but little. So likewise I seldom employ and quietly embusy myself. Whatever they intend and act, they do it with all their will and vehemency. There are so many dangerous steps that for the more security we must somewhat slightly and superficially slide through the world, [C]and not force it. [B]Pleasure itself is painful in its height.

You pass through fire (though unafraid)
Under deceitful ashes laid.

Hor. *Odes* II.i.7.

The town council of Bordeaux chose me mayor of their city, being far from France, but further from any such thought. I excused myself and would have avoided it; but they told me I was to blame, the more because the king's commandment was also employed therein. It is a charge should seem so much the more goodly, because it hath neither fee nor reward other than the honor in the execution. It lasteth two years, but may continue longer by a second election, which seldom happeneth. To me it was, and never had been but twice before: some years past the Lord of Lansac, and lately to the Lord of Biron, Marshal of France, in whose place I succeeded; and left mine to the Lord of Matignon, likewise Marshal of France, glorious by so noble an assistance.

> [C]Both, both in peace and war,
> Right serviceable are.
> Virg. *Aen.* XI.658.

[B]Fortune would have a share in my promotion by this particular circumstance, which she or her own added thereunto, not altogether vain. For Alexander disdained the Corinthian ambassadors, who offered him the freedom and burgess* of their city. But when they told him that Bacchus and Hercules were likewise in their registers, he kindly thanked them and accepted their offer.

At my first arrival, I faithfully deciphered and conscientiously displayed myself such as I am indeed: without memory, without diligence, without experience, and without sufficiency; so likewise without hatred, without ambition, covetousness, and without violence; that so they might be duly instructed what service they might or hope or expect at my hands. And forsomuch as the knowledge they had of my deceased father and the honor they bore upon his memory had moved them to choose me to that dignity, I told them plainly I should be very sorry that any thing should work such an opinion in my will, as their affairs and city had done in my father's while he held the said government, whereunto they had called me.

I remembered to have seen him, being an infant and he an old man, his mind cruelly turmoiled with the public toil, forgetting the sweet air of his own house, whereunto the weakness of his age had long before tied him, neglecting the care of his health and family, in a manner despising his life, which, as one engaged for them, he much endangered, riding long and painful journeys for them. Such a one was he, which humor proceeded from the bounty and goodness of his nature. Never was mind more charitable or more popular.

This course, which I commend in others, I love not to follow. Neither am I without excuse. He had heard that a man must forget himself for his neighbor; that in respect of the general, the particular was not to be regarded.

Most of the world's rules and precepts hold this train, to drive us out of ourselves into the wide world to the use of public society. They presumed to work a goodly effect in distracting and withdrawing us from ourselves, supposing we were by a natural instinct too, too much tied unto it, and to this end have not spared to say anything. For to the wise it is no novelty to preach things as they serve and not as they are. [C]Truth has her lets,* discommodities, and incompatibilities with us. We must often deceive others, lest we beguile ourselves, and seal our eyes and dull our understanding, thereby to repair and amend them. "For unskillful men judge, who must often even therefore be deceived, lest they err and be deceived." (Quintilian *Inst. Orat.* II.xvii.). [B]When they prescribe us to love three, four, yea fifty degrees of things before ourselves, they present us with the art of shooters, who, to come near the mark, take their aim far above the same. To make a crooked stick straight, we bend it the contrary way.

I suppose that in the temple of Pallas, as we see in all other religions, they had some apparent mysteries, of which they made show to all the people, and others more high and secret, to be imparted only to such as were professed. It is likely that the true point of friendship which every man oweth to himself is to be found in these. Not [C]a false amity, which makes us embrace glory, knowledge, riches, and such like with a principal and immoderate affection, as members of our being; nor [B]an effeminate and indiscreet friendship, wherein happeneth as to the ivy, which corrupts and ruins the walls it claspeth; but a sound and regular amity, equally profitable and pleasant. Who so understandeth all her duties and exerciseth them, he is rightly endenizened in the Muses' cabinet. He hath attained the type of human wisdom and the perfection of our happiness. This man, knowing exactly what he oweth to himself, findeth that he ought to employ the use of other men and of the world unto himself, which to perform, he must contribute the duties and offices that concern him unto public society. [C]He that lives not somewhat to others, liveth little to himself. "He that is friend to himself, know, he is friend to all" (Sen. *Ep.* VI.).

[B]The principal charge we have is every man his particular conduct. [C]And for this only we live here. [B]As he that should forget to live well and religiously, and by instructing and directing others should think himself acquitted of his duty, would be deemed a fool; even so, who forsaketh to live healthy, and merrily himself, therewith to serve another, in mine opinion, taketh a bad and unnatural course.

I will not that, in any charge one shall take in hand, he refuse or think much of his attention, of his labor, of his steps, of his speech, of his sweat, and, if need be, of his blood —

Not fearing life to end
For country or dear friend
Hor. *Odes* IV.ix. 51.

— but is only borrowed and accidentally, the mind remaining ever quiet and in health, not without action, but without vexation or passion. Simply to move or be doing costs it so little, that even sleeping it is moving and doing. But it must have its motion with discretion. For the body receiveth the charges imposed him, justly as they are. But the spirit extendeth them, and often to his hindrance makes them heavy, giving them what measure it pleaseth. Like things are effected by divers efforts and different contentions of will. The one may go without the other.[1] For how many men do daily hazard themselves in war which they regard not, and press into the danger of the battles, the loss whereof shall no whit break their next sleep? Whereas some man in his own house, free from this danger, which he durst not so much as have looked towards it, is for the war's issue more passionate, and therewith hath his mind perplexed than the soldier that therein employeth both his blood and life.

I know how to deal in public charges, without departing from myself the breadth of my nail; [C]and give myself to another, without taking me from myself. [B]This sharpness and violence of desires hindereth more than stead* the conduct of what we undertake, filling us with impatience to the events, either contrary or slow, and with bitterness and jealousy toward those with whom we negotiate. We never govern that thing well wherewith we are possessed and directed.

[C]Fury and haste do lay all waste,
Misplacing all, disgracing all,
Stat. *Theb*. X.704.

[B]He who therein employeth but his judgment and direction proceeds more cheerfully. He feigns, he yields, he defers at his pleasure according to the occasions of necessity; he fails of his attempt, without torment or affliction, ready and prepared for a new enterprise. He marcheth always with the reins in his hand. He that is besotted with this violent and tyrannical intention doth necessarily declare much indiscretion and injustice. The violence of his desire transports him. They are rash motions, and, if fortune help not much, of little fruit.

Philosophy wills us to banish choler in the punishment of offenses, not to the end revenge should be more moderate, but contrary, more weighty and surely set on, whereunto this violence seemeth to be a let.* [C]Choler doth not only trouble, but wearieth the executioners' arms. This passionate heat dulleth and consumes their force. "As in

[1] That is, action without "vexation or passion."

too much speed, hastiness is slow" (Quint.-Curt. IX.ix.12.) Haste makes waste, and hinders and stays itself. "Swiftness entangles itself" (Sen. *Ep.* XLIV.). [B]As for example, according as by ordinary custom I perceive covetousness hath no greater let* than itself. The more violent and extended it is, the less effectual and fruitful. Commonly it gathers wealth more speedily being masked with a show of liberality.

A very honest gentleman and my good friend was likely to have endangered the health of his body by an over-passionate attention and earnest affection to the affairs of a prince, who was his master.[2] Which master hath thus described himself unto me: that as another, he discerneth and hath a feeling of the burden of accidents; but such as have no remedy, he presently resolveth to suffer with patience. For the rest, after he hath appointed necessary provisions, which by the vivacity and nimbleness of his wit he speedily effects, he then attends the event with quietness. Verily, I have seen in him at one instant a great carelessness and liberty, both in his actions and countenance, even in important and difficult affairs. I find him more magnanimous and capable in bad than in good fortune. [C]His losses are to him more glorious than his victories, and his mourning than his triumphs.

[B]Consider how in mere vain and frivolous actions, as at chess, tennis, and suchlike sports, this earnest and violent engaging with an ambitious desire to win doth presently cast both mind and limbs into disorder and indiscretion, wherein a man doth both dazzle his sight and distemper his whole body. He who demeaneth himself with most moderation both in winning and losing is ever nearest unto himself, and hath his wits best about him. The less he is moved or passionate in play, the more safely doth he govern the same, and to his greater advantage.

We hinder the mind's seizure and holdfast* by giving her so many things to seize upon. Some we should only present unto her; others fasten upon her, and others incorporate into her. She may see and feel all things, but must only feed on herself and be instructed in that which properly concerneth her and which merely belongeth to her essence and substance. The laws of nature teach us what is just and fit for us. After the wise men have told us that, according to nature, no man is indigent or wanteth, and that each one is poor but in his own opinion, they also distinguish subtlely the desires proceeding from nature from such as grow from the disorders of our fantasy. Those whose end may be discerned are merely hers; and such as fly before us and whose end we cannot attain are properly ours. Want of goods may easily be cured, but the poverty of the mind is incurable.

2 Henri of Navarre.

CIf it might be enough, that is enough for man,
This were enough; since it is not, how think we can
Now any riches fill
My mind and greedy will?

Lucilius, in Non. Marc. V.98.

Socrates, seeing great store of riches, jewels, and precious stuff carried in pomp through the city: "Oh how many things," quoth he, "do not I desire!" BMetrodorus lived daily with the weight of twelve ounces of food, Epicurus with less. Metrocles in winter lay with sheep, and in summer in the cloisters of churches. C"Nature is sufficient for that which it requires" (Sen. *Ep.* XC.). Cleanthes lived by his hands, and boasted that, if Cleanthes would, he could nourish another Cleanthes.

BIf that which nature doth exactly and originally require at our hands for the preservation of our being is over-little (as in truth what it is, and how good cheap our life may be maintained cannot better be known or expressed than by consideration that it is so little, and for the smallness thereof, it is out of fortune's reach, and she can take no hold of it) let us dispense something else unto ourselves, and call the custom and condition of everyone of us by the name of nature. Let us tax and stint and feed ourselves according to that measure; let us extend both our appurtenances and reckonings thereunto. For so far, meseems we have some excuse. Custom is a second nature, and no less powerful. CWhat is wanting to my custom, I hold it a defect. BAnd I had well nigh lief one should deprive me of my life as refrain or much abridge me of my state wherein I have lived so long.

I am no more upon terms of any great alteration, nor to thrust myself into a new and unusual course, no not toward augmentation. It is no longer time to become other or to be transformed. And, as I should complain if any great adventure should now befall me, and grieve it came not in time that I might have enjoyed the same —

Whereto should I have much
If I to use it grutch?

Hor. *Epist.* I.v.12.

— I should likewise be grieved at any inward purchase. I were better, in a manner, never, than so late, to become an honest man, and well practiced to live, when one hath no longer life. I, who am ready to depart this world, could easily be induced to resign the share of wisdom I have learned concerning the world's commerce to any other man new-come into the world. It is even as good as mustard after dinner. What need have I of that good which I cannot enjoy? Whereto serveth knowledge, if one have no head? It is an injury and disgrace of fortune to offer us those presents which, forsomuch as they fail us when we should most need them, fill us with a just spite. Guide me no more. I can go no longer. Of so many dismemberings that sufficiency hath, patience sufficeth us. Give the capacity of an excellent treble to a singer that hath his lungs rotten, and of eloquence to a hermit confined into the deserts of Arabia.

[B]There needs no art to further a fall. [C]The end finds itself in the finishing of every work. My world is at an end, my form is expired. I am wholly of the time past, and am bound to authorize the same and thereto conform my issue.

I will say this by way of example: that the eclipsing or abridging of ten days which the Pope[3] hath lately caused, hath taken me so low that I can hardly recover myself. I follow the years wherein we were wont to count otherwise. So long and ancient a custom doth challenge recall me to it again. I am thereby enforced to be somewhat an heretic, incapable of innovation, though corrective. My imagination, mauger* my teeth, runs still ten days before or ten behind, and whispers in mine ears: "This rule toucheth those which are to come."

If health itself, so sweetly pleasing, comes to me but by fits, it is rather to give me cause of grief than possession of itself. I have nowhere left me to retire it. Time forsakes me, without which nothing is enjoyed. How small account should I make of these great elective dignities I see in the world, and which are only given to men ready to leave the world, wherein they regard not so much how duly they shall discharge them, as how little they shall exercise them. From the beginning they look to the end.

[B]To conclude, I am ready to finish this man, not to make another. By long custom, this form is changed into substance, and fortune into nature.

I say, therefore, that amongst us feeble creatures, each one is excusable to count that his own which is comprehended under measure. And yet all beyond these limits is nothing but confusion. It is the largest extension we can grant our rights. The more we amplify our need and possession, the more we engage ourselves to the crosses of fortune and adversities. The cariere* of our desires must be circumscribed and tied to strict bounds of nearest and contiguous commodities. Moreover, their course should be managed, not in a straight line having another end, but round, whose two points hold together and end in ourselves with a short compass. The actions governed without this reflection, I mean a near and essential reflection, as those of the covetous, of the ambitious, and so many others, that run

[3] The Gregorian calendar, named after Pope Gregory XIII, was adopted in France in 1582.

directly point-blank, the course of which carrieth them away before them, are erroneous and crazed actions.

Most of our vacations* are like plays. "All the world does practice stage-playing" (Petronius in Justus Lipsios, *De constantia,* I.viii.). We must play our parts duly, but as the part of a borrowed personage. Of a vizard* and appearance, we should not make a real essence, nor proper* of that which is another. We cannot distinguish the skin from the shirt. [C]It is sufficient to disguise the face, without deforming the breast. [B]I see some tranform and transubstantiate themselves into as many new forms and strange beings as they undertake charges, and who emprelate themselves even to the heart and entrails, and entrain their offices even sitting on their close-stool.* I cannot teach them to distinguish the salutations and cappings of such as regard them from those that respect either their office, their train, or their mule. "They give themselves so much over to fortune, as they forget nature" (Quint-Curt. III.ii.18.). They swell in mind and puff up their natural discourse, according to the dignity of their office.

The mayor of Bordeaux and Michael, Lord of Montaigne, have ever been two, by an evident separation. To be an advocate or a treasurer, one should not be ignorant of the craft incident to such callings. An honest man is not countable for the vice and folly of his trade and therefore ought not to refuse the exercise of it. It is the custom of his country, and therefore is profit in it. We must live by the world, and such as we find it, so make use of it. But the judgment of an emperor should be above his empire, and to see and consider the same as a strange accident. He should know how to enjoy himself apart, and communicate himself as James and Peter, at least to himself.

I cannot so absolutely or so deeply engage myself. When my will gives me to any party, it is not with so violent a bond that my understanding is thereby infected. In the present intestine trouble of our state, my interest hath not made me forget neither the commendable qualities of our adversaries nor the reproachful of those I have followed. [C]They partially extol whatever is on their side. I do not so much as excuse the greater number of my friends' actions. A good orator loseth not his grace by pleading against me.

[B]The intricateness of our debate removed, I have maintained myself in equanimity and pure indifferency. [C]"Nor bear I capital hatred when I am out of the necessity of war." [B]Wherein I glory, for that commonly I see men err in the contrary. Such as extend their choler and hatred beyond their affairs, as most men do, show that it proceeds elsewhence, and from some private cause, even as one being cured of an ulcer and his fever remaineth still, declareth it had another more hidden beginning. [C]It is the reason they bear none unto the cause in general, and forsomuch as it concerneth the interest of all and of the state. But they are vexed at it only for this, that it toucheth them in private. And therefore are they distempered with a particular passion, both beyond justice and public reason. "All did not so much find fault with all, as every one with those that appertained to every one" (Livy XXXIV.xxxvi.).

[B]I will have the advantage to be for us, which, though it be not, I enrage not. [C]I stand firmly to the sounder parts. But I affect not to be noted a private enemy to others and beyond general reason. I greatly accuse this vicious form of obstinate contesting: He is of the League, because he admireth the grace of the Duke of Guise; or he is a Huguenot forsomuch as the King of Navarre's activity amazeth him; he finds fault in the king's behaviors; therefore, he is seditious in his heart. I would not give the magistrate[4] my voice that he had reason to condemn a book, because a heretic was therein named and extolled to be one of the best poets of this age. Dare we not say that a thief hath a good leg, if he have so indeed? If she be a strumpet, must she needs have a stinking breath?

In wiser ages, revoked they the proud title of Capitolinus they had formerly given to Marcus Manlius, as the preserver of religion and public liberty? Suppressed they the memory of his liberality, his deeds of arms, and military rewards granted to his virtues, because, to the prejudice of his country's laws, he afterward affected a royalty?

If they once conceive a hatred against an orator or an advocate, the next day he becometh barbarous and uneloquent. I have elsewhere discoursed of zeal, which hath driven good men into like errors. For myself I can say: that he doth wickedly and this virtuously. Likewise, in prognostics or sinister events of affairs, they will have every man blind or dull in his own cause, and that our persuasion and judgment serve not the truth, but the project of our desires. I should rather err in the other extremity, so much I fear my desire might corrupt me. Considering I somewhat tenderly distrust myself in things I most desire.

I have, in my days, seen wonders in the indiscreet and prodigious facility of people, suffering their hopes and beliefs to be led and governed as it hath pleased and best fitted their leaders, above a hundred discontents, one in the neck of another, and beyond their fantasies and dreams. I wonder no more at those whom the apish toys of Apollonius and Mohammed have seduced and blinded. Their sense and understanding is wholly smothered in their passion. Their

4 Montaigne is referring to the Vatican censor who examined the *Essays* when Montaigne was in Rome in 1581. One of the objections made against his book was that he had mentioned the heretic poet, Théodore de Bèze. See Introduction.

discretion hath no other choice but what pleaseth them and furthereth their cause, which I had especially observed in the beginning of our distempered factions and factious troubles.[5] This other[6] which is grown since, by imitation surmounteth the same.

Whereby I observe that it is an inseparable quality of popular errors, the first being gone, opinions intershock* one another, following the wind, as waves do. They are no members of the body, if they may renounce it, if they follow not the common course. But truly they wrong the just parts, when they seek to help them with fraud or deceits. I have always contracted* the same. This mean is but for sick brains. The healthy have surer and honester ways to maintain their resolutions and excuse all contrary accidents.

[B]The heavens never saw so weighty a discord and so harmful a hatred, as that between Caesar and Pompey, nor ever shall hereafter. Meseemeth, notwithstanding, I see in those noble and heroical minds an exemplar and great moderation of the one toward the other. It was a jealousy of honor and emulation of command which transported them, not to a furious and indiscreet hatred, without malice or detraction. In their sharpest exploits, I discover some relics of respect and cinders of well-meaning affection. And I imagine that, had it been possible, either of them desired rather to effect his purpose without overthrowing his competitor than by working his utter ruin. Note how contrary the proceeding was between Sulla and Marius.

We must not run headlong after our affections and private interests. As in my youth I ever opposed myself to the motions of love, which I felt to usurp upon me, and labored to diminish its delights, lest in the end it might vanquish and captivate me to his mercy, so do I now in all other occasions which my will apprehendeth with an over-great appetite. I bend to the contrary of my disposition, as I see the same plunged and drunk with its own wine. I shun so far forth to nourish her pleasure, as I may not revoke it without a bloody loss.

Those minds which, through stupidity, see things but by halves, enjoy this happiness, that such as be hurtful offend them least. It is a spiritual leprosy that hath some show of health, and such a health as philosophy doth not altogether contemn. But yet it may not lawfully be termed wisdom, as we often do. And after this manner did, in former times, somebody mock Diogenes who, in the dead of winter, went all naked, embracing an image of snow to try his patience; who, meeting him in this order, said thus unto him: Art thou now very cold? Nothing at all, answered Diogenes. What thinkest thou to do then

[5] Florio mistranslates Montaigne's phrase, which refers to the Protestants and should read "the first of our feverish factions."

[6] The League (the Catholic party).

that is either hard or exemplar by standing in the cold? replied the other. To measure constancy, we must necessarily know sufference.

But such minds as must behold cross events and fortune's injuries in their height and sharpness, which must weigh and taste them according to their natural bitterness and charge, let them employ their skill and keep themselves from embracing the causes, and divert their approaches. What did King Cotys? He paid liberally for that goodly and rich vessel which one had presented unto him, but forsomuch as it was exceeding brittle, he presently brake it himself that so betimes he might remove so easy an occasion of choler against his servants. [C]I have in like sort shunned confusion in my affairs and sought not to have my goods contiguous to my neighbors and to such as I am to be linked in strict friendship, whence commonly ensue causes of alienation and unkindness.

[B]I have heretofore loved the hazardous play of cards and dice. I have long since left it only for this, that, notwithstanding any fair semblance I made in my losses, I was inwardly disquieted. Let a man of honor, who is to take a lie or endure an outrageous wrong, [C]and cannot admit a bad excuse for payment or satisfaction, [B]avoid the progress of contentious altercations.

I shun melancholic complexions and froward men as infected. And in matters I cannot talk of without interest and emotion, I meddle not with them, except duty constrain me thereunto. [C]"They shall better not begin than leave off" (Sen. *Ep.* LXXII.). [B]The surest way is, then, to prepare ourselves before occasion.

I know that some wise men have taken another course, and have not feared to engage and vehemently to insinuate themselves into divers objects. Those assure themselves of their own strength, under which they shroud themselves against all manner of contrary events, making mischiefs to wrestle one against another, by vigor and virtue of patience:

> Much like a rock which butts into the main,
> Meeting with wind's rage, to the sea laid plain,
> It does the force of skies and seas sustain,
> Endure their threats, yet does unmov'd remain.
>
> Virg. *Aen.* X.693.

Let us not imitate these examples. We shall not attain them. They opinionate themselves resolutely to behold and, without perturbation, to be spectators of their country's ruin, which whilom possessed and commanded their full will. As for our vulgar minds, therein is too much effort and roughness. Cato quit thereby the noblest life that ever was. We silly* ones must seek to escape the storm further off.

We ought to provide for apprehension, and not for patience, and avoid the blows we cannot withstand.

[C]Zeno, seeing Chremonides, a young man whom he loved, approach to sit near him, rose up suddenly; Cleanthes asking him the reason, "I understand," saith he, "that physicians above all things prescribe rest and forbid emotion in all tumors."

[B]Socrates saith not, "Yield not to the allurements of beauty; maintain it; enforce ourselves to the contrary." "Shun her," saith he, "run out of her sight and company, as from a violent poison that infecteth and stingeth far off." [C]And his good disciple,[7] feigning or reciting (but in mine opinion rather reciting than feigning) the matchless perfections of that great Cyrus, describeth him distrusting his forces to withstand the blandishments or allurings of the divine beauty of that famous Panthea, his captive, commiting the visitation and guard of her to another that had less liberty than himself.

[B]And likewise the Holy Ghost saith, "and lead us not into temptation" (Matthew VI.13.). We pray not that our reason be not encountered and vanquished by concupiscence, but that it be not so much as essayed therewith, that we be not reduced to an estate where we should but suffer the approaches, solicitations, and temptations of sin. And we entreat our Lord to keep our conscience quiet, fully, perfectly free from all commerce of evil.

[C]Such as say they have reason for their revenging passion, or any other mind-troubling perturbation, say often truth as things are, but not as they were. They speak to us when the causes of their error are by themselves fostered and advanced. But retire further backward; recall their causes to their beginning: there you surprise and put them to a *non-plus.* Would they have their fault be less, because it is more ancient, and that of an unjust beginning the progress be just?

[B]He that, as I do, shall wish his country's welfare, without fretting or pining himself, shall be grieved but not swoon to see it threatening either his own downfall or a continuance no less ruinous. Oh silly,* weak bark, whom both waves, winds, and pilot hull* and toss to so contrary designs.

Master, the wave and wind
So divers ways do bind.
Buchanan, *Franciscanus* 13.

Who gapes not after the favor of princes, as after a thing without which he cannot live, nor is much disquieted at the coldness of their entertainment or frowning countenance, nor regardeth the inconstancy of their will; who hatcheth not his children or huggeth not honors with

[7] Xenophon.

a slavish propension, nor leaves to live commodiously, having once lost them; who doth good, namely for his own satisfaction, nor is much vexed to see men censure of his actions against his merit — a quarter of an ounce of patience provideth for such inconveniences. I find ease in this receipt, redeeming myself in the beginning as good cheap as I can. By which means, I perceive myself to have escaped much trouble and manifold difficulties. With very little force, I stay these first motions of my perturbations, and I abandon the subject which begins to molest me, and before it transport me. [C]He that stops not the loose* shall hardly stay the course. He that cannot shut the door against them shall never expel them being entered. He that cannot attain an end in the beginning shall not come to an end of the conclusion; nor shall he endure the fall that could not endure the starts of it. "For they drive themselves headlong, when once they are parted and past reason, and weakness soothes itself and unawares is carried into the deep, nor can it find a place to tarry in "(Cic. *Tusc.* IV.xviii.). [B]I feel betimes the low winds, which are forerunners of the storm, buzz in mine ears and sound and try me within.

> As first blasts in the woods perceived to go,
> Whistle, and darkly speak in murmurs low,
> Foretelling mariners what winds will grow.
> Virg. *Aen.* X.97.

How often have I done myself an apparent injustice to avoid the danger I should fall into by receiving the same, haply worse, from the judges, after a world of troubles and of foul and vile practices, more enemies to my natural disposition than fire or torment? [C]"As much as we may, and it may be more than we may, we should abhor brabling* and lawing; for it is not only an ingenious part, but sometimes profitable also at some times to yield a little of our right." (Cic. *De off.*, II.xviii). If we were wise indeed, we should rejoice and glory, as I heard once a young gentleman, born of a very great house, very wittily and unfeignedly rejoice with all men that his mother had lost her suit, as if it had been a cough, an ague, or any other irksome burden. The favors which fortune might have given me, as alliances and acquaintances with such as have sovereign authority in those things, I have, in my conscience, done much instantly* to avoid employing them to other prejudice and not over-value my rights above their worth.

To conclude, [B]I have so much prevailed by my endeavors (in a good hour I may speak it) that I am yet a virgin for any suits in law, which have, notwithstanding, not omitted gently to offer me their service, and, under pretense of lawful titles, insinuate themselves into my allowance, would I but have given ear unto them. And as a pure maiden from quarrels, I have, without important offense, either passive or active, lingered out a long life, and never heard worse than mine own name: a rare grace of heaven.

Our greatest agitations have strange springs and ridiculous causes. What ruin did our last duke of Burgundy run into for the quarrel of a cart-load of sheepskins? And was not the graving of a seal the chief cause of the most horrible breach and topsy-turvy that ever this world's frame endured?[8] For Pompey and Caesar are but the new buddings and continuation of two others. And I have seen in my time the wisest heads of this realm assembled with great ceremony and public charge about treaties and agreements, the true deciding whereof depended, in the meanwhile, absolutely and sovereignly of the will and consultations held in some ladies' pate or cabinet, and of the inclination of some silly woman. [C]Poets have most judiciously looked into this, who but for an apple have set all Greece and Asia on fire and sword. [B]See why that man doth hazard both his honor and life on the fortune of his rapier and dagger; let him tell you whence the cause of that contention ariseth: he cannot without blushing, so vain and so frivolous is the occasion.

To embark him, there needs but little advisement; but being once in, all parts do work. Then are greater provisions required, more difficult and important. [C]How far more easy is it not to enter than to get forth! [B]We must proceed contrary to the briar, which produceth a long and straight stalk at the first springing; but after, as tired and out of breath, it makes many and thick knots, as if they were pauses, showing to have no more that vigor and constancy. We should rather begin gently and leisurely, and keep our strength and breath for the perfection of the work. We direct affairs in the beginning, and hold them at our mercy, but being once undertaken, they guide and transport us, and we must follow them.

[C]Yet may it not be said that this counsel hath freed me from all difficulties, and that I have not been often troubled to control and bridle my passions, which are not always governed according to the measure of occasions, whose entrances are often sharp and violent. So is it that thence may be reaped good fruit and profit, except for those who, in well doing, are not satisfied with any benefit, if their reputation be in question. For in truth, such an effect is not counted of but by everyone to himself. You are thereby better satisfied, but not more esteemed, having reformed yourself before you come into action or the matter was in sight. Yet not in this only, but in all other duties

[8] Sulla had a seal engraved to celebrate his victory over Jugurtha in 107 B.C. and this caused a bitter rivalry between him and Marius.

of life, their course, which aim at honor, is divers from that which they propound unto themselves that follow order and reason.

[B]I find some that inconsiderately and furiously thrust themselves into the lists, and grow slack in the course. As Plutarch saith, that such as by the vice of bashfulness are soft and tractable to grant whatsoever is demanded, are afterward as prone and facile to recant and break their word. In like manner, he that enters lightly into a quarrel is subject to leave it as lightly. The same difficulty which keeps me from embracing the same should incite me, being once moved and therein engaged, to continue resolute. It is an ill custom. Being once embarked, one must either go on or sink. [C]Attempt coldly, said Bias, but pursue hotly. [B]For want of judgment, our hearts fail us, which is also less tolerable.

Most agreements of our modern quarrels are shameful and false. We only seek to save appearances, and therewhilst betray and disavow our true intentions. We salve* the deed. We know how we spake it, and in what sense the bystanders know it, yea, and our friends, to whom we would have our advantages known. It is to the prejudice of our liberty and interest of our resolution's honor that we disavow our thoughts, and seek for starting-holes in falsehood to make our agreements. We belie ourselves to salve* a lie we have given to another.

We must not look whether your action or word may admit another interpretation; but it is your own true and sincere construction that you must now maintain, whatsoever it cost you. It is to your virtue and to your conscience that men speak, parts that ought not to be disguised. Leave we these base courses, wrangling shifts, and verbal means to pettifogging lawyers.

The excuses and reparations or satisfactions, which daily I see made, promised, and given to purge indiscretion, seem to me more foul than indiscretion itself. Better were it for one to offend his adversary again than, in giving him such satisfaction, to wrong himself so much. You have braved him, moved by choler, and now you seek to pacify and flatter him in your cold and better sense. Thus you abase yourself more than you were before exalted. I find no speech so vicious in a gentleman, as I deem any recantation he shall make dishonorable, especially if it be wrested from him by authority, forsomuch as obstinacy is in him more excusable than cowardice.

Passions are to me as easy to be avoided as they are difficult to be moderated. [C]They are more easily rooted out of the mind than brought to good temper. [B]He that cannot attain to this noble Stoical impassibility, let him shroud himself in the bosom of this my popular stupidity. What they did by virtue, I inure myself to do by nature. The middle region harboreth storms. The two extremes contain philosophers and rural men: they concur in tranquillity and good hap.*

> Happy is that could of things the causes find,
> And subject to his feet all fearfulness of mind,
> Inexorable fate, and noise of greedy hell.
> And happy he with country gods acquainted well,
> Pan and old Sylvan knows,
> And all the sister shrows.*
>
> Virg. *Georg.* II.490.

The beginnings of all things are weak and tender. We must, therefore, be clear-sighted in beginnings. For, as in their budding we discern not the danger, so in their full growth we perceive not the remedy. I should have encountered a thousand crosses daily, more hard to be digested, in the course of ambition, than it hath been uneasy for me to stay the natural inclination that led me unto them.

> I have been much afraid for causes right,
> To raise my foretop far abroad to sight.
>
> Hor. *Odes* III.xvi.18.

All public actions are subject to uncertain and divers interpretations, for too many heads judge of them. Some say of this my city employment (whereof I am content to speak a word, not that it deserves it, but to make a show of my manners in such things) I have demeaned myself like one that is too slowly moved, and with a languishing affection. And they are not altogether void of reason. I strive to keep my mind and thoughts quiet. [C]"Both ever quiet by nature, and now because of years." (Q. Cicero, *De Petit. Cons.* II.). [B]And if at any time they are debauched* to some rude and piercing impression, it is in truth without my consent. From which natural slackness one must not therefore infer any proof of disability. For, want of care and lack of judgment are two things, and less unkindness and ingratitude toward those citizens who, to gratify me, employed the utmost of all the means they could possibly, both before they knew me and since, and who did much more for me in appointing me my charge the second time than in choosing me the first. I love them with all my heart and wish them all the good that may be. And truly, if occasion had been offered, I would have spared nothing to have done them service. I have stirred and labored for them as I do for myself. They are good people, warlike and generous, yet capable of obedience and discipline, and fit for good employment, if they be well guided.

They say likewise that I passed over this charge of mine without any deed of note or great show. It is true. Moreover, they accuse my cessation, whenas all the world was convicted of too much doing.

I have a most nimble motion where my will doth carry me. But this point is an enemy unto perseverance. Whosoever will make use of me, according to myself, let him employ me in affairs that require vigor and liberty, that have a short, a straight, and therewithal a hazardous course. I may peradventure somewhat prevail therein. Whereas if it be tedious, crafty, laborious, artificial, and intricate, they shall do better to address themselves to some other man.

All charges of importance are not difficult. I was prepared to labor somewhat more earnestly, if there had been great need. For it lies in my power to do something more than I make show of and than I love to do. To my knowledge, I have not omitted any motion that duty required earnestly at my hands. I have easily forgotten those which ambition blendeth with duty and cloaketh with her title. It is they which most commonly fill the eyes and ears and satisfy men. Not the thing itself, but the appearance payeth them. If they hear no noise, they imagine we sleep.

My humors are contrary to turbulent humors. I could pacify an inconvenience or trouble without troubling myself, and chastise a disorder without alteration. Have I need of choler and inflammation, I borrow it, and therewith mask myself. My manners are musty, rather wallowish* than sharp. I accuse not a magistrate that sleepeth, so they that are under it sleep also, so sleep the laws. For my part, I commend a gliding, an obscure, and reposed life, [C]"neither too abject and submiss,* nor vaunting itself too much" (Cic. *De Off.* I.xxxiv.). [B]But my fortune will have it so. I am descended of a family that hath lived without noise and tumult, and of long continuance particularly ambitious of integrity.

Our men are so framed to agitation and ostentations, that goodness, moderation, equity, constancy, and such quiet and mean qualities are no more heard of. Rough bodies are felt; smooth ones are handled imperceptibly. Sickness is felt; health little or not at all; nor things that anoint us, in regard of such as sting us. It is an action for one's reputation and private commodity, and not for the common good, to refer that to be done in the market place which a man may do in the council-chamber, and at noonday what might have been effected the night before, and to be jealous to do that himself which his fellow can perform as well. So did some surgeons of Greece show the operations of their skill upon scaffolds, in view of all passengers, thereby to get more practice and custom. They suppose that good orders cannot be understood but by the sound of a trumpet.

Ambition is no vice for petty companions and for such endeavors as ours. One said to Alexander, "Your father will leave you a great command, easy and peaceful." The boy was envious of his father's victories and of the justice of his government. He would not have enjoyed the world's empire securely and quietly. [C]Alcibiades in Plato loveth rather to die young, fair, rich, noble, learned, and all that in excellence, than to stay in the state of such a condition.

[B]This infirmity is happily excusable in so strong and full a mind. When these petty, wretched souls are therewith inveigled, and think to publish their fame, because they have judged a cause rightly, or continued the order in guarding of a city's gates, by how much more they hoped to raise their head, so much more do they show their simplicity. This petty well-doing has neither body nor life. It vanisheth in the first month and walks but from one corner of a street to another. Entertain therewith your son and your servant, and spare not, as that ancient fellow who, having no other auditor of his praises and applauding of his sufficiency, boasted with his chambermaid, exclaiming, "Oh Perrette, what a gallant and sufficient man thou hast to thy master!" If the worst happen, entertain yourselves in yourselves, as a counselor of my acquaintance, having degorged a rabble of paragraphs with an extreme contention and like foolishness, going out of the council-chamber to a pissing place near unto it, was heard very conscientiously to utter these words to himself: "Not unto us, O Lord, not unto us, but unto thy name give the glory" (Psalms CXIII.1.). He that cannot otherwise, let him pay himself out of his own purse.

Fame doth not so basely prostitute itself, nor so cheap. Rare and exemplar actions, to which it duly belongeth, could not brook the company of this innumerable multitude of vulgar, petty actions. Well may a piece of marble raise your titles as high as you list, because you have repaired a piece of an old wall or cleansed a common ditch, but men of judgment will never do it. Report followeth not all goodness, except difficulty and rarity be joined thereunto. Yea, simple estimation, according to the Stoics, is not due to every action proceeding from virtue. Neither would they have him commended who, through temperance, abstaineth from an old blear-eyed woman. [C]Such as have known the admirable qualities of Scipio the African renounce the glory which Panaetius ascribeth unto him, to have abstained from gifts, as a glory not his alone, but peculiar to that age.

[B]We have pleasures sortable to our fortune. Let us not usurp those of greatness. Our own are more natural. They are the more solid and firm by how much the meaner. Since it is not for conscience, at least for ambition let us refuse ambition. Let us disdain this insatiate thirst of honor and renown, base and beggarly, which makes us so suppliantly to crave it of all sorts of people, [C]"What praise is this, which may be fetched out of the shambles?" (Cic. *De fin.* II.xv.), [B]by abject means and at what vile rate soever. To be thus honored is merely a dishonor. Learn we to be no more greedy of glory than we are capable of it. To be proud of every profitable and innocent action is fit for men to whom it is extraordinary and rare. They will value it for the price it cost them. According as a good effect is more resounding, I abate of its goodness. The jealousy I conceive, it is produced more because it is so resounding than because it is good. What is set out to show is half sold. Those actions have no more grace which, carelessly and under silence, pass from the hands of a workman, and which some honest man afterward chooseth, and redeemeth them from darkness to thrust them into the world's light only for their worth. [C]"All things in sooth seem to me more commendable that are performed with no ostentation and without the people to witness" (Cic. *Tusc.* II.xxvi.), said the most glorious man of the world.

[B]I had no care but to preserve and continue, which are deaf and insensible effects. Innovation is of great luster, but interdicted in times when we are most urged and have to defend ourselves but from novelties. [C]Abstinence from doing is often as generous as doing, but it is not so apparent. My small worth is in a manner all of this kind.

[B]To be short, the occasions in this my charge have seconded my complexion, for which I con* them hearty thanks. Is there any man that desireth to be sick, to see his physician set at work? And should not that physician be well whipped who, to put his art in practice, would wish the plague to infect us? I was never possessed with this impious and vulgar passion, to wish that the troubled and distempered state of this city might raise and honor my government. I have most willingly lent them my hand to further, and shoulders to aid, their ease and tranquillity. He that will not thank me for the good order and for the sweet and undisturbed rest which hath accompanied my charge cannot, at least, deprive me of that part which, by the title of my good fortune, belongeth unto me. This is my humor, that I love as much to be happy as wise, and attribute my successes as much to the mere grace of God as to the mean or furtherance of my operation.

I had sufficiently published to the world my insufficiency in managing of such public affairs. Nay, there is something in me worse than insufficiency, which is that I am not much displeased therewith and that I endeavor not greatly to cure it, considering the course of life I have determined to myself. Nor have I satisfied myself in this employment, but have almost attained what I had promised unto myself. Yet have I much exceeded what I had promised those with whom I was to negotiate. For I willingly promise somewhat less than I can perform or hope to accomplish. Of this I am assured: I have never left offense or hatred among them. To have left either regret or desire of me, this know I certainly, I have not much affected it.

> Should I this monster trust? Should I not know
> The calm sea's counterfeit dissembling show,
> How quietly sometimes the floods will go?
>
> Virg. *Aen.* V.849.

Of Physiognomy

❧ III. 12 ✧ 1585–88 ☙

[B]Almost all the opinions we have are taken by authority and upon credit. There is no hurt: we cannot choose worse than by ourselves in so weak an age. This image of Socrates his discourse which his friends have left us, we only approve it by the reverence of public approbation. It is not of our own knowledge; they are not according to our use. Might such a man be born nowadays, there are but few would now esteem him. We discern not graces inly or aright; we only perceive them by a false light set out and puffed up with art. Such as pass under their natural purity and simplicity do easily escape so weak and dim a sight as ours is. They have a secret, unperceived, and delicate beauty: [w]e ha[ve] need of a clear, far-seeing, and true-discerning sight that should rightly discover this secret light. Is not ingenuity (according to us) cousin-german* unto sottishness, and a quality of reproach? Socrates maketh his soul to move with a natural and common motion. Thus saith a plain countryman, and thus a silly* woman; [C]he never hath other people in his mouth than coachmakers, joiners, cobblers, and masons. [B]They are inductions and similitudes drawn from the most vulgar and known actions of men; everyone understands him. Under so base a form, we should never have chosen the noble worthiness and brightness of his admirable conceptions — we that esteem all those but mean and vile that learning doth not raise and who have no perceiving of riches, except set out in show and pomp. Our world is framed but unto ostentation. Men are puffed up with wind and moved or handled by bounds, as balloons. This man proposeth no vain fantasies unto himself. His end was to store us with things and furnish us with precepts, which really more substantially and jointly serve our life:

To keep a mean, to hold the end,
And nature's conduct to attend.
Lucan II.381.

So was he ever all one a like, and raised himself to the highest pitch of vigor not by fits, but by complexion. Or to say better, he raised nothing, but rather brought down and reduced all difficulties or sharpness to their original and natural state, and thereunto subdued vigor. For in Cato it is manifestly seen to be an outright proceeding, far above and beyond the common: by the brave exploits of his life, and in his death, he is ever perceived to be mounted upon his great horses. Whereas this man keeps on the ground, and with a gentle and ordinary pace treateth of the most profitable discourses, and addresseth himself both unto death and to the most thorny and crabbed crosses that may happen unto the course of human life.

It hath indeed fortuned that the worthiest man to be known, and for a pattern to be presented to the world, he is the man of whom we have most certain knowledge. He hath been declared and enlightened by the most clear-seeing men that ever were; the testimonies we have of him are in faithfulness and sufficiency most admirable.

It is a great matter that ever he was able to give such order unto the pure imaginations of a child, that without altering or wresting them, he hath thence produced the fairest effects of our mind. He neither represents it rich nor high-raised, but sound and pure, and ever with a blithe and undefiled health. By these vulgar springs and natural wards,* by these ordinary and common fantasies, sans* moving or without urging himself, he erected not only the most regular, but the highest and most vigorous opinions, actions, and customs that ever were. [C]He it is, that brought human wisdom from heaven again, where for a long time it had been lost, to restore it unto man, where her most just and laborious work is. [B]See or hear him plead before his judges; mark with what reasons he rouseth his courage to the hazards of war, what arguments fortify his patience against detraction, calumniation, tyranny, death, and against his wife's peevish head: therein is nothing borrowed from art or from learning. The simplest may there know their means and might; it is impossible to go further back or lower. He hath done human nature a great kindness to show what and how much she can do of herself.

We are every one richer than we imagine, but we are taught to borrow and instructed to shift, and rather to make use of others' goods and means than of our own. There is nothing whereon man can stay or fix himself in time of his need. Of voluptuousness, of riches, of pleasure, of power, he ever embraceth more than he can grasp or hold. His greediness is incapable of moderation. The very same I find to be in the curiosity of learning and knowledge: he cuts out more work than he can well make an end of, and much more than he need, [C]extending the profit of learning as far as his matter. "We are sick of a surfeit, as of all things, so of learning also" (Sen. *Epist.* CVI.). And Tacitus hath reason to commend Agricola's mother to have bridled in her son an overburning and earnest desire of learning. It is a good, being nearly* looked unto, that containeth, as other human goods, much peculiar vanity and natural weakness, and is very chargeable.

The acquisition and purchase whereof is much more hazardous than of all other viands and beverage. For, whatsoever else we have bought, we carry home in some vessel or other, where we have law[1] to examine its worth, how much, and at what time we are to take it. But sciences, we cannot suddenly put them into any other vessel than our mind; we swallow them in buying them and go from the market either already infected or amended. There are some, which instead of nourishing, do but hinder and surcharge us, and other some which, under color of curing, empoison us.

BI have taken pleasure in some place to see men who, for devotion's sake, have made a vow of ignorance, as of chastity, poverty, and penitence. It is also a kind of gelding of our inordinate appetites to muzzle this greediness which provoketh us to the study of books and depriveth the mind of that voluptuous delight which, by the opinion of learning, doth so tickle us. CAnd it is richly to accomplish the vow of poverty to join that of the mind unto it. BWe need not much learning for to live at ease. And Socrates teacheth us that we have both it and the way to find and make use of it within us. All our sufficiency that is beyond the natural is well-nigh vain and superfluous. It is much if it charge and trouble us no more than it steads* us. C"We have need of little learning to have a good mind" (Sen. *Epist.* CVI.). BThey are febricitant* excesses of our spirit, a turbulent and unquiet instrument. Rouse up yourself and you shall find forcible arguments against death to be in yourself, most true and very proper to serve and stead you in time of necessity. 'Tis they which induce a peasant swain, yea, and whole nations to die as constantly as any philosopher. Should I have died less merrily before I read the *Tusculanes*?[2] I think not. And when I find myself in my best wits, I perceive that I have somewhat enriched my tongue, my courage but little. It is even as nature framed the same at first. And against any conflict it shields itself but with a natural and common march. Books have not so much served me for instruction as exercitation. What if Blearning, assaying to arm us with new wards* and fences against natural inconveniences, hath more imprinted their greatness and weight in our fantasy than her reasons, quiddities, and subtleties therewith to cover us? CThey are subtleties indeed, by which she often awaketh us very vainly. Observe how many slight and idle arguments the wisest and closest authors frame and scatter about one good sound, which, if you consider

1 I.e., an opportunity, occasion.
2 Cicero's *Tusculan Disputations.*

nearly,* are but vain and incorporal. They are but verbal wiles, which beguile us. But forsomuch as it may be profitable, I will not otherwise blanch* them. Many of that condition are scattered here and there in divers places of this volume, either borrowed or imitated. Yet should a man somewhat heed [to] call not that force which is but quaintness, or term that which is but quipping sharp, solid, or name that good which is but fair: "which more delight us being but tasted, than swilled and swallowed down" (Cic. *Tusc.* V.5.). All that which pleaseth feedeth not; "where it is no matter of wit, but of courage" (Sen. *Epist.* LXXV.).

BTo see the struggling endeavors which Seneca giveth himself to prepare himself against death; to see him sweat with panting; to see him bathe* so long upon this perch, thereby to strengthen and assure himself, I should have made question of his reputation, had he not most undauntedly maintained the same in his death. His so violent and frequent agitation Cshoweth that himself was fervent and impetuous. "A great courage speaks softly but securely" (Sen. *Epist.* CXV.). "Wit hath not one color and courage another" (Sen. *Epist.* XCV.). He must be convicted at his own charges. And Bshoweth in some sort that he was pressed by his adversary. Plutarch's manner, by how much more disdainful and far-extending it is, in my opinion so much more manlike and persuasive is it; I should easily believe that his soul had her motions more assured and more regular. The one more sharp, pricketh and suddenly starts us, toucheth the spirit more. The other, more solid, doth constantly inform, establish, and comfort us, toucheth more the understanding. CThat ravisheth our judgment: this doth gain it.

I have likewise seen other compositions and more reverenced which, in portraying the combat they endure against the provocations of the flesh, represent them so violent, so powerful and invincible that ourselves, who are cast in the common mold of other men, have as much to admire the unknown strangeness and unfelt vigor of their temptation as their constant resistance. BTo what purpose do we so arm and steel ourselves with these laboring efforts of learning? Let us diligently survey the surface of the earth, and there consider so many silly* poor people as we see toiling, sweltering, and drooping about their business, which never heard of Aristotle, nor of Plato, nor ever knew what examples or precepts are. From those doth nature daily draw and afford us effects of constancy and patterns of patience, more pure and forcible than are those we so curiously study for in schools. How many do I ordinarily see that misacknowledge poverty; how many that wish for death, or that pass it without any alarm or affliction? A fellow that dungeth my garden hath haply this morning buried his father or his child. The very names whereby they call diseases do somewhat milden and diminish the sharpness of them. With them a phthisic or consumption of the lungs is but an ordinary cough; a dysentery or bloody flux, but a distemper of the stomach; a pleurisy, but a cold or murr*; and as they gently name them, so they easily endure them. Grievous are they indeed when they hinder their ordinary labor or break their usual rest. They will not take their beds but when they shall die. ᶜ"That plain and clear virtue is turned into obscure and cunning knowledge" (Sen. *Epist.* XCV.).

ᴮI was writing this about a time that a boisterous storm of our tumultuous broils and bloody troubles did for many months' space, with all its might and horror, hang full over my head. On the one side, I had the enemies at my gates; on the other, the *picoreurs* or freebooters, far worse foes. ᶜ"We contend not with armor, but with vices." ᴮAnd at one time felt and endured all manner of harm-bringing military injuries:

> A fearful foe on left hand and on right,
> Doth with his neighbor harms both sides afright.
> Ovid. *Pont.* I.iii.57.

Oh monstrous war! Others work without; this inwardly and against herself; and with her own venom gnaweth and consumes herself. It is of so ruinous and malign a nature that together with all things else, she ruineth herself, and with spiteful rage doth rent, deface, and massacre itself. We do more often see it, by and through herself to waste, to desolate and dissolve herself than by or through want of any necessary thing or by enemies' force. All manner of discipline doth shun and fly it. She cometh to cure sedition, and herself is throughly therewith infected. She goeth about to chastise disobedience, and showeth the example of it; and being employed for the defense of laws, entereth into actual rebellion against her own ordinances. Aye me, where are we? Our physic bringeth infection.

> Our evil is empoison'd more
> By plaster they would lay to th' sore.
> Anon.

> It rises higher, quicker,
> And grows by curing sicker.
> Virg. *Aen.* XII.46.

> Lawful unlawful deeds with fury blended,
> Have turn'd from us the god's just mind offended.
> Catul. *Epithal.* 406.

In these popular diseases, one may in the beginning distinguish the sound from the sick; but if they chance to continue any time, as ours hath done and doth still, all the body, yea head and heels feel themselves the worse; no part is exempted from corruption. For, there is no air a man draws so greedily, or sucks so gluttonously, and that more spreads itself, or penetrates more deeply, than doth licentiousness. Our armies have no other bond to tie them, or other cement to fasten them, than what cometh from strangers. It is now a hard matter to frame a body of a complete, constant, well-ordered, and coherent army of Frenchmen. Oh what shame is it! We have no other discipline than what borrowed or auxiliar soldiers show us. As for us, we are led on by our own discretion and not by the commanders; each man followeth his own humor and hath more to do within than without. It is the commandment should follow, court, and yield unto; he only ought to obey: all the rest is free and loose. I am pleased to see what remissness and pusillanimity is in ambition and by what steps of abjection and servitude it must arrive unto its end. But I am displeased to see some debonaire* and well-meaning minds, yea such as are capable of justice, daily corrupted about the managing and commanding of this many-headed confusion. Long sufferance begets custom; custom, consent and imitation. We had too, too many infected and ill-born minds, without corrupting the good, the sound, and the generous. So that, if we continue any time, it will prove a difficult matter to find out a man unto whose skill and sufficiency the health or recovery of this state may be committed in trust, if fortune shall haply be pleased to restore it us again.

Forbid not yet this youth at least,
To aid this age more than oppress'd.
Virg. *Geor.* 1.500.

[C]What is become of that ancient precept that soldiers ought more to fear their general than their enemy? And of that wonderful exampleless example, that the Roman army having upon occasion enclosed within her trenches and round-beset an apple-orchard, so obedient was she to her captains that the next morning it rose and marched away without entering the same or touching one apple, although they were full-ripe and very delicious; so that when the owner came, he found the full number of his apples? I should be glad that our youths, instead of the time they employ about less profitable peregrinations and less honorable apprenticeships, would bestow one moiety* in seeing and observing the wars that happen on the sea under some good captain or excellent commander of Malta; the other moiety in learning and surveying the discipline of the Turkish armies. For it hath many differences and advantages over ours. This ensueth, that here our soldiers become more licentious in expeditions, there they prove more circumspect and fearfully wary. For, small offenses and petty larcenies, which in times of peace are in the common people punished with whipping and bastinadoes, in times of war are capital crimes. For an egg taken by a Turk without paying, he is by their law to have the full number of fifty stripes with a cudgel. For every other thing, how slight soever, not necessary for man's feeding, even for very trifles, they are either thrust through with a sharp stake, which they call impaling, or presently beheaded. I have been amazed, reading the story of Selim, the cruellest conqueror that ever was, to see, at what time he subdued the country of Egypt, the beauteous gardens round about Damascus, all open and in a conquered country; his main army lying encamped round about, those gardens were left untouched and unspoiled by the hands of his soldiers, only because they were commanded to spoil nothing and had not the watch-word of pillage.

[B]But, is there any malady in a commonwealth that deserveth to be combated by so mortal drug? No, said Favonius, not so much as the usurpation of the tyrannical possession of a commonwealth. [C]Plato likewise is not willing one should offer violence to the quiet repose of his country, no, not to reform or cure the same; and alloweth not that reformation which disturbeth or hazardeth the whole estate and which is purchased with the blood and ruin of the citizens, establishing the office of an honest man, in these causes, to leave all there, but only to pray God, to lend his extraordinary assisting hand unto it. And seemeth to be offended with Dion, his great friend, to have therein proceeded somewhat otherwise.

I was a Platonist on that side before ever I knew there had been a Plato in the world. And if such a man ought absolutely be banished our commerce and refused our society[3] (he who, for the sincerity of his conscience, deserved by mean of divine favor, athwart the public darkness and through the general ignorance of the world wherein he lived, so far to enter and so deeply to penetrate into Christian light) I do not think that it befitteth us to be instructed by a pagan. Oh, what impiety is it, to expect from God no succor simply his, and without our cooperation! I often doubt whether, amongst so many men that meddle with such a matter, any hath been found of so weak an understanding that hath earnestly been persuaded he proceeded toward reformation by the utmost of deformations; that he drew toward his salvation by the most express causes that we have of undoubted damnation; that [by] overthrowing policy, disgracing magistrates, abusing laws, under whose tuition God hath placed him, [by] filling brotherly minds and loving hearts with malice, hatred, and murther,

[3] I.e., the commerce and society of Christians.

[by] calling the devils and furies to his help, he may bring assistance to the most sacred mildness and justice of divine law. BAmbition, avarice, cruelty, and revenge have not sufficient [proper] and natural impetuosity; let us allure and stir them up by the glorious title of justice and devotion. There can no worse estate of things be imagined, than where wickedness cometh to be lawful, and with the magistrates' leave to take the cloak of virtue: C"There is nothing more deceitful to show than corrupt religion, when the power of Heaven is made a pretense and cloak for wickedness" (Livy XXXIX.16.). The extreme kind of injustice (according to Plato) is that that which is unjust should be held for just.

BThe common people suffered therein greatly then;[4] not only present losses,

> Such revel and tumultuous rout
> In all the country round about,
> Virg. *Bucol.* I.2.

but also succeeding damages. The living were fain to suffer, so did such as then were scarce born. They were robbed and pilled* (and by consequence so was I, even of hope), spoiling and depriving them of all they had to provide their living for many years to come.

> They wretchless* spoil and spill what draw or drive they may not,
> Guilty rogues to set fire on guiltless houses stay not.
> Ovid. *Trist.* III.x.65.

> In walls no trust, the field
> By spoil grows waste and wild.
> Claud. *In Eutrop.* I.244.

Besides these mischiefs, I endured some others. I incurred the inconveniences that moderation bringeth in such diseases. I was shaven on all hands: to the Ghibelline I was a Guelph, to Guelph a Ghibelline. Some one of my poets expresseth as much, but I wot not where it is. The situation of my house and the acquaintance of such as dwelt round about me presented me with one visage;[5] my life and actions with another.[6] No formal accusations were made of it; for there was nothing to take hold of. I never opposed myself against the laws; and who had called me in question, should have lost by the bargain. They were mute suspicious that ran under hand, which never want apparance* in so confused a hurly-burly, no more than lack of envious or foolish wits. CI commonly afford aid unto injurious presumption that

[4] At the time mentioned by Montaigne several pages earlier, when he had "enemies at my gates."
[5] Protestant. [6] Catholic.

fortune scattereth against me by a fashion I ever had to avoid justifying, excusing, or interpreting myself, deeming it to be a putting of my conscience to compromise to plead for her. "For the clearing of a cause is lessened by the arguing" (Cic. *De nat. deor.* III.4.). And, as if every man saw into me as clear as I do myself, in lieu of withdrawing, I advance myself to the accusation and rather endear* it by an erroneous and scoffing confession; except I flatly hold my peace, as of a thing unworthy any answer. But such as take it for an over-proud confidence do not much less disesteem and hate me for it, than such as take it for weakness of an indefensible cause, namely the great, with whom want of submission is the extreme fault, [and who are] rude to all justice that is known or felt, not demiss,* humble, or suppliant. I have often stumbled against that pillar. So it is that by the harms which befell me, ^Ban ambitious man would have hanged himself, and so would a covetous churl. I have no care at all to acquire or get.

> Let me have that I have, or less, so I may live
> Unto myself the rest, if any rest God give.
> Hor. *Epist.* I.xviii.107.

But losses that come unto me by others' injury, be it larceny or violence, pinch me in a manner as one sick and tortured with avarice. An offense causeth undoubtedly more grief and sharpness than a loss. A thousand several kinds of mischiefs fell upon me, one in the neck of another; I should more stoutly have endured them had they come all at once. I bethought myself, amongst my friends, to whom I might commit a needy, a defective and unfortunate old age. But after I had surveyed them all, and cast mine eyes everywhere, I found myself bare and far to seek. For one to souse* himself down headlong, and from so great a height, he should heedily forecast that it may be in the arms of a solid, steadfast, vigorous, and fortunate affection. They are rare, if there be any. In the end I perceived the best and safest way was to trust both myself and my necessity unto myself. And if it should happen to be but meanly and faintly in fortune's grace, I might more effectually recommend myself unto mine own favor, more closely fasten and more nearly look unto myself. ^CIn all things men rely upon strange props to spare their own, only certain and only powerful, knew they but how to arm themselves with them. Every man runneth out and unto what is to come, because no man is yet come into himself. ^BAnd I resolved that they were profitable inconveniences; forsomuch as when reason will not serve, we must first warn untoward scholars with the rod; ^Cas with fire and violence of wedges we bring a crooked piece of wood to be straight.

[B]It is long since I call to keep myself unto myself and live sequestered from alien and strange things; notwithstanding, I daily start out and cast mine eyes aside. Inclination, a great man's favorable word, a kind look, doth tempt me. God he knows whether there be penury of them nowadays, and what sense they bear. I likewise, without frowning, listen to the subornings framed to draw me to some town of merchandise or city of traffic; and so coldly defend myself, that it seems I should rather endure to be overcome than not. Now to a spirit so indocile, blows are required; and this vessel that of itself is so ready to warp, to unhoop, to escape and fall in pieces, must be closed, hooped, and strangely knocked with an adze. Secondly, that this accident served me as an exercitation* to prepare myself for worse, if worse might happen, if I, who both by the benefit of fortune and condition of my manners hoped to be of the last, should by this tempest be one of the first surprised; instructing myself betimes to force my life and frame it for a new state. True, perfect liberty is for one to be able to do and work all things upon himself. [C]"He is of most power that keeps himself in his own power" (Sen. *Epist.* XC.).

[B]In ordinary and peaceful times a man prepares himself for common and moderate accidents; but in this confusion, wherein we have been these thirty years, every Frenchman, be it in general or in particular, doth hourly see himself upon the point of his fortune's overthrow and downfall. By so much more ought each one have his courage stored and his mind fraughted with more strong and vigorous provisions. Let us thank Fortune, that hath not made us live in an effeminate, idle, and languishing age: some, whom other means could never bring unto it, shall make themselves famous by their misfortunes.

[C]As I read not much in histories these confusions of other states without regret that I could not better them present, so doth my curiosity make me somewhat please myself with mine eyes to see this notable spectacle of our public death, her symptoms and forms. And since I could not hinder the same, I am content to be appointed as an assistant unto it, and thereby instruct myself. Yet seek we evidently to know in shadows and understand by fabulous representations upon theatres, to show of the tragic revolutions of human fortune.

It is not without compassion of that we hear, but we please ourselves to rouse up our displeasure by the rareness of these pitiful events. Nothing tickles that pincheth not. And good historians avoid calm narrations as a dead water or mort-mere* to retrieve seditions and find out wars whereto they know we call them. I doubt whether I may lawfully avow at how base a rate of my life's rest and tranquillity[7] I have passed it more than half in the ruin of my country. In

[7] I.e., "at how little cost to my life's rest and tranquillity."

accidents that touch me not in my freehold I purchase patience very cheap; and to complain to myself, I respect not so much what is taken from me as what is left me both within and without. There is comfort in sometimes eschewing one and sometimes another of the evils that one in the neck of another surprise us and elsewhere strike us round about. As matters of public interests, according as my affection is more universally scattered, she is thereby more enfeebled. Since it is half true: "We feel so much of common harms as appertain to our private estate (Livy XXX.44.); and that the health whence we felt was such that herself solaceth the regret we should have for her. It was health, marry, but in comparison of the contagion which hath followed the same. We are not fallen very high. The corruption and the brigandage which now is in office and dignity seems to me the least tolerable. We are less injuriously robbed in the midst of a wood than a place of security. It was an universal coherency of members spoiled avie* one another; and most of them with old-rankled ulcers which neither admitted nor demanded recovery.

BTruly this shaking-fit did therefore more animate than deter me, only by the aid of my conscience, which not only quietly but fiercely carried itself; and I found no cause to complain of myself. Likewise, as God never sends men either evils or goods absolutely pure, my health held out well for that time, yea against her ordinary. And as without it I can do nothing, so with it there are few things I cannot do. She gave me means to summon and rouse up all my provisions and to bear my hand before my hurt, which happily would have gone further; and proved in my patience that yet I had some hold against fortune, and that to thrust me out of my saddle, there was required a stronger counterbuff. This I speak not to provoke her to give me a more vigorous charge. I am her servant, and yield myself unto her. For God's sake, let her be pleased! Demand you whether I feel her assaults? I do indeed. As those whom sorrow possesseth and overwhelmeth do notwithstanding at one time or other suffer themselves by intermissions to be touched by some pleasure and now and then smile, I have sufficient power over myself to make mine ordinary state quiet and free from all tedious and irksome imaginations; but yet I sometimes suffer myself by starts to be surprised with the pinchings of these unpleasant conceits which, whilst I arm myself to expel or wrestle against them, assail and beat me.

Lo here another huddle or tide of mischief that on the neck of the former came rushing upon me. Both within and round about my house, I was overtaken, in respect of all other, with a most contagious pestilence. For, as soundest bodies are subject to grievous diseases because they only can force them, so the air about me being very healthy, where in no man's memory infection (although very near) could ever take footing, coming now to be poisoned, brought forth strange effects.

> Of old and young thick funerals are shared;
> By cruel Proserpine no head is spared.
>
> Hor. *Odes* I.xxviii.19.

I was fain to endure this strange condition, that the sight of my house was irksome unto me. Whatever was therein lay all at random (no man looked thereunto) and was free for any that had a mind unto it. I, who have so long been a good housekeeper and used to hospitality, was much troubled and put to my shifts how to find out some retreat for my family: a dismayed and scattered family, making both herself and her friends afraid and breeding horror where it sought to retire for shelter, being now to shift and change her dwelling so soon as any of the company began to feel his finger ache, all the rest were dismayed. Every sickness is then taken for the plague: none hath leisure to consider them. And the mischief is that, according to rules of art, what danger soever approacheth, a man must continue forty days in anxiety or fear of that evil; in which time your own imagination doth perplex you as she list* and infect your health. All which had much less touched me had I not been forced to bear other men's burthens and partake all their grievances, and for six months' space, in miserable manner, to be a woeful guide to so great-confused a caravan. For I ever carry my preservatives about me, which are resolution and sufferance. Apprehension doth not greatly press me, which is particularly feared in this sickness. And if being alone I should have taken it, it had been a stronger and further flight. It is a death, in mine opinion, not of the worst: it is commonly short and speeding, void of lingering giddiness; without pain, comforted by the public condition; without ceremony, without mourning, and without thronging. But, for the people about us, the hundredth part of souls cannot be saved.

> Kingdoms of shepherds, desolate, forlorn,
> Parks far and near lie waste, a state all torn.
>
> Virg. *Georg.* III.476.

In that place, my best revenue is manual. What a hundred men labored for me lay fallow for a long time. What examples of resolution saw we not then in all this people's simplicity? Each one generally renounced all care of life. The grapes (which are the country's chief commodity) hung still and rotted upon the vines untouched — all indifferently preparing themselves and expecting death, either that night or the next morrow, with countenance and voice so little daunted that they seemed to have compromitted* to this necessity, and that it was an universal and inevitable condemnation. It is ever such. But what slender hold hath the resolution of dying? The difference and distance of some few hours, the only consideration of the company, yields the apprehension diverse unto us. Behold these because they die in one same month, children, young, old; they are no more astonied,* they are no longer wept for. I saw some that feared to stay behind, as if they had been in some horrible solitude. And commonly I knew no other care amongst them, but for graves: it much grieved them to see the dead carcasses scattered over the fields, at the mercy of wild beasts which presently began to flock thither. [C]Oh how human fantasies differ and are easily disjoined! The Neorites, a nation whilom subdued by Alexander the Great, cast out their dead men's bodies into the thickest of their woods, there to be devoured; the grave only esteemed happy among them. [B]Some in good health digged already their graves; othersome yet living did go into them. And a day-laborer of mine, as he was dying, with his own hands and feet pulled earth upon him, and so covered himself. Was not this a lying down in the shade to sleep at ease? [C]An enterprise in some sort as highly noble as that of some Roman soldiers who, after the battle of Canna, were found with their heads in certain holes or pits, which themselves had made and filled up with their hands, wherein they were smothered. [B]To conclude, a whole nation was presently by use brought to a march, that in undauntedness yields not to any consulted and fore-meditated resolution.

The greatest number of learning's instructions, to encourage us, have more show than force and more ornament than fruit. We have forsaken nature, and yet we will teach her her lesson — she that led us so happily and directed us so safely. And in the meanwhile the traces of her instructions and that little which, by the benefit of ignorance, remaineth of her image, imprinted in the life of this rustical troop of unpolished men, learning is compelled to go daily a-borrowing, thereby to make her disciples a pattern of constancy, of innocency, and of tranquillity. It is a goodly matter to see how these men, full of so great knowledge, must imitate this foolish simplicity; yea, in the first and chief actions of virtue. And that our wisdom should learn of beasts the most profitable documents belonging to the chiefest and most necessary parts of our life: how we should live and die, husband our goods, love and bring up our children, and entertain justice. A singular testimony of man's infirmity. And that this reason we so manage at our pleasure, ever finding some diversity and novelty, leaveth unto us no manner of apparent track of nature. Wherewith men have done as perfumers do with oil: they have adulterated her with so many argumentations and sophisticated her with so diverse far-fetched discourses that she is become variable and peculiar to every man and hath lost her proper, constant, and universal visage, whereof we must seek for a testimony of beasts, not subject to favor or corruption, nor to diversity of opinions. For it is most true that themselves march not always exactly in nature's path, but if they chance to stray, it is so little that you may ever perceive the track. Even as horses led by hand do sometimes bound and start out of the way, but no further than their halter's length, and nevertheless follow ever his steps that leadeth them. And as a hawk takes his [C]flight but under the limits of her cranes,* or twine. "Banishments, torments, wars, sicknesses, shipwrecks, all these forecast and premeditate, that thou mayest seem no novice, no freshwater soldier to any misadventure" (Sen. *Epist.* XCI and CVII).

[B]What availeth this curiosity unto us to pre-occupate* all human nature's inconveniences, and with so much labor and toiling against them to prepare ourselves, which peradventure shall nothing concern us? [C]"It makes men as sad that they may suffer some mischief, as if they had suffered it" (Sen. *Epist.* LXXIV.). Not only the blow, but the wind and crack* strikes us. Or [B]as the most febricitant,* for surely it is a kind of fever now to cause yourself to be whipped because fortune may one day chance to make you endure it, [C]and at midsummer to put on your furred gown because you shall need it at Christmas? [B]Cast yourselves into the experience of all the mischiefs that may befall you, namely of the extremest; there try yourself (say they) there assure yourself. Contrariwise, the easiest and most natural were even to discharge his thought of them. They will not come soon enough, their true being doth not last us long enough, our spirit must extend and lengthen them and before-hand incorporate them into himself, as if they lay not sufficiently heavy on our senses. [C]They will weigh heavy enough when they shall be there, saith one of the masters,[8] not of a tender, but of the hardest sect; meanwhile favor thyself; believe what thou lovest best. What avails it thee to collect and prevent thy ill fortune; and for fear of the future, lose the present; and now to be miserable, because in time thou mayest be so? They are his own words. [B]Learning doth us willingly one good office, exactly to instruct us in the dimensions of evils.

> Men's cogitations whetting,
> With sharp cares inly fretting.
> Virg. *Georg.* I.123.

[8] Seneca.

It were pity any part of their greatness should escape our feeling and understanding.

It is certain that preparation unto death hath caused more torment unto most than the very sufferance. [C]It was whilom truly said, of and by a most judicious author: "Weariness less troubleth our senses, than pensiveness doth" (Quint. I.12.). The apprehension of present death doth sometimes of itself animate us with a ready resolution no longer to avoid a thing altogether inevitable. Many gladiators have in former ages been seen, having at first fought very cowardly, most courageously to embrace death, offering their throat to the enemy's sword, yea, and bid them make haste. The sight distant from future death hath need of a slow constancy, and by consequence hard to be found. [B]If you know not how to die, take no care for it; nature herself will fully and sufficiently teach you in the nick; she will exactly discharge that work for you; trouble not yourself with it.

Of death th' uncertain hour you men in vain
Inquire, and what way death shall you distrain:*
Propert. II.xxvii.1.

A certain sudden ruin is less pain
More grievous long what you fear to sustain.
Pseudo-Gallus I.277.

We trouble death with the care of life, and life with the care of death. [C]The one annoyeth, the other affrights us. [B]It is not against death we prepare ourselves; it is a thing too momentary. [C]A quarter of an hour of passion without consequence and without annoyance deserves not particular precepts. [B]To say truth, we prepare ourselves against the preparations of death. Philosophy teacheth us ever to have death before our eyes, to foresee and consider it before it come; then giveth us rules and precautions so to provide that such foresight and thought hurt us not. So do physicians, who cast us into diseases that they may employ their drugs and skill about them. [C]If we have not known how to live, it is injustice to teach us how to die and deform the end from all the rest. Have we known how to live constantly and quietly, we shall know how to die resolutely and reposedly. They may brag as much as they please. "The whole life of a philosopher is the meditation of his death" (Cic. *Tusc.* I.30.).[9] But methinks it is indeed the end, yet not the scope of life. It is her last, it is her extremity, yet not her object. Herself must be unto herself, her aim, her drift, and her design. Her direct study is to order, to direct, and to suffer herself. In the number of many other offices which the general and principal chapter to know how to live containeth, is this special article,

[9] Cf. the first sentence of *That to Philosophy Is to Learn How to Die.*

to know how to die. And of the easiest did not our own fear weigh it down. BTo judge them by their profit and by the naked truth, the lessons of simplicity yield not much to those which doctrine preacheth to the contrary unto us. Men are different in feeling, and diverse in force: they must be directed to their good according to themselves and by diverse ways:

> CWhere I am whirl'd by wind and weather;
> I guest-like straight am carried thither.
> Hor. *Epist.* I.i.15.

BI never saw mean paisant* of my neighbors enter into cogitation or care with what assurance or countenance he should pass this last hour. Nature teacheth him never to muse on death but when he dieth. And then hath he a better grace in it than Aristotle, whom death perplexed doubly, both by herself and by so long a premeditation. Therefore was it Caesar's opinion that the least premeditated death was the happiest and the easiest. C"He grieves more than he need, that grieves before he need" (Sen. *Epist.* XCVIII.). The sharpness of this imagination proceeds from our curiosity. Thus we ever hinder ourselves, desiring to forerun and sway natural prescriptions. It is but for doctors[10] being in health to fare the worse by it, and to frown and startle at the image of death. The vulgar sort have neither need of remedy nor comfort but when the shock or stroke cometh; and justly considers no more of it than he feeleth. BAnd is it not as we say, that the vulgar's stupidity and want of apprehension afford them this patience in private evils and this deep carelessness of sinister future accidents? CThat their mind, being more gross, dull, and blockish, is less penetrable and agitable? BIn God's name, if it be so, let us henceforth keep a school of brutality. It is the utmost fruit that sciences promise unto us, to which she so gently bringeth her disciples.

We shall not want good teachers, interpreters of natural simplicity. Socrates shall be one. For, as near as I remember, he speaketh in this sense unto the judges that determine of his life:

"I fear me my masters (saith he) that if I entreat you not to make me die, I shall confirm the evidence of my accusers; which is, that I profess to have more understanding than others, as having some knowledge more secret and hid of things both above and beneath us. I know I have neither frequented nor known death, nor have I seen anybody that hath either felt or tried her qualities to instruct me in them. Those who fear her, presuppose to know: as for me, I neither know who [or] what she is, nor what they do in the other world. Death may peradventure be a thing indifferent, haply a thing de-

[10] I.e., the learned.

sirable. [C]Yet is it to be believed that, if it be a transmigration from one place to another, there is some amendment is going to live with so many worthy famous persons that are deceased, and be exempted from having any more to do with wicked and corrupted judges. If it be a consummation of one's being, it is also an amendment and entrance into a long and quiet night. We find nothing so sweet in life as a quiet rest and gentle sleep, and without dreams.

[B]"The things I know to be wicked, as to wrong or offend one's neighbor, and to disobey his superior, be he god or man, I carefully shun them. Such as I know not whether they be good or bad, I cannot fear them. [C]If I go to my death and leave you alive, the gods only see whether you or I shall prosper best. And therefore, for my regard, you shall dispose of it as it shall best please you. But according to my fashion, which is to counsel good and profitable things, this I say, that for your own conscience you shall do best to free and discharge me — except you see further into mine own cause than myself. And judging according to my former actions, both public and private, according to my intentions, and to the profit that so many of our citizens, both young and old, draw daily from my conversation, and the fruit all you reap by me, you cannot more justly or duly discharge yourselves toward my deserts than by appointing (my poverty considered) that I may live, and at the common charge be kept in the Prytaneum — which, for much less reasons, I have often seen you freely grant to others. Impute it not to obstinacy or disdain in me, nor take it in ill part that I, according to custom, proceed not by way of entreaty and move you to commiseration. I have both friends and kinsfolk (being not, as Homer saith, begotten of a block or stone, no more than other men) capable to present themselves humbly suing with tears and mourning, and I have three desolate wailing children to move you to pity. But I should make our city ashamed, of the age I am in, and in that reputation of wisdom as now I stand in prevention, to yield unto so base and abject countenances. What would the world say of other Athenians? I have ever admonished such as have heard me speak never to purchase or redeem their life by any dishonest or unlawful act. And in my country's wars, both at Amphipolis, at Potidaea, at Delium, and others in which I have been, I have shown by effects how far I was from warranting my safety by my shame. Moreover, I should interest your duty, and prejudice your calling, and persuade you to foul unlawful things; for, not my prayers, but the pure and solid reasons of justice should persuade you. You have sworn to the gods so to maintain yourselves. Not to believe there were any might seem I would suspect, recriminate, or retort the fault upon you. And myself should witness against myself not to believe in them as I ought, distrusting their conduct, and not merely remitting my affairs into their hands. I wholly trust and rely on them, and certainly hold that in this they will dispose as it shall be meetest for you and fittest for me. Honest men, that neither live nor are dead, have no cause at all to fear the gods."

[B]Is not this a childish pleading, of an inimaginable courage; and in what necessity employed? [C]Verily it was reason he should prefer it before that which the great orator Lysias had set down in writing for him, excellently fashioned in a judiciary style but unworthy of so noble a criminal. Should a man have heard an humbly-suing voice out of Socrates his mouth? Would that proud virtue have failed in the best of her show? And would his rich and powerful nature have committed her defense unto art, and in her highest essay renounced unto truth and sincerity the ornaments of his speech to adorn and deck himself with the embellishment of the figures and fictions of a fore-learned oration? He did most wisely, and according to himself, not to corrupt the tenure of an incorruptible life and so sacred an image of human form to prolong his decreptitude for one year, and wrong the immortal memory of so glorious an end. He [owed] his life not to himself, but to the world's example. Had it not been a public loss if he had finished the same in some idle, base, and obscure manner? [B]Truly, so careless and effeminate a consideration of his death deserved posterity should so much more consider the same for him; which it did. And nothing is so just in justice, as that which fortune ordained for his commendation. For the Athenians did afterward so detest and abhor those which had furthered and caused his death, that of all they were loathed and shunned as cursed and excommunicated men: whatsoever they had but touched was held to be polluted; no man would so much as wash with them in baths or hot houses: no man afford them a salutation, much less accost or have to do with them. So that, being in the end no longer able to endure this public hatred and general contempt, they all hanged themselves.

If any man thinks that, amongst so many examples I might have chosen for the service of my purpose, in Socrates his sayings I have chosen or handled this but ill, and deemeth this discourse to be raised above common opinions, I have done it wittingly: for I judge otherwise and hold it to be a discourse in rank and sincerity much shorter and lower than vulgar opinions. It representeth, [C]in an un-artificial boldness and infantine security, [B]the pure impression [C]and first ignorance [B]of nature. Because, it is credible that we naturally fear pain, but not death, by reason of her. It is a part of our being, no less essential than life. To what end would nature have else engendered the hate and horror of it, seeing it holds therein and with it a rank of most great profit to foster the succession and nourish the vicissitude of her works; and that in this universal commonwealth it steadeth* and serveth more for birth and augmentation, than for loss, decay, or ruin.

So doth the sum of all,
By courses rise and fall.
Lucr. II.74.

[C]We thousand souls shall pay,
For one soul made away.
Ovid. *Fast.* I.380.

[B]The decay of one life is the passage to a thousand other lives. [C]Nature hath imprinted in beasts the care of themselves and of their preservation. They proceed even to the fear of their empairing,* to shock or hurt themselves, and that we should not shackle or beat them — accidents subject to their sense and experience. But that we should kill them, they cannot fear it, nor have they the faculty to imagine or conclude their death. Yet is it reported, that [B]they are not seen only to embrace and endure the same joyfully (most horses neigh in dying, and swans sing when it seizeth them), but moreover, they seek it when they need it; as by divers examples may be proved in the elephants.

Besides, the manner of arguing which Socrates useth here, is it not equally admirable both in simplicity and in vehemency? Verily it is much easier to speak as Aristotle, and live as Caesar, than speak and live as Socrates. Therein consists the extreme degree of difficulty and perfection; art cannot attain unto it. Our faculties are not now so addressed. We neither assay nor know them; we invest ourselves with others, and suffer our own to be idle.

As by some might be said of me: that here I have but gathered a nosegay of strange flowers, and have put nothing of mine unto it but the thread to bind them. Certes, I have given unto public opinion that these borrowed ornaments accompany me; but I mean not they should cover or hide me: it is contrary to mine intention, who would make show of nothing that is not mine own, yea mine own by nature. And had I believed myself, at all adventure I had spoken alone. [C]I daily charge myself the more beyond my proposition and first form, upon the fantasy of time and through idleness. If it misseem me as I think it doth, it is no great matter; it may be profitable for some other. [B]Some allege* Plato, some mention Homer, that never saw them, or as they say in English, many a man speaks of Robin Hood that never shot in his bow.[11] And I have taken divers passages from others than in their spring. Without pain or sufficiency, having a

11 The English saying is Florio's addition.

thousand volumes of books about me where I now write, if I please I may presently borrow from a number of such botcherly-patchcoats* (men that I plod not much upon) wherewith to enamel this treaty of physiognomy. I need but the liminary epistle of a German to store me with allegations*; and we go questing that way for a fading greedy glory, to cozen and delude the foolish world.

ᶜThese rhapsodies of commonplaces wherewith so many stuff their study serve not greatly but for vulgar subjects, and serve but to show and not to direct us — a ridiculous, fond* fruit of learning that Socrates doth so pleasantly inveigh and exagitate* against Euthydemus. I have seen books made of things neither studied nor ever understood, the author committing to divers of his learned and wise friends the search of this and that matter that so he might compile them into a book, contenting himself for his own part to have cast the plot and projected the design of it, and by his industry to have bound up the fagot of unknown provisions. At least is the ink and paper his own. This may be said to be a buying or borrowing, and not a making or compiling of a book. It is to teach men, not that one can make a book, but to put them out of doubt that he cannot make it. ᴮA president of the law,[12] in a place where I was, vaunted himself to have huddled up together two hundred and odd strange places in a presidential law-case of his, ᶜin publishing of which he defaced the glory which others gave him for it. ᴮA weak, childish, and absurd boasting, in my opinion, for such a subject and for such a man. ᶜI do clean contrary, and amongst so many borrowings am indeed glad to filch some one, disguising and altering the same to some new service. On hazard, to let men say that it is for lack of understanding its natural use, I give it some particular addressing of mine own hand, to the end it may be so much less merely* strange. ᴮWhereas these put their larcenies to public view and garish show. So have they more credit in the laws than I. ᶜWe other naturalists suppose that there is a great and incomparable preference between the honor of invention and that of allegation.* ᴮWould I have spoken according to learning, I had spoken sooner. I had written at such times as I was nearer to my studies, when I had more wit and more memory; and should more have trusted the vigor of that age than the imperfection of this, had I been willing to profess writing of books. ᶜAnd what if this gracious favor, which fortune hath not long since offered me by the intermission of this work, could have befallen me in such a season in lieu of this, where it is equally desirable to possess and ready to lose?[13]

ᴮTwo of mine acquaintance (both notable men in this faculty)

12 I.e., a magistrate.
13 Probably an allusion to Mlle. de Gournay. Cf. Introduction.

have, in my conceit, lost much because they refused to publish themselves at forty years of age, to stay until they were three-score. Maturity hath her defects as well as greenness, and worse. And as incommodious or unfit is old age unto this kind of work as to any other. Whosoever puts his decrepitude under the press committeth folly, if thereby he hopes to wring out humors that shall not taste of dotage, or foppery, or of drowsiness. Our spirit becometh costive and thickens in growing old. Of ignorance I speak sumptuously and plenteously, and of learning meagerly and piteously: [C]this accessorily and accidentally; that expressly and principally. And purposely I treat of nothing but of nothing, nor of any one science but of unscience. [B]I have chosen the time where the life I have to set forth is all before me; the rest holds more of death. And of my death, only should I find it babbling, as others do, I would willingly, in dislodging, give the world advice.

Socrates hath been a perfect pattern in all great qualities. I am vexed that ever he met with so unhandsome and crabbed a body as they say he had, and so dissonant from the beauty of his mind, [C]himself so amorous and so besotted on beauty. Nature did him wrong. [B]There is nothing more truly semblable as the conformity or relation between the body and the mind. [C]"It is of great import in what body the mind is bestowed; for many things arise of the body to sharpen the mind, and many things to dull and rebate it" (Cic. *Tusc.* I.32.). This man speaks of an unnatural ill-favoredness and membral deformity; but we call ill-favoredness a kind of unseemliness at the first sight, which chiefly lodgeth in the face and by the color worketh a dislike in us. A freckle, a blemish, a rude countenance, a sour look, proceeding often of some inexplicable cause, may be in well-ordered, comely, and complete limbs. The foulness of face, which invested a beauteous mind in my dear friend La Boétie, was of this predicament. This superficial ill-favoredness, which is notwithstanding the most imperious, is of less prejudice unto the state of the mind and hath small certainty in men's opinion. The other, by a more proper name called a more substantial deformity, beareth commonly a deeper inward stroke. Not every shoe of smooth-shining leather, but every well-shapen and handsome-made shoe, showeth the inward and right shape of the foot.

[B]As Socrates said of his, that it justly accused so much in his mind had he not corrected the same by institution. [C]But in so saying, I suppose that, according to his wonted use, he did but jest. And so excellent a mind did never frame itself.

[B]I cannot often enough repeat how much I esteem beauty, so powerful and advantageous a quality is she. He named it *a short tyranny;* [C]and

Plato *the privilege of nature.* [B]We have none that exceeds it in credit. She possesseth the chief rank in the commerce of society of men. She presents itself forward; she seduceth and preoccupates* our judgment with great authority and wonderful impression. [C]Phyrne had lost her plea, though in the hands of an excellent lawyer, if with opening her garments, by the sudden flashing of her beauty, she had not corrupted her judges. And I find that Cyrus, Alexander, and Caesar, those three masters of the world, have not forgotten or neglected the same in achieving their great affairs. So hath not the first Scipio. One same word in Greek importeth fair and good.[14] And even the Holy Ghost calleth often those good, which he meaneth fair. I should willingly maintain the rank of the goods, as employed the song which Plato saith to have been trivial, taken from some ancient poet: health, beauty, and riches. Aristotle saith that the right of commanding doth of duty belong to such as are fair; and if haply any be found whose beauty approached to that of the gods' images, that veneration is equally due unto them. To one that asked him why the fairest were both longer time and oftener frequented, "This question (quoth he) ought not to be moved but by a blind man." Most, and the greatest, philosophers paid for their schooling and attained unto wisdom by the intermission of their beauty and favor of their comeliness.

[B]Not only in men that serve me, but in beasts also, I consider the same within two inches of goodness. Yet methinks that the same feature and manner of the face and those lineaments by which some argue certain inward complexions and our future fortunes, is a thing that doth not directly nor simply lodge under the chapter of beauty and ill-favoredness, no more than all good favors or clearness of air do not always promise health, nor all fogs and stinks, infection, in times of the plague. Such as accuse ladies to contradict the beauty by their manners, guess not always at the truth. For, in [an] ill-favored and ill-composed face may sometimes harbor some air of probity and trust. As, on the contrary, I have sometimes read between two fair eyes the threats of a malign and dangerous, ill-boding nature. There are some favorable physiognomies; for in a throng of victorious enemies, you shall presently amidst a multitude of unknown faces make choice of one man more than of others to yield yourself unto and trust your life; and not properly by the consideration of beauty.

A man's look or air of his face is but a weak warrant; notwithstanding it is of some consideration. And were I to whip them, I would more rudely scourge such as maliciously belie and betray the promises which nature had charactered in their front. And more severely would I punish malicious craft in a debonaire appearance and in a mild-prom-

14 Καλοκαγαθός.

ising countenance. It seemeth there be some lucky and well-boding faces, and other some unlucky and ill-presaging. And I think there is some art to distinguish gently-mild faces from niais* and simple, the severe from the rude, the malicious from the froward, the disdainful from the melancholic and other neighboring qualities. There are some beauties not only fierce-looking, but also sharp-working; some others pleasing-sweet and yet wallowishly tasteless. To prognosticate future successes of them be matters I leave undecided.

I have (as elsewhere I noted) taken for my regard this ancient precept, very rawly and simply: that "We cannot err in following nature"; and that the sovereign document is for a man to conform himself to her. I have not (as Socrates) by the power and virtue of reason corrected my natural complexions, nor by art hindered mine inclination. Look how I came into the world; so I go on: I strive with nothing. My two mistress parts live of their own kindness in peace and good agreement; but my nurse's milk hath (thanks be to God) been indifferently wholesome and temperate.

[C]Shall I say thus much by the way? That I see a certain image of bookish or scholastical *prud'homie,** only which is in a manner in use amongst us, held and reputed in greater esteem than it deserveth, and which is but a servant unto precepts, brought under by hope, and constrained by fear? I love it such as laws and religions make not, but overmake and authorize, that they may be perceived to have wherewith to uphold herself without other aid, sprung up in us of her own proper roots, by and from the seed of universal reason imprinted in every man that is not unnatural. The same reason that reformeth Socrates from his vicious habit yields him obedient both to gods and men that rule and command his city, courageous in his death, not because his soul is immortal, but because he is mortal. A ruinous instruction to all commonwealths, and much more harmful than ingenious and subtle, is that which persuadeth men that only religious belief, and without manners, sufficeth to content and satisfy divine justice. Custom makes us see an enormous distinction between devotion and conscience.

[B]I have a favorable appearance, both in form and in interpretation,

> I have; what did I say?
> I had what's now away.
> Alas, you only now behold
> Bones of a body worn and old,
> Ter. *Heaut.* I.i.42.

and which makes a contrary show to that of Socrates. It hath often betided me that by the simple credit of my presence and aspect some that had no knowledge of me have greatly trusted unto it, were it about their own affairs or mine. And even in foreign countries, I have thereby reaped singular and rare favors. These two experiments are haply worthy to be particularly related.

A quidam* gallant determined upon a time to surprise both my house and myself. His plot was to come riding alone to my gate and instantly* to urge entrance. I knew him by name, and had some reason to trust him, being my neighbor and somewhat allied unto me. I presently caused my gates to be opened, as I do to all men. He comes in all affrighted, his horse out of breath; both much harassed. He entertains me with this fable, that within half a league of my house he was suddenly set upon by an enemy of his, whom I knew well and had heard of their quarrel; that his foe had wondrously put him to his spurs; that being surprised unarmed, and having fewer in his company than the other, he was glad to run away, and for safety had made haste to come to my house, as to his sanctuary; that he was much perplexed for his men, all which he supposed to be either taken or slain. I endeavored friendly to comfort and sincerely to warrant and refresh him. Within a while came galloping four or five of his soldiers, amazed, as if they had been out of their wits, hasting to be let in. Shortly after came others, and others, all proper men, well mounted, better armed, to the number of thirty or thereabouts, all seeming distracted for fear, as if the enemy that pursued them had been at their heels. [C]This mystery began to summon my suspicion. [B]I was not ignorant of the age wherein I lived, nor how much my house might be envied, and had sundry examples of others of my acquaintance that had been spoiled, beset, and surprised thus and thus. So it is that, perceiving with myself there was nothing to be gotten, though I had begun to use them kindly, if I continued not, and being unable to rid myself of them and clear my house without danger and spoiling all, as I ever do I took the plainest and natural well-meaning way, and commanded they should be let in and bid welcome. And to say truth, I am by nature little suspicious or mistrustful; I am easily drawn to admit excuses and incline to mild interpretations. I take men according to common order and suppose every one to mean as I do, and believe these perverse and treacherous inclinations, except I be compelled by some authentical testimony, no more than monsters or miracles. Besides, I am a man that willingly commit myself unto fortune and carelessly cast myself into her arms, whereof hitherto I have more just cause to commend myself than to complain. And have found her more circumspect [C]and friendly-careful of my affairs [B]than I am myself. There are certain actions in my life, the conduct of which may justly be termed difficult or, if any be so disposed, prudent. And of those, suppose the third part of them to be mine own; truly the other two are richly hers. [C]We are to blame and, in my conceit, we err that we do not sufficiently and so much as we ought trust the heavens with ourselves. And pretend more in our own conduct than of right appertains unto us. Therefore do our designs so often miscarry and our intents so seldom sort to wished effect. The heavens are angry and, I may say, envious of the extension and large privilege we ascribe unto the right of human wisdom, to the prejudice of theirs; and abridge them so much the more unto us, by how much more we endeavor to amplify them.

[B]But to come to my former discourse. These gallants kept still on horseback in my court and would not alight; their captain with me in my hall, who would never have his horse set up, still saying that he would not stay, but must necessarily withdraw himself so soon as he had news of his followers. He saw himself master of his enterprise; and nothing was wanting but the execution. He hath since reported very often (for he was no whit scrupulous or afraid to tell this story) that my undaunted looks, my undismayed countenance, and my liberty of speech made him reject all manner of treasonable intents or treacherous designs. What shall I say more? He bids me farewell, calleth for his horse, gets up, and offereth to be gone, his people, having continually their eyes fixed upon him to observe his looks and see what sign he should make unto them, much amazed to see him be gone and wondering to see him omit and forsake such an advantage.

Another time, trusting to a certain truce or cessation of arms that lately had been published through our camps in France, as one suspecting no harm, I undertook a journey from home through a dangerous and very ticklish country. I had not rid far, but I was discovered, and behold three or four troops of horsemen all several ways made after me with purpose to entrap me. One of which overtook me the third day; where I was round beset and charged by fifteen or twenty gentlemen, who had all vizards and cases, followed aloof* off by a band of argoletiers.* I was charged, I yielded, I was taken and immediately drawn into the bosom of a thick wood that was not far off; there pulled from my horse, stripped with all speed, my trunks and cloak-bags rifled, my box taken; my horses, my equipage, and such things as I had dispersed and shared amongst them. We continued a good while amongst those thorny bushes, contesting and striving about my ransom, which they racked so high that it appeared well I was not much known of them. They had long contestation among themselves for my life. And to say truth, there were many circumstances threatened me of the danger I was in.

> [C]Of courage then indeed,
> Then of stout breast is need.
> Virg. *Aen.* VI.261.

[B]I ever stood upon the title and privilege of the truce and proclamation made in the king's name, but that availed not. I was content to quit them whatever they had taken from me, which was not to be despised, without promising other ransom. After we had debated the matter to and fro the space of two or three hours, and that no excuses could serve, they set me upon a lame jade, which they knew could never escape them, and committed the particular keeping of my person to fifteen or twenty harquebusiers* and dispersed my people to others of their crew, commanding we should all divers ways be carried prisoners; and myself being gone two or threescore paces from them,

Pollux and Castor's aid,
When I had humbly prayed,
Catul. LXVI.65.

behold a sudden and unexpected alteration took them. I saw their captain coming toward me with a cheerful countenance and much milder speeches than before: carefully trudging up and down through all the troops to find out my goods again, which as he found all scattered he forced every man to restore them unto me, and even my box came to my hands again. To conclude, the most precious jewel they presented me was in liberty; as for my other things, I cared not greatly [C]at that time. [B]What the true cause of so unlooked-for a change and so sudden an alteration was, without any apparent impulsion and of so wonderful repentance, at such a time, in such an opportunity, and in such an enterprise, fore-meditated, consulted, and effected without controlment, and which through custom and the impiety of times was now become lawful (for at the first brunt I plainly confessed, and genuinely told them what side I was of, where my way lay, and whither I was riding), I verily know not yet, nor can I give any reason for it. The chiefest amongst them unmasked himself, told me his name, and repeated divers times unto me that I should acknowledge my deliverance to my countenance, to my boldness and constancy of speech, and be beholding to them for it, insomuch as they made me unworthy of such a misfortune; and demanded assurance of me for the like courtesy. It may be that the inscrutable goodness of God would use this vain instrument for my preservation. For, the next morrow it also shielded me from worse mischief or ambuscados, whereof themselves gently forewarned me. The last is yet living, able to report the whole success himself; the other was slain not long since.

If my countenance had not answered for me, if the ingenuity of mine inward intent might not plainly have been deciphered in mine eyes and voice, surely I could never have continued so long without quarrels or offenses, with this indiscreet liberty, to speak freely (be it right or wrong) whatever cometh to my mind, and rashly to judge of things. This fashion may in some sort (and that with reason) seem uncivil and ill-accommodated in our customary manners; but outrageous or malicious I could never meet with any would so judge it, or that was ever distasted at my liberty if he received the same from my mouth. Words reported again have as another sound, so another sense. And to say true, I hate nobody; and am so remiss to offend, or slow to wrong any, that for the service of reason itself I cannot do it. And if occasions have at any time urged me in criminal condemnations to do as others, I have rather been content to be amerced* than to appear. [C]"So as I had rather men should not offend, than that I should have courage enough to punish their offenses" (Livy XXIX.21.).

Some report that Aristotle being upbraided by some of his friends that he had been over-merciful toward a wicked man, "I have indeed (quoth he) been merciful toward the man, but not toward his wickedness."

Ordinary judgments are exasperated unto punishment by the horror of the crime. And that enmildens me. The horror of the first murther makes me fear a second. And the ugliness of one cruelty induceth me to detest all manner of imitation of it. [B]To me, that am but a plain fellow and see no higher than a steeple, may that concern which was reported of Charillus, king of Sparta: "He cannot be good, since he is not bad to the wicked." Or thus; for Plutarch presents it two ways, as he doth a thousand other things diversely and contrary: "He must needs be good, since he is so to the wicked." Even as in lawful actions it grieves me to take any pains about them when it is with such as are therewith displeased, so to say truth, in unlawful I make no great conscience to employ myself or take pains about them, being with such as consent unto them.

Of Experience

III. 13 ✧ 1587–88

[B]There is no desire more natural than that of knowledge. We attempt all means that may bring us unto it. When reason fails us, we employ experience —

> [C]By diverse proofs, experience art hath bred,
> Whilst one by one the way examples led.
>
> Manil. I.59.

—[B]which is a mean by much more weak and vile. But truth is of so great consequence that we ought not disdain any induction* that may bring us unto it. Reason hath so many shapes that we know not which to take hold of. Experience hath as many. The consequence we seek to draw from the conference* of events is unsure, because they are ever dissemblable.

No quality is so universal in this surface of things as variety and diversity. The Greeks, the Latins, and we use for the most express examples of similitudes, that of eggs. Some have nevertheless been found, especially one in Delphos, that knew marks of difference between eggs and never took one for another, [C]and having divers hens, could rightly judge which had laid the egg. [B]Dissimilitude doth of itself insinuate into our works; no art can come near unto similitude. Neither Perozet nor any other cardmaker can so industriously smooth or whiten the backside of his cards but some cunning gamester will distinguish them only by seeing some other player handle or shuffle them. Resemblance doth not so much make one, as difference maketh another. [C]Nature hath bound herself to make nothing that may not be dissemblable.

[B]Yet doth not the opinion of that man greatly please me that supposed by the multitude of laws to curb the authority of judges, in cutting out their morsels. He perceived not that there is as much liberty and extension in the interpretation of laws as in their fashion. And those but mock themselves who think to diminish our debates and stay them by calling us to the express word of sacred Bible. Because our spirit finds not the field less spacious to control and check the sense of others, than to represent his own, and, as if there were as little courage and sharpness, to gloss as to invent.

We see how far he was deceived. For we have in France more laws than all the world besides; yea more than were needful to govern all the worlds imagined by Epicurus. [C]"As in times past we were sick of offenses, so now are we of laws" (Tac. *Ann.* III.25.). [B]As we have given our judges so large a scope to moot, to opinionate, to suppose and decide, that there was never so powerful and so licentious a liberty.

What have our lawmakers gained with choosing a hundred thousand kinds of particular cases, and add as many laws unto them? That number hath no proportion with the infinite diversity of human accidents. The multiplying of our inventions shall never come to the variation of examples. Add a hundred times as many unto them, yet shall it not follow that of events to come there be any one found that, in all this infinite number of selected and enregistered events, shall meet with one to which he may so exactly join and match it, but some circumstance and diversity will remain that may require a diverse consideration of judgment. There is but little relation between our actions, that are in perpetual mutation, and the fixed and immovable laws. The most to be desired are the rarest, the simplest and most general.

And yet I believe it were better to have none at all than so infinite a number as we have. Nature gives them ever more happy than those we give ourselves. Witness the image of the Golden Age that Poets feign, and the state wherein we see divers nations to live which have no other.

Some there are who, to decide any controversy that may rise amongst them, will choose for judge the first man that by chance shall travel alongst their mountains; others that upon a market day will name some one amongst themselves who, in the place, without more wrangling, shall determine all their questions. What danger would ensue if the wisest should so decide ours, according to occurrences and at the first sight, without being tied to examples and consequences? Let every foot have his own shoe.

Ferdinand, King of Spain, sending certain colonies into the Indies, provided wisely that no lawyers or students of the laws should be carried thither, for fear lest controversies, suits, or processes should people that new-found world, as a science that of her own nature engendereth altercation and division; judging with Plato, that lawyers and physicians are an ill provision for any country.

Wherefore is it that our common language, so easy to be understood in all other matters, becometh so obscure, so harsh, and so hard to be understood in law cases, bills, contracts, indentures, citations, wills, and testaments? And that he who so plainly expresseth himself whatever he spake or writ of any other subject, in law matters finds no manner or way to declare himself or his meaning that admits not some doubt or contradiction? Unless it be that the princes of this art, applying themselves with a particular attention to invent and choose strange, choice, and solemn words and frame artificial, cunning clauses, have so plodded and poised* every syllable, canvassed and sifted so exquisitely every seam and quiddity, that they are now so entangled and so confounded in the infinity of figures and so several-small partitions, that they can no more come within the compass of any order, or prescription, or certain understanding. [C]"Whatsoever is sliced into very powder is confused" (Sen. *Epist.* LXXXIX.).

[B]Whosoever hath seen children laboring to reduce a mass of quicksilver to a certain number, the more they press and work the same and strive to force it to their will, so much more they provoke the liberty of that generous metal, which scorneth their art and scatteringly disperseth itself beyond all imagination. Even so of lawyers, who in subdividing their subtleties or quiddities, teach men to multiply doubts; and by extending and diversifying difficulties, they lengthen and amplify, they scatter and disperse them. In sowing and retailing* of questions, they make the world to fructify and abound in uncertainty, in quarrels, in suits, and in controversies; [C]as the ground, the more it is crumbled, broken, and deeply removed or grubbed up, becometh so much more fertile. "Learning breeds difficulty" (Quint. X.3.).

[B]We found many doubts in Ulpian; we find more in Bartolus and Baldus. The trace of this innumerable diversity of opinions should never have been used to adorn posterity and have it put in her head, but rather have been utterly razed out. I know not what to say to it; but this is seen by experience, that so many interpretations dissipate and confound all truth.

Aristotle hath written to be understood — which, if he could not, much less shall another not so learned as he was; and a third, than he who treateth his own imagination. We open the matter and spill it in distempering it. Of one subject we make a thousand. And in multiplying and subdividing we fall again into the infinity of Epicurus his atoms.

It was never seen that two men judged alike of one same thing. And it is impossible to see two opinions exactly semblable, not only in divers men but in any one same man at several hours. I commonly find something to doubt of, where the commentary haply never deigned to touch, as deeming it so plain. I stumble sometimes as much in an even, smooth path; as some horses that I know who oftener trip in a fair plain way than in a rough and stony. Who would not say that glosses increase doubts and ignorance, since no book is to be seen, whether divine or profane, commonly read of all men, whose interpretation dims or tarnisheth not the difficulty? The hundred[th] commentary sends him to his succeeder, more thorny and more crabbed than the first found him. When agreed we amongst ourselves to say, "This book is perfect; there's now nothing to be said against it"?

This is best seen in our French-peddling law. Authority of law is given to infinite doctors, to infinite arrests,* and to as many interpretations. Fnd we, for all that, any end of need of interpreters? Is there any advancement or progress towards tranquillity seen therein? Have we now less need of advocates and judges than when this huge mass of law was yet in her first infancy? Clean contrary; we obscure and bury understanding. We discover it no more but at the mercy of so many courts, bars, or plea-benches.

Men misacknowledge the natural infirmity of their mind. She doth but quest and ferret, and uncessantly goeth turning, winding, building, and entangling herself in her own work, as do our silkworms, and therein stifleth herself. "A mouse in pitch" (Eras. *Adag.* II.iii.68.). He supposeth to note afar off I wot not what appearance of clearness and imaginary truth; but whilst he runneth unto it, so many lets* and difficulties cross his way, so many impeachments and new questings start up, that they stray loose and besot him. Not much otherwise than it fortuned to Aesop's dogs, who far-off discovering some show of a dead body to float upon the sea and being unable to approach the same, undertook to drink up all the water, that so they might dry up the passage; and were all stifled. ^C^To which answereth that which Crates said of Heraclitus his compositions, that they needed a reader who should be a cunning swimmer, lest the depth and weight of his learning should drown and swallow him up.

^B^It is nothing but a particular weakness that makes us [contented] with that which others or we ourselves have found in this pursuit of knowledge. A more sufficient man will not be pleased therewith. There is place for a follower, ^C^yea and for ourselves, ^B^and more ways to the wood than one. There is no end in our inquisitions. Our end is in the other world. ^C^It is a sign his wits grow short when he is pleased, or a sign of weariness. No generous spirit stays and relies upon himself. He ever pretendeth and goeth beyond his strength. He hath some vagaries beyond his effects. If he advance not himself, press, settle, shock, turn, wind, and front himself, he is but half alive. ^B^His pursuits are termless and formless. His nourishment is ^C^admiration, questing, and [B]ambiguity; which Apollo declared sufficiently, always speaking ambiguously, obscurely, and obliquely unto us; not feeding but busying and amusing us. It is an irregular, uncertain motion, perpetual, patternless, and without end. His inventions inflame, follow, and interproduce one another.

As in a running river we behold
How one wave after the other still is rolled,
And all along as it doth endless rise,
The one the other follows, the one from the other flies.
By this wave, that is driven; and this again,
By the other is set forward all amain:
Water in water still, one river still,
Yet divers waters still that river fill.

La Boétie

There's more ado to interpret interpretations than to interpret things, and more books upon books than upon any other subject. We do but inter-gloss ourselves. [C]All swarmeth with commentaries; of authors there is great penury.

Is not the chiefest and most famous knowledge of our ages to know how to understand the wise? Is it not the common and last scope of our study? Our opinions are grafted one upon another. The first serveth as a stock* to the second, the second to the third. Thus we ascend from step to step. Whence it followeth that the highest-mounted hath often more honor than merit. For he is got up but one inch above the shoulders of the last save one.

[B]How often and peradventure foolishly have I enlarged my book to speak of himself? [C]Foolishly if it were but for this reason: that I should have remembered that what I speak of others, they do the like of me; that those so frequent glances on their works witness their heart shivereth with their love they bear them; and that the disdainful churliness wherewith they beat them are but migniardises* and affectations of a motherly favor; following Aristotle, in whom both esteeming and disesteeming himself, arise often of an equal air of arrogancy. For mine excuse: that in this I ought to have more liberty than others, forsomuch as of purpose I write both of myself and of my writings, as of my other actions; that my theme doth turn into itself. I wot not whether every man will take it.

[B]I have seen in Germany that Luther hath left as many divisions and altercations concerning the doubt of his opinions, yea and more, than himself moveth about the Holy Scriptures.

Our contestation is verbal. I demand what nature, voluptuousness, circle, and substitution is? The question is of words, and with words it is answered. A stone is a body; but he that should insist and urge, "And what is a body?" "A substance." "And what a substance?" and so go on, should at last bring the respondent to his calepin* or wit's end. One word is changed for another word, and often more unknown. I know better what *Homo* is than I know what *Animal* is, either mortal or reasonable. To answer one doubt, they give me three; it is Hydra's head. Socrates demanded of Memnon what virtue was. "There is," answered Memnon, "the virtue of a man, of a woman, of a magistrate, of a private man, of a child, of an old man. What virtue mean you?" "Yea marry, this is very well," quoth Socrates; "we were in search of one virtue, and thou bringest me a whole swarm."

We propose one question, and we have a whole huddle of them made unto us again. As no event or form doth wholly resemble another, so doth it not altogether differ one from another. [C]O ingenious mixture of nature! If our faces were not like, we could not discern a man from a beast. If they were not unlike, we could not distinguish one man from another man. [B]All things hold by some similitude; every example limpeth. And the relation which is drawn from experience is ever defective and imperfect. Comparisons are nevertheless joined together by some end. So serve the laws, and so are they sorted and fitted to all our suits or affairs, by some wiredrawn,* forced, and collateral interpretation.

Since the moral laws, which respect the particular duty of every man in himself, are so hard to be taught and observed, as we see they are, it is no wonder if those which govern so many particulars are more hard. Consider the form of this law by which we are ruled. It is a lively testimony of human imbecility, so much contradiction and so many errors are therein contained. That which we think favor or rigor in law (wherein is so much of either that I wot not well whether we shall so often find indifferency in them) are crazed, infected parts and unjust members of the very body and essence of law.

Certain poor countrymen came even now to tell me in a great haste that but now in a forest of mine they have left a man wounded to death, with a hundred hurts about him yet breathing, and who for God's sake hath begged a little water and some help to raise himself at their hands; but that they durst not come near him, and ran all away for fear some officers belonging to the law should meet and catch them; and as they do with such as they find near unto a murdered body, so they should be compelled to give an account of this mischance, to their utter undoing, having neither friends nor money to defend their innocency. What should I have said unto them? It is most certain that this office of humanity had brought them to much trouble.

How many innocent and guiltless men have we seen punished? — I say without the judge's fault — and how many more that were never discovered? This hath happened in my time. Certain men are condemned to death for a murder committed; the sentence, if not pronounced, at least concluded and determined. This done, the Judges are advertised* by the officers of a subalternal court not far off that they have certain prisoners in hold that have directly confessed the foresaid murder, and thereof bring most evident marks and tokens. The question and consultation is now in the former court, whether for all this they might interrupt or should defer the execution of the sentence pronounced against the first. They consider the novelty of the example and consequence thereof, and how to reconcile the judgment. They conclude that the condemnation hath passed according unto law, and therefore the judges are not subject to repentance. To be short, these miserable wretches are consecrated to the prescriptions of the law. Philip, or some other, provided for such an inconvenience in this manner. He had by an irrevocable sentence condemned one to pay another a round sum of money for a fine. A while after, the truth being discovered, it was found he had wrongfully condemned him. On one side was the right of the cause, on the other the right of judiciary forms. He is in some sort to satisfy both parties, suffering the sentence to stand in full power, and with his own purse recompensed the interest of the condemned. But he was to deal with a reparable accident; my poor slaves were hanged irreparably. CHow many condemnations have I seen more criminal than the crime itself?

BAll this put me in mind of those ancient opinions: that he who will do right in gross must needs do wrong by retail, and unjustly in small things, that will come to do justice in great matters; that human justice is framed according to the model of physic, according to which whatsoever is profitable is also just and honest; and of that the Stoics hold, that nature herself in most of her works proceedeth against justice. CAnd of that which the Cyreniacs hold, that there is nothing just of itself; that customs and laws frame justice. And the Theodorians, who in a wise man allow as just all manner of theft, sacrilege, and paillardise,* so he think it profitable for him.

BThere is no remedy. I am in that case as Alcibiades was, and if I can otherwise choose, will never put myself unto a man that shall determine of my head; or consent that my honor or life shall depend on the industry or care of mine attorney, more than mine innocency. I could willingly adventure myself and stand to that law that should as well recompense me for a good deed as punish me for a misdeed, and where I might have a just cause to hope, as reason to fear. Indemnity is no sufficient coin for him who doth better than not to trespass. Our law presents us but one of her hands, and that is her left hand. Whosoever goes to law doth in the end but lose by it.

CIn China, the policy, arts, and government of which kingdom having neither knowledge or commerce with ours, exceed our examples in divers parts of excellency; and whose histories teach me how much more ample and diverse the world is than either we or our forefathers could ever enter into. The officers appointed by the prince to visit the state of his provinces, as they punish such as abuse their charge, so with great liberality they reward such as have uprightly and honestly behaved themselves in them or have done anything more than ordinary and besides the necessity of their duty. There, all present themselves not only to warrant themselves but also to get something; not simply to be paid but liberally to be rewarded.

BNo judge hath yet, God be thanked, spoken to me as a judge in any cause whatsoever, either mine or another man's, criminal or civil. No prison did ever receive me, no not so much as for recreation to walk in. The very imagination of one maketh the sight of their outside seem irksome and loathsome to me. I am so besotted unto liberty that should any man forbid me the access unto any one corner of the Indies, I should in some sort live much discontented. And so long as I shall find land or open air elsewhere, I shall never lurk in any place where I must hide myself. O God, how hardly could I endure the miserable condition of so many men, confined and immured in some corners of this kingdom, barred from entering the chiefest cities, from access into courts, from conversing with men, and interdicted the use of common ways, only because they have offended our laws. If those under which I live should but threaten my finger's end, I would presently go find out some others, wheresoever it were. All my small wisdom, in these civil and tumultuous wars wherein we now live, doth wholly employ itself that they may not interrupt my liberty to go and come wherever I list.

Laws are now maintained in credit not because they are essentially just but because they are laws. It is the mystical foundation of their authority — they have none other — Cwhich avails them much. They are often made by fools — more often by men who in hatred of equality have want of equity — but ever by men, who are vain and irresolute authors. There is nothing so grossly and largely offending nor so ordinarily wronging as the laws. BWhosoever obeyeth them because they are just, obeys them not justly the way as he ought.

Our French laws do in some sort, by their irregularity and deformity, lend a helping hand unto the disorder and corruption that is seen in their dispensation and execution. Their behest is so confused and their command so inconstant, that it in some sort excuseth both the disobedience and the vice of the interpretation, of the administration, and of the observation. Whatsoever then the fruit is we may have of experience, the same which we draw from foreign examples will hardly stead our institution much if we reap so small profit from that we have of ourselves, which is most familiar unto us and truly sufficient to instruct us of what we want.

I study myself more than any other subject. It is my supernatural metaphysic, it is my natural philosophy.

> This world's great house by what art God doth guide;
> From whence the monthly moon doth rising ride,
> How wane, how with clos'd horns return to pride,
> How winds on seas bear sway, what the eastern wind
> Would have, how still in clouds we water find;
> ᶜIf this world's towers to raze a day be sign'd.
>
> Prop. III.v.26.

> ᴮAll this do you inquire
> Whom this world's travails tire.
>
> Lucan. I.417.

ᶜIn this universality I suffer myself ignorantly and negligently to be managed by the general law of the world. I shall sufficiently know it when I shall feel it. My learning cannot make her change her course. She will not diversify herself for me; it were folly to hope it. And greater folly for a man to trouble himself about it, since it is necessarily semblable,* public, and common. The governor's capacity and goodness should throughly discharge us of the government's care.

Philosophical inquisitions and contemplations serve but as a nourishment unto our curiosity. With great reason do philosophers address us unto nature's rules. But they have nought to do with so sublime a knowledge. They falsify them, and present her to us with a painted face, too high in color and over-much sophisticated; whence arise so many different portraits of so uniform a subject. As she hath given us feet to go withal, so hath she endowed us with wisdom to direct our life; a wisdom not so ingenious, sturdy, and pompous as that of their invention, but yet easy, quiet, and salutary, and that in him who hath the hap* to know how to employ it orderly and sincerely, effecteth very well what the other saith, that is to say, naturally. For a man to commit himself most simply unto nature is to do it most wisely. Oh, how soft, how gentle, and how sound a pillow is ignorance and incuriosity to rest a well-composed head upon!

[B]I had rather understand myself well in myself than in [C]Cicero. [B]Out of the experience I have of myself, I find sufficient ground to make myself wise, were I but a good, proficient scholar. Whosoever shall commit to memory the excess or inconvenience of his rage or anger past, and how far that fit transported him, may see the deformity of that passion better than in Aristotle, and conceive a more just hatred against it. Whosoever calleth to mind the dangers he hath escaped, those which have threatened him, and the light occasions that have removed him from one state to another state, doth thereby the better prepare himself to future alterations and knowledge of his condition.

Caesar's life hath no more examples for us than our own. Both imperial and popular, it is ever a life that all human accidents regard. Let us but give ear unto it, we record all that to us that we principally stand in need of. He that shall call to mind how often and how several times he hath been deceived and misaccounted his own judgment, is he not a simple gull if he do not forever afterward distrust the same? When by other's reason I find myself convicted of a false opinion, I learn not so much what new thing he hath told me and this particular ignorance, which were but a small purchase, as in general I learn mine own imbecility and weakness and the treason of my understanding; whence I draw the reformation of all the mass. The like I do in all my other errors. By which rule I apprehend and feel great profit for and unto my life. I regard not the *species* or *individuum* as a stone whereon I have stumbled; I learn everywhere to fear my going and endeavor to order the same. [C]To learn that another hath either spoken a foolish jest or committed a sottish act is a thing of nothing. A man must learn that he is but a fool, a much more ample and important instruction.

[B]The false steps my memory hath so often put upon me at what time she stood most upon herself, have not idly been lost. She may swear and warrant me long enough, I shake mine ears at her; the first opposition made in witness of her makes me suspect. And I durst not trust her in a matter of consequence, nor warrant her touching others' affairs. And were it not that what I do for want of memory others more often do the same for lack of faith. I would even in a matter of fact rather take the truth from another's mouth than from mine own.

Would every man pry into the effects and circumstances of the passions that sway him as I have done of that whereunto I was allotted, he should see them coming and would somewhat hinder their course and abate their impetuosity. They do not always surprise and take hold of us at the first brunt; there are certain forethreatenings and degrees as forerunners.

As when at sea, floods first in whiteness rise,
Sea surgeth softly, and then higher plies
In waves, then from the ground mounts up to skies.
Virg. *Aen.* VII.528.

Judgment holds in me a presidential seat; at least he carefully endeavors to hold it. He suffers my appetites to keep their course, both hatred and love, yea and that I bear unto myself, without feeling alteration or corruption. If he cannot reform other parts according to himself, at least he will not be deformed by them; he keeps his court apart.

That warning-lesson given to all men, to know themselves, must necessarily be of important effect, since that God of wisdom, knowledge, and light caused the same to be fixed on the frontispiece of his temple as containing whatsoever he was to counsel us. [C]Plato saith also that wisdom is nothing but the execution of that ordinance. And Socrates doth distinctly verify the same in Xenophon.

[B]Difficulties and obscurity are not perceived in every science but by such as have entrance into them. For some degree of intelligence is required to be able to mark that one is ignorant, and we must knock at a gate to know whether it be shut. [C]Whence ensueth this Platonical subtlety, that neither those which know have no further to inquire, forsomuch as they know already; nor they that know not, because to inquire it is necessary they know what they inquire after. [B]Even so in this, for a man to know himself. That every man is seen so resolute and satisfied, and thinks himself sufficiently instructed or skillful, doth plainly signify that no man understands anything, [C]as Socrates teacheth Euthydemus [in Xenophon].

[B]Myself, who profess nothing else, find therein so bottomless a depth, and infinite variety, that my apprentisage hath no other fruit than to make me perceive how much more there remaineth for me to learn. To mine own weakness, so often acknowledged, I owe this inclination which I bear unto modesty, to the obedience of beliefs prescribed unto me, to a constant coldness and moderation of opinions, and hatred of this importunate and quarrelous arrogancy, wholly believing and trusting itself, a capital enemy to discipline and verity.

Do but hear them sway and talk. The first fopperies they propose are in the style that religions and laws are compose[d] in. [C]Nothing is more absurd than that avouching and allowance should run before knowledge and precept" (Cic. *Acad. Qu.* I.12.). [B]Aristarchus said that in ancient times there were scarce seven wise men found in the world; and in his time, hardly seven ignorant. Have not we more reason to say it in our days than he had?

Affirmation and self-conceit are manifest signs of foolishness. Some one who a hundred times a day hath had the canvas* and been made a stark coxcomb, shall notwithstanding be seen to stand upon his *Ergos,* and as presumptuously resolute as before. You would say he hath since some new mind and vigor of understanding infused into him. And that it betides him, as to that ancient child of the earth who, by his falling to the ground and touching his mother, still gathered new strength and fresh courage.[1]

> Whose failing limbs with strength renew'd regrow,
> When they once touch his mother earth below.
>
> Lucan. IV.599.

Doth not this indocile, blockhead ass think to reassume a new spirit by undertaking a new disputation? It is by my experience I accuse* human ignorance, which (in mine opinion) is the surest part of the world's school. Those that will not conclude it in themselves by so vain an example as mine or theirs, let them acknowledge it by Socrates, CThe master of masters. For the philosopher Antisthenes was wont to say to his disciples, "Come on, my masters, let you and me go to hear Socrates. There shall I be a fellow disciple with you." And upholding this doctrine of the Stoics' sect, that only virtue sufficed to make a life absolutely happy, and having no need of anything, "but of Socrates his force and resolution," he added moreover.

BThis long attention I employ in considering myself enableth me also to judge indifferently of others. And there are few things whereof I speak more happily and excusably. It often fortuneth me to see and distinguish more exactly the conditions of my friends than themselves do. I have astonied* some by the pertinency of mine own description and have warned him of himself. Because I have from mine infancy inured myself to view mine own life in others' lives, I have thereby acquired a studious complexion therein. And when I think on it, I suffer few things to escape about me that may in any sort fit the same, whether countenances, humor, or discourses. I studiously consider all I am to eschew and all I ought to follow. So by my friends' productions I discover their inward inclinations; not to marshal or range this infinite variety of so divers and so distracted actions to certain genders or chapters, and distinctly to distribute my parcels and divisions into forms and known regions.

> But not how many kinds; nor what their names:
> There is a number of them (and their frames).
>
> Virg. *Georg.* II.103.

CThe wiser sort speak and declare their fantasies more specially and distinctly. But I, who have no further insight than I get from com-

[1] Antaeus.

mon use, without rule or method, generally present mine own but gropingly. As in this: [B]I pronounce my sentence by articles, loose and disjointed; it is a thing cannot be spoken at once and at full. Relation and conformity are not easily found in such base and common minds as ours. Wisdom is a solid and complete frame, every several piece whereof keepeth his due place and beareth his mark. [C]"Only wisdom is wholly turned into itself" (Cic. *De fin.* III.7.). [B]I leave it to artists, and I wot not whether in a matter so confused, so several, and so casual, they shall come to an end, to range into sides this infinite diversity of visages and settle our inconstancy and place it in order. I do not only find it difficult to combine our actions one unto another; but take every one apart, it is hard by any principal quality to design the same properly, so double, so ambiguous and parti-colored are they to divers lusters.

[C]Which in Perseus, the Macedonian King, was noted for a rare matter — that his spirit, fastening itself to no kind of condition, went wandering through every kind of life, and representing so new-fangled and gadding manners that he was neither known of himself nor of others what kind of man he was — methinks may well-nigh agree and suit with all the world. And above all, I have seen some other of his coat or humor to whom (as I suppose) this conclusion might also more properly be applied. No state of mediocrity, being ever transported from one extreme to another by indivinable occasions; no manner of course without cross and strange contrarieties; no faculty simple; so that the likeliest a man may one day conclude of him shall be that he affected and labored to make himself known by being not to be known.

[B]A man had need of long-tough ears to hear himself freely judged. And because there be few that can endure to hear it without tingling, those which adventure to undertake it with us show us a singular effect of true friendship. For that is a truly perfect love which to profit and do good feareth not to hurt or offend. I deem it absurd to censure him in whom bad qualities exceed good conditions. [C]Plato requireth three parts in him that will examine another's mind: learning, goodwill, and boldness.

[B]I was once demanded what I would have thought myself fit for, had any been disposed to make use of me when my years would have fitted service:

> While better blood gave strength, nor envious old years
> O'erlaid with wrinkled temples grew to hoary hairs.
>
> Virg. *Aen.* V.415.

I answered, "For nothing." And I willingly excuse myself that I can do nothing which may enthrall me to others. But had my fortune made me a servant, I would have told my master all truths and, had he so willed it, controlled his manners. Not in gross, by scholastical lessons, which I cannot do — besides, I see no true reformation to ensue in such as know them — but fair and softly and with every opportunity observing them, and simply and naturally judging them distinctly by the eye. Making him directly to perceive how and in what degree he is in the common opinion; opposing myself against his flatterers and sycophants. There is none of us but would be worse than kings if, as they are, we were continually corrupted with that rascally kind of people. But what? If Alexander, that mighty king and great philosopher, could not beware of them?

I should have had sufficient fidelity, judgment, and liberty for that. It would be a nameless office, otherwise it should lose both effect and grace; and is a part which cannot indifferently belong to all. For truth itself hath not the privilege to be employed at all times and in every kind. Be her use never so noble, it hath his circumscriptions and limits. It often cometh to pass, the world standing as it doth, that truth is whispered into princes' ears not only without fruit but hurtfully and therewithal unjustly. And no man shall make me believe but that an hallowed admonition may be viciously applied and abusively employed, and that the interest of the substance should not sometimes yield to the interest of the form.

For such a purpose and mystery I would have an unrepining man and one contented with his own fortune,

> Willing to be as him you see,
> Or rather nothing else to be,
> Mart. X.xlvii.12.

and born of mean degree. Forsomuch as on the one side he should not have cause to fear lively and nearly* to touch his master's heart, thereby not to lose the course of his preferment. And on the other side, being of a low condition, he should have more easy communication with all sorts of people. [C]Which I would have in one man alone, for to impart the privilege of such liberty and familiarity unto many would beget a hurtful irreverence. Yea, and of that man I would above all things require trusty and assured silence.

[B]A king is not to be credited when for his glory he boasteth of his constancy in attending his enemy's encounter, if for his good amendment and profit he cannot endure the liberty of his friend's words, which have no other working power than to pinch his learning, the rest of their effect remaining in his own hands. Now, there is not any condition of men that hath more need of true, sincerely free, and open-hearted advertisements than princes. They undergo a public life, and must applaud the opinion of so many spectators, that if they be once inured to have that concealed from them which diverteth them from their course, they at unawares and insensibly find themselves deeply engaged in the hatred and destestation of their subjects, many times for occasions which, had they been forewarned and in time gently reformed, they might no doubt have eschewed, to no interest or prejudice of their private delights. Favorites do commonly respect themselves more than their masters. And surely it toucheth their freehold, forsomuch as in good truth the greatest part of true friendship's offices are towards their sovereign in a crabbed and dangerous essay. So that there is not only required much affection and liberty, but also an undaunted courage.

To conclude, all this gallimaufry* which I huddle up here is but a register of my life's essays, which, in regard of the internal health, are sufficiently exemplary to take the instruction against the hair.[2] But concerning bodily health, no man is able to bring more profitable experience than myself, who present the same pure, sincere, and in no sort corrupted or altered, either by art or self-willed opinion. Experience in her own precinct may justly be compared to physic, unto which reason giveth place.

Tiberius was wont to say that whosoever had lived twenty years should be able to answer himself of all such things as were either wholesome or hurtful for him, and know how to live and order his body without physic. [C]Which he peradventure had learned of Socrates, who, industriously advising his disciples (as a study of chief consequence) to study their health, told them moreover that it was very hard if a man of understanding, heedfully observing his exercises, his eating and drinking, should not better than any physician discern and distinguish such things as were either good or bad or indifferent for him.

[B]Yet doth physic make open profession always to have experience for the touchstone of her operation. And Plato had reason to say that to be a good physician, it were requisite that he who should undertake that profession had passed through all such diseases as he will adventure to cure, and known or felt all the accidents and circumstances he is to judge of. It is reason, themselves should first have the pox if they will know how to cure them in others. I should surely trust such a one better than any else. Others but guide us as one who, sitting in his chair, paints seas, rocks, shelves, and havens upon a board, and makes the model of a tall ship, to sail in all safety; but put him to it in earnest, he knows not what to do, nor where to begin. They make even such a description of our infirmities as doth a town-

[2] *à contrepoil;* that is, as an example of what one should not be.

crier who crieth a lost horse or dog and describeth his hair, his stature, his ears, with other marks and tokens, but bring either unto him, he knows him not. O God, that physic would one day afford me some good and perceptible help, how earnestly would I exclaim,

> I yield, I yield at length,
> To knowledge of chief strength.
> Hor. *Epod.* XVII.1.

The arts that promise to keep our body and mind in good health promise much unto us, but therewith there is none performeth less what they promise. And in our days such as make profession of these arts amongst us do less than all others show their effects. The most may be said of them is that they sell medicinable drugs; but that they are physicians, no man can truly say it.

I have lived long enough to yield an account of the usage that hath brought me to this day. If any be disposed to taste of it, as his taster I have given him as assay.* Lo here some articles, digested as memory shall store me with them. [C]I have no fashion but hath varied according to accidents. I only register those I have most been acquainted with, and hitherto possess me most.

[B]My form of life is ever alike, both in sickness and in health — one same bed, the same hours, the same meat, the same drink, doth serve me. I add nothing to them but the moderation of more or less, according to my strength or appetite. My health is to keep my accustomed state free from care and trouble. I see that sickness doth on the one side in some sort divert me from it, and if I believe physicians, they on the other side will turn me from it. So that both by fortune and by art I am clean out of my right bias.

I believe nothing more certainly than this, that I cannot be offended by the use of things which I have so long accustomed. It is in the hands of custom to give our life what form it pleaseth; in that it can do all in all. It is the drink of Circe diversifieth our nature as she thinks good.

How many nations near bordering upon us imagine the fear of the *serein** or night-calm to be but a jest, which so apparently doth blast and hurt us? And whereof our mariners, our watermen, and our country men make but a laughing-stock? You make a German sick if you lay him upon a mattress, as you distemper an Italian upon a featherbed, and a Frenchman to lay him in a bed without curtains or lodge him in a chamber without a fire. A Spaniard cannot well brook to feed after our fashion, nor we endure to drink as the Switzers. A German pleased me well at [Augsburg] to rail against the commodity of our chimneys, using the same reasons or arguments that we ordinarily employ in condemning their stoves. For to say truth, the same close-smothered heat and the smell of that oft-heated matter, whereof they are composed, fumeth in the heads of such as are not accustomed unto them; not so with me. But on the other side, that heat being equally dispersed, constant, and universal, without flame or blazing, without smoke, and without that wind which the tunnels of our chimneys bring us, may many ways be compared unto ours.

Why do we not imitate the Romans' architecture? It is reported that in ancient times they made no fire in their houses but without and at the foot of them. Whence by tunnels, which were conveyed through their thickest walls and contrived near and about all such places as they would have warmed, so that the heat was conveyed into every part of the house. Which I have seen manifestly described in some place of Seneca, though I cannot well remember where.

This German, hearing me command the beauties and commodities of this city (which truly deserveth great commendation), began to pity me because I was shortly to go from it. And the first inconvenience he urged me withal was the heaviness in the head which chimneys in other places would cause me. He had heard some other body complain of it, and therefore alleged the same against me, being wont by custom to perceive it in such as came to him. All heat coming from fire doth weaken and dull me. Yet said Evenus that fire was the best sauce of life. I rather allow and embrace any other manner or way to escape cold.

We fear our wines when they are low, whereas in Portugal the fume of it is counted delicious and is the drink of princes. To conclude, each several nation hath divers customs, fashions, and usages which to some others are not only unknown and strange but savage, barbarous, and wondrous.

What shall we do unto that people that admit no witness except printed, that will not believe men if not printed in books, nor credit truth unless it be of competent age? [C]We dignify our fopperies when we put them to the press. [B]It is another manner of weight for him to say, "I have seen it," than if you say, "I have heard it reported." But I, who misbelieve no more the mouth than the hand of men, and know that men write as indiscreetly as they speak unadvisedly, and esteem of this present age as of another past, allege* as willingly a friend of mine as Aulus Gellius or Macrobius, and what myself have seen as that they have written.

[C]And as they account virtue to be nothing greater by being longer, so deem I truth to be nothing wiser by being more aged. [B]I often say it is mere folly that makes us run after strange and scholastical examples. The fertility of them is now equal unto that of Homer and

Plato's times. But is it not that we rather seek the honor of allegations than the truth of discourses? As if it were more to borrow our proofs from out the shop of Vascosan or Plantin[3] than from that we daily see in our village. Or verily that we have not the wit to blanch,* sift out, or make that to prevail which passeth before us, and forcibly judge of it, to draw the same into example. For if we say that authority fails us to add credit unto our testimony, we speak from the purpose. Forsomuch as in my conceit, could we but find out their true light, nature's greatest miracles and the most wonderful examples, namely upon the subject of human actions, may be drawn and formed from most ordinary, most common, and most known things.

Now, concerning my subject, omitting the examples I know by books, [C]and that which Aristotle speaketh of Andron of Argos, that he would travel all over the scorching sands of Lybia without drinking, [B]a gentleman who hath worthily acquitted himself of many honorable charges, reported where I was that in the parching heat of summer he had traveled from Madrid to Lisbon without ever drinking. His age respected, he is in very good and healthy plight, and hath nothing extraordinary in the course of custom of his life, saving (as himself hath told me) that he can very well continue two or three months, yea a whole year, without any manner of beverage. He sometimes finds himself thirsty but lets it pass, and holds that it is an appetite which will easily and of itself languish away. And if he drink at any time, it is more for a caprice or humor than for any need or pleasure.

Lo here one of another key. It is not long since that I found one of the wisest men of France (among those of [n]o mean fortune) studying hard in the corner of a great hall, which for that purpose was hung about with tapestry, and round about him a disordered rabble of his servants, grooms, and lackeys, prattling, playing and hoiting,* who told me [C](as Seneca in a manner saith of himself) [B]that he learned and profited much by that hurly-burly of tintamarre;* as if, beaten with that confused noise, he did so much the better recall and close himself into himself for serious contemplation, and that the said tempestuous rumors did strike and repercuss his thoughts inward. Whilst he was a scholar in Padua, his study was ever placed so near the jangling of bells, the rattling of coaches, and rumbling tumults of the market place, that for the service of his study he was fain, not only to frame and inure himself to contemn, but to make good use of that turbulent noise.

[C]Socrates answered Alcibiades, who wondered how he could endure the continual tittle-tattle and uncessant scolding of his wife: "Even as those who are accustomed to hear the ordinary creaking of the squeak-

3 Two printers.

ing wheels of wells." [B]Myself am clean contrary, for I have a tender brain and easy to take snuff in the nose or to be transported. If my mind be busy alone, the least stirring, yea the buzzing of a fly doth trouble and distemper the same.

[C]Seneca, in his youth, having earnestly undertaken to follow the example of Sextius to feed on nothing that were taken dead, could with pleasure (as himself averreth) live so a whole year. And left it only because he would not be suspected to borrow this rule from some new religions that instituted the same. He therewithal followed some precepts of Attalus not to lie upon any kind of carpets or bedding that would yield under one, and until he grew very aged he never used but such as they were very hard and unyielding to the body. What the custom of his days makes him account rudeness, ours makes us esteem wantonness.

[B]Behold the difference between my varlets' life and mine. The Indians have nothing further from my form and strength. Well I wot that I have heretofore taken boys from begging and that went roguing up and down, to serve me, hoping to do some good upon them; who have within a very little while after left me, my fare, and my livery, only that they might without control or check follow their former idle, loitering life. One of which I found not long since gathering of mussels in a common sink* for his dinner, whom (do what I could) I was never able, neither with entreaty to reclaim nor by threatening, to withdraw from the sweetness he found in want and delight he felt in roguing laziness. Even vagabondine rogues as well as rich men have their magnificences and voluptuousness, and (as some say) their dignities, pre-eminences, and politic orders.

They are effects of custom and use, and what is bred in the bone will never out of the flesh. Both which have power to inure and fashion us, not only to what form they please (therefore, say the wise, ought we to be addressed to the best and it will immediately seem easy unto us), but also to change and variation. Which is the noblest and most profitable of their apprenticeages.

The best of my corporal complexions is that I am flexible and little opinionative. I have certain inclinations, more proper and ordinary and more pleasing than others. But with small ado and without compulsion I can easily leave them and embrace the contrary. A young man should trouble his rules to stir up his vigor; and take heed he suffer not the same to grow faint, sluggish, or reesty.* For there is no course of life so weak and sottish as that which is managed by order, method, and discipline.

> List he ride in coach but to Mile-end,
> By the almanac he doth the hour attend:

If his eye corner itch, the remedy,
He fets from calculation of nativity.
Juven. VI.576.

If he believe me, he shall often give himself unto all manner of excess. Otherwise the least disorder will utterly overthrow him, and so make him unfit and unwelcome in all conversations. The most contrary quality in an honest man is nice-delicateness and to be tied to one certain particular fashion; it is particular if it be not supple and pliable. It is a kind of reproach through impuissance not to do or not to dare what one seeth his other companions do or dare. Let such men keep their kitchen. It is undecent in all other men, but vicious and intolerable in one professing arms, who (as Philopoemen said) should fashion himself to all manner of inequality and diversity of life.

Although I have (as much as might be) been inured to liberty and fashioned to indifferency, yet in growing aged I have through carelessness relied more upon certain forms (my age is now exempted from institution* and hath not anything else to look unto but to maintain itself) which custom hath already, without thinking on it, in certain things so well imprinted her character in me that I deem it a kind of excess to leave them. And without long practice, I can neither sleep by day, nor eat between meals, nor break my fast, nor go to bed without some intermission [C](as of three hours [B]after supper), nor get children but before I fall asleep and that never standing, nor bear mine own sweat, nor quench my thirst either with clear water or wine alone, nor continue long bare-headed, nor have mine hair cut after dinner. And I could as hardly spare my gloves as my shirt, or forbear washing of my hands both in the morning and rising from the table, or lie in a bed without a tester* and curtains about it, as of most necessary things.

I could dine without a tablecloth but hardly without a clean napkin, as Germans commonly do; I foul and sully them more than either they or the Italians, and I seldom use either spoon or fork. I am sorry we follow not a custom which according to the example of kings I have seen begun by some, that upon every course or change of dish, as we have shift of clean trenchers, so we might have change of clean napkins. We read that that laborious soldier Marius, growing old, grew more nicely delicate in his drinking and would taste no drink except in a peculiar cup of his. As for me, I observe a kind of like method in glasses and of one certain form, and drink not willingly in a common glass no more than of one ordinary hand. I mislike all manner of metal in regard of a bright, transparent matter; [C]let mine eyes also have taste of what I drink, according to their capacity. [B]I am beholden to custom for many such nicenesses and singularities.

Nature hath also on the other side bestowed this upon me, that I cannot well brook two full meals in one day without surcharging my stomach, nor the mere abstinence of one without filling myself with wind, drying my mouth, and dulling my appetite. And I do find great offense by a long *serein** or night-calm. For some years since, in the outroads or night-services that happen in times of wars, which many times continue all night, five or six hours after my stomach begins to qualm, my head feeleth a violent aching, so that I can hardly hold out till morning without vomiting. When others go to breakfast, I go to sleep, and within a while after I shall be as fresh and jolly as before.

I ever thought that the *serein** never fell but in the shutting in of night, but having in these latter years long time frequented very familiarly the conversation of a gentleman possessed with this opinion — that it is more sharp and dangerous about the declination of the Sun, an hour or two before it set, which he carefully escheweth, and despiseth that which falls at night — he hath gone about to persuade and imprint into me not only his discourse but also his conceit. What if the very doubt and inquisition woundeth our imagination and changeth us? Such as altogether yield to these bendings draw the whole ruin upon themselves. And I bewail divers gentlemen who, being young and in perfect health, have by the ignorant foolishness of their physicians brought themselves into consumptions and other lingering diseases, and as it were in physics' fetters. Were it not much better to be troubled with a rheum than forever through discustom, in an action of so great use and consequence, lose the commerce and conversation of common life? [C]O irksome learning! O science full of molestation, that wasteth us the sweetest hours of the day. [B]Let us extend our possession unto the utmost means. A man shall at last, in opinionating himself, harden and inure himself for it and so correct his complexion, as did Caesar the falling sickness, with contemning and corrupting the same. A man should apply himself to the best rules but not subject himself unto them, except to such (if any there be) that duty and thralldom unto them be profitable.

Both kings and philosophers obey nature and go to the stool, and so do ladies. Public lives are due unto ceremony; mine, which is obscure and private, enjoyeth all natural dispensations. To be a soldier and a Gascon are qualities somewhat subject to indiscretion. And I am both. Therefore will I say thus much of this action, that it is requisite we should remit the same unto certain prescribed night hours, and by custom (as I have done) force and subject ourselves unto it. But not (as I have done, growing in years) strictly tie himself to the care of a particular convenient place and of a commodious

Ajax* or easy close-stool* for that purpose, and make it troublesome with long sitting and nice observation. Nevertheless in homeliest matters and foulest offices, is it not in some sort excusable to require more care and cleanliness? C"By nature man is a cleanly and neat creature" (Sen. *Epist.* XCII.). Of all natural actions, there is none wherein I am more loath to be troubled or interrupted when I am at it. BI have seen divers great men and soldiers much troubled and vexed with their bellies' untune and disorder, when at untimely hours it calleth upon them; whilst mine and myself never miss to call one upon another at our appointment, which is as soon as I get out of my bed except some urgent business or violent sickness trouble me.

Therefore (as I said) I judge no place where sick men may better seat themselves in security than quietly and wish to hold themselves in that course of life wherein they have been brought up and habituated. Any change or variation soever astonieth* and distempereth. Will any believe that chestnuts can hurt a Périgordin or a Luquois, or that milk or white meats are hurtful unto a mountain-dwelling people? Whom if one seek to divert from their natural diet, he shall not only prescribe them a new but a contrary form of life, a change which healthy man can hardly endure. Appoint a Breton of threescore years of age to drink water, put a seaman or mariner into a stove, forbid a lackey of Basque to walk — you bring them out of their element, you deprive them of all motion, and in the end, of air, of light and life.

> Do we reckon it so dear,
> Only living to be here?
> Anon.[4]

> From things erst used we must suspend our mind,
> We leave to live that we may live by kind.
> Do I think they live longer, whom doth grieve
> Both air they breathe, and light whereby they live:
> Maxim. I.155, 247.

If they do no other good, at least they do this, that betimes they prepare their patients unto death by little undermining and cutting off the use of life.

Both in health and in sickness, I have willingly seconded and given myself over to those appetites that pressed me. I allow great authority to my desires and propensions. I love not to cure one evil by another mischief. I hate those remedies that importune more than sickness. To be subject to the colic and to be tied to abstain from the pleasure I have in eating of oysters, are two mischiefs for one.

4 "*An vivere tanti est?*" The author of this phrase is unknown. Montaigne relates in a letter that his friend La Boétie quoted these words on his deathbed.

The disease pincheth us on the one side, the rule on the other. Since we are ever in danger to misdo, let us rather hazard ourselves to follow pleasure. Most men do contrary, and think nothing profitable that is not painful; facility is by them suspected.

Mine appetite hath in divers things very happily accommodated and ranged itself to the health of my stomach. Being young, acrimony and tartness in sauces did greatly delight me, but my stomach being since glutted therewith, my taste hath likewise seconded the same. [C]Wine hurts the sick; it is the first thing that with an invincible distaste brings my mouth out of taste. [B]Whatsoever I receive unwillingly or distastefully hurts me, whereas nothing doth it whereon I feed with hunger and relish. I never received harm by any action that was very pleasing unto me. And yet I have made all medicinal conclusions largely to yield to my pleasures. And when I was young,

About whom Cupid running here and there,
Shined in the saffron coat which he did wear.
Catul. LXVI.133.

I have as licentiously and inconsiderately as any other furthered all such desires as possessed me;

A soldier of love's host,
I was not without boast.
Hor. *Odes* III.xxvi.2.

More, notwithstanding, in continuation and holding out than by snatches or by stealth.

I scarce remember past
Six courses I could last.
Ovid. *Amor.* III.vii.26.

It is surely a wonder, accompanied with unhappiness, to confess how young and weak I was brought under its subjection. Nay, shall I not blush to tell it?[5] It was long before the age of choice or years of discretion. I was so young as I remember nothing before. And fitly may my fortune be compared to that of Quartilla, who remembered not her maidenhead.

Thence goatishness, hairs over-soon a beard
To make my mother wonder and afeared.
Mart. XI.xxii.7.

Physicians commonly enfold and join their rules unto profit according to the violence of sharp desires or earnest longings that incidentally follow the sick. No longing desire can be imagined so

[5] This sentence is Florio's addition.

strange and vicious but nature will apply herself unto it. And then how easy is it to content one's fantasy? In mine opinion this part importeth all in all, at least more and beyond all other. The most grievous and ordinary evils are those which fancy chargeth us withal. That Spanish saying doth every way please me, "*Defiendame Dios de mí:* God defend me from myself."

Being sick, I am sorry I have not some desire may give me the contentment to satiate and cloy the same; scarcely would a medicine divert me from it. So do I when I am in health. I hardly see anything left to be hoped or wished for. It is pity a man should be so weakened and enlanguished that he hath nothing left him but wishing.

The art of physic is not so resolute that whatsoever we do we shall be void of all authority to do it. She changeth and she varieth according to climates, according to the moons, according to Fernelius, and according to Scala.[6] If your physician think it not good that you sleep, that you drink wine or eat such and such meats, care not you for that; I will find you another that shall not be of his opinion. The diversity of physical arguments and medicinal opinions embraceth all manner of forms. I saw a miserable sick man, for the infinite desire he had to recover ready to burst, yea and to die with thirst, whom not long since another physician mocked, utterly condemning the other's counsel as hurtful for him. Had not he bestowed his labor well? A man of that coat[7] is lately dead of the stone who during the time of his sickness used extreme abstinence to withstand his evil; his fellows affirm that contrary, his long fasting had withered and dried him up and so concocted the gravel in his kidneys.

I have found that in my hurts and other sicknesses earnest talking distempers and hurts me as much as any disorder I commit. My voice costs me dear and wearieth me, for I have it loud, shrill, and forced. So that when I have had occasion to entertain the ears of great men about weighty affairs, I have often troubled them with care how to moderate my voice.

This story deserveth to be remembered and to divert me. A certain man in one of the Greek schools spake very loud, as I do; the master of the ceremonies sent him word he should speak lower. "Let him (quoth he) send me the tune or key in which he would have me speak." The other replied that he should take his tune from his ears to whom he spake. It was well said, so he understood himself, "Speak according as you have to do with your auditory." For if one say, let it suffice that he heareth you, or govern yourself by him, I do not think he had reason to say so. The tune or motion of the voice hath

6 Fernel and L'Escale were two doctors of the time.

7 I.e., a doctor.

some expression or signification of my meaning. It is in me to direct the same, that so I may the better represent myself. There is a voice to instruct, one to flatter, and another to chide. I will not only have my voice come to him, but peradventure to wound and pierce him. When I brawl and rate my lackey with a sharp and piercing tune, were it fit he should come to me and say, "Master, speak softly. I understand and hear you very well"? C"There is a kind of voice well applied to the hearing, not by the greatness of it, but by the propriety" (Quint. XI.3.). BThe word is half his that speaketh and half his that hearkeneth unto it. The hearer ought to prepare himself to the motion or bound it taketh. As between those that play at tennis, he who keeps the hazard doth prepare, stand, stir, and march according as he perceives him who stands at the house to look, stand, remove, and strike the ball, and according to the stroke.

Experience hath also taught me this, that we lose ourselves with impatience. Evils have their life, their limits; Ctheir diseases and their health. The constitution of diseases is framed by the pattern of the constitution of living creatures. They have their fortune limited even at their birth, and their days allotted them. He that shall imperiously go about or by compulsion (contrary to their courses) to abridge them, doth lengthen and multiply them, and instead of appeasing, doth harsell* and wring them. I am of Crantor's opinion, that a man must neither obstinately nor frantically oppose himself against evils, nor through demissness of courage faintingly yield unto them, but according to their condition and ours, naturally incline to them.

BA man must give sicknesses their passage; and I find that they stay least with me, because I allow them their swing and let them do what they list. And contrary to common received rules, I have without aid or art rid myself of some that are deemed the most obstinately lingering and unremovably obstinate. Let nature work; let her have her will. She knoweth what she hath to do and understands herself better than we do. "But such a one died of it," will you say. So shall you, doubtless; if not of that, yet of some other disease. And how many have we seen die when they have had a whole college of physicians round about their bed and looking in their excrements? Example is a bright looking-glass, universal and for all shapes to look into. If it be a luscious or taste-pleasing potion, take it hardly; it is ever so much present ease. CSo it be delicious and sweetly tasting, I will never stand much upon the name or color of it. Pleasure is one of the chiefest kinds of profit.

BI have suffered rheums, gouty defluxions, relaxations, pantings of the heart, migraines, and other suchlike accidents to grow old in me and die their natural death; all which have left me when I half inured and framed myself to foster them. They are better conjured by courtesy than by bragging or threats.

We must gently obey and endure the laws of our condition. We are subject to grow aged, to become weak, and to fall sick, in spite of all physic. It is the first lesson the Mexicans give their children. When they come out of their mother's wombs, they thus salute them: "My child, thou art come into the world to suffer; therefore suffer and hold thy peace."

It is injustice for one to grieve that anything hath befallen to anyone which may happen to all men. [C]"Then take it ill if anything be decreed unjustly against thee alone" (Sen. *Epist.* XCI.). [B]Look on an aged man who sueth unto God to maintain him in perfect, full, and vigorous health, that is to say he will be pleased to make him young again:

> Fool, why dost thou in vain desire,
> With childish prayers thus to aspire?
> Ovid. *Trist.* III.viii.11.

Is it not folly? His condition will not bear it. [C]The gout, the stone, the gravel, and indigestion are symptoms or effects of long-continued years, as heats, rains, and winds are incident to long voyages. Plato cannot believe that Aesculapius troubled himself with good rules and diet to provide for the preservation of life in a weak, wasted, and corrupted body, being unprofitable for his country, inconvenient for his vocation, and unfit to get sound and sturdy children; and deem[s] not that care convenient unto divine justice and heavenly wisdom, which is to direct all things unto profit. [B]My good sir, the matter is at an end. You cannot be recovered. For the most you can be but tampered withal and somewhat underpropped, [C]and for some hours have your misery prolonged.

> [B]So he that would an instant ruin stay
> With divers props strives it underlay,
> Till all the frame dissolv'd a certain day,
> The props with the edifice doth oversway.
> Maximianus I.171.

A man must learn to endure that patiently which he cannot avoid conveniently. Our life is composed, as is the harmony of the world, of contrary things; so of divers tunes, some pleasant, some harsh, some sharp, some flat, some low and some high. What would that musician say that should love but some one of them? He ought to know how to use them severally and how to intermingle them. So should we both of goods and evils, which are consubstantial to our life. Our being cannot subsist without this commixture, whereto one side is no less necessary than the other. To go about to kick against natural necessity were to represent the folly of Ctesiphon, who undertook to strike or wince* with his mule.

I consult but little about the alterations which I feel, for these kind of men are advantageous* when they hold you at their mercy. They glut your ears with their prognostications, and surprising me heretofore, when by my sickness I was brought very low and weak, they have injuriously handled me with their doctrines, positions, prescriptions, magistral fopperies and prosopopoeial* gravity; sometimes threatening me with great pain and smart, and other times menacing me with near and unavoidable death. All which did indeed move, stir, and touch me near, but could not dismay or remove me from my place or resolution. If my judgment be thereby neither changed nor troubled, it was at least hindered. It is ever in agitation and combating.

Now I entreat my imagination as gently as I can, and were it in my power, I would clean discharge it of all pain and contestation. A man must further, help, flatter, and (if he can) cozen and deceive it. My spirit is fit for that office. There is no want of apparencies* everywhere.

Did he persuade as he preacheth, he should successfully aid me. Shall I give you an example? He tells me it is for my good that I am troubled with the gravel, that the compositions of my age must naturally suffer some leak or flaw; it is time they begin to relent and gainsay themselves. It is a common necessity, and it had been no new wonder for me. That way I pay the reward due unto age, and I could have no better reckoning of it. That such company ought to comfort me, being fallen into the most ordinary accident incident to men of my days. I everywhere see some afflicted with the same kind of evil, whose society is honorable unto me forsomuch as it commonly possesseth the better sort of men, and whose essence hath a certain nobility and dignity connected unto it.

That of men tormented therewith, few are better cheap quit of it, and yet it costs them the pain of a troublesome diet, tedious regiment, and daily loathsome taking of medicinal drugs and physical potions. Whereas I merely owe it to my good fortune, for some ordinary broths made of eryngo* or sea-holme, and burstwort* — which twice or thrice I have swallowed down at the request of some ladies who, more kindly than my disease is unkind, offered me the moiety* of theirs — have equally seemed unto me as easy to take as unprofitable in operation. They must pay a thousand vows unto Aesculapius and as many crowns to their physician for an easy profluvion* or abundant running of gravel, which I often receive by the benefit of nature. [C]Let me be in any company, the decency of my countenance is thereby nothing troubled, and I can hold my water full ten hours, and, if need be, as long as many man that is in perfect health.

[B]The fear of this evil (saith he) did heretofore affright thee, when yet it was unknown to thee. The cries and despair of those who through their impatience exasperate the same, bred a horror of it in thee. It is an evil that comes and falls into those limbs by and with which thou hast most offended; thou art a man of conscience:

> The pain that comes without desert,
> Comes to us with more grief and smart.
>
> Ovid. *Heroid.* V.8.

Consider but how mild the punishment is in respect of others, and how favorable. Consider his slowness in coming. He only incommodeth that state and encumbreth that season of thy life which (all things considered) is now become barren and lost, having as it were by way of composition given place unto the sensual licentiousness and wanton pleasures of thy youth.

The fear and pity men have of this evil may serve thee as a cause of glory. A quality whereof, if thy judgment be purified and thy discourse perfectly sound, thy friends do notwithstanding discover some sparks in thy complexion. It is some pleasure for a man to hear others say of him, "Lo there a pattern of true fortitude; lo there a mirror of matchless patience." Thou art seen to sweat with labor, to grow pale and wan, to wax red, to quake and tremble, to cast and vomit blood, to endure strange contractions, to brook convulsions, to trill down brackish and great tears, to make thick, muddy black, bloody, and fearful urine, or to have it stopped by some sharp or rugged stone which pricketh and cruelly wringeth the neck of the yard;* entertaining in the meanwhile the bystanders with an ordinary and undaunted countenance, by pauses jesting and by intermissions dallying with thy servants, keeping a part in a continued discourse, with words now and then excusing thy grief and abating thy painful sufferance.

Dost thou remember those men of former ages who to keep their virtue in breath and exercise, did with such greediness seek after evils? Suppose nature driveth and bringeth thee into that glorious school into which thou hadst never come of thine own accord and free will. If thou tell me it is a dangerous and mortal evil, what others are not so? For it is a kind of physical cozenage to except any and so they go [not] directly unto death. What matter is it whether they go by accident unto it, and easily slide on either hand toward the way that leadeth us thereunto? [C]But thou diest not because thou art sick; thou diest because thou art living. Death is able to kill thee without the help of any sickness. Sicknesses have to some prolonged their death, who have lived the longer inasmuch as they imagined they were still dying. Seeing it is of wounds as of diseases, that some are medicinal and wholesome.

[B]The colic is often no less long-lived than you. Many are seen in whom it hath continued even from their infancy unto their extremest age, who, had they not forsaken her company, she was like to have assisted them further. You oftener kill her than she doth you. And if she did present thee with the image of near-imminent death, were it not a kind office for a man of that age to reduce it unto the cogitations of his end? [C]And, which is worse, thou hast no longer cause to be cured. Thus and howsoever, common necessity calls for thee against the first day.

[B]Consider but how artificially and how mildly she brings thee in distaste with life and out of liking with the world, not forcing thee with a tyrannical subjection, as infinite other diseases do wherewith thou seest old men posssessed — which continually hold them fettered and ensnared and without release of weakness nor intermission of pains — but by advertisements and instructions, reprised by intervals, intermixing certain pauses of rest, as if it were to give thee mean at thy ease to meditate and repeat her lesson. To give thee leisure and ability to judge soundly and like a man of a courage to take a resolution, she presents thee with the state of thy condition perfect, both in good and evil, and in one same day, sometimes a most pleasing, sometimes a most intolerable life. If thou embrace not death, at least thou shakest her by the hand once a month. [C]Whereby thou hast more cause to hope that she will one day surprise thee without threatening; and that being so often brought into the haven, supposing to be still in thy accustomed state, one morning at unawares both thyself and thy confidence shall be transported over. [B]A man hath no reason to complain against those diseases which so equally divide time with health.

I am beholden to fortune that she so often assails me with one same kind of weapon; she by long use doth fashion and inure me unto it, harden and habituate me thereunto. I now know within a little which way and how I shall be quit. [C]For want of natural memory I frame some of paper. And when some new symptom or accident cometh to my evil, I set it down in writing. Whence it proceedeth that having now (in a manner) passed over and through all sorts of examples, if any astonishment threaten me, running and turning over these my loose memorials (as Sibylla's leaves), I miss no more to find to comfort me with some favorable prognostication in my former past experience. [B]Custom doth also serve me to hope the better hereafter. For the conduct of this distribution, having so long been constituted, it is to be supposed that nature will not change this course and no other worse accident shall follow than that I feel. Moreover, the condition of this disease is not ill-seeming to my ready and sudden complexion. When it but faintly assails me it makes me afraid, because it is like to continue long. But naturally it hath certain vigorous and violent excesses. It doth violently shake me for one or two days.

My reins* have continued a whole age without alteration; another is now well-nigh come that they have changed state. Evils as well as goods have their periods; this accident is haply come to his last. Age weakeneth the heat of my stomach; his digestion being thereby less perfect, he sendeth this crude matter to my reins.* Why may not, at a certain revolution, the heat of my reins* be likewise enfeebled, so that they may no longer p[e]trify my phlegm and nature address herself to find some other course of purgation? Years have evidently made me dry up certain rheums, and why not these excrements that minister matter to the stone or gravel?

But is there anything so pleasant in respect of this sudden change, when by an extreme pain I come by the voiding of my stone to recover, as from a lightning, the fair sunshine of health so free and full, as it happeneth in our sudden and most violent colics? Is there anything in this pain suffered that may be counterpoised* to the sweet pleasure of so ready an amendment? By how much more health seemeth fairer unto me after sickness, so near and so contiguous that I may know them in presence one of another in their richest ornaments, wherein they attire themselves avie,* as it were confront and countercheck one another. Even as the Stoics say, that vices were profitably brought in to give esteem and make head unto virtue, so may we with better reason and bold conjecture affirm that nature hath lent us grief and pain for the honor of pleasure and service of indolency.

When Socrates (after he had his irons or fetters taken from him) felt the pleasure or tickling of that itching which their weight and rubbing had caused in his legs, he rejoiced to consider the near affinity that was between pain and pleasure, how they combined together by a necessary bond so that at turns they interengender and succeed one another. And cried out to good Aesop that he should from that consideration have taken a proper body unto a quaint fable.

The worst I see in other diseases is that they are not so grievous in their effect as in their issue. A man is a whole year to recover himself, ever full of weakness, always full of fear. There is so much hazard and so many degrees before one can be brought to safety that he is never at an end. Before you can leave off your coverchief* and then your night-cap, before you can brook the air again or have leave to drink wine or lie with your wife, or eat melons, it is much if you fall not into some relapse or new misery. The gravel hath this privilege, that it is clean carried away, whereas other maladies leave ever some impression and alteration which leaveth the body susceptible or undertaking of some new infirmity, and they lend one another their hands. Such are to be excused as are contented with the possession they have over us, without extending the same and without introducing their sequel.

But courteous, kind, and gracious are those whose passage brings us some profitable consequence. Since I have had the stone colic, I find myself discharged of other accidents more (as methinks) than I was before, and never had ague since. I argue that the extreme and frequent vomits I endure purge me; and on the other side, the distastes and strange abstinences I tolerate, digest my offending humors, and nature voideth in these stones and gravel whatsoever is superfluous and hurtful in her. Let no man tell me that it is a medicine too dear sold. For what avail so many loathsome pills, stinking potions, cauterizings, incisions, sweatings, setons, diets, and so divers fashions of curing, which because we are not able to undergo their violence and brook their importunity, do often bring us unto our graves? And therefore when I am surprised I take it as physic, and when I am free I take it as a constant and full deliverance.

Lo here another particular favor of my disease, which is that he in a manner keeps his play apart and lets me keep mine own, or else I want but courage to do it. In his greatest emotion I have held out ten hours on horseback with him. Do but endure, you need no other rule or regiment. Play, dally, dine, run, be gamesome, do this, and if you can, do the other thing; your disorder and debauching will rather avail than hurt it. Say thus much to one that hath the pox, or to one that hath the gout, or to one that is bellybroken* or cod-burst.* Other infirmities have more universal bonds, torment far otherwise our actions, pervert all our order, and engage all the state of man's life unto their consideration, whereas this doth only twitch and pinch the skin. It neither meddleth with your understanding nor with your will, tongue, feet nor hands, but leaves them all in your disposition. It rather rouseth and awaketh you than deter and drowsy you. The mind is wounded by the burning of a fever, suppressed by an epilepsy, confounded by a migraine, and in conclusion, astonied and dismayed by all the diseases that touch or wound the whole mass of his body and its noblest parts. This never meddleth with it. If therefore it go ill with it, his be the blame; she betrayeth, she forsaketh, and she displaceth herself.

None but fools will be persuaded that this hard, gritty, and massy body which is concocted and petrified in our kidneys, may be dissolved by drinks. And therefore after it is stirred there is no way but to give it passage. For if you do not, he will take it himself.

This other peculiar commodity I observe, that it is an infirmity wherein we have but little to divine. We are dispensed from the trouble whereinto other maladies cast us by the uncertainty of their causes, conditions, and progresses; a trouble infinitely painful. We have no need of doctoral consultations or collegial interpretations. Our senses tell us where it is and what it is.

By and with such arguments, forcible or weak (as Cicero doth the infirmity of his old age), I endeavor to lull asleep and study to amuse my imagination and supple or anoint her sores. If they grow worse tomorrow, tomorrow we shall provide for new remedies or escapes.

[C]That this is true, lo afterward again haply the lighest motion wrings pure blood out of my reins.* And what of that? I omit not to stir as before, and with a youthful and insolent heat ride after my hound. And find that I have great reason of so important an accident which costs me but a deaf heaviness and dumb alteration in that part. It is some great stone that wasteth and consumeth the substance of my kidneys and my life, which I void by little and little, not without some natural pleasure, as an excrement now superfluous and troublesome. [B]And feel I something to shake? Expect not that I amuse myself to feel my pulse or look into my urine, thereby to find or take some tedious prevention. I shall come time enough to feel the smart without lengthening the same with the pain of fear. [C]Who feareth to suffer, suffereth already because he feareth.

Seeing the doubt and ignorance of those who will and do meddle with expounding the drifts and shifts of nature, with her internal progress, and so many false prognostications of their art should make us understand her means infinitely unknown. There is great uncertainty, variety, and obscurity in that she promiseth and menaceth us. Except old age — which is an undoubted sign of death's approaching — of all other accidents I see few signs of future things whereon we may ground our divination. [B]I only judge myself by true-feeling sense and not by discourse. To what end? since I will add nothing thereunto except attention and patience. Will you know what I gain by it? Behold those who do otherwise and who depend on so many divers persuasions and counsels, how oft imagination presseth them without the body. I have divers times, being in safety and free from all dangerous accidents, taken pleasure to communicate them unto physicians as but then coming upon me. I endured the arrest or doom of their horrible conclusions and remained so much the more bounden unto God for his grace and better instructed of the vanity of this art.

Nothing ought so much be recommended unto youth as activity and vigilancy. Our life is nothing but motion. I am hardly shaken, and am slow in all things, be it to rise, to go to bed, or to my meals. Seven of the clock in the morning is to me an early hour. And where I may command, I neither dine before eleven nor sup till after six. I have heretofore imputed the causes of agues or maladies whereinto I have fallen, to the lumpish heaviness or drowsy dullness which my long sleeping had caused me, and ever repented me to fall asleep again in the morning. [C]Plato condemns more the excess of sleeping than the surfeit of drinking.

[B]I love to lie hard and alone, yea and without a woman by me, after the kingly manner, somewhat well and warm-covered. I never have my bed warmed, but since I came to be an old man, if need require, I have clothes given me to warm my feet and my stomach. Great Scipio was taxed to be a sluggard or heavy sleeper (in my conceit) for no other cause but that men were offended he only should be the man in whom no fault might justly be found.

If there be any curiosity in my behavior or manner of life, it is rather about my going to bed than anything else, but if need be, I generally yield and accommodate myself unto necessity as well and as quietly as any other whosoever. Sleeping hath possessed a great part of my life, and as old as I am, I can sleep eight or nine hours together. I do with profit withdraw myself from this sluggish propension and evidently find myself better by it. Indeed I somewhat feel the stroke of alteration, but in three days it is past. And I see few that live with less (when need is), and that more constantly exercise themselves, nor whom toiling and labor offend less.

My body is capable of a firm agitation, so it be not vehement and sudden. I avoid violent exercises and which induce me to sweat; my limbs will sooner be wearied than heated. I can stand a whole day long and am seldom weary with walking. [C]Since my first age I ever loved rather [B]to ride than walk upon paved streets. Going afoot, I shall dirty myself up to the waist, and little men going alongst our streets are subject (for want of presential* appearance) to be jostled [C]or elbowed. [B]I love to take my rest, be it sitting or lying along, with my legs as high or higher than my seat.

No profession or occupation is more pleasing than the military; a profession or exercise both noble in execution (for the strongest, most generous, and proudest of all virtues is true valor) and noble in its cause. No utility either more just or universal than the protection of the repose or defense of the greatness of one's country. The company and daily conversation of so many noble, young, and active men cannot but be well-pleasing to you: the daily and ordinary sight of so divers tragical spectacles, the liberty and uncontrolled freedom of that artless and unaffected conversation, masculine and ceremoniless manner of life, the hourly variety of a thousand ever-changing and differing actions, the courageous and mind-stirring harmony of warlike music, which at once entertaineth with delight and inflameth with longing both your ears and your mind, the imminent and matchless honor of that exercise — yea the very sharpness and difficulty of it, [C]which Plato esteemeth so little that in his imaginary commonwealth he imparteth the same both to women and to children. As a voluntary soldier [B]or adventurous knight [B]you enter the lists, the bands or particular hazards, according as yourself judge of their successes or importance, and you see when your life may therein be excusably employed.

And nobly it doth come in mind,
To die in arms may honor find.
Virg. *Aen.* II.317.

Basely to fear common dangers that concern so numberless a multitude and not to dare what so many sorts of men dare, yea whole nations together, is only incident to base, craven, and milksop hearts. Company and good fellowship doth hearten and encourage children. If some chance to exceed and outgo you in knowledge, in experience, in grace, in strength, in fortune, you have third and collateral causes to blame and take hold of. But to yield to them in constancy of mind and resolution of courage, you have none but yourself to find fault with.

Death is much more abject, languishing, grisly, and painful in a down bed than in a field-combat; and agues, catarrhs, or apoplexies as painful and mortal as an harquebusade. He that should be made undauntedly to bear the accidents of common life should not need to bombast his courage to become a man at arms. [C]"Friend mine, to live is to go on warfare" (Sen. *Epist.* XCVI.).

I cannot remember that ever I was scabbed; yet is itching one of nature's sweetest gratifications, and as ready at hand. But repentance doth over-importantly attend on it. I exercise the same in mine ears (and by fits), which within do often itch.

[B]I was born with all my senses sound, almost in perfection. My stomach is commodiously good and so is my head, both which, together with my wind, maintain themselves athwart* my agues. I have outlived that age[8] to which some nations have not without some

[8] Florio here follows the text of 1588. Montaigne later changed this to read: "I have outlived [C]by six years now my fiftieth year, [B]which some nations . . ."

reason prescribed for a just end unto life, that they allowed not a man to exceed the same. I have notwithstanding some remisses or intermissions yet, though unconstant and short, so sound and neat that there is little difference between them and the health and indolency of my youth. I speak not of youthly vigor and cheerful blitheness; there is no reason they should follow me beyond their limits:

> These sides cannot still sustain
> Lying without doors, showering rain.
> Hor. *Odes* III.x.19.

My visage [C]and eyes [B] do presently discover* me. Thence begin all my changes, and somewhat sharper than they are in effect. I often move my friends to pity ere I feel the cause of it. My looking-glass doth not amaze me, for even in my youth it hath divers times befallen me so to put on a dusky look, a wan color, a troubled behavior and of ill presage, without any great accident; so that physicians, perceiving no inward cause to answer this outward alteration, ascribed the same to the secret mind or some concealed passion which inwardly gnawed and consumed me. They were deceived. Were my body directly by me, as is my mind, we should march a little more at our ease. I had it then not only exempted from all trouble but also full of satisfaction and blitheness, as it is most commonly, partly by its own complexion and partly by its own design:

> Nor doth sick mind's infection,
> Pollute strong joints' complexion.
> Ovid. *Trist.* III.viii.25.

I am of opinion that this her[9] temperature* hath often raised my body from his fallings; he is often suppressed, whereas she, if not lasciviously wanton, at least in quiet and reposed estate. I had a quartan argue which held me four or five months and had altogether disvisaged and altered my countenance, yet my mind held ever out not only peaceably but pleasantly. So I feel no pain or smart, weakness and languishing do not greatly perplex me. I see divers corporal defailances,* the only naming of which breed a kind of horror, and which I would fear less than a thousand passions and agitations of the mind, which I see in use. I resolve to run no more. It sufficeth me to go on fair and softly; nor do I complain of their natural decadence or empairing* that possesseth me.

> Who wonders a swollen throat to see,
> In those about the Alps that be?
> Juven. *Sat.* XIII.162.

9 In this sentence *her* and *she* refer to the mind, *his* and *he* to the body.

No more than I grieve that my continuance is not as long and sound as that of an oak.

I have no cause to find fault with my imagination. I have in my life had very few thoughts or cares that have so much as interrupted the course of my sleep, except of desire, to awaken without dismay or afflicting me. I seldom dream, and when I do it is of extravagant things and chimeras, commonly produced of pleasant conceits, rather ridiculous than sorrowful. And think it true that dreams are the true interpreters of our inclinations; but great skill is required to sort and understand them.

> [C]It is no wonder if the things which we
> Care for, use, think, do oft, or waking see,
> Unto us sleeping represented be.
> Accius, in Cic. *De div.* I.22.

Plato saith, moreover, that is the office of wisdom to draw divining instructions from them against future times. Wherein I see nothing but the wonderful experience that Socrates, Xenophon, and Aristotle relate of them, men of unreprovable authority. Histories report that the inhabitants of the Atlantic Isles never dream, who feed on nothing that hath been slain. Which I add because it is peradventure the occasion they dream not. Pythagoras ordained therefore a certain method of feeding, that dreams might be sorted of some purpose.

Mine are tender and cause no agitation of body or expression of voice in me. I have in my days seen many strangely stirred with them. Theon the philosopher walked in dreaming, and Pericles his boy went upon the tiles and top of houses.

[B]I stand not much on nice choice of meats at the table, and commonly begin with the first and nearest dish, and leap not willingly from one taste to another. Multitude of dishes and variety of services displease me as much as any other throng. I am easily pleased with few messes,* and hate the opinion of Favorinus, that at a banquet you must have that dish whereon you feed hungrily taken from you and ever have a new one set in the place, and that it is a niggardly supper if all the guests be not glutted with pinions and rumps of divers kinds of fowl, and that only the dainty bird *beccafico,* or snapfig, deserveth to be eaten whole at one morsel.

I feed much upon salt cates,* and love to have my bread somewhat fresh[10]; and mine own baker makes none other for my board, against the fashion of my country. In my youth my overseers had much ado to reform the refusal I made of such meats as youth doth commonly love best, as sweetmeats, confets,* and marchpanes.* My tutor was

10 I.e., unsalted.

wont to find great fault with my loathing of such dainties, as a kind of squeamish delicacy. And to say truth, it is nothing but a difficulty of taste, where it once is applied. Whosoever removeth from a child a certain particular or obstinate affection to brown bread, to bacon, or to garlic, taketh friandise* from him. There are some that make it a labor and think it a patience to regret a good piece of powdered beef or a good gammon of bacon amongst partridges. Are not they wise men in the meantime? It is the chief dainty of all dainties. It is the taste of nice, effeminate fortune that will be distasted with ordinary and usual things. [C]"Whereby the lavishness of plenty plays with tedious pleasure" (Sen. *Epist.* XVIII.). [B]To forbear to make good cheer because another doth it, for one to have care of his feeding, is the essence of that vice.

> If in a sorry dish to sup
> You brook not all the herb pottage up.
> Hor. *Epist.* I.v.2.

Indeed there is this difference, that it is better for one to tie his desires unto things easiest to be gotten; yet is it a vice to tie himself to any strictness. I was heretofore wont to name a kinsman of mine over-delicate because whilst he lived in our galleys he had unlearned and left to lie upon a bed and to strip himself to go to bed.

Had I any male children, I should willingly wish them my fortune. That good father it pleased God to allot me (who hath nothing of me but thankfulness for his goodness, which indeed is as great as great may be) even from my cradle sent me to be brought up in a poor village of his, where he kept me so long as I sucked and somewhat longer, breeding me after the meanest and simplest common fashion: [C]"A mannerly belly is a great part of a man's liberty" (Sen. *Epist.* CXXIII.). [B]Never take unto yourself, and much less never give your wives, the charge of your children's breeding or education. Let fortune frame them under the popular and natural laws. Let custom inure them to frugality and breed them to hardness, that they may rather descend from sharpness than ascend unto it.

His conceit aimed also at another end; to acquaint and re-ally me with that people and condition of men that have most need of us. And thought I was rather bound to respect those which extend their arms unto me than such as turn their back toward me. And that was the reason he chose no other gossips* to hold me at the font than men of abject and base fortune, that so I might the more be bound and tied unto them. His purpose hath not altogether succeeded ill. I willingly give and accost myself unto the meaner sort, whether it be because there is more glory gotten by them, or through some natural compassion, which in me is infinitely powerful. [C]The faction which I condemn in our civil wars, I shall more sharply condemn when it prospers and flourisheth. I shall in some sort be reconciled unto it when I see it miserably depressed and overwhelmed.[11]

[B]Oh, how willingly do I remember that worthy humor of Chelonis, daughter and wife to king[s] of Sparta. Whilst Cleombrotus, her husband, in the tumultuous disorders of his city had the upper hand of Leonidas, her father, she played the part of a good daughter, allying herself with her father in his exile and in his misery, mainly opposing herself against the conqueror. Did fortune turn? So changed she her mind, courageously taking her husband's part, whom she never forsook, whithersoever his ruin or distress carried him. Having (in my seeming) no other choice than to follow that side where she might do most good, where she was most wanted, and where she might show herself most truly pitiful. I do more naturally incline toward the example of Flamineus, who more and rather yielded to such as had need of him than to those who might do him good, than I bend unto that of Pyrrhus, who was ever wont demissly* to stoop and yield to the mighty and insolently to grow proud over the weak.

Long sitting at meals doth much [C]weary and [B]distemper me, for be it for want of better countenance and entertainment, or that I used myself unto it when I was a child, I feed as long as I sit at the table. And therefore being in mine own house, [C]though my board be but short and that we use not to sit long, [B]I do not commonly sit down with the first but a pretty while after others. According to the form of Augustus; yet I imitate him not in his rising before others. Contrary, I love to sit a great while after and to hear some discourse or table talk. Always provided I bear not a part myself, for if my belly be full, I shall soon be weary and hurt myself with talking. And I find the exercise of loud-speaking and contesting before meat very pleasant and wholesome. [C]The ancient Grecians and Romans had better reason than we, allotting unto feeding, which is a principal action of man's life (if any other extraordinary business did not let or divert them from it), divers hours and the best part of the night, eating and drinking more leisurely than we do, who pass and run over all our actions in post-haste, and extending this natural pleasure unto more leisure and use, intermixing therewith divers profitable and mind-pleasing offices of civil conversation.

[B]Such as have care of me may easily steal from me whatsoever they

[11] In the edition of 1588 Montaigne had employed less prudent tenses here and had written: "In our troubles I condemn the cause of one of the parties, but more when it flourishes and prospers; at times I have been more reconciled to it when I saw it miserable and crushed."

imagine may be hurtful for me, inasmuch as about my feeding I never desire or find fault with that I see not. That proverb is verified in me: "What eye seeth not, the heart rueth not."[12] But if a dish or anything else be once set before me, they lose their labor that go about to tell me of abstinence. So that when I am disposed to fast I must be sequestered from eaters and have no more set before me than may serve for a stinted and regular collation, for if I but sit down at a set table, I forget my resolution. If I chance to bid my cook change the dressing of some kind of meat or dish, all my men know I infer my appetite is wallowish* and my stomach out of order and I shall hardly touch it.

I love all manner of flesh or fowl, but green-roasted and raw-sodden, namely, such as may bear it without danger; and love to have them thoroughly mortified* and, in divers of them, the very alteration of their smell. Only hardness or toughness of meat doth generally molest me (of all other qualities I am as careless and can as well brook them as any man that ever I knew), so that (contrary to received opinion) even amongst fishes I shall find some both too new and over-hard and firm. It is not the fault or want of teeth, which I ever had as perfectly sound and complete as any other man and which but now, being so old, begin to threaten me. I have from my infancy learned to rub them with my napkin, both in the morning when I rise, and sitting down and rising from the table.

God doth them a grace from whom by little and little he doth subtract their life. It is the only benefit of old age. Their last death shall be so much the less full languishing and painful; it shall then kill but one half or a quarter of a man. Even now I lost one of my teeth, which of itself fell out, without struggling or pain; it was the natural term of its continuance. That part of my being, with divers others, are already dead and mortified in me; others of the most active, half dead, and which during the vigor of my age held the first rank. Thus I sink and escape from myself. What foolishness will it be in my understanding to feel the start of that fall, already so advanced, as it were perfectly whole? I hope it not; [C]verily I receive a special comfort in thinking on my death and that it shall be of the most just and natural, and cannot now require or hope other favor of destiny concerning that than unlawful.

Men persuade themselves that, as heretofore they have had a higher stature, so their lives were longer. But they are deceived. For Solon, of those ancient times, though he were of an exceeding high stature his life continued but seventy years. Shall I that have so much and so universally adored that ἄριστον μέτρον (a mean is best) of former

12 This sentence is added by Florio.

times, and have ever taken a mean measure for the most perfect, therefore pretend a most prodigious and unmeasurable life? Whatsoever cometh contrary to nature's course may be cumbersome, but what comes according to her should ever please. "All things are to be accounted good that are done according to nature" (Cic. *De Senect.* XIX.). And therefore (saith Plato) is that death violent which is caused either by wounds or sicknesses, but that of all others the easiest and in some sort delicious, which surpriseth us by no means of age. "A forcible violence takes their life from the young, but a ripe maturity from the old" (Cic. *De Senect.* XIX.).

[B]Death intermeddleth and everywhere confounds itself with our life; declination doth preoccupate her hour and insinuate itself in the very course of our advancement. I have pictures of mine own that were drawn when I was five and twenty, and others being thirty years of age, which I often compare with such as were made by me as I am now at this instant. How many times do I say, "I am no more myself." How much is my present image further from those than from that of my decrease? It is an over-great abuse unto nature to drag and hurry her so far that she must be forced to give us over, and abandon our conduct, our eyes, our teeth, our legs, and the rest to the mercy of a foreign help and begged assistance, and to put ourselves into the hands of art, weary to follow us.

I am not overmuch or greedily desirous of salads or of fruits except melons. My father hated all manner of sauces; I love them all. Overmuch eating doth hurt and distemper me, but for the quality I have yet no certain knowledge that any meat offends me. I never observe either a full or waned moon, nor make a difference between the springtime or autumn. There are certain inconstant and unknown motions in us. For (by way of example) I have heretofore found radish roots to be very good for me, then very hurtful, and now again very well agreeing with my stomach. In divers other things I feel my appetite to change and my stomach to diversify from time to time. I have altered my course of drinking, sometimes from white to claret wine, and then from claret to white again.

I am very friand* and gluttonous of fish, and keep my shroving days upon fish days and my feasts upon fasting days. I believe as some others do that fish is of lighter digestion than flesh. As I make it a conscience* to eat flesh upon a fish day, so doth my taste to eat fish and flesh together. The diversity between them seems to me overdistant.

Even from my youth I was wont now and then to steal some repast,[13] either that I might sharpen my stomach against the next day

[13] I.e., omit a meal.

(for as Epicurus was wont to fast and made but sparing meals, thereby to accustom his voluptuousness to neglect plenty, I, contrary to him, to inure my sensuality to speed the better and more merrily to make use of plenty), or else I fasted, the better to maintain my vigor for the service or performance of some bodily or mental action; for both are strangely dulled and idled in me through overmuch fullness and repleteness. (And above all I hate that foolish combination of so sound and buxom a goddess[14] with that indigested and belching god[15] all puffed with the fume of his liquor.) Or to recover my crazed stomach, or because I wanted some good company. And I say as Epicurus said, that a man should not so much respect what he eateth as with whom he eateth. And commend Chilon, that he would not promise to come to Periander's feast before he knew certainly who were the other bidden guests. No viands are so sweetly pleasing, no sauce so tasteful, as that which is drawn from conversable and mutual society.

I think it wholesome to eat more leisurely and less in [quantity] and to feed oftener. But I will have appetite and hunger to be endeared.* I should find no pleasure, after a physical manner, to swallow three or four forced and spare meals a day. CWho can assure me, if I have a good taste or stomach in the morning, that I shall have it again at supper? Let us old men, let us, I say, take the first convenient time that cometh. Let us leave hopes and prognostics unto almanac makers.[16] BThe extreme fruit of my health is pleasure. Let us hold fast on the present and to us known. I eschew constancy in these laws of fasting. Whoso will have a form to serve him, let him avoid continuance of it. But we harden ourselves unto it and thereunto wholly apply our forces; six months after you shall find your stomach so inured unto it that you shall have gotten nothing but this, to have lost the liberty to use it otherwise without damage.

I use* to go with my legs and thighs no more covered in summer than in winter, for I never wear but one pair of single silk stockings. For the easing of my rheum and help of my colic, I have of late used to keep my head and belly warm. My infirmities did in few days habituate themselves thereunto and disdained my ordinary provisions. From a single nightcap I came to a double coverchief,* and from a bonnet to a lined and quilted hat. The bombasting* of my doublet serves me now for no more use than a stomacher; it is a thing of nothing unless I add a hare or a vulture's skin to it, and some warm wrapping about my head. Follow this gradation and you shall go a fair pace. I will do no such thing. If I durst I could find in my

14 Venus. 15 Bacchus.
16 Montaigne says "almanac makers and doctors."

heart to revoke the beginning I have given unto it. Fall you into any new inconvenience? This reformation will no longer avail you. You are so accustomed unto it that you are driven to seek some new one. So are they overthrown that suffer themselves with forced formalities or strict rules to be entangled and do superstitiously constrain themselves unto them. They have need of more, and of more after that; they never come to an end.

It is much more commodious both for our business and for our pleasure (as did our forefathers) to lose our dinner and defer making of good cheer unto the hour of withdrawing and of rest, without interrupting the day. So was I wont to do heretofore. I have for my health found out since by experience that, on the contrary, it is better to dine, and that one shall digest better being awake.

Whether I be in health or in sickness, I am not much subject to be thirsty; indeed my mouth is somewhat dry but without thirst. And commonly I use* not to drink but when with eating I am forced to desire it, and that is when I have eaten well. For a man of an ordinary stature I drink indifferent much. In summer and at a hungry meal, I not only exceed the limits of Augustus, who drunk but precisely three times; but not to offend the rule of Democritus, who forbade us to stay at four, as an unlucky number, if need be, I come to five; three demisextiers,* or thereabouts. I like little glasses best; and I love to empty my glass, which some others dislike as a thing unseemly.

Sometimes, and that very often, I temper my wine one half, and many times three parts with water. And when I am in mine own house, from an ancient custom which my father's physician ordained both for him and himself, look what quantity of wine is thought will serve me a meal, the same is commonly tempered two or three hours before it be served in, and so kept in the cellar. [C]It is reported that Cranaus, king of the Athenians, was the first that invented the mingling of wine with water. Whether it were profitable or no, I will not now dispute or stand upon. I think it more decent and more wholesome that children should drink no wine until they be past the age of sixteen or eighteen years.

[B]The most usual and common form of life is the best. Each particularity doth in mine opinion impugn it. And I should as much detest a German that should put water in his wine, as a Frenchman that should drink it pure. Public custom giveth law unto such things.

I fear a foggy and thick air, and shun smoke more than death (the first thing I began to repair when I came to be the master of mine own house was the chimneys and privies, which in most of our buildings is a general and intolerable fault), and among mischiefs and difficulties attending on war there is none I hate more than in hot, sweltering weather to ride up and down all the day long in smoky dust, as many times our soldiers are fain to do. I have a free and easy respiration, and do most commonly pass over my murrs* and colds without offense to my lungs or without coughing.

The sultry heat of summer is more offensive to me than the sharpness of winter. For besides the incommodity of heat, which is less to be remedied than the inconvenience of cold, and besides the force of the sun's beams, which strike into the head, mine eyes are much offended with any kind of glittering or sparkling light; so that I cannot well sit at dinner over against a clear-burning fire. To allay or dim the whiteness of paper when I was most given to reading, I was wont to lay a piece of green glass upon my book, and was thereby much eased. Hitherto I never used spectacles, nor know not what they mean, and can yet see as far as ever I could and as any other man. True it is that when night comes I begin to perceive a dimness and weakness in reading, the continual exercise whereof, and specially by night, was ever somewhat troublesome unto mine eyes. [C]Lo here a step back, and that very hardly sensible. I shall recoil one more, from a second to a third, and from a third to a fourth, so gently that before I feel the declination and age of my sight. I must be stark blind. So artificially do the Fates untwist our life's-thread.

Yet am I in doubt that my hearing is about to become thick, and you shall see that I shall have lost it half when yet I shall find fault with their voices that speak unto me. The mind must be strained to a high pitch to make it perceive how it declineth.

[B]My going is yet very nimble, quick, and stout, and I wot not which of the two I can more hardly stay at one instant, either my mind or my body. I must like that preacher well that can tie mine attention to a whole sermon. In places of ceremonies, where every man doth so nicely stand upon countenance, where I have seen ladies hold their eyes so steady, I could never so hold out but some part of mine would ever be gadding; although I be sitting there, I am not well settled. [C]As Chrysippus the philosopher's chambermaid said of her master, that he was never drunk but in his legs, for wheresoever he sat he was ever accustomed to be wagging with them — and this she said at what time store of wine had made his companions cupshotten* and yet he felt no alteration but continued sober in mind — it might likewise have been said of me that even from mine infancy I had either folly or quicksilver in my feet, so much stirring and natural inconstancy have I in them, wherever I place them.

[B]It is unmannerliness and prejudicial unto health, yea and to pleasure also, to feed grossly and greedily as I do. I shall sometimes through haste bite my tongue and fingers' ends. Diogenes, meeting with a child that did eat so, gave his tutor a whirret* on the ear. [C]There were men in Rome that, as others teach youth to go with a good grace, so they taught men to chew with decency. [B]I do sometimes lose the leisure to speak, which is so pleasing an entertainment at the table, provided they be discourses short, witty, and pleasant.

There is a kind of jealousy and envy between our pleasures, and they often shock* and hinder one another. Alcibiades, a man very exquisitely skillful in making good cheer, inhibited all manner of music at tables because it should not hinder the delight of discourses, [C]for the reason which Plato affords him, that it is a custom of popular or base men to call for minstrels or singers at feasts, and an argument they want witty or good discourses and pleasing entertainment, wherewith men of conceit and understanding know how to interfeast and entertain themselves. [B]Varro requireth this at a banquet: an assembly of persons, fair, goodly, and handsome of presence, affable and delightful in conversation, which must not be dumb nor dull, sullen nor slovenly; cleanliness and neatness in meats; and fair weather.

[C]A good mind-pleasing table-entertainment is not a little voluptuous feast nor a meanly artificial banquet. Neither great or stern commanders in wars, nor famous or strict philosophers have disdained the use or knowledge of it. My imagination hath bequeathed three of them to the keeping of my memory, only which fortune did at several times yield exceedingly delightsome unto me. My present state doth now exclude me from them. For everyone, according to the good temper of body or mind wherein he finds himself, addeth either principal grace or taste unto them.

[B]Myself who but grovel on the ground, [B]hate that kind of human wisdom which would make us disdainful and enemies of the body's reformation. I deem it an equal injustice either to take natural sensualities against he heart or to take them too near the heart. [C]Xerxes was a ninny-hammer* who, enwrapped and given to all human voluptuousness, proposed rewards for those that should devise such as he had never heard of. And he is not much behind him in sottishness that goes about to abridge those which nature hath devised for him. [B]One should neither follow nor avoid them, but receive them. I receive them somewhat more amply and graciously, and rather am contented to follow natural inclination. [C]We need not exaggerate their inanity; it will sufficiently be felt and doth sufficiently produce itself. Godamercy* our weak, crazed, and joy-diminishing spirit which makes us distate both them and himself. He treateth both himself and whatsoever he receiveth sometimes forward and other times backward, according as himself is either insatiate, vagabond, newfangled, or variable.

In no sweet vessel all you pour,
In such a vessel soon will sour,
Hor. *Epist.* I.ii.54.

Myself who brag so curiously to embrace and particularly to allow the commodities of life, whensover I look precisely into it I find nothing therein but wind. But what? We are nothing but wind. And the very wind also, more wisely than we, loveth to bluster and to be in agitation, and is pleased with his own offices, without desiring stability or solidity, qualities that be not his own.

The mere* pleasures of imagination as well as displeasure (say some) are the greatest, as the balance of Critolaus did express it.[17] It is no wonder she composeth them at her pleasure and cuts them out of the whole cloth. I see daily some notable precedents of it, and peradventure to be desired. But I that am of a commixed condition, homely and plain, cannot so throughly bite on that only and so simple object, but shall grossly and carelessly give myself over to the present delights of the general and human law, intellectually sensible and sensibly intellectual. The Cyrenaic philosophers are of opinion that as griefs, so corporal pleasures are more powerful; and as double, so more just. [B]There are some [C](as Aristotle saith) who with a savage kind of stupidity [B]will seem distasteful or squeamish of them. Some others I know that do it out of ambition. [B]Why renounce they not also breathing? Why live they not of their own [C]and refuse light because it cometh of gratuity and costs them neither invention nor vigor? [B]That Mars, or Pallas, or Mercury should nourish them to see, instead of Ceres, Venus, or Bacchus? [C]Will they not seek for the quadrature of the circle even upon their wives?

[B]I hate that we should be commanded to have our minds in the clouds whilst our bodies are sitting at the table; yet would I not have the mind to be fastened thereunto, nor wallow upon it, [C]nor lie along thereon, but to apply itself and sit at it. Aristippus defended but the body as if we had no soul; Zeno embraced but the soul as if we had no body. Both viciously. Pythagoras (say they) hath followed a philosophy all in contemplation; Socrates altogether in manners and in action; Plato hath found a mediocrity between both. But they say so by way of discourse. For the true temperature* is found in Socrates; and Plato is more Socratical than Pythagorical, and it becomes him best.

[17] In the scales of Critolaus, spiritual goods weighed more than material goods. (Cf. Cicero, *Tusculanes* V.17.)

[B]When I dance, I dance; and when I sleep, I sleep. And when I am solitary walking in a fair orchard, if my thoughts have awhile entertained themselves with strange occurrences, I do another while bring them to walk with me in the orchard and to be partakers of the pleasure of that solitariness and of myself.

Nature hath, like a kind mother, observed this, that such actions as she for our necessities hath enjoined unto us should also be voluptuous unto us. And doth not only by reason but also be appetite invite us unto them. It were injustice to corrupt her rules. When I behold Caesar and Alexander, in the thickest of their wondrous great labors, so absolutely to enjoy human and corporal pleasures,[18] I say not that they release thereby their mind but rather strengthen the same; submitting by vigor of courage their violent occupation and laborious thoughts to the customary use of ordinary life. [C]Wise had they been had they believed that that was their ordinary vocation and this their extraordinary.

What egregious fools are we! "He hath passed his life in idleness," say we; "Alas I have done nothing this day." What? Have you not lived? It is not only the fundamental but the noblest of your occupation[s]. "Had I been placed or thought fit for the managing of great affairs, I would have showed what I could have performed." Have you known how to meditate and manage your life? You have accomplished the greatest work of all. For a man to show and exploit himself, nature hath no need of fortune; she equally shows herself upon all grounds, in all suits, before and behind, as it were, without curtains, welt,* or guard. Have you known how to compose your manners? You have done more than he who hath composed books. Have you known how to take rest? You have done more than he who hath taken empires and cities. The glorious masterpiece of man is to live to the purpose. All other things, as to reign, to govern, to hoard up treasure, to thrive, and to build, are for the most part but appendixes and supports thereunto.

[B]It is to thee a great pleasure to see a general of an army at the foot of a breach, which ere long intendeth to charge or enter, all whole, undistracted, and carelessly to prepare himself whilst he sits at dinner with his friends about him to talk of any matter. [C]And I am delighted to see Brutus, having both heaven and earth conspired against him and the liberty of Rome, by stealth to take some hours of the night from his other cares and walking of the round, in all security to read, to note, and to abbreviate Polybius. [B]It is for base and petty minds, dulled and overwhelmed with the weight of affairs, to be

[18] Montaigne later changed this to read: "[C]pleasures that are natural and therefore necessary and just."

ignorant how to leave them and not to know how to free themselves from them, nor how to leave and take them again.

> Valiant compeers, who oft have worse endured
> With me, let now with wine your cares be cured:
> Tomorrow we again
> Will launch into the main.
>
> Hor. *Odes*. I.vii.30.

Whether it be in jest or earnest that the Sorbonnical or theological wine and their feasts or gaudy days are now come to be proverbially jested at, I think there is some reason that by how much more profitably and seriously they have bestowed the morning in the exercise of their schools, so much more commodiously and pleasantly should they dine at noon. A clear conscience to have well employed and industriously spent the other hours is a perfect seasoning and savory condiment of tables. So have wise men lived. And that inimitable contention unto virtue which so amazeth us in both Catos, their so strictly severe humor, even unto importunity, hath thus mildly submitted [it]self and taken pleasure in the laws of human condition and in Venus and Bacchus. CAccording to their sect's precepts, which require a perfectly wise man to be fully expert and skillful in the true use of sensualities as in all other duties or devoirs* belonging to life. "Let his palate be savory whose heart is savory" (Cic. *De fin.* II.8.).

BEasy yielding and facility doth in my conceit greatly honor and is best befiitting a magnanimous and noble mind. Epaminondas thought it no scorn to thrust himself amongst the boys of his city and dance with them, Cyea and to sing and play Band with attention busy himself, were it in things that might derogate from the honor and reputation of his glorious victories and from the perfect reformation of manners that was in him. And amongst so infinite admirable actions of Scipio, Cthe grandfather, a man worthy to be esteemed of heavenly race,[19] Bnothing addeth so much grace unto him as to see him carelessly to dally and childishly to trifle in gathering and choosing of cockle-shells, and play at cost-castle* along the seashore with his friend Laelius. And if it were foul weather, amusing and solacing himself, to represent in writing and comedies the most popular and base actions of men. CAnd having his head continually busied with that wonderful enterprise against Hannibal and Africa, yet he still visited the schools in Sicily and frequented the lectures of philosophy, arming his enemies' teeth at Rome with envy and spite.

19 In 1588 Montaigne had written: "Scipio the Younger (all things considered, the first man of the Romans)." His earlier attribution was actually the correct one.

[B]Nor anything more remarkable in Socrates than when, being old and crazed, he would spare so much time as to be instructed in the art of dancing and playing upon instruments, and thought the time well bestowed. Who notwithstanding hath been seen to continue a whole day and night in an ecstasy or trance, yea ever standing on his feet in presence of all the Greek army, as it were surprised and ravished by some deep and mind-distracting thought. He hath been noted [C]to be the first, amongst so infinite valiant men in the army, headlong to rush out to help and bring off Alcibiades, engaged and enthronged by his enemies, to cover him with his body and by main force of arms and courage, bring him off from the rout. And in the Delian battle, to save and disengage Xenophon, who was beaten from his horse. And in the midst of all the Athenian people, wounded as it were with so unworthy a spectacle, headlong present himself to the first man to recover Theramenes from out the hands of the officers and satellites of the thirty tyrants of Athens, who were leading him to his death, and never desisted from his bold attempt until he met with Theramenes himself, though he were followed and assisted with two more. He hath been seen (provoked thereunto by a matchless beauty, wherewith he was richly endowed by nature)[20] at any time of need to maintain severe continency. He hath [B]continually [C]been noted [B]to march to the wars on foot, [C]to break the ice [B]with his bare feet, to wear one same garment in summer and winter, to exceed all his companions in patience of any labor or travail, to eat no more or otherwise at any banquet than at his ordinary. [C]He hath been seen seven and twenty years together with one same undismayed countenance patiently to bear and endure hunger, poverty, the indocility and stubbornness of his children, the frowardness and scratchings of his wife, and in the end, malicious detraction, tyranny, imprisonment, shackles, and poison.

[B]But was that man invited to drink to him by duty of civility, he was also the man of the army to whom the advantage thereof remained. And yet he refused not nor disdained to play for nuts with children, nor to run with them upon a hobby-horse, wherein he had a very good grace. For all actions (saith philosophy) do equally beseem well and honor a wise man. We have good ground and reason, and should never be weary to present the image of this incomparable man unto all patterns and forms of perfections.

[C]There are very few examples of life absolutely full and pure. And our instruction is greatly wronged in that it hath certain weak, defec-

[20] Florio mistranslates here. Socrates' ugliness was, of course, proverbial. What Montaigne says is: "He was seen, when courted by a beauty with whom he was taken, to maintain when necessary a strict chastity."

tive, and imperfect forms proposed unto it, scarcely good for any good use, which divert and draw us back, and may rather be termed corrupters than correcters. [B]Man is easily deceived. One may more easily go by the sides, where extremity serveth as bound, as a stay, and as a guide, than by the midway, which is open and wide, and more according unto art than according unto nature, but therewithal less nobly and with less commendation.

[C]The greatness of the mind is not so much to draw up and hale forward, as to know how to range, direct, and circumscribe itself. It holdeth for great whatsoever is sufficient. And showeth her height in loving mean things better than eminent. [B]There is nothing so goodly, so fair, and so lawful as to play the man well and duly. Nor science so hard and difficult as to know how to live this life well.[21] And of all the infirmities we have, the most savage is to despise our being. Whoso will sequester or distract his mind, let him hardily do it, if he can, at what time his body is not well at ease, thereby to discharge it from that contagion. And elsewhere contrary, that she may assist and favor him and not refuse to be partaker of his natural pleasures and conjugally be pleased with them, adding thereunto, if she be the wiser, moderation, lest through indiscretion they might be confounded with displeasure. [C]Intemperance is the plague of sensuality, and temperance is not her scourge but rather her seasoning. Eudoxus, who thereon established his chief felicity, and his companions, that raised the same to so high a pitch by means of temperance, which in them was very singular and exemplar, savored the same in her most gracious sweetness.

[B]I enjoin [C]my mind [B]with a look [C]equally regular [B]to behold both sorrow and voluptuousness, [C]"As faulty is the enlarging of the mind in mirth as the contracting it in grief" (Cic. *Tusc.* IV.31.), and equally [B]constant. But the one merrily and the other severely. And according to that she may bring unto it, to be as careful to extinguish the one as diligent to quench the other. [C]To have a perfect insight into a good, draws with it an absolute insight into evil. And sorrow hath in her tender beginning something that is unavoidable; and voluptuousness in her excessive end, something that is evitable. Plato coupleth them together and would have it to be the equal office of fortitude to combat against sorrows and fight against the immoderate and charming blandishments of sensuality. They are two fountains at which whoso draweth, whence, when, and as much as he needeth — be it a city, be it a man, be it a beast — he is very happy. The first must be taken for physic and necessity, and more sparingly. The second for thirst but not unto drunkeness. Pain, voluptuousness, love, and hate are the

21 Montaigne adds: "[C]and naturally."

first passions a child feeleth. If reason approach and they apply themselves unto it, that is virtue.

[B]I have a dictionary severally and wholly to myself. I "pass the time" when it is foul and incommodious. When it is fair and good I will not pass it; I run it over again and take hold of it. A man should run the bad and settle himself in the good. This vulgar phrase of *pastime* and *to pass the time* represents the custom of those wise men who think to have no better account of their life than to pass it over and escape it; to pass it over and balk it, and so much as in them lieth, to ignore and avoid it as a thing of an irksome, tedious, and to be disdained quality. But I know it to be otherwise, and find it to be both prizable and commodious, yea in her last declination, where I hold it. And nature hath put the same into our hands, furnished with such and so favorable circumstances that if it press and molest us, or if unprofitably it escape us, we must blame ourselves. [C]"A fool's life is all pleasant, all fearful, all fond of the future" (Sen. *Epist.* XV.).

[B]I therefore prepare and compose myself to forgo and lose it without grudging; but a thing that is losable and transitory by its own condition, not as troublesome and importunate. [C]Nor beseems it a man [not] to be grieved when he dieth except they be such as please themselves to live still. [B]There is a kind of husbandry in knowing how to enjoy it. I enjoy it double to others. For the measure in jovissance* dependeth more or less on the application we lend it. Especially at this instant that I perceive mine to be short in time, I will extend it in weight. I will stay the readiness of her flight by the promptitude of my hold-fast* by it, and by the vigor of custom, recompense the haste of her fleeting. According as the possession of life is more short, I must endeavor to make it more profound and full. Other men feel the sweetness [of a] contentment and prosperity. I feel it as well as they, but it is not in passing and gliding; yet should it be studied, tasted, and ruminated, thereby to yield it condign* thanks that it pleased to grant the same unto us. They enjoy other pleasures, as that of sleep, without knowing them. To the end that sleep should not dully and unfeelingly escape me, and that I might better taste and be acquainted with it, I have heretofore found it good to be troubled and interrupted in the same.

I have a kind of contentment to consult with myself, which consultation I do [not] superficially run over but considerately sound the same and apply my reason to entertain and receive it, which is now become froward, peevish, and distasted. Do I find myself in some quiet mood? Is there any sensuality that tickles me? I do not suffer the same to busy itself or dally about senses, but associate my mind unto it. Not to engage or plunge itself therein, but therein to take delight; not to lose, but therein to find itself. And for her part I employ her to view herself in that prosperous state, to ponder and esteem the good fortune she hath, and to amplify the same. She measureth how much she is beholden unto God for that she is at rest with her conscience and free from other intestine* passions, and hath in her body her natural disposition, orderly and competently enjoying certain flattering and effeminate functions with which it pleaseth him of his grace to recompense the griefs wherewith his justice at his pleasure smiteth us. Oh, how availful is it unto her to be so seated that wherever she casteth her eyes, the heavens are calm round about her, and no desire, no fear or doubt troubleth the air before her. Here is no difficulty, [C]either past or present or to come, [B]over which her imagination passeth [not] without offense.

This consideration takes a great luster from the comparison of different conditions. Thus do I in a thousand shapes propose unto myself those to whom either fortune or their own error doth transport and torment. And these nearer who so slackly and incuriously receive their good fortune, they are men which indeed pass their time. They overpass the present and that which they possess, thereby to serve their hopes with shadows and vain images which fancy sets before them,

> Such walking shapes we say, when men are dead,
> Dreams, whereby sleeping senses are misled,
>
> Virg. *Aen.* X.641.

which hasten and prolong their flight, according as they are followed. The fruit and scope of their pursuit is to pursue. As Alexander said, that the end of his travail was to travail.

> Who thought that nought was done,
> When ought remained undone.
>
> Lucan. II.637.

As for me, then, I love my [life] and cherish it, such as it hath pleased God to grant it us. I desire not he should speak of the necessity of eating and drinking. [C]And I would think to offend no less excusably in desiring it should have it double. "A wise man is a most eager and earnest searcher of those things that are natural" (Sen. *Epist.* CXIX.). Nor [B]that we should sustain ourselves by only putting a little of that drug into our mouth wherewith Epimenides was wont to allay hunger and yet maintained himself. Nor that we should insensibly produce children at our fingers' ends or at our heels, [C]but rather (speaking with reverence) that we might with pleasure and voluptuousness produce them both at our heels and fingers' ends. Nor

[B]that the body should be void of desire and without tickling delight. They are ungrateful [C]and impious [B]complaints. I cheerfully [C]and thankfully and with a good heart [B]accept what nature hath created for me, and am therewith well pleased and am proud of it. Great wrong is offered unto that great and all-puissant Giver to refuse his gift, which is so absolutely good, and disannul or disfigure the same, [C]since he made perfectly good. "All things that are according to nature are worthy to be esteemed" (Cic. *De fin.* III.6.).

[B]Of philosophy's opinions, I more willingly embrace those which are the most solid and that is to say, such as are most human and most ours. My discourses are suitable to my manners, low and humble. [C]She then brings forth a child well [dis]pleasing me when she betakes herself to her quiddities and ergos to persuade us that it is a barbarous alliance to marry what is divine with that which is terrestrial, wed reasonable with unreasonable, combine severe with indulgent, and couple honest with unhonest. That voluptuousness is a brutal quality unworthy the taste of a wise man. The only pleasure he draws from the enjoying of a fair young bride is the delight of his conscience, by performing an action according unto order; as to put on his boots for a profitable riding. Oh that his followers had no more right, or sinews, or pith, or juice at the dismaidening of their wives than they have in his lesson.

It is not that which Socrates, both his and our master, saith. He valueth rightly, as he ought, corporal voluptuousness, but he preferreth that of the mind, as having more force, more constancy, facility, variety, and dignity. This, according to him, goeth nothing alone — he [is] not so fantastical — but only first. For him, temperance is a moderatrix and not an adversary of sensualities.

[B]Nature is a gentle guide, yet not more gentle than prudent and just. [C]"We must enter into the nature of things and throughly see what she inwardly requires" (Cic. *De fin.* V.16). [B]I quest after her track; we have confounded her with artificial traces. [C]And that academical and peripatetical *summum bonum,* or sovereign felicity, which is to live according to her rules, by this reason becometh difficult to be limited and hard to be expounded. And that of the Stoics, cousin-german* to the other, which is to yield unto nature.

[B]Is it not an error to esteem some actions less worthy forsomuch as they are necessary? Yet shall they never remove out of my head that it is not a most convenient marriage to wed pleasure unto necessity. [C]With which (saith an ancient writer) the gods do ever complot* and consent.

[B]To what end do we by a divorce dismember a frame contexted* with so mutual, coherent, and brotherly correspondency? Contrariwise, let us repair and renew the same by interchangeable offices, that the spirit may awake and quicken the dull heaviness of the body, and the body stay the lightness of the spirit, and settle and fix the same. [C]"He that praiseth the nature of the soul as his principal good, and accuseth nature of the flesh as evil, assuredly he both carnally affecteth the soul, and carnally escheweth the flesh, since he is of this mind not by divine verity but human vanity" (Aug. *De Civ. Dei* XIV.5.). [B]There is no part or parcel unworthy of our care in that present which God hath bestowed upon us; we are accountable even for the least hair of it. And it is no commission for fashion's sake for any man to direct man according to his condition; it is express, natural, [C]and principal. [B]And the Creator hath seriously and severely given the same unto us. [C]Only authority is of force with men of common reach and understanding, and is of more weight in a strange language. But here let us charge again. "Who will not call it a property of folly to do slothfully and frowardly what is to be done, and one way to drive the body and another way the mind and himself to be distracted into most diverse motions?" (Sen. *Epist.* LXXIV.).

[B]Which, the better to see, let such a man one day tell you the amusements and imaginations which he puts into his own head and for which he diverteth his thoughts from a good repast and bewaileth the hour he employeth in feeding himself. You shall find there is nothing so wallowish* in all the messes* of your table as is that goodly entertainment of his mind (it were often better for us to be sound asleep than awake unto that we do), and you shall find that his discourses and intentions are not worth your meanest dish. Suppose they were the entrancings of Archimedes himself. And what of that? I here touch not nor do I blend with that rabble or rascality of men, as we are, nor with that vanity of desires and cogitations which divert us, only those venerable minds which through a fervency of devotion and earnestness of religion, elevated to a constant and conscientious meditation of heavenly divine things, [C]and which by the violence of a lively, and virtue of a vehement hope, preoccupating* the use of eternal soul-saving nourishment, the final end, only stay, and last scope of Christian desires, the only constant delight and incorruptible pleasure, disdain to rely on our necessitous, fleeting, and ambiguous commodities, and easily resign the care and use of sensual and temporal feeding unto the body. [B]It is a privileged study.

[C]Super-celestial opinions and under-terrestrial manners are things that amongst us I have ever seen to be of singular accord. [B]Aesop, [C]that famous man, [B]saw his master piss as he was walking. "What? (said he) Must we not etc. when we are running?" Let us husband time as well as we can. Yet shall we employ much of it both idly and ill. As if our mind had not other hours enough to do her business, without dissassociating herself from the body in that little space which she needeth for her necessity.

They will be exempted from them and escape man. It is mere folly. Instead of transforming themselves into angels, they transchange* themselves into beasts; in lieu of advancing, they abase themselves. CSuch transcending humors affright me as much as steepy, high, and inaccessible places. And I find nothing so hard to be digested in Socrates his life as his ecstasies and communication with daemons; nothing so human in Plato as that which they say he is called divine. BAnd of our sciences, those which are raised and extolled for the highest, seem to me the most basest and terrestrial.

I find nothing so humble and mortal in Alexander's life as his concepts about his immortalization. Philotas by his answer quipped at him very pleasantly and wittily. He had by a letter congratulated with him and rejoiced that the oracle of Jupiter Ammon had placed him amongst the gods; to whom he answered that in respect and consideration of him, he was very glad, but yet there was some cause those men should be pitied that were to live with a man and obey him, who outwent others Cand would not be contented with Bthe state and condition of mortal man.

CSince thou less than the gods
Bear'st thee, thou rul'st with odds.
Hor. *Odes* III.vi.5.

BThe quaint inscription wherewith the Athenians honored the coming of Pompey into their city, agreeth well and is conformable to my meaning.

So far a God thou mayest accounted be
As thou a man dost reacknowledge thee.
Plut. *Vit. Pomp.* (tr. Amyot)

It is an absolute perfection, and as it were divine for a man to know how to enjoy his being loyally. We seek for other conditions because we understand not the use of ours, and go out of ourselves forsomuch as we know not what abiding there is. CWe may long enough get upon stilts, for be we upon them yet must we go with our own legs. And sit we upon the highest throne of the world, yet sit we upon our own tail.

BThe best and most commendable lives and best-pleasing men are (in my conceit) those which Cwith order Bare fitted and with decorum are ranged to the common mold Cand human model, Bbut without wonder or extravagancy.

Now hath old age need to be handled more tenderly. Let us recommend it unto that god who is the protector of health and fountain of all wisdom, but blithe and social:

> Apollo grant, enjoy health I may
> That I have got, and with sound mind, I pray:
> Nor that I may with shame spend my old years,
> Nor wanting music to delight mine ears.
>
> Hor. *Odes* I.xxxi.17.

Glossary

Abuttings: boundaries
Accrease: increase
Accuse: affirm
Advantageous: domineering, taking advantage of
Advertise: inform
Affected to: inclined towards
Affiance: trust
Ajax: privy
Allegation: quotation
Allege: quote
Aloof off: at a distance
Amerced: fined
Anatomy: skeleton
Antic: bizarre, grotesque
Apparence, Apparency: justification
Appay: satisfy, pay
Argoletiers: a kind of horse soldier
Arrests: legal decisions
Assay: sample, attempt
Assistance: those in attendance
Astonieth: stuns, stupefies
Astonish: stun, stupefy
Astonishment: stupefaction
Athwart: across, all over
Avie: in emulation, vying with each other

Bandels: swaddling-clothes
Bandy: band together
Bar: barrier
Bare-conned: merely memorized
Bathe: bustle, hop around
Battle: battalion, army
Beavers: drinking times, snacks between meals
Bedrell: bedridden
Bellybroken: ruptured
Blanch: expose, examine
Blazoned: disagreed, decried
Blinding-board: blinkers
Bombasting: cotton padding
Boscage: foliage
Botcherly-patchcoats: authors whose works consist merely of an assemblage of quotes from others, the sort of anthologists Rabelais called "patchers together of old Latin junk"
Brables: quarrels
Brabling: quarreling
Broaches: spits
Burgess: citizenship
Burstwort: rupture wort

Calepin: dictionary
Caliver: musket
Canvas (had the canvas): been discredited
Canvass: to labor
Cariere: [a term from tournaments] a course
Cark: trouble, anxiety
Carking: worrying
Casting-lots: places where dice are thrown
Cates: delicacies, meats
Cawcy: causeway
Champaign: flat
Champain: flat, open

Chap: split
Chirugeon: surgeon
Chuck: charge
Chuff-penny: miserly
Climate: region
Close-stool: water-closet, toilet
Closely: tacitly
Cock'ring-kind: Pampering
Cod-burst: ruptured
Cog: trick
Coil (keep a coil): make a fuss
Colewort: cabbage
Complot: conspiracy; conspire
Compromitted to: compromised with
Con (I con thanks): I owe thanks
Condign: worthy, deserved
Conference: resemblance
Confets: confections
Conscience (make it a conscience): troubled, to scruple
Contexted: put together, fabricated
Contracted: opposed
Convince: convict
Cope: vault
Copesmate: partner
Cost-castle: a children's game
Counterpeising: weighing, comparing
Counterpoise: weigh, compare
Counter-roll: catalogue
Cousin-german: akin
Coverchief: head-covering, kerchief
Crack: noise
Cranes: jesses
Cranishes: chasms, fissures
Cranks: winding paths
Crotesko: grotesque
Cue: direction
Cunny: rabbit
Cup-shotten: drunk

Debauched: diverted
Debonaire: courteous
Defailances: faintnesses
Demised: leased, conveyanced
Demiseness: cowardice
Demisextiers: half-pints
Demiss: cowardly, humble, faint
Demissly: cowardly
Devoir: duty
Diapred: diversified
Difficile: difficult
Discover: reveal
Dissemblable: unlike [us]
Dissociable: unsociable
Distrain: compel
Domification: the astrological art of dividing the heavens into "houses" in order to predict the future at the hour of birth
Dumpish: sad, moping, quiet

Eftsoons: again, afterwards; also; recently
Emmet: ant
Empairing: growing worse
Emprise: motto, device
Enable: strengthen
Endear: enhance, justify, to value at a high (or over-high) rate
Enhoney: beguile sweetly
Ens entium: being of beings
Eryngo or sea-holme: sea-holly
Essays: attempts
Estridge: ostrich
Exagitate: censure
Exercitation: exercise

Fardle up: gather together in a bundle
Febricant: feverish
Fets: roams about
Fixly: fixedly
Flirting at: turning up one's nose at, scoffing at
Fond: foolish
Fondhardness: foolhardiness
Fondhardy: foolhardy
Fondly: foolishly
Foord: current
Friand: fond of
Friandise: squeamishness about food
Frication: friction, rubbing
Fustian: bombastic

Galimatias: gibberish
Galiot: a small galley
Gallimaufry: hodge-podge
Genuity: nature
Glaive: sword
Godamercy: thanks to
Gossips: godmothers
Grievous: gravely ill
Gudgeon: a kind of fish [one who swallows gudgeons is one who will swallow anything]

Hap: fortune, luck
Harquebusiers: soldiers armed with harquebuses, an early type of gun
Harsell: torment
Herb-wife: flower-girl
Heteroclite: extraordinary
Hine-boy: peasant boy
Hoised-full: well-hoisted
Hoiting: romping
Hold-fast: grasp
Hulling: tossing
Husband: manager

Impresa: device, motto
Induction: means
Instantly: insistently, urgently
Institution: training, education
Inter-bearing: putting up with
Interessed: wronged
Intershock: jostle one another
Intestine: internal, civil

Jovissance: enjoyment
Jump to speak truth: agree with this

Kenning: seeming

Laver: bowl for washing
Leasing: falsehood
Let: hindrance
List: wish, wished
Lively: vivid; natural; notable
Long of: because of
Loose: departing
Louting: bowing
Lurking: retreat
Luxurious: lustful

Makes for: is good for
Malapertness: effrontery
Mammocks: pieces
Maquerelage: pandering
Marble-sounds: shining seas
Marchpane: marzipan
Marrish: marshy
Mauger: in spite of
Meacock: an effeminate person, a coward
Mean: moderate
Mere: pure, absolute, sheer
Merely: purely, closely
Messes: dishes
Mignardises: caresses
Milt: spleen
Moiety: half, part, portion

Morbidezza: softness
Mortified: "high" [meat]
Mort-mere: dead sea
Mows: faces, mouths
Mum-chance: a game of chance played silently
Murr: bad cold

Nearly: closely
Niais: silly, foolish
Ninny-hammer: oaf, blockhead
Nunchions: meals, luncheons

Oppugn: fight against
Ought: owed
Overpeering: high, overlooking

Paillardize: lewdness, debauchery, lechery
Paisant: peasant
Pavesado: shield
Peiseth upon: lays weight on
Penitentiaries: shriving priests
Perflable: allowing air to pass through
Petty: little
Philosophy: philosophize
Piece: harquebus
Piercent: sharp, penetrating
Pilled: pillaged
Piot: magpie
Pirling: rippling
Plunges (put to his plunges): have a hard time, be put in difficulty
Poise: weigh
Poiseth upon: lays weight on
Pommada (to make the pommada): to walk on one's hands
Porterly rascal: a porter, a man who carries things
Pourcontrel or many-feet: octopus
Preallable: preliminary
Preoccupate: anticipate
Presential appearance: good presence
Primely: perfectly, strictly
Profluvion: flowing forth
Propense discourse: reflection
Proper: one's own
Proprieties: properties
Prosopopoeial: epic
Prud'homie: sincerity, uprightness
Punies: younger children

Quick: alive
Quidam: certain

Rabble case-canvassing: pettifogging litigations
Rechlessness: recklessness, carelessness
Reesty: rusty
Reins: kidneys
Require: ask for
Retailing: cutting up

Saciety: satiety
Salve: pass over, conceal
Sans: without
Scald: scurvy
Scantling: a portion
Screen: litter
Searce: sieve
Seld: seldom
Semblable: similar
Serein: a light rain or dew falling from a cloudless sky in summer after sunset
Sets: shoots planted in the ground
Shock: jostle

Shrow: shrew
Silly: simple
Sink: sewer, dump
Sithence: since
Slops: loose trousers
Sortable: suitable
Souse: plunge
Spawling: watering
Spiny: thin
Stead: succour, help, avail
Stern: rudder
Stoccado: a thrust in fencing
Stock: support
Store: a great quantity, abundance
Submiss: submissive
Success of time: course of time
Suffragant: secondary
Swathing clothes: swaddling clothes
Symbolize: compare

Table: painting
Temper: moderation, temperance
Temperature: temperateness
Tennons: joinings
Tester: canopy
Thirled: hurled
Tintamarre: racket, hubbub, clamor
Tipple-square: drink a great deal
To-rent: cut to pieces
Transchange: alteration; alter
Trilling: rolling
Trunk-sleeves: wide sleeves

Uberty: fertility
Unhaunted: solitary
Ure: use
Use: am accustomed

Vacation: occupation
Veil: body, carcass
Vented: put into circulation
Verdugales: farthingales
Vizards: masks, visors
Voil: of open space, wide
Vulgar: common, common people; vernacular

Wallowish: insipid
Ward: guard, defense, spring
Welt: ornament
Whirret: a box on the ear
Wince: kick
Wire-draw: extend
Wishly: earnestly
Wretchless: reckless

Yard: penis
Yonker: young man

A B C D E F G H I J – R – 7 3 2 1 0 / 6 9 8 7 6 5 4